THE MODERN WORLD-SYSTEM II

Mercantilism and the Consolidation of the
European World-Economy, 1600 –1750

"World Map," by Joan Blaeu, 1638, from the *Atlas Major*. Joan Blaeu and his father Willem were the most respected cartographers of their time. Their maps were required on all Dutch ships engaged in trade with the Indies. Atlases replaced sheet maps as the dominant cartographic form in the seventeenth century. In 1670, Joan Blaeu was appointed Map Maker in Ordinary to the Dutch East India Company (VOC).

THE

MODERN WORLD-

SYSTEM II

Mercantilism and the Consolidation of the
European World-Economy, 1600–1750

Immanuel Wallerstein

ACADEMIC PRESS

A Subsidiary of Harcourt Brace Jovanovich, Publishers

New York   London   Toronto   Sydney   San Francisco

ACADEMIC PRESS, INC.
111 Fifth Avenue, New York, New York 10003

United Kingdom Edition published by
ACADEMIC PRESS, INC. (LONDON) LTD.
24/28 Oval Road, London NW1 7DX

Library of Congress Cataloging in Publication Data

Wallerstein, Immanuel Maurice, Date
    The modern world-system.

    (Studies in social discontinuity)
    Includes bibliographies and indexes.
    CONTENTS: v. 1. Capitalist agriculture and the
origins of the European world-economy in the sixteenth
century.——v. 2. Mercantilism and the consolidation of
the European world-economy, 1600—1750.
    1. Europe——Economic conditions. 2. Economic history
——16th century. 3. Capitalism. I. Title. II. Series.
HC45.W35 1974   330.94   73—5318
ISBN 0—12—785923—3 (v. 2) (hardcover)
ISBN 0—12—785924—1 (v. 2) (paperback)

To Fernand Braudel

CONTENTS

LIST OF ILLUSTRATIONS

The illustrations were selected and annotated with the assistance of Sally
Spector.

ACKNOWLEDGMENTS

The following persons read one or more chapters of the manuscript and gave me the benefit of their detailed comments and/or objections: Perry Anderson, Sven-Erik Åström, Nicole Bousquet, Stuart Bruchey, Aldo de Maddalena, Emiliano Fernández de Pinedo, André Gunder Frank, Walter Goldfrank, Terence K. Hopkins, Hermann Kellenbenz, E. H. Kossmann, Witold Kula (and associates), Hans Medick, Birgitta Odén, and C. H. Wilson. I thank them all.

Previous versions of the following chapters have appeared elsewhere: Introduction and Chapter 1, in French, in *Annales E.S.C.* (1979); Chapter 2, in Maurice Aymard, ed., *Capitalisme hollandais et capitalisme mondiale* (1980); part of Chapter 1, in *Caribbean Yearbook of International Relations* (1978).

INTRODUCTION:
CRISIS OF THE
SEVENTEENTH CENTURY?

Figure 1: "The Old Exchange at Amsterdam," by Adianesz Job Berckheyde, an artist from Haarlem. This scene was described thus in 1747 by Charles Louis Pollnitz:

> I went to see the square where the merchants assemble about the affairs of their trade from noon till half past one o'clock. This square, which is longer than it is broad, is surrounded by a large open gallery or corridor, supported by stone pillars, which serves as shelter in case of rain. This place is called the Exchange, and here are to be seen merchants of all nations, the diversity of whose clothes and language is no less pleasing than the beauty of the place. Above all, nothing is more interesting than to witness the hurrying of those who are called brokers, who are the men employed by the great merchants to traffic for the bills of exchange, or to transact their other affairs to see them scurrying from one part to another all over this square, anyone would think that they were mad.

The work of historians of European price trends between the two world wars[1] along with the theory of secular economic cycles (trends that go up and down over approximately 250 years) with its two phases (A and B), elaborated by François Simiand[2] have bequeathed us a generalization about early modern European history that still seems largely accepted: There was expansion in the sixteenth century (phase A) and contraction, depression, or "crisis" in the seventeenth (phase B). The dates that demark these phases, the nature of the changes that occurred (even if we limit the discussion to economic matters), the regional variations, and above all, the consequences and causes of the flows are matters of much debate; but the generalization remains.

In 1953, Roland Mousnier wrote a large tome on these two centuries (which has since seen four revised editions), and he opened the part on the seventeenth century, defined as the period between 1598 and 1715, in a dramatically tremolent tone:

> The seventeenth century is the epoch of a crisis that affected man in his entirety, in all his activities—economic, social, political, religious, scientific, artistic—and in all his being, at the deepest level of his vital powers, his feelings, and his will. The crisis may be said to be continuous, but with violent ups and downs.[3]

A year after this was written, E. J. Hobsbawm published an article in *Past and Present* that launched an important scholarly debate. The thesis was that "the European economy passed through a 'general crisis' during the seventeenth century, the last phase of the general transition from a feudal to a capitalist economy."[4]

The same theme is found in the major surveys of European agriculture by Wilhelm Abel and B. H. Slicher van Bath. For Abel, "the dominant tendency of prices in Europe, during the second half of the seventeenth and the first half of the eighteenth centuries, was downward."[5] To be sure, Slicher van Bath hesitates at using the word *crisis*, asserting that the period between 1650 and 1750 was "more truly an unusually prolonged depression";[6] but is that so much less? In any case, he does not disagree with Abel's assertion that the period represented a "reversal of the secular trend."[7] We could enlarge the scholarly consensus further if we used still

[1] See the bibliography accompanying the article by Braudel and Spooner (1967, 605–615).

[2] See Simiand (1932b).

[3] Mousnier (1967, 161).

[4] Hobsbawm (1965, 5).

[5] Abel (1973, 221). The first German edition of Abel's survey appeared in 1935 and the second, revised and augmented, in 1966. Abel says that the "general framework was kept" but that "the depressions of the fourteenth-fifteenth and of the sixteenth-seventeenth centuries are interpreted as periods of slowdown, and subdivided as much as

possible" (1973, 6). Presumably, Abel believes there was an upturn between the two depressions.

[6] Slicher van Bath (1963a, 206). Two more recent surveys (Cipolla, 1974, 12; Davis, 1973b, 108) are equally reluctant to use the word *crisis*, although, as Cipolla adds: "At the bottom of every simplification there is always a grain of truth."

[7] This wording appears in the title of Part II, ch. V (Abel, 1973, 206). Pierre Chaunu uses a similar phrase, "the reversal of the principal tendency of prices and activities," in the title of an article on the seventeenth century (1962b).

more cautious language. Pierre Vilar speaks of "the relative retreat (*recul*) of the seventeenth century";[8] and Pierre Chaunu defines the difference between periods A and B not as "growth [versus] decline (*décroissance*)" but rather as "growth [versus] less growth."[9] René Baehrel is the most reluctant to see any crisis at all; but even he accepts the concept for the very limited period between 1690 and 1730.[10] As the terms get weaker and the time shorter, we may wonder if much is left. Ivo Schöffer begins his article on this period on a note of doubt:

> It sometimes seems as if the seventeenth century, wedged between the sixteenth and eighteenth centuries, has no features of its own. With Renascence and Reformation on the one side, Enlightenment and Revolution on the other, for the century in between we are left with but vague terms like "transition" and "change."[11]

Perhaps this is only because, as Jean Meuvret argued in 1944, "we have much less information" about the period between the two moments of clear price rise.[12] Shall we then refuse to characterize this period and allow it to slip away in the complexities of blurred and sometimes confusing data? Or shall we say, with Schöffer: "It may be traditionalism, against our better judgment, but we simply have to give the seventeenth century a place of its own. Our imagination needs it."[13]

We could leave such a decision to the whims of literary fashion were it not for the important theoretical issues behind the fuss about nomenclature. There is, first of all, the question of whether such things as "secular trends" of the economy exist at all,[14] and if so, how they relate to politics and culture. If there are secular trends, does each successive pair of phases (from the Middle Ages to the present) reflect a different kind of economy,

[8] Vilar (1974, 46), who defines his period as starting between 1598 and 1630 and ending between 1680 and 1725.

[9] Chaunu (1962b, 224). This comes close to Simiand's original description of phase B: "not the inverse of what occurred in phase A, but . . . an attentuated increase or a stabilization, and no longer a continuation of the rise" (1932b, 649).

[10] Baehrel (1961, 29), who, like Chaunu, notes that phase B is not necessarily a decline and can simply be a lower rate of growth (1961, 51). Others agree that this period is particularly severe. Le Roy Ladurie specifies "the two or three last decades of the [seventeenth] century" (1973, 431). Jacquart dates it from 1680 to 1710 (1978a, 385). Morineau, however, finds "a large number of signs that are positive (*de bon allant*)" between 1660 and 1700 (1978f, 523).

[11] Schöffer (1966, 82). Vague terms can always be rejected as the historian's dramatic flourish. "It is a telling comment on the historian's attachment to change that almost every historical period has, at one time or another, been categorized as 'a time of transition'" (Supple, 1959, 135).

[12] Meuvret (1944, 110). See the similar complaint that opens Murdo MacLeod's book on Spanish Central America: "The seventeenth century was characterized some time ago as 'Latin America's forgotten century'" (1973, xi)—a reference to the article by Leslie Boyd Simpson entitled "Mexico's Forgotten Century" (1953). J. V. Polišenský, in the same vein, observes that "historians of the social, economic and Marxist schools have been concerned primarily with the 'more revolutionary' sixteenth and eighteenth centuries and have cast little light on the seventeenth" (1971, 2). William Bouwsma calls the seventeenth century "in an historiographical sense . . . an underdeveloped borderland between two overdeveloped areas" (1970, 1).

[13] Schöffer (1966, 83).

[14] François Crouzet referred in 1971 to "obsolete concepts like Simiand's A and B phases" (1971, 147). A similar attack, this time from the left, was made by Gilles Postel-Vinay: "A and B phases . . . have proved to be a sure way of ignoring the real problems posed by the analysis of ground rent" (1974, 78).

as Gaston Imbert argues?[15] or are they all part of one long period of "indirect agricultural consumption" running from about 1150 to about 1850, as Slicher van Bath argues?[16] or is there a crucial rupture somewhere in the middle? If there is a crucial rupture, we are faced with the additional question of when it occurs.

There are several familiar positions on this last question. One is that the fundamental break, the significant rupture, occurs with the Industrial Revolution in the late eighteenth century. To Carlo Cipolla both this "event" and the Agricultural Revolution of the eighth millenium B.C. represent "deep breaches in the continuity of the historical process."[17] D. C. Coleman makes the same point in a different way and says there is more continuity than change in European economic development from 1500 to 1750: "Where light breaks through, the technology of 1500–1750 is revealed to be, on the whole, more static than mobile."[18] Similarly a whole school of Marxist thought arrives at the same conclusion regarding the timing of any rupture, insisting, as does Balibar, that period between 1500 and 1750 is the period of the "transition to capitalism" and that after 1750 is the period of capitalism proper.[19] In the same spirit as Balibar is G. N. Clark's distinction

---

[15] G. Imbert, in his book on long waves (1959), distinguishes four secular trends, each corresponding to a form of economy:

> 1250—medieval economy
> 1507/1510—mercantilist economy
> 1733/1743—capitalist economy
> 1896—planned economy

[16] Slicher van Bath (1963a, Pt. III).

[17] Cipolla (1964, 31).

[18] Coleman (1959, 506). This is an article reviewing the third volume of *History of Technology*, which Coleman offers as evidence for his proposition. See also Le Roy Ladurie (1977) on "motionless history" between 1300–1320 and 1720–1730.

[19] Many Marxists *assume* this periodization. But Etienne Balibar self-consciously makes the theoretical distinction between a "period of transition" and one in which a mode of production prevails or is "dominant" (1968, 217–226).

An intra-Marxist debate that discussed this question of periodization with clarity appeared in *Labour Monthly* in 1940–1941. The debate revolved around one of Christopher Hill's earliest writings on the English revolution. Peter Field criticizes Hill's assessment of pre-1640 England as "still essentially feudal." For Field, Marx had said quite clearly that sixteenth-century England was "definitely bourgeois, that is capitalist," and "Marx is right: the sixteenth-century society is a bourgeois society." Indeed Queen Elizabeth "was the most prominent capitalist in capitalist bourgeois society—comparable to Leopold of Belgium" (Field, 1940a, 558). Douglas Garman replies that Field "mistakes

the egg for the chicken" and that if the bourgeois revolution had already occurred before 1640, "one can only ask, When?" (Garman, 1940, 652). Field responds that Mr. Garman "forgets that conception and birth are not identical" and that "beginning with the War of the Roses—the mass-suicide of the feudalists which the bourgeoisie utilised to implant its roots firmly—[and] proceeding by way of peasant revolts, the confiscation of the Church lands, the Pilgrimage of Grace, [and] the rising of the northern earls, bourgeois society came into being" (Field, 1940b, 654–655).

Thereupon, Dona Torr takes up the cudgels with a very explicit theorization of stages. Field's error, she says, is to assume that society goes straight from feudalism to capitalism, thus "ignoring the intermediate stages of small commodity production, essential to capitalist development." She says that the "final form of capitalist society" exists only with the Industrial Revolution, 400 years after the "breaking down" of English manorial economy in the fourteenth century (Torr, 1941, 90).

Maurice Dobb, writing on the same issue as Dona Torr, takes an intermediate position. On the one hand, he does not agree with Torr on dating capitalism as of the Industrial Revolution. If one did this, he says, "how could the seventeenth-century struggle be treated as a bourgeois democratic revolution when it came a century and a half before the rise of capitalist production?" Furthermore, he says, to argue that "Tudor and Stuart England was an epoch of 'merchant capitalism' by contrast with later 'industrial capitalism' is to evade

between the "early capitalism" of the later Middle Ages and the "fully developed capitalism" of the nineteenth century, the limits of the first stage being clearly demarked "from Machiavelli to Burke, from Columbus to Warren Hastings, from the Fuggers to the decline of Amsterdam, from Giotto to Tiepolo. It stops short of Adam Smith, James Watt, the Rothschilds, Napoleon, Robert Owen."[20]

To another school of thought, the rupture involves not the Industrial Revolution, but the expansion of Europe, the creation of a world market, and the emergence of capitalism—occurring more or less in the long sixteenth century. Simiand, for example, marks the sixteenth century as the beginning of the period of long waves.[21] Paul Sweezy attacks the Marxist tradition represented by Balibar and argues that for Marx "the period of manufacture proper" (from about 1500 to 1750) and "the period of modern industry" were not "two different social systems but rather two phases of capitalism."[22] The rupture thus comes in the sixteenth century. Fernand Braudel makes essentially the same point, although spreading the period over more time:

> It is clear, in fact, that from an economic point of view, the thirteenth to the seventeenth centuries constitute more or less a period of European and world history which effectively challenges [*met en cause*] a kind of economic *Ancien Régime*.[23]

A third group offers a point of rupture between the period marked by the Industrial Revolution and the French Revolution, on the one hand, and that marked by the long sixteenth century, on the other. They suggest the mid-seventeenth century as the turning point of modernity. Hobsbawm seems to be in this camp, and Pierre Chaunu makes this position virtually the theme of his synthesis regarding "classical Europe." In the introduction to his book, he specifically rejects the points of view of scholars who fail to see that the "intellectual origins of the French Revolution" are to be found in Spinoza and who forget that the "quantitative and spatial expansion" of

the issue." Dobb's solution is to argue that at this time, "the *relations* of production [may be said to have changed] even if the *productive forces* retained their medieval shape." Ergo it would be correct to characterize sixteenth-century England as one whose "mode of production was *already in process of transformation* into a capitalist one" (Dobb, 1941, 92). While Dobb's formulation avoids the crude trap into which Dona Torr's formulation readily leads, it is ultimately not really different from her idea, as Dobb's own subsequent work reveals.

Hill published an article several years later on Marx and Engels's views on the English Revolution; he argues that the "Marxist concept of bourgeois revolution" is one wherein "the feudal state is overthrown by the middle class that was grown up inside it, and a new state created as the instrument of bourgeois rule." Hill lists as examples, both successful and unsuccessful, the German reformation ("first onslaught of the bourgeois spirit on the old order"); the Netherlands Revolt ("first successful bourgeois revolution on a national scale"); the English Revolution of 1640; the French Revolution of 1789; the abortive German Revolution of 1848; and the Russian revolutions of 1905 and February 1917 (1948, 135). This article concentrates on political manifestations and power, skirting direct description of the economy. It thus fails to come to grips with the position put forward by Field.

[20] G. N. Clark (1960, 10–11).
[21] Simiand (1932a, 3).
[22] Sweezy (1972a, 129).
[23] Braudel (1974, 6).

the sixteenth century was not a truly profound change but merely the "end result of a revolution begun in the twelfth century." For Chaunu, "the most important qualitative changes occurred in the seventeenth century," the first among them being the "mathematization of the world."[24] As proof that one can find Marxists on every side of every question, one advocate of this third possible rupture point is Academician E. M. Zhukov of the USSR, who asserted to assembled world historians in Stockholm in 1960:

> The conventional and terminal boundary of the medieval era, in the opinion of Soviet historical Science, is the middle of the seventeenth century. This is because feudalism began outliving itself economically by that time and was already a handicap to the development of productive forces.[25]

Three dates, then, for a rupture: around 1500, 1650, and 1800; three (or more) theories of history: 1800, with an emphasis on industrialism as the crucial change; 1650, with an emphasis either on the moment when the first "capitalist" states (Britain and the Netherlands) emerge or on the emergence of the presumably key "modern" ideas of Descartes, Leibnitz, Spinoza, Newton, and Locke; and 1500, with an emphasis on the creation of a capitalist *world*-system, as distinct from other forms of economies. It follows that the answer one gives to the query, "crisis of the seventeenth century?", is a function of one's presuppositions about the modern world. The term *crisis* ought not to be debased into a mere synonym for *cyclical shift*. It should be reserved for times of dramatic tension that are more than a conjuncture and that indicate a turning point in structures of *longue durée*.

Crisis would then describe those infrequent historical moments in which the usual mechanisms of compensation within a social system prove so ineffective from the point of view of so many important social actors that a major restructuring of the economy begins to occur (not a mere redistribution of advantage within the system), which is later seen in retrospect as having been inevitable. Of course a given crisis was not truly inevitable; but the alternative was a collapse of the old system such that many (most?) social actors considered this even more traumatic or disagreeable than the structural revolution which did take place. If this is what we mean by crisis, then "crisis of the seventeenth century?" becomes a significant intellectual question. It really means, from this perspective: When and how did the world-historic "transition from feudalism to capitalism" occur? The answer requires a definition of capitalism as a social system, as a mode of production, and, indeed, as a civilization as well. As we choose our dates, so we choose our scale of similarities and differences.

The argument of this work is that the modern world-system took the form of a capitalist world-economy that had its genesis in Europe in the long

[24] Chaunu (1966a, 20–21).
[25] Zhukov (1960, 85). Zhukov specifically takes note that some Marxists fix the French Revolution as the turning point and says that the Russians do not agree.

sixteenth century and that involved the *transformation* of a particular redistributive or tributary mode of production, that of feudal Europe (Braudel's "economic *Ancien Régime*") into a qualitatively different social system. Since that time, the capitalist world-economy has (*a*) geographically expanded to cover the entire globe; (*b*) manifested a cyclical pattern of expansion and contraction (Simiand's phases A and B) and shifting geographical locations of economic roles (the rise and fall of hegemonies, the movements up and down of particular core, peripheral, and semiperipheral zones); and (*c*) undergone a process of secular transformation, including technological advance, industrialization, proletarianization, and the emergence of structured political resistance to the system itself—a transformation that is still going on today.

In such a perspective, the seventeenth century, taken to cover a period running approximately from 1600 to 1750, is primarily an example of the cyclical pattern of expansion and contraction. In terms of the overall geography of the world-system, the boundaries created circa 1500 did not significantly change until after 1750. As for the ongoing secular processes of change, no marked qualitative leap is observable in the period from 1600 to 1750. We are arguing, therefore, for the essential *continuity* between the long sixteenth and the seventeenth centuries, with the one great difference of expansion (a) and contraction (B), of growth and less growth. How shall we provide evidence for this way of summarizing reality? At one level the answer is quite simple. We shall try to identify the empirical differences between expansion and contraction, to suggest why this cyclical pattern occurs, and to outline the consequences in terms of class-formation, political struggles, and cultural perceptions of the turn in economic fortune. From this empirical description, we shall try to specify more clearly the theory of capitalist development as part of a larger theory of sociohistorical change.

We are arguing that although the boundaries of the world-economy remained largely the same in the period from 1500 to 1750, there was a difference between the periods of 1450 (or 1500) to 1650 and 1600 to 1750 (the overlap in dates is deliberate) regarding allocation of resources, economic roles, and wealth and poverty and location of wage employment and industrial enterprise. To demonstrate this assertion is not easy; a convincing proof requires the construction of several entirely new series of economic indicators, which would be intrinsically difficult and extrinsically perhaps impossible. We might want a series of successive synchronic maps at intervals of 25 years that would show the volume, value, and direction of trade in both luxuries and essentials and "cumulative" maps for 1500–1650 and 1600–1750. Presumably, if our guesses are correct, such maps should show that European trade involving primarily essentials rather than luxuries was carried on within boundaries that lay between eastern Europe, on the one side, and Russia and the Turkish Balkans on the other, and between the

Christian and the Moslem Mediterraneans; and these boundaries would include the Americas but exclude Africa and Asia.

Above all, the maps should show no significant differences of pattern between the period of 1500 to 1650 and that of 1600 to 1750 with regard to external boundaries, except for the inclusion of the Caribbean, as we shall see. On the other hand, we should find certain significant changes with regard to economic, political, and cultural patterns *within* the boundaries of the European world-economy between the two periods. The location and concentration of industries should be different (or at least in the process of changing), as should the terms of trade between industry and agriculture, the percentages of wage employment in the various zones, and the real wages of wage earners. Different state-machineries should be getting stronger and weaker, and the rates of increase in agricultural, industrial, and demographic production should shift. The areas that were core, semiperipheral, and peripheral should change somewhat, and most importantly, the relative degree of world surplus appropriated by each of the regions should shift.

Even before specifying the anticipated directions of change, given our theory of capitalist development, it should be clear to the reader that quantitative data of the kind required are scarce—at best, partial and sporadic. Particularly lacking are *overall* data on the world-economy that would permit testing *relational* statements. If one dreams of making firm statements regarding variables of the social structure, the situation is even worse. We ought to find shifting patterns of class-formation and changes in the definition of ethno–national boundaries between the two periods of 1500 to 1650 and 1600 to 1750, especially within the world-economy as a whole rather than within the boundaries of particular states, and here our data are even thinner. At this point, all we can do is analyze scattered data, sketch out what seems more and less solid, review explanatory models that encompass the data, suggest a theoretical view, and arrive at some notion of our empirical lacunae and theoretical conundrums. It is in this spirit that we look at what the historical literature has meant by the "crisis," the "relative retreat," or the "lesser growth" of the seventeenth century.

NÉ POUR LA PEINE

Reueille matin de Campagne

But des gens de Campagne Tailles payee'

Collecteur

L'ABEILLE qui mouche à miel Chacun a part à ses trauaux

animaux

par son moyen bon boit et mange

LA VACHE

du paysan

LE COCHON

Il est meprise' et necessaire

Attributs

LA POULE

sa journée est d'un petit prix

L'acquisition

qui ne nourrit rien n'a rien

N. Guerard inu et fecit

L'homme de Village

Tous les jours au milieu d'un champ.   Trauailler tant que lanneé dure.
Par la chaleur par la froidure.   Pour amasser par son labeur.
L'on voit le pauure paysan.   Dequoy payer le collecteur

Se Vend à paris chez N. Guerard Graueur rüe St Jacques à la Reyne du Clergé proche St Yues   C.P.R.

1

THE B-PHASE

For Slicher van Bath, the fundamental distinguishing characteristic of the periods of *agricultural* expansion and contraction in Europe since the Carolingian era is the rise and fall in the price of cereals, vis-à-vis other merchandise and wages. It was a question of favorable or unfavorable terms of trade for cereals. He sees a contraction, meaning *unfavorable terms of trade*, for cereals in the period from 1600 (or 1650) to 1750.[1] It is important to underline this definition of contraction, because the relative decline of the price of wheat in Slicher van Bath's belief, is far more important than its absolute decline.[2] Side by side with a shift in the terms of trade (avoiding, for the moment, all suggestion of causal sequence) is what K. Glamann calls a turning point around 1650 in "the great east–west grain trade," apparently occurring because "southern and western Europe [seemed] to have become more self-sufficient in grain."[3] This self-sufficiency is attributed to an "increased production of foodstuffs in western Europe during the second half of the seventeenth century, coinciding with a general stagnation of population,"[4] resulting presumably in oversupply. However, Glamann also notes that at this same time "Europe was glutted with pepper."[5]

But how can oversupply be suggested when the problem of the times was presumably too little food? Schöffer speaks of "permanent, sometimes latent, structural phenomena" existing in Europe "from the disasters of the fourteenth century until far into the eighteenth century," primarily "the continuous tension between food production and food distribution on the one hand and the population's food requirements on the other." The result was "a situation where malnutrition was endemic, hunger often epidemic."[6] Domenico Sella sees the well being of the early modern period as dependent "on whether food supplies kept pace with population,"[7] yet others

---

[1] Slicher van Bath (1965a, 38), who in a later piece noted "This by no means precludes prosperity in other sectors of economic life, as in the flourishing breweries, distilleries, textile and tobacco industries during this period" (1977, 53).

[2] "What is most important are the shifting price ratios between cereals and livestock produce such as butter, cheese and wool over a long period. Of great significance also is the relation between wheat prices and industrial crops such as flax, coleseed, tobacco, etc.; also between wheat and wine, between wheat and industrial foods such as textiles, brick, for example, and finally between wheat prices and rent" (Slicher van Bath, 1965b, 144). In this connection, see Perry Anderson's rebuff to Duby's unwillingness to denote Europe's economy of the late Middle Ages as an economy in crisis. Duby sees certain continuing signs of economic progress in some regions, and Anderson comments: "This is to confuse the concept of crisis with that of retrogression" (1974b, 197).

[3] Glamann (1974, 464).

[4] Glamann (1974, 465). See also Slicher van Bath (1965a, 208). On the overall decline of cereal production that followed, see Jacquart (1978a, 352, 360). Jacquart points out (p. 378) that there can only be three possible reasons for an overall decline in production—changes in the costs of production, changes in the level of the harvests, and changes in the market value of the product. He rejects the first as implausible for the period, which leaves the other two explanations. He thinks lowered yield is the primary explanation. See, however, Slicher van Bath's arguments against climate as a valid explanation in fall of yield. "If all other factors had remained constant, *ceteris paribus*, grain prices during this period should have shown a tendency to rise. In fact, in most countries they showed a tendency to fall. The implication is that changes must have taken place which affected demand" (1977, 63).

[5] Glamann (1974, 485).

[6] Schöffer (1966, 90).

[7] Sella (1974, 366).

speak of production rising faster than population. Clearly we have an anomaly that can only be resolved with a clearer notion of the sequence of
events. Let us see first what other events occurred.

Certain agronomic shifts are reported for the seventeenth century: the
process of land reclamation was at least slowed down, probably stopped,
possibly reversed. Unlike the sixteenth and eighteenth centuries, which
"invented land" (in Chaunu's felicitous image), the seventeenth century,
especially after 1650, was a time of "consolidation," but a consolidation
"without merit."[8] In addition to the cessation of expansion of land area, the
average yield ratio of cereals fell throughout Europe in the period between
1600 and 1699, to a greater degree for barley and oats than for wheat and
rye, and fell more sharply in central, northern, and eastern Europe than in
western Europe.[9] De Maddalena calls this fall of yield ratios "a remarkable
phenomenon."[10] Another major agronomic shift was in the choice of crops
to be cultivated: first, a shift in the use of land for cereals to its use for
pasturage in the cooler areas and for wine in the warmer areas;[11] second, a
shift from the cultivation of cereals to increased production of forage crops,
vegetables that require intensive labor, and commercial crops (flax, hemp,
hops, rapeseed, madder, and pastels);[12] and third, a shift from high-priced
cereals (rye and wheat) to low-priced ones (barley, oats, and buckwheat)[13]
and a reduction in the purchase of fertilizer (both humus and marl) for the
production of cereals.[14]

Alongside the purely agronomic changes, a number of shifts in the social
organization of agricultural production occurred. De Maddalena speaks of
a general "degredation of the peasant class"[15] during the seventeenth century, during which "the landowners, adducing *'urgens et improvisa necessitas'*
proceeded to confiscate farms formerly owned by peasants."[16] He notes also
the "expropriation—it might better be termed usurpation—of a third of the

[8] Chaunu (1966a, 272). See also Slicher van Bath
(1963b, 18). Deserted villages are to be found during the seventeenth century not only in war-
devastated areas like Bohemia, the Germanies, Poland, and Burgundy, but in areas outside the main
arenas of fighting, such as the Campagna and Tuscany in Italy and Salamanca in Spain. See Slicher
van Bath (1977, 68).

[9] See Slicher van Bath (1963b, 17); see also Jacquart (1978a, 363–368).

[10] De Maddalena (1974a, 343). Slicher van Bath
argues that there is a necessary link between yield
ratios and cereal prices. "Increased fertilization,
which required the purchase of manure, led to a
higher yield. But this was done only if cereals production was remunerative." (1965a, 32). Obviously,
he does not believe it was remunerative, since he
also argues: "Reductions in the quantity or quality
of manuring were probably responsible for the
slight fall in the yield ratios of cereals between 1600
and 1750 in most of the countries of Europe for

which we have evidence" (1977, 95).

[11] See Romano (1962, 512–513). See also Slicher
van Bath (1965a, 33–34), who offers this list for
areas turning from arable use to pasturage between
1650 and 1750: Castille, Schwerin, Vorarlberg,
Allgau, Bregenzerwald, Pays d'Enhaut, Emmenthal,
Savoie, Jura, Gruyères, Pays d'Hervé, Bourgogne,
Thiérarche, Pays d'Auge, Bessin, Cotentin, Mid-
lands, Ireland. New vinyard areas between 1630
and 1771 were Les Landes, Périgord, Sète, Montpel-
lier, Alsace, Catalonia, Vaud, Hallwil, the Canton of
Zurich.

[12] Slicher van Bath (1965a, 33, 39), who cites
shifts in the Moselle, Harz, Erfurt, and the Low
Countries.

[13] Slicher van Bath (1965a, 39).

[14] Slicher van Bath (1965a, 15, 39).

[15] De Maddalena (1974a, 288); cf. Jacquart
(1978a, 346; 1978b, 427–428; 1978c, 462).

[16] De Maddalena (1974a, 292); cf. Jacquart
(1978b, 391–392).

communal property (hence the term 'triage')," which affected the peasants by reducing the area in which they had rights for pasturage and wood gathering.[17] Slicher van Bath agrees that the rural population suffered for the most part more than the urban population, but he distinguishes between the small farmers and the cottagers on the one hand and the laborers and house servants on the other; the former pair having "had it relatively worse" than the two wage-earning categories.[18] Meuvret finds a very obvious explanation for this:

> For every cultivator-owner/tenant (*laboureur*) who complains of his small profit because of the price of wheat, how many laborers (*manoeuvriers*) or artisans rejoice at the lower price they have to pay on those few occasions when they must purchase it.[19]

In general, Slicher van Bath argues that the unfavorable financial position of the peasant owners and tenants (*fermiers-propriétaires*) went along with a reduction in tenancies (*fermages*) and especially in the number of small tenant-farmers (*petits fermiers*).[20] The two reductions were paralleled by the fact that in general the size of the agricultural unit (*exploitation agricole*) became larger.[21] Nonetheless, despite larger units and more costly labor there was less improvement in agricultural equipment in the seventeenth century than in the sixteenth, although there were more innovations in the tools used in dairy farming, such as the improvement in the churn.[22]

Industry, like agriculture, is said to have lost its "force of acceleration" in the seventeenth century, although somewhat later.[23] It is not clear what this meant in terms of total European production. Sella argues that the fluctuations were relatively small because when population expanded in the sixteenth century, real wages declined, and thus things were "basically unchanged"; when there was a rise in per capita incomes after 1650, however, the increased individual demand "may have been offset [globally] in part by sagging population figures."[24] The uncertainty of such an analysis is stated bluntly by Hobsbawm: "What happened to production? We simply do not know."[25]

What we do seem to know is that there was a shift in the *location* of industry. For Slicher van Bath, it is "well known that during periods of agricultural contraction—end of the Middle Ages and of the seventeenth

[17] De Maddalena (1974a, 294).

[18] Slicher van Bath (1965b, 147). The terms in German are *Kleinbauern*, *Kätner*, and *Häusler* versus *Knechte* and *Magde*. Jacquart similarly emphasizes the relative decline of the "middle peasantry," whom he defines as those "possessing or exploiting a small family holding," and who he says were "proletarianized" in the crisis (1978c, 466).

[19] Meuvret (1944, 116).

[20] Slicher van Bath (1965a, 38).

[21] Slicher van Bath (1965a, 37–38).

[22] Slicher van Bath (1965a, 15, 34, 39).

[23] Romano (1962, 520). In recapitulating the essence of this article later, Romano said: "The first, most important, determining breakdown—in agriculture—comes at the end of the sixteenth century; the commercial and industrial breakdown comes later: it is set in 1619–1622 in the sense that *after* the short crisis of those years commercial and 'industrial' activity enters into a longer crisis" (1974, 196).

[24] Sella (1974, 366–367).

[25] Hobsbawm (1965, 9).

century—rural industry appears on the scene, especially the textile industry."[26] This occurred, it is argued, because of the cheapness and attractive-
ness to industry of underemployed rural labor. Since such industry was
based on a low ratio of fixed capital, at least until the mid-eighteenth century, Romano argues that "consequently, it was extremely easy to liquidate
a business, taking out one's capital";[27] this may have been true of the textile
industry, but the argument is difficult to apply to the other two of the three
major industries of the time (according to Romano's own list)—mineral
extraction and shipbuilding.[28] This shift of textile production to the rural
areas was combined with the installation of the only significant new
industries—brewing, distilling, and paste manufacture, which were all
bared on the transformation of cereals.[29]

Apparently, the counterpart of declining cereal prices were rising real
wages. "In the second half of the seventeenth century, . . . as food prices
tended to fall . . . wage-rates held their own or failed to drop to quite the
same extent."[30] This is of course the inverse of what happened in the long
sixteenth century.[31] Presumably, this resulted in part from the relative
"stickiness" in wages, but even more because "all over Europe there was a
marked labor shortage from 1625–1750."[32] If this is so, how do we reconcile
it with the fact that the seventeenth century has been thought to be a period
of relatively high unemployment of underemployment? As Glamann notes:

> The wage-earning labourer may have enjoyed some increase in real wages. This
> presupposes, however, that he was in employment, which cannot be assumed in an
> age such as this which is characterised by disturbed economic conditions. Many of the
> economic writers of the seventeenth century, at any rate, based themselves on the
> assumption that large-scale under-employment prevailed in their communities.[33]

Any discussion of prices (whether of cereals or wage labor) is especially
bedeviled in this period by the relation of nominal prices to prices in bullion.[34] It is generally agreed, as Mousnier notes, that "the decline is greater
than it seems for many countries, if instead of looking only at nominal
prices calculated in money of account, one calculates the price in its corresponding weight in precious metals."[35] Therefore, if we look at metallic

[26] Slicher van Bath (1965a, 37), who lists the fol-
lowing areas: Ireland, Scotland, Maine (France),
Flanders, Twente, Westphalia, the surroundings of
Munster, Saxony, and Silesia.

[27] Romano (1962, 520).

[28] Romano (1962, 500).

[29] Slicher van Bath (1965a, 39).

[30] Sella (1974, 366); see also Vigo (1974, 390).

[31] See my discussion in Wallerstein (1974, 77–84).

[32] Abel (1973, 225).

[33] Glamann (1974, 431). See the similar observation of Léon: "In the seventeenth century, the rise of
real wages was thwarted by the agricultural crisis,
which generated brusque and violent thrusts of

cereal prices, a crushing increase in the cost of living, and also strong industrial depressions, which
involved long and severe unemployment. Thus, for
the larger part of the working classes, it was a catastrophe" (1970e, 674).

[34] See my brief discussion in Wallerstein (1974,
271).

[35] Mousnier (1967, 167). The argument for using
a bullion measure is made persuasively by Le Roy
Ladurie, who cites the pointed question of René
Baehrel (1961): "There can not exist a single correct
measure of monetary value. Why would we think it
should be a gram of silver?" To which Le Roy
Ladurie responds: "Correct. But *a fortiori* why

prices, as Vilar says, there is "one sure fact: internationally, prices, in terms of silver, collapsed around 1660 and hit a first low point in 1680 and doubtless a second about 1720–1721."[36] The decline in metallic prices must be set beside a decline in the quantity of bullion in circulation.

Geoffrey Parker summarizes the overall situation:

> On balance it seems safe to assume that Europe's net stock of precious metals augmented moderately between 1500 and 1580; that it increased rapidly between 1580 and 1620; and that it *probably declined from the 1620s,* when silver mining in Europe collapsed and the remittances of American silver fell sharply, until the arrival of the Brazil gold after 1700.
>
> There is no doubt that the growth in the volume of money available in Europe was extremely important. Europe's trade in 1700 could clearly not have been carried on with the slender monetary resources of 1500. A crucial question, however, remains: was it enough? Was the net increase in Europe's monetary stock, substantial as it was, equal to the rapidly rising demand for means of payment? There are several indications that it was not, *particularly after 1600.*[37]

Not only was there a shortage of monetary stock, but there was a corresponding shortage of credit such that for at least the half-century running from 1630 to 1680, as Spooner notes, the total available quantity of "silver, copper, gold, credit [taken together] barely suffice, resulting in an uneasy and mediocre monetary life that was both reflection and consequence of a general slowdown of material life in the world."[38] This explains the wave of counterfeit money, the "pervasive plague of the seventeenth century."[39] What did this shift of prices mean for the global *quantity* of trade? As in the case of European industrial production, virtually no global data are available.

A construct by Frédéric Mauro of what he calls intercontinental trade relations divides the world into five continents: Europe, Africa, Temperate America, Tropical America, and Asia. In our terms, these are not entirely appropriate geographic categories because Africa and Asia are external to the world-economy while the Americas are peripheral to it and because Mauro places in one category both the core and peripheral areas of Europe and thereby loses crucial data.[40] Nonetheless, it is useful to look at his estimates in Table 1; the layout has been altered by me in the interest of clarity. Assuming the correctness of the comparisons in the table we note that trade to and from Europe and worldwide trade moved in parallel

would we think it should be the *livre tournois*, which adds to the relativity of the metal the supplementary instability of the money of account? . . . I criticize the meter measured in iridium, in the name of a certain relativity of the universe. Am I going to replace it with a meter in rubber, just as relative, but in addition annoyingly elastic?" (1964, 83).

[36] Vilar (1974, 246); but Vilar adds, "except in France, it is hard to ignore a rise in the curve be-

tween 1683–1689 and 1701–1710."

[37] Parker (1974a, 529–530, italics added).

[38] Spooner (1956, 8).

[39] Spooner (1956, 35–36).

[40] See Mauro (1961a, especially 16–17). A criticism of Mauro's treatment of Europe as a single category is to be found in Mata and Valério (1978, especially 118–120).

TABLE 1

Comparison of the Extent of Intercontinental Trade to and from Five Areas and Worldwide
in Relation to the Previous Century[a]

	Century		
Area	Sixteenth	Seventeenth	Eighteenth
Europe	Rising	Constant	Rising
Africa	Constant	Rising	Rising
Temperate America	(Near zero)	Rising	Rising
Tropical America	Rising	Constant	Constant
Asia	Rising	Falling	Falling
Worldwide	Rising	Constant	Rising

[a] Adapted from Mauro, 1961a.

directions, and in the seventeenth century, both indicate an interim of
stability as opposed to earlier and later periods of expansion.

Turning to the one remaining significant variable, population, we find
that estimates of demographers tend to vary within narrow limits. The
seventeenth century was characterized by Reinhard and Armengaud as
"stagnation, if not . . . slight decline (*recul*)" but *not* a "catastrophic [crisis]
of the kind that occurred in the fourteenth century";[41] and Fr. Roger Mols
says that "despite the terrible crises which wracked it, the seventeenth seems
also to have experienced a slight gain in population."[42] Slight decline, slight
gain—in short, a leveling off.

What emerges from this survey of general European economic patterns
for 1600 to 1750 (period B) in comparison with the period from 1450 or
1500 to 1650 (period A) and indeed with the period following 1750 is a
picture of an economic plateau, a time of respite, concern, reshuffling; but
was it a "crisis" in the sense that there was a "crisis of feudalism" from 1300
to 1450?[43] It seems not, for although "its chief symptoms were the same,"
the 1650–1750 "depression was of a far milder sort than the serious economic decline of the late Middle Ages."[44] If this is true, this is precisely what
must be explained, and the explanation we offer is that the contraction
between 1600 and 1750, unlike that between 1300 and 1450, was *not* a
"crisis" because the hump had already been passed, the corner turned, and
the crisis of feudalism essentially resolved. The contraction of the seventeenth century was one that occurred *within* a functioning, ongoing
capitalist world-economy. It was the first of many worldwide contractions or

[41] Reinhard and Armengaud (1961, 114).

[42] Mols (1974, 39); J. de Vries calculates an index
of 106 in 1700 for 100 in 1600 (and one of 123 for
1750); but he omits eastern Europe from his calculations, which surely must further reduce the index

(1976, 5, Table I).

[43] See my discussion in Wallerstein (1974, chap.
1).

[44] Slicher van Bath (1963a, 206).

depressions that this system would experience; but the system was already
sufficiently ensconced in the interests of politically dominant strata within
the world-economy, and the energies of these strata turned *grosso modo* and
collectively not to undoing the system, but instead to discovering the means
by which they could make it work to their profit, even, or perhaps especially, in a period of economic contraction.

The capitalist strata were in the seventeenth century a mixed bag, hardly
yet a coherent class formation and certainly not yet constituting a class that
was totally conscious of itself and certain of its right to rule, to reign as well
as to gain; but they were very capable of making a profit against great odds.
As Jeannin says of the Danzig merchants, after explaining some of the very
complex calculations they had to make circa 1600: their "mode of reckoning shows that the merchants understood the profit-mechanisms. They
traded in such a way that one can actually ascribe to them an understanding
of the concept of the 'terms of trade' in its most concrete meaning."[45] A
consideration of the profits that could be derived from the shifting terms of
trade leads us to the central explanation for the economic behavior of this
period. As Vilar suggests, it is less on the ups and downs of prices that we
should focus than on the "disparity in the movements" of prices.[46]

These disparities involve both time sequences and geographical locations, and their significance is not merely in the profits that could be made,
but in their effect on the system as a whole. Topolski says that the contraction was not a "general economic crisis in the sense of a stagnation, lull, or
recession caused by a weakening of economic activity"; it was rather a period marked by an "increasing disequilibrium"[47] within the system as a
whole. Increasing disequilibrium is not something to be placed in contrast
to contraction; in a period of contraction disequilibrium is in fact one of the
key mechanisms of capitalism, one of the factors permitting concentration
and increased accumulation of capital. Vilar's explanation is a good one:
"In every general conjuncture, different countries react differently, whence
the inequalities of development which, in the end, make history."[48]

[45] Jeannin (1974, 495).

[46] Vilar (1961, 114).

[47] Topolski (1974a, 140). Ralph Davis says virtually the same thing: "Much more striking than
general economic decline was the way in which lines
of development came to diverge" (1973b, 108).
Compare Topolski's rejection of the term "stagnation" with that of Ruggiero Romano: "What is
the seventeenth century? . . . While definitions
abound, they can readily be reduced to a single one:
it is the century of 'economic stagnation'. It is only
an impression, but I am firmly convinced that behind this facile argumentation lies only one datum:
the history of prices. . . . But is this a good criterion? I don't believe so" (1962, 481–482).

[48] Vilar (1974, 52). This is why I cannot accept
Morineau's attempt to refute the whole concept of a

phase B for the seventeenth century. He says:
"Hesitations of growth? This is the title chosen for
this [collective] volume. It is full of postulates and of
many vague notions. It supposes an adherence to a
Rostowian-type growth, to an optimistic vision of
the sixteenth century, to a uniformly pessimistic vision of the seventeenth. . . . If one is Dutch or English, rather than Spanish or Portuguese, the geographic rise of Europe after 1598 seems quite clear.
It was a question of a redistribution of the cards"
(1978g, 575). If, however, one is not uniformly pessimistic in one's vision, if one *assumes* that a phase B
involves *precisely* a redistribution of the cards, and if
one asserts the opposite of a Rostowian-type theory
of growth, then one is less affected by the force of
the objection.

Let us turn to what Sella calls the "dramatic shifts in the geographical distribution of economic activity,"[49] but not in the conventional mode of scholarly despair whereby we must "avoid generalizations."[50] Rather let us bear in mind Fernand Braudel's adjunction to precision; "for there is no single conjuncture: we must visualize a series of overlapping histories, developing simultaneously."[51] The main geographical distinctions are a matter of general agreement, albeit there is much scholarly nit-picking about details. Hobsbawm's discussion of "general crisis" notes "the relative immunity of the States which had undergone 'bourgeois revolution',"[52] by which he means the United Provinces and England. In another discussion, however, he divides "the European economy" into four zones, three of which are said to have declined economically in some sense (there is no attempt to rank them vis-à-vis each other). The zones are "the old 'developed' economies of the Middle Ages—Mediterranean and South-West German"; the "overseas colonies"; the "Baltic hinterland"; and the "new 'developed' areas." In this fourth zone, which has a "more complex" economic situation, we find not only Holland and England, but France as well.[53]

Romano's geography is more stratified:

> In England and the Low Countries the crisis had essentially liberating effects; in France, it did not release energies, but it certainly sowed the seeds which were to bear fruit later; in the rest of Europe, it meant nothing but involution. Italy is undoubtedly to be included in this last part of Europe, under the label of involution.[54]

Cipolla adds a nuance to Romano's geography: "The seventeenth century was a black century for Spain, Italy and Germany and at least a grey one for France. But for Holland it was *the* golden age, and for England, if not golden, at least silver."[55] Topolski draws the map of stratification in a slightly different way, distinguishing between zones of great dynamism (England the the United Provinces), less rapid development (France, Scandinavia, Germany, and Bohemia and the other states in eastern and central Europe, with the exception of Poland), and stagnation or regression (Spain, Portugal, Italy, and Poland).[56] As a group, the geographical classifications seem concordant, although varying in detail.

Let us now look at the temporal classifications, where the confusion is greater: dates for the contraction vary among countries and there is varia-

[49] Sella (1974, 390).
[50] De Maddalena (1974a, 274).
[51] Braudel (1973, **II**, 892). This overlap of processes, it seems to me, Pierre Chaunu's certainty: "The downturn does not normally occur in one movement, but in two, three, four moments, moments which are those of cyclical crisis. . . . The chronology of these crises is, more or less, the same everywhere in Europe, give or take two or three years. But the relative importance and meaning of these crises varies from one place to another"

(1962b, 231).
[52] Hobsbawm (1965, 13).
[53] Hobsbawm (1958, 63).
[54] Romano (1974, 194).
[55] Cipolla (1974, 12). Schöffer speaks of the reluctance of Dutch historians to contribute to the discussion on the concept of a general European crisis: "How can this general crisis be made to square with the Dutch Golden Age?" (1966, 86).
[56] As reported by Geremek (1963).

tion in nominal and silver prices; and even for particular countries and
particular kinds of prices, the analysts seem to disagree. In Braudel and
Spooner's review of the price data, their theme is simple: "The end of the
sixteenth century is as hard to ascertain as its beginning."[57] For bullion
prices, they find a reversal of the upward secular trend "in the south between 1590 and 1600; in the north, between 1620 and 1630 and perhaps
even by 1650." But for nominal prices they find a quite different pattern of
three successive movements: one around the 1620s in Germany; one
around mid-century for cities as different as Siena, Exeter, Ragusa, Naples,
Amsterdam, Danzig, and Paris; and one in 1678 for Castile, which is "very
much out of line." "Nominal prices," they say, "exactly followed silver prices
only in the case of England, and very closely in the case of Holland." Note
how our pair of countries reappears. In all other countries there is a gap
ranging from a decade to as high as three-quarters of a century for Castile.
"Successive inflations . . . are what kept nominal prices up in these various
countries."[58]

Here we have a precious clue to pursue. Can inflation be one of the
modes of relative decline when there is contraction in the world-economy?
Can one say that the degree of nominal inflation, especially if measured in
relation to bullion-prices, is a measure of relative decline? This question
should be borne in mind as we review the various datings (for which the
criteria of placement are often not explicit). According to Slicher van Bath,
depression began in Spain around 1600, in Italy and part of central Europe
in 1619, in France and part of Germany in 1630, in England and the
United Provinces in 1650. It was worst in central Europe between 1640 and
1680 and in the United Provinces between 1720 and 1740. It ended in
England and France in 1730, in Germany in 1750, and in the United
Provinces in 1755. "The economically more highly developed lands like
England and Holland could resist longer. The primary producers—in the
seventeenth century these were the cereal-producing areas in the Baltic
zone—were almost completely defenseless."[59]

Vilar, using silver prices, finds two main patterns—one in Spain and
Portugal, whose decline started earlier (between 1600 and 1610) and also
ended earlier (between 1680 and 1690), and one in northern Europe, which
started between 1650 and 1660 and went on until between 1730 and 1735.
France appears in this classification as a split country, where the Midi,
"linked to the conjuncture of Marseilles, of the Mediterranean, was closer to
Spain than to the Beauvaisis."[60] Chaunu sees the same two patterns: a
"precocious trend of the Mediterranean and Hispano-America, and a tardy

---

[57] Braudel and Spooner (1967, 404).
[58] Braudel and Spooner (1967, 405).
[59] Slicher van Bath (1965b, 136). A similar time
period for the depression in the Baltic zone is found
in Maczak and Samsonowicz (1965, 82), who date it

from the 1620s to the 1760s.
[60] Vilar (1974, 303). Thus Vilar attempts to make
the otherwise dissonant arguments of Baehrel
(1961) fit in with general theses of and about the
French.

one, that of the North and the Baltic, to which is linked, rather paradoxically, Brazil and the Indian Ocean."[61]

Abel, however, comes up with a somewhat different grouping on the basis
of 25-year averages of silver-prices for cereal, which he summarizes as, in
general, a downward trend "during the second half of the seventeenth and
the first half of the eighteenth centuries."[62] This, he says, holds true for
England, the Spanish Netherlands, France, northern Italy, the United Provinces, Denmark, and Poland, but not for Germany and Austria, whose
"price curves are upward from the last quarter of the seventeenth century."[63] In fact, a close look at Abel's chart shows a far more complex
picture, in which two facts stand out. First, the largest price gap may be
seen to occur in 1650, when Poland is markedly high and Germany is
markedly low. Second, Poland shows the widest variation in prices over
time, going from the highest prices anywhere in 1650 to the lowest anywhere in 1725. (The degree of Germany's deviation from the norm is much
smaller.) This remarkable swing of Poland should not be overlooked in
seeking a general framework for an explanation; but for the moment, let us
deal with Germany, since a large literature has emerged on the question of
the role of the Thirty Years' War in the "decline" of Germany.

Theodore Rabb, in reviewing the literature as of 1962, described two
schools of thought, the "disastrous war" school and the "earlier decline"
school (who see the Thirty Years' War as merely the final blow).[64] Friedrich
Lütge stands as a good example of the former school. For him, Germany's
economy between 1560 and 1620 was flourishing. She was involved in overseas trade, and manufactures were extensive and profitable. After 1620,
this was no longer so, and hence he concludes that the Thirty Years' War
was the key intervening variable.[65] To this the response of Slicher van Bath
is typical: "The Thirty Years' War cannot be responsible, since the decline in
Germany started already in the second half of the sixteenth century."[66]
Several attempts have been made to settle this debate. Carsten, for example,
throws a skeptical eye on the thesis of prewar decline:

> Even if it could be established that the majority of German towns declined already
> before 1618, this would not necessarily entail a general decline, for economic activity
> might have shifted from the towns to the countryside. Indeed this was the case in
> north-eastern Germany where the sixteenth century was a period of peace and pros-
> perity, of growing corn exports and quickly rising corn prices.[67]

The decline of towns is thus not necessarily to be taken as a negative
economic sign. Of course not! It is a sign of peripheralization.[68] Carsten

---

[61] Chaunu (1962b, 251–252).
[62] Abel (1973, 221).
[63] Abel (1973, 222, 223, chart no. 37).
[64] Rabb (1962b, 40).
[65] See Lütge (1958, 26–28).
[66] Slicher van Bath (1963b, 18); see the same argument in Abel (1967, 261).

[67] Carsten (1956, 241).
[68] To Carsten himself, this is well known, although
he does not use this language. He speaks of "the rise
of the landed nobility and their direct trading with
foreign merchants, which killed many of the smaller
towns" (1956, 241).

finds, in addition, that the period before 1608 in Upper Bavaria, an area he has looked at closely, was "a time of slowly growing prosperity." He advised prudence, therefore, until there was "more detailed investigation and research."[69] Whereas Carsten mediates by insisting on our collective ignorance, Rabb mediates by insisting that our collective knowledge "shows both absolute prosperity and decline within Germany [prior to the Thirty Years' War], often side by side." He also concludes on a note of prudence.

> The fact that areas of decline were in a decided minority . . . makes it impossible to conclude that the struggle before 1618 was any worse than diverse. . . . At best, the Thirty Years' War started a general decline that had not previously existed; at worst it replaced prosperity with disaster.[70]

A third variant of mediation is Kamen's. He acknowledges that "there can be no doubt at all that the war was a disaster for most of the German-speaking lands," but he argues that "the controversy is to some extent a false one" because there was "no single economic or political unit called Germany" and it was "often unrealistic to distinguish between prewar and wartime decline."[71]

All these national "economic" measurements fail to take into direct account the degree to which the Thirty Years' War was itself both the political consequence and the sign of a general economic contraction throughout Europe. One major attempt to view this war in a totally European context has been made by J. V. Polišenský, who says the war is to be

> seen as an example of two civilizations in ideological conflict. The clash of one conception, deriving from the legacy of Humanism, tinged with Protestantism and taking as its model the United Netherlands, with another, Catholic-Humanist, one which followed the example of Spain, becomes thus the point of departure for the development of political fronts and coalitions of power.[72]

This war throughout Europe might then be thought of as the first world war of the capitalist world-economy. Polišenský makes the point, albeit in somewhat prudent terms.

> A precondition for the generalizing of the conflict was the presence in early seventeenth century Europe, if not of an economic unity, at least of a framework for exchange and the first signs of a world market, whose centre of gravity was the whole area between Baltic, Atlantic and Mediterranean.[73]

[69] Carsten (1956, 241).

[70] Rabb (1962b, 51).

[71] Kamen (1968, 44, 45, 48).

[72] Polišenský (1971, 9). Parker similarly suggests an analogy to the first World War. (1976a, 72); but note the very next sentence in Polišenský warning against misinterpretation: "It would be a crass oversimplification to contend that the War was a collision between the champion of capitalism and the bourgeoisie on the one hand, and the representative of the 'old regime' and feudal aristocracy on the other."

[73] Polišenský (1971, 258). It followed thus that "the War acted as a catalyst to accelerate certain socio-economic changes which were already in progress before it broke out." (p. 259). It was *not* a turning point. "The Thirty Years' War underlined an *already existing* inequality of economic develop-

To his central argument that "what is beyond dispute" is Vajnshtejn's thesis that "the Thirty Years' War belongs intimately with the story of the Dutch revolution and the movement for liberation from Spain," Polišenský adds: "We need to know precisely how an internal bourgeois-led revolution could become a bogy for its adversaries throughout Europe."[74] For him, not only did the "Dutch factor" play a key role in the generalization of the conflict, but the most important outcome was in fact the victory of the Dutch throughout Europe. He notes that the war wound up precisely when the Dutch were ahead:

> In 1645 the Dutch fleet, for the first time, gained control of the Sound and the trade routes of the Baltic. The merchant patriciate of the province of Holland and the city of Amsterdam could now see no reason for continuing a war with Spain from which only France could be the victor. . . .
> The separate peace [of the United Provinces and Spain in January 1648] was at once a triumph of the Republic over Spain and of Holland over the Prince of Orange and the rest of the Netherlands. It can equally be seen as an outright victory of Amsterdam over all other Dutch interests and the ending of the war confirmed the privileges of that same urban oligarchy which Maurice of Orange had brought low thirty years earlier.[75]

A crucial question intervenes regarding how we explain that the Dutch war of independence, the Netherlands Revolution, which began as early as 1566, did not spill over into a conflagration throughout Europe until 1621—the beginning of what Polišenský called the "Dutch period of the war" (from 1621 to 1625).[76] Has it not something to do with Romano's crisis of 1619–1622?[77] It is more than likely that it does. For the contraction throughout Europe that was signaled by the acute crisis of those years[78] meant that the stakes of political control were higher; and the costs of military destruction seemed lower to the participants than the potential losses from a weak commercial position at a moment of contraction. In this sense, the United Provinces gambled and won. Especially since many of the costs of the war, in terms of destruction, were in fact paid by Germany and, let us not forget, by Bohemia.[79] Kamen is thus correct in seeing the controversy about Germany as a "false one." The question is not whether Germany would or would not have declined if the Thirty Years' War had

ment. It did not alter the basic direction of trade routes or the intensity of commercial contracts" (p. 260, italics added). Hroch also analyzes the Thirty Years' War as the result of the contradiction between "the developing forces of production and the stagnating relations of production," in turn the outcome of the development of commodity production for a "Europe-wide market" (1963, 542). However, he sees the conflict as one "within the feudal class" (p. 541).

[74] Polišenský (1971, 264).

[75] Polišenský (1971, 236–237).

[76] This is the title of Polišenský's fifth chapter (1971).

[77] See Romano (1962).

[78] See my discussion in Wallerstein (1974, 269–273).

[79] "The extent of the [economic] tragedy [of Bohemia] is clear" (Polišenský, 1971, 294). It is true of Switzerland as well; see the discussion in Kamen (1968, 60).

not intervened—this is a largely meaningless hypothetical consideration. Its intervention was one response to a reversal in trend in the world-economy, and hence the war became one of the modalities by which reallocations of economic roles and intensifications of economic disparities occurred.

Summarizing the various studies and syntheses, we have the following picture. In the years around 1600 to 1650 (as in those around 1300 to 1350), a period of economic expansion seemed to end. Descriptions of this expansion primarily in price terms, the approach of the price historians of the interwar period, are not wrong, but they are very misleading because prices are, by definition, relative. A price has significance only within the context of the whole synchronic series of prices of a given market. Prices never go up or down in general; *some* prices go up, which therefore means that others go down. The expansions that came to an end did not involve merely the ethereal measure of nominal prices; they involved real material products. The first and perhaps central expansion was in the production of cereals both in the yield per acre and in the total acreage devoted to cereals. This latter expansion was achieved by the reclamation (*bonification*) of land and also by the shift from the use of land from pasturage and wine growing to its use for cereals. These various expansions took place, of course, because the terms of trade became more profitable for cereals vis-à-vis other products.

In addition, there were expansions in at least four other real areas: (*a*) population, whose rise and fall in that era could not long be out of line with food supply; (*b*) *urban* "industry", relatively monetized in both its forward and backward linkages, creating high rates of wage employment, and never too far out of line, therefore, with relatively low or at least declining real wages; (*c*) the stock of money in its multiple forms (bullion, paper, credit); (*d*) the number of *marginal* entrepreneurs, rural and urban. All these involve expansions in terms of measures of the economy as a whole, and they are never uniform throughout the many sectors of the economy. Measuring them within the boundaries of political units rather than within the boundaries of global economic markets will therefore give only a partial picture in which economic meaning is incomprehensible; and political consequences are thus inexplicable unless one takes into account the larger whole.

In about 1300/1350 and 1600/1650 these expansions came to an end for largely similar reasons. What differed greatly, however, were the systemic responses to the end of expansion. In quantitative terms, we can see the difference quite easily. The period from 1300 to 1450 involved a *fall* in the various measures, roughly comparable to the previous rise, whereas the period from 1600 to 1750 represented a *stabilization* in the measures. The curve for 1450 to 1750 looks like a step rather than like the mountain peak of the curve for 1150 to 1450. This is only the outer shell of the difference in structure, however. The recession of 1300 to 1450 led to the crisis of a social structure, that of European feudalism, whereas that of 1600 to 1750 led to "a period of solidifying and organizing," in Schöffer's phrase;[80] it marked what Chaunu called the "end of easy growth and the beginning of fertile difficulties."[81] Solidification and fertile difficulties regarding what? The capitalist world-economy as a system is the only plausible answer.

Let us note some of the systemically constructive features of the contraction between 1600 and 1750. In the first place, and overemphasizing this fact is difficult, this period saw a *strengthening* of the state structures, at least in the core states and in the rising semiperipheral ones, as a way of coping with the contraction; the comparable contraction between 1300 and 1450, on the other hand, led precisely to acute internecine warfare among the landed nobility, a virtual *Götterdammerung* of feudal Europe. Not that wars and destruction were unknown in the seventeenth century, quite the contrary; but they did not have the same character of massive bleeding of the ruling strata. The modes of warfare had changed; the use of mercenaries was widespread; and above all, the struggles of the seventeenth century were interstate rather than interbaronial and thus could serve to the accretion of someone's economic strength. As Elliott put it in his discussion of the so-called crisis: "The sixteenth and seventeenth centuries did indeed see significant changes in the texture of European life, but these changes occurred within the resilient framework of the aristocratic monarchical state."[82] Resilience is precisely what keeps contractions from becoming crises.

In the second place, there was constant economic activity somewhere, activity that from close up seemed to be the sign of prosperity. I pass over the most obvious instances: Holland's Golden Age, the German upturn from the late seventeenth century, the steady improvement in English agronomy, and in short, "throughout this somber and difficult seventeenth century, the accumulation of an infinity of minor improvements."[83] Such less frequently observed phenomena include the fact that land reclamation never really ceased, as Romano reminds us:

> Land reclamation (*bonifiche*)? It still went on in the seventeenth century; it was simply not paid for with money, but rather by means of corvées, service, abusive exactions (*soprusi*), etc. It is in this sense that it can well be said that "agricultural production, unlike other kinds, hardly diminished in the seventeenth century."[84]

It should not surprise us that there seemed to many entrepreneurs in the seventeenth century "an absence of safe and productive outlets for investment";[85] this is, after all, one of the meanings of contraction. When Chaunu describes the seventeenth century as one in which "profit retreats but . . .

[80] Schöffer (1966, 106).
[81] Chaunu (1967, 263).
[82] Elliott (1969, 55).
[83] Chaunu (1967, 265).

[84] Romano (1962, 512); the internal quote is Bulferetti (1953, 44, n. 77).
[85] Minchinton (1974, 160).

victorious rent triumphs,"[86] he is thus misleading us. He is, in fact, describing the shift *toward* agricultural investment in the *core* countries of the capitalist world-economy.

Hobsbawm finds a paradox in the history of capitalism:

> We are therefore faced with the paradox that capitalism can only develop in an economy which is already substantially capitalist, for in any which is not, the capitalist forces will tend to adapt themselves to the prevailing economy and society, and will therefore not be sufficiently revolutionary.[87]

But is it really a paradox that a predominantly *industrial* capitalist world-economy can only emerge out of a capitalist world-economy already in existence—which is exactly what happened? The way in which the capitalist world-economy persisted and stabilized in the period between 1600 and 1750 it was unable to do between 1300 and 1450 (precisely because the expansion between 1150 and 1300 had not yet broken the binds of the feudal structure of Europe); and for this reason the seventeenth century could prepare the way for the spurt of the so-called industrial revolution—economically, politically, intellectually, and socially.[88]

We must not overlook the revolution of mores, for example, which had no counterpart in the late Middle Ages, the steady rise of an ascetic sexual morality from the sixteenth to the eighteenth centuries and all that it imposed on family structures to make them adapt to a capitalist world. Chaunu, as usual, is a bit swept away with his idealist imagery; but he is not really off the mark in his argument:

> The seventeenth century is, in terms of mores, the great, perhaps the only revolutionary century, with respect to traditional civilization, the iconoclastic century *par excellence*! It thus achieved, paradoxically, one of the preconditions for the Malthusian revolution.[89]

Again we ask, wherein is the paradox? Indeed we can raise the question of whether the Industrial Revolution was not already going on in the seventeenth century. Charles Wilson is daring enough to suggest this:

> Was there an absolute difference between the economic development of the later, so-called, Industrial Revolution and that of seventeenth-century Holland? Most historians would probably say yes there was. But can we be so sure? . . . Dutch shipbuilding was itself, in contemporary terms, a basic industry, as transport engineering was to be in the nineteenth century.[90]

---

[86] Chaunu (1967, 264). Spooner points out that land was only one of the outlets for commercial fortunes at this time. He also lists the Thirty Years' War, the states, the great companies, and new technology (1970, 100–103).

[87] Hobsbawm (1960, 104).

[88] The accomplishment of this period as opposed to the earlier period is caught by Chaunu: "With a range of tools, of which the most perfected date from the thirteenth century, European man in the sixteenth threw the net of the first global economy. The paradox is not there. Is it not rather that, from 1550 to 1750, classical Europe managed to maintain this miracle? Before the transport revolution of the mid-eighteenth century." (1966a, 277–278).

[89] Chaunu (1966a, 209).

[90] Wilson (1973, 331).

Let us not forget that the period from 1600 to 1750 *continued* and *furthered* one crucial process of the world-economy: the steady breakdown, as the survey by Braudel and Spooner demonstrates, of price differentials in the three basic price zones of Europe.

> The unmistakeable closing of the gap between [maximum and minimum prices] from the early eighteenth century shows how far prices throughout Europe had begun to converge. . . . By over-exploiting . . . price differentials, merchant capitalism contributed to a process of levelling out, to the creation of channels of communication, and in turn to a diversion of interests looking elsewhere for more favourable conditions.[91]

That is the point. There was a capitalist process going on from the sixteenth to the eighteenth century that made possible the industrial spurt, and the leveling of prices was an essential element in this.

One crucial difference remains, it seems to me, between the period from 1450 to 1750, when a capitalist world-economy was created and alternative historical possibilities progressively eliminated, and the period from 1150 to 1450, when, it might be argued, a similar attempt was made but failed because the political coherence of the feudal economy had not yet fallen apart through its internal contradictions. This crucial difference is to be found in the pattern of distribution of income within the overall economy.

Wilhelm Abel's major point in his book on mass poverty in preindustrial Germany was that Friedrich Engels's argument in *Conditions of the Working Class in England in 1844* that conditions of the workers deteriorated with industrialization was totally wrong. According to Abel, who cites the work of Bruno Hildebrand, "poverty was greatest [in Germany] precisely in those regions where there was no industry."[92] In fact, says Abel, mass poverty predated industrialism, going back to the sixteenth century:

> The severest decline [in real wages] occurred in the sixteenth century. Subsequently real wages rose in Germany soon after the Thirty Years' War and elsewhere in the beginning of the eighteenth century. Nonetheless, these wages . . . were not much higher than those of the second half of the sixteenth century (and very much lower than the wages of the fifteenth century). The Age of Pauperism (1791–1850) completes this series with a renewed decline, but least of all in early-industrializing England.[93]

The point of Abel's book was to argue that the Industrial Revolution meant a rise in the standard of living for the working classes. This question falls outside our present context, although his own reference to the period between 1791 and 1850 indicates that this might not be so for the world-

---

[91] Braudel and Spooner (1967, 395). Achilles speaks of the Amsterdam price for wheat having become "standard for all Europe" (1959, 52).

[92] Abel (1972, 7).

[93] Abel (1972, 63), who illustrates this phenomenon with a graph showing the real wages of a mason in kilograms of wheat (used for bread) in England, Strasbourg, Vienna, and Leipzig.

economy as a whole. What is pertinent to our present discussion is his argument that there was an overall decline in the income of the lower strata in the period from 1450 to 1800. This argument finds confirmation in other writings. Minchinton, taking the period between 1500 and 1750, hazarded a few generalizations about the "structure of demand" in Europe: "It was better to be rich in 1750 than in 1500," he says, and "the gulf between rich and poor widened."[94] Braudel and Spooner came up with similar conclusions by looking at the price data:

> From the late fifteenth century until well into the beginning of the eighteenth century, the standard of living in Europe progressively declined. It would be interesting to make a close analysis, where possible, of conditions before this time, in the fourteenth and fifteenth centuries. Broadly speaking, conditions then were better. Did this time constitute a golden age for labour, as so many excellent historians have claimed, before the repeated and violent upsets which we have noted?[95]

In a table that I constructed from Slicher van Bath's data, the real wages of an English carpenter from 1251 to 1850[96] show *a steady rise from 1251 to 1450,* with a doubling over that period and a *more or less steady decline after that,* returning in the end to the starting point (with one exceptionally low period between 1601 and 1650). To interpret this, we must look again at the so-called crisis of feudalism. Perry Anderson has correctly stated that "a full awareness of the dynamism of the feudal mode of production has been one of the most important gains of medieval historiography in the last decades." This crisis then does not build on failure but on success, on "the remarkable overall economic and social progress that [feudalism] represented."[97] Yet by the thirteenth century, following three to four centuries of steady expansion, the system found itself in crisis.

I have previously explained[98] why I believe this resulted from a conjuncture of a cyclical economic regression, climatological changes, and secular exacerbations of the basic contradictions of a feudal structure. Anderson's subsequent and somewhat detailed analysis of this historical conjuncture places central emphasis on the fact that "the basic motor of rural reclamation, which had driven the whole feudal economy forwards for three centuries, eventually overreached the objective limits of both terrain and social structure."[99] While emphasizing what might be called the socio-

[94] Minchinton (1974, 168).

[95] Braudel and Spooner (1967, 429). See also Teuteberg on the "depecoration" (increasing meatlessness) of Europe in the period between the late Middle Ages and 1800 (1975, 64–65).

[96] See Wallerstein (1974, 80, Table I). Le Roy Ladurie reports that M. Baulart shows that the highpoint for a Parisian worker's salary over the fifteenth through eighteenth centuries was from 1440 to 1498. (1973, 434). Fanfani asserts that Italian real wages declined by 50% in the sixteenth century

(1959, 345).

[97] P. Anderson (1974b, 182).

[98] See Wallerstein (1974, 21–37).

[99] P. Anderson (1974b, 197), for whom the crisis was not exclusively agricultural: "At the same time, the urban economy now hit certain critical obstacles to its development. . . . There was a pervasive scarcity of money which inevitably affected banking and commerce." This scarcity is explained by Anderson in terms of a "technical barrier" in mining (1974b, 199).

economic exhaustion of the system, Anderson criticizes the "empirically questionable and theoretically reductionist" explanation advanced by Dobb and Kosminsky that the crisis resulted from "a linear escalation of noble exploitation," because it "does not seem to square with the general trend of rent relationships in this epoch."[100]

The confusion here is worth taking some time to untangle. Some empirical evidence for the hypothesis of linear escalation is in fact to be found in Anderson's own book, where he noted, for example, that the average size of peasant holdings in medieval Europe dropped "from perhaps some 100 acres in the ninth century to 20 or 30 acres in the thirteenth century."[101] He also noted that the stratum of smaller nobles and ministerial intermediaries between magnates and the peasantry "tended to rise steadily [in social and economic importance] throughout the whole medieval period."[102] Presumably, this must have meant an increased percentage of the economic surplus was going to nonproductive workers and, therefore, that there was a linear escalation of noble exploitation. In this case it would be the combination of the steady socioeconomic exhaustion and the increased exploitation (did not the former lead to the latter partly as a way of equilibrating the individual incomes of members of the upper strata?) that brought on (along with reinforcement, as I noted, from other factors) the famous crisis of seigniorial revenues resulting from the "widening scissors in the relationship between urban and agricultural prices."[103]

One of the *consequences* of this "scissors" was the general change in rent relationships that occurs precisely in the period of economic downturn. Anderson says:

> Far from the general crisis of the feudal mode of production worsening the conditions of the direct producers in the countryside, it thus ended by ameliorating it and emancipating them. It proved, in fact, the turning point in the dissolution of serfdom in the West.[104]

The impression here is of economic "scissors" followed by seigniorial reaction followed by relatively successful peasant resistance that ended in the dissolution of serfdom. "The demesne tilled by servile labour was an anach-

[100] P. Anderson (1974b, 198). I risk falling into this camp myself insofar as I associated myself with Hilton's version of this hypothesis; see Wallerstein, 1974, 23–24.

[101] P. Anderson (1974b, 186), who suggested in a private communication that this may have been due to partible inheritances and not escalation of exploitation.

[102] P. Anderson (1974b, 185), who suggests that this could be the result of increase in global output, again not of escalation of exploitation. But see the careful empirical study by Herlihy of rural Pistoia in the thirteenth century. In refutation of a Malthusian explanation of a population decline in the four-

teenth century, he points out that in the thirteenth, the peasants were "supporting a staggering level of rents"; they had sold perpetual rents on their land to investors in order to raise capital, and after 1250, "with the debasement of the coinage and a rapidly rising price of wheat, the value of perpetual rents also spurted, reaching their peak in the 1280s." In addition, the "countryside of Pistoia was supporting a tax six times as high as that paid by the city" (1965, 238, 240, 242).

[103] P. Anderson (1974b, 200–209), whose empirical description of the consequences is set forth pithily and with admirable clarity.

[104] P. Anderson (1974b, 204).

ronism in France, England, Western Germany, Northern Italy, and most of Spain by 1450."[105] I see the sequence somewhat differently. The socio-economic crisis weakened the nobility such that the peasants steadily increased their share of the surplus from 1250 to 1450 or 1500. This was true *throughout* Europe, west and east.[106] It was the increase in the standard of living of the lower strata moving in the direction of relative equalization of incomes, rather than the prior condition of "exhaustion," that for the upper strata represented the real crisis and the dilemma they had to face.

There was no way out of it without drastic social change. This way, as I have previously argued, was the creation of a capitalist world-system, a *new* form of surplus appropriation.[107] The replacement of the feudal mode by the capitalist mode was what constituted the seigniorial reaction; it was a great sociopolitical effort by the ruling strata to retain their collective privileges, even if they had to accept a fundamental reorganization of the economy and all the resulting threats to familiar modes of stratification. There would be some families, it was clear, who would lose out by such a shift; but many would not.[108] Additionally, and most importantly, the principle of stratification was not merely preserved; it was to be reinforced as well.

Does not the discovery that the standard of living of the European lower strata went *down* from 1500 to at least 1800 despite the fact that this period included both expansion (phase A) and contraction (phase B)? demonstrate how successful was the strategy, if such it could be called, of economic transformation? It should be noted that the empirical argument for income decline is made *not* by a critic of capitalism, but by an Abel *correcting* Engels. (Abel's mistaken belief that this decline was arrested after 1800 indicates only that he failed, for whatever reasons, to make his post-1800 calculations within the correct unit of analysis, that is, for the capitalist world-economy as a whole, the outer boundaries of which had expanded precisely at that point.)

We now return to our interpretation of the contraction between 1600 and 1750. To analyze the period from 1450 to 1750 as one long "transition" from feudalism to capitalism risks reifying the concept of transition, for we thus steadily reduce the periods of "pure" feudalism and "pure" capitalism and sooner or later arrive at zero, being left with nothing but transition. Fair enough—all is transition; but whenever we expand a partitive into a universal attribute, we merely displace the issue terminologically. We still

[105] P. Anderson (1974b, 209).

[106] Although one of the major themes of the pair of books by P. Anderson is the *divergent* paths of western and eastern Europe, even he admits that the "relative impact [of the crisis of feudalism] may if anything have been even greater" in eastern than in western Europe. Of course, he proceeds to argue that the cause of the crisis in the two areas was different (1974b, 246–248). But its reality was the same, and the beneficial consequences for the peasantry the same.

[107] See Wallerstein (1974, 37–38).

[108] P. Anderson himself indicates one of the ways of reducing the risk or slowing down the pace of the circulation of elites. He calls it *vincolismo*, referring to various juridicial devices introduced in the late seventeenth century and in the eighteenth to preserve large landed property within families "against the disintegrating pressures and vagaries of the capitalist market" (1974a, 56).

want to know *when* and *how* and *why* major alterations in social structures occurred. The ideological descriptions that systems convey about themselves are never true. It is always easy to find presumed instances of "noncapitalist" behavior in a capitalist world—all over Europe in 1650 and 1750 but also in 1850 and 1950. The mixture of such "noncapitalist" behavior, firms, and states with "capitalist" behavior, "capitalist" firms, or (the least happy usage of all) "capitalist" states within a capitalist world-economy is neither an anomaly nor transitional. The mixture is the essence of the capitalist system as a mode of production, and it accounts for how the capitalist world-economy has historically affected the civilizations with which it has coexisted in social space.

I have said that capitalism represented a solution for the crisis of feudalism; but solutions are the result of choices that have rallied the majority by overcoming resistance in individuals and groups who stand to lose by any given solution. Since losers are many and manifold, strange alliances are made, and the process is drawn out and unclear. Other "solutions" may be attempted. Charles V tried to recreate the universal monarchy, but he did not succeed.[109] The lower strata might have taken advantage of the cyclical downturn from 1600 to 1750 to create havoc with the system, thereby achieving a major reallocation of a now much bigger absolute surplus; but this did not happen because of the strengths of the state-machineries in the now core countries of the capitalist world-economy. Seeking in complicated ways to reconcile opposing forces, they survived and flourished in the long run only to the extent to which they promoted the interests of dominant economic strata in the world-economy as a whole. For Anderson, "absolutism was essentially . . . *a redeployed and recharged apparatus of feudal domination,* designed to clamp the peasant masses back into their traditional social position—despite and against the gains they had won by the widespread commutation of dues."[110]

I could accept Anderson's entire statement if the adjective *feudal* were dropped. To me, the redeployment precisely involved substituting capitalist domination for feudal domination, whatever the outer shell of public terminology. Even Anderson himself admits that there is an "apparent paradox of Absolutism"; he states that while absolutism was protecting "aristocratic property and privileges," it "could *simultaneously* ensure the basic interests of the nascent mercantile and manufacturing classes." To explain this paradox, Anderson invokes the fact that in the period before "machine industry" (thus, before about 1800), "merchant and machine capital" did not need a "mass" market and could therefore avoid a "radical rupture with the feudal agrarian order."[111] This is true; however, within the

---

[109] See Wallerstein (1974, 165–181); see also Yates (1975).

[110] P. Anderson (1974a, 18), who provides another formulation of the same argument: "The rule of the Absolutist State was that of the feudal nobility in the epoch of transition to capitalism" (1974a, 42).

[111] P. Anderson (1974a, 40).

capitalist world-economy taken as a whole, it remains true in the twentieth century. That is, the "need" of the mass market still encompasses less than the entire world population.

From the foregoing, we can understand why not all absolute monarchies were strong states and not all strong states were absolute monarchies. The key element is how strong the state was and not how absolute the form of government was. Of course we must explain the form, and we will then notice that in the seventeenth century the *strongest* states were those which dominated *economically*: the United Provinces were in first place, England was second, and France was only in third place. The English Revolution strengthened the English state, while the assertion by Louis XIV, *l'Etat c'est moi*, was a sign of the relative weakness of the state.

The seventeenth-century contraction was not a crisis in the system. Quite the contraty, it was a period of its consolidation. Schöffer catches the spirit of this when he suggests there was a positive side to the decline in the import of silver from Hispanic America in the late sixteenth century. The result, he suggests, is that in the seventeenth century "in general the price *average* remained at the same level," and this was "a stabilizing factor for economy, which had been ravaged by an all too extravagant inflation."[112]

The long sixteenth century had not merely been an inflationary era. It had been a structurally revolutionary one, not the least of which was the willingness of large groups of people to adopt new and radical ideas. The ideas of humanism and the Reformation had a heady quality to them that risked getting out of hand. The seventeenth century represented a period of calming down and cooling off. Classicism, like absolutism, was not a description of reality, but a program—a program of returning the political and cultural initiatives to the upper strata, the better to digest the fundamental social change that was represented by the genesis of a capitalist world economy. William Bouwsma characterizes the essential intellectual thrust of the seventeenth century as

> the *recovery* everywhere of the systematizing mentality, which rested on a positive estimate of man's intellect very different from the view that underlay the secularizing movement, and which insisted on relating all aspects of human experience to a central core of universal and therefore abstract truth.[113]

Politically and culturally, the seventeenth century represented a search for stability in form and structure that was concomitant with the moment of slowdown in the rate of development of the world-economy. Without such a period, the next qualitative leap forward would not have been possible. This makes the seventeenth century not a "crisis" but a needed change of

[112] Schöffer (1966, 97).
[113] Bouwsma (1970, 10, italics added). Bouwsma explains this concern for the "systematic rationality of the universe" in turn by going back to the "material conditions of the age: to the prolonged depression of the century, to its social dislocation, its wars and revolutions (p. 14)."

pace, not a disaster but an essential element in furthering the interests of those who benefited most from a capitalist system.[114] Because the period from 1600 to 1750 was so important in the *consolidation* of the European world-economy, it is worthwhile to make a careful analysis of why this was so. We will then be able to understand what mechanisms the capitalist strata use to cope in recurrent periods of contraction in the world-economy.

[114] Rabb speaks of the "colossal scope, the vast canvas" of the intellectual systems constructed between 1610 and 1660 (Bacon, Descartes, Spinoza, Hobbes), which he sees precisely as a response to crisis. "When that kind of aspiration lost its centrality in European culture, as it did from the 1660s on, one could tell yet again, that the uncertainties and thus the 'crisis' had been left behind" (1975, 58–59).

2

DUTCH HEGEMONY IN THE WORLD-ECONOMY

Figure 3: "Jan Uytenbogaert, Receiver-General," by Rembrandt van Rijn. The 1639 etching is more popularly known as "The Goldweigher." The style is one of affluent solemnity, almost sanctity; compare this with portraits of money-changers by sixteenth-century artists, who portrayed them as pince-nosed and dour-faced.

The core of the European world-economy was by 1600 firmly located in
northwest Europe, that is, in Holland and Zeeland; in London, the Home
Counties, and East Anglia; and in northern and western France.[2] The political units in which these core areas were located were rather different in
size, form, and politics, and they underwent significant changes in the following century and a half; but economically these zones were more alike
than different. As observed in the previous chapter, 1600 to 1750 was a
period of consolidation in which there was a slowdown in the rate of the
development of the world-economy. This was true overall; but the hallmark
of a capitalist economic system is that the overall central tendency is the
composite of strikingly different trends of the component sectors. With
slowdown and consolidation, difficult economic decisions are forced, and
hence political (and cultural) convolutions are fostered. Nowhere was this
truer than in the core countries of the seventeenth century, among whose
entrepreneurial strata there was acute competition for survival in a situation
where some had to be eliminated to leave enough profit for the others.

History books call the period from 1600 to 1750 the age of *mercantilism.* I
have no intention of reviewing the multiple meanings given to this term or
the definitions that constitute its "essence."[3] The debate about mercantilism
largely concerns the truth-value of arguments put forward by theorists of
the seventeenth century. Obviously, their themes in some ways reflected
reality and in some ways were designed to act on reality. This is true of all
theories. But in the present context we are interested in the actual practices
of the states of the time, whatever the ideological justification. These practices are not unique to the time but were utilized by *some* states at almost
every moment of the history of the capitalist world-economy, although the
ideological justifications have varied. In the vast welter of explanations of
mercantilism in the seventeenth century, two aspects of this concept are
agreed upon by virtually everyone. Mercantilism involved state policies of
economic nationalism and revolved around a concern with the circulation
of commodities, whether in terms of the movement of bullion or in the
creation of balances of trade (bilateral or multilateral). What the facts were

[1] Geyl (1961, 37–38).

[2] J R Jones singles out these specific zones for
comparison between Britain and the United Provinces (see 1966, 40).

[3] A good overview of this debate is found in Coleman (1969). However, I cannot agree with Coleman's view that although mercantilism is a "red-
herring of historiography" as a label for policy, it is
useful as a description of economic theories (1957,
24). I should have thought the exact opposite was
true, that the theories were inconsistent because
they were apologia but that countries in certain positions tend to adopt policies that we call mercantilist.

37

regarding the true relation of "profit and power" is what the debate is about—among men of the time and among analysts of today.

To argue that economic nationalism is the state policy of the weaker against the stronger and of competitors against each other is merely to accept an orthodoxy. What will perhaps be somewhat different in this book is the assertion that success in mercantilist competition was primarily a function of productive efficiency and that the *middle*-run objective of all mercantilist state policies was the increase of overall efficiency in the sphere of production. The story must start with the United Provinces because for at least part of the seventeenth century this "sand and mud dump left over from the ice age"[4] with a jerry-built and seemingly ineffectual state machinery was the hegemonic power of the capitalist world-economy. The United Provinces (or should we say Holland?) was the first such hegemonic power after the collapse of the attempt on the part of Charles V to convert the world-economy into a world-empire. Hegemony is a rare condition; to date only Holland, Great Britain, and the United States have been hegemonic powers in the capitalist world-economy, and each held the position for a relatively brief period, Holland least plausibly because it was least of all the military giant of its era.

Hegemony involves more than core status. It may be defined as a situation wherein the products of a given core state are produced so efficiently that they are by and large competitive even in other core states, and therefore the given core state will be the primary beneficiary of a maximally free world market. Obviously, to take advantage of this productive superiority, such a state must be strong enough to prevent or minimize the erection of internal and external political barriers to the free flow of the factors of production; and to preserve their advantage, once ensconced, the dominant economic forces find it helpful to encourage certain intellectual and cultural thrusts, movements, and ideologies. The problem with hegemony, as we shall see, is that it is passing. As soon as a state becomes truly hegemonic, it begins to decline; for a state ceases to be hegemonic not because it loses strength (at least not until after a long time has elapsed), but because others gain. To be at the summit is to be certain that the future will not be yours, however much the present is; but it is sweet nonetheless. The pattern of hegemony seems marvelously simple. Marked superiority in agro-industrial productive efficiency leads to dominance of the spheres of commercial distribution of world trade, with correlative profits accruing both from being the entrepôt of much of world trade and from controlling the "invisibles"—transport, communications, and insurance. Commercial primacy leads in turn to control of the financial sectors of banking (exchange, deposit, and credit) and of investment (direct and portfolio).

These superiorities are successive, but they overlap in time. Similarly, the

[4] Van Veen (1950, 11). A good brief description of the geological conditions of the Netherlands be- fore its modifications as the result of human intervention is found in Schöffer (1973, 9–13).

loss of advantage seems to be in the same order (from productive to commercial to financial), and also largely successive. It follows that there is probably only a short moment in time when a given core power can manifest *simultaneously* productive, commercial, and financial superiority *over all other core powers*. This momentary summit is what we call hegemony. In the case of Holland, or the United Provinces, that moment was probably between 1625 and 1675. Dutch productive efficiency was first achieved in the historically oldest form of food production, that of gathering, in this case the gathering of fish, particularly (but not only) salted herring, the "Dutch Gold Mine."[5] The origins of this efficiency are to be found in the invention around 1400 of the *haringbuis,* or buss,[6] a fishing boat whose high length-to-breadth ratio offered "greater maneuverability, seaworthiness and speed without great losses in cargo space."[7] The two great advantages to the buss were that its design made possible the use of a large dragnet for herring, first noted at Hoorn in West Friesland in 1516,[8] and that its wider decks made curing possible on board. The new technology of curing, or gutting and salting the fish immediately and thus ensuring its preservation, had been developed in the thirteenth century.[9] The creation of this "factory ship"[10] enabled ships to go far from Dutch shores, staying out from six to eight weeks. The busses transferred their cargo to *ventjagers,* or sale-hunters, fast ships that returned to shore with the produce.[11]

Not only did the Dutch dominate the North Sea herring fishery, the so-called Grand Fishery,[12] but they dominated the Iceland cod fishery and the Spitzbergen whale fishery as well.[13] Whales were in fact not wanted as food but as an industrial product. The whales supplied "train oil", used for soap and lamp fuel, and bone, used in connection with clothing.[14] The

[5] See Wilson (1941, 3). Andrews traces the expression to a proclamation of the States-General on July 19, 1624 (1915, 541). Meynert Semeyns wrote in 1639: "The Dutch catch more herrings and prepare them better than any other nation ever will; and the Lord has, through the instrument of the herring, made Holland an exchange and staple-market for the whole of Europe. The herring keeps Dutch trade going, and Dutch trade sets the world afloat", *Corte beschryvinge over de Haring vischerye in Hollandt,* cited in Beaujon (1884, 60–61). The French analyst Luazc wrote in 1778 that fishing was "the cradle of [Dutch] commerce" (**I,** 19).

[6] See H. P. H. Jansen (1978, 13). R. W. Unger's more precise date for the boat's first appearance, in Hoorn, is 1415 (1978, 30).

[7] R. W. Unger (1978, 30). In the beginning the ratio was 2.5 : 1. By 1570, it was 4.5 : 1, "markedly greater than even that for the most advanced sailing ships." There was, however, a technical limit on the ratio: "The pull on the net could not be too great."

[8] See R. W. Unger (1978, 29–30).

[9] See Schöffer (1973, 72–73). Spoilage occurred within 24 to 48 hours. See Michell (1977, 142).

[10] Michell (1977, 148), who notes that this ship was "of a sort only recently reintroduced into fishing." On board were three kinds of workers: gippers (removers of the intestines), curers (adders of the salt), and fishermen.

[11] See Parry (1967, 172).

[12] They could thus exploit three herring-fishing seasons: one in June and July, around the Orkneys, Shetlands, and the north of Scotland; one in August, from Dunbar in Scotland to Yorkshire; and one in September to November, off Yarmouth. See Michell (1977, 139). Herring was known as the "poor man's steak." In Holland and West Friesland "the first herrings of the season were rushed inland by carts which raced one another to get to the market first" (Michell, 1977, 180).

[13] See Parry (1967, 167–173).

[14] Michell points this out and says: "The course of the whale fishery should therefore reflect the industrial rather than the demographic history of Europe. The failure of the English to achieve self-sufficiency (let alone a surplus) of whale products at

fishing industry was important not only for such forward linkages, but also for backward linkages such as net making, creating a situation "unique in Europe" in the proportion of the population "involved with fishing at least tangentially."[15] In the seventeenth century, it was "galling"[16] to the English that the Dutch could fish off English shores and sell fish competitively in English ports and, upon this advantage, build their "mother trade" in the Baltic. The English were very aware of this at the time. Sir George Downing wrote to Clarendon on July 8, 1661: "The herring trade [of the Dutch] is the cause of the salt trade, and the herring and salt trade are the causes of this country's having, in a manner, wholly engrossed the trade of the Baltic Sea for they have these bulky goods to load their ships with thither."[17] The control of the Baltic trade being precisely one of the factors that contributed to the efficiency of Dutch shipbuilding, the Dutch found themselves for some time in the happy circumstance of the spiral effect: circular reinforcement of advantage.

Despite Sir George Downing, herring cannot explain everything. The Dutch showed equal superiority in agriculture, the most fundamental productive enterprise of the time; and this was a prodigious achievement, both in the breadth of the consequences[18] as well as in the depth of effort, for the Netherlands was not at all well suited geologically for cereal growing[19] nor for most other forms of agriculture. Weakness was turned to strength in two ways, however. First, the process of pumping water out of the country in order to create land (poldering) led to the invention of windmills and the flourishing of the science of engineering, so that in many ways Holland became "the centre of the wood mechanical era."[20] Poldering went back to 1250, but its highpoint was during 1600–1625, when there was a sudden quantitative spurt; this high level was largely maintained from 1625 to 1675.[21] Hence Andrew Marvell's ill-placed sneer in *Character of Holland:* "So rules among the drownèd he that drains." The second result of difficult natural conditions was perhaps still more important. Necessity pushed the Dutch into intensified agriculture, first in about 1300, when earlier hard times and low prices had led to inventiveness, and later, be-

---

the height of their mercantile supremacy, while the Dutch maintained their position despite general economic decline, is interesting" (1977, 171).

[15] Michell (1977, 180).

[16] Wilson (1968, 64). The response to this was, as Cunningham noted in 1887, the "conscious imitation of the Dutch," words that served as the title of his second chapter in Book V of the first edition of *The Growth of English Industry and Commerce* (cited in Clark, 1960, 15).

[17] Cited in Wilson (1957a, 3).

[18] "How can we ignore the relationship between the remarkable development of Dutch agriculture

and the pre-eminence of the Low Countries in the seventeenth-century economic scene?" (De Maddalena, 1974a, 313). How indeed?

[19] See E. L. Jones (1967, 47).

[20] Van Veen (1950, 145).

[21] See Van Veen's chart (1950, 65). Slicher van Bath traces a positive correlation between agricultural prices and polder-making. "It stands out clearly that after 1664 the great period of polder-making had come to an end, at exactly the same time that the price of corn was going down and the general economic situation was deteriorating" (1977, 69; also 70, Table 4).

tween 1620 and 1750, when a greater expansion of intensive agriculture occurred.[22]

Since the soil was particularly bad for arable agriculture,[23] increased production could most easily be achieved by shifting to industrial crops such as flax, hemp, hops, horticulture, fruit culture, and to the very important production of dyes, of which, in the sixteenth and seventeenth centuries, the Dutch were the "most advanced growers in the world, meeting little competition."[24] Along with horticulture and arable crops went a sizeable increase in livestock husbandry.[25] Part of what made this concentration on industrial crops possible was the very large import of grain, which was no marginal matter. De Vries estimates that in the mid-seventeenth century, half the inhabitants of the provinces of Holland, Utrecht, Friesland, and Groningen were being fed from grain imports.[26] The other contributing factor was improvement in agricultural techniques—the disappearance of fallow,[27] the related cultivation of fodder crops, bed and row cultivation, the use of simple and inexpensive tools, and high yields through heavy fertilizing and much careful labor devoted to small areas.[28] The sowing of grasses and systematic fertilization also permitted larger herds and higher milk yields.[29] All this intensified agriculture both permitted and was fostered by increased urbanization and industrialization. "By the mid-seventeenth century most cities had franchised men to collect [industrial] refuse [such as ash] and sell and deliver it to farmers."[30] No wonder Romano calls the period from about 1590 to 1670 the "Dutch agricultural

[22] See Davis (1973b, 112–115), Slicher van Bath (1960, 153), and Wilson (1977a, 23–24). For Slicher van Bath, the intensification was the necessity to make a living for an increased and dense population during the period of relatively low grain-prices." But why could not others have done as much? Davis offers the argument that England and France did not match Dutch advances because, when the Dutch improvements of the thirteenth and fourteenth centuries diffused to them in the fifteenth and sixteenth centuries, Europe was in its expansionist phase and thus less hospitable to techniques of intensification, especially since between 1450 and 1650 peasants were at a highpoint of control over cultivated land and good pasture and were the class least open to innovation. He argues that the English and French were not at the same starting point in the seventeenth century as the Dutch.

[23] Land was unsuitable except for "a few favored districts where the soil lay relatively high and dry, such as the dune coast of Holland, parts of the islands south of the river Maas, and the coastal clays of Friesland" (J. de Vries, 1974, 71).

[24] Gibbs (1957, 693).

[25] J. de Vries (1974, 136–144).

[26] J. de Vries (1974, 172). This was, above all, a question of optimizing profit: "A tentative conclusion can be offered that the growth of trade cheapened the price of grain, which in the northern Netherlands could be produced only at high cost. If this is so, the region's economy enjoyed large savings in the form of relatively lower grain prices which, given grain's importance in any economy of that time, liberated funds for other purposes" (p. 182). See also van der Wee, who says that the rising trend of productivity in the northern Netherlands between 1500 and 1670 "was principally the result of pronounced specialisation: grain was imported *en masse* from the Baltic so that coastal areas could concentrate on dairy produce, horticulture, and industrial crops for the rapidly increasing, affluent population of the growing towns" (1978, 15).

A note of skepticism on the importance of the Baltic grain trade is sounded by Glamann, who objects on the grounds of hinterland trade, defined, however, as the Rhine, Flanders, northern France, and England (*sic!* 1977, 231–232).

[27] Slicher van Bath (1955, 181).

[28] Slicher van Bath (1960, 132, 147–148; 1955, 176–178).

[29] J. de Vries (1974, 142–144).

[30] J. de Vries (1974, 150).

century" as compared with the European agricultural sixteenth century.[31] The gap grew wider as the Dutch became ever more efficient and most of the rest of Europe stood relatively still in agricultural techniques.

The United Provinces not only was the leading agricultural producer of this time; it was also, and at the same time, the leading producer of industrial products. So much ink has been spilled to explain why Holland did not industrialize that we tend to overlook the fact that it did do so. To his credit, Charles Wilson has consistently insisted on this point throughout his large corpus of writings on the Netherlands.[32] Industrial advance is to be noticed first of all in textiles, the traditional leading sector. The northern Netherlands began to profit in the 1560s from the flow of refugees northward, brought about by the Netherlands Revolution. Textile production centered in Leiden,[33] where the "new draperies" (bays, says, camelots, fustians, etc.) for which England became famous, got their start. Over a hundred-year period, industrial production surged forward, and it reached a peak in the 1660s. (An index calculated for 1664 is 545 as compared with 100 for 1584, and 108 for 1795).[34] Not merely did production expand quantitatively, but until the 1660s, the chief industrial textile rival of Leiden, the "new draperies" of East Anglia, "had to fight an uphill battle."[35] Åström, assess-

---

[31] Romano (1962, 519).

[32] See for example Wilson's summary statement: "It is sometimes suggested that [the Dutch Republic] was a purely commercial economy that somehow failed to change gear into a phase of industrialism. . . . [As] far as seventeenth century conditions are concerned it is an exaggeration. . . . Much of the technology . . . was rationally concentrated on those economically highly profitable processes for finishing or refining raw materials or semi-manufactured products; this stimulated the flow of goods through the warehouses and markets" (1968, 30).

Contemporaries saw this clearly. J. J. Becher, economic advisor to Emperor Leopold I in Vienna, advocating the encouragement of manufactures, wrote in 1673: "Dutchmen produce silk, and yet it does not grow in the country; they buy flax and hemp from foreigners and produce lace and beautiful linen which they export again; they work up foreign wool into cloth which they export; they produce leather from foreign raw materials and export it" (*Politischer Discours*, 2nd ed., Frankfurt, 1673, p. 173, cited in Klima, 1965, 97).

[33] Leiden was an important producer of textiles for export after 1350. See H. P. H. Jansen (1978, 11). Jansen argues that the industries of Holland got a crucial boost in the period from 1350 to 1400; having been less affected by depopulation due to the lesser impact of the Black Death, Holland was "better able to compete against the surrounding areas with their decimated populations and their occa-

sionally hostile guild organizations" (p. 17).

[34] Faber *et al.* (1974, 7).

[35] Wilson (1965, 55). Glamann sees the situation more in terms of a division of labor: "A glance at the period 1620–1700 shows that while woollens are in decline in England and worsteds are prosperous, the converse is true of Leiden. The woollens of Leiden, known as *lakens,* do very well in competition with the English product, while England leads in the worsteds group" (1974, 505). Notice, however, that Wilson is speaking of roughly 1570 to 1670.

The end of the Truce in 1621, which cut off Spanish-controlled territories as textile export markets, is seen by Israel as a clear setback for Dutch production of cheap, light draperies. "Leiden managed to compensate for its losses by expanding the production of old draperies, the celebrated *lakens* which were more suited to northern European markets; but although the overall value of textiles produced at Leiden undoubtedly increased between 1621 and 1648 (old draperies being costlier than new draperies), in terms of quantity of cloth produced and of labour required, Leiden in fact declined" (1977, 61). For Deyon, this shift, which he dates after 1650, is the consequence of the competition of Tilburg, Verviers, and Bois-le-Duc, in relation to which Leiden was at a disadvantage because of its high cost of living and high wage levels. Leiden "abandoned the most labor-intensive manufactures . . . [and] devoted herself once again to luxury products, thick cloths, camelots mixed with goat and camel skin" (1978d, 267).

ing the source of Dutch strength in seventeenth-century Baltic trade, gives efficiency of textile production as his *first* explanation and the fact that they were intermediaries for *English* cloth (and southern European salt) as his *second*[36]—a productive advantage first and a commercial advantage second, following upon and abetted by the first.

This advantage is clearly demonstrated in the history of the Alderman Cockayne's Project, by which England sought to reverse a situation where English undyed and undressed cloth was sent to Holland for finishing. In 1614 James I forbade the export of cloth "in the white," and the Dutch retaliated by prohibiting the import of finished goods; to which James I retorted by prohibiting, once again, the export of wool. It was, as Supple says, a "gigantic gamble"[37] and one that abysmally failed. Over a three-year period, English exports fell by a third, and the Project died in 1617. The stake had been high. Wilson has calculated that 47% of the value added was in the process of dyeing, and this was done in Holland.[38] The reason England could not have won this gamble leaps into view, for we have already noted the enormous advantage Holland enjoyed at this time in the production of dyes and hence the cost of dyeing. In the first half of the seventeenth century, therefore, English competition with the United Provinces in cloth trade, as with fisheries, reflected "mercantilist hopes unfulfilled."[39]

The second great industry of early modern times was shipbuilding, and here too the lead of the United Provinces is common knowledge.[40] Less widely acknowledged but essential to a clear analysis is the fact that the Dutch shipbuilding industry was "of modern dimensions, inclining strongly toward standardised, repetitive methods."[41] It was highly mechanized and used many labor-saving devices—wind-powered sawmills, powered feeders for saws, block and tackles, great cranes to move heavy timbers—all of which increased productivity.[42] The linkage with an industrial-commercial complex is striking. There were a series of ancillary industries in Amsterdam—rope yards, biscuit bakeries, ship chandlering, and the construction of nautical instruments and sea charts.[43] To build the ships themselves, wood was required—a lot of wood. It is estimated that one warship required 2000 oak trees that needed a century of maturation so the wood would not split too easily; and 2000 oak trees required at the time 50 acres of woodland.[44] One major source of this timber was the Baltic, and one

[36] Åstrom (1963, 61). The third factor listed is "colonial products."

[37] Supple (1959, 34).

[38] Wilson (1965, 71). In general, says Wilson, "the biggest profit margins" lay in "the refined technology of dyeing and dressing the cloth which [in turn] provides the key to the control of the markets" (1968, 29).

[39] Wilson (1957a, 40).

[40] See Kellenbenz (1977a, 531).

[41] Wilson (1973, 329). See also Michell: "The real

Dutch achievement was not in building large ships, but in achieving a consistent quality in their product" (1977, 152).

[42] See R. W. Unger (1978, 7) and Kindleberger (1975, 618).

[43] See van Klaveren (1969a, 183).

[44] See Naish (1957, 493), see also Sella (1974, 392–394). Barbour attributes the lower cost of Dutch as compared with English shipbuilding to the fact that the English could not import timber and other materials cheaply—the cost of materials in

major reason the Dutch cornered this trade was their efficiency in textile production. The consequence, of course, was efficiency in shipbuilding, which, as we shall see, was largely the reason the Dutch could dominate world commerce. Furthermore, since other Dutch industries in addition to shipbuilding were "wholly dependent" on supplies brought by water, the ships "must be seen as a genuine factor of *production*."[45] Hence, shipbuilding was production of the means of production.

Textiles and shipbuilding were not the only industries of significance. Holland was a leading center of sugar refining, at least until 1660.[46] There was a "powerful boom" in distilleries beginning shortly after 1600 and lasting through the century. Other industries were a paper industry; sawmills; book production; a brick and lime industry, expanding about 1500 and still "reasonably prosperous" in the eighteenth century; crockery; tobacco and pipe-making factories; very large tanneries directed toward export, especially in the seventeenth century; breweries, reaching their height at the turn of the seventeenth century; oil and soap production, whose greatest prosperity was in the middle of the seventeenth century; of course a chemical industry, whose primary function was to provide dyestuffs;[47] and one must not omit the munitions industry. Spurred by the Eighty Years' War and the Thirty Years' War, the import of war materials was encouraged by the government, and the industry steadily expanded. A large export trade existed by the end of the sixteenth century; as of 1600, the structure of production had shifted from artisanal guilds to manufacture and the putting-out system.[48]

It is not that in the hundred years between 1575 and 1675, the United Provinces excelled in every industrial field or had no effective competition; but if it is to be asserted, as it is by North and Thomas, that the Netherlands was the "first country to achieve self-sustained growth,"[49] it is primarily because no other country showed such a coherent, cohesive, and integrated agro-industrial production complex—and this despite the economic complications of fighting an eighty-year war of independence.[50] There were no

shipbuilding being eight times the cost of labor. The Dutch advantage was "cheap purchasing, low freights, and low duties" (1954, 238).

[45] Wilson (1977a, 39).

[46] Amsterdam had 60 refineries in 1661. Most French and English colonial sugar was refined there until the English Navigation Act of 1660 and similar restrictions enacted by Colbert. See Masefield (1967, 293).

[47] See Faber *et al.* (1974, 4–10); Deyon (1978d, 289); Supple (1977, 429). On book production, see Hazard (1964, 112), who points out that as late as 1699, five of the ten major book-printing centers were in Holland and there were 400 printers in Amsterdam alone.

[48] See Klein (1966, 195–197) and Barbour (1963,

35–41).

[49] North and Thomas (1973, 145). Speaking of twentieth-century circumstances, Stephen Hymer and Stephen Resnick say: "In our view a major substitution that occurs in the process of development is not the replacement of leisure or idleness by work, but rather the shift from inferior methods of home production to superior methods based on specialization and exchange" (1969, 503). Does this not summarize well what occurred in the United Provinces at this time?

[50] G. Parker tries to assess the positive and negative economic effects of the Dutch Revolt and concludes that on the whole, it brought more loss than gain, though not by much (1974b, 11–15). Wilson on the other hand says: "After forty years of war the

more careful observers of the Dutch scene in the seventeenth century than the English. In 1673, Sir William Temple, the English Ambassador, published his *Observations upon the United Provinces,* in which he said:

> I conceive the true origin and ground of trade to be great multitudes of people crowded into small compass of land, whereby all things necessary to life are rendered dear, and all men who have possessions are induced to parsimony; but those who have none are forced to industry and labor. Bodies that are vigorous fall to labor; such as are not supply that defect by some sort of invention and ingenuity. These customs arise first from necessity and grow in time to be habitual in a country.[51]

Sir William wished that as much might have been said of the English.

Confirmation of this vitality can be found in the figures of population movement and urbanization. It is well known that there was a major migration, especially of artisans and burgesses, from the southern to the northern Netherlands, above all from Antwerp[52] to Amsterdam and Leiden[53] in the late sixteenth century. In 1622, 60% percent of the population of the United Provinces were townsfolk; and of these, three-quarters were in towns with over 10,000 people.[54] The population of Amsterdam quadrupled—from 50,000 in 1600 to 200,000 in 1650,[55] and it served as a veritable "melting pot," turning Flemings, Walloons, Germans, Portuguese and German Jews, and French Huguenots into "true Dutchmen."[56] Most writers concentrate on the merchant and artisanal strata who migrated; it is at least as important to observe the growth, especially but not only in Leiden, of a mass of urban proletarians who were living in slums, many of the workers employed being female and child labor. As Jeannin says so aptly, "the tensions and the conflicts have a modern resonance."[57] Of course they do, because we are in the presence of industrial capitalism. In summary, it can be said that in the late sixteenth century, the northern Netherlands was set firmly on the path of a productive efficiency that enabled the United Provinces to flower in about 1600 into the principal (though of

underlying economic strength of the northern Netherlands had never been greater than it was at the Truce of 1609" (1968, 22). The two assessments are not necessarily contradictory if Wilson's statement is taken as an assessment of the Dutch *relative* position in the world-economy.

[51] London, 1673, p. 187, cited in Furniss (1957, 102).

[52] See the analysis of the stages of the decline of Antwerp in Van Houtte (1962, 707–712).

[53] See the striking map prepared by Mols (1974, 63). See also Jeannin (1969, 71).

[54] See Helleiner (1967, 46).

[55] Kossmann (1970, 366).

[56] Verlinden (1964, 329). On the attraction of Holland for lower strata people of Westphalia seeking to make their fortune, see Beutin (1939, 131–132); for the whole northwest of Germany, see

Kuske (1956, 255).

[57] Jeannin (1969, 75). We even see urban planning similar to that of the twentieth century as a response to the conflicts. Between 1585 and 1622, the three great canals of Amsterdam were built—the Heerengracht, the Keisergracht, and the Prinsengracht. Thereupon, the polluting industries—breweries, metalworking, dyeworks, glassmaking, soapmaking, sugar refineries—were forbidden in the center of the city. "They were confined to a workers' quarter outside the city to the west, the Jordaan, where speculators had built small low houses for the immigrants and where the social security agency (*prévoyance*) of the Regents had installed several charitable institutions. It was the first example of systematic zoning, heavily segregationist and bourgeois" (Deyon, 1978e, 299).

course not the only) production center of the European world-economy. In the agricultural sector it specialized in products that required high skills and made high profits[58] and in the industrial sector, Holland took a commanding lead in textiles and shipbuilding, the two major industries of the era, and played a major, sometimes dominant, role in other industries as well. It is on the basis of this productive efficiency that the United Provinces was able to build its commercial network and establish itself as the "packhouse of the world."[59] It is to this somewhat more familiar story that we now turn.

Dutch shipping dominated the world carrying trade in the seventeenth century. It grew tenfold from 1500 to 1700. As of 1670, the Dutch owned three times the tonnage of the English, and more than the tonnage of England, France, Portugal, Spain, and the Germanies combined. The percentage of Dutch-*built* ships was even greater. Dutch shipping reached its heyday, in fact, only in the second half of the seventeenth century, the Dutch having used the occasion of the English Civil War to establish "undisputed ascendancy in the world's carrying trade." While Dutch ships carried all Dutch textiles, English ships, despite monopolies and chartered companies, had to share with Dutch ships the carrying of English textiles, indeed had the lesser share.[60] As late as 1728, Daniel Defoe was still referring to the Dutch as "the Carryers of the World, the middle Persons in Trade, the Factors and Brokers of Europe."[61] What is so impressive about the Dutch in the seventeenth century is that they "spread everywhere"[62]—to the East Indies, the Mediterranean, Africa, and the Caribbean, while still holding on to the Baltic (Eastland) trade; they expanded their share of the trade of northwest Europe and seized the river trade inland to the continent.

The story of the East Indies trade is of course the story of the *Vereenigde Oost-Indische Compagnie* (VOC). It was a model of a capitalist trading company, part speculative enterprise, part long-term investment, part colonizer.[63] It had sober directors in Amsterdam, *De Heeren Zeventien*, the seventeen gentlemen, and hard-to-control proconsuls in Batavia, first among them Jan Pieterszoon Coen.[64] In some ways the Dutch backed into the East Indies trade. When Antwerp fell to the Spanish in 1585, the Euro-

---

[58] Even among grains, which were a relatively minor agricultural product, there was a shift in the seventeenth century from barley to wheat, "a crop of more exacting production requirements" (J. de Vries, 1974, 148).

[59] This expression of the time is reported in Clark (1960, 14).

[60] The quote is from Lipson (1956, **II**, liii). See also Lipson (1956, **III**, 10–11), Parry (1967, 176, 210), Glamann (1974, 452), and Minchinton (1974, 164). Bowman says that as of 1650, Dutch ships numbered 15,000–16,000 out of the 20,000 ships in

the world carrying trade (1936, 338).

[61] From *A Man of the English Commerce*, p. 192, cited in Wilson (1941, 4).

[62] Coornaert (1967, 244).

[63] For a description of the legal structure of the VOC, see Rabe (1962, 351–366).

[64] Despite the claim of Werner Sombart and the outward similarity of names, Coen is not Cohen, and he was *not* Jewish. For the speculation about why Coen's father changed the family name from van Twisk to Cöen, see Masselman (1963, 229–230).

pean spice market was transferred to Amsterdam. But since Spain had annexed Portugal in 1580 and Lisbon was the European port of entry for spices, the Dutch sought to bypass the Spanish.[65] Thus Cornelis de Houtman was sent on his mission to the Indies in 1592, the first trading fleets sailed in 1598, and by 1602 the States-General had chartered the VOC, in part to contain ruinous competition among the Dutch, in part to provide a stable outlet for the smaller investor, in part to create an economic and political weapon against Spain, and in part simply to get more spices than were available then in Europe.[66]

It was, in fact, a good moment to get into the sea-borne spice trade; the most important blockages of the overland trade across the Levant occurred not, as is often said, between 1450 and 1500, but rather between 1590 and 1630.[67] The opportunity was therefore great, and the Dutch seized it. The principal shipping lanes of the Indian Ocean shifted from the northern half (the Red Sea and the Persian Gulf) to the southern half (the Cape route). The Dutch were able to exploit this opportunity because they had the technology with which to do so. As Parry puts it, "the square sail triumphed over the lateen, the trade wind over the monsoon";[68] but as soon as the Dutch were into this trade, they encountered the basic problem of trade with an external arena. Because it was a trade in luxuries, profits were high and competition keen; but because it was a trade in luxuries and not necessities, the market was inherently small, and glutting the market was a serious possibility—Scylla and Charybdis.[69] There were only two ways to handle the dilemma. Either one transformed the nature of the trade by incorporating the Indies as a peripheral zone of the capitalist world-economy or one had to resort to "administered" trade in the traditional fashion of the long-distance commerce between world-empires. Which path to follow was in fact the subject of the ongoing debate between Coen and *De Heeren Zeventien*. Coen, the "partisan of a strong manner in Asia,"[70] pushed for the first option; his superiors in Amsterdam for the second.

Coen said that the peripheralization of the East Indies would require a policy of colonization in two senses: establishing political control in order to

[65] They would bypass the Spanish-Portuguese not only by skipping Lisbon, but by skipping India as well and going to the Indonesian source of the trade. See Parry (1967, 195).

[66] See Masselman (1963, *passim,* but especially 62–66 and 141–179). Morineau emphasizes the fact that there was a penury of spices in Europe with consequent high prices. (1978c, 133).

[67] See Duncan (1975, 512); also Glamann (1974, 477), who notes: "So convincing was the victory of 'Atlantic' pepper [over 'Mediterranean' pepper] that it was even re-exported to the Levant." For the earlier period, see the discussion in Wallerstein (1974, 215–216, 325).

[68] Parry (1967, 199).

[69] The metaphor is used by Glamann (1974, 483), who emphasizes limited demand for spices in Europe. Rich notes the parallel problem on the other side of the dyad: "[The] spice trade was conditioned by the fact that the Spice Islands wanted very little of the produce of Europe save firearms. . . . Here the Dutch came up against the same problem as their fur-traders were to meet in North America. Once their immediate wants were satisfied, the islanders were indifferent to trade" (1967, 368). Meilink-Roelofsz similarly states: "There was hardly any demand for European products in Asia" (1968, 66).

[70] Morineau (1978e, 170).

constrain relatively strong Asian potentates and reorganize the system of production; and exporting a white settler class, both to help with supervising cash-crop production and to provide a secure initial market for European exports other than bullion. He said that such a policy was incompatible with administered trade, and required the operation of a market principle. The terminology in which this was discussed is often referred to, somewhat misleadingly, as free trade versus monopoly;[71] but in fact Coen was not opposed to the VOC monopolizing *in the market* (and indeed with a judicious assist from time to time of brute force); nor were *De Heeren Zeventien* unaware of the limits of their ability to restrict access to their administered trade over such great distances.[72] It was a matter of what made most sense to capitalist entrepreneurs in the short run—the profits of exploitation or the profits of speculation. In the short run, those who were in favor of speculation prevailed;[73] but in the long run, as we have previously argued,[74] the profits of productive exploitation are the only solid base on which to stay ahead in the capitalist world-economy. The core powers (not only the Netherlands, but also Britain and France) launched in the eighteenth century the peripheralization of the Indian Ocean arena, which really took root after 1750.[75]

[71] See the discussion, by no means untypical, in Masselman (1963, 433–442).

[72] Coen wrote in a letter to *De Heeren Zeventien*: "There is nothing in the world that gives one a better right than power and force added to right." Cited in Boxer (1965, 98–99). Indeed, according to an assessment by Geyl, the VOC was, "in the Indian world, the power of the sword" (1961, 188). As for *De Heeren Zeventien,* Boxer notes that they "explicitly recognized" that there were three categories of trade: areas (few in number) where they had territorial control; areas where they had monopoly contracts; "free-trade" areas. The last category, as Boxer observes, "was nearly always the most important" (1965, 94). Parry notes that except for the "long-haul trade," the Dutch faced the active competition of Chinese, Malay, Arab, and non-Dutch European traders (1967, 197).

One of the reasons the English could compete with the Dutch in the Indies trade but not in the Baltic trade had precisely to do with the nature of "rich" trades versus "bulk" trades. The cost of shipbuilding mattered more in bulk trades, and for this reason, the English wrote them off at the time as "lost trades." In the Indies (and in the Mediterranean), the goods carried tended to be of small size and weight in proportion to value, and arming the ships was more important than speed and efficiency. Dutch comparative advantage was thinner in this domain (Barbour, 1954, 230–231). Indeed, R. W. Unger speaks of the English having a "comparative advantage in dangerous trades"—and not only in

the Far East—because they used "strong and well-armed merchantmen" (1978, 110). In the Mediterranean, privateering was so much the route to profit that it was in the early seventeenth century a "vast . . . industry, partly large-scale and organized on business-like lines by rich merchants" Davis (1961, 127). As of 1618, corsair fleets were stronger than those of all the Mediterranean powers combined.

[73] As Glamann notes: "This divisibility of pepper in conjunction with its durability . . . rendered it an excellent object for speculation. It could be kept a long time: instances are known of pepper lying in store for over thirty years, which of course did affect the quality, but this could be improved by an admixture of fresh pepper" (1974, 475). However, Klein argues that more generally, "the success of Dutch real trade in the seventeenth century was in part due to the adroit speculation of rich merchants, playing the market with their stocks of goods" (1970, 33).

[74] See Wallerstein (1974).

[75] Coornaert notes the reluctance of the Europeans to create "continental establishments" in the seventeenth century. It was only toward the end of this period and during the eighteenth century "that the Dutch, English and French Empires began to take shape" (1967, 265). Similarly, Schöffer speaks of the fact that "the native population was initially hardly touched by the influence of the Company." Until the *nineteenth* century, says Schöffer, Dutch presence meant primarily that for coastal populations their merchants and administrators replaced

Were the policies of the VOC in the seventeenth century "shortsighted,"[76] as Masselman asserts? I do not think so, because one has to look at the alternatives. Were there greater exploitative profits to be had elsewhere, especially in an era of relative overall stagnation of the world-economy? The answer is surely yes—in the Eastland trade, in northwest Europe itself, in the Americas, all nearer at hand. Why bother with the East Indies at all? One wonders whether the overall century-long negative balance of the VOC did not mask a gigantic process of internal transfer of income and concentration of capital *within* the United Provinces, from small investors to big.[77] If so, the VOC could be said to have functioned as a kind of stock exchange, very useful for those with superior access to information, such as *De Heeren Zeventien* themselves; but then its history, at least until the turn of the eighteenth century, belongs more properly to the financial side of the story than to the commercial and distributional side. Nonetheless, the story of the VOC illustrates well how dominance in one area is linked to dominance in the other.

The East Indian trade may have been the most dramatic and even spectacular branch of Dutch commercial expansion in the seventeenth century, but it is not the most important, nor does it account for Dutch hegemony. At the time Dutch traders appeared in the Indian Ocean, they first began to ply the Mediterranean. The turning point seems to have been shortly after the Dutch–Spanish Truce of 1609.[78] Two areas of trade ought to be distin-

Arab and Chinese traders (1973, 75). This is, of course, basically similar to the role of the Portuguese in sixteenth-century Asia as described in Wallerstein (1974, chap. 6). For Perak, who makes the same point (1973, 60–61). There was, it is true, a limited use of Dutch "coffee-sergeants" after 1680 in charge of indigenous cultivators in outlying areas; but it was limited. See Rich (1967, 370).

F. Gaastra notes a shift in trade patterns in the eighteenth century with an increase in the outflow of bullion, but also a shift toward textiles, tea, and colonial products as imports (1976, 18–19). Paradoxically, it is the decline of the Dutch role in *intra*-Asian trade that explains the increase in bullion outflow. This is, in fact, a sign of peripheralization, as is the increased outflow of bullion as a result of the increased need to use it as money rather than as a luxury decoration.

[76] Masselmann (1963, 460). The argument is that monopolies involved a kind of pillage that killed off trade: "Deprived of the two main sources of their former prosperity, the cultivation of spices and free shipping, the renowned principalities of the Middle Ages, Ternate, Tidore, Matjan, and Batjan, were reduced to little more than subsistence level. Such was the penalty for having a valuable product that was coveted by a determined group of European entrepreneurs. . . . Towards the end of the seventeenth century, the natives had become so poor that

they could no longer afford to buy [calicoes and they] turned to weaving their own" (p. 461).

[77] Masselman notes that spices were sold at a profit of two and a half to three times their cost and paid an average annual dividend in the seventeenth century of 18.7%. Despite this, after 90 years, the Company was four million guilders in debt. Masselman says that this "points up the fact that the cost of maintaining the monopoly absorbed all but a fraction of the gross profits" (1963, 466). This is true from the company's collective viewpoint, but was it true for the large investors in the company? In a fascinating article by Morineau (1975) about the so-called unfavorable balances of trade with far-off countries, he suggests that "one equals two"; that is, the merchants simply doubled prices on the return trip, and therefore the bullion was not flowing out in the quantities it seemed to be. It represented, in fact, an internal transfer of income in Europe.

[78] See Parry (1967, 189) and Israel (1977, 37). Romano dates the turning point rather as 1611–1612, noting that a Consul for Syria, Palestine, Cyprus, and Egypt was named for the first time in 1611 (1962, 489–491). Parry sees 1612 as the moment when Dutch trade was "fully legitimized" as a result of the Dutch having secured their own capitulations with the Turks. Romano notes that by 1612 the tonnage is greater than that of the VOC.

guished, however. There was first of all the trade with the Christian
Mediterranean in general and northern Italy in particular, where it was a
matter of supplying grain, chronically needed but now even scarcer due to
bad Italian harvests, epidemics, and political cut-offs from the Levant, while
simultaneously, northern Italian industry was undercut by the export of
cloth to this formerly textile-exporting area and Venetian shipping was
displaced.[79] In the late sixteenth and early seventeenth centuries, along with
the Dutch, English, French, and Hanseates all competed for the Mediterranean trade; but the Dutch came to carry the largest share, primarily because of their superiority in "technical matters of ship design and commercial organization,"[80] which gave them the double advantage of being able to
carry grain (and other products) from northern Europe to the Mediterranean and to secure the grain in the first place in the Eastland trade.

After obtaining the larger part of the trade with northern Italy, "the
Dutch stayed to seize a great part of [a second area of commerce, that of] the
'rich trades,' also, accompanying their commerce by acts of violence as
efficient as they were ruthless."[81] One followed upon the other, for the
commerce in "rich trades" in the Mediterranean was not new. Essentially,
the Dutch were taking over the traditional Venetian role in the trade with
the Levant. In this era, the Levant was ready to import more real goods (as
distinct from bullion as luxury goods) from northwestern Europe than was
the East Indies, but they probably exported more luxury items over the
period 1600–1750 than did the Indian Ocean area, where, as the period
progressed, there was an increased export of tea, coffee, calicoes, and other
items that eventually became staples rather than luxuries. Was the Levant
still then part of the external arena? It is hard to say; the transition to
peripheral status was beginning, though perhaps it would await the late
eighteenth century to be fully realized.

The Atlantic trade—to both the Western Hemisphere and to West Africa,
which was its appendix—moves us still closer into the heart of the Dutch
commercial network. Much has been made of the difference between the
two great Dutch companies, the VOC and the "much later and less successful" West India Company.[82] For one thing, their social basis of support was

[79] See Rapp (1975). See also Parry (1967, 188),
who notes that 73 of 219 ships arriving at Leghorn
in 1593 were carrying grain. If one asks what northern Italy exchanged for its imports, the answer has
to be the accumulated capital of prior periods. Thus
grain import had a fundamentally different significance for Venice than for Amsterdam at this time.
For Amsterdam it meant not wasting energy producing grain when it was more profitable to produce textiles, ships, and other forms of agriculture,
thereby reaping the advantages of unequal exchange. For Venice it meant largely eating up capital for current consumption, a good operational
definition of "decline."

[80] Parry (1967, 189) and Davis (1975, 10, 14).
Rapp, in his discussion of the success of Holland
(and England) in displacing Venice in the Mediterranean, points out that the northern powers introduced no novelties in commercial practices which
could account for their success. What they had to
offer was their competitive advantage in industrial
production, with which they could *impose* "decline"
on Venice (see 1975, 499–501).
[81] Parry (1967, 189).
[82] Wilson (1968, 206), who discusses the differences between the VOC and the West India Company (chap. 12, 206–229).

different. The VOC (the East India Company) was controlled by Amsterdam merchants—who were Remonstrants and partisans of peace.[83] But the West India Company was largely the fruit of the efforts of their opponents—the "party" of Orangists, Calvinists, Zeelanders, and southern Netherlander migrants resettled in the north—who were Gomarian, colonizing, and warlike.[84] When it was founded, on June 3, 1621, a few weeks after the Truce ended, Amsterdam capital entered the company too; and the idea of a "missionary-colonizing corporation" became transformed into a "privateering institution."[85] The struggle between different interests took place inside the West India Company, largely between the economically weaker Zeelanders, with their reliance on the Company's monopoly in privateering, and the Amsterdam merchants, who were willing to take a cut off the privateering of any Dutch entrepreneur.[86]

The West India Company was thus a "belligerent mixture of trade and religion" and consequently, we are told, "a dreary tale of muddle and near bankruptcy."[87] No doubt this is so; but this allegedly political effort in fact laid the basis of one central pillar of capitalist trade in the seventeenth and eighteenth centuries: the so-called triangular trade, which provided Europe with its cotton, sugar, and tobacco, all grown of course with African slave labor plus the silver Europe used to obtain the spices and tea from the East Indies.[88] The Dutch were the pioneers of this structure, and if the profits went largely to the English and the French, it was primarily because the initial "social investment" was heavy and time consuming and, in bookkeeping terms, borne by the Dutch, with the profit just ready to be reaped after the end of Dutch hegemony in the 1670s by the subsequently productively more efficient English (and to some extent by the French)

What happened was simply that after the founding of the West India Company in 1621, the Dutch sought to expand in the Atlantic during the next quarter century. They founded New Amsterdam, conquered north

---

[83] One should remember, however, that although the Amsterdam policy was "traditionally peace-loving, . . . when business interests were threatened, as in 1645, 1657, and 1668, or when the existence of the Republic (and with it their trade) was at stake, as in 1672, the powerful city no longer remained passive, but advocated a policy that was forceful and aggressive" (Franken, 1968, 6–7).

[84] See Chaunu (1961, 1200–1202). Goslinga says it was "regarded as a stronghold of Calvinism and of Contra-Remonstrantism" and that in 1629 the Amsterdam City Council "complained that northerners were being victimized in favor of the Brabanders, i.e., refugees from the South" (1971, 287).

[85] Goslinga (1971, 39).

[86] See Wansink (1971, 146) and Goslinga (1971, 109).

[87] Wilson (1968, 210). J. R. Jones labels the Dutch West India Company "an aggressive and semipiratical body" and attributes to its attitudes a good deal of responsibility for the three Anglo–Dutch wars (1968, 44–45). Dutch historians also emphasize its political nature. Van Hoboken says: "Ultimately the fortunes of the [Dutch West India] Company, its rise and decline, were to a large extent determined by political factors" (1960, 42). Goslinga emphasizes that this was merely a difference in the method of the two companies in the search for profit. "Gains were sought by trade in the East, aided by force if necessary, whereas in the West profit came from privateering" (1971, 91).

[88] Spooner makes the point that one of the advantages the Dutch had over the English in the East Indies was the fact they controlled silver (more desired) while the English only had gold to offer (1956, 68).

east Brazil, taking it from the Portuguese (Spanish), and on a second try captured, Elmina in West Africa and then Luanda in Angola. In the first Anglo-Dutch War (1652–1654), however, the Portuguese (now free again from the Spanish) recaptured Brazil; and in the second Anglo-Dutch War, the Dutch lost New Amsterdam and some West African forts. What was accomplished then during this brief period corresponding with Dutch world hegemony? First, the Dutch held the Spanish at bay in the Americas, providing the "naval screen"[89] behind which the English (plus the Scots) and the French built up colonies of settlement. Second, sugar cultivation was launched in the Americas in Brazil, being shifted, after the expulsion of the Dutch, to Barbados, the first great English Caribbean plantation colony. Third, the Dutch conducted the first serious slave trade in order to furnish the manpower for the sugar plantations; when they lost the plantations, they tried to remain in the field as slave traders, but by 1675, Dutch primacy ended, yielding place to the newly founded Royal African Company of the English.[90]

The Atlantic era of the Dutch no doubt made a great contribution to the growth of the European world-economy; but how much did it do for the Dutch? Surely not as much as was done by the Baltic trade, which had already been the "mother trade" in the sixteenth century, when Dutch ships were carrying about 60% of the total. In the seventeenth century, at least until 1660, the Dutch continued to maintain the same dominance[91] despite the serious efforts of the English to break into their market. Here then is the evidence for Dutch commercial supremacy. In a key arena, where both the English and Dutch and indeed even the French (not to speak of the northern countries) all considered control of shipping to be important and lucrative, the Dutch alone carried off the lion's share.[92] Looking closely at the impact of the emerging stagnation of the world-economy on Anglo-Dutch competition in the Baltic, both Supple and Hinton, explain the Dutch advantage by the same two factors: cheap freights and the control of a sufficient supply of silver for export.[93] Morineau attributes their advantage in addition to their willingness to buy more grain than the Eastland Company bought.[94] Perhaps their ability to sell fish at such a low price that it virtually constituted dumping played a role too.[95]

---

[89] Parry (1967, 204). Sluiter (1948) makes essentially the same point. See the discussion of the background in Wallerstein (1974, 342, n. 197).

[90] See Emmer (1972) and Rich (1967, 333).

[91] See W. S. Unger (1959, 206). Indeed the relative dominance increased from 1600 to 1660, and the profit went up correspondingly from 100% to 200–300%. See Bogucka (1973, 439).

[92] While English ships carried only English goods, Dutch ships plied between all the western countries from Spain north and the Baltic. See Dunsdorfs (1947, 20).

[93] Supple (1959, 83) and Hinton (1959, 19). Hinton adds a third factor, Dutch "sharp practice," which might have played some role, but also may simply be a perception left to us by the English who used it as a rationalization to themselves of Dutch success.

[94] Morineau (1978d, 144–145). "Grain represented quantitatively by far the most important single commodity in which the Dutch traded with the Baltic" (Faber, 1966, 115).

[95] See Michell (1977, 177).

Having silver to export was an advantage acquired through productive efficiency in shipping and textiles, which made it possible to obtain silver from the Spanish and others. Why was it an advantage to have silver in the Baltic trade? It was because economic contraction plus the Thirty Years' War resulted in what the English called the "rising of the moneys" (and the Germans the *Kipper- und Wipperzeit*), which involved a devaluation of small coins vis-à-vis silver. The rixdollar, a transportable silver coin whose silver content remained constant, was worth 37 groschen in 1600 and 90 by 1630; its biggest jump, from 45 to 75 occurred between 1618 and 1621. These shifts came about by reducing the silver content of the groschen while proclaiming a change in its value in terms of the rixdollar.[96] The question is why the effect of this on the Dutch was different from its effect on the English. Presumably both could now obtain products in the Baltic at a lower cost in silver; but to do this, one had to have "ready money" to export, which the Dutch had and the English did not. In addition, when there was a depression in trade generally, having cheap imports mattered less than having cheaper imports.

The basic problem for the English was that Dutch merchants could sell Baltic goods in *England* more cheaply than English merchants could.[97] The Eastland merchants in England thought the solution might be to obtain permission to reexport Baltic corn to the Mediterranean as the Dutch did; but they ran afoul of the strong opposition of the English wheat merchants, who succeeded in maintaining the ban on export whenever price was above a rather low figure because of the fear that English cereals were not sufficiently competitive internationally.[98] As a result, the English could not earn the silver in the Mediterranean that they could have used to take advantage of the cheap prices of the Baltic, which in turn would have enabled them to obtain the products to earn more silver, and so on. The devaluation in the Baltic was therefore more profitable to the Dutch than to the English in terms of their domination of Baltic trade and thereby of Mediterranean trade; and it also permitted the Dutch to begin "to encroach on English merchants' trade in England itself."[99]

The one last element in this picture is the river trade inward, which had belonged to Antwerp until the Revolt of the Netherlands. When the Dutch closed off the River Scheldt, the trade passed to Amsterdam, after which there were two ways by which it might have returned once more to Antwerp: by extending the United Provinces to include Antwerp or through peace and free trade. The first never occurred. Smit suspects that, despite the proclaimed objectives of the United Provinces (and the real intent of the Orangists and the Calvinists), the failure was due to lack of

---

[96] See Hinton (1959, 14–16).
[97] See Supple (1959, 86). Wilson says that the *Kipper- und Wipperzeit* posed to English merchants only a "short-term soluble problem"; the "larger" prob lem was caused by Dutch competition (1965, 55).
[98] See Hinton (1959, 29–30).
[99] Hinton (1959, 9–10).

effort: "Holland did not want a restitution of the southern provinces, with the accompanying risk that trade would flow back to a liberated Antwerp."[100] When peace finally came in 1648, prohibitive taxes on any trade that would pass the Scheldt estuaries to Antwerp were written into the treaty.[101] So much political effort was the consequence of the importance of the entrepôt trade in general; one would have thought that by 1648 Amsterdam would have felt secure against a resurgence of Antwerp, but there was one crucial item needed for production on which no chances could be taken: peat. Originally dug for Antwerp and the Brabant market, it was reoriented after the 1570s to the area between the Ij and the Maas Rivers in Holland proper. The use of peat was a key to the efficiency of the urban industries of Holland, and it "had an impact on the economy that can be compared to the impact of coal in nineteenth-century Europe."[102] In addition, the river trade carried urban manure in the other direction, which helped achieve the "uniquely high yields of Dutch cereal farming."[103]

From the 1580s on, a network of regular services on the improved canal system linked the cities of Holland with each other and with the hinterland of the other provinces and Brabant as well—all centered on Holland. Beginning in 1632, a further technological advance occurred with the construction of the first *trekvaart,* a straight canal with a towpath for passenger boats that required much capital.[104] Dutch shipbuilders created vessels that were able to distribute and assemble cargoes on the streams and lakes with great dispatch.[105] The result was the most efficient internal transportation network in Europe; it reached a peak of traffic in the 1660s. If we put the pieces together, we can conclude that the furthest trade routes—the East Indies, the Levant, and even the Christian Mediterranean and the Atlantic trade—were important, to be sure; but they were secondary. The key to Dutch commercial hegemony in the European world-economy from the 1620s (perhaps already from the 1590s) to the 1660s "remained the ancient trade between northern and western Europe";[106] and the reason the Dutch could achieve commercial supremacy had to do with their prior agro-

---

[100] Smit (1968, 21).

[101] See Schöffer (1973, 89), who observes that "this was to remain Flanders' never-ending grudge against the north." See also Boxer (1965, 92). The Scheldt remained closed through the seventeenth and eighteenth centuries. For the many negotiations about it, see Hubert (1909, 641–646). The restrictions were finally lifted in the Treaty of The Hague, May 16, 1795.

[102] J. de Vries (1974, 204) and Kuske (1956, 232–233). De Zeeuw points out that the availability of peat was a geological accident in that the peat was "very near to, partly even just below the overall water table" and that this was caused by "the rising of the sea level during the holocene" (1978, 5). The peat gave the Dutch "cheap fuel" with which to "run

industries based on *thermal* processes" and they thus "were able to produce goods that could easily compete on the international market" (p. 23). The decline of the world competitiveness of the Dutch was directly related to later events. First, turf became more expensive as a result of using zones of easy access and being forced to acquire it in more distant areas by deeper dredging and by extending approach canals; and second, transport became more difficult because harbors and rivers silted up (see p. 25).

[103] Wilson (1977a, 24).

[104] See J. de Vries (1974, 202–209) and (1978).

[105] See R. W. Unger (1978, 52).

[106] Wilson (1957a, 2).

industrial efficiency. This was transposed into commercial efficiency mainly through freight rates, insurance costs, and general overhead.

Why were Dutch freight rates so cheap? The biggest factor was the low cost of ship construction. Parry lists six cost advantages: skill of Dutch shipwrights, economy in the use of materials, labor-saving devices, large-scale standardized production, large-scale purchasing of materials, cheap transportation of construction materials in Dutch ships. The result was an overall cost of production, as late as the mid-seventeenth century, that was 40–50% cheaper than in England, their nearest competitor.[107] Of these advantages, the first three may be seen as the technological advance of the Dutch, and the second three as the cumulative advantage of being ahead on the first three. In addition to being constructed more economically, Dutch ships were constructed in such a way as to require a smaller crew—normally 18 hands instead of the 26–30 used on ships of other countries.[108] This enabled the Dutch to feed their crews well, probably better than other shippers;[109] they thereby presumably obtained higher productivity for a lower overall wage outlay. The higher productivity was to be seen in port as well as at sea. The "greater durability and speed" of Dutch ships was a function of "regular maintenance"[110] as well as of design. Furthermore, the fact that Dutch ships were "cleaner, cheaper, and safer"[111] had a spiral effect: cheaper freights led to control of the Baltic trade, which led to cheaper timber, which led to cheaper costs in shipbuilding, which led to cheaper freights. Cleaner, cheaper, and safer ships also meant an increase in total shipping, which made it possible to have lower insurance rates—in part a function of scale, in part the result of a more efficient financial structure,[112] which we will shortly discuss. Lower insurance costs are also cumulative; they lead to lower freight rates, which leading to increases in scale and in transactions skills, which lead to lower insurance costs.

In "the foundation of [Dutch] trade was shipping,"[113] the biggest profits were made through marketing and stapling[114] in the great Amsterdam entrepôt, the success of which was due to the superiority of the Dutch form

---

[107] See Parry (1967, 211).

[108] Wilson (1941, 6).

[109] Morineau is skeptical of this, and suggests that sailors on southern French ships were equally well fed (1970b, 118). For a discussion of the high caloric outlay provided on Dutch shipping in the seventeenth century, see Morineau (1970a, 114). Boxer, nonetheless, makes a point of low wages for Dutch sailors as a factor which explains low freight rates (1965, 66–67).

[110] R. W. Unger (1978, 4; see also p. 183, n. 7).

[111] Wilson (1957a, 42).

[112] At least it can be said that in the seventeenth century in Amsterdam "insurance was transacted less amateurishly than elsewhere." (Barbour, 1929, 580). Barbour reports that English ships commonly obtained their insurance in Holland in the seventeenth century "in spite of premium rates that were normally higher than those obtainable in London" (p. 581). This is puzzling on the face of it. If Barbour is empirically correct, it must be that nominal rates and real rates were different, which could be explained by greater efficiency in Dutch commercial organization, which was a significant variable in general, as we shall shortly see. In any case, Barbour later writes of the general European attraction for Dutch marine insurance. (See 1963, 33–35).

[113] Wilson (1967, 518).

[114] Wilson (1941, 10). This is so, claim North and Thomas, because the "market, or transactions sectors, . . . was the sector where at this time large gains in productivity could occur" (1973, 135).

of commercial organization. Heckscher says the "greatest peculiarity" of the Netherlands of the seventeenth century was its "capacity . . . to make shift with *fewer* and *simpler* commercial organizations" as compared with those of other nations.[115] But what did this mean? First, it meant the pooling of savings in the partnership system,[116] which of course was not original with the Dutch; but they extended it to encompass, along with a thin commercial aristocracy, a large number of smaller merchants.[117] Second, it meant the creation of a system of buffer stocks, which considerably reduced risks for the merchant, especially since it was organized monopolistically, and which reduced the dependence of the staple market on fluctuating supply (and costs) while enabling the merchants to make speculative profits on the sales.[118] Thirdly, it meant a network of commission agents, who found the customer for the producer, obtaining goods on consignment and receiving a commission on the bill paid by the purchaser to the producer.[119] Thus the Dutch entrepôt trade developed in the wake of Dutch shipping, itself the outgrowth of Dutch industrial efficiency.[120] Once again we have the spiral effect: the strength of the Dutch entrepôt trade "tended to ruin"[121] English shipping. Of course, being the entrepôt created a large amount of steady employment[122] which, especially in the seventeenth century, sustained the internal demand for Dutch products.

[115] Heckscher (1935, **I**, 352).

[116] For Sella, it was these partnership shipping companies, the *reederij*, "that made possible the spectacular, ten-fold growth of the Dutch commercial fleet between 1500 and 1700" (1974, 411).

[117] Glamann speaks of the "massive scale" of participation by "ordinary merchants" in the "Dutch commercial expansion of the seventeenth century," citing, in particular, their role in the corn, salt, herring, timber, and brick trades (1974, 519). Moreover, a shipping industry was particularly suited for small investors in a land-short country. Scammell, speaking of England, says: "With the competition for land intense in the sixteenth and early seventeenth centuries, and *on analogy with what happened in Holland,* a ship, or more likely a boat, may have been the only outlet for such capital as humble and obscure owners had" (1972, 404, italics added).

[118] Klein believes that this system "contributed substantially to the growth of the Dutch economy" in the seventeenth century. He argues that it was the enforcement of monopolistic practices—"horizontal or vertical price agreements, domestic or foreign monopoly concessions"—which made possible the "hazardous undertaking" of creating essential buffer stocks; for otherwise "the successful merchant [would have been] an open target for profit-hunting competitors" (1966, 188–189). These monopolies were effective. Glamann notes of grain that "indeed, it is no exaggeration to say that in the seventeenth and eighteenth centuries, the celebrated corn ex-

change of the Dutch metropolis [fixed] the grain prices of Europe" (1974, 457). For evidence on how Liège prices were dependent on those of Amsterdam between 1630 and 1738, see Ruwet (1957, 101).

[119] In the eighteenth century, the consignment system would shift to one in which the Agent paid three-quarters of the likely price (estimated low), but received moderate interest on his advance payment until the goods were sold. Wilson thinks of this as a "slippery slope." As Agents moved from a commission business proper to shipping and cargadooring, and offering acceptance credit, they moved from banking to speculation and gambling. "As the commission trade became increasingly indirect, the element of uncertainty and fraud became stronger" (1941, 12).

[120] "Indeed," as Davis remarks of the Netherlands in the seventeenth and eighteenth centuries, 'it is difficult to distinguish between commercial and industrial capital" (1973b, 232); but as Supple notes, "it was a perfectly normal and anticipated practice for commercial entrepreneurs to invest in and manage manufacturing enterprises" (1977, 424).

[121] The phrase is from Hinton, who sees Dutch entrepôt trade as the "most important single factor in shaping English economic policy in the seventeenth century" (1959, 10–11).

[122] Glamann speaks of the grain trade spreading like "ripples in a pond." Not only was the grain loaded and discharged, but the system of buffer

We have argued that the sequence of Dutch advantages in the world-economy is productive, distributional, financial. If the first part of the sequence is controversial, the second is conventional wisdom; but it is often presented as something a bit shameful, the transformation of the noble, ascetic (commercial) entrepreneur into an ignoble, luxury-loving rentier, the betrayal of the Protestant Ethic in Zion itself, the explanation why Holland was cast out from the Garden of Eden. There has been a healthy reaction against such nonsense in recent years, but I wish to go further. The turn to finance is *not* a sign of decline, much less of decadence; it is, in fact, a sign of capitalist strength that the Amsterdam stock exchange can be considered "the Wall Street of the seventeenth century."[123] What was the origin of such strength? It was the result of three steps in a sequence: One, productive and commercial strength in the world-economy created the basis for sound public finances. Two, sound public finances, combined with a worldwide commercial network, allowed Amsterdam to become the locus of the international payments system and money market, especially given the world-economic slowdown and hence monetary instability. Three, productive and commercial strength, combined with control over the international money market, permitted the *export* of Dutch capital that brought in remittances, which enabled the Dutch to live off productive surplus far beyond what they created themselves, and for long after the epoch of their own major productive contributions.

In a world-economy whose expansion had slowed, the fact that the United Provinces was "always solvent"[124] and was the major exception in the seventeenth century to "the dismal succession of defaults"[125] is both cause and effect of general economic hegemony. It is effect insofar as the commercial advantages in maritime freight and insurance alone sufficed to create a surplus in the balance of payments;[126] and it is cause because the reputation of sound finances enabled the Dutch government to borrow more cheaply,[127] because the excellence of Dutch state credit accounted for "a good part of [its] military success,"[128] and because it could therefore probably attract sufficient financial flows as a safe place of deposit to enable the United Provinces to have an overvalued currency. This last advantage meant that the United Provinces could balance a deficit of current account

---

stocks led to the building of warehouses, some three-quarters of which were devoted to grain storage. Further employment was then created by the need to toss the grain regularly "to prevent germination and spontaneous combustion" (1974, 461). Briggs points out that between shipping and warehousing needs, Amsterdam began in 1610 a "remarkable and ambitious scheme of concentric expansion which . . . quadrupl[ed] the habitable area" (1957, 294).

[123] Goubert (1970c, 27).
[124] Carsten (1961, 13). Compare this with the

French budget, which between 1610 and the French Revolution was in surplus *only* for the decade between 1662 and 1671. See Parker (1974a, 575).
[125] Homer (1963, 98).
[126] See Vilar (1974, 249).
[127] See Parker (1974a, 573). The one state that was still better off "for a time" in this regard was Genoa.
[128] Homer (1963, 124). Among other things, as Homer suggests, "with good credit, German mercenaries could be hired for land defense" (p. 125).

with incoming financial flows.[129] Sound finances are, however, only a prerequisite for the level of general capitalist confidence that is needed for an
effective flow of financial operations. Sound finances permit large-scale
credit operations at low rates and make possible the profit of high overall
income composed of low returns per financial operation.

In 1609, the Year of the Truce, *De Wisselbank van Amsterdam* was founded;
it quickly became the great center of European deposit and exchange because it "provided a security and convenience rare in the annals of
seventeenth-century banking." Over the century, deposits rose from under
1 million to over 16 million florins,[130] and it became the place of retreat for
owners of capital who feared for the safety of their wealth.[131] Once enough
bullion and coin was deposited, Amsterdam held "the key, so to speak, to
Europe's international payments system."[132] With the currencies largely in
its coffers, Amsterdam developed a system of bills of exchange that permitted multilateral settlements to expand. It took time, of course, to develop the confidence and the flows; but by 1660, at the latest, Amsterdam
played an undisputed role as the center of a multilateral payments system,
and it would remain so at least until 1710.[133] Regarding restrictions placed
on the export of bullion, the United Provinces was the great exception
among states in the era of mercantilism: bullion could flow out of the
United Provinces quite as easily as it could flow in. This is precisely why so
much of it flowed in,[134] and of course this policy was only possible when
bullion did flow in. The phenomenon then, like so many others, was spiral
in form, each act contributing to making the next more possible, until a
peak was eventually reached.

Solidity in deposit and exchange made possible a credit function that

[129] This is the tentative suggestion of Grantham
(1975, 65). Van der Wee offers another motive:
"The Dutch Republic [deliberately overvalued]
silver in the seventeenth century so as to supply the
great Amsterdam market in precious metals with
white metal urgently needed for export to the Baltic
and the Far East" (1977, 297).

[130] Barbour (1963, 44–45).

[131] See Barbour (1963, 46), who notes that in both
English political crises of the century, individuals
shifted funds to the Netherlands. Similarly Castillo
notes the "curious event" of the arrival in Amsterdam of four vessels in 1649 with more than three
million ducats in unminted form (*en barras y piñas*).
He says these were probably the property of Marranos repatriating money because of the bankruptcy of Spain in 1648. "Capitalism, when important interests are at stake, knows how to ignore
ideologies and frontiers" (1964, 314). De Roover
says that "in the second half of the seventeenth century, Amsterdam displaced Genoa as the world
market for precious metals" (1974b, 227).

[132] Glamann (1974, 510).

[133] Parker (1974a, 550–551). His chart shows the
clear advantage of Amsterdam over London as such
an exchange center circa 1700. Vilar thinks this remains true until 1763 (1974, 257). See also Homer
(1963, 174) and Glamann (1977, 261). The gener-
ality of the confidence, and therefore of the flows, is
illustrated by the fact that Amsterdam was the *sole*
financial center until 1763 on which merchants
could draw or accept bills of exchange from Russia.
See Knoppers (1977a, 13–14).

[134] See Deyon (1969, 38). See also Vilar: "For the
Dutch, precious metals were a commodity like any
other, whose 'export-import' was profitable" (1974,
251). Morineau points out, however, that once this
system was established, very little bullion actually
needed to be exported, at least to peripheral areas
of the world-economy, such as the Baltic, as distinguished from external arenas, such as the East Indies and the Levant. "In the last analysis, then it is
indeed to the *economic* [as opposed to the financial]
functioning of the *economy* of the United Provinces,
both externally and internally, to which we have to
return" (1972, 4).

began for the *Wisselbank* in 1683. First there were "advances" for depositors and later, "acceptance credits," operations no longer tied to the entrepôt functions of Amsterdam and essentially credit on operations in distant centers.[135] The Dutch developed credit based on specific deposits that was "uncommonly stable" because the "costs of replacing bills of exchange by a shipment of precious metals in any desired coinage were much reduced"[136] since the *Wisselbank* was precisely the storehouse of such precious metals. Finally, the stability of Dutch currency made its trade coins (*negotiepenningen*), both silver and gold, to be of such "guaranteed quality" that they became the preferred specie of world trade, making a dent even on the Spanish *reales de ocho*.[137] The financial flows in turn created and sustained the low interest rates, which attracted further flows. The rate in Holland declined by more than half over the course of the seventeenth century, forcing rates down in England, France, and even Sweden; but these latter never came down low enough to compete effectively.[138] Low interest rates, in turn, lead us to the subject of investments, the other source of financial profit. Being both the chief money market of Europe and the chief commercial entrepôt, Amsterdam was able to lower significantly the search, negotiation, and enforcement costs of lending capital, and thereby to encourage investment in general.[139] Being the most technologically advanced society of the time, the United Provinces could also export its technologies, another facet in assuring inward financial flows.[140]

[135] See Van Dillen (1974b, 179–185) and Klein (1970, 39–40). See also Barbour (1963, 53), who says: "Freedom to export the monetary metals, rare elsewhere in the seventeenth century, helped to stabilize exchange rates in Amsterdam and so encouraged the circulation of bills of exchange as in general, instruments of credit, the discounting and sale of which became a lively business in the city." Amsterdam's centrality for bills of exchange not only facilitated trade in general; it proved highly profitable as a banking operation. Bogucka points out that the transfer of large sums by Dutch bankers to Gdańsk merchants by bills of exchange "did not constitute only a means of transferring funds, but gave rise to independent operations of speculation, called arbitrage, which . . . in the first half of the seventeenth century, realized profits in a few weeks of up to 6.5 to 8 percent, sometimes 10 to 12 percent of the capital invested. At this time, the rate of interest in Holland itself barely reached 3–4 percent" (1972, 10).

[136] Van der Wee (1977, 342).

[137] Van der Wee (1977, 340).

[138] See Klein (1970, 38) and Homer (1963, 137, 179). Homer compares Dutch, English, and French rates for both the first and second halves of the seventeenth century for three kinds of loans: census annuities, mortgages, other long-term debts; short-term commercial loans; and short-term deposits. In five of the six comparisons, the reported Dutch rate is the lowest; in one, it is slightly edged out by the English. Ringrose suggests that the origin of the low interest rates comes from the "tremendous concentration of liquid capital for military purposes in the Low Countries" over the period of 1566 to 1648 (1973, 291).

[139] See North and Thomas (1973, 139, 142) and Reed (1973, 182–183). See Klein (1969, 14) on investments in buffer stocks. There is a survey of Dutch loans and investment abroad in Barbour (1963, 104–129). On investments in the rising debts of European countries in the eighteenth century, see Wilson (1977a, 27): the money was channeled "above all [to] England, where the Dutch investors' decisions were large enough to be an important consideration with successive First Lords of the Treasury."

[140] Already in 1628, Cornelius Vermuyden entered into an agreement with Charles I to drain Hatfield Chase. See Cunningham (1897, 209–210). Dickens speaks of the Dutch "technical colonization of England" in the seventeenth century (1976, 8). See also Wilson on the export of the technology of drainage, ship construction, and agricultural techniques (1968, 77–91). On land drainage and reclamation, see the article by L. E. Harris. It is only by

The expansion of investment at home and abroad was profitable to Dutch capitalists and aided the balance of payments of the state; but did it aid the overall economy of the state? There has been a curious debate in recent years, with mercantilist overtones, suggesting that the "decline" of the Dutch was due in some way to the placing of investments outside the United Provinces, especially in England. This is to neglect the fact that the concern of the investor is to maximize profits, not to support the state.[141] We shall talk of this again in discussing the rise of English finance. For the moment, let us content ourselves with Van Dillen's reminder that the creation of capital was of "great importance . . . to the political and economic position of the Republic. One need only think of the acquisition of allies by means of subsidies,"[142] a form of state investment that reinforced that of private parties. Indeed, we cannot complete this story of Dutch hegemony without looking directly at the role of the state. The United Provinces seemed to be the great exception to the predominance of mercantilist ideology in the seventeenth century. From this fact, many persons draw the curious inference that the Dutch state was weak. It seems to me that exactly the inverse was true: in the seventeenth century, the Dutch state was the *only* state in Europe with enough internal and external strength such that its need for mercantilist policies was minimal.

Let us review, briefly, the nature of the ideology and practices and then look at these internal and external strengths of the United Provinces. At earlier points in history, Amsterdam had of course pursued a vigorously protectionist line,[143] which at the level of the towns did not disappear entirely even in the seventeenth century.[144] Furthermore, there were many who raised objections to the lack of protectionism at the level of the federation. As the century went on, the agro-industrial sectors lost their edge and appealed for tariffs, albeit with limited success.[145] Nor were the Estates-General above tariff retaliation in their struggles with the English and the French.[146] The role of the state was clear in matters other than protection; it created the conditions for the success of private enterprise. As

the end of the seventeenth century that "the draining of the [English] fens . . . ceased to be the prerogative of Netherlanders" (1957, 322).

[141] Marx, describing Holland's investments abroad in the eighteenth century as the consequence of the loss of mercantile supremacy, said: "Its fatherland had begun to lie there where the best interest for its capital was paid" (1969, 93).

[142] Van Dillen (1974a, 207).

[143] See Glamann (1974, 457).

[144] "The towns protected and subsidized industry. Shipbuilding is an excellent example. Construction of shipbuilding facilities were one form of subsidy. The regulations of the shipcarpenters' guilds included a number of other forms" (R. W. Unger, 1978, 114).

[145] Nonetheless these interests had to be appeased. In 1681, at a moment of economic difficulty, a compromise was reached between the grain merchants of Amsterdam and the agricultural producers of Zeeland. The former obtained the abolition of export (and reexport) duties, but the latter obtained an augmentation of import duties. See Jeannin (1969, 74), who has informed me that two Dutch articles by Van Dillen (1917 and 1923) contain the details of the controversy and the political compromise. Also note that "through the seventeenth and eighteenth centuries the export of raw materials for shipbuilding, such as ropes and masts, was at times made illegal" (R. W. Unger, 1978, 115).

[146] See Deyon (1969, 38).

soon as there was an autonomous government in the Netherlands, "the fisheries came in for the Government's most earnest solicitude."[147] In order to control quality, William of Orange in 1575 called together the representatives of the five fishing ports and by a series of statutes from 1580 to 1582 created a collegiate organization to control the herring industry.[148] Even more important was the creation of the Dutch East India Company, which was to an important degree a response to the anarchy of the free world market in colonial goods and to the dumping that ensued. Stols argued that their key importance was the "intervention of the State in trade and economies" and that the creation of the two Companies "could almost be called nationalization 'avant la lettre'," a mode of seeking to unite a previously international trade under one national monopoly.[149]

The Dutch state defended the interests of its entrepreneurs and worried little about ideological consistency in doing so. The ideology of Dutch hegemony was *mare liberum,* most cogently expressed by Grotius in his book published in 1609, the Year of the Truce. However, as Sir George Downing bitterly wrote to Lord Clarendon on November 20, 1663: "It is *mare liberum* in the British seas but *mare clausum* on the coast of Africa and in the East Indies."[150] There is nothing surprising in all this.[151] The United Provinces were dominant, and "liberalism suits dominant economies well";[152] but whenever liberalism conflicts with the possibility of continued dominance, it has a way of not lasting. This is why the "liberal" decentralized structure of the Dutch state can be taken as an indicator of strength rather than of weakness. It is not that decentralized structures are always a sign of strength. In a peripheral zone such as Poland, the rise of the local diets and the kinglets was the measure of peripheralization. In the hegemonic power, however, such a structure is the sign of strength *relative to other core powers,*

---

[147] Beaujon (1884, 30).

[148] Michell (1977, 148).

[149] Stols (1976, 39).

[150] Cited in Geyl (1964, **II,** 85). See Meilink-Roefolsz (1968, 71). See also Goslinga on the Caribbean: "The Dutch colonial empire, built in the first half of the seventeenth century, began with a broom in the mast, i.e., with the principle of a free sea. As soon as the sea was cleaned, however—as soon as Spanish sea power was no longer a real danger for the Dutch—the latter lost interest in the high principles expounded by their finest philosopher, and not even reluctantly, accepted the Iberian thesis of a *mare clausum* [vis-à-vis the English]" (1971, xiv).

[151] Heckscher is nonetheless surprised. "The paradoxical situation now arises that the Netherlands, although the ideal of all mercantilists, were yet at the same time, less affected by mercantilist tendencies than most other countries. The only explanation is that the Netherlands were idealized" (1935, **I,** 359). This is of course the only explanation one can imagine if one wears the ideological blink-

ers of economic liberalism and refuses to think in terms of relational rather than attributive characteristics. Compare Heckscher's view to that of Schmoller: "The heroic struggle of the Dutch for religious liberty and for freedom from the Spanish yoke displays itself, when looked at in a 'dry light' as a century-long war for the conquest of the East Indian colonies, and an equally long privateering assault on the silver fleets of Spanish and Spanish-American trade. These Dutch, so lauded by the naif free-trader of our day on account of the low customs-duties of their early days, were from the first the sternest and most warlike of monopolists after the monopolist fashion that the world has ever seen" (1897, 65).

[152] Deyon (1969, 40). Glamann calls liberalism a "passive attitude" of the state, and says that "inasmuch as government policy is in a sense never neutral in the economic process" it is clear that "this passive attitude was exactly the right one to chime in with the growth of the staple in Amsterdam" (1977, 273–274).

who precisely need to increase their administrative centralization in order to try to overcome the economic advantage of the hegemonic power.

What was the structure of the United Provinces? The details changed from the time of the Union of Utrecht in 1579 to the time of downfall of the decentralized state with the creation of the Batavian Republic in 1795; but the reality of each successive variation was not too different. Already in 1576, seven states (or Provinces)—Gelderland, Holland, Zeeland, Utrecht, Friesland, Overijssel, and Groningen—had agreed to send delegates to an Estates-General. Each state had one vote therein, and decisions had to be unanimous. There was in addition a rather weak executive organ called the Council of State. The fleet, the key military institution, was under the daily direction of five separate Admiralty Colleges. The most important state, Holland, itself had a cumbersome governmental structure; its central legislature, the States of Holland, were composed of 18 representatives of the various towns and one representative of the nobility as a whole. There was no monarch in the United Provinces. The nearest equivalent was the Stadholder, a provincial official. The princes of Orange were usually the stadholder of various (but not all) provinces simultaneously, except of course in the two so-called "stadholderless periods." One would be hard pressed to invent a structure seemingly less likely to work efficiently or indeed to work at all.

In fact, it did work quite well, although not without frictions and violences. (On an individual level, few events of the time match the lynching of Johan de Witt in The Hague in 1672, a year known in Dutch history as the "Year of Disaster.") Still, if we compare the internal dissensions of the United Provinces to those of England and France, no reasonable analyst can fail to see that the Netherlands was less turbulent than the other two; the internal divisions of the ruling strata rent the society apart far less, and the lower strata were less rebellious. To explain this, we note, first of all, that the formal structure of government masked (and only lightly) another real structure. Financially, Holland paid almost 60% of the costs of government, and Amsterdam half of that. The chief provincial administrative official of the States of Holland was the Land's Advocate. The office was later renamed the Council Pensionary and called the Grand Pensionary by foreigners, and the official came to be a virtual prime minister of the United Provinces as a whole and acted as president in the "stadholderless periods."[153]

The power of this official resulted from the fact that the Estates-General and the States of Holland met in the same building in The Hague, from a continuity provided by the unusual practice whereby the Grand Pensionary

---

[153] See Kossmann (1970, 362–365), van Hoboken (1960, 46), Renier (1944, 52), Burke (1974, 44), and Wansink (1971). "Paradoxically Holland strongly supported the federal government, but it meant in practice that Holland could rule the Republic to a great extent in a complicated semi-centralized way" (Schöffer, 1973, 92).

stayed in the Estates-General year after year, from Holland's being the economic and cultural heart of all Dutch activity, and from Amsterdam's control of the import of grain, which fed nearly half the population.[154] If there was any doubt of Amsterdam's preeminence in the beginning of the seventeenth century, it disappeared entirely in the first "stadholderless period" of 1650–1672, when the ascendancy of Holland became "the cement that held the state together" and when foreign policy "was made subordinate to the interests of trade,"[155] as befits a hegemonic power. Amsterdam paid the piper, and in this period especially, she "felt entitled to call the tune."[156] Why then should one worry about centralizing the state if one gets what one wants without it? What Renier, and Wilson after him, called the "social dictatorship of the upper middle class"[157] was no doubt jostled occasionally by its internal opponents—the Contra-Remonstrants versus the Remonstrants, the Orangists versus the Loevesteiners; and it was perhaps sapped by a slow process of "aristocratization,"[158] although the interests of the ruling stratum were never really threatened by more socially conservative peers. As Kossmann correctly perceives: "the princes of Orange were rarely willing and never able to supersede the Holland plutocracy."[159]

Nor was this stratum really threatened from below; its members paid the price of social peace. Dutch social welfare, and that of Amsterdam in particular, aroused the "unqualified admiration" of foreign visitors, who were perhaps unaware that the money came in good part from the confiscated properties of the Roman Catholic Church.[160] No matter—other countries also confiscated Church properties in the seventeenth and eighteenth centuries, even without having "provided so amply for the poor."[161] We should be under no illusions about the social reality of the Dutch welfare state. The overall profits of Dutch capitalism "hardly benefited the majority of the people." Real wages, which at most rose slightly at first, declined over the century;[162] national prosperity went hand in hand with "greater poverty among many groups of workers," and about half the population of

---

[154] "Great was Amsterdam's power in the years when there was scarcity of grain in the country," for example, in 1628–1630 (Van Dillen, 1964, 145).

[155] Franken (1968, 2, 4). See also Burke (1974, 42–43), Carter (1975a, 1), and Riemersma (1950, 39). On the limits, however, to Amsterdam's (and Holland's) ability to determine policy, see Rowen (1974).

[156] Boxer (1965, 90). Amsterdam's tune was very profitable for her. Albers notes that after 1650 "the trade with the Mediterranean and the Baltic became increasingly concentrated in Amsterdam until, eventually, that town monopolized them" (1977, 86).

[157] Renier (1944, 16–24) and Wilson (1968, 47). Boxer specifically indicates agreement with Renier on this point (1965, 11).

[158] See the discussion in Roorda (1964, 119, and 1967, 196 197). Van Dijk and Roorda warn against overstating this phenomenon. "There was no question of a continuing aristocratization preventing all social mobility until the end of the eighteenth century" (1976, 101–102).

[159] Kossman (1970, 365). Haley similarly notes that though the Orangist struggle with the "plutocracy" drew support from lower-class urban elements and therefore had "all the makings of civil war and social revolution," the Orangists in the end drew back. "In the last resort they were themselves aristocrats and upholders of the existing social order" (1972, 83).

[160] Boxer (1965, 55).

[161] Wilson (1968, 53).

[162] Klein (1969, 9); see also J. de Vries (1978, 303).

Amsterdam were living in "squalid back premises, cellars, and base-ments."[163]

How was it possible that there was nonetheless relative social peace? One major factor was that for some people, declining real income was balanced by social welfare payments, which were *higher than elsewhere* in the core states.[164] A second factor was that the reputation of Amsterdam for its benefits made it a "lode-star to the unemployed and underemployed of neighboring countries." This secret was rediscovered in a later era by New York. Once the belief was allowed to develop that "the streets of Amster-dam were paved with gold,"[165] workers migrated from everywhere—just enough to worsen the labor situation for working-class residents in the city of light, to make those with a few extra crumbs cherish them, and to make every migrant concentrate on the possibilities of individual advancement. All that was needed was power, prosperity, a small amount of largesse, and a *soupçon* of social mobility—in short, the typical social policy of a hegemonic power.

Strength at home was paralleled by strength abroad. In the first half of the seventeenth century the Dutch fleet ruled the seas, to the extent that it is possible for a fleet to rule seas.[166] Spain, of course, had been the previous dominant naval power. The Dutch had assisted the English in bringing to an end the "invincibility" of Spain in 1588; still, as of 1600, Spanish naval strength remained stronger than that of the Dutch and English com-bined.[167] Successive naval victories changed that. The "naval screen" in the Caribbean, mentioned earlier, was anchored in 1634, when the Dutch seized Curaçao. In 1645 the Dutch fleet gained control over the Sound for the first time.[168] Thus it was, as the great theorist of sea power Admiral Mahan wrote, that "the United Provinces owed their consideration and power to their wealth and their fleets."[169] This power, to be sure, was chal-

---

[163] Boxer (1965, 54–55).

[164] See Klein (1969, 9).

[165] Boxer (1965, 58).

[166] In a private discussion the late Stein Rokkan suggested to me a major factor in the ability of the European world-economy to resist transformation into a world-empire: it was built around the seas rather than the land, and the seas are inherently more difficult to conquer than a land mass. For this interesting suggestion, I leave him the entire re-sponsibility for the moment. Regarding this matter, see the assessment by P. Anderson of the English choice of options: "For although higher per unit, the total costs of naval construction and maintenance were far below those of a standing army. . . . Yet the yields throughout the next centuries were to be far higher" (1974a, 135).

[167] See Cooper (1970, 227). By 1659, in both the Atlantic and the Mediterranean, the Spanish fleet was weaker than either the fleet of the United Prov-

inces or that of England (and soon thereafter weaker than that of France as well).

[168] Polišenský (1971, 236).

[169] Mahan (1889, 97). Franken argues further that this was the *only* route to power available: "It is also certain that the financial reserves were not large enough to pay for an army which in the long run would be necessary for an active land policy, besides a powerful navy to guard the coast and the long trade routes" (1968, 6). Still, one mustn't forget the Dutch army. During the period of the Truce, 1609–1621, "increasing wealth enabled the Dutch to acquire, besides the world's largest navy, the only standing army in Europe remotely comparable in strength to that of Spain" (Israel, 1977, 38). This was the consequence of the Maurician reforms, in-volving the better use of manpower, the smaller tac-tical unit, and innovations in siege warfare. Roberts points out these reforms had two preconditions: "The first was that Dutch armies should be paid

lenged in the period between 1651 and 1678, at the height of Dutch hegemony; and by the time of the wars of the turn of the eighteenth century, the Dutch had become a secondary military power in comparison to France and England. But this was precisely the consequence of Dutch economic hegemony. There came a point in the mid-seventeenth century when cumulative economic advantage seemed so incapable of being undercut that both England and France decided that the "Dutch must be driven from the field by force."[170] In fact, of course, even in purely economic terms, hegemony cannot last in a capitalist system; but one cannot blame the English and the French for chafing at the bit. We contend, then, that the state was an essential instrument used by the Dutch bourgeoisie to consolidate an economic hegemony that they had won originally in the sphere of production and had then extended to commerce and finance. The states of competing core and semipheripheral powers would be equally essential instruments in the later process of destroying this hegemony.

What of the cultural sphere? Was there no place for ideas, values, science, art, religion, language, passion, and color? Of course there was, for cultures are the ways in which people clothe their politico-economic interests and drives in order to express them, hide them, extend them in space and time, and preserve their memory. Our cultures are our lives, our most inner selves but also our most outer selves, our personal and collective individualities. How could there not be a cultural expression of hegemony? Such expression would not be in all cases cultural dominance. Core powers often dominate peripheral areas, imposing a sense of inferiority on people regarding their own culture; it is, however, unlikely that a hegemonic power would be able to do the same with other core powers. At most, in the latter case, the culture of a hegemonic power can serve as a model,[171] especially a technological model; but cultures are precisely arenas where resistance to hegemony occurs, where appeals are made to the historical values of established "civilizations" against the temporary superiorities of the market. This is true today and was no less true in the seventeenth century.

On the other hand, hegemonic powers do tend to shine culturally, and their critics often proceed from sour grapes. First of all, they have the material need and material means to be productive scientifically, and such productivity carries over into the arts. Second, the politics of liberalism is nourishing to a cultural explosion, and all the more so because the resulting open door policies often lead to the arrival of cultural personalities from elsewhere. Third, wealth breeds luxury, which feeds on cultural artifacts even as it undermines the material base of the wealth itself. Obviously,

---

well, and above all punctually. . . . The second condition was an efficient system of training and drill." To contemporaries, the Dutch reforms "seemed to transform the art of war" (1958, 185, 187).

[170] Andrews (1915, 542).

[171] "However cautious the gentlemen regents might view the fact, the United Provinces were by 1621 a great power, the striking model of a civilization which by its very existence became the ideal of tens of thousands of thinking people throughout Europe." (Polišenský, 1971, 162).

applied science was of central concern to Holland. The technological advances of previous centuries were precisely one of the key factors in Dutch agro-industrial efficiency. Indeed, in the seventeenth century, the Dutch were busy exporting this technology, and we have already mentioned this transfer as a source of inward financial flows. It was, of course, also a sign of cultural impact. All over the European world, in England, France, Italy, Denmark, Prussia, Poland, there were "Hollandries," villages of Dutch migrants working on dikes and drainages.[172] As they exported their agricultural skills, the Dutch invested much energy in improving their shipping technology—seeking to reduce costs, especially by improving the techniques of navigation.[173]

In describing how English sovereigns encouraged Dutch skilled artisans to migrate to England between 1669 and 1750, Clark says one reason the Dutch came was that they faced the heavy competition of peers at home, which compared unfavorably to "the easier opportunities of a backward country" like England. For it was the case in the seventeenth century that "however obscure the employment, if it demand[ed] ingenuity, . . . we are not surprised if we find a Dutchman in it."[174] Nor are we surprised, if we think about it, that there were "special bonds" with Scotland.[175] Commercial ties were reinforced by religious affinities, with the result that generations of Scotsmen went to the Netherlands for their university education. This is another link in the chain that explains the Scottish Enlightenment of the late eighteenth century, itself a crucial factor in the British industrial surge forward. Scientific advance is not dependent on intellectual liberty; but that is surely one mode of nourishing it, and it is a mode congenial to hegemonic powers. A curious paradox, however, is that intellectual liberalism always has its dangerous side, and most especially internally. Its logic may not respect political compromises among factions of the ruling strata; its slogans may encourage rebellion by the lower strata. So it is the way of hegemonic powers to encourage a culture of liberty but to constrain it, to indicate its limits (particularly internally) by erecting untouchable ideological flagstones in order to garner the political and economic advantages for the prevailing dominant interests without reaping the whirlwind.

Let us look at what this meant for the United Provinces. On the one hand, Holland was "a haven for philosophers"[176]—including Descartes, Spinoza, and Locke, the three great luminaries of seventeenth-century thought. Descartes found a tranquility and certainty in Holland that had

---

[172] See the map in Van Veen (1950, 56).

[173] Wilson points out that this task required achievements in many branches of technology simultaneously, calling together "the talents of mathematicians, engravers, printers, cartographers, instrument makers, lens grinders" (1968, 92).

[174] Clark (1960, 16). Glamann notes that from a third to a half of the inhabitants of towns like Nor-

wich and Colchester, which specialized in new draperies, were of "Netherlands origin" (1977, 253). It is surely true, as Wilson suggests, that "economic innovations are invariably short-lived, fatally easy to imitate" (1968, 39); but the issue is who makes the innovations.

[175] Wilson (1968, 178).

[176] Wilson (1968, 165–177).

escaped him in France. Spinoza was driven by excommunication from the *Jodenbreestraat,* the quarters of the Sephardic Jews, to the friendlier districts of Dutch burghers. Locke sought refuge from the wrath of James II until the happier era when a Dutchman sat on the English throne. Of course, there were many more persecuted intellectuals, such as Comenius, Jurieu, and Bayle, who blessed the existence of Amsterdam and Rotterdam.[177] It was a land of exile for French Huguenots to be sure; but the Dutch were liberal and welcomed both Huguenots and Jansenists; Puritans, Royalists, and Whigs; and even Polish Socinians. All were beneficiaries of Holland's commercial axiom: "forbid as little as possible, accept inputs from everywhere."[178] Nor did this attitude represent merely gratuitous appreciation by the Dutch of high culture; it was good business, and for everyone involved. On the one hand, Holland attracted intellectuals by its "large salaries and good working conditions"[179]—the brain drain being no recent invention.[180] On the other hand, the freedom of the multiple national oppositions of the European world-economy to print whatever they wanted in Holland[181] meant that the Regents "realized the economic advantages to be derived from the sale of books and pamphlets"[182]; thus the "providential alternative medium of expression"[183] of the ones was the commercial profit of the others.

There was another side to this coin, however. In 1592, just when the transition of the United Provinces to the status of world power began, the first Arminian controversy broke out. In the high days of Protestant theology when all was grace and all was salvation, Jacobus Arminius was to grasp the most nettlesome branch of the Calvinist logic, the paralogic[184] or psycho-logic of predestination, the doctrine of positive reprobation. Arminius rejected the view that grace is salvation, a view espoused by his chief opponent, François Gomar. He proposed as an alternative that grace is the indispensable prerequisite for salvation, the necessary instrument of salvation. This may seem, to the jaundiced eyes of twentieth-century persons, a picayune distinction, but it led to the greatest theological debate of

[177] On the different ways in which Jurieu and Bayle reacted to their exile, see E. Labrousse (1967).

[178] Jeannin (1969, 103).

[179] Jeannin (1969, 102).

[180] "The semi-laissez-faire of the Dutch Republic [with its policy of free immigration] . . . brought to the new 'state' vital increments of manufacturing, mercantile and financial skill, a network of personal business relationships and a vast addition of capital and ships. . . . Without them the progress of the Dutch would have been slower and smaller" (Wilson, 1977a, 18).

[181] Beutin says it was the only place in Europe in the eighteenth century with a "relatively free press" (1939, 110).

[182] Haley (1972, 124).

[183] Wilson (1968, 163). As Vilar says: "The spirit of liberty expressed Dutch superiority of the time in matters of commerce" (1974, 251). It would take us into a long detour to argue the relationship of the marvelous period of Dutch art, the "middle-classness" and "naturalism" of the style, and the prevailing conditions. Suffice it to bear in mind the crass aspect of the situation, underlined by Wilson: "What kept the [art] profession going was the steady persistence of demand, rather than any expectation of high rewards" (1968, 124).

[184] The phrase is found in Chaunu. See his discussion of "Dordrecht, the greatest affair of the century" (1966a, 470–474). "Tout va se jouer en Hollande."

seventeenth-century Holland, and probably of Christian Europe.[185] Despite the strong support the Arminians seemed to have had at first in political and economic circles in Holland, it was a debate they lost in the short run when, at the Synod of Dordrecht in 1619, the Contra-Remonstrants (Gomarians) carried the day against the Remonstrants (Arminians) and had the latter excluded from the state. Of course, the Arminians didn't really lose in the long run. The whole story is there.

What was at issue? According to the Dutch historian G. J. Renier, the Arminian formulation meant that an individual could withstand grace or lose it, and thus "a fragment of human freedom and dignity was preserved by the Remonstrants. They were the true children of humanism." Perhaps, but who supported humanism?[186] The Arminians were clearly a social minority, but a powerful one because their political base was the product of social links to the merchant-patricians.[187] On the other side were the orthodox puritanical *predikants* recruited from modest homes and backed by the petty bourgeoisie in the consistories and excited crowds in the towns, with the support of Prince Maurice and the Orangist camp.[188] The Gomarians accused the Arminians of being "soft" on Catholicism, and this perhaps brought the Arminians some tacit Catholic support; but Catholics were oppressed, and being in the "lowest strata of society,"[189] could offer little in the way of political strength.

[185] In my view, Chaunu is quite correct to say that this debate, at least in the seventeenth century, is more fundamental than that between Catholics and Protestants. The Arminian–Gomarian debate was paralleled, as Chaunu reminds us, by the Molinist–Jansenist controversy within the Catholic Church. He is also correct to call Arminianism the "ancestor of the liberal heresy of the nineteenth century" (1962a, 119).

[186] Renier (1944, 46). See Pieter Geyl's description of the view of Samuel Coster, Arminian and Amsterdam literary figure: "By means of a parable—the world is a vicious horse ridden by authority and curbed by the whip of the law and the bridle of religion; put the bridle into the hands of a secular rider, the Church, and the horse will bolt—Coster develops the pure Remonstrant theory of relations of Church and State. It was a theory which appealed to the cultivated all over Europe. Their fear of the unreasonable multitude and its excesses of religious excitement everywhere redounded to the claims to absolute authority put forward by the secular magistrates; by the monarchs elsewhere; here by the States" (1961, 70).

[187] Though this statement refers to the moment of the original controversy, the social cleavages remained constant through the century. Jeannin says that: "In Amsterdam, in 1672, there were complaints that the Arminians—a term that had become more political than religious—were in the majority among the magistrature, although they represented

less than 5% of the population" (1969, 111). But how serious were these complaints? Roorda notes that a compromise had been reached in the period of Dutch hegemony with slow "aristocratization" of the clergy. "The Church was exposed to the world and assimilated with the powers of that world. . . . The regents became more churchy too. . . . The most heated conflicts between Church and State were things of the past [by 1672]" (1967, 201).

[188] Chaunu gives this description of the social cleavage: "A social opposition: the Regents of Holland, on the one hand, constituted the Arminian party; the landed nobility of the east, the middle classes, and a minority of recently arrived grand bourgeois, on the other hand, the cadres of the Gomarian party. Gomarians, the six provinces other than Holland, and especially the agricultural provinces recently conquered; Gomarians, the newly-converted beyond the frontier of 1590. Arminians, the bourgeoisie of the coastal cities of Holland, with the revealing exception of Amsterdam, more recently Protestant than that part of Holland on the back side of the dunes" (1966a, 128–129).

[189] Roorda (1967, 204). Renier suggests secret Catholic sympathy despite outward "indifference" (1944, 49). E. H. Kossmann, in a private communication, says he doubts that Catholics could be described in the early seventeenth century as the lowest strata of society since many patricians were still Catholics.

This locating of social groups in the two camps is crude but not inaccurate. What does it tell us about the meaning of the debate? First we must see why the debate turned against the Arminians. The second Arminian controversy began in 1602 and reached a climax in 1608. The second debate caused much more fuss than the first one, although both the main protagonists and the theological issues were identical. What had changed was the *political* situation. What was to become the Truce of 1609 was then under discussion between the camp of continued war and the camp of truce. The first included the Orangists, who wished to strengthen further the hero-stadholder and achieve glory; the Protestant proselytizers, who still hoped to incorporate the southern Netherlands and extirpate Catholicism; some merchants, who drew their profits from privateering; and segments of the popular strata, attracted by opportunity and xenophobia. The camp of truce was led by the Land's Advocate of Holland, Johan van Oldenbarnevelt, who spoke for all those who saw the possibilities of hegemony. Their point of view was to be summed up later in the century by William Bareel, who wrote to the moral successor of Oldenbarnevelt, Jacob de Witt, on December 18, 1654: "The best possible maxim and wish for the sovereign Republic seems to me to be Peace in our days and Peace everywhere, since our Trade extends everywhere."[190]

On October 30, 1608, when the political debate about the truce was at its "intense peak,"[191] Arminius delivered his Declaration of Sentiments. The two debates became inextricably intertwined. Oldenbarnevelt got his Truce, but Gomarus was to get his Synod of Dordrecht. Was one the price of the other? It is surely true, as Boxer suggests, that the regent class was able to keep Calvinist zealots from "sacrificing gain to godliness." Since their attitude to religious tolerance was "essentially utilitarian and self-interested,"[192] a few Arminians thrown to the wolves in a timely way might not seem an unreasonable price—if not to Oldenbarnevelt (who was executed in 1619, the same year as the Synod of Dordrecht), at least to others of his class.[193] This particular dramatic plot is a familiar scenario of the modern world-system. Cultural tolerance had its limits, particularly its internal limits. It could not be permitted to sow subversion. It could not

---

[190] Cited in Franken (1968, 5).

[191] Bangs (1970, 481), whose article is an excellent analysis of the interrelation between theological, economic, and political phenomena. See also Geyl (1961, 13–14).

[192] Boxer (1965, 131).

[193] Haley agrees: "[The Regents] were inclined to tolerant views and strongly disinclined to become simply the secular arm of an intolerant church. But their main concern was to damp down controversy in the interests of peace and harmony" (1972, 104). Conversely, as Roorda points out, the degree to which the Orange Stadholder was really ready to offer the common man protection against "aritocratic malpractices" was limited, the "stadholder's ac-

tions only rarely com[ing] up to the expectations of lower middle-class Orangists" (1967, 189).

The "truce" party was also beginning to find fewer virtues in the truce at this time. In 1621 Philip III laid down three conditions for extending the truce: freedom of worship for Catholics, opening of the Scheldt, and evacuation of the East and West Indies. The Orangists and the Amsterdam merchants found their interests harmonious once more (see Geyl, 1961, 84). Presumably what the Spanish would win out of 26 more years of war was a *Catholic* Southern Netherlands; but Dutch *economic* interests prevailed (see Parker, 1972, 263). Hence in the *longer* run, the *predikants* did not gain what *they* wanted.

even be permitted to create a fundamental split among the ruling strata. Descartes and Locke were welcomed, but Grotius was imprisoned for life. A ban was placed on the principal works of Spinoza, who was an internal exile, although he was allowed to live and write; and when he died, his funeral was accompanied "by six carriages and a large number of well-to-do people."[194] Not merely liberalism but liberality.

In 1618 a Venetian remarked that Amsterdam was "the mirror-image of the early days of Venice."[195] By 1672 a lifetime had passed. The fruit of hegemony is "decline," but the process is not painful as one might think because it is scarcely perceived until long past the peak. In later centuries, we may argue about when decline set in. At the time, however, the English and French as well as the Dutch saw Holland as the kingpin, and at least until 1763, if not until the French Revolution, it was materially very satisfying, and no doubt morally too, to be a Dutch burgher. Decline can only be analyzed as rise, the rise of others within the framework of the efficiencies of profit. To pursue further our discussion of the limits of hegemony, we must thus turn from this hitherto Hollandocentric presentation to a systematic discussion of the parallel developments and interrelations between the United Provinces, England, and France.

The situation began to change in mid-century. The Thirty Years' War ended; the Eighty Years' War ended. The United Provinces at last began to feel the pinch of economic contraction, which the other states had been feeling for from 30 to 50 years. The English Civil War was over—not yet liquidated, but over. The century-long period of acute internal strife in France had just about ended. The battles between Reformers and Counter-Reformers, between the "puritan" and the "proto-liberal" (or "tolerant") versions of Christianity, were publicly contained and largely privatized. The states breathed again, and public administration could begin to be the central concern of rulers.[196]

In a sense we move from an era where the cleavages were primarily *intra*state, the turning inward of European wars and politics after Cateau-Cambrésis, to an era when the cleavages were once again primarily *inter*state. This latter period runs from 1651, the time of the start of the first Anglo–Dutch War, to 1763 and the close of the Seven Years' War. In a sense, the distinction between intrastate and interstate cleavages is both arbitrary and fuzzy; but nonetheless, it may be useful in underlining the dominant tone of an epoch. Class struggles in a capitalist world-economy are complex affairs and appear sinuously under many guises. The period leading up to the dominance of a hegemonic power seem to favor the intrastate form, as those that seek class advantage on the market seek to eliminate *internal* political constraints left over from earlier eras. The period

---

[194] Haley (1972, 128).
[195] Visconti (1958, 301).
[196] E. Barker begins his history of modern administration in 1660 "somewhat arbitrarily and yet with some reason" (1966, 1).

of the decline of hegemony seems to favor the interstate form, as those who seek class advantage on the market strive to eliminate *interstate* political constraints left over from earlier eras.[197]

In the mid-seventeenth century, it was clear that both England and France were interested in forcibly eliminating certain Dutch advantages and substituting their own. Because the market superiority of the one over the other was not so clear-cut and the Dutch were still very strong, and because rising semiperipheral powers such as Prussia, Sweden, and Austria sought to profit from the absence of a militarily preponderant state, it took over 100 years to clarify this situation. By 1763 the English edge over France (and the Dutch) would be clear and Britain could move forward to becoming the next hegemonic power. By 1763 the success of Prussia in the semiperipheral game of moving to the head of the line was clear, and it determined the future course of central European politics; the contraction and reorganization of the periphery was complete and the world-economy was ready for further geographic and economic expansion.

---

[197] P. Anderson's comments are similar: "For if the seventeenth century is the noon of turmoil and disarray in the relationship between class and State within the total system of aristocratic political rule, the eighteenth century is by comparison the golden evening of their tranquility and reconciliation" (1974a, 55).

3

STRUGGLE IN THE CORE –
PHASE I: 1651–1689

Figure 4: "Louis XIV Visiting the Gobelins Factory," a Gobelins Tapestry after a drawing by Charles Le Brun, First Painter to the King, Curator-General of Drawings, and Director of the Gobelins Tapestry Factory. The tapestry celebrates a visit by Louis XIV in 1677. He was accompanied by the young Duke d'Enghein and the Prince of Condé. Colbert is behind him.

Dutch hegemony was first really challenged in 1651. Why only then? Surely not because England and France did not want to do it earlier. It was rather because they were too preoccupied with their internal problems to carry through "any vigorous effort at breaking the hegemony of Holland."[2]

The half-century after 1650 throughout Europe was a period of cessation in population growth only, either through decline or leveling off, and the curves started to go up again at the end of the century.[3] No doubt this can be explained by the combination of the ravages of the Thirty Years' War, the ecological stress that led in some areas to local shortages (and therefore epidemics), and the overproduction of cereals in the world-economy *as a whole* leading to declining *world* prices.[4] It is, however, the regional variation that is most pertinent. It is quite striking that at the beginning of the seventeenth century the areas of the highest population density tended to be located primarily in the old dorsal spine of Europe (from Flanders to northern Italy) and in the new core areas of the European world-economy (western part of the United Provinces, southeast England, and northeast and west of France).[5] The main impact of the Thirty Years' War, the Eighty Years' War, and the epidemics of the early seventeenth century was to dramatically reduce the population of the old dorsal spine, and of northern and central Spain, which was previously a medium density area.[6]

By contrast, in the new core states there was little decline. In the United Provinces the situation was confused from 1650 to 1680 and generally stable after that, until an upswing occurred around 1750.[7] In northern

---

[1] Cited in Plumb (1950, 71).

[2] Geyl (1961, 161–162), who says: "Richelieu might have his moments of annoyance, but his life-work of bringing Huguenots and nobles to order and of uniting the forces of France against the Hapsburgs . . . left him no freedom of action."

[3] See Chaunu's chart with various regional curves placed side by side (1966a, 181).

[4] Pentland cogently argues that the causal sequence, in general, is from economic opportunity to population increase and not the other way around; but this sequence applies at the beginning of a secular upward curve. At other times, "population growth, by itself, and in the absence of other supports, produces distress and stalemate" (1972, 179). For example, in discussing English population growth in the eighteenth century, he inverses the usual analysis, asserting that it "stagnated in the first part of the century *because* food was too plentiful, and agriculture depressed; and grew later because, among other things, agricultural prices were higher and rural populations more prosperous" (1972, 180). See also van der Woude (1972), who has a similar hypothesis.

[5] Chaunu's map on population density for 1620 makes this extremely visible (1966a, Graph 23).

[6] See Reinhard and Armengaud (1961, 141–142, 144–146), who discuss the Germanic "catastrophe" (including Czechia) and the "slow but durable decline" of southern Europe in the seventeenth century. Furthermore, as Chaunu points out, hunger led to increased human circulation, which led to increased virulence of epidemics. "Each food shortage recreated, *mutatis mutandis*, the conditions of a *Conquista* of America" (1966a, 233).

[7] See van der Woude and Mentink (1966, 1189).

France, there was an "absence of major catastrophes."[8] England's picture is considered "unclear"[9] and "still little known," but there may have been a "modest" increase in population at this time.[10]

It is quite understandable, given this link between core status and resistance to population decline, that the "optimistic" theory of population should prevail in the seventeenth century, the belief that populousness leads to national strength whereas sparse habitation means that a country is "necessarily poor and weak."[11] How to strengthen their state as compared with others was what preoccupied the core states. It was the Depression of 1622 that inspired Sir Thomas Mun's mercantilist classic, *England's Treasure by Foreign Trade*.[12] To be sure, mercantilism was nothing new in England. Grampp dates it back to 1500,[13] and Unwin describes an extensive protectionist movement under James I;[14] but as the crunch came to England and France, mercantilist policies were adopted with "more force and coherence."[15] Yet, as we discussed before, the Alderman Cockayne's Project turned out to be premature. What had changed by mid-century that made it possible for mercantilist policies to succeed? What in fact made it *essential* that they succeed?[16]

In the acute struggle of the core, the English Navigation Act of 1651 was the opening gun. What precipitated it? The end of the Thirty Years' War and the final recognition of Dutch independence by the Spanish both occurred in 1648. The English Commonwealth was proclaimed in 1649, and the stadholderless period of the United Provinces began in 1651. In terms of Europe's great religious struggle, the bounds of Reformation and Counter-Reformation had more or less been reached (with the exception of the expulsion of the French Huguenots). Hence there was peace, and yet there were wars—or really a long "cold war" that occasionally involved

---

[8] Le Roy Ladurie (1975a, 360).

[9] Slicher van Bath (1965b, 145).

[10] Reinhard and Armengaud (1961, 147); but *London's* population went steadily up, from 200,000 in 1600 to 400,000 in 1650 to 575,000 in 1700. That of Paris went up only from 400,000 in 1600 to 500,000 in 1700. See Wrigley (1967, 44).

[11] Hutchison (1967, 94), who discusses the ideas themselves (chap. 5) and their origin and spread (chap. 3) and also notes the simultaneous rise of "political arithmetik," the ancestor of modern demography. One general caveat must be made about the link between core status and population density. As Habakkuk notes, "before the nineteenth century, our knowledge of population movements is partly inferred from economic evidence—that is, from the behavior of wages, prices, and rents—which the population movements are then invoked to account for" (1965, 148–149).

[12] The dating of this pamphlet, which was not publicly distributed until much later, was once thought uncertain; but it now seems well-established in the 1620s (see Gould, 1955a,b; Supple, 1954).

[13] Grampp (1952, 465).

[14] Unwin (1904, 172–195). This movement met extensive opposition, the exact sources of which are the subject of a sprightly controversy revolving around the English Parliament's debate on free trade in 1604. See Rabb (1964 and 1968), Ashton (1967 and 1969), and Croft (1975).

[15] Deyon (1969, 31). Hinton reminds us that, although the mercantilists "did not believe in Progress, . . . their contrary idea, Degeneration, was an equally potent spur to action" (1955, 286).

[16] See Deyon (1969, 43), who says: "In the difficult world of the years 1650–1750, when stagnation of demand and of prices exacerbated competition, the prosperity of manufacturers *presumed* a rigorous tariff protectionism, and therefore a political power able to resist the pressures of foreign diplomats and merchants" (italics added).

interludes of fighting to punctuate the "venomous trade-rivalry" of the core powers.[17] The end of the various continental wars was no advantage to England. Quite the contrary, for English shipping had benefited from England's neutral status, and "the coming of peace meant a reversion to the Dutch entrepôt."[18] Furthermore, after 1632, because of wartime insecurity, the Spanish *asientistas* used English ships to carry their bullion to Flanders. This had a very important side advantage for England because, by agreement, two-thirds of the bullion was unloaded at Dover and coined at the Mint in London before proceeding. This provided significant state revenue, useful to Charles I and later to the Long Parliament.[19]

On the Dutch side, the war's end was followed by the Redemption Treaty between the Dutch and the Danish in 1650, allowing the Dutch to farm the Sound tolls on their own ships for a fixed annual sum, which saved money and, "no less important," time.[20] On April 7, 1652, Jan van Riebeeck established the first Dutch outpost on the Cape of Good Hope, which dominated the route to the East Indies. In general, Dutch prosperity was reaching a new peak and by contrast, "the English position had never been worse."[21] Corn prices had reached their peak for the century in 1649. The French were prohibiting English imports. The merchants were paying the costs of civil war, at home (via taxation) and abroad (because of the absence of a diplomatic corps and the coastal preoccupations of the navy). It was under these circumstances that the arch-Protestant regime of the Commonwealth was to break the historic, closely interwoven pattern of Protestantism and patriotism.[22] Indeed, Lichtheim sees Cromwell as having made "the decisive break" in the history of British overseas expansion. He secularized foreign policy, as he "nationalized" the Puritans.[23]

Since the Dutch were in fact hegemonic, there were only two possible ways of enhancing English commerce: state assistance to English merchants or state constraint on foreign merchants. In 1621 the English, fearing to antagonize the Dutch by adopting the latter policy, opted for the former, in the form of regulated companies.[24] This served the companies well, but did not serve the English bourgeoisie as a whole. Over the objec-

---

[17] This modern terminology is used with reference to Dutch–British relations by Franken (1968, 8). Wilson also underlines the venom: "In the interval between the declining threat of a Spanish, and the later rise of a French, hegemony, Englishmen allowed themselves the luxury of a temporary but virulent campaign against the Dutch" (1965, 41).

[18] H. Taylor (1972, 260), who says that the "coincidence of the crisis after 1648 and the Navigation Act of 1651 seems too close to be purely accidental."

[19] See Kepler (1972); see also H. Taylor on this role of supplier to the Spanish in Flanders as the "new dynamic stem" of English trade in the 1630s (1972, 240).

[20] Hinton (1959, 85).

[21] J. R. Jones (1966, 21).

[22] See the discussion in C. Hill (1969, 42). See also Roberts, who argues that Cromwell did *not* subordinate English trade to Protestant concerns and that his policies in the Baltic, "even if influenced by religious considerations, [were] right from a strictly secular point of view" (1961, 405).

[23] Lichtheim (1974, 24).

[24] See Hinton (1959, 63).

tions of the regulated companies,[25] but in the line of "the forward march of economic forces as a whole,"[26] the English moved directly against the Dutch by putting restrictions on imports in 1651. The Navigation Act of 1651 decreed that goods entering England had to be shipped either in English ships or in ships of the country of production (defined as being the country of first port). This was designed precisely "to cripple the carrying and entrepôt trade of the Dutch."[27] Must we then choose between Adam Smith's interpretation that the Act was a result of the interested counsel of merchants and Schmoller's that it was an aspect of state building?[28] Not at all—since what was of interest at this point to merchants (some merchants) and manufacturers was precisely the strengthening of the state in ways that could help them engross not merely the Baltic trade but also the about-to-expand and ultimately more important transatlantic trade.[29]

It is difficult to see how a military test of strength could have been avoided. The provocation to the Dutch was too great, even if the English thought they were being defensive. In early 1651, the Dutch rejected a proffered treaty, and relations with England rapidly deteriorated.[30] Once a war started in 1652, it rapidly turned against the Dutch, largely because their navy was in surprisingly bad shape.[31] One war in a sense led to another. The "jingoists" in England were waiting for "another smack against the Dutch."[32] Their chance would come—years later, and this time as quite

[25] See Hinton (1959, 165); see also M. P. Ashley (1934, 19–20, 163) on the varying attitudes of English merchant groups.

[26] Wilson (1965, 184).

[27] Harper (1939b, 49). One of the side effects of this new English thrust illustrates this well. In 1597 the Dutch Estates-General issued a new charter in favor of "the Portuguese Nation residing in these lands." This meant both New Christians and, indirectly, professing Jews. The motive was to attract the financial resources of the Jews, which, Baron argues, "the Prince of Orange and his associates greatly overestimated" (1973, 20; 3–73, *passim*). Shortly after the passage of the Navigation Act in 1651, Oliver Cromwell began negotiations, ultimately successful, with Amsterdam's Sephardi Jews about their readmission to England (Jews having been banished by Edward I in 1290). From the point of view of the Jewish entrepreneurs, readmission meant that "the crippling intentions of the Navigation Act could by bypassed." From the point of view of Cromwell, readmission was a "minor element in a more general policy of expanding overseas trade: permitting Jewish merchants to settle in London strengthened England in her commercial rivalry with Holland" (Endelman, 1979, 15, 17).

[28] See discussion of these two interpretations in Farnell (1964, 439–440).

[29] Davis (1962, 297).

[30] See Geyl (1964, 25–28). Hinton points out that the Dutch basically wanted economic union, which was to their advantage, whereas the English preferred political union, which was to theirs (1959, 88). One can see how the participants, starting from such contrary positions, could move rapidly from a discussion of unity to the "unleashing of hatred" (P. de Vries, 1950, 46). A proposal to consider unification of the Dutch and English East India Companies had prefigured the political discussion. It occurred between 1610 and 1618 and failed because of Dutch demands considered exorbitant by the English. See Dermigny (1970b, 453).

[31] Admiral Mahan's explanation was that "the Dutch government, averse to expense, unmilitary in its tone, and incautious from long and easy victory over the degenerate navy of Spain, had allowed its fleet to sink into a mere assembly of armed merchantmen. Things were at their worst in the days of Cromwell" (1889, 126). Recent scholarship confirms this judgment. See Wilson, who says that "during the long period of land warfare in the Thirty Years' War, the Dutch navy had been relatively neglected (1975a, 65). For a brief account of the war itself, see Wilson (1968, 190–194), who concludes that the "war had nevertheless revealed the critical weaknesses of a Dutch economy which had evolved in terms of economic efficiency, peace, and business as usual."

[32] Wilson (1968, 194).

open aggression. If "Cromwell wished to defend himself against the Dutch, Charles II wished to make himself their master."[33] But by the time of Charles II, the Dutch fleet had improved, having learned its lesson, and English morale was low (because of administrative incompetence and the plague in London); hence there was stalemate and peace.

In some ways, the Treaty of Breda in 1667 was a Dutch victory, or at least a compromise. The Dutch exchanged the "expensive liability" of New Amsterdam for Surinam, and for Pulo-Run in the East Indies.[34] The English agreed that goods from the natural hinterland of the United Provinces (such as the German linens treated and/or stapled in Holland) would be considered Dutch. Since they were the bulk of Dutch exports to England, this vitiated some of the point of the Navigation Acts.[35] Nonetheless, Breda is seen by Wilson as "a real turning-point in Anglo–Dutch relations" and by Carter as the "downturn of the Dutch Republic's prosperity."[36] Obviously, something must have been going on below the political surface, and it must have been more than the mere advantage the English obtained by acquiring New Amsterdam and thereby plugging a major Dutch smuggling hole in English mercantilist restrictions.[37] Was it not that English hatred of the Dutch had in fact been coordinate with a "reluctant admiration for Dutch economic skill"[38] and "a desire to emulate them?"[39] and that important changes in the agro-industrial efficiencies of England were taking place that could render the setback of Breda essentially unimportant and turn the Dutch into England's junior partner?

No doubt France's entry into the rounds of warfare was the consequence of, and also facilitated, this shift. The French invasion of the Spanish Netherlands in 1667 was a "crucial event,"[40] hastening the Treaty of Breda and promptly leading to the Triple Alliance of England, the United Provinces, and Sweden (the fourth significant military power in Europe at that point). Louis XIV was forced to backtrack and the Dutch boasted with some justification in 1668 of being the arbiter of Europe and of having subdued five kings." No wonder Louis would have a "Dutch obsession."[41]

In 1672 matters came to a head. The Dutch found themselves in separate wars with the English and the French. The Third Anglo–Dutch (naval) War

---

[33] Hinton (1959, 145). Haley agrees that all three Anglo–Dutch wars were "unwelcome to the Dutch." He says that "the first two took place when they did essentially because jealous English commercial interests were able, for brief moments, to press the government to attack to break Dutch commercial and naval strength by force" (1972, 177). This view is made plausible by the fact that "one of Admiral Blake's three major directives when the first war began in 1652 was to destroy the Dutch fishing fleet assembling in Scottish waters" (Michell, 1977, 179).

[34] See Carter (1975a, 6).

[35] See Wilson (1941, 6).

[36] Wilson (1957a, 154); see also Farnie (1962, 206) and Carter (1975a, 6).

[37] See Wilson (1968, 213–214); see also Williamson (1929, 252).

[38] This is the attitude Wilson ascribes to Sir George Downing, the "architect" of the English mercantile system (1965, 168).

[39] Hinton (1959, 106).

[40] J. R. Jones (1966, 75).

[41] Goubert (1970b, 112); see also J. R. Jones (1966, 60–61). On the Dutch efforts "to maintain the status quo," see Franken (1968, 7).

was relatively inconclusive, although the English won their way on the symbolic salute issue.[42] The French land campaign, by contrast, seemed to be spectacularly successful, at least at first. In the Year of Disaster, 1672, all of Holland was nearly conquered by the French; in the consequent political turmoil, Johan de Witt was murdered and the regime of the Dutch Republic was terminated. Yet the near victory turned to failure. (Hence the other Dutch appellation for 1672, the Year of the Miracle.) Far from the French taking over the Dutch trading system, the Treaty of Nijmegen that finally terminated the long and ultimately inconclusive war in 1678 and required that the French revoke the tariff of 1664.[43]

The real significance of 1672 is that from 1651 to then, both the English and the French saw the Dutch as the great rival. They now turned primarily on each other, and the Dutch suddenly became a secondary factor despite continuing Dutch economic strength.[44] In a sense, what was happening was that the cost of warfare was steadily rising. Although the technology of weapons would remain basically similar throughout the early modern period, there was a steadily declining role for the cavalry[45] and for the siege warfare in which the Dutch excelled.[46] By the end of the seventeenth century, the demographic consequences of the partition of the Burgundian state had begun to take their military toll. The United Provinces, despite its wealth, was "too small to carry indefinitely the insupportable burden of military and naval defence they had to bear."[47] The English navy surpassed that of the Dutch in the end largely because England "commanded larger

[42] For some time the English had been demanding that other ships at sea salute English ships. This chronic demand was reiterated forcefully in 1672. J. R. Jones remarks that for the Dutch, the Scandinavians, the Hanse, and the French, "this would amount to the establishment of what contemporaries called a United Monarchy at sea"; and it was seen as parallel to Louis XIV's pretensions on the land (1968, 48).

[43] See Wilson (1968, 202–204).

[44] Until this time, Louis XIV regarded England as "a weak pro-French country," which judgment, Goubert argues, "was permissible in 1661: it was unfortunate that Louis pronounced it in 1670" (1970d, 72–73). Rule similarly says that Louis "underestimated the power of England." No doubt this is why, in part, the Dutch war turned out to be "puzzling to French statesmen" (1969, 59).

As for England, a shift in perspective was a matter of political debate. C. Hill says that, as of 1674, it was the "Whigs and the monied interests [who] saw France as England's main competitor for world trade and world power" (1969, 163). The Tories were less decided, and it is only after 1689 that England would willingly accept the role of great power. Until then, Horn feels that England's appearances on the continent in this role "had usually

been involuntary, short-lived and ineffective" (1967, 2). I am not sure I agree with the adjective involuntary, but the other two seem true enough. Horn offers as an elementary indicator that it is only after 1689 that the English cease to be a receiver of subsidies and become a payer, as the Dutch and French already were.

[45] See A. R. Hall (1957a, 347, 349). The absence of significant change in weapons technology should not lead us to neglect the "great improvement in the organization of military forces, and a large increase in their size." On changes in the structure of armies, as opposed to their weaponry, see Finer (1975, 99–102). On reservations concerning how much of a military revolution occurred, see Parker (1976b). Hall dates the decline of the cavalry after the mid-seventeenth century. Barnett points out that two inventions between 1660 and 1714, the bayonet and the flintlock musket, made for "the greater effectiveness of infantry" (1974, 129).

[46] "From the time of Prince Maurice of Nassau, the Dutch had a special reputation for siege warfare which enabled them to deploy their varied talents in engineering, mining and countermining, ballistics, explosives, etc." (Wilson, 1968, 100).

[47] Wilson (1970, 125).

resources."[48] France did too, of course, but they used their resources on land and not at sea; and in the long run they got less return for their military investment.[49]

The growing English and French military strength had its roots in important shifts in the economic base. One of the problems of discussing the comparative efficiencies of the agro-industrial production of the core powers between 1650 and 1750, and especially the comparison of England/Britain with France, is that almost all the research has been done within national bounds. Such works often contain comparative statements, which quite frequently represent prejudices rather than sober assessments. The scholars of the world, including the French, tend all too often to read the differences of the nineteenth century back into the earlier period, and thereupon make assiduous efforts to explain facts they have not yet empirically verified. My strong suspicion is that there was far less of a difference between the real agro-industrial efficiencies of England and France in this period than we tend to assume. The small differences that emerged as of 1763 were magnified *politically* into the significant differences of a century later, by which time they had been economically institutionalized. It is the first half of this argument that we shall try to outline at this point.

One of the basic problems of comparison is what areas to compare. The political unit of France was about four times that of England in size and population (hence roughly the same density). If we add Scotland and Wales, to use Great Britain as a unit of comparison, this a little less than doubles the area and reduces the population ratio. Considering only the Five Great Farms of France, which represented a unified tariff zone, gives us roughly the same area as Great Britain. If we had the data neatly divisible by these various units, which we do not, we would come up with different results depending on our choices. The outer political boundaries are quite meaningful for assessing military possibilities and indicating areas within which government policy could affect economic life, even though, in each of the three core powers, the central government was constrained, in varying ways, by the nature of its constitutional structure (not to speak of its internal politics).

Jacquart says of France that agriculture was in the seventeenth century

---

[48] Fischer and Lundgreen (1975, 541).

[49] For Goubert, 1672 was "the great turning point of the reign" of Louis XIV, in that the French–Dutch war marked the victory of Louvois over Colbert and the end of financial stability. "[By] 1673 the king was running out of money and the edifice which Colbert had built up began to fall apart at all sides" (1970a, 140).

Admiral Mahan, needless to say, thought the same: "Of all the great powers [France] alone had a free choice [between land and sea]. In 1672 she definitively chose expansion of land. Why [in 1715] was France miserable and exhausted while England was smiling and prosperous? Why did England dictate, and France accept, terms of peace? The reason apparently was the difference in wealth and credit." Mahan cites Campbell (*The Lives of Admirals*) on English successes in naval war and trade: "Such were the fruits of the increase of our naval power, and the manner in which it was employed." Mahan comments: "It is needless to add more" (1889, 226–227, 229).

"the most important source of wealth, and by far."[50] Is this not equally true of England? In the period of economic stagnation, part of the arable land was used for animal husbandry in England, but for wine growing in France. In each case it was a return to the usage of the period prior to the sixteenth-century expansion. The variation in response between the two countries was primarily a function of climate and pedology. Goubert paints a dark picture of France's agriculture in the seventeenth century in comparison with England's, Holland's and some of Europe's other areas as well; but Le Roy Ladurie sees France's agricultural expansion, at least in the far north (the best arable area), as starting at precisely the same point as England's—in 1690. Imbert argues, from a third position, that French cereal production improved only slightly, but wine production much more.[51]

A century-long decline in the prices of cereals occurred in all three core countries from 1650 to 1750. Prices of other agricultural products declined as well, but not always at the same rate.[52] In each of the countries, the response was to try to maintain profit levels by turning to other enterprises or lowering the costs of production through increased efficiency and organizational restructuring. The Dutch had long led the way in agricultural diversification. The others would now emulate them.[53] For Fussell the "most important novelty" in England was the introduction of turnips and clover in arable rotation, and for Jones the "crucial innovation pertained to the supply of fodder." Wilson stresses the role of assarting, the "process of winning new land from old waste and heath," whereas for Habbakuk, it was less the use of new techniques that mattered than "the spread of the best existing [ones]."[54] Whichever of these four emphases is correct, two main facts are noticeable. The "improvements" essentially made possible the cultivation of areas that had been previously low in productivity or totally unused;[55] and they were a direct response to the weakness of the cereals market since, in order to maintain profit levels, farmers had to obtain a larger share of a relatively stagnant market[56] or turn to other products.

The story of English agricultural improvements in this period is the

[50] Jacquart (1973, 172).
[51] See Goubert (1970f, 150), Le Roy Ladurie (1975a, 416), and J. Imbert (1965, 339).
[52] For the United Provinces, see van der Woude (1975, 240); for England, Thirsk (1970, 149); for France, Goubert (1970g, 334, 338–340).
[53] "Contemporaries in England began to be aware very early in the seventeenth century that in many branches of social organization the Dutch were far ahead of them. Pamphlets began to point out Dutch practices which the English ought to imitate or Dutch gains which the English ought to contest" (Clark, 1960, 14).
[54] See Fussell (1959, 613–614), E. L. Jones (1967, 7), Wilson (1965, 33), and Habakkuk (1965d, 328).

"In England, . . . the new fodder crops were merged to produce mixed farming systems from about 1630" (Jones and Woolf, 1969, 7).
[55] See Chambers (1960, 21) and Darby (1973, 330–344).
[56] See E. L. Jones (1965, 14), who contradicts his own point when he says (p. 1) that between 1660 and 1750 the "transformation in [the] techniques [of English agriculture were] out of all proportion to the rather limited widening of its market." What is a proper proportion? and when? When markets *expand*, it is often most profitable to maintain current techniques rather than to pay the costs of improvements.

subject of a vast literature, so persuasive as perhaps to cause us to lose perspective. De Vries reminds us that at least for the seventeenth century English agricultural improvement "served mainly to bring her up to a standard already achieved in the Netherlands and Northern Italy and not to leave them behind in a trail of smoke."[57] In a somewhat bold statement in light of the hesitancies of even the French scholars,[58] Roehl insists:

> Modern [agricultural] techniques were introduced *as early in France as elsewhere.* Particularly the area west of Paris toward the Channel and north toward Flanders is structurally and climatically quite similar to the best agricultural regions of England. It is not surprising, therefore, to note that the 'agricultural revolution', which was as uneven in its incidence in France as in England, began in and was for long largely confined to these same types of agricultural regions in the two countries.[59]

What do we know about the increase in productivity? Slicher van Bath puts England, the Netherlands, and France *all* in his phase C (average yield ratio on grains being 6.3–7.0), dating the period for the first two at between 1500 and 1699 and that for France as between 1500 and 1820—the same starting date but a different terminal one. For England and the Netherlands, he calculates a move into his phase D (average yield above 10.0) after 1750 (leaving us uncertain what he believes occurred between 1700 and 1750.[60] Hoskins sees no discernible rise in yields in England from 1680 to the end of the eighteenth century, and Wrigley estimates a 10% rise in per capita yield from 1650 to 1750; but Fisher says that as of the later years of Charles II, presumably circa 1680, "the flow of produce from the land was to become so great as to inflict upon men the horrors of plenty."[61] As for Scotland, commercialization of agriculture (arable and pastoral) was "one of the most striking characteristics in the seventeenth century."[62] In France, cereal productivity remained stable from the fifteenth century to 1840

---

[57] J. de Vries (1975, 89)

[58] Le Roy Ladurie, for example, talks of England's "stroke of genius" in adapting Flemish methods designed for small farm units to large-scale agriculture. He says that a similar attempt in France involving open fields between the Somme and the Loire, succeeded only partially and quite late (1975a, 416–417).

[59] Roehl (1976, 262, italics added). He specifies: "New crops, especially from North America, were introduced into the rotations—potatoes, clover and other forage crops, Indian corn, sugar beets. They performed the function of simultaneously 'cleaning' and resting the soil and allowed for the suppression of the fallow; stall feeding of cattle, and the consequent expansion of arable, also resulted." Roehl offers Bloch as reference (1966, 213–219), but notes that Morineau (1968) offers a contrasting view.

[60] Slicher van Bath (1963b, 16).

[61] Hoskins (1968, 27), Wrigley (1967, 57), and F. J. Fisher (1961, 4).

[62] Smout and Fenton (1965, 78); but they see innovation (liming for the acid soils) and reclamation as slowing down as of 1650 because of the "weak rule of the central government" and because of a decline of returns due to low prices (pp. 56–87). This is different from what presumably happened in England, and can probably be explained as follows: Although politically Scotland was located within a core power (and indeed only partially until 1707), it was, in *economic* terms, part of the periphery; thus in viewing the impact of the contraction we may see a greater similarity between Scottish and Polish producers than between Scottish and English producers.

when measured by yield ratio or production per hectare,[63] but not in terms of the workday or workyear, both of which grew longer.[64]

If we look at cereals production in isolation, we miss part of the point, for the "crux of agricultural improvement was the *combination* of animal and arable husbandry."[65] This was what the new grasses—hay, lucerne, clover—permitted. This was what the English learned from the Dutch.[66] This was what permitted the substitution of labor power for space and allowed for high productivity pastoralism without nomadism.[67] While this was going on in England, a similar flourishing of wine production was going on in France. In the seventeenth century, Chaunu remarks somewhat austerely, the Occident began to catch up with the Orient "on the road of artificial paradises."[68]

Taking the European world-economy as a whole between 1650 and 1750, there was a striking shift of the locus of cereals production, from the periphery to the core. We shall discuss this at length when we treat what happened to the eastern European periphery; but since much of the southern half of France was really semiperipheral, or even peripheral, the same phenomenon occurred there.

Perhaps the way to picture what happened is to say that although England and northern France as core areas both significantly increased their percentage of world cereals production at this time, in the case of England, the new surplus was exported across national boundaries,[69] but in the case of northern France the new surplus was "exported" internally.[70] If this

[63] See Morineau (1968, 326). Le Roy Ladurie specifies that this is true "in the world of the peasants" (1973, 425).

[64] Le Roy Ladurie (1968, 83), referring only, however, to Languedoc.

[65] Wilson (1965, 143).

[66] See Fussell (1968, 33–34).

[67] See Meuvret (1968, 17).

[68] Chaunu (1966a, 310).

[69] The significant rise in grain exports began as of 1700, which therefore indicates, says Bairoch, that the process started perhaps "a quarter of a century earlier" (1973, 459). This date fits in with the date changes began in governmental policies. The Act of 1673 initiated corn bounties—not merely allowing, but encouraging export; see Lipson, (1956, **II,** lxx–lxxii, 451–452). It is quite probable that the United Provinces increased its percentage of world cereals production too; but since it started with a low percentage, it was less noticeable. See, for example, the response of Franken to E. L. Jones's suggestion that the increase of grain production at a time of poor prices was a "uniquely English feature" (1967, 159). Nonsense, says Jansen: the same thing happened in Limburg and elsewhere. Franken attributes this expansion to pressure from the towns, and says it led to soil exhaustion (1971, 165): but the question is

why, especially in the light of the ecological factors, the grain wasn't imported from farther away. The question of profit possibilities must enter into the explanation.

[70] According to Jacquart (1974, 181–182), "the bulk of agricultural output in seventeenth-century France was consumed at home or processed on the spot." Although other agricultural products were exported, "commerce in grains was usually forbidden unless the harvest was good." For example, just when England was initiating corn bounties, the *Conseil du Roi* was issuing strict edicts against export—more than 30 between 1675 and 1683. Usher, in his classic treatment of the grain trade, assessed the issue differently (1913, 273, 294). He saw "the one element of originality in Colbert's treatment of the grain trade" to be *free* trade and argued that Colbert was governed by the principle of "prohibition in times of dearth; permission if there is plenty." Usher points out that *two* freedoms were involved, export and interprovincial trade. What was happening between 1675 and 1683 in the relative freedom of this latter trade?

One should perhaps observe in this regard that Basse-Provence and Languedoc grain production was still expanding until about 1680. The explanation of this is different, but the consequence is that it

analysis is correct regarding the broad outlines, the explanation of later differences between England and France are not to be found in differing levels of agricultural productivity in the seventeenth century. They can perhaps be located rather in the different organization of agricultural production. To make a sensible comparison of developments in English and French land tenure in this period, we must bear in mind that they each had two major modes of utilizing the land, but they only had one in common—cereals. The second mode in England was animal husbandry, which lent itself more to economies of scale than did wine production, the second mode in France; and animal husbandry required more capital investment. This simple economic fact may explain more about the differences in land tenure developments than is explained by laws, traditions, attitudes, prior class structure, or the presumed heritage of "feudal" rights.

Both in England and France, the complex interweaving of jurisprudence, politics, and the oscillations of the market created a veritable kaleidoscope of relationships to the land. One can cut through this complexity by visualizing four major categories in terms of primary sources of income: landlords, usually large, often nobles, who received rental payments from producers; prosperous producers, quite often "tenants," controlling medium-to large-scale units, and employing laborers; nonprosperous producers, having small units, occasionally proprietors, often needing to supplement their incomes by other employment; and landless laborers (or almost landless). Usually, marvelously ambiguous terms such as peasants and yeomen farmers principally designate the second category, and frequently the third as well. When authors write of the disappearance of the yeoman farmer in England and the survival of the peasant in France, it is this third category that seems to be the referent. What in fact was happening in the seventeenth century in England and France? We shall see this most clearly if we proceed category by category.

One of the basic phenomena of modern capitalism is the slow but steady growth of the large estate, a process of increasing concentration.[71] A principal method was the enclosure of commons, which seems not to have abated significantly in this period.[72] It took money and effort to create such

---

took up some of the slack of other regions. Chaunu argues that the "anomaly" of this continued expansion in a noncore area is "the importance of previously uncultivated land (*l'incult*)," which implied "a limit that was reached later" than elsewhere (1963b, 354). See also Goubert (1970c, 49–54). Le Roy Ladurie sees in the years 1655–1675 only a "momentary upsurge" for Languedoc (1974a, 149).

Of course, the English exported "internally" too, especially to London, (see Everitt 1968, 64). The point is to see the limits of foreign trade as a measure of productive processes—a point emphasized by Morineau (1965, 171). The United Provinces,

England, and France are on an upward continuum in terms of geographic size. The smaller the country, the larger will external trade loom as a percentage of total trade, other things being equal.

[71] See F. M. L. Thompson (1966, 512); Goubert (1970e, 102); Le Roy Ladurie (1975b, 1412); and Jacquart (1968, 66), who stresses that the growth of large estates occurred in France only north of the Loire valley.

[72] Hoskins speaks of "a vast amount of hitherto unsuspected enclosure" in seventeenth-century open-field England (1955, 220). See also Darby (1973, 321). In seventeenth-century France the

estates in difficult times. Increasingly, land was transferred by sale into
non-noble hands, although in France, this fact is less noticeable in retrospect because the same wealth that enabled a non-noble to purchase land
enabled him to purchase also a title of nobility (with significantly more
facility than in England). These large estates were in part put together
piecemeal, and therefore some of the concentration of ownership was just
"bookkeeping centralization."[73] By definition, such bookkeeping centralization entailed consequently increased absenteeism. In addition, with a decline in grain prices, there was a decreased advantage to direct farming and
an increased advantage to leasing.[74] The steady growth of the state attracted more and more of these landlords to life in the capital. Whether
they left to be courtiers or to be participants in the money market, there was
an increase in their physical distance from agricultural production.[75]

To preserve large estates, individuals had to be competent entrepreneurs; there was ample room for such talents, but families sought to
protect themselves against the incompetence of particular heirs. In England this gave rise to a new juridical form—the strict settlement.[76] This was
helpful, as were lowered interest rates, which made it more possible to carry
debts and were reinforced by the constraints on borrowing that the strict
settlement entailed.[77] In France, family inheritance faced the additional
problem of compulsory partibility of estates. But the French estate owners
were as astute as the English and used the legal loophole of *rentes constituées,*
which could be assigned to heirs, as distinguished from *rentes foncières,* which
could not. They were willing to accept low rates of interest rather than to
recover capital for the purposes of creating perpetual lineage property.
Venality of office provided a key form of such investment.[78]

The next two categories, the prosperous and nonprosperous producers,
are confused because although some were owners, most were tenants, and
because some tenants *de jure* were owners *de facto;*[79] the owner–tenant dis-

great plains were being preempted by the seigniors
such that having even a tiny pastureland was for a
peasant "a blessing of Heaven" (Goubert, 1970e,
102). Bloch reports widespread enclosure in the
west and center of France by 1700 (see 1930, 332).

[73] Meuvret (1960, 346). Tapié says that many a
great seignior in seventeenth-century France "had
become a sort of capitalist entrepreneur, his holding
being dispersed and administered by stewards or
tenants" (1959, 138).

[74] Roebuck (1973, 15). Slicher van Bath says that
after 1665, however, "the lessor's situation deteriorated" (1977, 107).

[75] This phenomenon is widely observed for
France; but the same thing happened in England.
See Roebuck (1973, 11–14). The employment of
full-time officials specialized in estate management
added to the distance. See Mingay (1963, 59).

[76] Strict settlements were mechanisms by which

the heir to an estate was legally constrained in the
ways he could sell or mortgage it (see Habakkuk,
1967b, 2–3). This system forced newly rich families
to look to the smaller gentry, freeholders, and
copyholders as sellers of land, which thus further
contributed to concentration. See Mingay (1968,
28).

[77] See Mingay (1960, 375–376) and Habakkuk
(1960, 160–165).

[78] This very complex system is fully outlined in
Giesey (1975). Goubert argues that the rates of
interest on *rentes constituées* in seventeenth-century
France were not in fact low compared to other
sources of revenue (see 1970g, 343–345).

[79] Meuvret argues that a *censive,* a perpetual
tenure akin to English copyhold, was a "veritable
property," whose holder could "rent, exchange, sell,
or share" it, so long as he paid seigniorial dues,
"which constituted a sort of tax system" (1960, 343).

tinction did not correlate with groupings of economic strength, social standing, or political outlook. Below the level of the great estate owner, it was
possibly better in a time of economic difficulties to be a tenant than to be an
owner.[80] The evolution of these two categories should be seen as a process
in two stages. In the first half of the seventeenth century, rents were still
rising and taxes had begun to rise, but profits from wheat production were
already declining.[81] This created a squeeze on the smaller products of cereals. Many independent producers had to yield their independent status.[82]
So did *smaller* tenant-farmers.[83]

The consequence seems to have been the rise of the prosperous tenant
cereals-farmer in the subsequent period of stagnation at the expense of the
nonprosperous farmers, whether owners or tenants. This was equally true
in England[84] and in northern France.[85] It was also true to some extent of

However Goubert points out it could be a very expensive tax for exercising the privilege of ownership
(1970f, 130). Kerridge makes a similar point for
England when he argues that a copyholder with a
life lease was a freeholder in respect of the land, if
not the law (1969, 60).

[80] For example, Mingay points out quite correctly
that the term yeoman as used by Adam Smith was
"merely a mark of social status." A yeoman was a
farmer above the status of husbandman and below
the status of larger farmers; but he might be, indif-
ferently, a freeholder, a copyholder, or a leaseholder
(1963, 88). Slicher van Bath agrees that, in general,
it was not always a mark of advantage to be an
owner. "The densely populated and more fertile
regions were farmed by tenants more prosperous
than the poorer sort of owner-occupier. Landownership and wealth were far from always going
hand in hand" (1977, 109).

[81] For France, 1660 seems to be the turning point.
It marks the end of the period of "immobilism and
catastrophes," the title Jacquart (1975) gives to a
chapter on rural France from 1560 to 1660. Le Roy
Ladurie, however, argues that ground rent augmented until 1675 (1973, 430).

[82] After the mid-century, "the independent small
farmer (*laboureur*), proud of his accounts-books and
of his few acres (*arpents*) and his relative independence, had to throw in the sponge. In the regions of
large-scale production (*grande culture*), his land is
attached to some large tenancy-unit (*quelque grosse
ferme*). He is happy if he can bet back his old holding
on lease" (Jacquart, 1975, 264). See also Dupâquier
(1973, 171) and C. E. Labrousse (1970, 703).

[83] Lawrence Stone says: "In the *early* seventeenth
century rents increased more rapidly than prices,
and profits flowed back to the landlord and away
from the tenant" (1972, 68, italics added). He must
mean the *small* tenant primarily, because he says
that this fact, plus engrossing, accounts for the
tripartite pattern of the latter period: landlord,

prosperous tenant-farmer, and landless *laboureur*.
Habakkuk tends to confirm this when he makes
overall size of capital a crucial factor in the explanation of the decline of the small peasant. A rich landlord in this period of stress "had a [capital] reserve
from which to draw, whenever the goods of peasants were placed on sale in the vicinity" (1965a,
660). Habakkuk precisely distinguishes this 1660–
1740 period from the 1540–1640 period, when it
was more frequent for *large* estates to be sold. Regarding the decline of the small landowner in
seventeenth-century England because of the need
for capital, see Thirsk (1970, 157).

Jacquart speaks of the bankruptcies after 1675 of
the small producer, whether *laboureur* (independent) or *fermier* (tenant) (1975, 210–211). In another
text, he refers to the disappearance in northern
France between 1680 and 1700 of a "good number
of dynasties of merchant-*laboureurs*" (1978c, 467).

[84] Mingay speaks of a "dramatic" decline of small
owner-occupiers in the period 1660 to 1750. (1968,
14–15, 31). In this same period, Mingay says, the
group of "substantial squires," a middle group between the small owner-occupier and the great estate
owner "held their own" (1960, 375). Lavrovsky
dates this decline of small landowning and peasant
farming as occurring "in the eighteenth century,
following the bourgeois revolution of the seventeenth century" (1960, 354).

[85] Dupâquier describes the powerful social group
at the village level as being composed of big tenant-
farmers (*gros fermiers*) and medium-sized "owners"
(*grands laboureurs*) as well as of merchants (1973,
169). The Duke of Sully was fond of repeating in
the early seventeenth century that *"labourage* and
pasturage were the two breasts at which France is
suckled, its true mines and treasures of Peru" (cited
by Larraz, 1943, 201). Meuvret refers to the particularly acute impact, after 1660, of subsistence crises
"in the rich countryside of cereals production"
(1971b, 122).

dairying, the other main agricultural activity of these areas.[86] One of the reasons for the rise of the prosperous tenant-farmer was precisely the growth of the great estate as a capitalist structure that needed intermediaries to oversee the direct producers, whether they were laborers or subtenants.[87] Such intermediaries were not easy to find, and the period of low cereals prices enabled these intermediaries to get better terms from the landlords. The better terms might be in reductions in real rents[88] or in the degree to which the landlord would assume the cost of improvements.[89]

In the period of 1660 to 1750, it is generally agreed the small peasant or yeoman farmer or "owner-occupier" was disappearing in England; but was he surviving in France? We have been suggesting that in very broad outlines, the answer is negative for northern France (or at least as negative as for England) but positive for southern France. What kind of evidence is there concerning France? Let us start with terminology. The nearest French term for a yeoman farmer is *laboureur*, which connoted not land tenure but capital stock. A *laboureur*, says Goubert, "habitually designates someone [in eastern and northern France] who possesses the farming implement known as the great northern *charrue*."[90] Now a *charrue* is to be distinguished from an *araire*, although in English both are often translated as *plow*.[91] In the seventeenth and eighteenth centuries in France, a *charrue* was a far heavier instrument than an *araire*, plowing more deeply and containing more iron. Hence it required horses or oxen to pull it. A *laboureur* therefore was "a rather large owner or controller of land (*exploitant*) who stood out among the population of the village by the importance of his means and by the number of persons he could employ."

Moving south to lands with only an *araire* and not a *charrue*, instead of *laboureurs* we find smaller and weaker farmers called *métayers* and *closiers*.[92] Dupâquier and Jacquart calculate that between 1685 and 1789 in the *Vexin francais*, a northern area, the percentage of the population who were *petits laboureurs*, called *haricotiers* or *sossons*, went from 9.9% to 3.0%, whereas the

---

[86] Fussell describes the phenomenon of "letting dairies" in various parts of western Europe in the seventeenth century (1968, 31–32).

[87] See Meuvret on the economic role of *fermiers généraux* and *amodiateurs* (1960, 347–349). Le Roy Ladurie reports that 39% of the tenures of all of France (but how many of northern France?) were "great estates" (1975a, 421).

[88] In bad times, landlords wrote off arrears of rent and reshouldered land taxes in order to compete for suitable tenants. See E. L. Jones (1965, 8).

[89] See Mingay (1960, 378–379). The initiative for improvements seems to have come largely from the tenant-farmers and the group of persons controlling medium-sized units in general (see Habakkuk, 1965d, 327, 330; and Mingay, 1963, 166); but in this period, landlords could be pressured to bear a larger part of the cost.

[90] Goubert (1973, 135).

[91] See, for example, Quencez (1968, 118–119), who in this technical dictionary translates *charrue* (French) as "plow" and *araire* as "scratch plow, primitive plow." The same difficulty occurs for German (*Pflug* and *Hakenpflug*), Italian (*aratro* and *aratro di legno*), Spanish (*arado de labor profunda* and *arado* or *arado primitivo*) and Dutch (*ploeg* and *primitive ploeg*).

Haudricourt and Delamarre (1955) devote an entire book of 506 pages essentially to explaining not merely the differences between the *charrue* and the *araire*, across the world and from ancient times to today, but the enormous misperceptions that have occurred because of linguistic confusion and false translations.

[92] Goubert (1973, 135–136).

percentage of more wealthy *fermiers laboureurs* only changed from 10.2% to 8.4%. We find, by contrast, that in wine country, "small peasant property is clearly dominant," five times as important as in the northern areas of large-scale cultivation.[93] As these *petits laboureurs* were squeezed, many crossed the line to become primarily *manoeuvriers* (laborers). Le Roy Ladurie suggests, and I agree, that we should not overdo this distinction even for the sixteenth century, since the real line was between both these groups taken together and the *gros fermier*, the large tenant-farmers.[94] This is true for England, too. However, what happened in the period of stagnation is that although this line became socially and politically more distinct in England, the situation was less clear-cut in the areas of rural France that did not grow cereals.

What, then, of the argument that Brenner puts forth (and he is not alone) that it was "the predominance of petty proprietorship in France in the early modern period which ensured long-term agricultural backwardness." We have suggested our skepticism about both assumptions—the predominance of petty proprietorship (not true of northern France), and the agricultural backwardness of France relative to England (doubtfully true of northern France, at least up to 1750). Brenner says that in England, agrarian advance was possible because "the landlords were able to engross, consolidate and enclose, to create large farms and to lease them to capitalist tenants who could afford to make capitalist investments."[95]

Jacquart, describing changes in northern France as the old families begin to sell their lands in the "second" sixteenth century, says:[96]

> What matters . . . is the behavior of the new controllers of the land (*maîtres du sol*). Of bourgeois origin, they retained something of the profit mentality of their merchant ancestors, even if they sought to make them forgotten. They understood the key role of the reserve in seigniorial revenue, the advantage of the concentrated large estate, the greater revenue furnished by woodlands and meadows. There was a whole conscious policy which involved, over generations, the acquisition of lands, their improvement, their development (*mise en valeur*).

Side by side, Jacquart notes, there also developed medium-sized, market-oriented farms of 15–50 hectares, which represented typical *modest bourgeois investments*, "viable and profitable." This growth of both large es-

---

[93] Dupâquier and Jacquart (1973, 171). They define a *haricotier* as a *"laboureur* with a poor horse" and a *sosson* as a "peasant possessing only one team." Jacquart estimates that three-quarters of the French peasants did not have enough for their basic needs and he sees a steady growth of medium-sized holdings throughout the seventeenth century, medium being defined as at least 30 hectares (1966, 22–26). G. Durand defines the southern vineyard, with its peasant owner, as "the place of extremely hard work and unlimited poverty," the profits going primarily to the merchants and to the state bureaucracy via taxation (1977, 133).

[94] Le Roy Ladurie (1975b, 1405–1407).

[95] Brenner (1976, 43, 63). Croot and Parker are skeptical: "The peasant, far from being an obstacle to economic development, may actually have supplied its impetus by adopting new practices or new crops or just by showing landlords the profits that good husbandry can bring" (1978, 39).

[96] Jacquart (1975, 273–275).

tates and medium-sized units involved a "slow process of peasant expropriation" that resulted in a "real pauperization of the rural masses." Is this really different from England?

Brenner admits that French landlords might have wished "to consolidate holdings" as much as their English confrères. But alas they could not! For if in England the laws permitted the landlords to "raise rents or fines to impossible levels and thus evict the small tenant," in France they might instead have had "to *buy* up countless small peasant holdings in order to amass a consolidated unit." This, we are led to infer, was an impossible burden on French protocapitalist landlords. But we have seen that buying up properties, far from being implausible, was a prime method of concentration *both in England and in France.* Indeed, Brenner implicitly admits it when he says that in France, "throughout the early modern period, many peasants were indeed forced deeply into debt and were ultimately obliged to sell their holdings."[97] If so, then who bought these holdings? Brenner concludes that at the end of the seventeenth century, "some 40–50 percent of the cultivated land was still in peasant possession" in France, but "no more than 25–30 percent" in England. What, however, was the percentage in *northern* France?

Our argument is that in land organization and agricultural productivity differences between England and northern France in the period of 1650 to 1750 were relatively minor. Seen from the point of view of the capitalist world-economy as a whole, the two areas were more alike than different. They were *both* expanding their percentage of the world's production of cereals in order to maintain overall profit levels in a time of stagnation; this enabled them to catch up partially with Holland's net advantage. Regarding the industrial sector, the seventeenth century was a time when the protection of industry was a prime concern of both the English and the French government. This protection in England is considered by Lipson to be one of the three pillars of English mercantilism, along with the Navigation Acts and the Corn Laws; the "Age of Mercantilism," he says, was the "Age of Enterprise."[98] As for France, "Colbertism" stands out as one of the major phenomena of the century, although in fact protectionist intervention is already important in the days of Richelieu.[99]

Efforts at industrial protection, or perhaps we should say promotion,

---

[97] Brenner (1975, 72–73). In any case, the English landlords acquired extensively by purchase. See T. S. Ashton (1969, 36). Croot and Parker say: "Just as Professor Brenner passes over the contribution of the English peasant and minimizes his independence, so he exaggerates the independence of the French peasantry" (1978, 41). Jacquart also argues that the modes of acquisition of peasant lands by large landowners were the same on the continent as in England (see 1978b, 409).

[98] Lipson (1956, **II,** lxxxix, cxliv). How important

was patent protection, a central English governmental policy of the seventeenth century? Opinions are divided. North sees it as of "prime importance" (1973, 228), encouraging innovation. Clark says that it is "doubtful" that it encouraged very many inventors, because so many were cheated of their rewards (1936, 152).

[99] Following the collapse of cloth production in Reims, Amiens, and Beauvais, the tariff of June 15, 1644 doubled the duty on Dutch and English cloth. See Deyon (1969, 77; 1966, 54).

were focused primarily in textiles. Let us look first at the results and second at the explanations. French textiles were located essentially in the far
north and to a lesser extent, in the Midi.[100] The traditional silk industry of
Lyon had a "remarkable rise" in the seventeenth century.[101] Wool and cottons did less well. They were at their height from 1625 to 1635, then
declined, then were "stagnant at a lower level"[102] under Colbert (and despite Colbert?) and finally picked up and were partially reconverted in the
period of 1680 to 1705,[103] (as a result of Colbert?). The reconversion involved a significant "ruralization" of industry.[104] England's crisis in textiles
started earlier, and was perhaps overcome earlier, with the rise of the new
draperies. From 1660 to 1700, cloth production increased, exports doubled, and there was a growing variety in the cloth products.[105] Here too,
textile production was ruralized, perhaps "more precociously and more
radically than in continental Europe."[106]

Compared to England and even to France, the Dutch textile industry
in the second half of the seventeenth century was running into trouble. For
one thing it was located in the towns, and labor costs were high.[107] The
Dutch therefore declined in all fields of worsteds except camelots (*greinen*),
but not in woollens. In camelots and woollens, they retained the advantage
of privileged access to the necessary raw materials—Spain for wool, and
Turkey for the material needed for camelots; and they maintained the
advantage of techniques of dyeing with indigo and cochineal. The camelots
and the woollens were high-value, high-quality goods, but they were *not*
intended for a wide market. Such a shift in orientation was the consequence
of a "generally weaker position,"[108] and thus it is quite understandable that
in the second half of the seventeenth century, Dutch capital was shifting out
of industrial investment to mercantile enterprises with a higher rate of
return.[109]

In other industries, less was happening. However, English shipbuilding
did rise "more or less steeply, perhaps about 1670,"[110] at the very moment
that Dutch shipbuilding was reduced in volume.[111] What really must be
kept in the forefront of one's attention is that in the world-economy as a

---

[100] See map for 1703–1705 in Léon (1970b, 236).
[101] Deyon (1966, 60).
[102] Goubert (1970g, 336).
[103] "[We] do not hesitate to assert that the progress momentarily achieved [in the *sayetterie* of Amiens] from 1680 to 1705 prepared the way for, indeed launched, the impetuous rise of the first part of the eighteenth century" (Deyon, 1963, 955).
[104] See Deyon (1963, 952) and Kellenbenz (1965, 389–390).
[105] See Wilson (1965, 185).
[106] This is the view of Deyon (1972, 31); but Kellenbenz's survey (1965) does not seem to indicate this.
[107] See Glamann (1974, 506) and Wilson (1977a,

26–27).
[108] Wilson (1960a, 221).
[109] See Smit (1975, 62).
[110] Hinton (1959, 101).
[111] See Romano (1962, 519), who dates the Dutch reduction at 1671 to 1701. See also Faber *et al.* (1965, 108). R. W. Unger notes that Dutch design leadership, already rare by the 1630s, had faded by the 1670s, and that by the eighteenth century, Dutch shipyards contracted or disappeared. He offers a number of factors in explanation: French protectionism; wars causing an increasing Dutch tax burden and public debt; shrinking home market; the general decline of piracy; the longer life of ships (see 1978, 109–110).

whole, demand was lethargic. Even in sectors in which demand was expanding, it could not keep pace with the agro-industrial efforts of the United Provinces and its mercantilist rivals, England and France. The major concern of England and France was to *find* employment for its workers; that of the United Provinces was to *keep* it.[112] So long as the mercantilist could create such employment, says Pares, he was "indifferent to the productivity of the labour employed."[113]

This struggle of core powers to export unemployment to each other is a recurrent phenomenon of the capitalist world-economy in its moments of stagnation. What made it even more acute in the period of 1660 to 1763 is that England and France both faced, in addition, a "chronic problem of poverty" affecting one-quarter to one-half their population, including not only the paupers proper, but the large (and growing) number of part-time workers. Wilson says of England that there was "an army of workers partly or wholly dependent on a great but unstable manufacturing export industry."[114] The same was true of France, with perhaps a lesser emphasis on the export. The question, then, was what would maximize the desired employment. Here the controversy was acute about the role of wages. On the one hand, it is said, and was said at the time, that a disadvantage of the Dutch was high wages, which "were unique in resisting the massive erosion of purchasing power experienced elsewhere."[115] This may be attributed to the urban location of industry and hence to the syndical strength of the workers, which led to the social welfare policies of the government, one explanation of high taxes. High wages and high taxes presumably were making Dutch products relatively less competitive, and this explains the relative decline.

However, English and French wages may in fact have been rising. There is some suggestion of this for France, both in agriculture and industry.[116] On the other hand, to know what was really happening, we would have to know more about labor productivity and the percentage of wages that were paid in money. Hill says that in the seventeenth century "English laziness

---

[112] Speaking of England in the early seventeenth century, Supple says: "The most critical element of instability as far as the government was concerned was the problem of chronic unemployment" (1959, 234). Speaking of the early eighteenth century, D. George says: "There is a belief that irregularity of employment is a modern disease. This is indeed far from the truth" (1953, 53).

[113] Pares (1937, 120). Furniss says that trade connections were judged not only in terms of their contributions to the balance of trade but also on the "extent to which the trade in question could be depended upon to furnish employment to the native labourer" (1957, 52).

[114] Wilson (1969a, 125).

[115] J. de Vries (1974, 183). As of 1690, Romein estimates that Dutch wages were 16% higher than

English (cited in Wilson, 1969b, 118).

[116] Jacquart talks of the lack of agricultural workers in the post-Fronde period of forcing up the wages of rural labourers (1973, 178); see also Goubert (1970d, 64). Regarding industry in the period from 1665 to 1688, despite recession, "the wage-rate (by the piece and the day) seems to have remained stable, both in town and in the country" (Goubert, 1970g, 348). This represents a relative rise. See also C. E. Labrousse (1970, 370). Léon points out that "from 1660 to 1750 there was a veritable invasion of the guilds," which would explain both rising urban rates and the increasing transfer of industry to rural areas where the workers were "over-abundant and docile, used to low salaries" (1970b, 251).

was a bye-word with foreigners."[117] Presumably the chief comparison was with the Dutch. Lipson tells us that in these harder times, artisans were often obliged either to take part of their wages in kind at an overvalued rate or to have wages deferred in the form of a promissory note, which the worker then sought to transform into cash by selling it at discount.[118] The last is particularly interesting since this would mean that rising wages, although a real cost to the employer, benefited not the worker but some petty banker.

We come thus to the contradictory needs of the mercantilist core powers fighting the hegemonic core power in a time of contraction. On the one hand, they had to try to be cost-competitive. On the other hand they had to locate demand for their products. The pressure to be cost-competitive put pressure on the workers regarding labor discipline. Furniss describes the rise of this concept in England in the context of ideas about the "duty to labor," said to be a correlate of the "right to employment."[119] Thompson speaks of the image of clockwork that spread during the seventeenth century "until, with Newton, it . . . engrossed the universe."[120] Nef notes that in this same period Scottish coal miners and salters were "reduced to slavery" as a result of early industrialism.[121] We are so used to associating the rise of free wage labor with the rise of capitalism, especially in the core, that the word *slavery* startles, even amazes. The same thing happened in the royal manufactures of France, where the workers were virtually imprisoned in their work places; yet they received relatively high wages.

Let us put this side by side with the debate on high wages. The majority of mercantilists, like most capitalist entrepreneurs, were in favor of *low* wages as a way of improving competitive costs; but the most sophisticated mercantilists were not. In 1668 Josiah Child in his new *Discourse on Trade* explained Dutch advantage in the following way: "Whenever wages are high, universally throughout the whole world, it is an infallible evidence of the riches of that country; and wherever wages for labour run low it is proof of the

---

[117] C. Hill (1969, 98).

[118] Lipson (1956, **III**, 278).

[119] See Furniss (1957, 76–78). The same pressure existed in France. See Martin Saint-Léon (1976, 13, 501–504).

[120] E. P. Thompson (1967, 57), who notes (p. 64) the simultaneous rise of the English clock-making industry.

[121] Nef (1968, 233). Duckham says of "collier serfdom": "No one statute actually 'enslaved' the colliers. Yet nothing is plainer in Scottish social history of this period than that most masters assumed that their miners were bondsmen *in the fullest sense* and that virtually all colliers accepted this status" (1970, 243). This did not prevent them, nonethe-

less, from periodically engaging in strike action, which was possible because "skilled hewers were in short supply" (Hughes, 1952, 253).

Rusche and Kirchheimer note that at just this time and precisely in Holland, England, and France, we see the rise of houses of correction, serving principally as "manufactures, turning out commodities at a particularly low cost because of their cheap labor" (1939, 50; see also 24–52, *passim*). In addition, this was the era when the juridical punishment of galley slavery was invented—"the most rational way to procure labor for tasks for which free labor could never be found, even when economic conditions were at their worst" (pp. 57–58).

poverty of that place."[122] Thus Josiah Child anticipated by 300 years the argument of Arghiri Emmanuel.[123] Although to be sure Child did not persuade everyone, his views reflected structural pressures.

Labor discipline and increased wages are *complementary* in a time of world economic stagnation, and the two thrusts combined increase employment regardless of true unit productivity: that is, labor discipline (even including near slavery) as a way to increase output (was this not the real motivation in the Scottish coal mines and the *Gobelins* in Paris?) plus increased wages to attract *skilled* workers (the *Gobelins* again) and also to expand the internal market and thereby expand demand. A system in which increased "wages" transfer income to the petty banker instead of to the worker might have done as much, perhaps more, to increase demand as a system in which the workers were truly well paid. However, too much of an increase in labor costs too early (regardless of who benefited) would have jeopardized competition with the Dutch; so a balance had to be reached.

We can now evaluate the success of efforts in the second half of the seventeenth century to promote agriculture and industry in England and France. The classic comparison of liberal historiography is that made between Whig England as it moved toward privately controlled mass industries of the future and bureaucratic Colbertist France as it fell into a luxury-industry rut. As a consequence, it is argued, England was moving towards liberalism, Parliamentary controls, and progress; whereas France was reinforcing aristocracy, "feudalism," and waste—in short, the *Ancien Régime*. As in so many other arguments concerning this period, the modern *locus classicus* of these prejudices is Heckscher:

> Not only was there no counterpart in England to the *établissements* of the luxury industry in the hands of the [French] state, but also—and what is much more important—the numerous and extensive private *manufactures royales* endowed with every possible privilege . . . were absent in England. . . .
> *This difference is vital.* Thus if the technical changes had consisted, as those of the previous period did, mainly in improved manual dexterity, cultivated taste, and artistic plasticity, in other words if it had belonged to that technical sphere in which production was determined by the Royal Family, the Court, the aristocracy and other wealthy producers, France would then have had every prospect of beoming the leading industrial country north of the Alps. But things turned out differently. "Industrialism" or "capitalism" meant mass production for mass consumption, and here the luxury industries were entirely subordinate. The leadership was thus transferred to England.[124]

The first question to ask about Heckscher's explanation is whether the facts are correct. Pierre Léon, for one, although agreeing that Colbert promoted some luxury industries, doubts its accuracy.

[122] Cited in Wilson (1969a, 122). See also Heckscher (1935, **II,** 169), Lipson (1956, **III,** 273–274), Coats (1958, 35, 46), and Wiles (1968, 115, 118).
[123] Emmanuel (1972).
[124] Heckscher (1935, **I,** 221, italics added).

The main thrust was, in fact, directed towards mass industries, woollen and linen textiles (Elbeuf, Sedan, Languedoc); steel, the basis of the armaments industry (Valenciennes, Cambrai); paper-manufacturing. More than 400 endowments (*fondations*), including 300 in textiles, were created through his efforts. No doubt [Colbert] did not create an "industrial base," which had already existed for centuries, but he did try to reinforce it and to concentrate it. . . . There is no doubt that the Royal Manufactures . . . first implanted . . . the "form" of the factory of the future.[125]

As for the stifling effect of Colbertism on capitalist enterprise, we must not forget that, like the venality of office and mercenary soldiers, Colbertism represented a step toward nineteenth-century forms, not a step away from it. Colbertism had originated with Richelieu, and John Nef argues that two of its positive effects must be appreciated:

First, within the system, economic adventurers gained more freedom than they had been ordinarily allowed before the time of Richelieu. . . . Second, the mercantile system of regulation . . . actually constituted a step toward granting merchants the political recognition, the rank, which Eon [a cleric whose writings became influential in the time of Colbert] had insisted they so badly needed.[126]

If there is less of a difference between the seventeenth-century mercantilist efforts of England and France than is frequently contended, why does Goubert (like so many others) talk of the "global failure of Colbert"?[127] Why is it said that the main effect of Colbert's tariffs was merely "to retard for a while" the upward trend of English cloth production?[128] If the context was unfavorable, as Deyon suggests,[129] it was as unfavorable for England as for France. Wilson hints that the French were not mercantilist *enough*, that their mercantilism, unlike England's, "was to remain relatively incoherent and unformulated, even in Colbert's day," because France lacked "that combination of expanding commercial capital and government influence represented by the Westminster-City axis in London."[130] This suggestion pushes us to see how interest groups pursued their economic objectives within the framework of the two mercantilist core states—remembering that France was four times the size of England and contained within its frontiers very large regions that were not core regions.[131]

[125] Léon (1970a, 113). Furthermore, state investment in industry between 1660 and 1789 only amounted to 2 million francs a year, "a derisory figure in fact" since industrial revenue averaged 100 million francs (Léon, 1970b, 225).

[126] Nef (1968, 215).

[127] Goubert (1970g, 354–356), who reminds us that, in the Treaty of Nijmegen (1678), Colbert had to make concessions on his high tariff policy under Dutch and English pressure. Meuvret claims that the failure of the Companies was more important than the failure of tariffs and Fouquet's tax of 50 sous per ton on foreign shipping, France's equiva-

lent of the Navigation Acts, (1971a, 32). See also Deyon (1966, 55).

[128] Priestly (1951, 47).

[129] Colbert's efforts "were inscribed from the outset as a difficult enterprise" (Deyon, 1963, 951).

[130] Wilson (1965, 65).

[131] While it is said that France was in some ways too big, it has also been argued that the Dutch had the opposite problem. "Had all the Netherlands been united, the further stages of economic progress, which were to develop in Britain, might have taken place earlier. Belgian steel and coal, the vital water power that was available in the Ardennes,

To compare them adequately, we must first survey the commercial and financial scenes, beginning with overall assessments. It is generally thought that 1660 to 1700 was the period of England's "commercial revolution,"[132] at a time when England was first becoming "a world entrepôt on its own."[133] What is usually emphasized about this period is the percentage of world trade the English gained vis-à-vis the Dutch, reflection of the successful aspects of the Navigation Acts.[134] But what of France? According to Crouzet, "there is no parallel in France [for] the fast and prolonged growth during the seventeenth century [especially after 1660] of English foreign trade;"[135] but Delumeau, surveying the whole period of 1590 to 1690, presents the quite different picture of a distinct strengthening of French foreign trade: "progress . . . was slow, unequal, beset by setbacks, but decisive."[136] Richet agrees with this, seeing an "absolute growth" that had an effect "well beyond the coastal regions" and enabled textile producers and others to "reach, in the years 1680–1690, a level they had never known even in the best years of the previous century."[137]

What explains the failures, if there indeed was one, of French companies and the greater reluctance of French capitalists to invest as compared with their English and Dutch counterparts? Explanations that say it was because of "the French temperament and its defects"[138] or because the offspring of French merchants gave up being businessmen[139] are answers I cannot take very seriously. Even if truer than elsewhere, which is doubtful, why should either have been so? In any case, one would still have to account for the investment patterns of the fathers of the offspring in question. Perhaps a closer look at world trade by sector will clarify matters for us.

We begin with the total tonnage and the value of English shipping by geographical sector, which have been calculated in Table 2. (Unfortunately, I know of no parallel calculation for France.)

Three facts stand out in this table. Areas of nearby Europe, which are largely those of the other core powers, accounted for more than a third of the tonnage and nearly half of the value. Baltic trade accounted for another good third of the tonnage but for very little of the value, which was good for the shippers, but not too important for the traders. The East Indies

could have provided the essential elements for an industrial revolution, but the Dutch lacked them" (Plumb, 1965, xxv).

[132] See Davis (1954, 161, 163), who notes, however, that "the one period of good trade runs from the lifting of the depression in 1677 to the Revolution of 1688."

[133] Wilson (1965, xii). However, Klein says that "by about 1670 the Amsterdam staple market was already of little importance as a central world market" (1966, 208–209).

[134] Harper thinks the acts had a "real effect in restraining the Dutch from serving as third-party carriers" (1939b, 300). Åström says that the change in the Baltic trade between 1633 and 1685 was "substantial" (1960, 7), although Holland's loss was often a gain for Baltic as well as for English shipowners. Franken cites the City Fathers of Amsterdam in 1684, who called attention to the fact that the English had "in their crops and manufactures in themselves a greater fund of commerce" than did Amsterdam, whose trade was "artificial" by comparison (1968, 10).

[135] Crouzet (1972, 62).

[136] Delumeau (1966, 105).

[137] Richet (1972, 205).

[138] Meuvret (1971a, 33).

[139] Kulischer (1931, 16–17).

TABLE 2
English Foreign Shipping in 1700[a]

Sector	Tonnage	Millions of Pounds	Pounds per 1000 tons
East Indies	5,000	0.9	.180
Mediterranean	} 71,000	1.5	} .046
Spain and Portugal		1.7	
West Indies	43,000	1.3	.030
North America	33,000	0.7	.021
Northern Europe	218,000	0.9	.004
Areas of nearby Europe	224,000	5.1	.023
Total	594,000	12.1	

[a] This table is reconstructed from Wilson's (1965, 162); Wilson based his on the work of Ralph Davis.

accounted for very little shipping and very little total value, but the value per ton for this area is by far the highest (whereas the Baltic trade is by far the lowest), and high value per ton means a high profit ratio per ship. In the case of Asian trade, these facts imply that although it may have been important to the East India Company, it was not *yet* very important for the world-economy as a whole. This perhaps explains the ability of the East India Company to resist attacks on its violations of mercantilist logic through its unfavorable balance of trade.[140] The damage such trade really cost was limited. The counterpart, of course, was that the English government was expected by the East India Company "to fund for itself in Asia."[141]

Imports were on the rise—861,000 pieces of calico in the year 1700 (of which two-thirds were reexported), compared to 240,000 in the year 1600,[142] but the export market for European goods in Asia was still so limited that "any attempt to overstock the goods led to a drastic shortage in demand and fall in the prices."[143] At a time when demand was the chief collective concern of the mercantilist powers, East Indian trade offered no solution. Indeed, to make this trade "useful," India would have to be peripheralized, and to do this was considered not worth the effort by the English, and even less so by the French, until the post-1750 upturn. It was, in fact, at that time that the British began the political conquest of India and

[140] See P. J. Thomas on the "acrimonious" discussions about the East Indian trade in the seventeenth century (1963, 6). As for profitability, see Glamann, who says "the profit by the Dutch Asiatic trade was moderate as compared with the receipts won by the Dutch by shipping and commerce in Europe" (1958, 11); see also Morineau (1978e, 175).

[141] Bassett (1968, 85).

[142] Wilson (1965, 170). Asian cloth was particu-

larly valued at the time for its lightness, elegance, and fine texture. P. O. Thomas reminds us that in 1727 the *Atlas Maritime* said "India and China were able to clothe the whole world with their manufactures" (1963, 31).

[143] Chaudhuri (1968, 486), who adds that as of 1700 "the terms of trade seem to have deteriorated against European goods."

its economic peripheralization.[144] Mediterranean trade was in many ways in between on all the dimensions, that is, in the degree to which the Mediterranean was a periphery rather than an external arena,[145] in the quantitative importance of the trade,[146] and in its decisiveness in terms of English–French rivalry.[147]

When we speak of Anglo–Dutch rivalry and England's rise at Holland's expense, we think primarily of two things, the English home market, in which the Dutch had had a significant role, and Baltic shipping, which was Holland's "mother trade." What can get lost from view when we emphasize the flag of the ships is the nature of the cargo, which changed radically in the course of the seventeenth century. In the long sixteenth century, Baltic trade consisted primarily of the westward flow of grain (and here Gdańsk was crucial) and the eastward flow of textiles. The stagnation of the seventeenth century brought this trade to an end, but only in the middle decades, which saw a veritable "disintegration of the Baltic area."[148] The decline of grain exports was the consequence of the collapse in world prices and, consequently, the withdrawal from the international market of the Polish and east Elbian grain-producing areas. This meant, in turn, a decline in the market for cloth in precisely these grain-producing areas, because of less hard currency being available (remember the *Kipper- und Wipperzeit*) and because of the reemergence of local artisanal production in eastern Europe,

---

[144] Mukherjee dates the shift from the fourth decade of the eighteenth century when, because of the disintegration of the Mughal Empire, Anglo–French rivalry could take the form of "a serious contest with a view to controlling India for the supreme 'trading' advantages of one company at the expense of others" (1974, 110).

[145] Davis argues the case for peripheralization in his analysis of English trade (1961, 125, 137). In the case of Italy, he says that by 1700 it had become "yet another country which exchanges its agricultural products for English manufactures." He describes the Levant trade as "the exchange of English manufactures for foreign raw materials" and says "the trade can be reduced, in fact, to the exchange of broadcloth for raw silk." I agree with the evaluation on Italy but reserve judgment on the Levant. Issawi (1974) describes a steady process of increasing involvement of the Ottoman Empire in the world-economy between 1600 and 1914; but is unclear about when a decisive change occurred. He seems to suggest the eighteenth century as a turning point.

[146] Rapp says that the seventeenth-century rise of England "rested upon the conquest of the southern market, and more precisely upon the elimination of Mediterranean rivals in industry and trade" (1975, 522–523). This seems to me a considerable over-

statement despite the immediate usefulness to England (and to the United Provinces) of the expansion of trade with the *Christian* Mediterranean in the *early* seventeenth century. The fact is that after 1660, Mediterranean trade played an ever-smaller part as a percentage of the total, even though it continued to expand in absolute terms. For France, trade with the Levant went down from being half of all foreign trade in the late sixteenth century to being one-twentieth in the 1780s. For England, the decline was even sharper: from a peak of 10% in the mid-seventeenth to 1% at the end of the eighteenth. Furthermore, as a source of raw cotton and a market for textiles, the Levant lost its importance as other sources and market emerged. See Issawi (1974, 114–115).

[147] Parry says that the eighteenth century would later produce "that unlikely paradox, an English Mediterranean" (1967, 191). Léon and Carrière say that over the period from 1661 to 1789, Mediterranean trade represented 30% of France's total (1970, 194); and Issawi says that in the 1780s France accounted for 50–60% of Ottoman trade (1974, 114). French trade included a dominant role in *Barbarie*, which corresponded more or less to Tunisia (Léon and Carrière, 1970, 193).

[148] Åström (1963, 29).

by which the landlords sought to redress somewhat their losses from the collapse of their grain markets.[149]

The marginal efficiency of English textiles vis-à-vis Dutch textiles and locally produced textiles was not so great that it could survive in the Baltic zone, where demand was reduced, "short of out-and-out price cutting, which was out of the question."[150] The Eastland Company had received vital support from the Crown precisely because it exported dyed and dressed cloth and thus provided employment.[151] When it shifted its emphasis from export to import, it doomed its privileged role, especially as England turned more and more to reexport and the entrepôt role. But import what? Grain, the traditional import, had collapsed. Since the cause of the collapse of grain trade, stagnation of the world-economy, led to acute commercial rivalry among the three core powers, and since their rivalry degenerated frequently into wars (especially naval wars), a double demand arose that the Baltic zone could supply: naval stores and iron.

Naval stores, of course, had been imported for a long time from the Baltic, but "the problem of supply before 1650 [had] never [been] acute."[152] Now it was, and for three reasons: shipbuilding expanded, house building expanded (especially after the Great Fire of London), and previous construction had so depleted English timber supply (and by the end of the century, Irish timber supply), that the shortage had "reached . . . the dimensions of a national crisis."[153] Here we come to a crucial difference between England and France: Because France was so much larger in size, it had a considerably larger supply of timber, and as late as the time of Colbert, it seemed comfortably ahead of England in this regard.[154] To be

---

[149] Åström adds another factor, arguing that the social groups in the Baltic zone that bought broadcloth (rather than silk and velvet) were the lesser nobility and gentry, the clergy, the officials, and the burghers, and that their demand remained reasonably constant. "Thus the big fluctuations in the consumption of cloth were represented only by one group of clothing-wearers, the military. Warlike preparations stimulated the demand, while demobilization restrained it" (1963, 71). The "Lull in the North" following the end of the Thirty Years' War is thus rendered responsible for the sharp decline in cloth purchase.

I wonder if this is enough to account for it. First of all, I don't believe the nonmilitary demand was all that constant. Åström himself notes that the English at the time accounted for their cloth-export crisis in terms of three factors: "the competition of the Dutch, the increase of cloth manufactures in Northern and Eastern Europe, and the reduction in the purchasing power of the Polish market" (1963, 69). The second and third explanations precisely

involve the inconstancy of nonmilitary demand. The first factor related to the Thirty Years' War not to military demands but to the fact that because of the war, Dutch ships had "disappeared from English trade" in the Baltic from 1623 to 1649 (Hinton, 1959, 37).

[150] Hinton (1959, 45).

[151] See Hinton (1959, 59).

[152] Hinton (1959, 99).

[153] Wilson (1965, 80). Darby says that by the time of "the Restoration in 1660, the amount of woodland had been much reduced" (1975, 328). One policy consequence was that the Navy Board was alarmed and consulted the Royal Society. In 1664, John Evelyn wrote a report in which he appealed to the landed gentry to plant trees. The advice was widely followed and eventually paid off in terms of a larger internal supply. It is clear that "trees planted during those years came to maturity in time to sustain the British navy through the wars of the eighteenth century" (Darby, 1973, 329).

[154] See Bamford (1956, 206–207).

sure, the French timber suffered from being of poor quality in terms of shipbuilding, whereas northern European masts were of top quality; but France did have its own timber. The question for the French was whether the difference in the quality of masts was sufficient to make it worth the extra effort in time, money, and politico-military resources to obtain timber from elsewhere. The answer seems to have been largely negative.[155] The English did not have the luxury of this choice; they *had* to obtain the timber from outside. Hence they made a great effort in the Baltic and a *greater* effort than the French in North America.

France's greater internal supply of timber had two important far-reaching side effects. It pushed the Baltic trade geographically eastward, from Gdańsk to Königsberg, then to Riga, then to Narva, eventually beginning to incorporate Russia and Finland via the ports of Stockholm and Viborg.[156] The second, more far-reaching consequence was that England was pushed to develop its coal resources. A recent conservative estimate says that coal production rose about 60% over the century as a whole and rose 370% from the low point in 1650 to the high point in 1680.[157] The impulse to replace wood by coal for heating and cooking was first made fashionable by James I, but it got its real impetus as a result of the interruptions of imports caused by the Anglo–Dutch wars. Later, manufacturers began to look for processes that would permit the use of coal, and by 1738 a French observer wrote that coal was "the soul of English manufactures."[158]

In addition to naval stores, the other new import from the Baltic was iron. At the beginning of the seventeenth century, iron represented 2% of Eng-

[155] "The reluctance of French entrepreneurs to venture capital and ships in northern shipping enterprises, for which they were often criticized, appears to have been founded on a realistic appreciation of their own limitations and of the risks involved in competition with the formidable Dutch" (Bamford, 1954, 219). Bamford suggests that a second source of reluctance to secure northern masts, in addition to cost, was the fear of "incurring grave strategic disabilities that dependence upon them involved in wartime" (1956, 113). French trade in the Baltic was at this time only 7% of the total (see Léon and Carrière, 1970, 194). Of French North American efforts, Bamford says: "Masting trees were abundant and cheap in Canada, but their exploitation required the employment of local labor for which wages were notoriously high" (1956, 120).

It is crucial to see that the initial reluctance of the French (as compared with the *need* of the English) to seek out North American timber resources was self-reinforcing. Bamford notes that one of the French arguments for halting all importation of North American masts in 1731 was poor quality. But Bamford says the poor quality of the masts was in fact the result of their being cut in the vicinity of the St. Lawrence River rather than further inland,

and of laying them on the ground for two years or so before shipping. "Had the French, instead of discontinuing importations, undertaken to expand their Canadian exploitation, the results could certainly have been as fruitful for them as later Canadian cuts were for Britain" (1956, 127–128).

[156] See Åström (1963, 41–44). This was true not only in the search for timber, but for flax, hemp, pitch, tar, and potash as well.

[157] Langton (1972, 51), who suggests that this figure is conservative vis-à-vis Nef's estimate of a 15-fold increase. He therefore concludes that "no clear-cut 'revolution' occurred." To each his own required quantity for a revolution!

[158] Cited in Minchinton (1974, 151). On the timber shortage and the rise of coal in England, see Wilson (1965, 80–85), who adds a characteristic caution: "The success with which coal was substituted for wood as fuel, and the growing output of the coal industry, must not be regarded as a *deus ex machina* which can be involved to expain every development of British industry outside textiles." Nonetheless, he adds: "It was probably the factor in the economy of the early seventeenth century most favourable to expansion."

lish imports from the Baltic, at the end 28%.[159] Iron meant Sweden, and iron was an industrial product, the result of the transformation of ore. Why did Sweden at this time have such an important role in the production of iron? One must remember that before the end of the eighteenth century, charcoal was the crucial source of energy in iron smelting. Since both the metal and the energy were expensive to transport, the optimal situation was to have both elements in one place. (Iron was in fact more widely available and abundant than forests.) In Sweden there was both a good *quality* of the mineral and a large *quantity* of the charcoal.[160] England and France also had major smelting operations—France's probably larger, primarily because of a "lesser penury of fuel." The result was that England became a major importer of Swedish iron in order to supplement its own production, whereas France "neither imported nor exported this metal."[161] That is, France produced what it needed and therefore did not "need" the Baltic trade. Swedish iron played a major role in her rise as a semiperipheral power in the world-economy. We shall discuss this part of the story later. For the moment, the point we are trying to underline is the consequences of the comparative sizes and resources of England and France for their patterns of foreign trade. Manufacturing was expanding in both countries; more and more iron was needed,[162] and more iron required, in turn, more fuel. The reason England had to turn to coal as fuel and to the import of iron earlier than France did[163] was more a matter of different ecologies than different levels of industrialization.

It is perhaps in the Atlantic trade that the most striking and important differences between England and France developed. The quantity of trans-atlantic trade was far greater for England than for France. In addition, England developed settler colonies in the Western Hemisphere during this period, whereas French settlement was comparatively dilatory and unsuccessful. The two phenomena are in fact linked. By 1700 England was the country "with the greatest stake in the Atlantic."[164] Why was this so? We have already discussed how the Dutch dominated European trade; and it seemed more sensible for them to pursue their strong suit rather than to

[159] Åström (1963, 32).

[160] Heckscher (1932, 139), says that, "it was the quantity [of charcoal] more than the quality [of the mineral] to which [Sweden] owed her privileged position."

[161] Léon emphasizes a growing shortage of raw iron in France through the eighteenth century. He asserts that already in 1685 France was importing 8.5 million pounds a year (and in 1787 it was 42 million) from Germany, Russia, Spain, and especially England and Sweden. He talks of growing complaints in the eighteenth century "about the threats of deforestation and the increasing cost of fuel," mentioning peasant revolts in 1731 in Franche-Comté against the metallurgists who were

destroying the forests (1970b, 231–232).

[162] Flinn attacks the old view that iron manufactures was a stagnant industry in England between 1660 and 1760. He believes that the rising import reflected, on the contrary, rising demand at home and in the colonies. (1958, 145). Bairoch shows that while British home production of steel remained stable from 1660 to 1760, imports rose 130%. He believes the major use was located in agriculture (1966, 8–10).

[163] The parallel expansion in France eventually forced her to enter the "era of coal" circa 1735 (Léon, 1970b, 232).

[164] K. G. Davies (1974, 314).

cultivate new and difficult ones. Why was it, however, that the French did not turn, along with the English, to the Atlantic trade? Or rather, why, especially from 1660 to 1700, did the English do so much better than the French? The facts seem to be clear. In the seventeenth century, 28 new separate units of colonization were established in the Western Hemisphere; 3 Dutch, 8 French, and 17 English; as of 1700, the English had 350,000–400,000 subjects (including slaves) as against 70,000 for the French, and in the flourishing Caribbean colonies there were twice as many Englishmen as Frenchmen.[165] French Canada and Louisiana could not begin to match British settlements in North America in terms of size of population or production output. Between 1600 and 1700, a major European *reexport* trade of colonial products was developed by England, a vast new profitable entrepôt trade.[166] Indeed one of the most important results of the Navigation Acts was the success with which English carriers monopolized the trade to their own colonies, to which must be added their widespread success in smuggling in Spanish America.[167]

The French, of course, shipped tobacco and sugar across the Atlantic just as the English did, except that the total quantity was less and the French home market largely absorbed what was imported, leaving less over for reexport. As compared with the English, the French had fewer producers in the Americas—colonists, indentured servants, and slaves; and hence they produced less.[168] The question of why they had fewer producers is not easy to answer. We know that the two countries had somewhat different attitudes toward the emigration of dissident religious groups. In effect the British encouraged such emigration, or at least did not discourage it, whereas Louis XIV forbade the Huguenots to settle in the Americas, saying he "had not made his realm Catholic in order to deliver up his colonies to heretics."[169]

We seem to be back to the usual explanation of differences between the two countries—England was constitutional and relatively liberal and France was absolutist and authoritarian. A curious fact, however, intrudes. In 1687–1688, shortly after the Revocation of the Edict of Nantes, the King of France *threatened* that Huguenots caught "escaping" across the borders (presumably to other European countries) would be deported to Mississippi, Canada, Martinique, or elsewhere in the Americas. This was a meaningful threat, according to Scoville at least, because "the threat of transportation across the Atlantic appalled Huguenots and converts much more than the possibility of being chained to the galleys for life."[170] In view of

---

[165] K. G. Davies (1974, 45, 80, 85). Of course, the number of separate units of colonization depends on how one defines a unit. Davies gives a list and a justification.

[166] See Davis (1954, 131) and Wilson (1965, 161).

[167] Parry (1967, 206).

[168] The English made "fuller use of the device of indentured labor." As of 1700, 250,000 Englishmen but only 20,000 Frenchmen had migrated to North

America (K. G. Davies, 1974, 80, 96). Curtin's estimate indicates a higher number of slaves in British colonies, especially before 1700 (1969, chap. 3).

[169] Dehio (1962, 89). The Huguenots were not necessarily anxious to go; as Dehio says, they "could only expect to find the same authoritarian forms of social, political and ecclesiastical life on the other side" of the Atlantic.

[170] Scoville (1960, 103).

these facts, it seems that religious considerations were not what was keeping the French from sending more settlers. Perhaps it was that the French weren't as interested in settler colonies as the English.

What causes an interest in settler colonies? Here I think we come to the crux of the issue. Colonies in the Americas served two purposes. First, they were a source of so-called tropical produces—sugar, cotton, tobacco—that required a climate not available in most of Europe. The extended Caribbean (including Brazil and the southern part of North America) was ecologically appropriate, and both Britain and France acquired colonies in this region for this end. The differences in this regard were relatively minor, although Britain may have been more successful than France. The second and quite different function of colonies was as a market for manufactures and reexports. The tropical colonies were a weak market precisely because they tended to use coerced labor to keep down the costs of production. It took European settlers with a relatively high standard of living to create a large enough net collective income to serve this function.

England developed such colonies and France did not. Is the explanation that France needed markets less or that she found her markets in different places? Once again, we return to the factor of size. Was not France able to sell more of its products internally?[171] England needed Europe as a market (for a long time via the United Provinces),[172] and also needed to create its North American colonies.[173] It is all a relative matter. Faced with the same problem of worldwide contraction, both England and France had mercantilist reactions, directed first against the United Provinces, then against each other; but everything in England pushed toward some concentration on foreign trade. This was self-reinforcing: as a result of their need

[171] "There can be no doubt that in quantitative terms the volume of internal trade [in France] exceeded overwhelmingly the volume of external trade" (Léon and Carrière, 1970, 165).

Indeed, in the seventeenth century, we have the turning inward of the trading port—what Morineau calls the "northernization" of Marseille, which "dissociated itself from the Mediterranean." He explains that in the early seventeenth century, Marseille knew an "authentic expansion," one that was "more brilliant than the expansion [of] the sixteenth century" (1970b, 163, 169). One wonders how this could be, since Marseille had just lost the profitable spice trade due to the capture of this trade by the Dutch and its consequent rerouting. Morineau's answer: Marseille served as a point of import for leather and especially for raw silk and supplied the silk manufactures of Lyon, who were just at that point taking over the markets in France that previously were supplied by the northern Italians. Which markets were these? The luxury markets of the Court, which thrived despite overall decline. The market derived from three sources: the reorienting

of existing demand, the expansion of seigniorial revenues, and the expansion of the revenue of courtiers, that resulted from increased taxation. "Thus was stimulated a luxury trade, rivaling that of weapons and that of leather, for the seventeenth century was, let us not forget, a booted century. Marseille pumped the juices of its development into the internal resources of France. She could thus escape the reverberations of the depression of bullion (1970, 168–169).

[172] Despite England's "spectacular colonial ventures [in the seventeenth century], trade was [still] primarily intra-European" (Supple, 1959, 7). However, trade with Holland declined as trade with the colonies rose (Wilson, 1965, 271–272).

[173] See F. J. Fisher (1950, 156). Jeannin argues that in the period from 1650 to 1750, the two chief markets for western Europe's manufactures were the North American colonists and the various states themselves (1964, 338–339). Once again, the fact that France as compared with England had a larger state with more extensive needs meant a correlatively lesser need for a North American market.

for trade, they needed ships, then naval stores, then products with which to buy the naval stores, then colonial purchasers of expanding manufactures. Quantity may even explain why the British developed the triangular trade and the French did not. More ships led to more concern with one-way traffic and with the underutilization of ships, to which the triangular trade was a solution;[174] this, of course, further reinforced the usefulness of the settler colonies. As a final twist, the larger Atlantic trade of Britain led to a larger reexport trade, which created a significant antimercantilist pressure group in England;[175] this perhaps explains different developments in the eighteenth century.

It is often argued that another major factor in England's economic advance was the combination of an absence of tolls, and improvement of the internal transport system (removing weirs, strengthening banks, deepening beds, constructing locks, and shortening routes by digging cuts).[176] Although the increase in costs resulting from tolls in France was relatively small, and let us not forget that this applied only to trade outside the Five Great Farms, on the whole transport in France was costly, say Léon and Carrière. They are puzzled: "It is difficult for us to say more about a very difficult question."[177]

Would it not be proper to look at the problem this way? The costs of transport within England may not have differed greatly from the costs of transport within the northern tariff zone of France. Since from England one went out by sea, and from France's northern tariff zone one went at least in part, if not primarily, by land, and since it is just at this time that sea transport became significantly less expensive then land transport, England's dilemma about the lack of a sufficient market internal to its frontiers turned into an advantage.[178] Perhaps the point is that France was *better off* economically than England. It had fewer needs pushing it into the development of "foreign" trade. The development of foreign trade may have made no real difference in the long period of contraction, but it may be what prepared Britain better—economically, politically, and militarily—for taking advantage of the renewed economic expansion of the mid-eighteenth century.[179]

---

[174] See Davis (1956, 71).

[175] See Wilson (1967, 513).

[176] See T. S. Ashton (1969, 72–74).

[177] See Léon and Carrière (1970, 178).

[178] See previous discussion in Wallerstein (1974, 264–266).

[179] Let us not forget that in the long period of contraction, even for England, foreign trade was not everything. Reed, for example, argues: "It is the total volume of transactions that is important in lowering transactions costs, irrespective of the national origin of the traders involved. While [English] foreign trade expanded in [the seventeenth century], its level was lower than that of internal trade, and there is no evidence to show that it grew faster.

Domestic commerce, therefore, may very well have played the dominant role" (1973, 184). The point is well taken. It remains to be seen, however, whether the total volume of transactions in France was indeed less than that in England, especially given France's far larger size.

We may want to look, therefore, not at the *national* volume of transactions but at the volume in given markets. Paris, of course, never combined administrative and economic functions in the way that London did, once again due to the size and consequent geographic structure of France. The growth of London as a city and a market between 1650 and 1750 is widely discussed in the literature (see Wrigley, 1967, 63); and it may be the case that transac-

We must now turn to the question of how England and France coped with the problem of financing the flow of production and trade. Discussion is required regarding three knotty problems: the role of bullion in trade in this era (presumably the great mercantilist concern); the availability and flows of bullion in this era; and the impact of public finances on the operation of the system as a whole. Geoffrey Parker argues that the period from 1500 to 1730 saw a "financial revolution" that was the essential prelude to the Industrial Revolution and that meant two things in terms of private finance—the concentration of credit facilities in a few centers and, "associated with this, the evolution of an international system of multilateral payments."[180] Behind the ambiguous meanings of *evolution*, a noun denoting process, lies a major controversy. To what extent were payments in fact multilateral? Or perhaps more accurately, when did the multilaterality of payments become sufficiently prevalent such that traders, and governments as well, counted on it in their calculations?

The debate was formulated in a well-known exchange that started because Charles Wilson was unhappy with Eli Heckscher's dismissal of mercantilist logic (as indeed he had every right to be). Wilson argues that since the shift from a bilateral to a multilateral system of payments occurred only in the *eighteenth* century, the mercantilists' concern in the *seventeenth* century with the availability of coin had been a rational one.[181] Heckscher replies that "multilateral trade and arbitrage existed already in the Middle Ages—perhaps even before then"—and that the means "by which . . . this multilateral trade was effected" is a "subordinate question."[182] The flow of bullion was only one means of achieving multilateral settlement; there was also the flow of bills of exchange, without the "universal use" of which multilateral trade "could not go on." Wilson's response is as follows: of course there had been *some* multilateral trade and *some* use of bills of exchange, but it was on the "link" of bullion or specie that the volume of trade depended (notably in the Baltic), and, without bullion, trade would have been "restricted by a relapse into more or less bilateral conditions."[183]

Commenting on this debate, Jacob Price accuses both sides of "imprecise

tion costs in *London* were lower than those in Paris and other French centers. If North and Thomas are correct that in the period from 1500 to 1700 technological change was too small to account for productivity gains and the only plausible source of such gains was in the "reduced cost of using the market" (1973, 150), this would perhaps explain an English *edge*, but no more than that, over France.

[180] Parker (1974a, 532).

[181] Wilson (1949).

[182] Heckscher (1950, 221–222).

[183] Wilson (1951, 232), who insisted that the debate was real: "Agreement that the use of precious metals as a medium of international payments constitutes one kind of multilateral settlement will, I hope, narrow down the field of argument. It does not, however, entirely dispose of it. For I cannot help feeling that there remains a difference of conception as to the normal pattern of international trade and payments in the mercantilist age. Prof. Heckscher appears to me to suggest too small a *role* for bullion, too large a *role* for the bill of exchange. Was the world of Thomas Mun *really* as much like the world of Alfred Marshall as Prof. Heckscher suggests? Is the financing of international trade a subject without a history? I do not think so. [There were] bullion movements on a scale markedly different from the 'driblets' of the nineteenth and early twentieth centuries" (1951, 233).

historicity" and of seeing the whole mercantilist period as static. Bills of exchange he said, had originated in the Middle Ages not simply for reasons of security or simplicity of payment, "but in part to compensate for the relative scarcity of currency." He argues that from the mid-sixteenth century to 1660, the world silver supply boomed, allowing trade to expand, but that after 1660, the silver supply contracted, which led to both the increased use of bills of exchange and to the expansion of commodity flows in order "to balance the trade."[184] Price thus offers to split the difference, awarding the first half of the seventeenth century to Wilson and the second half to Heckscher. For Price, the difference is explained by the quantity of bullion available. Sperling seconds Price, agreeing that 1660 is the crucial moment of the shift, after which there existed an Amsterdam–London international clearing center that "expanded to meet the needs of a growing system of world trade"[185] and thereby made possible the Industrial Revolution. Into this controversy Rudolph Blitz adds the useful reminder that bullion is a commodity as well as a currency:

> If one country produces nothing but gold, which it exports to the rest of the world in exchange for consumption and investment goods, it is more meaningful to regard these gold exports as "gold commodity exports" than as a measure of an unfavorable balance.[186]

This statement is entirely correct, and therefore the question of why bullion flowed in some channels more than in others in the seventeenth century is as important as where it flowed. Reviewing the different trading zones, we note that the original Wilson–Heckscher debate centered around the Baltic trade, Wilson arguing that "the Baltic was the drain down which disappeared much of American silver which Spain mortgaged to Amsterdam for Dutch exports."[187] On closer look, however, it was not true that Baltic trade *as a whole* required silver export. Hinton sees three English trades as requiring silver export circa 1660—East India, Turkey, and Norway—a requirement "not necessarily true of the Eastland trade."[188] Commenting precisely on Wilson's statements about the Baltic, Åström argues that silver coin was exported to Norway and Russia but not at all, or much less so, to the areas of high trade turnover, the East Country and Sweden proper.[189] Furthermore, Sperling insists that there is "abundant evidence" for the use of bills

---

[184] J. M. Price (1961a, 273–274).
[185] Sperling (1962, 468).
[186] Blitz (1967, 41).
[187] Wilson (1949, 154). Supple supports Wilson against Heckscher in this (1959, 86), and cites a 1641 work written by Lewes Roberts and entitled *The Merchant's Map of Commerce:* "The Eastland population are noted to have so little gold and silver, as despising all in respect of it [sic], they sell their rich commodities . . . at a low rate, especially

those which are for daily food" (1951, 176).
[188] Hinton (1959, 115).
[189] See Åström (1963, 82). Heckscher also insisted, regarding Sweden: "To put it mildly, there is not the slightest trace of a continuous influx of silver to [Sweden]" (1950, 225). But Attman, speaking of trade with Russia, says, "down to the middle of the seventeenth century, at least, every country had to pay for its trade deficit with precious metals" (1973, 160).

of exchange in the Baltic, and both Hroch and Glamann suggest that the Baltic trade deficit may have been compensated for by a reverse trade balance on the overland east–west trade.[190] Where, then, did bullion flow? It seems to have flowed to Norway and Russia and perhaps to Turkey and, most importantly, to East India and to one other place—to Holland. East India and Holland—a curious pair! These two bullion flows were quite different in form and purpose.

Dales argues that Wilson is right, but not about the Baltic; he says Wilson's arguments hold true primarily about trade between Europe and the "Orient."[191] Chaudhuri's work seems to leave little doubt that there was a persistent outflow of bullion from England to India between 1600 and 1750. But what did this mean? About the early seventeenth century, Chaudhuri says:

> Since the Company had become local traders in the markets of Asia, it may be argued that the export of treasure was half in the nature of export of capital, which when invested in the Company's Asiatic factories produced a high profit from which at least part of the purchases for Europe could be made.[192]

However, the subsequent import presumed that some goods (primarily spices) would be purchased cheap in Asia and sold dear in Europe. In currency terms, Chaudhuri finds "the root cause for the drain of precious metal . . . in a marked and wide disparity in the value of gold and silver in terms of commodities in the two Continents."[193] But why this disparity?

When Chaudhuri comes to discuss the period from 1660 to 1720,[194] he suggests that the East India trade was "also becoming multilateral in character." Nonetheless, the data he presents show no significant decline of bullion export—indeed, quite the contrary. In general, he says, treasure continued to be 70–90% of the total annual export value, which suggests that "the basic economic factors underlying the trade between Europe and the Indies did not fundamentally change in the seventeenth and early eighteenth centuries." As for Holland, figures indicate that from 1672 to 1695, she received 70–90% of all the bullion and coin exported from Eng-

---

[190] Sperling (1962, 461). Some of the silver that went to the Baltic was spent by the Poles in the Levant in exchange for "oriental luxury goods" (Mączak, 1976b, 2, and see also 1974, 507). See also Hroch (1971, 26) and Glamann (1977, 262).

[191] Dales (1955, 142–143).

[192] Chaudhuri (1963, 26) and see Singh (1977, chap. VII). About the outflow from Spain to the Philippines, see Chaunu (1960b, 268–269); about that from Holland to the East Indies, see Schöffer (1966) and van der Wee (1977, 310). Raychaudhuri summarizes Dutch imports to Coromandel thus: "The major items of import, other than bullion and

specie, were in the nature of luxury items" (1962, 197). In the case of Holland, however, its ability to take over intra–Asian sea trade running between India, China, and Japan, "permitted [her] to reduce the volume of gold and silver specie that the West allowed to flow out to the Orient to balance payments. Thus, up to 1668, Japanese silver permitted the Dutch to dispense in part with Spanish piasters and gave them a certain advantage over their English competitors" (Deyon, 1978b, 229).

[193] Chaudhuri (1963, 27).

[194] Chaudhuri (1968, 484, 495).

land[195] and that from 1699 to 1719 she still received England's "largest movements of treasure."[196]

An additional detail to be noted is that bullion means both silver and gold, and these clearly did not move indiscriminately. There were gold–silver ratios, and they varied; but are there any patterns to observe? Herbert Lüthy suggests a very important one in which both gold and silver arrived from outside Europe proper, at least for the most part. Europe then reexported its largely American silver to Asia, "almost entirely monometallist-silver."[197] Gold played, however, a different role in the European world-economy. It "arrived in Europe to remain there, serving primarily as a mass of maneuver for large-scale commercial clearance and payments by States among European countries."[198]

Let us now return to the distinction between trade within the capitalist world-economy and trade between any particular world-system and its external arena. In this case, the world-system is the European world-economy and the external arena is primarily the East Indies, and also Norway, Russia, and perhaps Turkey. To facilitate exchanges for trade within the system, *currency* is required (in the case of the European world-economy, silver and copper on a daily basis, backed by gold). Obviously, paper (bills of exchange) also serves this purpose. We would expect such exchanges to be basically multilateral and to be conducted primarily by paper with occasional settlements by gold transfers in the international financial center (which in the seventeenth century was Amsterdam). In an exchange between two economic arenas, each external to the other, "currency" is not used. Exchange is relatively bilateral and is conducted in commodities that are inversely valued—in this case, the silver of Europe was exchanged first for the spices, and later for the calicoes of the East Indies. The coin or

---

[195] See Åström (1963, 82).

[196] Chaudhuri (1968, 496).

[197] Lüthy (1961, 34). Lüthy says "*almost* entirely monometallist-silver, which is not the same as *entirely.*" Chaudhuri notes that in the period from 1662 to 1680 the East India trade absorbed the gold desired by the southeast of India, which was then in the forefront of trade, but that "in 1676, for some reason—which still remains obscure—the silver price of gold suddenly broke in the Indian bullion markets" (1968, 488).

Ruiz Martín notes the "supremacy" of silver over gold on the European financial markets "from 1609 . . . up to the eighteenth century." He says part of the explanation is the demand in the East. "The Dutch and the English, in their diplomatic contacts with Algerians and Persians, for example, repeatedly heard the themes of a single condition for the capitulations to be applied: pay in Castilian *reales* [silver]" (1970, 56). Sperling, however, speaking of the "silver crisis," c. 1680 to 1703, asks why gold

was not substituted for silver in shipments to the East Indies. "Silver went eastward, *not because the trade depended upon it* in any ultimate sense, but because it was profitable. Second, . . . gold could have been used but the profits would have been less because of the terms of trade would have worsened for the Europeans" (1962, 466–467, italics added). He notes that the silver–gold ratios of the time were 17:1 in Spanish America, 15:1 in Europe, 12:1 in India, and 9:1 in Japan. But whence come these different ratios, if not from the different evaluations of the use to made of the bullion?

[198] Lüthy (1961, 35). Of course, silver was used within Europe, but for market exchange rather than for clearance. Lüthy adds the following illuminating linguistic footnote: "If, in French, silver (*argent*) became the term used to denote money, specie-point was translated gold-point (*point-or*)." (Lüthy uses "specie-point" in English in the French text.)

bullion brought into Asia (and Russia) was largely used "for hoarding or
jewelry";[199] and the "balance of trade" (if one refuses to think of silver as a
commodity) was *persistently* unfavorable and largely bilateral for a long period of time. These two facts are precisely evidence that the East Indies
remained *external* to the European world-economy. The fact that the trade
of western Europe with the Eastland (and Sweden) was largely regulated
multilaterally and in bills of exchange is on the other hand evidence that
both trading zones were part of one economic system.

The production of gold and silver as a commodity made the Americas a
peripheral area of the European world-economy insofar as this commodity
was essential to the operation of this world-economy, and it was essential to
the extent that it was used as *money*. Had the bullion of the Americas *all*
flowed out to Asia, the Americas would have been just another external
arena and Europe would have been merely an axis of three arenas—
America, Europe, and Asia—obtaining its Asian luxuries at the price of the
goods sent to the Americas. But the Americas were not interested in ex-
changing their bullion, and surely not in mining it. Therefore, the Europeans first seized Inca gold, then mined Potosí and Mexican silver, seeking
ever-new mining areas (of which Brazilian gold would soon be the most
important). They sent settlers to control the area of the Americas politically
and to supervise the economic operations, and they imported labor as well.
In short, they incorporated the Americas into their world-economy, primarily because they needed a solid currency base for an expanding capitalist
system and secondarily to use the surplus in trade with Asia. When in 1663
the English revoked penalties on the export of bullion to the Baltic,[200] was it
not because the Baltic was in fact safely encapsulated in a system of multilateral payments?

Was there then any justification for mercantilist concern with the flow of
bullion? Yes there was—because the flow of bullion as *currency* was one of
the mechanisms by which the hegemonic power assured extra advantage to
itself. By worrying about the flows of bullion, were the English mercantilists
(and to a lesser extent the French) not worrying about the flows of currency
to Holland and the flows of commodities through Holland?[201] If the silver
flowing out to the East Indies were the real problem, why was there never a
serious attempt to stem it? The flows of bullion *internal* to the European
world-economy depended, in turn, not only on the mechanisms of financial
clearance, but also on the control of the creation of the commodity as well as

[199] Sperling (1962, 450).

[200] See Wilson (1967, 509).

[201] Supple argues that the *real* problem for governments was that of speedy readjustment to shifts
in bullion flows, that is, liquidity difficulties. "In this
light, 'mercantilism', as it is generally understood,
more readily takes on the appearance of a

defense-mechanism than an aggressive, fallacious
and self-defeating hunt for treasure. Worried by
quantitative and qualitative loss of money, the authorities quite rightly wished to control the outflow
before it produced chronic maladjustments in the
economy" (1959, 194).

the total available supply. It is in this regard that the issue of the so-called penury of precious metals in the seventeenth century presents itself to us.

It is argued that world production of silver declined in the seventeenth century and that production of gold stagnated while imports of bullion from the Americas to Spain dropped precipitously.[202] Morineau, in a re-evaluation of the Spanish bullion flows, is skeptical of the received facts, and even more doubtful of the interpretations built on these facts:

> In any case, . . . we can no longer envisage the seventeenth century in terms of a general and generalized crisis; and even less in terms of a famine of gold and silver, either at the source in America or upon arrival in Europe. The true problems are different.[203]

Morineau does not wish to deny a fall in the quantity of bullion that arrived in Spain, although he believes the usual figures are exaggerated; but he doubts that this was the result of a long-term trend. He argues that it was the result of a series of accidental economic factors, and he doubts even more that the economic contraction of the European world-economy (to the extent that he admits there was one) can be accounted for by shifting bullion supply.

Both issues are worth discussing. Why did the bullion imports decline? Obviously, it had to be because of a decline in either supply or demand. The most frequent explanation is a decline in supply. The easy sources of bullion had been exhausted, overexploited. It was now more costly to mine the precious metals. It would take time to uncover new sources. One argument is that sixteenth-century expansion had used up this key resource at a certain level of technology, and that there was, consequently, a shortage capital and hence a depression. To this, Morineau responds that around 1620, "when the arrivals of gold and silver started to become scarce," it was men "in conjunction with . . . the elements, who created this trend."[204] To him it was a case of men "perhaps following upon the elements," and not vice versa.

Bullion, like any other commodity, has its price, and a general price inflation, the major financial characteristic of the sixteenth century, often means a lowering of the price of bullion. But bullion as money is only one

---

[202] See the summarizing discussion in Vilar (1974, 237–244).

[203] Morineau (1969a, 346–347; also 1978b, 80–85).

[204] Morineau (1969a, 311). For example, in accounting for the "swelling" of arrivals to Spain in the last two decades of the sixteenth century, Morineau refers to the fact that the king repatriated more bullion from the Americas (which presumably was mined anyway but would otherwise not have crossed the Atlantic) and to his taking a larger cut from the Indians and the Spaniards (1969a, 334). But the Indians did not get bullion in pay, and the Spanish settlers would presumably have wanted to use it for purchases in Spain, and hence the bullion would have crossed the Atlantic in any case. Deyon expresses a skepticism similar to Morineau's: "No one dreams of denying the role of unexpected discoveries, but how can we fail to express our reservations with regard to an interpretation that would bury in the depths of American mines the destiny of Europe?" (1967, 84).

element in a real exchange.[205] Bullion import at the time slowed down. It was the "Drake effect," says Morineau "the 'modern' version of the sword of Damocles."[206] If the privateers intercepted relatively few convoys, they had nonetheless, as Morineau says, a "more subtle, more efficacious, more pernicious" impact: they caused delays, which ultimately caused bankruptcies. In addition to the "Drake effect" of the late sixteenth, there was the "Blake effect" of the mid-seventeenth century, which "killed off the *Carrera*."[207]

However, these military depredations merely raised the cost of bullion. If bullion was needed as much as before, why could this cost not be passed on to the consumer? Why weren't more ships sent out? It will not do to ignore the realities of the contraction; it was not primarily caused by declining bullion supplies, but by a lessening demand for these supplies. A declining supply served the hegemonic power well in the early seventeenth century because Holland, by its productive and commercial advantage, could attract the existing bullion disproportionately.[208] When the supply became really short, bullion became the base of a system of lucrative investments. By mid-century, Dutch merchants were leaving in London the bullion they were receiving in payment from their English clients, and they were beginning to lend it out at rates of 5–7%, thereby creating a mechanism "which in time was to relieve the pressure on capital in its 'solid' forms."[209]

We have taken a circuitous path to come to our subject, the availability of bullion in the second half of the seventeenth century and its meaning in terms of the Anglo–French rivalry. Since the production rate was less for bullion than for other commodities, the scarcity of precious metals grew as the century went on. The shortage was beginning to be felt, which led to a renewed search for gold and silver."[210] Lúthy doubts that France was any worse off than other countries in this time of shortage, and notes that, in the years of peace, France had a very positive balance of trade. He says that considering France both as a state and as an arena of monetary exchange,

[205] Using the historical data of this period, René Baehrel argues that bullion or money is a "secondary phenomenon" (1953, 309). I would state it differently. It is a commodity like wheat or textiles, and we must be concerned about the terms of trade of all these commodities in relation to each other.

[206] Morineau (1969a, 331–332), who adds that the Drake effect was "above all the holy wafers of the insurance companies." On the Drake effect, see also Parry (1961, 127) and Lynch (1969, 190).

[207] Morineau (1969a, 346). The reference is to Admiral Blake of England, who in 1656 attacked eight Spanish galleons off Cádiz, sinking two and capturing two.

[208] Vilar says "it is a certainty that, as of mid-century, the capital of the Republic of Holland was at least equal to that of all the rest of Europe" (1974, 241).

[209] Wilson (1949, 160). Stone notes the drop in interest rate in London from 10% to 5% in the period from 1620 to 1650, saying they were the equal of any in Europe except in Holland. "This dramatic reduction in interest rates was both cause and consequence of the growth of fluid capital and [of] the development of institutional facilities for its employment, such as joint-stock companies and deposit banking with scriveners and goldsmiths" (1972, 69). If it was really Dutch-owned bullion that was causing the drop in interest rates, may it not in fact be better explained by the reduction in global liquid capital, notwithstanding the increase in liquid capital available through banks for loans.

[210] "First of all, one must always remember that a time of very low prices for commodities as a whole means a time of high purchasing power for precious metals, and thereby an incitement to discover them" (Vilar, 1974, 247).

its specie hunger was, unlike that of Holland and England, "not tempered by any institution that could mobilize for it readily and in insignificant quantities the other means of circulation or savings or—not least important—hoarded wealth."[211]

As usual, such an explanation only pushes us one step back. The old dorsal spine of Europe had long since developed banking structures. In the seventeenth century, Holland followed suit, the natural outgrowth of her hegemony. Why was England more capable than France of going down this path in the late seventeenth century? I have no clear answer, but I offer two observations side by side. First, within the European world-economy, the social usage of the three currency metals was (indeed still is) more or less as follows: gold for international clearance and affairs of state (also for hoarding), silver for large-scale internal commerce, and copper for household and petty commercial needs. Since, as we have already explained, French production was largely sold on a French market and English (and Dutch) production were sold more in export markets, the two rivals moved toward "*de facto* monometallism"—silver for France and gold for England.[212]

The second observation has to do with the role of copper coin, or rather with its multiplication, "the nightmare of the century."[213] Spooner argues that there was an inverse relationship between the degree to which gold and silver circulated (as opposed to their being hoarded) and the circulation of copper coin and credit. The latter two went hand in hand,[214] in terms of the world-economy; but were they not alternatives in terms of a national policy? The French state throughout the seventeenth century sought to avoid devaluation of the *livre tournois* at all costs,[215] but was relatively successful only during the era of Colbert.[216] May we not have here one more example of how the size of a state is a factor in the world-economy? The French state, looking inward economically but outward politically, was oriented to silver; and it was unable to stem a plague of copper expansion at a time of silver shortage, except at the one point when it tried to shift politico-economic gear (the era of Colbert). The English state, looking outward economically (because it had to) but inward politically, was oriented to gold; it was open, therefore, to an international gold banking network, and was able to utilize paper rather than copper.

Which, then, was the "strong" state? The question is not normally in doubt. Was not Louis XIV the absolute monarch incarnate? And did not France's dilemmas result because state and aristocracy jointly stifled

[211] Lüthy (1959, 95), who wonders if penury of bullion is the right concept and suggests rather a lack of liquidity, pointing out that at the time the word *resserrement* (contraction) meant both hoarding and scarcity of money.

[212] Lüthy (1959, 97). This had continuing implications. Vilar points out that, in the first half of the eighteenth century, "England founded her monetary circulation on her relations with Brazil and Por-

tugal, and hence, on gold; France concentrated on her relationship with Spain and the Caribbean, and hence was counting on silver as the basis of her currency" (1974, 324).

[213] Vilar (1974, 287).

[214] See Spooner (1956, 3–4).

[215] See Pillorget (1966, 129).

[216] See Lüthy (1959, 98).

bourgeois enterprise? I see the situation quite differently, however. At the beginning of our period, in 1651, the United Provinces was the "strong" state. By the end, in 1689, England and France were both "stronger" than the United Provinces and about equal to each other. In the eighteenth century, Britain would become stronger than France, and it would be the weakness of the French state and not its strength that would impel the revolutionaries of 1789. To be sure, this argument revolves around what one means by the strength of a state.

In a capitalist world-economy, owner-producers wish the state to perform two key functions on their behalf. They want it to help them gain or maintain advantage in the market by limiting or expanding the "freedom" of this market at a cost less than the increased profit, regardless of whether this is a positive or negative intervention by the state. This is the interest of an owner vis-à-vis other owners. The owner-producers in addition want the state to help them extract a larger percentage of the surplus than they could do otherwise, once again at a cost less than the resulting increased profit, and with indifference in this case too as to whether the state's role is active or passive. Hence, for the owner-producer, the strong state is not necessarily the one with the most extensive state-machinery nor the one with the most arbitrary decision-making processes. Quite often the exact opposite is true.

Needless to say, a state's strength correlates with the economic role of the owner-producers of that state in the world-economy; but if these assertions are not to be mere tautologies, we must have some independent *political* measures of this strength. We suggest five possible such measures: the degree to which state policy can directly help owner-producers compete in the world market (mercantilism); the degree to which states can affect the ability of other states to compete (military power); the degree to which states can mobilize their resources to perform these competitive and military tasks at costs that do not eat up the profits (public finance); the degree to which states can create administrations that will permit the swift carrying out of tactical decisions (an effective bureaucracy); and the degree to which the political rules reflect a balance of interests among owner-producers such that a working "hegemonic bloc" (to use a Gramscian expression) forms the stable underpinnings of such a state. This last element, the politics of the class struggle, is the key to the others.

All these measures are political and not economic because they are not measures of productive efficiency. Ultimately, of course, political and economic measures are linked reciprocally because productive efficiency makes possible the strengthening of the state and the strengthening of the state further reinforces efficiency through extramarket means. States where the *most* efficient producers are located have less need to intervene actively in the world market than states where moderately efficient producers are located. Since efficiency of production is linked to the ability of the state-machinery to intervene in the world market, states where the least efficient producers are located are incapable of being "strong." The role of the state in the world market (which of course includes the internal market) is in *curvilinear* relationship to the economic role of the owner-producers located within the state. The state is most "active" in states of moderate strength. The rhetoric of strength ("l'Etat, c'est moi") is frequently a substitute for the reality.

The Whig interpretation of history sees modern times as encompassing one long historical quest for the weak state, a quest viewed as synonomous with the advance of human liberty. This perspective stops short of theoretically embracing anarchism, but only just. Insofar as many Marxist historians have seen the English Revolution in this same light, they share the mystification.[217] I see the modern history of the state rather as one long quest to create structures sufficiently *strong* to defend the interests of one set of owner-producers in the world-economy against other sets of owner-producers as well as, of course, against workers.

Military strength is one key to efficacity in this regard. J. H. Plumb rightfully reproaches those Dutch historians who see the extension of Dutch power in the period from 1580 to 1640 as a "miracle" because of the absence of centralized state-machinery. He very correctly observes:

> The miracle lies in the fact that in spite of intense rivalry between state and cities, and the constant obstacle of entrenched rights and privileges, the Dutch were able to mount great navies and armies and pay for them mainly out of taxation. And this was achieved largely through the dedication of the Calvinist oligarchies who possessed a strong and viable sense of their own destiny as a class and as a nation.[218]

It was a miracle only if one regards absolutism as the optimal road to a strong state rather than a *pis aller*. A self-aware and self-confident bourgeois class can *agree* to the necessary collective adjustments that elsewhere require a strong king to impose, with none of the dangers of the latter format whereby the strong king might delude himself into the possibility of re-creating the "universal monarchy" in the capitalist world-economy. It was precisely of this sin, that of imitating Charles V, that Burckhardt accused Louis XIV, and later Napoleon.[219] It was a folly that derived from weakness.

We have already discussed how and why the three core powers turned upon each other as a result of the economic difficulties of the seventeenth century and how, once England and France turned their energies to reinforcing their military structures, England confounded the United Provinces at sea and France confounded her on land. The Dutch suffered from two problems. They were *defending* an advantage rather than seeking one,

[217] Ashton accuses Christopher Hill of precisely this: "For him, as for the Whig, the seventeenth century is indeed the great heroic age of the emergence of modern liberalism" (1965, 581).

[218] Plumb (1965, xxii). J. R. Jones similarly argues that before 1640 the powerlessness of England "in relation to the Dutch was crucial" (1968, 41).

[219] See Burckhardt (1965, 144–145, 152–153, 180), who says: "The *increase* in his power and possessions was first and foremost for Louis XIV a way to *preserve* them."

which meant that for at least a good part of the Regent class, the costs of military preparation often seemed more horrendous than the potential losses from lack of preparation.[220] This is the perpetual dilemma of the wealthy vis-à-vis insurance policies; and in military affairs, one has to run even to remain in place. Worse yet, this particular period was one of significant upgrading in the size of military units.[221] This created a major problem of provisioning these enlarged armies since "the numerical growth of the armies far exceeded progress in the means of production."[222] It became much more demanding for the United Provinces to compete with England and France at a moment when Dutch will was perhaps sliding.

Quite aside from previously discussed considerations of what pushed France toward a continental (land) perspective and the English and the Dutch towards a maritime one, the purely demographic advantage of France tended to confirm such a military orientation, particularly since the absolute size of armies was growing throughout Europe. This purely military consideration also explains the inevitability of the Anglo–Dutch reconciliation at the expense of the French.[223] The shock of 1672 is what seems to have led to a Dutch perception that France was the primary enemy,[224] and the accession of William III to the English throne in 1688 finally reconciled the merchants of Amsterdam to the junior partnership with England.[225]

The seeming military strength of France notwithstanding, Tapié talks of France's having reached its apogee in 1679[226] and Bourde, reproaching Louis XIV for fixating on a southern continental axis rather than attending to a northern maritime one, speaks of the "failure of Louis XIV" that resulted therefrom.[227] It is then to nonmilitary factors that we must turn— the question of mercantilism and its vagaries—if we are to explain the ultimate[228] military defeat of the French.

---

[220] Wilson accounts for the high rate of Dutch taxation by the costs of defense. He says of the period after independence: "To fight in one's own defence may have been more satisfying than to owe helpless allegiance to a dynastic overlord. It was not less expensive" (1968, 235). Smit notes that the increasing costs of warfare in the last quarter of the seventeenth century "exceeded the capacity of the tax basis, or the population basis, of the country." To keep up with the competition, the Dutch would have had to expend "staggering sums . . . in a country already taxed at the highest rate" (1975, 62).

[221] Finer says that "the sharp increases come, in every case, after the close of the Thirty Years' War, in 1648" (1975, 101).

[222] Perjés (1970, 3). Glamann points out that at the end of the seventeenth century the British Navy had 20,000 men in sea service, "a figure comparable to the contemporary populations of cities such as Bristol and Norwich" (1977, 200).

[223] Carswell argues that, as of 1685, English and Dutch military powers were "comparatively even" in strength, each depending for warfare on a "specially assembled effort," but that France had a "large professional force" (1969, 24).

[224] See Carter (1975a, 12, 33).

[225] On the resistance as late as 1683 of the Amsterdam merchants and on their change of view in 1688, see Smit (1968, 33). On the Anglo–Dutch "hostile symbiosis" leading to an English-dominated partnership, see Hobsbawm (1960, 112). On the fact that it took Louis XIV awhile to appreciate that England had become his "principal rival," see Bourde (1960, 54).

[226] Tapié (1960, 12).

[227] Bourde (1960, 63).

[228] See Hobsbawm, who says: "The impressive thing about late seventeenth-century France is not Colbertism, but its relative failure; not the reform of the monarchy, but its failure, *in spite of much greater resources*, to compete economically—*and therefore in*

Mousnier says that from the time of Henry IV to that of Louis XIV, Colbertism was a permanent feature of French policy, the objective of which was "above all, political."[229] What can this possibly mean? Presumably, the strengthening of a state is seen by Mousnier as an end in itself, an objective that a sovereign can in fact pursue. No doubt he can, as an aberration, but will he in fact succeed? The French kings clearly did not. In fact, the states in Restoration England and Colbertian France both sought consciously and actively to support their producing classes against foreign competitors, to build up their merchant marine, to work out a viable sharing of the total national product between the state and the owner-producers. Léon and Carrière note the increase in the number of large ships under Colbert but say we should not credit him alone since it in fact resulted from "the importance of the wars."[230] Delumeau notes the general improvement of the economic situation under Colbert but says that it is less to his credit than due to the "political stabilization" resulting from the defeat of the Fronde.[231] In short, these authors are suggesting that the deliberate policy of a small group was not the key factor, that we should turn to underlying pressures. I agree; but then we could apply the same analysis to England, which also had the spur of wars to stimulate shipbuilding and which also experienced a calming of political violence after 1660.

Wilson suggests a *difference* between England and France in the form of a metaphor: "Between English 'mercantilism' and Colbertism and its derivatives, there was all the difference between a tailor-made suit and a ready-made."[232] Let us look at this metaphor as it might apply to the system of public finance and to administration in general. The "institutionalisation of war"[233] in the seventeenth century meant a greatly increased scale of public expenditure for the core powers. It was eventually too much for the Dutch Republic. But what about for England and France? The increased money had to come from somewhere, and that somewhere had to be the moneyed classes. The reason was simple. Insofar as capitalism as a system already involved an increased levy on the productive output of the worker, any increase in public taxes on the worker meant, in fact, less profit for the moneyed classes, either because they would not obtain the same rents on their land or because they would have to pay higher wages in consequence.[234]

the end, militarily—with its maritime rivals, and its *consequent* defeat by those rivals" (1960, 111, italics added).

[229] Mousnier (1967, 269).

[230] Léon and Carrière (1970, 190).

[231] Delumeau (1966, 94).

[232] Wilson (1965, 57). Is this what Hinton means when he speaks of the quality of flexibility in the English mercantile system? See Wilson (1959, 71–83) and compare Harper (1939b) on the importance of the role of administrative decisions in in-

terpreting the Navigation Acts.

[233] The phrase is Minchinton's (1974, 111). See also Parker (1974a, 561).

[234] This reality of the relationship between public finance and private profit can be seen as having its effect in many ways. De Maddalena, for example, points out that in France and western Germany, concentration of property by the new bourgeois landowners was pursued "circumspectly, since the incorporation of peasant farms meant assuming the tax obligations that went with them" (1974a, 293).

The problem for the state was a double one: raising the money and spending it well. Spending it well did not mean spending it honestly, but spending it productively, using as a gauge the degree to which the increased profits of the national bourgeoisie in the world market exceeded the indirect costs to the bourgeoisie of such state expenditures. The problem was the same for the English and French states; and for the period of Restoration England and Colbertian France it is not clear that there was much difference in their ability to respond.

It was not only necessary to raise the money; it had to be raised rapidly, which meant borrowing from somewhere. This was still the forte of the United Provinces, whose "healthy public credit . . . lay in the fact that the chief investors ran the government."[235] Both England and France were searching in this period for ways of coping with the need to borrow.

Febvre says of Colbert that he was "an alchemist, who had to find gold for his king. And who searched, who never ceased to search."[236] But Colbert felt that the state was already borrowing too much, in the form of tax-farming. To increase total revenue, he reduced the role of the tax-farmers (which in reality transferred a larger percentage of the taxation of the peasants to the state) and simultaneously kept "nonproductive" state expenditure in check (which reduced the amount of tax money simply redistributed to the same moneyed classes) in order to spend it on mercantilist ends.[237]

Colbert was moderately successful. He probably doubled the king's revenue.[238] The state of Louis XIV was possibly the only one in the period able to support major military efforts without excessive difficulty.[239] Yet Colbert's suit was ready-made, if you will, in its clarity and visibility: tax more directly and balance the budget (that is, redistribute more directively). His methods were not popular, and geared as France still was to an expensive continental military expansion, they could not be sustained.

The English suit was tailor-made, creating new mechanisms of long-term public borrowing that involved less visible taxation and was no less heavy on the moneyed classes in the long run. This met less resistance and was to become in the eighteenth century more productive of state income that was

This is why Jacquart can talk of the state's being "the true profiteer of the seventeenth century" (1978b, 406).

[235] Parker (1974a, 572).

[236] Febvre (1933, 270).

[237] On Colbert's hostility to the *traitants,* see Marsin (1970, 269). Lüthy notes, however, that the *fermiers* and *traitants* were a necessary evil because they could advance the state its revenue (1959, 109). The mercantilist ends were not exclusively in the industrial arena. See Le Roy Ladurie: "The state played the same role of sugar daddy vis-à-vis the large 'seigniorial' domains of capitalist vocation as it played elsewhere vis-à-vis Colbertian manufactures"

(1974b, 16). Dessert and Journet (1975) describe what they call a "Colbert lobby," which represented the *financiers* who from 1663 to 1687 occupied *la Ferme générale;* that is they creamed taxes off the land for their industrial and export–import enterprises. In this sense, Colbertism represented a shift of resources from the low-level unproductive *traitants* and *fermiers* to high-level productive persons.

[238] See Rule (1969, 32) and Goubert (1970f, 123).

[239] "Colbert had done his work well, and although the French had certainly paid dearly, this was probably because they were able to do so" (Goubert, 1970f, 124).

to a greater degree well spent. Although England, as late as the Protectorate, was "relatively backward"[240] in its modes of public borrowing compared not only to the United Provinces but to France, the base of the
so-called financial revolution after 1689 was created during the Restoration.
The experiments of Sir George Downing in 1665, which involved appeals
to small individual investors to lend directly to the government, only lasted
until 1672, but they created an important precedent for the ascendancy of
the Treasury as the controlling department of finance and they prepared
for later techniques.[241]

The more straightforward approach of the French, as it may be described, extended to various aspects of administration. Once again, effective
administration does not necessarily mean absolutist administration. To
Swart's assertion that the Dutch government was ineffective, an "an-
tiquated, semi-medieval patchwork" that was an obstacle to further economic advance, Smit responds with total disagreement (as do I):[242] "In the
seventeenth century, it was precisely the decentralization of the Dutch government that made it efficient compared to the centralized monarchies."
Indeed, a sign of the *decline* of administrative efficiency is to be found in the
"aristocratization" of the Dutch burghers, which led some of their supporters to propound absolutist political theories for the Dutch *Republic* and
gave rise to complaints that the Regents had lost interest in overseas
trade.[243]

The French path to strengthening the state is well known: centralization
and uniformity. Indeed, this has come to be considered the classic path. Of
course, centralization did not only involve the mere creation of the central
administration *per se,* which was the accomplishment of an earlier era; it also
involved the creation of direct lines of authority from center to locality, the
system of *intendants.* This new mode of *local* administration was "the true
absolutist revolution."[244] We may call it a revolution, but Colbert created a
unified tariff only in the Five Great Farms. Heckscher says that this "proves
that he never intended a general unification."[245] How uncharitable. I believe Meuvret to be more fair when he says: "Probably it was better that
Colbert was only a hard-working and tenacious administrator and not an
audacious and original innovator. Neither the situation nor the attitudes of
the time permitted radical changes."[246] To realize the upward battle Colbert
fought to bureaucratize the state, one has only to look at the resistance of
both the *gens de mer* and the naval officer corps to Colbert's desire to create a
reserve of naval sailors that, in times of peace, could serve the merchant

[240] M. P. Ashley (1934, 97).

[241] See Roseveare (1969, 61; 1976).

[242] Swart (1975, 45) and Smit (1975, 63).

[243] See Roorda (1964, 126–127). On absolutist
political theories in the Dutch Republic, see
Kossmann (1976, 13–17) and Bouwsma (1970, 9).

[244] E. Barker (1966, 7).

[245] Heckscher (1935, **I**, 104).

[246] Meuvret (1971a, 29). Furthermore, it is absurd
to compare this unfavorably with Britain, whose unified tariff zone was only slightly larger than that of
the Five Great Farms. As Crouzet says, Britain's unification "should not be overestimated" (1972, 78).

marine.[247] During the same period of time, the 1670s and 1680s, "the core of the [English] government was growing both stronger and more efficient in spite of the wild conflicts of political life,"[248] but with far less fanfare and therefore far less opposition.

Why did the French and English affect such seemingly different styles in the parallel search for the strong state? Why was the English path more fruitful? It is in the *minor* variations in the class structure that we will find our answer. We must start with what was the same in England and in France. Both countries were thriving centers of agricultural and industrial production in the European world-economy of the time. In both countries the feudal aristocracies had largely reconverted themselves into capitalist farmers and were playing a large role in nonagricultural activities. In both countries those who were not aristocrats also played significant roles as capitalist entrepreneurs in agriculture, commerce, and industry, and the economic success of these nonaristocratic bourgeois was sooner or later rewarded with access to higher status. Because the line one drew between noble and commoner was lower in France than in England, technically, persons of medium-high status who would be nobles in France (*noblesse de robe*) were commoners in England (gentry); but the social status and social roles of the two were in fact comparable. Because the French state was historically *weaker* than the English (more because of its size than anything else and because of the consequent centrifugal economic forces), the *noblesse de robe* were incorporated into the political structure as national officials, the gentry more frequently as local officials; but in both cases their new roles represented real, if limited, political participation in the government.

Furthermore, both countries were the arena of a fundamental political conflict within the upper strata that went on from the sixteenth century to at least the eighteenth, and perhaps the nineteenth. The struggle was between those who had high status, in terms of the surviving juridical structures of feudal times, and those who were more or less successful capitalists. The key to the struggle is the fact that at any moment in time, the majority of the members of each group demonstrated both traditional status and high achievement in the economy, and they could therefore opt to think of themselves either as aristocrats or as capitalists, depending on their immediate interests. If one adds to this the constant historical process of translating market achievement into social status by means of "aristocratization," there were bound to be many ambiguities. It must be said, however, that the men of the time navigated these ambiguities and understood the realities of the struggles better than do the scholars of later times looking back at the struggles.[249]

[247] See Asher (1960, 48), whose explanation as to why Colbert's system of naval requirement, which was far more equitable than the system of the press, failed is that the absolute monarchy was not strong enough (see pp. 91–95).

[248] Plumb (1967, 13).

[249] For example, James Harrington in the *Commonwealth of Oceana* (1656) says: "*Nobility*, in which style . . . I shall understand the *Gentry* also, as the French do by the term *Noblesse*" (cited by Wilson,

In all of this, I repeat again, there was no significant difference between England and France in the whole period of around 1500 to 1800. R. H. Tawney is credited with the sally, "Bourgeois revolution? Of course it was a bourgeois revolution. The trouble is the bourgeoisie was on both sides."[250] But this was as true of the Glorious Revolution of 1688–1689 as it was of the revolution of 1640; and it was true of the Fronde as well, and even of the French Revolution in 1789. This takes away none of their "revolutionary" character. It means we must do away with the ahistorical idea that the bourgeoisie and the aristocracy were two radically different groups, particularly in this period of time. They were two heavily overlapping social groups that took on somewhat different contours depending on whether one defined the dominant stratum in terms of social status or in terms of social class. It made a lot of difference which definition was used. The social and political struggles were real, but they were *internal* to the ruling strata.[251]

Having emphasized the similarities between England and France, we must note that there were differences of detail that must be analyzed in order to understand the divergent paths of the two countries in the *nineteenth* century. For it is the *small* differences of the earlier period that enabled England after 1763 to pull ahead of her rival significantly in terms of economic productivity and dominance.

In a book revolving around the concept of political stability, Theodore Rabb draws a picture in which early modern Europe is essentially politically unstable after 1500, the "balance" between king and noble, central government and region being "uncertain" until the mid-seventeenth century, "when the problems ceased to polarize society for over a hundred years." Rabb says that although there were "after-tremors" following mid-century, no one "fundamentally questioned . . . the very organization of politics. *That* was the crucial change."[252] Is that a reasonable description of political reality? If it is, what would it imply for the struggle between England and France? We notice immediately that Rabb's dates correlate roughly with the long-term economic trends. It appears at first glance to be the classic Weberian correlation: expansion and political instability, stagnation and political stability.

I do not think Rabb is wrong, provided we specify more clearly what kind

---

1965, 109). It is not fair to suggest that no subsequent scholars recognized this. For example, Habakkuk says that English aristocracy plus gentry were "a single, if not very homogeneous, social class" (1967, 2). See also C. E. Labrousse's assertion that the owning class (*la classe propriétaire*), which includes the nonannual, nonpeasant world of the nobility, the clergy and the well-to-do (*bonne*) bourgeoisie, "confounds the three orders. It in no way denies their existence. Class, here, does not contradict order" (1970, 474).

[250] Cited by C. Hill (1975a, 281).
[251] "The real division in English landed society was not between old landed families and new, but between those proprietors of severely limited estates and interests who found the times out of joint and their grievances neglected, and those more enterprising or fortunate who found only advantage in economic expansion and social fluidity" (Mingay, 1963, 107).
[252] Rabb (1975, 71).

of stability we are talking about and what our timing is. I think what happened is that the economic expansion of the sixteenth century permitted the clear emergence of the bourgeoisie as a social class whose relationship to the dominant status-group was unclear. It was a situation that did not need to be clarified as long as the rate of expansion stayed high. Once the economic limits of the expansion were in view, the struggle of defining who had a right to control the state-machinery became acute. However, the *continuing* economic difficulties forced a *de facto* compromise between the two factions, lest the political strife get out of hand, and the lower strata (both urban and rural) begin to assert themselves, not only vigorously, but independently and directly. Hence there followed, as Rabb suggests, a period of relative stability in which the *internal* conflicts of the dominant strata were put under wraps, or institutionally contained.

I have no intention of analyzing here the complex story of the political struggles of the mid-seventeenth century in England and France; but let us quickly outline where matters stood when they ended. The monarchy was challenged in both countries, more dramatically, to be sure, in England. In the end, the Fronde was put down in France, the monarchy restored in England. To be sure, there was a major constitutional difference in the role of Parliament, which was augmented in England and eliminated in France. In England the "administrative absolutism of a king" was replaced by the "legislative omnipotence of a Parliament."[253] But what was the *content* of the social compromise? We can find remarkably different summary statements of the upshot of the English Revolution. Two will suffice. Stone says: "England at the end of the revolution in 1660 was barely distinguishable from England at the beginning in 1640."[254] Hill says, "the old state was not restored in 1660, only its trappings."[255]

May I suggest that neither summary strikes the right note. There was a real difference between 1660 and 1640, but I believe, contrary to most arguments, that it was the *social* difference and not the *political* difference that mattered. The open social warfare came to an end. The bourgeoisie as a social *class* gained its *droit de cité,* but the leading position in this class were in fact securely in the hands of the old families. The basis of the social

---

[253] E. Barker (1966, 31). The continuation of this was in 1688. What seemed to be the triumph of Parliament over the monarchs would in fact mean in the eighteenth century "the growth of the executive, which . . . achieved the subjugation of the legislature that the Stuarts had frequently attempted but never achieved" (Plumb, 1967, 65).

[254] Stone (1972, 49). Similarly, Zagorin says that "no great social change followed" (1959, 400).

[255] C. Hill (1969, 135). Besides the changes in political structures, which no one denies, Hill points to the abolition of feudal tenures and the end of governmental efforts to check enclosure. He says:

"In trade, colonial and foreign policy, the end of the Middle Ages in England came in 1650–[16]51, when the republican government was free to turn its attention outward" (p. 155). For Hill, the Middle Ages is like a spigot; in different faucets, it seems to get turned off at different exact moments: "The Middle Ages in industry and internal trade . . . ended in 1641, when the central government lost its power to grant monopolies and to control the administration of poor relief" (p. 169). "In finance the Middle Ages in England ended in 1643, when two new modern taxes, the excise and the land tax, were introduced" (p. 180).

compromise was the working out of a policy of economic nationalism that could serve former Cavaliers and Roundheads alike: "Nothing is more typical of this quest than the government committees and boards of the trading companies of the Restoration, where princes and tradesmen sat side by side in conspiracy that was expected to be mutually advantageous."[256] Nothing proves better that this solution was a compromise than the murky complexities in which the issue of restoration of confiscated lands was shrouded. It was a hot potato that Charles II tossed to Parliament and that Parliament tossed to a committee, and finally, the issue was largely resolved by private arrangements.[257]

Lawrence Stone suggests that preindustrial England's reputation as an "unusually mobile society is largely an illusion,"[258] except possibly for the period from 1540 to 1640. Is not the compromise of 1660 an agreement to halt, to *stabilize* the unsettling mobilities of the sixteenth century, to freeze matters more or less where they were?[259] Was not the great social change in England in 1660 the agreement among the dominant strata that there was to be no more internal *social* change, that the English state (whether king or Parliament, it mattered little) was to concentrate on promoting economic development at the expense of the rest of the world-economy?[260] And did not the Glorious Revolution of 1688–1689 confirm this?[261] For a whole host of minor reasons, did not some groups in the 1680s threaten to reopen the questions that the Restoration had resolved? These groups were squelched.

If the Marxist Whigs look to the English Revolution as the moment of great triumph over "feudalism," the Glorious Revolution was always the preferred moment of the liberal Whigs. As Trevelyan says,[262] the "keynote of the Revolution Settlement was personal freedom under the law, both in religion and in politics. The most conservative of all revolutions in history was also the most liberal." Is Trevelyan caught short by the suggestion that the revolution was aristocratic? Not so, he says: "It was effected by the whole nation, by a union of all classes"; it is just that an additional factor has to be considered:

> In a society still mainly agricultural, where the economic and social structure rendered the landlords the natural and accepted leaders of the countryside, noblemen and squires like the Tories Danby and Seymour, the Whigs Devonshire and Shrewsbury took the lead when resistance to government had to be improvised.

---

[256] Wilson (1957a, 153).

[257] See Thirsk (1954).

[258] Stone (1966, 51).

[259] After 1660, "barriers were being erected against social mobility which bore the hallmarks of counterrevolution" (Thirsk, 1976, xx).

[260] Supple says that the "very characteristics of the market environment which distinguished Britain's position from that of other European countries were in large part a function of state action." Nevertheless, he adds that this state action was indirect. First on the list for Supple are the political stability and social harmony after the civil strife of the seventeenth century, (1973, 314–316).

[261] "The Revolution [of 1688] demonstrated the ultimate solidarity of the propertied class" (Hill, 1961a, 276).

[262] Trevelyan (1963, 45).

Behind the rhetoric of a union of all classes lies the reality of these "natural and accepted leaders of the countryside." To be sure, an "arbitrary" king was forever eliminated from the scene; but as Pinkham says, what this fundamentally meant was that

> the royal powers which the king had hitherto been able to use in the interests of whatever group he pleased, sometimes even—God save the mark—the common people, those powers now passed into the control of the landed aristocracy which could control Parliament.[263]

This triumph of the landed aristocracy was in fact the triumph of the capitalist classes. The political compromise would hold until the mid-nineteenth century, and it would serve England well because it would permit aristocrat and squire to join with merchant and financier in order to outstrip their French rivals in the race to exploit the riches of the European world-economy.

In what way did the story differ in France? We come back once again to the peculiar geography of France. England had its peripheral regions and *a fortiori* Great Britain. These peripheral regions, located within a core state, were fearful of two trends: the gradual strengthening of this English–British state, which threatened them politically, and the triumph of capitalist elements, which threatened them economically. In Great Britain these two threats were coordinate; and it is no surprise that peripheral areas tended to be more hostile to the English Revolution[264] or that "the revolutionary decades completed the unification of England."[265] The situation in France was quite different, as we have discussed previously.[266] There, the forces of centralization and the forces of capitalist enterprise were not as geographically coordinated as in England, and the forces of the center found themselves facing resistance, not necessarily coordinated, both from economically peripheral and from economically central but politically peripheral zones. This made the internal strife of the dominant strata much more drawn out (going from the Religious Wars to the Fronde) and far more politically unclear.

Whereas the Restoration involved a calming of the tensions, if you will, because a compromise seemed to be evolving between the two factions, the equivalent period in France, the Colbertian era of Louis XIV, involved a sort of imposed truce. The truce depended on the political strength of the

[263] Pinkham (1963, 85). See also J. R. Jones: "Nevertheless James's attempt to use the urban middle classes as a replacement for the landowning class should make historians hesitate before sweepingly describing the Revolution as a bourgeois revolution. Strictly speaking it was exactly the opposite" (1972, 15).

[264] See Trevor-Roper: "In Ireland and Scotland, the King had begun by appealing to the old royalist classes, the secular, tolerant 'official' aristocracy and gentry on whose support his father's union would have rested. . . . But as these parties proved insufficient, he fell back, in both countries, on the Celtic fringe. He became the leader of the 'Old Irish' against the English planters and of the Scottish Highlanders against the settled Lowlands" (1967, 710). The link with the Highlanders was to survive later in the form of Jacobitism.

[265] C. Hill (1969, 137).

[266] See Wallerstein (1974, 293–297).

monarchy to contain forces still playing for high stakes, or let us say more
ready and able to play dangerous games than their equivalents in England.
The political structure of the country reflected this: The west, the south,
and the borderlands of the northeast were all juridically (and economically)
outside the "center." Not only were these areas deprived then of the advantages of being in customs union with the rest, although there were disadvantages as well, to be sure, but they were taxed more heavily.[267] Those
bourgeois who were not aristocrats gained access to high status as individuals,[268] but not collectively, which left them permanently uncomfortable
and potentially restive.[269]

   The contradictions come out in the whole question of the Huguenots.
Presumably the Edict of Nantes had been a step toward the resolution of
the internal divisions of the dominant strata. Why was it revoked in 1685?
There is no really good answer to this question in the literature. The
Huguenots were not particularly antiroyalist.[270] Why should the king have
been anti-Huguenot? Lüthy sees it as the act of a France "dedicated to the
cult of the State" in reaction to the humiliations of the earlier civil wars.[271]
Robert sees it as the act of a king waiting for his chance, which came after
the glorious peace of Nijmegen: "This great success in foreign policy . . .
convinced the king that henceforth he could try almost anything."[272] Le Roy
Ladurie sees it as the way to get the Church at last on the side of the throne.
"Fair exchange (*donnant donnant*). The parish priests, so ready for confron-
tation under the League and the Fronde, became thereafter, despite the
Jansenist quarrels, pillars of the established order."[273] None of these explanations suffice. Perhaps it was like a pointless exchange in chess, a hope that
by reducing the pieces, one might improve one's position. In chess, if an
exchange is not clearly advantageous, it simply brings stalemate closer. The
king sought to strengthen the state. It was harder to do than in England.
The Revocation of the Edict of Nantes did not help matters, but it may not
have hurt them either.

[267] See Pillorget (1975, 879). Of course these regions would often lose economically as well. On how
this affected the Basque country, see Goyhenetche
(1975, 5–32).

[268] This is perfectly clear from a series of studies
on the policies of Louis XIV toward his bureaucratic
personnel. Whether we are considering Secretaries
of State or military officers or judicial officials, it is
clear that wealthy and competent persons were actively recruited and rewarded with advancement on
their personal status. See Bluche (1959, 18–22),
Corvisier (1959, 45–46), and Goubert (1959, 73).

[269] "Nonetheless, the bourgeoisie remained . . .
unsatisfied. The power they lusted after with so
much ardor, they possessed and did not possess at
the same time. If, since Colbert, a large part of the
ministers were of more or less distant bourgeois origins, they largely renounced their origins from the

moment they sat in the councils of government and
attached themselves to the nobility" (Léon, 1970d,
643).

[270] See the discussion in Adams (1974). This is so
much the case that some modern Protestants argue
that the Revocation constituted the salvation of
French Protestantism from its royalism and conformity, forcing a return to its "original characteristics" after the Revocation (Léonard, 1940, 11).

[271] Lüthy (1959, 12).

[272] Robert (1967, 47).

[273] Le Roy Ladurie (1971, 28), who explicitly
compares England and France: "The English
monarchy, new style, made its peace [in 1688] with
the former opposition; just as did Louis XIV, with
the clergy which had previously supported the *Ligue*
and the *Fronde*" (1975c, 36).

There is one more important piece of evidence for the general explanation we are giving of stabilization in England and France as of the mid-seventeenth century. The stabilization, which was more effective in England than in France but which occurred in both countries nonetheless, was the result of a compromise *within* the dominant strata. If this be so, then we should see a shift in attitude of the lower strata, for the split in the ruling classes offered them space whereas a compromise would have constricted their political margin. We have some evidence of the latter. There was a decline in the frequency of peasant revolts, and such as there were tended to be more moderate.[274] Since this was presumably a time of some economic difficulty, it seems probable that the explanation lies in the political difficulty of rebellion rather than a lack of incentive.

In the earlier period, peasants were able to attach themselves to a fraction of the dominant strata in revolt. In the late seventeenth century this was no longer possible.[275] How bitter for the peasants and the urban workers must have been the great compromises! A Chartist in 1837 looking back on the English Revolution said: "For the millions it did nothing."[276] To be sure, there was unrest, especially in the towns, where it was difficult to suppress;[277] but once the compromise among the bourgeoisie was achieved, they turned to holding back the unrest. It was at this time that the two concepts *working classes* and *dangerous classes* began to be linked, developing "in the minds of the ruling classes" an association "between poverty and crime."[278]

One can, if one so desires, repeat old saws about commerce being incompatible with absolutism because the merchant might "eclipse the Roi Soleil."[279] But Schumpeter's adjunction is more to the point: "[Feudal] fetters not only hampered [the bourgeois], they also sheltered."[280] They did so in England and they did so in France;[281] but for the various reasons we have adumbrated, the policy was slightly more successful in England.

---

[274] See Jacquart (1975, 344–345; 1978c, 492), Le Roy Ladurie (1974c, 8–9), and C. S. L. Davies (1973, 125–127).

[275] On the "docility" of the notables in Provence after 1661, see Pillorget (1975, 863–866). See also Busquet *et al.*: "[This docility] is a proof, perhaps the best one, of the success achieved by the royal government in the work of unification to which it had set itself" (1972, 79).

[276] Cited in C. Hill (1975b, 204). Hill agrees: "What after all did the multitude get from the Revolution? Excise, free-quarter, pillage, conscription; not stable copyholds, abolition of titles, or protection of industrial craftsmen against their employers." As J. R. Jones says, the smaller men, the militants who fought for the revolution "did not turn out to be its beneficiaries" (1972, 16). This was true of the smaller country gentry in the years 1688 to 1689 in England—as it had been of the Calvinist militants, the sea-beggars, the urban poor, and the petty bourgeoisie after the Revolt of the Netherlands.

[277] See Léon (1970e, 684).

[278] Léon (1970e, 686).

[279] Grassby (1960, 38). Far from being incompatible, the French aristocracy was, as Supple points out, "to some extent forced [to contribute] capital and prestige to the joint-stock businesses of the seventeenth and eighteenth centuries" (1977, 450).

[280] Schumpeter (1943, 135).

[281] Citing instances from both England and France, Supple says: "Aristocratic enterprise was . . . nowhere more active than in mining and heavy industry" (1977, 499). On the role of the aristocracy in French manufacturing, see also Deyon (1978d, 277).

4

PERIPHERIES IN AN ERA OF SLOW GROWTH

Figure 5: "Morgan's Invasion of Puerto del Principe," by John Esquemelin, published in *De Americaensche zee-roovers* in 1678, and republished in *Bucaniers of America* in 1684. It is not sure if Esquemelin was French, Flemish, or Dutch. Esquemelin served as a barber-surgeon for the buccaneers for six years. His book remains the principal source of information about pirates, and its descriptions are substantiated by the State Papers of the time.

Periods of expansion of the world-economy are relatively easy to summarize. Production is expanding overall and in most places. Employment is extensive. Population is growing. Prosperity is the sign of the time. That real wages for large numbers of people may in fact be declining is less visible in the steady inflation of nominal prices. There is considerable social ferment, but it is a ferment nourished by optimism, even daring. Individual mobility seems to be the order of the day. Progress seems to be the gift of Providence.

Periods of downturn are much more complex. First of all, they are much more visibly uneven. There is regression, stagnation, withdrawal, bad times—but not bad for everyone. Total production, that of the world-economy taken as a whole, may remain steady in some calculation of overall value or per capita quantity; but this may be the result of a rise in some areas of the volume of production or the rate of productivity or both, balanced by a decline in other areas. The real wages of those employed may rise, but the percentage of unemployed may rise as well.

A particularly somber picture may be expected in the peripheral areas of the world-economy. They are the politically weakest arenas. It is to be expected that the ruling groups in core and semiperipheral areas will seek to maintain their levels of production and employment at the expense of the peripheral areas. And yet the periphery does not drop out of the world-economy entirely—for many reasons. For one thing, its capitalist cadres wish to remain in the world-economy; they struggle to remain there. For a second, the cadres in the core must be concerned with the eventual cyclical upturn of the world-economy as a whole, for which they will need the physical areas and energies represented by the land and population of the peripheries. For a third thing, the core countries continue to need, even at moments of downturn, certain of the products of the periphery—partly because due to ecological considerations they cannot be supplied elsewhere, partly because the cost of labor is more than ever lower than in the core.

What needs to be underlined most of all is that a downturn is a slowdown of activity, not a stoppage. It represents, in economic terms, a set of obstacles in the search for profit that, if you will, weeds out the capitalist sheep from the goats. The strong not only survive; they frequently thrive. For the peripheries, therefore, a downturn in the world-economy occasions both involution and evolution; both a seeming decline in the monetarization of economic activity and the emergence of new enterprises; both abandonment and restructuring or relocation; both a decline in their specialized role in the world-economy and a deepening of it. To evalute this apparent paradox, we must start at the beginning. What causes a secular reversal of trends in the world-economy? A capitalist system involves the market mechanism. The market is not free—far from it—since the market is affected by political adjustments and cultural slownesses and preferences. If, however, there is no market response whatsoever, it is difficult to talk of a capitalist system.

The market responds, as we know, to variations in supply and demand. To be sure, these are not some mystical forces that meet in unpredictable ways in the agora. Supply and demand are reciprocally and institutionally determined; but if there is too great a disparity over too long a time, the market is bound to take notice of it. An era of expansion tends to create, over time, more supply than demand—for the very simple reason that supply is determined by the individual entrepreneur (for whom, in an era of expansion, increased production shows good prospects of profit) and demand is collectively determined (via the political machinery that has arranged the distribution of income). Sooner or later, given the existing worldwide distribution, there comes to be insufficient worldwide demand for the constantly expanding production. Two things can eliminate the disparity: The expansion of production can be reversed, stopped, or at the very least slowed down; and the distribution of income can be rearranged such that there is increased global demand, permitting eventually a new expansion.

Both things do in fact occur, and in that order. Production stagnates, and then later there is a political redistribution of income. This is the social profile of an era of downturn, but specifications must be added immediately. Production stagnates more in the old peripheries than elsewhere; and the political redistribution of income occurs more in core and semiperipheral areas (or at least in some of them) than in the peripheries. This, as we shall see, is precisely the story of the long era of downturn of the seventeenth century, of the period from 1600/1650 to 1750. There is another specification of this model based on lack of effective demand. We have dated this period of downturn as beginning between 1600 and 1650. This ambiguity, found throughout the book, is not an ambiguity of inadequate knowledge, but the expression of the normal mode of shift from expansion to downturn. Normally, there is a long moment during which expansion continues but downturn has already begun, and this therefore is part of the story of both eras.

We have already discussed that this particular reversal of secular trends seems to have been composed of three successive commercial shockwaves: one in the 1590s, one in the 1620s, and one in the 1650s.[1] This is the same period when the European world-economy was affected with monetary instability—the Rising of the Moneys in the Baltic, the inflation of copper coin in Spain, the sudden decline in the production of precious metals in the Americas. It was also the moment of various population disasters caused by wars, epidemics, and famines. The combination was not fortuitous. What does a producer of export crops in the periphery do when there is suddenly

[1] See Wallerstein (1974, 269–271).

an unfavorable market? There are two responses that make sense from his point of view. He can try to maintain his net income by expanding the volume of his export and/or by diminishing his production costs. Either or both often work in the short run for the individual entrepreneur, but they worsen the collective situation of peripheral producers in a given area in the medium run. Expansion of production of the export crop increases global production still more in a market where demand is already stretched. Diminishing production costs exhausts the potential of future production if it is achieved, as is most likely in peripheral areas, by intensification of exploitation of natural or human resources.

We shall try to show that in the principal peripheries of the sixteenth-century world-economy, this is precisely what happened. The weak markets of the 1590s and the 1620s led to increased volume of production and/or increased rate of exploitation of resources. By the 1650s, if not earlier, peripheral producers were forced by the consequences of this first tactic to turn to the only other sensible response, partial withdrawal from production for the market—at least for that particular part of the world market in which they had found their niche in the sixteenth century.[2] Let us start with the eastern European periphery. Its export products fell in price, in productivity, and in total value and quantity exported in the seventeenth century, most notably (but not only) for Polish grains and Hungarian cattle. The story of prices is the most familiar because it is on the break in agricultural prices that the basic image of a seventeenth-century depression is built. Polish wheat prices fell as of 1615–1620, then saw a temporary rise followed in the mid-seventeenth century "by a violent drop and price depression of long duration."[3] The rise in Hungarian cattle prices slowed down as of the beginning of the seventeenth century, only "to stop altogether after another brief boom in the 1620s."[4] By the middle of the seventeenth century, the price of Hungarian cattle in Vienna had declined "considerably."[5] For Czech agriculture too, the 100 years following 1650 was "a century of stagnation."[6]

Not only did the prices of the exports go down in absolute terms, but they may have gone down relatively, that is, the terms of trade became "more and more disadvantageous" for the peripheral exporters.[7] At the same time, there was a "rapid increase of the volume of imports of luxury articles," especially in the second quarter of the seventeenth century[8]—a kind

[2] There is a good description of this sequence for Poland in Wyczański (1967). As to the first half of the sequence, Gould notes that "there are numerous historical sequences of the response of farmers to a fall in prices being to *expand*, not to curtail, production, in an effort to maintain gross incomes at a conventionally acceptable level" (1962, 332).

[3] Wyczański (1967, 68–69).

[4] Pach (1970b, 254).

[5] Zimányi (1973, 327).

[6] Matejek (1968, 210).

[7] Topolski (1971, 62). See Table 4.1 for the specification by Kula of terms of trade for different strata of the population. Kula's comments on Topolski can be found in 1970, 164–165, n. 164. Even Kula accepts the hypothesis generally for the subperiod of 1650 to 1700.

[8] Bogucka (1972, 1).

of last fling of the peripheral gentry. The combination of declining exports
and increasing imports (at least in the period of transition) resulted in a
dramatic shift in the balance of trade. For example, Poland's sea trade in
the Baltic shifted from a 52% surplus in 1565–1585 to 8% in 1625–1646
and then to an adverse balance of trade in the second half of the seventeenth century.[9] Mączak speaks of Poland's passive trade balance resulting
from "the fateful decade of the 1620s."[10] The shifting trade balance was
aggravated by the inability of Poland's weakly protected economic enterprises to resist the negative effects of the monetary instability resulting from
price inflation. Dutch merchants required Gdańsk merchants to accept part
of their payment in weak money (for example, Loewenthalers) alongside
the harder ducats and thalers. Of course, this money could have been
barred by political authorities; but there was much opposition to any such
preventive measures by the Gdańsk merchants themselves, who both
"feared grave pertubations in external trade"[11] and did not find such protection essential, since they could pass along this burden, foist upon them by
the Dutch, "onto the shoulders of the middle bourgeoisie, the nobles, and
the peasants."[12]

The measurements of eastern European grain yield ratios have been
extensive, and the consensus is that there was a definite fall in the seventeenth century. How much is a matter of some debate. The more optimistic
see grain yields as merely stagnant at the time the yields of northwest
Europe were rising. The less optimistic see a significant drop.[13] The general
explanation of the decline of wheat yields is the "domination of commodity
production by landlords using forced labor to the utmost," the same explanation Pach gives to explain the decline of Hungary's cattle exports.[14] But
why should this domination lead to a decline in yield ratios? Two reasons
are offered. One is that the increasing exigencies of corvée labor "led many
a peasant to stop keeping draught animals and pass over to the rank of
cottars"; and since the yield ratios of peasant farms was generally higher
than that of the aristocracy, the overall yield fell.[15] The second reason is that

[9] Mączak and Bogucka, cited in Pach (1970b,
258). See also Mączak (1970, 139, Table 16).

[10] Mączak (1975, 3).

[11] Bogucka (1972, 4). The local money changers
also were opposed to such a measure as they shared
in the profits of international speculators (p. 5).

[12] Bogucka (1972, 13).

[13] Zytkowicz sees a generally "low yield of rural
husbandry" in Poland, Hungary, Slovakia, and
Bohemia, but not particularly lower from 1655 to
1750 than from 1500 to 1655 (1971, 71). Slicher van
Bath sees "stagnation or even a decline" in eastern
Europe in the seventeenth century. For Czechoslovakia, Poland, Latvia, Estonia, and Russia combined, he shows a fall from 4.3 to 3.9 between the
period of 1600 to 1649 and the period of 1650 to
1699 (1969, 175–176). Mączak is skeptical of Zyt-

kowicz's low figures for the sixteenth century
(1976b, 23), and suggests there was indeed a *fall*,
"already visible in the first half of the seventeenth
century" (1968, 77). Wyczański shows a fall for one
domain (Korczyn) from 4.8 in 1569, to 4.1 in 1615,
to 4.4 in 1660, to 3.2 in 1765 (1960, 589). Topolski
talks of an overall decline from around 5 at the end
of the sixteenth century to around 3–4 at the end of
the eighteenth (1974a, 131). Szczygielski uses the
strongest language; he speaks of Polish yields being
among the highest in Europe in the fifteenth and
sixteenth centuries and among the lowest in the
seventeenth and eighteenth (1967, 86–87).

[14] Pach (1970b, 262).

[15] Mączak (1968, 77), who says that "the contraction of market surplus caused by the shrinkage of
the farms is hardly questionable" (p. 78).

production was increased "by deviating from the fundamental principles of rotation in tilling the soil,"[16] which over time exhausted the soil. Exhausting the men and the soil maintained a level of total production for 50–60 years, but it was a self-consuming method. This can be seen since, despite all these efforts to increase production and lower costs, the total of exports declined. In the end of the sixteenth century, 100,000 lasts of wheat were shipped from Gdańsk annually; in the seventeenth, 30,000; in the beginning of the eighteenth, only 10,000.[17] Abel shows a break point in 1620,[18] but Jeannin points out that the records of the Sund show 1649 or 1650 as "a record year, outdoing 1618," and suggests we think of the turning point as 1650 rather than 1620.[19]

The story on cattle export is the same. In Hungary, 1550–1600 was the "Golden Age,"[20] after which there was a decline. The Polish cattle trade to Silesia, Saxony, and the Rhine "lost its importance" with the beginning of the Thirty Years' War because of the dangers of cattle driving.[21] The same was true of Danish cattle export, which in this context is part of the same picture.[22] Pach argues that the decline in cattle trade was more severe than the decline of the wheat trade, and hence that Hungary suffered even more than Poland because whereas the wheat was sold to "the Atlantic centre of the rising modern-type international trade," the cattle was sold to the South German towns who "fell themselves victims to the shift of international trade routes."[23] The third major export of eastern Europe in the sixteenth century had been copper. Here too there was a marked decline as of the 1620s.[24] In each of these cases—wheat, cattle, copper—the explanation lies in worldwide overproduction. In the case of wheat, there had been a rise, albeit "a small rise," in cereals production in southern and western Europe, but large enough, says Faber, to account for "the disastrous recession of the

---

[16] Szczygielski (1967, 94), who says this was true of the harvest of wood as well: "During the seventeenth century, reckless exploitation produced a desert in the woods" (p. 97).

[17] Leśnodarski (1963, 24).

[18] Abel (1973, 251 Graphic 45). See also Slicher van Bath, who says the highest export was in 1617 (1977, 87).

[19] Jeannin (1964, 320, 322). This has confirmation at the other end of the trading process. In considering Baltic wheat imports into Scotland, Smout and Fenton find an "unmistakeable" break in the mid-seventeenth century—that is, a sharp decline in such imports—which they explain by "a partial replacement of the Baltic [suppliers] by English and Irish suppliers." In fact, they add, between 1675 and 1685, Scottish grain was "even shipped *into* the Baltic" (1965, 76).

[20] Makkai (1971, 483). See also Prickler (1971, 143–144). Wiese uses the same term for European

cattle trade in general "before the outbreak of the Thirty Years' War" (1974, 454).

[21] Mączak (1972, 679). Mączak speaks of "the disastrous decline of cattle, including draught animals (mostly oxen, also horses)," going from about 77 heads per 100 hectares of peasant land in 1549 to 53 in 1630 and a continuous declining trend thereafter (1976b, 23).

[22] Abel speaks of a "weakening" of Danish cattle export in the seventeenth century (1973, 249). See also Glamann (1977, 236–237).

[23] Pach (1968, 316). Some confirmation of Pach's argument is found in the observation by Wiese that in the Germanies from 1640 to 1820 meat prices were always less favorable than those of rye (see Wiese, 1966, 105). Hungarian and Polish cattle went to south German towns, but Danish cattle went in large part to Holland (see Glamann, 1977, 216, 233).

[24] See Pach (1970b, 257).

Dutch grain trade" in the second half of the seventeenth century.[25] For cattle, it was the "decreased demand which brought down the prices."[26] In the case of copper, the main factor was the "glut of Swedish copper [that] came on the market."[27]

In each case the export situation was worsened, but not caused, by war and devastation at home—in particular by the Swedish invasion of Poland (1655–1660), by the century of intermittent fighting in Hungary, going from the Fifteen Years' War (1591–1606) to Rákóczi's war of independence (1703–1711), and by the Danish–Swedish war (1643–1645).[28] But the devastations of war, which involve the reduction of total supply, are no explanation in themselves. As Vera Zimányi reminds us: "The sixteenth century knew, throughout Europe, wars that were no less devastating, but in that era they served only to stimulate production, to create favorable conjunctures, etc., and consequently to raise prices."[29] What then had changed from the sixteenth century? The European world-economy had moved from a situation of less total supply than demand to the reverse. In the former, destruction tended to make the demand more acute. In the latter, destruction tended to offer a good excuse to reduce overall production.

How was such an overall reduction distributed? This is the key issue, as it determined, or rather restructured, the social relations of the peripheral zones. We have already seen that in eastern Europe, coerced cash-crop labor (the so-called second serfdom) had spread in the sixteenth century as a mechanism of labor control of the expanding capitalist domains. What we must now explain is why the demands on the serfs grew *even more intensive* in the receding export markets of the seventeenth century. We must begin with the fact that in the sixteenth century, cash crops were produced both on the seigniorial domain and on the peasant's plot at approximately the same level of efficiency.[30] Nonetheless, the seventeenth century is marked by a considerable concentration of land throughout eastern Europe, that is, more of the total cultivated area and more of the crops produced for the market were in the hands of seigniors and less were in the hands of peas-

[25] Faber (1966, 131). Topolski explains the decline of Polish grain exports in the seventeenth century as resulting from the decline of productivity and therefore the decline of "quasi-comparative" advantage (1974c, 435). We are arguing the inverse relationship—the increase in wheat production elsewhere indirectly caused the decline of productivity in Poland.

[26] Zimányi (1973, 330).

[27] Kellenbenz (1974, 262) and Vlachovič (1971, 626). There was also competition from Japanese and Chilean copper (Pach, 1970b, 257).

[28] On the effect of the Swedish invasion on Poland, see Baranowski *et al.* (1966, 79) and Gieysztorowa (1958); on Hungary, see Makkai

(1971, 493–494) and Várkonyi (1970, 272); on Denmark, see Jørgensen (1963, 79).

[29] Zimányi (1973, 309).

[30] Żytkowicz gives this as his tentative conclusion in comparing the productivity of peasant farms and the *folwark* (domains) of Masovia in the seventeenth century. "In any case, the main reason for the emergence of this [seigniorial] system was not that it produced more food, but that it enabled the feudal landowning class to increase its revenues" (1968, 118). Kirilly, however, studying cereals production in Hungary, notes a "turnabout" in the first half of the eighteenth century: "In contrast to preceding centuries, seigniorial wheat is henceforth characterized by a higher yield-ratio" (1965, 621).

ants. This is reported for Poland,[31] Czechia,[32] and Livonia.[33] Indeed for Poland, Mączak specifically contrasts the seventeenth and eighteenth century with the sixteenth, noting that "the small group of prosperous yeomen-peasants . . . completely disappeared . . . as a direct victim of the avarice of the landowners."[34]

Let us be clear on what happened. The expansion of total cultivated land area, a phenomenon of the sixteenth century in response to a favorable world market, ceased, even was partially reversed; but within the land area under cultivation, an increasing share was held by the direct reserve of the seigniors. That is to say, the challenge to expand market production had been met in two ways in eastern Europe in the sixteenth century: by the farming of the large domains of the magnates with coerced labor and also by *some* development of farming by rich peasants. "By the early seventeenth century, however, the fight ended with the victory of the '*Gutsherr*' trend relying on the use of forced serf labor."[35]

The advantages of the large domain over the peasant farm, indeed over the medium-sized domain, were several. Unpredictability of crops favored larger units because they had a kind of internal insurance against bad harvests by the variety of areas they controlled.[36] In addition to this advantage on the supply side of the equation, there was an advantage on the

[31] Topolski says that following the destructive wars of the mid-seventeenth century, the production of the reserves were able eventually to resume their prewar levels; but the peasant plots only resumed 60–65% of their former production (1967, 114). For one region, Gniezno, he says that the total area of the reserves equalled 13% of the peasant land area in the beginning of the sixteenth century, 16% in the middle, 20% in the end, and 25% by the eighteenth century (1970, 90). Rusiński speaks of the "diminution of the average area of the peasant units, especially in central and southern areas, as a process beginning in the sixteenth century and intensifying in the seventeenth, and leading to pauperization" (1972, 112–13).

Rutkowski had made the mid-seventeenth century a turning point because of the wars: "The farms of the larger peasants (*laboureurs*) disappeared and were replaced by smaller ones . . . or by parcels cultivated by *closiers*, by *chałupnicy* and by day-workers/renters (*komornicy*)." He spoke of "the process of proletarianization of the rural population" and the "absolute concentration of agricultural production" (1927b, 119–120). While later Polish historians contested Rutkowski's causal explanation (the wars), they did not contest the observations. See the various studies cited in Gierowski (1965, 244).

[32] Špiesz dates this for Czechia as of 1620, but says that in Moravia, the ratio of rominical (lord's) land to rustical (peasant) land remained about the same

(1969, 43–44). Łom notes increased "concentration of land" in Bohemia from 1650 to 1750 and the rise in percentage of *Gutsherrschaften* (1971, 9–10). Mejdricka says that the "greatest expansion of large domains using corvée-labor is to be observed in the second half of the seventeenth century" (1971, 394).

[33] Although Dunsdorfs sees this as a process especially true for the eighteenth and nineteenth centuries, "one can also demonstrate an increase in the size of the seignorial reserves (*gutsherrlichen Wirtschaften*) for the seventeenth century" (1950, 115).

[34] Mączak (1972, 673). Dworzaczek reports the gradual aggrandizement of the domains of the lesser nobility by the magnates in this same period (see 1977, 159); whereas, for the sixteenth century, Rusiński speaks of "a tendency toward the concentration of land in the hands of the richer peasants who bought it from their poorer neighbors" (1972, 104). See also Małowist (1972, 203–204) on the role of the well-off peasants.

[35] Pach (1970b, 261). In Poland, there were a few areas where emphyteusis survived. Explaining one such area, near the town of Elblag in Old Prussia, Żytkowicz says this exception was possible because of "the proximity of developed markets, the comparative ease with which surplus products could be disposed of, and also cheap transport to markets" (1974, 251).

[36] Kula (1961, 138) and see also Żytkowicz (1968, 109).

TABLE 3
Changes in Terms of Trade for Social Groups in Poland[a]

	1550	1600	1650	1700	1750
Magnates	100	276	385	333	855
Nobles	100	80	144	152	145
Peasants	100	205	169	118	51
Magnates		100	139	121	310
Nobles		100	180	190	181
Peasants		100	82	58	25

[a] Reprinted from Kula (1970, 94) with permission.

demand side. At that end, their direct access to the market, the fact that they could transport their goods to the port themselves without an intermediary, was "a considerable economic privilege," which Kula believes was "partially responsible" for the process of land concentration.[37] That these advantages became all the greater as times grew harder is made clear in the remarkable table (see Table 4.1) in which Kula calculates the terms of trade (the purchasing power of the products they sold in relation to those they bought) for three different social groups in Poland over time. While one shouldn't overinterpret such shaky data,[38] the use of two different index dates, 1550 and 1600, makes possible some tentative suggestions. The period of maximal expansion, 1550–1600, was good for the magnates but also good for the peasants—for both, it seems, at the expense of the nobles. As soon as bad times set in, the peasants felt the brunt of it. Both the nobles and the magnates did well. While starting from a 1600 index, it is clear that the nobles did relatively better than the magnates for a while (but only for a while); it is also clear, using the 1550 index, that in absolute terms the magnates were always way ahead of the nobles.

Why should this be so? May I suggest a very simple mechanism. When times are hard, there are two ways to maximize sales for a producer— reduce costs and eliminate competitors. The magnates (and the nobles) sought to reduce costs by increasing corvée labor, as opposed to wage labor.[39] This not only reduced average cost but *increased* total production, a

[37] Kula (1970, 91).

[38] Kula explains his methods of arriving at these figures and admits that "these results are certainly exaggerated" (1970, 94).

[39] But of course the opposite was true too. When harvests were inadequate, prices were high and corvée labor in high demand. Mączak says: "I suspect that at least in some estates landowners used to

press their tenants harder in more lean years, even if they came to the rescue of the drowning ones. . . . It emerges from [one study of an estate between 1550 and 1695] that in lean years—when prices were high—ducal stewards extracted relatively more grain from tenants" (1975, 16). Might there not have been a curvilinear relationship? When prices were relatively high, more corvée labor

second means of compensating for losses growing out of reduced market prices[40]; and to make sure the increased production on the seignior's land found a market, the seignior bought out the peasants and even the nobles,[41] many of whom were ready to sell because of *de facto* bankruptcy. Even if the seigniors didn't put the new land into production, they at least kept it from producing goods in competition with their old land. This very plausible process of investing in land, even if it was not intended that it immediately bring in money from export crops, was no doubt abetted by the financial crisis of the early seventeenth century, which pushed the magnates into a "psychologically understandable race to hoard goods as insurance against the insecurity of the money market."[42] Goods, including land, seemed safer as stored value than did coins if their "storage" was to extend over a longer time period.

What happened on these lands that were acquired to put them out of competition? They no doubt represented "a shift toward subsistence production,"[43] involution if you will, but not a negation of the capitalist mode of production. They represented precisely an intelligent adjustment to market conditions, a way for the capitalist entrepreneurs (the magnates and the nobles) to optimize profits (or minimize losses) in a weak market—a global reduction of inventory and an overall stagnation in production. The peasants may not have expanded or contracted their efforts in response to the fluctuations of the world market, but peasants were not the entrepreneurs; they were semi-proletarians, whose labor input was largely a function of the entrepreneurs' reactions to the world market.[44]

Retrocession did not mean abandonment of capitalist production as is shown by the survival, even the thriving, of regional markets as opposed to the decline in export of products to core countries. Špiesz points out that

was needed because more *labor* was needed; and peasants would not have responded to wages, since they preferred to produce their own goods for the high-price market. When prices were relatively low, more corvée labor was needed because more non-wage labor was needed. In the middle, there was the lowest demand for corvée labor. This alternation of reasons for the corvée would explain why it continued as a technique through secular upswing and downswing.

[40] Kula says: "There was no absurdity in the fact that the decision to invest [materials and labor] came not from an improvement of market conditions . . . but on the contrary because of its deterioration" (1970, 35). He says that this is noncapitalist behavior; but in the twentieth century, in periods of stagnation, do not multinational corporations sometimes follow the same tactic?

[41] Even when the nobles were not forced into outright sale to the magnates, the general lack of cash "turned the magnates into the bankers of the squirearchy and gave them an additional superiority which a banker often has over his customer" (Mączak, 1968, 88).

[42] Bogucka (1975, 147), who speaks of the hoarding of jewelry, luxury plate, precious metals, and solid coin; but the motive would have been the same in the hoarding of land, that is, protection against acute inflation, and both warrant her conclusion: "This hoarding . . . undoubtedly had unfavorable consequences for the country's economy, since it froze considerable capital for many years" (p. 148).

[43] Pach (1962, 234).

[44] Because peasants are presumed not to respond to the world market, Kula argues that "the methods of capitalist accounting are not applicable to this kind of 'enterprise'" (1970, 27). Similarly, Achilles (1959, 51–52) is skeptical that agricultural production was really responsive to prices in the sixteenth and seventeenth centuries. Neither is properly distinguishing between the large landlord who is a capitalist entrepreneur and the peasant/semi-proletarian.

already in the sixteenth century the territories of central Europe were producing for regional markets and that this accounts for the ways in which
they differed from the areas of eastern Europe exporting to western
Europe. He calls the productive relations in central Europe—Bohemia,
Moravia, Slovakia, Lower Silesia, Lower Lusatia, Austria (not including
Tyrol), Saxony, Thuringia, and western Hungary—*Wirtschaftherrschaft* as
opposed to second serfdom. Even in these countries, conditions worsened
for the peasants in the seventeenth century.[45] What is to be noted however is
that in the seventeenth century, some of the market centers in Poland that
formerly served transcontinental trade, such as Cracow and Poznań, ceased
this role because of the combined effects of the Thirty Years' War and the
Swedish wars; but they flourished nonetheless as regional market centers as
of the second half of the seventeenth century.[46] The increased concentration of land went hand in hand with an expanded extraction of days of
corvée labor. Obviously, if the seignoir had a larger reserve he needed more
labor; and if the peasant had less land, he had more time to devote to
corvée labor—that is, he presumably still tilled enough to feed himself,[47] but
no longer tilled very much of his own land for cash-crops. We have reports
of an *increase* in the amount of corvée labor in the *seventeenth* century for
Poland,[48] east Elbia,[49] Hungary,[50] Bohemia,[51] Rumania,[52] and Denmark.[53]

[45] Špiesz (1969, 61). Mejdricka makes the same
point, that is, Bohemia differed from Poland and
northern Germany in the geographic scope of its
market: "the market for agricultural products and
raw materials in the Czech lands was tied to interre-
gional exchange within the country and to some
extent with neighboring countries" (1971, 401).

[46] Cracow "proved to be much more permanent
and more solid" as a regional market than as a
transcontinental market (Malecki, 1970, 119; see
also 1971, 151). "In the second half of the seventeenth century, . . . Poznań trade came to have a
new life, now, however, serving exclusively as a regional market" (Grycz, 1967, 55; see also 1971,
119).

[47] Mączak reminds us that "poor as she was, Poland offered her inhabitants important advantages.
In comparison with other early modern countries,
Poland did not experience true universal famines"
(1972, 678). Makkai argues that "the peasants of
eastern Europe were better nourished than the
French, German, and Italian wage workers, but less
well nourished than the workers of rising western
countries where the bourgeois revolution had
triumphed" (1974, 207). Regarding the latter, he
specifies England and the United Provinces. Since
for France his only citation is Le Roy Ladurie, it may
be that what he says held true for southern France
but that northern France would fall with the "rising
western countries." In the terminology of this book,
his argument is that rural workers were worse off in

the semiperipheral regions than in the peripheral
ones, presumably because the latter kept greater
control over subsistence plots.

[48] See Mączak (1972, 677) and Rutkowski (1927b,
122). Zientara reports that peasant corvée labor was
introduced into large-scale iron mining in the
seventeenth century (see 1971, 284). Rutkowski says
that the dues (*redevances*) were not as high in the
eighteenth as in the sixteenth century (1927a, 89).
On the other hand, Rutkowski may be mismeasur-
ing. Kula points out that one of the ways in which
peasant dues were increased was to increase the
measure of wheat for peasant dues. A bushel (*bois-
seau, korzec*) in Cracow was 26.26 litres in the sixteenth century and 43.7 in the eighteenth; in
Warsaw it was 52.5 in the sixteenth and 64 in the
nineteenth (1962, 279).

The Polish aristocrats proved themselves sophisticated manipulators of capitalist mechanisms. They
realized that this redefinition of measures served
them well as rent receivers but not as sellers. So they
arranged that "the wholesale measure, the *laszt*, that
was especially used for exports, be stabilized and
unified relatively early, while the retail measure
that was used for dues payments (*prestations*)—the
bushel—went up continuously. It was simply that
over time the *laszt* had fewer and fewer bushels." It
should be noted that this is also a way of maintaining profit levels in a falling price market.

[49] See Lütge (1963, 123–127).

There is one final question about the relations of production. If an *increase* in corvée labor was rational in the seventeenth century, why was not the same high level already reached in the sixteenth? One answer might be that it took time. Another answer would be that a *high* rate of corvée labor was rational in times of market downturn for the various reasons adduced, but a *medium* rate more suitable for times of market expansion because there was a negative side to a high rate. After a certain point, corvée labor was exhausting and reduced productivity. Rusiński asks: "At what moment did corvée labor begin to show economically retrogressive features? . . . The latest research permits us to fix this moment with extreme precision." It is, he says, between 1580 and 1620 for central Poland and a little later for Silesia and Bohemia.[54] This brings us right back to our period of transition (1600 to 1650). We may resume the situation as follows: In the sixteenth century, corvée labor was economically productive. It involved the same labor in which the peasant would have engaged in any case because of the strong market; but the seignior appropriated part of the surplus for himself, from the peasant, by instituting corvée labor. As times became difficult, the seignior's demands on the peasant's labor time increased. At that point, the peasant was beginning to give labor that he might not have otherwise expanded at all. In the long run, this excess-output would tend to exhaust the peasant's labor potential and be counterproductive; but it would nonetheless in the medium-run ensure that the bulk of the loss from a weak world market was borne by the peasant and not by the seignior.

Naturally, the peasant was not happy with this situation. "The bigger the estate, the greater the contrast between the reserve and the peasant plot (*Guts- und Bauernwirtschaft*)."[55] The result was peasant flight and sabotage. We thereupon run into another seeming paradox. There occurred simultaneously an increase of both corvée labor and wage labor. This paradox is

---

[50] See Makkai (1963, 41), who says it holds true primarily in wheat production since "in cattle-breeding and wine-growing corvée-labor (*Fronarbeit*) cannot for technical reasons play as large a role as in wheat production." There was, however, an *increase* of cereals production in the seventeenth century in Hungary—perhaps because it lent itself to corvée-labor. See Kirilly and Kiss (1968, 1235).

[51] Małowist asserts that there was an intensification of the corvée in Bohemia, "mainly after the Habsburg victory at Biala Gora (White Mountain) in 1621 and the ravages suffered by Bohemia in the Thirty Years' War" (1974, 344). See also Klíma (1957, 87), Kavke (1964, 58), and Wright (1966, 14).

[52] See Stefanescu *et al.* (1962, 56), who date the increased extortion as of the late seventeenth century.

[53] See Nielsen (1933, 153) and also Tonnesson (1971, **I**, 304; **II**, 719–720), who insists that it is appropriate to "consider Denmark as a case of the

eastern type" (**II**, 719). There is a problem about Norway, then part of Denmark. Most Norwegian peasants were freed in the late seventeenth century. See Johnsen (1939, 392–393). Tonnesson explains this by the fact that "in a country with a weak aristocracy it was important [to the Danish crown] to preserve the loyalty of the peasant mass of the population in order to be able to defend the country against the Swedish neighbor" (1971, **I**, 311). But if this were so, the same logic should have prevailed in the Ukrainian areas of Poland. The Poles should have wanted to preserve Ukrainian peasant loyalty against Russian blandishments; and we know that this was not at all their attitude. It was probably rather the absence of export crops and of an early prospect for them in Norway that accounts for the differences between the Norwegian and Ukrainian attitudes.

[54] Rusiński (1974, 40–41).

[55] Rusiński (1960, 420).

not difficult to resolve if we remember that there were in fact *three* modes by which the east European seignior related to the rural laborer: corvée wages, and quit-rent (*cens*). It was quit-rent, as opposed to both corvée and wages, that was the principal formula of the fourteenth and fifteenth centuries in eastern Europe. In the sixteenth century the expansion of the world-economy led to the reinstitution and expansion of corvée labor in place of quit-rent. In fact, in those areas closest to export ports, for example, West Prussia, north "Great Poland" and Kujawy, the peasants had been better able to resist the institution of corvée labor in the sixteenth century and to keep more of the market profit for themselves by retaining the quit-rent system.[56] This was presumably because their nearness to ports made it relatively easy for them to dispose of their produce at competitive costs. In the seventeenth century, however, given the tighter market, the ability of the remaining east European tenant-farmers to resist the pressures of the seigniors crumbled, and quit-rent began to diminish even further—now to be replaced by *both* corvée and wage labor.[57]

From the rural laborer's point of view, wage labor was not necessarily preferable to a system of corvée labor. In fact, on the reserve, the wage laborers were largely either servants or day laborers, and the latter "found themselves in a still more dependent situation" than the serfs owing corvée labor.[58] The serfs not only had more security than the day laborers, in the sense that they could not be let go, but more status and more real income. Strange as it may seem, they also had more alternatives. The fact was that despite the legal constraints on them, "the serfs whose seigniors sought to impose too high dues could always change their seignior" because of the weakness of the public authorities.[59] In this conflict between seignior and peasant, which was really a class conflict between bourgeois and proletarian, the peasant was not totally bereft of ability to defend his interests, even in these hard times. The seignior/bourgeois thus had to find other means than the mere reduction of real wages via legal devices in order to extract surplus. He turned, as was logical, to industrial production so that the peasant would relate to him not merely as an employee but as a consumer as well.

If there was a pauperization of the peasants in the seventeenth century, what could they buy? Such urban industries as existed were dying out by the end of the sixteenth century because of "the pauperism, already widespread, of the principal masses of the population."[60] What then could the

---

[56] See Rusiński (1972, 112).

[57] Rutkowski says that, as of the mid-seventeenth century, "wage-labor begins to play, alongside corvée-labor, a more important role than previously in the organization of seigniorial reserves" (1926, 473). Kula agrees: after 1650 "the mobility of the peasant population, accentuated by the wars, increased the supply of wage-labor (*main-d'oeuvre de louage*)" (1970, 152).

[58] Rutkowski (1926, 503).

[59] Rutkowski (1926, 486), who says the "public powers of the time were incapable of introducing an 'adscriptus glebae' that was absolute and without frequent exceptions" (p. 485). Kula also speaks of "the extensiveness of peasant desertions and the impotence of the nobility in the face of this phenomenon" (1961, 145).

[60] Małowist (1972. 215).

seigniors produce that the peasants could afford? Occasional simple textiles, some glass and metalware, and grain in lean years. There seems in any case to have been a movement of artisans from the towns to large estates to work on the manufactures of the estates.[61] The most successful industry was unquestionably that which produced the perpetual standby of the poor who get poorer—alcohol.We associate gin with the new urban factories of England in the late eighteenth century, and whiskey with the uprooted indigenous populations of nineteenth-century frontier areas. Similarly, it was vodka and beer in Poland and wine in Hungary for the pauperized peasantry of the seventeenth century. The key institution was called the *propinatio,* the "invitation to drink," which meant in fact the monopoly of the seignior in the production and sale of alcoholic beverages.[62] In the period from 1650 to 1750, the *propinatio* often became the nobles' main source of income.[63]

The net result of the concentration of land, the further decline of quit-rent, plus the *propinatio* meant that despite the weak world market for their export crops, despite the destructions of wars, the east European upper strata managed to survive the period in reasonable shape. No doubt they may not have been as flourishing as the Amsterdam regent class or as the seigniors of northern France, but the severe reductions in net revenue of the eastern European periphery took its toll first of all on the lower strata.[64] The urban artisans and richer peasants went under, and the poor peasants got poorer. As the social cleavages polarized more, some also moved upward in status. These were the clientele of the courts—not so much of the king, as in France, but of the many seigniorial potentates.[65] This has been

---

[61] "The closed circuit of goods and currency secured the monopolist landlord substantial profits. He set up artisan workshops on his estates to supply both himself and his peasants" (Mączak, 1972, 672). Rostworowski points out that the latifundia were in effect princely states with mercantilist policies: "A magnate, with his own means of transport and his own brokers, concentrated the exports and imports of a large agricultural area in his own hands. Within this area there was no liberalism, but rather a system of compulsion and monopoly. . . . Those were the conditions which led to the establishment of manufactories in the latifundia" (1968, 307). Molenda reports that control of the lead mines was shifted in the seventeenth century from Cracow merchants to magnates who could smelt at lower costs because of their tax privileges (see 1976, 169). Could it have also been because of easier access to corvée labor?

[62] On Poland, see Szczygielski (1967, 97) and Kula (1970, 102–103). On Hungary, see Pach (1962, 262–263) and Makkai (1963, 41).

[63] Żytkowicz (1972, 149); see also Slicher van Bath (1977, 116). Leśkiewicz shows that on the royal domains in Poland, the percentage of the revenue from alcoholic drinks rose from 0.4% in 1661 to 37.5% in 1764 while that from agricultural products went down from 59.6% to 38.2% (1960, 414, Table III).

[64] Rostworowski, writing about the situation as of the middle of the eighteenth century, says that "Polish magnates were considered to be the richest private individuals in Europe, next to English aristocracy" (1968, 291). This was partly because of the lucrative sinecures available in the court of the Saxon Polish union, and it may not have been as true in the seventeenth century. Still, it is unlikely that they went suddenly from rags to riches.

[65] Małowist speaks of young nobles living at the courts of seigniorial and ecclesiastical nobles, serving, as of the first half of the seventeenth century, as "administrators of the various properties of the aristocracy, particularly in the private armies recruited by the grand seigniors" (1976, 15). Mączak suggests that Trevor-Roper's "remarks on royal courts' extravagant spending may be assigned also to Polish magnate's courts" (1975, 33, n. 16). This is no doubt what explains Rutkowski's observation that in the seventeenth and eighteenth centuries there was a "considerable increase" in the number of nobles living in the most important towns of the kingdom (1927b, 153).

termed *refeudalization,* but Makkai insists rightly that it is a misnomer; it should be called, he says, an "inflation of the nobility."[66]

In the previous chapter, we drew a picture of the social compromise reached in England and France between the new capitalists and the old aristocrats, two categories that overlapped far more than contemporary opinion or that of the times acknowledged; but they overlapped imperfectly and therefore with considerable friction in the era of expansion of the world-economy. The conflict grew most acute in the period of transition, the last period of inflation that went hand in hand with the levling off of the worldwide expansion; but in the period of 1650 to 1750, the realities of an era of downturn and mercantilism forced a coming to terms with each other of the two overlapping strata, which was crystallized by the end of the seventeenth century in new constitutional arrangements (using the expression broadly). Did anything comparable happen in the east European periphery? There were two factors present in the core that were absent in the periphery. First, for those strata located in the core, the prospects of capitalist profit remained on the whole relatively better, and this must have tempered the bitternesses of making mutual concessions. It was somehow worth it. Second, being in the core, the upper strata profited collectively, if not individually, from the strengthening of the state-machinery; but in turn this state-machinery could act as an institutional brake on internal conflicts among the upper strata.

The peripheral areas had neither the economic compensations nor the strong state-machinery. The monarchy was getting ever weaker in Poland. Hungary was divided into three parts, two of which were under foreign rule, and ultimately all three would be. Czech lands were also under foreign rule. Indeed, with the exception of Brandenburg-Prussia, a special case which we shall discuss subsequently, the seventeenth was a century of the further collapse of the indigenous national authorities. The Polish state, the only one to have an indigenous sovereign over all its ethnic territory, was in fact called the *Rzeczpospolita,* a term derived from the Latin *Respublica,* and it was commonly referred to as the Commonwealth of the Gentry. Foreign states, however, regularly interfered with the choice of the king, who was elected; and frequently, someone other than a native Pole was chosen. Three leaders in seventeenth-century Hungary (Gabor Bethlen, Zrínyi, and Ferenc Rákóczi II) sought to "create a Hungarian state strong enough to bear the burden of changed European conditions"[67] and tried to create a

---

[66] Makkai (1974, 198). Mączak similarly says that this does *not* represent "a continuation of medieval ways. . . . Old and new members of the upper strata of landowners . . . needed now more *noble* retainers than ever" (1975, 10). Kowecki (1972, 6) points out the large size of the Polish and Hungar- ian (as well as the Spanish) nobility, as compared with those in France. He gives the following figures: 8–10% in Poland (16% of the ethnic Poles); 5% in Hungary (more than the bourgeoisie); 0.7% in France (1.0% if one includes the clergy).

[67] Várkonyi (1970, 279).

strong army and, as a prerequisite, obtain taxes.[68] They failed because of the combined opposition of the Hungarian aristocracy and the Habsburg monarchs, who reached a mutually convenient and lasting arrangement after the failure of the Hungarian war of independence in 1711. "In Hungary, the tax exemption of the nobility was prolonged for another century, the copper trade fell into the hands of the Dutch, while the middleman's profit was invested by the Habsburg state into the modernization of Austrian mines."[69]

In the core countries, the newer, rising strata, whether gentry or *noblesse de robe*, could count on the fact that the state-machinery could place some check on the pretensions of the old aristocracy, and especially on those who could not perform well in the market. But in eastern Europe this possibility barely existed. These strata sought to substitute for the strong state the "commonwealth of the gentry," that is the imposition by legal and moral pressures of equality within the upper 5–10% of the population, although the social and economic inequality and conflict *within* this upper group was in fact quite marked[70] and was accentuated by the economic difficulties of the time.[71] In Poland, the efforts of the middle gentry to obtain justice in the tribunals against abuses of the magnates or legislative redress were nonetheless in vain. The magnates bribed the courts and broke up the Seym and the local diets whenever they got out of hand.[72] In Hungary, the

[68] Várkonyi cites Zrínyi: "Neque quies gentium sine armis, neque arma sine stipendiis, neque stipendia sine tributis haberi queunt" (1970, 281).

[69] Actually, the Dutch and others had been bidding for this trade for a whole century ever since the tenth(?) [...] German capitalists had been driven out. Várkonyi describes the role of early Western "tourists" who traveled in the seventeenth century to scout the terrain as "the reconnaissance-agents of western capitalism" (1970, 275).

[70] Várkonyi (1970, 299). This kind of foreign intrusion, which today we call inperialism, was not an isolated phenomenon. Mączak describes a parallel phenomenon in Poland. The hub of Poland's export trade was of course Gdańsk, which enjoyed the status of considerable autonomy; and vis-à-vis the king, "the corporation of Gdańsk played a role analogous to that of a magnate" (1976b, 12). Władysław IV, who came to power following the Swedish war (1626–1629) amidst "enthusiastic acclamation" (Tazbir, 1968a, 235) sought to strengthen the royal authority. Mączak describes what happened: "Just after the treaty signed in 1635 in Stuhmsdorf by Swedes and Poles, the King of Poland tried with some success to acquire a share of [Gdańsk's] revenue from customs. Danish men-of-war prevented the King from continuing a strongman's show, and the city of Gdańsk's sovereignty with regard to customs remained untouched" (1976b, 14).

[71] Rutkowski describes the differences between the upper nobility, that is, the seigniors (*panowie*) or magnates (*magnaci*); the middle nobility (*szlachta czastkowa*); and the lesser nobility (*drobna szlachta*). The latter were without serfs; they cultivated their own lands and were in fact peasants, comparable in income to rich peasants. There was even a small subgroup of lesser nobility, called quit-rent nobility (*szlachta czynszowa*), who rented land from the seigniors, having none of their own (1926, 498–499).

[72] The old distinction between magnates and gentry, always latent, but forgotten in the days of agricultural prosperity and social equality, had been revived in the seventeenth century, which saw the rise of vast estates in Lithuania and the Ukraine which not only overweighted the position of the owners of these *latifundia*, but brought into being a large sector of small squires ready to serve the magnates and helping them to destroy the old institutions based on equality" (Boswell, 1967, 159). In other words, the inflation of the nobility, linked to the phenomenon of clientele already referred to, was multiplying the number of lesser nobility attached to the magnates, thereby threatening the claims of the middle nobility and older lesser nobility to claims of equality with the magnates.

A similar situation is reported in Hungary. At the time of the Peace of Szatmár (1711), there were about 200 to 300 magnates and 25,000 gentry, each with a house in parliament. "It was the magnates'

"gentry" tried a war and lost. In Poland, they reshaped the Sarmatian myth—originally intended simply to argue that the ethnically diverse populations of the Polish–Lithuanian realms descended from a common proto-Slavonic ancestor, the Sarmatians—into one that accounted for the origins of a conquering nobility, founders of the ruling class.[73] In that way, "the gentry, and only they, were identified with the Polish nation, excluding other social classes, allegedly of different origin, from the national community."[74] Defenders of the Christian faith and xenophobic, the gentry pushed this doctrine zealously and in extreme ways[75] and were no doubt guilty of "megalomania"[76] and "morbid mythomania."[77] But if one has no possibility of a Glorious Revolution, one has to make do with Sarmatism, even if it implies "cultural stagnation and an atrophy of creative intellectual activity."[78]

While the period of world economic downturn led the core countries along the path of nationalism (mercantilism) and constitutional compromise within the upper strata, with the consequence of a lowered ability of the lower strata to rebel, the weakness of the east European states meant that they could neither seek the advantages of a mercantilist tactic nor *guarantee* any compromise within the upper strata. This led the peripheral areas in the direction of sharpening class conflict,[79] increased regionalism and decreased national consciousness,[80] the search for internal scapegoats,[81] and

heyday. Never before had a Hungarian oligarchy enjoyed such opportunities, not so much (after the redistribution ended) of acquiring wealth, but of keeping it. . . . A large proportion of [the latifundia of the magnates] lay in areas recovered from the Turks and unburdened with servitudes. Their owners could treat them as 'dominical' land, exempt from any obligation to the state whatsoever. Their production costs were thus extremely low, low enough to enable them to make capital investments which sometimes repaid themselves tenfold" (Macartney, 1967, 129).

[73] Tazbir (1968b, 259).
[74] Tazbir (1968b, 264). On the necessity for Lithuanian and Ruthenian magnates to "Polonize" themselves in language and religion, see Kersten (1977, 125–126).
[75] In the seventeenth century Fr. Wojciech Debolecki claimed that "the Poles were the direct descendents of Adam and Eve, and therefore, he considered them the oldest nation, predestined to rule the world" (Tazbir, 1966, 20).
[76] Tazbir (1968b, 265).
[77] P. Anderson (1974a, 292).
[78] Rostworowski (1968, 302). After the enormous physical and cultural destruction of the Swedish conquest in 1658, Warsaw was rebuilt as a "Sarmate" town and "orientalized"—its bourgeoisie ruined (see Tomkiewicz, 1967). Rostworowski is very caustic about Warsaw. "The decay of the capi-

tal was particularly harmful to cultural life. The Warsaw of the Saxon times not only did not fulfill the role of a patron of arts and culture, but could not even be a centre of social life. . . . Poland became one large province, and cultural life drifted idly along a parochial course" (1968, 302).

When Augustus III in 1733 moved the court of the union of Saxony and Poland to Dresden, nothing was left. "Up to that time, the monarch, in spite of all the limitations upon his power, had remained the keystone of the Commonwealth's political structure and the royal court had been an important institution in the cultural life of the country. After the collapse of Augustus II's ambitious plans, the Polish–Saxon union deprived Poland of that element" (Rostworowski, 1968, 275).

[79] "One of the important consequences of the monetary problems [of seventeenth-century Poland] was . . . the recrudescence of class hatred and antagonism between various groups, which developed into a merciless struggle among various sectors of the community" (Bogucka, 1975, 152). See also Slicher van Bath: "This was a period of frequent peasant wars and revolts in the whole of central and eastern Europe" (1977, 122).

[80] See Tazbir: "In the seventeenth century, the conception of the nation—as an ethnic unit—was pushed in the background by the ultra-subjective concept of the nation of the nobles (*nation nobiliaire*), based on the Sarmatian myth. . . . The triumph of

acute restiveness of the peasantry.[82] *Mutatis mutandis,* we shall see that the same thing was true of the old peripheral areas of southern Europe and the Americas. A rapid overview of the Christian Mediterranean shows that the same patterns prevailed for a seventeenth century that was characterized by "stagnation in business."[83] The prices of primary exports fell. In Spain, wheat prices declined after 1585, and they remained stagnant throughout the seventeenth century, as did prices for wine, rice, and oil.[84] In Sicily, the export of silk declined, as did the export of wheat and wine after 1640; but Aymard notes that the reduction in exports was compensated for by a continued increase in population that increased "internal" consumption.[85]

the Counter-Reformation took the form in the western regions (especially Silesia) not only of an almost exclusive use of Latin but also by the progress of Germanization which was favored by the Church. . . . The victory of the concept of a Sarmatian nation favored the renaissance of regionalisms characteristic of the various territories of Poland. In the seventeenth century, Masovia rediscovered its particularity" (1966, 14–15, 20).

Rostworowski, however, argues: "In spite of the paresis, or even atrophy, of its central government, regional particularism was not developed in the Commonwealth. A far-reaching differentiation among the peasant masses and burghers still prevailed in the multi-national State but the 'gentry nation' was growing more and more homogeneous in its outlook. The process of Polonizing the Ruthenian nobility was completed (in 1697, Ruthenian was abandoned in judicial records). The Polish, Lithuanian and Ruthenian gentry, interrelated by thousands of family ties, were assimilated into one big family of brother nobles" (1968, 907). The question, however, is the degree to which the *magnates* encouraged this sense of Polishness, as opposed to regional particularism.

[81] The Jews who made their entrée en masse to eastern Europe in the context of sixteenth-century expansion proved their lasting merits as convenient scapegoats as of the seventeenth-century recession. See Weinryb: "A large number of these Jews had settled in the [Polish] Ukraine . . . during the sixteenth and seventeenth centuries. . . . A sizeable number of these Jews . . . fulfilled economic functions as leaseholders of villages or whole towns as well as of inns, and as collectors of revenues for the nobility or the royal domain. Leaseholding was frequently associated with the exercise of certain powers, including jurisdiction over various sectors of the population. These activities and powers placed the Jews in the role of the Polish landlords, as it were, so that they often became de facto overlords in relation to the 'lowly' (as the chronicler Hanover called them) Ukrainians. In this way the Jew became iden-

tified with the Polish nobility" (1973, 185). Weinryb recounts the scapegoating by Polish nobles after the losses in the Swedish wars and the confiscations of property, especially in Cracow (1973, 190–191).

P. Anderson notes that the ethnic stratification in large parts of eastern and southeastern Poland consisted of Polish (or assimilated Lithuanian) aristocrats as landlords and non-Polish serfs, who were Orthodox in religion and Belorussian or Ruthenian in language (and, as we have just seen from Weinryb, Jews as intermediaries). This is, Anderson reminds us, a classic "colonial" situation (1974a, 285); and it should be added, colonial situations, in times of difficulties, are conducive to conflicts among ethnic groups.

[82] Tazbir talks of the response of peasants to the increase in number of days of labor-service. "The peasants replied by mass flight, refusal to work and, in some parts of the country, even armed resistance. In addition to the peasants' rebellion of 1651, mention should be made of the risings on the royal estates in the south-western part of the Cracow voivodship (1669–1672), in the Podhale, in the Kurpie region (on the frontiers of Ducal Prussia) and on the Suraz estate in the Podlasie" (1968b, 258–259). In addition, there was the continuing "Cossack question" in the Ukraine. See Tazbir (1968a, 237–241).

In Hungary, where there was a "nationalist" struggle against an external force, the peasants were in desperation pulled into the fight by the Hungarian gentry-bourgeoisie. From 1704 to 1706 Rákóczi sought strength in his struggles against the aristocracy and the Hapsburgs by liberating the serfs and arming them (Várkonyi, 1970, 292). One can well imagine that the peasants did not put away their arms too quickly.

[83] Braudel (1956, 196).

[84] For Valencia, see Castillo (1969, 251–252); for Andalusia and Castile, see Ponsot (1969, 105). Wittman compares Spanish agricultural decline to that of Hungary (1965).

[85] Aymard (1971b, 440).

This may mean, however, that the per capita grain production was falling, a phenomenon we have already encountered in eastern Europe.

What is the explanation? Cancila speaks of the "intensive works of colonization" in Sicily from 1573 to 1653.[86] DaSilva reports that a worried writer in Spain in 1609–1610 noted that abuses were multiplying, triennial rotation was no longer being observed, and thus the producers "were exhausting the fields."[87] DaSilva says that this situation led, in the years from 1570 to 1630, to the search for new domains, which were then similarly exhausted. This "aridification" of the land hit particularly the small producers[88] and led to further land concentration. While this process of exhausting the land led to inability to export, land concentration that resulted from it led to a further *monetarization* of productive relations, since "the inability of the peasants (*contadini*) and villagers to provide for their own subsistence by working their own land enlarged the internal market."[89] We saw the same expansion of the *regional* markets in eastern Europe as world trade declined. Demography followed suit. The Spanish population declined—plagues in the last years of the sixteenth century and the expulsion of the Moriscos. There was a 35% reduction of the population of Valencia from 1609 to 1638, but this "violent demographic crisis" followed rather than preceded the stagnation.[90]

Regarding southern Italy, there was population decline in Naples. Sicily, according to Aymard, experienced only a "slowing down" of demographic expansion (rather than a decline); but he adds that the figures for Sicily hide a "clear regional differentiation"; the island was split in two, with the north, northeast, and center stagnating and no longer self-sufficient in food supply.[91] One wonders if there wasn't, in addition, some hidden demographic decline. Verlinden reports that the incidence of slavery in southern Italy and Sicily declined in the seventeenth century from its high point in the fifteenth and sixteenth, because trade in African slaves (who were formerly imported to the Mediterranean by the Portuguese) was diverted to the Americas and the supply of Turkish and other Moslem slaves was much smaller.[92] Does this not imply a decline in overall population that may not be caught up in the other statistics? The "undoubted contraction" of the

---

[86] Cancila (1969, 25).

[87] DaSilva (1964b, 244).

[88] DaSilva (1964b, 248).

[89] DaSilva (1964b, 250).

[90] Castillo (1969, 242, 247, 273). Demographic decline also reflected repressive moves, which ended the current of immigration from southern France. See Nadal and Giralt (1960, 83–84, 198).

[91] Aymard (1968, 222, and see also 1971b, 427). For Naples, see Petraccone (1974, 40–41, 51).

[92] Verlinden (1963, 37). Larquié reports a similar decline in slavery in southern Spain in the second half of the seventeenth century and also its disappearance by the eighteenth. He explains this as

being the result of the weak economic conjuncture. "Finally the commercial currents become disorganized and the economic difficulties of Spain affect the consuming societies; little by little, they curtail their desire for luxury" (1970, 55). Although he speaks of slaves as a luxury item, he notes that many of them were "royal slaves," used in port maintenance, in the mines of Almadén, and on galleyships (see p. 67). This was scarcely luxury usage. Isn't it more that in times of contraction, in an old periphery, slaves are an *expensive* form of labor compared to coerced labor? (a matter to be discussed later in the context of Caribbean slavery).

economy is said to account for the *rise* of *local* manufactures from Aquila to Salerno in the state of Naples;[93] however, this was true not only for Naples but for all of Italy as well as Languedoc. Might this be, asks Braudel, "the demonstration of a discomfort, a diffuse reaction to the insufficiency of trade"?[94] The results of this squeeze on the small rural producers, who were the real losers in the period of regression, led to acute class conflict. Speaking of the peasant's revolt in 1647–1648 in Naples, Emilio Sereni writes that it was "the response of rural populations to feudal oppression and abuse, now aggravated by the mercantile avidity of the new barons." He says, "rather than speaking of 'refeudalization', we might properly talk of the commercialization of the fief."[95] Economic regression, increased pressures on land and labor power, concentration, further commercialization of land and labor—all in fact went hand in hand in southern as in eastern Europe.

Let us now turn to Hispanic America, where the "depression of the seventeenth century" has long been a subject of major controversy, and let us start with the rise of the hacienda as the key agricultural institution of this peripheral arena of the world-economy. How is the hacienda to be defined and perceived? When did it arise? We have already encountered a debate in the context of the sixteenth century about whether to describe land structures as "feudal"[96] or "capitalist." It is possible to argue, as does Frédéric Mauro, that whereas in Hispanic America the sixteenth and eighteenth centuries at least "increased the importance of the speculators, the merchants, the mine-owners, the urban bourgeois and . . . even the royal bureaucracy," the seventeenth and nineteenth centuries represented the triumph of "patriarchal society."[97] From this perspective, capitalism and

[93] Aymard (1971a, 11).

[94] Braudel (1956, 194).

[95] Sereni (1961, 195). There was in any case no *adscriptus glebae* in southern Italy at this time. "Refeudalization", here as in eastern Europe, meant the decline of the [Spanish] state in relation to the power of local landowning barons. See Villari (1962, 260, and also 1963 and 1965); see also Vivanti (1974, 422).

[96] Charles Verlinden's explanation is that a "feudal" land-tenure system was introduced not only in Spanish America, but also in Brazil, French Canada, and the Dutch Caribbean because of "the lack of resources of the central metropole," which "did not wish to assume the initial risks" (1971, 347). He sees the situation changing only with white settlement. In Spanish America, therefore, despite the "theoretical" abolition of feudalism "the seigniorial regime persisted as long as settlement was insufficiently dense to permit the state's revenues to increase sufficiently to make over all the aspects of public authority" (p. 348).

[97] Mauro (1974, 249), who specified that "the only influence the long-term conjuncture may have on a closed economy" such as that of Hispanic America is "to make it more closed . . . or more open" (p. 245). Since his "only" is in fact everything, one might wonder why Mauro uses the word. It is worth noting another distinction he makes about the seventeenth century: If, because of the importance of sugar production, "we are by and large partisan to the 'capitalist' thesis [for Brazil], for Hispanic America, we lean openly to the 'feudalist' thesis" (p. 245). Using this distinction to account for political differences in the late eighteenth century, he says that "feudalist" Hispanic America (like France) would be expected to have a more violent political upheaval than "capitalist" Brazil (which was like England). See p. 251.

Mauro applied this distinction to the tenure systems: "The *sesmaria* [in Brazil] was not a peasant tenure; it was a concession made [by the *donatário*] to a capitalist entrepreneur with a view to export agriculture. . . . It was not intended to create a closed economy in the manner of the Carolingian domain or *even* of the Mexican hacienda of the seventeenth century" (1971, 388). The *even*, which was not italicized in the original, suggests that Mauro sees *some* distinction nonetheless between the Carolingian domain and the Mexican hacienda.

feudalism are seen as competing tendencies linked with very long A and B cycles of the world-economy. The key debate thus turns out to be about the seventeenth not the sixteenth century. The triumph of a self-sufficient "noncapitalist" hacienda is the basic theme of François Chevalier's work, a triumph said to be the consequence of the retraction of the world-economy:

> In the early decades of the seventeenth century the silver boom collapsed, smothering in its passage the first stirrings of a barely nascent capitalism. Land became the sole source of income. . . . The largest estates were self-sufficient. The big sugar refinery, the plantation, the harvest estancia, and the smelter with its farm annexes supplied nearly all their own needs. . . . We have frequently had occasion to recall the Middle Ages. . . . [The hacienda owners] constituted an aristocracy in fact; some succeeded in obtaining titles. The state of the Marqueses del Valle, finally, is a pale replica of the Duchy of Burgundy.[98]

An alternative perspective on the Mexican hacienda in the seventeenth century is stated with great vigor by André Gunder Frank:

> The growth of the latifundium in seventeenth-century Mexico was not a depression-induced retrenchment of the economy into what has come to be called a feudal *hacienda,* but on the contrary the *hacienda* grew and flourished at this time, as at all other times and places in Latin America, because events elsewhere in the national and indeed in the world economy rendered latifundium production highly profitable.[99]

It would aid our ability to assess these contrary perspectives if we analyzed some of these historical processes in closer detail. The first issue is the timing of the downturn. Lynch says the peak of Mexican silver production was in the 1590s, and that "after this, the boom was over."[100] However, for the Indies trade in general, he accepts Chaunu's view that a mere "reversal of major trend" occurred between 1593 and 1622 and that the great depression occurred between 1623 and 1650.[101] MacLeod, in turn, speaking of Central America, calls the period between around 1576 and 1635 a "half century of transition" and dates the depression as occurring somewhere

---

[98] Chevalier (1970, 309, 311, 313). Note that Chevalier's quasi-lyrical prose refers to the *largest* estates. What then of the less large ones? How did they obtain food? Note also that there is no reference to the fact that while the hacienda may have sufficed unto itself, it also produced a surplus that then had to be sold somewhere. What was then done with the profits so realized?

[99] Frank (1979a, 38). See the brief review by Piel of the Chevalier–Frank debate (1975, 147–148). P. J. Bakewell, who analyzes the role of the silver mines in the Mexican economy picture, is essentially on Frank's side: "[The] economy of New Spain in the seventeenth century, in many respects, was plainly of a capitalist nature" (1971, 225).

[100] Lynch (1969, **II,** 204). Bakewell criticizes a similar dating with reference to Chevalier, who, he

says, "places the decline of mining 20 years too early, in the first decade of the seventeenth century" (1971, 117, n. 4).

[101] Lynch (1969, **II,** 184), who says: "The years 1592–1622 form a plateau between expansion and contraction, a high plateau to be sure, with continuing signs of prosperity but equally distinctive signs of hesitation which indicate a reversal of the previous trend" (p. 185). He calls New Spain "the sick man of the transatlantic economy from the 1620s to the 1650s" (p. 189). See also Chaunu (1959, **VIII,** 2/*bis, passim*). Chaunu argues that a downturn "absolutely in conformity [with] the Atlantic–Seville [conjuncture]" is to be found in the Philippines at this same time, there being an "immense breaking-point in the years 1630–1640" (1960b, 246, 250).

between 1635 and 1720.[102] Berthe dates the profound crisis for Mexican agriculture between 1630 and 1680.[103] Finally Mellafe, speaking of Spanish America in general and Chile in particular, says that "the *true* crisis begins after 1650," adding that "the fall of Cartagena, in the year 1595, was the first warning of the cruel and destructive struggle that would last two centuries."[104]

As usual, scholarly quibbles about dating reflect the complexity of a reality in which downturns seem to begin before upward cycles end. It seems fairly clear that there was a period of cyclical overlap (or transition) in Hispanic America beginning perhaps as early as the 1570s but more plausibly in the 1590s and ending somewhere between 1630 and 1650. What we should expect to find in such a period is a crisis in profits in the leading sectors and resultant efforts by large-scale proprietors and investors to recoup losses by short-run actions, which in fact make the long-run situation worse. This is what occurred. Silver, the major export of Hispanic America in the sixteenth century, reached a plateau between 1590 and 1630, and after that the figures show a sharp and sudden decline. The official trade statistics here may be misleading because there was a growing clandestine trade; nevertheless the descriptive evidence from the mining areas seems to indicate that there was indeed "a real fall in production."[105] Why should this have occurred? One argument is that it was caused by a labor shortage. However, despite the decline in overall population and the slightly higher costs of labor, the mine owners seemed to get the labor they needed. In Mexico they resorted to wage labor, and in Potosí they simply drew the forced labor from farther distances. The point is that production declined even when labor was available, as Davis argues. "Indeed in the mid-seventeenth century many Potosí mine operations were accepting Indian monetary tribute in place of the *mita* or forced labour they were entitled to, preferring this certain income to whatever profits mining might bring."[106]

Was it then the shortage of mercury? It is clear that there was such a shortage between the 1630s and the 1660s. Bakewell calls the difficulties of mercury supply the "single largest determinant of variations of [silver] output"; but Davis does not believe they were "decisive."[107] The question is why was more mercury available in the 1660s than in the 1630s. It must have been profitable to do what was necessary to get mercury in the 1660s but not in the 1630s. Let us remember again that although the supply of bullion was a principal factor in price formation in that epoch, "gold and silver too

[102] MacLeod (1973, 208), who speaks of the currency crisis reaching its height between 1655 and 1670 when the debasements, suspensions, and revaluations of coinage "damaged exports, destroyed internal trading, and even weakened security and confidence in the governmental order" (p. 286).

[103] See Berthe (1966, 103). This accords with Chevalier's view that the end of the first economic cycle in the Mexican production of silver was from

around 1630 to 1640 (1970, 4).

[104] Mellafe (1959, 207–208, italics added).

[105] Bakewell (1976, 224) and Davis (1973b, 158). Davis calls the evidence "ample."

[106] Davis (1973b, 159).

[107] Bakewell (1971, 188) and Davis (1973b, 159). M. F. Lang (1968, 632) also gives primacy of place to the quicksilver shortage.

[had] their price" and "moneys in general, and particularly in a metallic system, were but a commodity like any other."[108] André Gunder Frank agrees with the foregoing and explains the fall in production as the long-term *result* of price inflation:

> Did not, then, fixed prices for silver mean a falling return, even if costs had remained fixed as well? To say that in an inflation the prices of goods and services increased is to say, in other words, that the value or the price of money decreased. And was it not money that the mine-owners were producing in their mines since the price of silver was fixed? The implication is that they faced both an increase in costs *and* a decrease in returns—enough reason for any capitalist to reduce his output and put his money into some other business, if possible.[109]

The decline of bullion exports, the leading sector, affected the other "export crops" in turn. Regarding indigo production in Central America, MacLeod argues that the state of shipping technology in the seventeenth century created a shaky rate of profit for primary products shipped across the Atlantic. "In favorable times indigo survived on the margins of gold and silver. In harder times [indigo] was too far from Europe to show consistent profits."[110] This point about indigo can also be applied more generally.[111]

Two powerful groups suffered immediately from the decline in export prices: the Spaniards who controlled the productive enterprises and the state that taxed these Spaniards. The rate of taxation had already climbed remarkably in the second half of the sixteenth century;[112] but the onset of economic difficulties in Spain and its empire coincided with a period of great military activity (the Revolt of the Netherlands followed by the Thirty Years' War). Faced with the growing gap between diminished revenues and increased expenditures, the Spanish state resorted to "unbridled coinage of

---

[108] Romano (1970, 131, 140). See also Onody, who makes the same point about Brazilian gold and cites a nineteenth-century document of the Brazilian Ministry of Finance that reads: "We must consider our national currency in the present circumstances, within the Empire, as a veritable kind of merchandise, part of our coastal commerce or of our cabotage" (1971, 236, n. 2).

[109] Frank (1979a, 54). Davis too is in accord: "On the whole, however, rising costs were accommodated. Silver mining was checked because of the declining value of silver in terms of the goods it could buy. . . . [The fixed price of silver plus the rising prices of imported goods] made the purchasing price of silver so low that it was not worthwhile continuing to produce it at constant or rising real costs" (1973b, 159). Of course, we can then ask why the price of silver was prevented from rising, and here Romano supplies the answer: "The American mines reduced their production quite simply because European economic life in a phase of stagna-

tion did not need [the silver], or at least had a reduced need for it" (1972, 140). A reduced world demand (or in effect world overproduction) and a reduced rate of profit are two sides of the same coin. The two explanations of decreased production are the same.

[110] MacLeod (1973, 382). Indigo stagnated throughout the seventeenth century despite its low demands on labor and the fact that it did not require the best of soils (see p. 202).

[111] See the discussion by Lopez (1974) of the decline of the price of yerba mate, Paraguay's only link with the world-economy, in the course of the seventeenth century.

[112] José Larraz's table shows the index of prices rising steadily and tripling between 1504 and 1596 and the index of two key taxes, the *alcabala* and the *millones*, at first going up more slowly, then considerably exceeding the index of prices by 1575 and reaching 537 by 1596 (see 1943, 79).

vellon" in the beginning of the seventeenth century,[113] and when that was not enough it tried "to squeeze the last drops" from the empire.[114] Thus in Mexico and in Peru the Spanish state both increased taxes and sought to enforce taxation more efficaciously.[115] This was in fact self-defeating. When in 1620 Philip III confiscated one-eighth of the bullion shipped privately (offering in its stead vellon or *juros*), he most assuredly directly deprived merchants of their capital; but more importantly, they consequently became reluctant to ship back their bullion at all (no doubt another factor in reducing silver production). As a result, the Crown's income from the *avería*, the *ad valorem* tax that paid for the cost of escorts, went down. To maintain the fleets, the Crown had to raise the *avería* rate still higher, which was, as Lynch says, "a further incitement to fraud" and turned the Crown into a "parasite [living] on the American trade and colonies." The Crown also compensated by granting more *mercedes* to Spaniards. It was a spiral. "Plunder and parasitism made fraud and contraband a way of life"[116]—and the latter two, as we shall see, advanced still further the semiperipheralization of Spain.

While some of the Creoles were smarting from the effects of the economic difficulties and seeking salvation in public office,[117] thus multiplying the parasitism of the state bureaucracy, others were in fact adapting quite well to the vicissitudes of the world market. The production of bullion, up to then the major export crop, went down; and the production of grains went up. It is at this point that the confusion arises. Since American grain (unlike east European grain) did not serve as a peripheral export to core regions, it is often assumed that such production was noncapitalist. Bazant says that it was quite the contrary: "The production [of wheat] on a large scale was without doubt production for the market and using capital." He reminds us that although wheat was not consumed by peons who ate tortillas, "there was nonetheless an appreciable market: the white population of the cities."[118] Furthermore, this production required much capital in the form of mills, animals, and food for the work force.

It may be argued that this is true for wheat but not for maize. Here too, however, commercialization was central:

[113] E. J. Hamilton (1947, 12). Morineau suggests that we ask Charles Wilson's "unfashionable question." Was Spain's high rate of taxation, "ransom, in the sixteenth century, of a dubious preponderance . . . not the cause, in the seventeenth, of its misery and decadence?" (1978d, 158).

[114] Lynch (1969, **II,** 165).

[115] See Israel (1974a, 40). Ergo, says Israel, we should not consider the high tax levels as an "index of economic performance" of Hispanic America but as an "index of the pressure imposed by Spain" on its colonies. Spanish taxation needs affected economic production in other ways as well. The acute

shortage of mercury in the Mexican mines after 1630 was the result of a decision by the Crown that reduced shipments by half. Brading and Cross say that the royal decision was "taken presumably [because the] viceroyalty [of Peru] paid the *quinto* whereas Mexico only paid the *diezmo*" (1972, 574).

[116] Lynch (1969, **II,** 165–167).

[117] See MacLeod (1973, 311) on public office as the "only practical answer" to prevent the "falling in status" of many Creoles and Spaniards.

[118] Bazant (1950, 90), who adds that "a part of the total production was for export."

The workers (Indians, mulattos, Negroes, mestizos) as well as the mules and horses that moved the machines, the entire work force employed in the mines depended on corn (maize). To service them, beginning in the end of the sixteenth century, there grew up around the mines a belt of agricultural and cattle haciendas specially devoted to their provisioning.[119]

This is not to suggest that these haciendas were unaffected economically; bad times of the mining areas led to "difficult years, sometimes recession"[120] that was often exacerbated by the creation of new competitive haciendas. However, it is to suggest that the market had a regional limit and that it was not profitable to go beyond that limit in the world economic contraction.[121] This is no doubt the *conjunctural* origin of the classical description of the *structural* difference between haciendas, which supplied small-scale markets, and sugar plantations, which supplied large-scale ones.[122] Within the regional limits, hacienda production was quite profitable. One may call this self-sufficiency if one wishes, but to me it seems more plausible that it was, as Bakewell says, "the result of fashioning in the New World a diversified and, in contemporary terms, capitalist economy of the European type; and of using this economy to exploit the rich assets of Middle America for Middle America's advantage."[123] The resulting advantages could not affect an abstract entity called Middle America but they did affect a concrete social group who were the landowners of Middle America.

As in eastern Europe, however, the slowdown of the world-economy as a whole required intensified use of the basic resources (land and labor) to maintain the level of profit. The precipitous decline of the Indian popula-

[119] Florescano (1969, 150). See also Bakewell: "Perhaps the most striking feature of the process of grain supply to Zacatecas is the width over which the net was cast. . . . Zacatecas silver was carried on homeward-bound carts and mules in literally every direction, finding its way, in payment for grain, to Saltillo in the North and to Puebla in the South" (1971, 64). This description for Mexico is matched by that for Peru by Lynch: "The greatest markets for the product of the plantations, for sugar, wine and cotton were the mining settlements of Upper Peru. In one way or another the whole of Peru worked for Potosí and profited from its wealth" (1969, II, 217). Further evidence can be found in the impact of the earthquake in Peru in 1687. It led to a "wheat rush" in Chile, where producers shifted from pasturage and wine growing (Romano, 1969, 280; see also Carmagnani, 1973, 31–42, 265–266).

[120] Florescano (1969, 183).

[121] "[All the evidence] indicates that in a relatively short lapse of time the large hacienda succeeded in supplying regional consumption needs. Once this level was reached however, before the hacienda developed its maximum productive capacity, the regional structure of the markets, the enormous dis-

tances, the bad roads, the high freight costs, the commercial policies of the Crown, made it impossible to export its surpluses beyond the regional limit. The hacienda then was obliged, if not to reduce production, at least to maintain it at a stable level" (Florescano, 1969, 184).

[122] See Wolf and Mintz (1957, 380).

[123] Bakewell (1971, 235); see also Morner (1973, 191). Lynch goes even further and calls this "the first emancipation of Spanish America." He says: "It is tempting to attribute the great depression of the American trade to the collapse of the colonial economies. But it was the consequence of shift rather than collapse. If the colonies no longer fed the trade as of old, it was largely because they were employing their capital at home, in public and private investment" (1969, II, 139). Piel inverts the argument further, seeking to refute writers (see Romano, 1970) who speak of a low circulation of bullion based on reduced figures of transatlantic shipment: "If the trans-oceanic monetary flow slowed down, is this the sign of retraction of mining production, or rather that a growing proportion of the bullion is kept locally?" (1975, 151).

tion in all parts of Hispanic America is a tale now quite well known,[124] and the role of disease epidemics therein clearly established.[125] This decline created both opportunity and dilemma for the Spanish landowners. The decline of Indian producers (by death and by land ouster) along with the growth of the Spanish and mestizo population in the urban and mining areas, created the regional market and its high prices for the hacienda owner. On the other hand, the owner needed laborers. It is here that we find the crux of the struggle over who is to accumulate the capital. The fact that there was a slowdown worldwide in capital accumulation meant that the capitalist sectors in Hispanic America were in acute competition with those in Spain for a reduced economic pie. We have already mentioned increased taxation by the Crown which transferred surplus from the Americas. From the point of view of New Spain, the erstwhile most dynamic region of the Americas, what hurt most was the attempt by the Spanish Crown to reduce Mexico's direct ties with Peru and the Philippines. No doubt there was widespread smuggling but no doubt too the Crown's policy had "a serious adverse affect on Mexico City."[126]

The tension over profits manifested itself not merely in disputes about the control of trade routes but about control of labor supply. The system of *repartimiento* had been in effect from the middle of the sixteenth century, and it was quite frustrating from the point of view of large agricultural producers. While it amounted to forced wage labor, the laborers were transitory and returned regularly to maintain their traditional productive activities.[127] The supply was mediated by the Spanish bureaucracy, particularly by the *corregidores*, with the firm support of the friars, who argued for it as a means of protecting the Indians from Spanish rapacity. The interests of the "protectors" was quite transparent, as Israel explains it in the Mexican context:

---

[124] See, for example, Cook and Borah (1971). There was a parallel, but less severe, reduction of population in the Philippines. See Phelan (1959, 194) and Chaunu (1960b, 74, Table 1).

[125] On smallpox, see Crosby (1967). The Andes region seemed to escape the mortality figures of Middle America in the sixteenth century and was caught up in the late seventeenth (see Dobyns, 1963, 514). On Chile, see Mellafe (1959, 226), and on Central America, see MacLeod (1973, 204–205).

[126] Israel (1974a, 39), who points to "the many bitter Mexican protests of the 1630s and 1640s." M. F. Lang believes it evident "that the desire to restrict trade between New Spain and Peru was the prime motive in the Crown's reluctance to provide for a regular supply [of quicksilver to the Mexican mines] from Huancavelica" (1968, 639).

[127] See the definition of *repartimiento* given by Enrique Semo, which he admits is that made by the twentieth-century analyst and not necessarily the usage of contemporaries: "We consider *repartimiento* to be the system of rationed, rotated work on the economic enterprises of the Spanish, which affected both the Indians who had been given in *encomienda* and those who had not and which benefited a class of possessors far wider than that which had enjoyed the benefits of the *encomienda*. To this must be added the fact that, unlike the Indians in *encomienda*, given as rewards for service to the Crown and who were put to such use the recipient thought convenient, the *repartimientos* were authorized more frequently for well-defined *economic* purposes and with a prohibition to use the Indians for other ends. Under the new system, the priorities were fixed in the final instance by the viceroy. . . . The scale of priorities placed silver production among that of the needs of the *encomenderos*" (1973, 222).

> The *corregidores* . . . regularly made large fortunes by their various methods of
> extortion including the forced purchase of Indian crops at minimal prices in order to
> sell at great profit in the towns, conducting compulsory sales of goods at exorbitant
> prices, taking fees for favours from Spaniards, and making astute use of the *repar-*
> *timiento*. . . . Thus the Indians were in effect supporting two separate economies, that
> of the Spanish settlers on the one hand and that of the Indian districts functioning
> chiefly in the interests of the *corregidores,* friars, and Indian hierarchy on the other.[128]

This double burden on the Indians was surely part of the story of their
demographic decline; and it surely created, in addition, an impossible
strain on the political system as soon as there was an economic crunch.[129]

In 1632 the Crown finally brought about the suspension in New Spain of
compulsory wage labor outside the mines. Because of the continuing tension,
this merely speeded up the evolving tactic of the Spanish landowners (now
hacendados) of attracting permanent laborers known as *gañanes* or *laboríos*.
The *corregidores* responded at first by not exempting these *gañanes* from the
repartimiento, which meant *de facto* that, in order to weaken the Creoles as a
stratum, the *corregidores* forced an Indian to leave one Creole and move
under the control of another. When the Crown tried the alternate tactic of
abolishing compulsion altogether, the Indian faced the increased possibility
of not working at all; at which point, the large agricultural producer resorted to the creation of debt peonage as a way of holding labor on the
land.[130] Land expropriation reinforced this control even further;[131] thus the

[128] Israel (1974a, 47). Compare the situation described by MacLeod for Central America: "This period between 1630 and 1690 is the one par excellence of the *derrama* [additional tax], in which minor
government officials, often Creoles, forced Indians
to buy unwanted goods at inflated prices or forced
them to produce goods for nothing or for a pit-
tance" (1973, 384).

[129] Israel's whole article spells out the frictions in
Mexico among the ruling strata between 1620 and
1664 in terms of the conflict over the control of
scarce labor.

[130] See Zavala (1966, especially 79), Godinho
(1948), and Chevalier who writes: "Debt peonage
crept slowly—and irrevocably—into more and more
haciendas. By the end of the seventeenth century or
the beginning of the eighteenth, it was common
practice to refer to *gañanes* or *naboríos* as estate
property" (1970, 285). See also Phelan: "Attaching
the Indians to the *hacienda* through debt peonage
had several advantages over other forms of labor.
Negro slaves involved a large capital investment.
Repartimiento labor was inefficient in that there were
weekly changes of shifts and a steadily diminishing
number of Indians available (1959, 191). In the case
of miners, the owners tried initially to keep their
workers by a combination of salaries and the per-
quisite of doing some mining for their own profit.
This was called the *pepena* in Mexico, the *dobla* in

Peru. The extra silver that was mined, however,
could not be processed by an individual Indian; he
had to sell it cheaply to the mine owner. In some
cases, the salaried work became transformed *de facto*
into payment in kind. In any case, the mine owners
moved toward the use of debt mechanisms to maintain the worker in place. See Romano (1970, 132–
133 and Bakewell (1971, 125–126). Davis analyzes
the system of debt bondage as a response of the
employer to the *strength* of the laborer in the free
market "as population reached its lowest levels
around the end of the sixteenth century" (1973b,
167).

[131] "The best way to get *gañanes* and peons was to
take the lands away from the Indian towns. . . .
[The] monopolization of the essentially complementary resource, land, is one of the most important
and common causes (though largely unobserved)
for the growth and continuation of latifundium agriculture and its associated inefficiency of resource
utilization (this from the social though not from the
private monopoly point of view)" (Frank, 1979a,
70–71). See also MacLeod regarding the 1580–
1590 period: "For the first time, Spaniards [in Central America] were taking up the *tierras baldías* and
realengas which had been abandoned by dead or
'congregated' Indians. Now also, the first heavy in-
trusions on Indian lands began" (1973, 221).

encomienda became the hacienda,[132] and the forced laborer became the debt peon. In terms of remuneration, which is calculated on units of time, it is possible that the worker's situation might even have improved. The labor shortage had given the worker some bargaining power;[133] but did he not pay for this higher level of remuneration with the increased total time he was obligated to offer? Was there not, in fact, an increase in the rate of work and a probable shortening of his life span? Were they not here, as in eastern Europe, eating up the capital of the labor force itself to maintain the level of production?

The sequence was probably this: The high prices and short supply of agricultural goods at the end of the sixteenth century led to land appropriation and production speedup. Chevalier, for example, speaks of the degree to which cattlemen were willing "to sacrifice many animals even at the risk of depleting their herds."[134] The mine owners, the townsmen, the bureaucrats—in short, those who constituted the regional market for agricultural goods—tried to control the level of profit of the producers by using mechanisms of price control, such as the *alhóndiga,* a municipal granary with fixed prices from which, however, Indian produce was exempt.[135] The smaller Spanish agricultural producers tended to go under because of the squeeze, as did the mestizo producers, many of whom "were reduced to a miserable peasant existence."[136] Conversely, the larger ones became still larger, expanding at the very moment of price decline. The logic of such seeming perversity is caught by Morner:

> Haciendas often had to reduce their production due to the limitations of the market and the drastic fall of prices when harvests were plentiful. Why then did they bother to expand? Because by depriving their neighbors of their lands, the hacendados wiped out competing production or forced hitherto self-sufficient small producers to become consumers of hacienda products instead.[137]

[132] Lockhart demonstrates rather convincingly the following points: whatever the legal disjunctures, the sociological continuities from *encomienda* to hacienda are great; "the encomendero and the later hacendero were cut from the same cloth"; the vaunted self-sufficiency of the hacienda is "very hard to distinguish from diversification or integration of a commercial enterprise"; and, most importantly, life remained the same for the workers: "The villagers came to work on the estancias and later haciendas, first through encomienda obligations, then through the mechanism of the repartimiento, and finally through individual arrangements, but they were always the same people doing the same things" (1969, 419, 425–426). See also R. G. Keith (1971, 441) and Piel (1975, 161, 238).

The legal basis of the hacienda were two *cédulas* of the Spanish Crown in 1591 in which it declared its right to all land for which a legal title did not exist. This forced landowners to pay a fee, *composición,* to obtain title to these lands, which were denounced as *baldíos,* wastelands or abandoned lands. See E. M. Barrett (1973, 89–90) and Lira and Muro (1976, 143). By 1713, the Crown had become so desperate for funds that in Peru it was willing to sell *baldíos* even to Indians, when they had the money. See Piel (1975, 191).

[133] See MacLeod, who talks of a "marginal improvement in the conditions of some members of the lower classes" (1973, 227).

[134] Chevalier (1970, 107).

[135] See Bakewell (1971, 75), who notes, however: "The efficacy of the *alhóndiga* in regulating prices is unknowable" (p. 66). See also Guthrie (1939, 105) and Chevalier (1970, 62–65).

[136] MacLeod (1973, 153). Of course there was resistance. Osborn (1973) observes that the ability of Indians in Mexico to resist land appropriation at this time was a function of the strength of community organization.

[137] Morner (1973, 192).

The large, so-called self-sufficient hacienda was precisely a mechanism that enabled subtle adjustment to market forces. It could contract and expand production in function of shifting profitability and speed up or slow down resource utilization, thus maintaining the link between agricultural production and the world-economy over time. Furthermore, the hacienda was the locus of new textile production. Its emergence is analogous to what in later centuries would be known as import substitution, the notorious consequence of worldwide contractions. Bakewell argues that "trade probably declined, in large part, because New Spain no longer needed imports from Europe."[138] He draws the conclusion that "the economy of New Spain, far from suffering any decline in the early seventeenth century, became more healthy";[139] but this is to misconceive the situation. There is no such thing as an economy of New Spain that can be compared to an economy of Spain. Some entrepreneurs in Hispanic America transferred investment, *inter alia*, to textile production because of the shifting state of the market (the increase of the Spanish and mestizo populations, the decline of silver export, and the economies of labor scale of the hacienda system) and thereby hurt the export potential of Spanish textile producers.

Worldwide contraction did not imply a decline of capitalist economic activity. Indeed, it probably signaled the increased strength of locally-based bourgeois enterprise.[140] Furthermore, as with Europe, the point is not that there was any *decline* in overall textile production but that this production was moving to the rural areas, the haciendas and Indian villages, and that "fine clothes were being produced for the most part in *obrajes*."[141] Nor were textiles the only growing industry. The iron and bronze industries expanded at the beginning of the seventeenth century to provide for the building of "large churches, with Renaissance grating on doors and windows (*verjas y rejas*)."[142] When the chief export crops of Hispanic America (particularly silver) suffered a decline on the world market, the producers

[138] Bakewell (1971, 234).

[139] Bakewell (1971, 230). Phelan makes essentially the same point: "The Borah thesis about the Indian labor shortage is beyond dispute, but this very shortage may have contributed more to economic growth in the seventeenth century than it did to economic stagnation. The word, 'depression,' I suggest, is a misleading term to apply to the whole period" (1970, 213).

[140] "If the emergence of large landed property in Peru coincided chronologically with a decline of the monetary economy and of non-agricultural enterprises—mining, manufacturing, commercial—how would we explain the rise of the Peruvian *obrajes* in the seventeenth century whose volume of production would exceed . . . that of Spain in that epoch, and even more how would we

explain the prodigious rise of a Spanish–Peruvian merchant bourgeoisie capable, as of 1613, of forcing Madrid to share the colonial monopoly on commerce between Peru and Spain by the creation of the Tribunal of the Lima Consulate?" (Piel, 1975, 150). On the "increasing latitude" of the New Spain economic elite vis-à-vis that of Seville, see Boyer (1977, 457 and *passim*). For the increasing strength of the local *aviadores*, or outfitters, in Mexico vis-à-vis the Crown, who could force debtors to repay them before they paid taxes, see Bakewell (1976, 219).

[141] Pohl (1969, 448). Davis, however, emphasizes that "the goods that Mexico produced in quantity were the cheaper, low-quality ones, while the high-grade woollens, linens and metalwares continued to come from Europe" (1973b, 161–162).

[142] Bargalló (1955, 251).

in these old peripheral areas turned their attention to other ways of making profit. They focused their productive activities on growing regional markets, which, from the point of view of transatlantic trade, represented a relative withdrawal; but it can scarcely be described as the rise of autarky. Meanwhile, within core countries, the high level of demand created expanding markets for the export of sugar (and to a lesser extent of tobacco). To some extent, this meant involving new peripheral areas in the world-economy—the Caribbean islands and their extension, and the southern mainland colonies of British North America. It is to this story that we must turn to complete the picture.

Until the beginning of the seventeenth century, most Caribbean islands were not under European control. The Spanish had taken over primarily the large islands of Trinidad and the so-called Greater Antilles (Cuba, Jamaica, Hispaniola, Puerto Rico). They did some cattle raising and grew some food crops and a little tobacco and sugar; but their main concern was simply to control the trade routes to their areas of prime concern in the Americas. Suddenly, between 1604 and 1640, the English, French, and Dutch invaded the Caribbean and took over all the minor islands. From 1625 to 1654, the Dutch controlled part of Brazil. In 1655, the English seized Jamaica from the Spaniards. In 1629 some French buccaneers landed in Tortuga off Hispaniola, and by 1659 they controlled the latter definitively; they soon moved onto the western half of the larger island, today called Haiti (although France's sovereignty was not to be formally recognized until 1697). Then from the 1650s until 1763, there was a relative stability of colonial allocation. Why was there a sudden upsurge of intrusion by the northwest European powers into the extended Caribbean? Why did it stop substantially short of taking over the Spanish and Portuguese territories? And why was the Caribbean in the seventeenth century, and particularly in the 1660s and 1670s, the haven of pirates and buccaneers, the Wild West of the era, "promising far more in the way of glamor, excitement, quick profit, and constant peril than the prosaic settlements" of the rest of the Americas?[143]

Pierre Chaunu says that somewhere between 1619/1623 and 1680, "at a date it would be fruitless to seek to make too precise," there was a change in the very nature of the Spanish *Carrera*. Bureaucratic rigidities replaced the supple mechanisms that had characterized the triumphant *Carrera* of the sixteenth century. "From the second half of the seventeenth century, the Atlantic of Guadalquivir had become only one Atlantic among several."[144] Chaunu's dating is later than that of some men of the time. In 1619, Sancho de Moncada, Professor of Holy Scripture at the University of Toledo and a Spanish mercantilist thinker, asserted (no doubt with some exaggeration) that nine-tenths of the commerce to the Indies was in the hands of foreigners, "such that they have the Indies, and Your Majesty the

---

[143] Dunn (1972, 9–10).   [144] Chaunu (1959, 1539).

title.''[145] He would be proven essentially right. In the seventeenth century, the century of mercantilism, Spain and Portugal failed to be, were unable to be, mercantilist, and thus they became transformed into semiperipheral states, conveyor belts for the interests of the core powers in the peripheral regions. As a story of the semiperiphery we shall speak of this at some length in the next chapter; as a story of the periphery, we must tell it now.

In an era of overall contraction, *some* arenas of economic activity must be contracting. Seeking to minimize contraction in their economic activities, the core powers compete acutely among themselves, partly by seeking preemptive control of peripheral areas. They both colonize and seek to keep each other from colonizing, which leads to acute colonial wars, and they seek to shape the world market to favor more controllable areas over less controllable ones (the Americas versus eastern and southern Europe). In addition, they seek to feed off weaker colonial powers when it proves too expensive to seize their territory outright, as was largely the case for the Spanish and Portuguese empires.[146] Thus, as the world contraction began, the English, French, and Dutch all turned to the Caribbean to preempt it. They colonized the zones that were easy to take and then, by seizing the trade, sought to obtain the economic advantages they would have had by direct colonial rule in those areas still controlled by Spain and Portugal. The chief mechanism of doing this in the seventeenth century was contraband.

To understand how contraband worked, we must first look at the social origins of the buccaneers. In the sixteenth century, cattle roamed Central America and the Caribbean islands. Some of it was wild. Some of it was controlled by Indians, but less and less as the century went on, and some ranched by the Spaniards. We have already described the demographic shifts of Hispanic America: the steady decline of the Indian population, combined with a steady growth not only of Creoles, but of mulatto and mestizo groups. The seventeenth-century contraction of the mining areas caused a tightening of opportunities in the urban areas for the poorer Creoles and for the socially intermediate mulatto and mestizo populations. Many of them migrated to rural areas. Some found placement in the grow-ing network of haciendas and ranches. Others did not. Members of the

[145] Cited in Larraz (1943, 90).
[146] Charles Boxer summarizes the Dutch–Portuguese worldwide struggles in the first two-thirds of the seventeenth century as follows: "At the risk of oversimplification, it can be said that this lengthy colonial war took the form of a fight for the spice-trade of Asia, for the slave-trade of West Africa, and for the sugar-trade of Brazil. Similarly, it can be said that the final result was, in effect, a victory for the Dutch in Asia, a draw in West Africa, and a victory for the Portuguese in Brazil" (1961, 49). Is this the way to put it? In terms of *political* control, it is; but in terms of *economic* control, was this not a victory for the Dutch (later supplanted by the English) in all three areas—a victory that took differing forms depending on whether it occurred in the external arena (Asia) or in the periphery (Brazil), West Africa being an area in slow transition at this time from external arena to periphery? The difference is in the degree of Portuguese entrenchment in the processes of production, and Boxer himself gives us this clue: "[The] Portuguese, with all their faults, had struck deeper roots [in Brazil] as colonists; and so they could not, as a rule, be removed from the scene simply by a naval or a military defeat, or even by a series of such defeats" (1961, 54).

intermediate strata who did not find employment risked "inferiorization," reduction to the status of mere cultivators of food crops. In the frontier atmosphere, however, they did have an alternative. They became cowboys of wild animals, slaughtering what they needed for survival. Their ranks began to be swelled by runaways from ships. Dutch captains began to trade with them for the hides of cattle, and this increased the rate of slaughter even more. "Obviously such practices were very wasteful";[147] In time, from the point of view of settler populations, "this waste went too far."[148]

In roughly 1640, Spanish authorities began trying to clear the islands and Central American coastal areas of these *boucaniers*.[149] One way the Spanish did this was to kill the cattle themselves in order to discourage the cowboys. The English joined the game in order to discourage the Spanish. By now the cattle had virtually disappeared, at least from the islands, and the buccaneers in desperation took to the sea as pirates. The pirates would never have survived, however, had not the Dutch in Curaçao, the French in St. Dominigue (western Hispaniola), and especially the English in Jamaica "offered them secure outlets for their booty."[150] Jamaica was the key. It was under Cromwell that the island was seized from Spain and under the Restoration that it became so much the base of the buccaneers that one of their number, Henry Morgan, would rise to become Lieutenant-Governor and be knighted. Only with the Glorious Revolution did piracy die out completely. Cromwell's aim was to break Spain's monopoly of trade to the West Indies. He first tried diplomacy and failed, thereupon resorting to plunder. Strong writes: "Cromwell was Elizabethan. He belongs with Raleigh, Gilbert and Hakluyt. The whole aspect of the West Indian expedition is Elizabethan."[151] The policy was not only Cromwell's, however, for the career of Jamaica as a "state piratical venture" continued unabated under Charles II.[152] In theory, piracy was outlawed in the Anglo–Spanish Treaty of 1670, but in practice, it went on in great strength until at least 1685, and really until the earthquake that destroyed the great buccaneer redoubt of Port-Royal in 1692, finally being interred by the Treaty of Rijswijk in 1697.

[147] MacLeod (1973, 212).

[148] Pares (1960, 20).

[149] The word *boucaniers* originated because they sold their meat after smoking it on iron trellises or trays known as *boucan* in an Indian language. See Deschamps (1973, 40). It is not that buccaneers were unknown before this time. Rather, it was that "until about 1650, buccaneering in the West Indies was more or less accidental, occasional, in character" as compared with the "heyday" after that (Haring, 1964, 249).

[150] Davis (1973b, 169). In the early seventeenth century, Dutch pirates were the most "audacious and . . . persistent . . . in their pursuit of Spanish ships. . . . The name 'Hollander' became synonymous with 'corsair' and 'pirate'" (Peterson, 1975, 250).

[151] Strong (1899, 233). Strong adds: "The advisors of Charles II understood how far-reaching were Cromwell's plans in regard to conquest and colonization and perceived the real motives of his attack on the West Indies. 'A.B.' in writing to the King of Spain, January 1656, in behalf of Charles, lays great stress on the fact that Cromwell intended to colonize the West Indies and by his fleet cut off the Spanish trade. In fact on other grounds the entire enterprise has no meaning. To suppose that after such enormous preparations and expense the Protector would be content with a few square miles of territory falls hardly short of absurd" (1899, 244).

[152] Pares (1960, 3).

In Jamaica there was a growing contradiction between the island's role as a sugar colony and its role as a base for plunder and contraband; but even more there was a diminishing need in the core states for piracy as a way of primitive accumulation.

The pattern of contraband trade had been initiated by the Dutch in the last decade of the sixteenth century as a very practical matter. The wars with Spain cut off Dutch shipping to the Iberian peninsula and therefore interfered with the purchase of salt, so necessary for the herring industry. The Dutch turned to illicit purchase from the salt pans of Venezuela. This emergency procedure became permanent policy because of the basic structure of world prices. The United Provinces was a far more efficient agro-industrial producer than Spain. "The Seville monopoly could not supply sufficient goods [to Spanish America] at reasonable prices."[153] The Dutch could. Smuggling thereupon became a way of life that linked the merchants of the core countries to the producers of peripheral countries they did not directly control.[154] Each time relations between Spain and a core power were bad, and most of all in times of war, new colonies were founded "destined, in part, to serve as privateering bases," which, Pares observes, is a partial explanation of their chronology.[155] It may also explain why there were eventually more English than French colonies, since France was frequently in *alliance* with Spain against England.

Jamaica represented the culmination of the system of contraband. It became the emporium of Caribbean contraband trade, which "the English would not stop . . . and the Spaniards could not."[156] At first the existence of pirates aided this process. They were, after all, not true pirates since they pillaged only the Spanish and often did it with the authorization of their

[153] J. Lang (1975, 55). As a consequence, says Haring, "Spanish merchants often became in effect merely intermediaries, the agents or factors on a commission basis to which often they lent their Spanish names in order to elude the law." Ultimately this meant that "the trade of Spain with America became a more or less passive machine, a device by which was canalized under royal control the supply of goods from the rest of Europe" (1947, 314–315).

[154] It was a practice that transcended the Caribbean zone. The Dutch related in the same way to the Danish "colony" of Norway. See Lunde: "Smuggling was on the whole considered the great problem for the governing authorities in Copenhagen. That there was smuggling on a large scale throughout Norway was absolutely clear to everyone. The *Staatsloven* [vicegeral council] blamed the Dutch who were characterized as experts in this profession. Whenever there were customs, Norwegian merchants had to smuggle, wrote the *Staatsloven;* there was only one remedy for the traffic— reduction of the customs duties. This was what they

sought, but with few results, and the smuggling continued. . . . The merchants themselves asserted that they would be ruined if they were honest. . . . Smuggling was a direct consequence of the reigning economic system and operative commercial policies in Copenhagen" (1963, 38–39).

[155] Pares (1960, 12).

[156] Christelow (1942, 312). Sheridan's estimates show clearly why the contraband trade went on: "Prior to about 1763, Britain's informal empire trade was probably no less valuable than that with her formal empire" (1969, 24). He cites, as the two major components of Britain's informal empire the contraband trade via Jamaica and the indirect trade via Cádiz and Portugal. One should not forget the interloper trade via Buenos Aires. "Its location far from the centers of Spanish power in Lima and the West Indies and close to the Portuguese in Brazil made adquate control there almost impossible. And as the port was virtually closed in the interest of the galleon trade, the temptation was irresistible to secure by such means what was denied by Spain" (Haring, 1947, 329).

own government.[157] But sugar planting became more important on Jamaica, and when the Spanish in 1670 finally renounced their ancient claim to the exclusive right of settlement, the buccaneers came to be seen by the English as a nuisance, especially since their numbers were growing and their desperation increasing as poor whites were being forced off Jamaican land by expanding plantations.[158] Buccaneers were no longer needed. The producers on the Gulf of Honduras were happy to deal directly with the Jamaican merchants, who had taken "much of the risk out of smuggling goods into Central America."[159]

The buccaneers had *plundered*.[160] The English (and the French) were now ready to settle for *illegitimate trade*, since this involved the same transfer of surplus, but at the same time guaranteed continued production, which the plundering of the buccaneers did not. Once the bases of the buccaneers were closed down, "it was possible for Spanish planters again to begin flourishing in the islands and along the coastlands."[161] It was also possible for the English and French to negotiate directly with the Spanish for a "legitimate" trade in slaves, the so-called *asiento*.[162] Contraband in Spanish America was only the smaller part of the picture. The bigger part was sugar, which had long been one of the basic products of peripheral countries. Sugar production had steadily moved westward because of a continuing process of soil exhaustion,[163] and it had reached Brazil (and to a lesser extent, Mexico) in the late sixteenth century. It was to move to the Caribbean islands in the seventeenth. Unlike wheat, cattle, and silver, sugar was

---

[157] See Deschamps (1973, 44–45). This authorization, Haring reminds us, could be "real or pretended" (1964, 210).

[158] See Floyd (1967, 26–28). See also Farnie: "Sugar reduced ranching to a secondary role ending the 'buccaneering' phase of Caribbean history" (1962, 209).

[159] MacLeod (1973, 367–368).

[160] Davis (1973b, 169). There were in fact two forms of plunder. One was the plunder of treasure fleets. The other was the plunder of Spanish cities on the Caribbean and the Gulf of Mexico. The former was never really engaged in by the buccaneers, only by naval squadrons and then only three times, in 1628 by the Dutch and in 1656 and 1657 by the English. See Haring (1964, 235–247). Plunder of Spanish cities, however, was a buccaneer specialty. Between 1655 and 1671, eighteen cities were devastated; and it was this form of plunder that was decisive in transforming the patterns of transatlantic trade. "It was by such means, coupled with the trade of the interloper, that the fountains of Spanish–American trade were dried up, not by the destruction of the silver fleets" (Haring, 1964, 250). Ultimately, as Glamann says, the "pirate economy . . . [was not] particularly productive of growth. . . . Men-of-war, whether flying the black

flag or not, were sterile instruments of trade and prosperity compared with heavily-laden corn-barges or other coastal vessels with coal and bricks, casks of wine or salt and dried fish in their holds" (1977, 191).

[161] Davis (1973b, 169). See also Dunn, who says that at the end of the seventeenth century the English, French, and Dutch "tacitly agreed to let Spain, the Sick Man of America, keep the rest of its sprawling, undeveloped Caribbean empire. Indeed both the English and French authorities saw more profit in trading with Spanish colonists than in robbing them, and from 1680 onwards they tried their best to suppress the buccaneers" (1972, 22). Actually, after the Treaty of Nijmegen in 1678, the Dutch were no longer "a major factor to be reckoned with in the Caribbean" (Goslinga, 1971, 482). Dunn sees one further factor in this sift of policy, at least for England. The Glorious Revolution represented, he says, a decisive turning point and a victory for the sugar planters who henceforth "maintained convivial relations with the crown," which no longer ate up their profits as it had under the Restoration (1972, 162).

[162] See the discussion of the shift in policy in Nettels (1931b, 17–19).

[163] See Wallerstein (1974, 88, especially n. 70).

not involved in the problem of oversupply in the world-economy around 1600 that caused a basic contraction in peripheral exports to core areas. Sugar was more like wood, the continuing "growth" crop of the Baltic. Its eternal problem was ecological exhaustion and the necessity to find virgin zones to exploit; but the profits were consequently high.[164]

For sugar, absolute demand grew as the seventeenth century proceeded because of the creation of new food tastes in the core countries. In the Middle Ages, Europe's desire for sweets had been satisfied largely by honey and must (unfermented grape juice), both naturally sweet. Now, new drinks had been discovered and new desserts invented that required the addition of sugar to make them palatable.[165] Sugar production had shifted in a big way from the Atlantic islands to Brazil in about 1580.[166] As the signs of secular downturn began to appear in Hispanic America, there seems to have been an upturn in Brazil. Chaunu explains that this "tardy turning point" occurred in Brazil around 1630/1650 rather in 1580 due to the fact that in the period from 1570 to 1620, Brazil, unlike Hispanic America, "was still benefiting from the easy growth of youth."[167] This seems to me factitious. Is it not easier to explain this expansion by the previously discussed relationship between the fairly rapid rate of ecological exhaustion and world demand and conclude that as a product of the world-economy, sugar was less subject to secular swings than were wheat and silver? The downturn of 1630/1650 that Chaunu sees would then be precisely the factor of reduced productivity intruding itself once again.[168]

It is in any case the Dutch entrepreneurs who introduced sugar to Barbados at the very point when Dutch exports from Brazil were at their

[164] Chevalier, speaking of Mexico, says: "Estate owners were only too eager to replace their wheat with sugar cane whenever the climate permitted. . . . Wheat, considered a primary commodity, was subject to [governmental] price ceilings and requisitions by the authorities which often left producers only a narrow margin of profit; sugar, on the other hand, was a luxury product sold on the open market and fetching high prices because of the growing demand" (1970, 74).

Why then did not Mexico become a major sugar producer? Berthe finds the explanation in politically maintained labor-cost differentials. "Long excluded from the benefits of the *repartimiento* system, to the advantage of the wheat haciendas, [the sugar mills] couldn't even make exclusive use of Indian wage-workers and had to use, for the most part, slave manpower, both fragile and expensive" (1966, 103). Batie, on the other hand, emphasizes the *difficulties* of sugar production as compared with the production of tobacco and cotton: it required "a heavy capital outlay, sizeable labour force, and sophisticated knowledge . of manufacturing processes" (1976, 13).

[165] "The habit of taking sweetened drinks and eat-

ing sweet puddings and pies became more common during the seventeenth century" (Forbes, 1957, 7). See also Davis (1973b, 168) and Pares (1960, 23).

[166] Boxer calls the years from 1580 to 1680 Brazil's "century of sugar" (1952, 388).

[167] Chaunu (1961, 1193–1194). Mauro explains the "special case" of Brazilian sugar in the seventeenth-century conjuncture by the expansion of demand due to the shift from the use of sugar as a drug to its use as a foodstuff (1960, 233).

[168] See de Castro (1976). Pares, speaking of sugar production at a later point in time, in the eighteenth-century in the British West Indies, says: "The effects of soil exhaustion upon sugar planting can be seen clearly. Every decade it took more slaves to produce the same amount of sugar from the same acreage, or, where cultivation was advanced or output increased, it was only done at the cost of heavy additional labour" (1960, 41). Masefield speaks of the "see-saw fortunes" of the sugar industry resulting from repeated exhaustions of fertility (1967, 291). Batie suggests as an additional factor in the case of Brazil that the warfare with the Dutch (1630–1641) "largely destroyed" the sugar estates (1976, 15).

maximum and *before* the Pernambuco revolt of 1645 that was to lead to Dutch expulsion from Brazil. Why? Dunn offers two reasons for this: First, the craving of Europeans for sugar was presumably "great enough to warrant expanding the supply by adding Barbados to Brazil." Second, the Dutch were able to profit from middleman services at a point when "English overseas trade was distracted by the civil war at home."[169] Perhaps; but perhaps also the Dutch were knowledgeable about the exhaustibility of sugar cane plantations.[170] The fact that the Dutch were seeking *optimal* conditions is clear in the very choice of Barbados over other islands. Generally speaking, Barbados had better climate and better soil than other Caribbean islands and a better physical location in terms of security from plunder.[171] In fact, such considerations would apply to all the early sugar islands (of which Barbados was only *primus inter pares*), as Sheridan points out:[172]

> Small islands were initially favored over large islands in the establishment of plantations. From the standpoint of transport and defense, the distance from northern Europe was less, islands to windward were more easily defended than those to leeward, and the high ratio of coastline to land area enabled most plantations to have direct access to sea-going vessels.

And, Sheridan adds, there was more wind for windmills, a less enervating climate, and less possibility of slave insurrections and escape.

When sugar production reached Jamaica, a very large island, it stopped the process of territorial expansion, at least for England, because Jamaica provided substantial acreage and the English sugar interests feared that "any further cane fields would glut production and drive down prices."[173]

[169] Dunn (1972, 55–66); Sheridan argues that the English tobacco growers had a crisis of overproduction in 1636 that led to a search for alternatives. The Dutch came along in 1637 with sugar cane—and with technology, capital, and Negro slaves (see 1969, 11). Furtado, on the other hand, argues: "It is probable that changes bearing upon the Caribbean economy would have occurred much more slowly except for an external occurrence at the end of the first half of the seventeenth century—the final expulsion of the Dutch invaders from northern Brazil" (1963, 25).

[170] Edel attributes the shift to the fact that costs in Barbados were lower than those in Brazil because of the freshness and high quality of the soil. Thus it "rational for Dutch capitalists, despite their existing interests in Pernambuco, to have considered Barbados as a ground for new investments, even apart from the insecurity of Dutch control of northeast Brazil" (1969, 42). Batie adds a factor of passing conjuncture. After the Pernambuco revolt in 1645, the Dutch West India Company, thinking it short-lived, ordered its agents on the Gold Coast to continue sending slaves. When these slaves arrived, they were then sent on to the Lesser Antilles to be sold off on "lenient credit terms. Of the islands, Barbados lay nearest to Recife" (1976, 21).

[171] On climate and soil, see Dunn (1972, 26–30). On security, see Pares: "Barbados owed its exceptionally tranquil career (it had never changed flags, even for a day, since its foundation) to the fact that, lying a few miles to the east of the main group of islands, it was out of the track, not only of Spaniards, but of Caribs" (1960, 10). Batie says security was important because of the large investment required by sugar. "The threat of invasion particularly worried wealthy investors who stood to lose a fortune in slaves and equipment during even the briefest seaborne raid" (1976, 15).

[172] Sheridan (1969, 19). One of the disadvantages of Brazil was that the interior provided areas in which communities of escaped slaves could survive. This was particularly the case in Cairú and Camamú in Bahía. See Schwartz (1970).

[173] Dunn (1972, 21). See also Davies: "The half century which followed the capture of Jamaica in 1655 was characterized by the consolidation rather than by the expansion of the English interest in the West Indies" (1952b, 89).

In this sense, the absence of further expansion was an expression of newly acquired mercantilist strength. The same is true with the French attitude after their acquisition of St. Domingue.[174] Expansion at *Spanish* expense was no longer necessary because the sugar acreage under English and French rule was quite sufficient for another century. But mutual destruction of each other's property remained a major objective for England and France during the three Anglo–French wars in the Caribbean: 1666–1667, 1689–1697, and 1702–1713. If this mutual destruction died down after 1713, it was because world demand had by now expanded enough to accommodate the sugar industries of both countries, which were booming. "The sugar planters had discovered El Dorado after all."[175]

There is a sense in which tobacco was always the poor relative of sugar—an early starter and an early loser. It was an early starter because it was a beginner's crop. It came up within a year and required little special equipment. But it had certain great disadvantages, at least in the period we are discussing. Tobacco "murdered the soil,"[176] even more than sugar did. It had to move on every 25 years or so, and hence it was only really feasible to grow it on large islands or in areas with expanding hinterlands like Virginia and Maryland.[177] In addition, tobacco had a smaller world market and a smaller profit margin than sugar. It "did not lend itself to bonanza agriculture, as did sugar . . . where fortunes could be made in a decade."[178] Like sugar, it had been thought to have therapeutic properties; but sugar became a staple instead of a drug somewhere in the early seventeenth century, and tobacco did not seem to do this until a century later, perhaps even two centuries. Why this should have been so is not entirely clear, although there are two obvious facts: Sugar has nutritive value whereas tobacco does not, and expanding sugar consumption complemented the expanding consumption of coffee, tea, and cocoa.[179]

---

[174] See Dunn (1972, 21).

[175] Dunn (1972, 23). If the mutual destruction of the wars failed to check the growth rate of the sugar industry (a sign of a persistently growing demand), it did affect the social organization of production. "In the English islands the [long] War [from 1689 to 1713] undoubtedly hurt the peasant farmers and benefited the big planters" (Dunn, 1972, 147). See also Sheridan (1965, 299, Table 3) on the increasing concentration of land in Jamaica from 1670 to 1754.

[176] Pares (1960, 20).

[177] Pares curiously turns this disadvantage into a virtue: "[Both sugar and tobacco] planters suffered from the exhaustion of their soil. The tobacco colonies suffered least, because the owner of an exhausted plantation could easily obtain virgin soil—at most, a couple of hundred miles away—and could move his slaves to it. . . . The sugar planters were less able to help themselves. Many of the islands were small" (1960, 41). But this inverts the

cart and the horse. Why did sugar displace tobacco in the first place on the smaller islands and retreat, as it were, to the larger islands and the Chesapeake Valley? The shift from tobacco to sugar on the smaller islands was definitive by the 1660s. See Pares himself (1960, 22) and also Farnie (1962, 210). This was so despite the slump in sugar prices from 1645 to 1680. See Pares (1960, 40). The beginner's-crop advantage did have one spillover in relation to soil exhaustion, as Pares argues: "A sugar plantation was not so easy to transplant as a tobacco plantation—there was more heavy machinery, and more capital was invested in the acres already planted. For these reasons a sugar planter often had to stay put" (1960, 41).

[178] Land (1965, 647).

[179] On how tobacco was viewed primarily as physical therapy during this period, see Ortiz (1947, 242–245). On the growth of the taste for sugar, Nef offers this explanation: "During the sixteenth and

Furthermore, since tobacco, unlike sugar, could be grown in nontropical climates, it represented an agricultural option for much of Europe. Cane sugar production was only possible on the Mediterranean islands, and it had "passed through" these areas already. Hence, despite the rapid soil exhaustion tobacco caused, world supply exceeded world demand more frequently in tobacco production than in sugar production. The tobacco situation was further complicated by the policies of most European governments, which seized upon this luxury item as one easy to tax, indeed to tax farm through state monopolies. This was not true everywhere to be sure. The United Provinces, as befit the world's leading tobacco market, imposed no taxes,[180] and inland tobacco production flourished there, especially during the difficult years for cereals.[181] In addition to regulating and taxing tobacco, most countries tried to prohibit national production. This was particularly true of England and France, the most probable motive being fiscal control. "It was easier to collect customs duties on tobacco imported into London or La Rochelle than [to collect] excises upon an article grown in Gloucestershire or Gascony."[182]

At first, state taxation hurt the tobacco industry of the Americas. Its main result was "to raise prices and restrict the markets,"[183] especially since the imposition of customs duties in turn fostered domestic European production and thereby worsened the "besetting economic problem" of Western Hemisphere production, the "costs of labor and transportation."[184] However, by the early eighteenth century, a particular combination of factors turned the whole picture around. First, state suppression of European tobacco production had come to be relatively successful. Second, among Western Hemisphere producers, the English colonies in the Chesapeake Valley turned out to produce a superior crop at lower prices. Third, the English developed their *re*export of various tropical goods (including tobacco) as one of their central economic activities. Hence the English came to regard tobacco primarily as a source of commercial revenue instead of as a

---

early seventeenth centuries the Europeans developed a taste for sugar that had not existed among earlier civilized peoples. This is partly explained by the growth of economic civilization in the north. The northern fruits and vegetables had less succulence than those growing in the Mediterranean soil. To make them palatable it was necessary to sweeten them" (1968, 77).

[180] The only other major area in Europe that did not tax tobacco imports was the Spanish Netherlands. See Gray and Wyckoff (1940, 4).

[181] See Roessingh: "In the long term, the rise in tobacco cultivation may be interpreted as an accompaniment of the prolonged agricultural recession in the period from about 1650 to about 1750. The price ratio of inland tobacco to cereals shifted in favour of tobacco and the growers reacted to these economic changes by increasing the tobacco area" (1976, 500).

[182] Pares (1960, 26). It was not that easy, however, to stamp out European tobacco production. Beer observes: "The first prohibition against English tobacco was issued in 1620, and . . . it took seventy years of more or less constant effort and energetic measures to uproot this industry" (1912, 145). There was no ecological obstacle to tobacco growing in England. Thirsk calls the agricultural conditions in England "entirely suitable" and points out that its timing does not interfere with the cultivation of essential food crops (1974, 89).

[183] Gray and Wyckoff (1940, 4); but Breen attributes "the transformation of Virginia . . . [to] the rise of tobacco prices after 1684" (1973, 13).

[184] K. G. Davies (1974, 144).

source of fiscal revenue.[185] At the same time, France took precisely the opposite tack and turned tobacco duties into a "major branch of state revenues."[186] After 1720, with government encouragement, France became the largest single purchaser of the Virginia and Maryland tobacco reexported from England, purchasing in one fell swoop a quarter of the total production and thereby accounting in large part for the boom (at long last) and for the increasing concentration of production and merchandising.[187]

In the very last years of the seventeenth century, probably between 1693 and 1695, gold was "found" in Brazil.[188] This was the start of a gold export boom, and the official figures show an increase of from 725 kilograms in 1699 to 14,500 kilograms in 1712, the top year. Boxer estimates, however, that this was only one-tenth to one-third of the real export, the rest being contraband.[189] Why was Brazilian gold "discovered" just then? Vilar notes the coincidence of the onset of Brazil's "gold cycle" and the monetary inflation in England resulting from the wars from 1689 to 1713; he suggests, most pertinently, that it is not the discoveries that account for England's commercial expansion and inflation, but rather the other way round: the expansion, "requiring or favoring the exploitation of new mines, explains the onset of the 'gold cycle'."[190] Supporting this view is the fact that contraband trade was scarcely secret; rather, it was systematically organized to bring Brazil's gold to England, virtually bypassing Portugal's economy altogether.

> In war and peace alike Brazil gold went to England on board Royal Naval vessels and by the weekly Falmouth–Lisbon packet boat service. Both warships and packet boats were immune from search by the Portuguese customs and all other officials. Naturally, the merchants at Lisbon, both British and foreign, preferred to remit their gold to England by this means, since the export of specie and bullion from Portugal had been strictly forbidden since the Middle Ages.[191]

The foregoing events indicate that the long contraction of 1600 to 1750 did not involve a simple involution of peripheral areas. What occurred was a relocation of some former peripheral activities (particularly cereals production and pasturage) from the periphery to the core (thus forcing production in eastern Europe and Hispanic America to reorient itself toward

---

[185] In 1723, Walpole stimulated the reexport of tobacco by exempting it from duty (and thereby eliminating the price advantages of Dutch and German tobacco). See J. M. Price (1964, 504–505).

[186] J. M. Price (1964, 504). "Whereas the king of England had gained about twice as much revenue from tobacco as the king of France in 1700, by the 1760s, the king of France was getting about four times as much from that leaf as his Britannic cousin" (p. 503).

[187] J. M. Price relates this directly to "the pressure of the French monopsonistic buyer" (1964, 506).

[188] Boxer (1969b, 35).

[189] Boxer (1969b, 59).

[190] Vilar (1974, 279). Perhaps there is another side to this coin. Boxer points out that "with the decline in sugar prices in the last quarter of the seventeenth century, many Lisbon merchants insisted on being paid in cash [for slaves] rather than in kind [sugar or tobacco], and the resultant export of coin produced a serious financial crisis in Brazil" (1969b, 26). This would suggest a Brazilian as well as an English incentive for the gold "discoveries."

[191] Boxer (1969a, 460).

regional markets) plus the creation of a new peripheral region, partly directly colonized and producing only goods that could not be produced in core countries. This new peripheral region was the extended Caribbean, stretching from northeast Brazil to Maryland, and its three principal products were sugar, tobacco, and gold. The United Provinces, England, and France, the three core states, shared the economic benefits—the Dutch more so up to 1650, the English more so later on and especially after about 1690.

Let us look now to the process of class-formation in this new periphery, particularly to the forms the bourgeoisie and proletariat took. The bourgeoisie located in peripheral regions were primarily that classic duo of "merchants and planters." In the seventeenth century, in the "old" peripheries of the east and extreme south of Europe (Sicily plus the southern parts of Italy, Spain, and Portugal) and of Hispanic America, involution prevailed, manufacture regained a role, and the market orientation became regional. Thus it seems clear that the importance of the merchant class declined as compared with the importance of the productive entrepreneurs, that is, the planters, using as a measure the percentage of total capital concentrated in the hands of a group or the rate of profit of their activities or their political influence (both local and worldwide). The elimination of much of the long-distance trade must have hurt the merchant groups severely, particularly in their bargaining power vis-à-vis landowning cash-crop producers. The whole system of *international* debt peonage (of planters to merchants) must have declined, as *local* debt peonage (peasants to landowners) expanded.[192]

But what about the "new" periphery of the extended Caribbean? Is this not the locale par excellence of "merchant capitalism"? It is worth taking a careful look at what was happening, starting with the conclusion of Richard Pares's detailed analysis of capital investment and flows between the British West Indies and England in the seventeenth and eighteenth centuries:

> Thus it was the planter who was paying, so to speak, for his own enslavement. The profits of the plantations were the source which fed the indebtedness charged upon the plantations themselves. In this sense Adam Smith was wrong: the wealth of the British West Indies did not all proceed from the mother country; after some initial loans in the earliest period which merely primed the pump, the wealth of the West Indies was created out of the profits of the West Indies themselves, and, with some assistance from the British tax-payer, much of it found a permanent home in Great Britain.[193]

How did this system work? Let us be clear that what I am discussing is *not* how much the exploitation of labor in the Caribbean contributed to the accumulation of capital in England; the question is how the internal conflicts among the bourgeois strata affected the ways in which the surplus-

---

[192] For a discussion of international debt peonage as it worked in the sixteenth century, see Wallerstein (1974, 121–122).
[193] Pares (1960, 50).

value was distributed among them and eventually channelled from periphery to core.

The sugar "interest" shifted to England from the end of the seventeenth through the eighteenth century. Dunn, however, has skipped a step. Dunn notes that although the Caribbean sugar planter was "a large-scale entrepreneur" and a "combination farmer–manufacturer,"[194] by the end of the seventeenth century "absentee ownership was becoming a major problem."[195] In the beginning, the usual pattern was that planters with small landholdings and limited capital started in a region to which they had emigrated. They obtained needed investment capital from merchants in European port cities such as London and Dieppe. Instead of obtaining an unencumbered loan, a merchant entered into a partnership with a small planter (a mateship, or *matelotage* in French). The planter was given passage money for himself and his indentured servants, plus money for tools and initial provisions. The merchant thus placed his capital and received his returns in kind. This system, as opposed to one of direct ownership in which the "planter" would be an "agent," was of great advantage to the merchant, who "was partly protected against the unfaithfulness of agents— the chief risk in all colonial enterprise—by the partnership which gave the planter an honest interest in the prosperity of the business."[196]

Once the plantations had been launched in given islands, however, a process of concentration occurred because of the greater resilience of larger-scale producers in the face of acute world competition. As the plantations grew in scale, the planter's importance vis-à-vis his merchant partner also grew. This can be seen in the conflict over the Navigation Acts. Mercantilist legislation protects manufacturers and merchant reexporters. It is seldom useful to peripheral primary producers. In the mid-seventeenth century, when British Caribbean sugar production was strong relative to that in other regions and English home consumption was relatively small, the small planters of the British West Indies tried their best to circumvent English merchants by selling to the Continent via merchants in North America, the Dutch and French West Indies, and even Ireland and Scotland. By the eighteenth century the routing was reversed. Sugar production expanded in other areas, the English home market prices rose because of protection, and English demand increased because of a rising standard of living and population growth. It was the planters in non-English areas who then sought to pass their goods via merchants in the British West Indies. This weakened the position of English planters and strengthened that of London merchants.[197]

---

[194] Dunn (1972, 194). The manufacturing role included having mills for extracting juice from cane, boiling houses for evaporating cane juice to sugar crystals, curing houses for drying sugar and draining molasses, distilleries for transforming molasses into rum, and storehouses for keeping barreled sugar (see pp. 189–190).

[195] Dunn (1972, 200).

[196] Pares (1960, 5).

[197] See Sheridan (1957, 63–66).

We must thus distinguish three phases. In the first phase, the Caribbean planter was small and weak vis-à-vis a relatively large merchant. As a result of concentration, the planters grew stronger and bigger and achieved local political power in the islands.[198] Even more important, the commission system developed; instead of the planter being the "agent" of the merchant, the merchant now became the "agent" of the planter. The commission system worked to eliminate the small island-based merchants (as opposed to the large English factors).[199] This had the secondary advantage of reducing clandestine trade between the islands. By 1707 the West India interest was strong enough to create a "forced" market in Scotland and, by means of the notorious Molasses Act of 1732, in Ireland and British North America.[200] Through the direct relationship between planters in the Caribbean and merchants in England, the commission system eliminated the *peripheral* merchant middleman. It moved the location of the primary market for sugar from the Caribbean to Europe. Two factors created the conditions for the emergence of the commission system, which first appeared in connection with Barbados sugar production: the increasing strength of the planters through concentration and the pressure on them of falling prices since they needed a larger percentage of the profit to retain the same level of income.[201] The system spread to other islands, and by the 1690s, it was used in tobacco production as well.[202] It shifted the locus of entrepreneurial investment from merchant to planter. "The planter sent his produce home to Europe to be sold on commission by the merchant as his factor, and this same factor bought, once more on commission, the plantation stores at the planter's order."[203] The commission system was not universal. It was used by English sugar planters but not by French planters. In the case of Virginia tobacco, the shift to this system was temporary, and in the 1730s planters reverted to the type of arrangements they had used earlier. We must answer three questions: Why did this system occur in English and not in French islands? Why did Virginia tobacco planters revert? How do we interpret the shift in terms of the locus of profit?

Speaking to the question of why the system was used by the English and not the French, Pares first notes Davies's explanation that the commission

---

[198] "By the early years of the eighteenth century wealthy planters held a majority of seats in most of the island legislatures" (Sheridan, 1957, 67).

[199] "The resident merchants, as a class, began to languish or even to disappear in many parts of the colonies, although they survived at Kingston, Jamaica, which was closely connected with the Spanish Empire, at Bridgetown, Barbados, where big business was done in slaves, and at Martinique where the *commissionnaires* battened on the trade of other islands. Elsewhere, they declined much in importance. There were merchants, but they were mostly mere factors, selling North American pro

duce on commission" (Pares, 1960, 33).

[200] "The planters were so successful in their attempts to raise the price of sugar that [in 1753] buyers were forced to seek parliamentary assistance." Sheridan gives this as the primary explanation of the period of "excess profit" from the late 1730s to 1763 (1957, 81, 83).

[201] See K. G. Davies (1952b, 101, 103–104), who says: "The commission system was in origin the method of disposal for the sugar produced by the large, intensely cultivated, highly capitalized estate."

[202] See J. M. Price (1954, 506).

[203] Pares (1960, 33).

system originated because *large* planters had to pay for their slaves. In London, factors could utilize bills of exchange to make these payments, being repaid through consignments in sugar. The commission system thus created credit for the large planter–entrepreneur. Pares says, however, that since large French planters also needed credit for slaves and did not create a commission system, an additional factor was at work—the fact that owner absenteeism started earlier and was more extensive in the English islands than it was in the French islands.[204] But what does absenteeism signify? It came about because successful entrepreneurs were profiting from their good fortune, and it is evidence of the strength of their enterprise. Their role shifted from that of foreman to that of financial executive; and because of the scale of their accumulated capital, they could afford to specialize in the latter task (and incidentally to devote more personal time to consuming their profits). Absenteeism (and the resulting commission system) occurred in the English and not in the French islands, and more in connection with sugar than with tobacco, precisely because of the higher profitability of the English zones and of sugar.[205]

The question of why Virginia tobacco planters reverted is thus partially answered. Tobacco planters could not as easily be absentee entrepreneurs because of the emergence of the French monopsonistic buyer. French market purchasers sought large-scale suppliers, and Scottish firms on the west coast of Scotland offered themselves in this role. Although their sailing distance to French ports was no greater, they had the advantage (over other British merchants groups) of nearness to Virginia and lower labor costs (because of Glasgow's semiperipheral status). Scottish firms, having a large market to supply, sent their agents to the Chesapeake Valley, bypassing the large planters who had commission agents in London and reaching the smaller interior farmer with credit that could be repaid in kind.[206] Thus the balance of strength shifted back in this case to the buyer's end of the exchange. Finally, to answer the question about the shift of the locus of entrepreneurial risk and profit, we must look at the meaning of debt. Since the fall of sugar prices was one of the precipitants of this shift, Pares

[204] See K. G. Davies (1952b) and Pares (1960, 33–34). Pares then adds: "But there is one grave objection to this explanation: it was not only the absentee planter, but nearly every resident planter too, who, in the English colonies, consigned his sugars home on his own account." I do not see the force of this objection. Once the model was created, smaller owners jumped on the bandwagon and found London factors willing to have their business.

[205] Land points out that Chesapeake tobacco did not provide the fortunes of West Indian sugar. "Consequently the Chesapeake planters did not go 'back home' to dazzle the populace with their wealth. Their returns derived in the first instance from tobacco production, which afforded a compe-

tence, and secondarily from enterprise, which gave greater rewards" (1965, 647). In other words, they couldn't afford to "specialize"; they had to remain overseers. J. R. Ward however is skeptical that there was significant differences of profitability in the English versus the French islands in the *eighteenth* century (see 1978, 208).

[206] See J. M. Price: "If a [Glasgow] merchant wanted more tobacco, he had only to expand his credit to planters and the extra tobacco would flow in at the harvest. Thus, Scottish and other credit created its own tobacco supply much more efficiently than did the price mechanism. And behind Scots credit was the French buyer" (1964, 509).

suggests that "the position of entrepreneur was not a proud and profitable one which the planter had seized from the merchant, but a humble and unrewarding one into which the merchant had shoved him." However, the role was clearly *not* a humble and unrewarding one, as Pares himself notes: "The absentee sugar planters were, with the East India Nabobs, the most conspicuous rich men of their time."[207]

Let us put this fact together with a second one, the growing indebtedness of the English planter throughout the eighteenth century, increasingly to English merchants. Does this not represent a shift once again, now against the planter toward the merchant? Perhaps, but there is another way to interpret the financial arrangements. The usefulness of this structure of indebtedness to factors worked only while the sugar industry flourished. Clearly, however, absentee planters were beginning to live beyond their current income. "Nearly every great debt . . . started as a debt or account-current and ended as a mortgage. . . . In the end, . . . many West India estates proved to be worth less than the amount of their mortgages."[208] We know that sugar (and tobacco) exhaust themselves. After an initial stage of merchant-aided enterprise and a second stage of land concentration and planter domination of the realization of profit, was there not a third stage in which plantations, given their inevitable decline, were bled by absentee owners who failed to reproduce capital at the same level? To be sure, these owners shared these super profits with their factors; but such an arrangement is an instance not of the dominance of merchants in a preindustrial era, but of the form of profit in the period *following* that of maximum productivity and relative efficiency.[209]

We must now turn to the other half of this equation: the supply of labor that created increased efficiency of production. That sugar and slavery were "intimately linked"[210] is virtually a truism. The fact is, however, that the first attempts to grow sugar and tobacco in the Caribbean were almost always based on using indentured labor, not slaves. It was only toward the end of the seventeenth century that slaves became the characteristic labor force of the islands, and only in the early eighteenth century can this be said to have become the case for the southern mainland colonies of North America.[211] The degree of juridical difference between the two statuses is a matter

---

[207] Pares (1960, 35, 38).

[208] Pares (1960, 48–49).

[209] Thus when Sheridan says "it is evident that the plantation economy of Jamaica came to be directed by a group of London merchants and absentee planters, and that the great family fortunes were much more nearly allied to commerce and finance than they were to tropical agriculture" (1965, 309–310), he is right for the later period; but he fails to take into account that this *later* stage is only possible because of the earlier period of competitive efficiency of production.

[210] Masefield (1967, 290).

[211] See Davis (1973b, 134). Breen, however, argues that the turning point for Virginia was 1680, when "English companies developed the capacity to ship Negroes directly from Africa to the mainland colonies" (1973, 14). He also points out that in 1682 England passed new regulations for the recruitment of indentured servants requiring that all contracts have the signature of a magistrate in England and that contracts for children under 14 have parental consent.

of verbal jousting between scholars who emphasize that indentured service
was temporary *slavery,* such as Ralph Davis,[212] and those who remind us that
it was only *temporary* slavery, such as K. G. Davies.[213] The real issue is an
economic one. What were the long-term cost advantages and disadvantages
of each? It is easy to see why early Caribbean entrepreneurs would have
preferred indentured labor to slaves. The first and probably determining
reason was the much lower initial capital outlay. At the time, an indentured
servant had to be advanced from about 5 to 10 pounds for passage, whereas
an African slave cost 20 to 25.[214] Even if the subsequent expenditure for
food and clothing were less for a slave, and even if the outlay for the
indentured laborer were amortized over a period of only three or four years,
there was still the issue of initial capital liquidity.

Of course, there had to be a supply available. Who in fact came to the
Western Hemisphere as indentured laborers (*engagés*)? Generally speaking,
these persons were quite young, most often adolescents, children of wage
laborers or poorer middle strata. To the extent that they were not pressed
into service, what attracted them to the rigors of uncertain climes and
certain hard work was the possibility of upward social mobility via a grant of
land following their service. It is sometimes suggested that they were more
skilled than African slaves; but this is doubtful, considering their age and
experience. Indeed, one could make a case for the opposite position. It
would take several years to train a worker to be efficient, and just when
indentured laborers had "acquired some skill,"[215] they would leave their
employers. African slaves, on the other hand, would remain once they
were trained. Is this not what is at issue when we say that the decision of
Barbados to utilize slave labor is explained by the search for "a more settled,
more dependable work force?"[216]

What was it that shifted the balance of factors from favoring the use of
indentured labor? In the first place, "good unappropriated land," on which
the arrangement was based, gave out[217] because of the combination of land
turnover, due to soil exhaustion, and increasing land concentration. Slavery
thus came to sugar plantations earlier than to tobacco plantations and came
to the West Indies rather than to southern mainland North America.[218] If
an indentured laborer could not look forward to his reward, why would he
suffer the brutal service on the plantation? When the decline in labor supply
was matched by a simultaneous rise in demand, slavery was sure to be

[212] Davis (1973b, 130, italics added).

[213] See K. G. Davies (1974, 107).

[214] See Pares (1960, 19). See also Phelan: "Negro
slaves involved a large capital investment" (1959,
191).

[215] Pares (1960, 19).

[216] Dunn (1972, 72). Debien cites the fact that the
engagés were "a floating population" to explain the
shift in the French Antilles (1942, 74).

[217] Davis (1973b, 131). The fact that land did not

give out is exactly the reason that indentured labor
survived in French Canada and not in the French
Antilles. See Dermigny (1950, 236).

[218] Pares suggests at one point that tobacco was "a
free man's crop," because it required "nicety of
judgment" and therefore "could not so easily be en-
trusted to slaves working by routine"; but then he
admits that "the experience of Virginia shows that
tobacco could be grown on slave plantations too"
(1960, 21).

adopted. Even when it wasn't "necessarily the cheapest or most efficient mode of operating sugar plantations, . . . it was *the only one available* when white servants could no longer be attracted."[219] It is no accident then that the *substitution* of slaves is regularly associated with *boom* periods.[220] The reasons that slaves replaced European indentured servants as the labor force are relatively straightforward. But why Africans? Why not Indians as slaves? And why was the system of Indian (and mestizo) debt peonage not utilized in the extended Caribbean as it was in much of Hispanic America?

In fact, Indians *were* used as slaves in the beginning, but it is widely reported that they "died fast in captivity,"[221] showing "an inability to adapt . . . to the living conditions of sugar mills."[222] They were also used at first as slaves in mines in Chile,[223] but they were replaced after 1589 by African slaves, which Mellafe says was "one of the fundamental factors that permitted the survival of the [Spanish settlement] in Chile."[224] In areas where African slaves were used instead of Indian labor, either the Indian peoples had been primarily hunters and gatherers (as in the Lesser Antilles) or the agriculture had not yet developed clear class structures (such as the Arawak, or Taino, in the Greater Antilles). It was such peoples who were "inadapted" to disciplined labor and who "died out."[225] However, where redistributive modes of production had existed, the Indian populations stratified by class and lower strata were already producing a surplus that

---

[219] Davis (1973b, 133, italics added). Allen notes that there were ten popular and servant revolts or revolt plots in Virginia between the 1667 Servant Plots and the tobacco riots of 1682, the decisive one being Bacon's Rebellion in April, 1676. He argues that the planters saw a need to divide the working class by giving the white workers a different status. Hence, "the shift to African labor was precipitate after 1685" (1975, 49). Menard points out that "prices for indentured labor began to rise in the late 1670's" (1978, 24). The increased demand for slaves led to higher prices circa 1700, and to reduce prices, there followed "an increase in the proportion of younger slaves and females in total shipments" (Galenson, 1979, 247).

[220] See Dunn (1972, 59) on the effect of the sugar boom between 1640 and 1660 and Farnie (1962, 208) on the effect of the tobacco boom between 1680 and 1700. Curtin suggests a third factor in addition to the decline in the supply of European labor and the rise in demand for labor: differences in the rates of susceptibility to disease. Africans had "the enormous advantage of coming from a disease environment where both tropical diseases and a wide range of common Afro-Eurasian diseases were present" (1971, 253). He suggests that the death rate ratio of European to African laborers in the Caribbean was 3 : 1. In an earlier article, he had said

it was 4 : 1, calculating that if we assumed "the cost of maintaining [slaves and indentured servants] was about the same, the slave was preferable at anything up to three times the price of the European" (1968, 207).

[221] Boxer (1952, 223).

[222] Viana (1940, 11). In fact, of course, Africans showed the same "inability" and also died. Schwartz reminds us of the following: the Brazilian adjective describing the conditions of slaves in the period of the sugar boom (1570–1670) was "hellish"; four hours of sleep during the harvest period was the norm; and "the prevailing theory of slave management was to extract as much labor at as little cost as possible" (1970, 316).

[223] See Romano (1970, 133).

[224] Mellafe (1959, 252–253).

[225] Speaking of the situation in Hispaniola, Dupuy says: "The social formation and organization of production of the Arawaks was not one characterized by the exploitation and subjugation of one class by another. Production relations in Arawak society were characterized by the predominance of use values and total absence of exchange values, i.e., commodity production. . . . It was therefore better to die starving in the mountains rather than to die in bondage to foreign colonialists" (1976, 22).

was appropriated hierarchically. They could therefore be pressed with relative success into continuing this in a modified form on behalf of European
expropriators, especially if their previous overlords cooperated—hence the
repartimiento, the *mita,* and the eventual evolution of debt peonage, especially in New Spain, Guatemala, and Peru.[226]

If African slaves replaced Indian labor only where Indians could not be
successfully pressed into one version or another of coerced labor, then it
must be that slavery was a *pis aller;* and the only possible explanation is that
it *cost less* to use coerced cash-crop labor—whether in agriculture, mining, or
industry—than to use slaves.[227] How is it that labor that received "wages"
for only part of their work, such as coerced cash-crop labor, cost less than
labor that was only remunerated in kind, and not generously at that? If it
were only the difference in initial outlay on the part of the employer, this
might have been amortized over time; but it was also that the coerced
cash-crop workers and their cousins produced part of their "wages" in the
form of food crops on land outside the control of the employer, which were
thereupon deducted from the labor costs of the employer. The total of the
recurrent cost of labor was *higher* if one used slave labor than if one used
coerced cash-crop labor.[228]

---

[226] See Romano (1970, 130). Brading and Cross
point out that forced labor survived longer in the
mines of Peru (until 1812) than it did in the mines
of Mexico, where the Indian population declined
catastrophically. In consequence, by the eighteenth
century, Mexican mine workers came to be paid relatively high wages and were recruited from mestizos, mulattos, and acculturated Indians. "The reasons for this divergence are not entirely clear, . . .
but . . . it is tempting to locate such causes in the
disparate development of the two Indian peoples
and the different location of the principal sites responsive to sedentary populations" (1972, 557).
Bakewell claims that already in the seventeenth century, "the central relationship . . . between
Spaniard and Indian in Zacatecas was . . . one of
employer and employee" (1976, 217). By contrast,
Céspedes speaks of the "docile indigenous population of Peru" (1947, 39).

[227] Oberem asserts precisely this in comparing the
cost of using *conciertos,* or indebted workers, with the
cost of using African slaves in Ecuador. He defines
conciertos as "quasi slaves," since they could even be
"bought" (1967, 767–770).

[228] It is for this reason that I cannot agree with D.
Hall who sees slaves as "capital equipment" and says
that therefore one cannot compare the costs of slave
labor and free labor since it is really a matter of
substituting labor and capital costs (1962, 309). If it

were only that, it would have been irrational, as
Land in fact argues, for Virginia tobacco planters to
use slaves. Land says they had a "decided preference" in the seventeenth and eighteenth centuries
for enlarging production via additional slave labor
rather than via technological improvements,
thereby "inhibit[ing] technological change" (1969,
75, 79). This goes along with W. Barrett's observation about sugar plantations in the British West Indies: "there is no indication . . . that economies of
scale were practiced" (1965, 167).

This leaves, however, the preference itself unex-
plained, therefore "cultural", and therefore economically irrational. This strikes me as a failure to
analyze. In one sense, all labor costs are capital costs.
It is always a choice about the optimal combination
of machinery (dead labor) and living labor. We want
to know when it is optimal and politically possible
in the short run to use slave labor as an alternative to
(*a*) wage labor, (*b*) coerced cash-crop labor, (*c*) additional machinery. The answer is complicated still
further when we remember that slaves were able in
many areas to participate as sellers in the money
economy and to accumulate capital. As Schwartz
asks (see 1974, 628–629), how else could Brazilian
slaves pay for their own manumission? Mintz points
out that in Jamaica "by the early eighteenth century
slaves were actively selling and buying their own
produce in the market places" (1964, 251).

Thus it was that in the extended Caribbean, the new periphery of the period from 1600 to 1750, the basic form[229] in which proletarian labor was organized was slavery rather than wage labor, tenantry, or coerced cash-crop labor. Slavery, given the political conditions of the epoch, was economically optimal for the bourgeois producers who shaped, via the legal system as well as the market, the basic relations of production in the region.

[229] Basic form does not mean only form. The whole thrust of Schwartz's article on the *lavradores de cana* in Brazil's sugar areas is that their tenancy arrangements, and even proprietorship, represented for large landowners an alternative form of exploiting labor, the utility of which varied according to economic conditions. "The use of cane growers . . . in the period of economic expansion [was] a method for reducing capital costs and perhaps for providing intensive supervision of engenho property" (1973, 193–194).

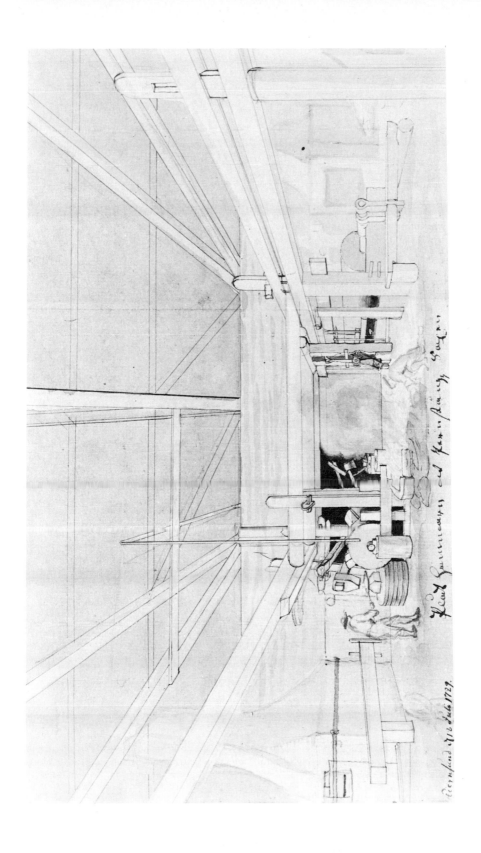

Ellenfurd d. 16 Juli 1727.

Plan Quvirirarijs ad Hammstuirij Bergen

5

SEMIPERIPHERIES AT THE CROSSROADS

Figure 6: Drawing of a Swedish forge, by Carl Johan Cronstadt (1709–1779), who studied mechanics and geometry as a background for architecture and became the most famous Swedish architect of his time.

One constant element in a capitalist world-economy is the hierarchical (and spatially distributed) division of labor. However, a second constant element is the shifting location of economic activity and consequently of particular geographic zones in the world-system. From the point of view of state-machineries, regular, but not continuous, alterations in the relative economic strength of localities, regions, and states can be viewed (and indeed most often are viewed) as a sort of upward or downward "mobility" of the state as an entity, a movement measured in relation to other states within the framework of the interstate system. In the twentieth century, one talks of the "development" of states. In the seventeenth century, one talked of the "wealth" of the kingdom, but the people of the seventeenth century often saw more clearly than we do today that the measurement was ordinal and not cardinal, at least within the constraints of the modern world-system. Alterations of status occur particularly in moments of overall downturn or stagnation; and for those in the middle of the hierarchical continuum, the semiperiphery, movement is primarily effected and affected by state action. Semiperipheral states are the ones that usually decline and ascend.

This sounds voluntaristic, and to some degree it is. Intelligent state policies have much to do with what happens. But two caveats must immediately be added. First, state policies are not prime movers but intervening processes. Secondly, not every state machinery can utilize any given set of policies with the same expectation of happy result. Indeed, quite the contrary. Many may try, but only a few succeed in significantly transforming the rank of their state in the world division of labor. This is because the very success of one eliminates opportunities and alternatives for others. In the seventeenth century, there were many semiperipheral areas which lost ground—Spain, Portugal, the old dorsal spine of Europe (from Flanders through the western and southern Germanies to northern Italy); but there were a few areas that gained ground: notably Sweden, Brandenburg-Prussia, and the "northern" colonies of British North America (New England and the Middle Atlantic colonies). The former set underwent many of the same processes we have already described for peripheral areas, although for various reasons they retained important structural differences from these areas. The latter set had only just begun their struggle to become part of the core areas of the world-economy in this epoch. For these latter entities, it was an achievement even to start on this path, let alone to be able to turn the overall difficulties of the world-economy to their own profit rather than suffer still more distancing from core areas, as happened to most peripheral and semiperipheral areas.

In this regard, the "decline" of Spain was the most spectacular phenomenon of the seventeenth century—visible even to the men of the time. As we have previously seen, the causes lay deep in Spain's economic and political

179

structures, and the relative weakness was already there to a considerable extent in the sixteenth century.[1] These weaknesses had been partially hidden by Spain's military power and sheer wealth in bullion; but the economic reversals of the world-economy as a whole tore the covering from the Spanish facade and exposed the weaknesses to the Spanish themselves as well as to the world. If we wish a date, perhaps 1596, the time of the second bankruptcy of Philip II, will do as well as any. This bankruptcy "meant more than the end of northern Castile's financial preeminence: it meant also the end of Philip II's imperial dreams."[2] The traditional historiographic picture of seventeenth-century Spain was one of economic decadence. For Earl Hamilton, this picture was an exaggeration, but nonetheless, he adds, the seventeenth century represented "one of the lowest ebbs in the economic annals of Spain."[3] What do we know of agricultural production in Spain during this period? Not as much as we might.[4] The seventeenth century became a period of "uncultivated and unirrigated fields [and] acute scarcity of livestock."[5] As of the first third of the seventeenth century, there was much contemporary discussion regarding the overuse of land, of annual planting instead of triennial rotation and the consequent exhaustion of the land. The coarser grains—millet, sorghum, and barley—as well as maize were substituted for wheat,[6] which reminds us of developments in the peripheral areas. The expansion of wine production at the expense of cereals, as in southern France, was so widespread that people began bartering wine for wheat.[7]

[1] See Wallerstein (1974, chap. 5, *passim*) for a discussion of sixteenth-century Spanish structures. For the self-perception of seventeenth-century Spanish thinkers of their *decadencia,* see Elliott (1977).

[2] Elliott (1966, 283). Ruiz Martín dates the "century of decadence" as going from 1586 to 1680 or 1690 (1970, 43). But it sometimes takes further events and another 50 years to persuade the participants of the realities. "The defeat of the Spanish infantry at Rocroi on 19 May 1643 seemed to symbolize the downfall of the military system which had sustained Spanish power for so long. The country now lacked both the armies and the leaders to turn the new international situation to account" (p. 345). For Stradling, it wasn't until 1668 that "a nadir of humiliation was reached with the formal concession of Portuguese independence. The world empire of Philip II thus ceased to exist" (1979, 182). By the end of the seventeenth century, says G. Desdevises de Dezert, "Spanish military might was no more than a memory" (1927, 354). See also E. J. Hamilton (1943, 192).

[3] E. J. Hamilton (1935, 111). Similarly, José Gentil da Silva argues that there was a "decline," although this might be "too simple" an expression (1965, 175–179). Two recent articles challenge this tradition from opposite points of view. For Kamen, the

seventeenth century was not a decline since Spain had been "dependent" since the fifteenth century and therefore "it is difficult to see how so undeveloped a country could have 'declined' before ever becoming rich" (1978, 35, 41). For Stradling, "Spanish power and power-systems [survived] into the 1660s," and at least until then "no enemy, or combination of enemies was sufficiently strong and organized to administer . . . the death-blow" (1979, 167, 171). Stradling is here repeating Henri Hauser's dating of the "Spanish preponderance"— 1560–1660.

[4] See J. H. Elliott's complaint on this subject, written in 1961 and cited and echoed by Weisser (1973, 615).

[5] E. J. Hamilton (1935, 111). Production curves that have been developed for Segovia "tend to confirm the . . . interpretations of the seventeenth century as the century of 'decadence' or 'stagnation'" (Anes and Le Flem, 1965, 16).

[6] See da Silva (1965, 156–158); see also Anes and Le Flem (1965, 18–19) on the relative increase of rye and oats production and the overuse of the land through exhaustion of the supply of humus and manure. They also point out that the cultivation of rye requires less manpower.

[7] da Silva (1965, 158–160).

Along with a shift in crops came a decline in the quantity of exports. In general, "as an exporter of raw materials, Spain's performance [in the seventeenth century] was not impressive."[8] However, Spain in the sixteenth century had not been a peripheral country, restricted to the export of raw materials. It had been a center of manufactures, and the decline was even more striking in this sector. Spain declined most severely in the textile industry. Toledo, the center of Spanish silk and linen production, was virtually wiped out in the 20 years from 1600 to 1620.[9] So were Segovia and Cuenca. It was not only the textile industry that declined but the metallurgical industries and shipbuilding as well. In all three of these "growth industries" of early modern Europe, Spain "lost her export markets, [and] also lost a large part of her domestic and colonial markets; she lost them to the English, the French, and the Dutch."[10] Thus, in this era of stagnation, Spain suffered not only the agricultural involution of peripheral areas but also deindustrialization. The consequences were twofold: on the one hand, there was increased polarization and regional conflict within Spain; on the other hand, Spain had to spend her colonial patrimony to survive.

Already in the sixteenth century, Spain had witnessed a widening gap between Castile and the other regions of Spain. "Everything conspired to give Castile an overwhelming, and increasing, predominance."[11] The economic difficulties in general, plus the expenditures required by Spain's heavy involvement in the Thirty Years' War, led to a steady increase in taxation. To be sure, Castile bore the burden as well as the rest of Spain, perhaps even more so; but as Jaime Vicens Vives notes, Castile had "colossal compensations . . . . : exploitation of the American continent; cultural and political primacy within the heart of Spain."[12] Probably the gap was growing wider still. In any case, Catalonia and Portugal, the two principal regions that had maintained relative economic parity with Castile up to the beginning of the seventeenth century, felt the breadth of new economic pressures on behalf of Castile.[13] Thus, when the government, in the person

[8] Lynch (1969, 153).

[9] See Weisser, who wishes to explain this not in E. J. Hamilton's terms of "the importance of *external* factors (i.e., treasure)," but in terms of "internal economic conditions in Castile." His three internal factors, however, turn out to be: one, a "lack of balance [between] the competing demands of subsistence versus industrial production," which began circa 1575 and which is in turn explained by "the shrinkage of Mesta herds and the rupture of trade with the North [which] forced Toledo to rely more heavily upon industrial strength in the tierra"; two, "the appearance of foreign goods, which . . . undersold locally produced commodities in wholesale quantities"; and three, the growth of Madrid, which drew population from Toledo, whose depopulation was the result of "the imperial ambitions of the Crown" (1973, 614–615, 637–

640). Weisser also attributes the decline of urban population to the expulsion of the Moriscos (p. 632), the factor cited as well by Warden (1864, 261) in accounting for the near extinction of linen manufactures in Toledo—from 50 factories in 1550 to 13 in 1665.

[10] Lynch (1969, 152, and see 149–151).

[11] Elliott (1963, 11). "The medieval divisions—has this been sufficiently stressed?—did not weaken as one might have expected, but became more accentuated across the centuries" (Vilar, 1962b, **I**, 191).

[12] Vicens Vives (1970, 107).

[13] "In spite of the success [as of 1637] of the Conde Duque's [that is, Olivares's] efforts to squeeze more money from Castile, he was as well aware as anyone that there was bound to come a moment when Castile would be squeezed dry. This meant that the Union of Arms must be made effective, and

of Olivares, wanted more money, "it was quite logical for [the Catalans] to fortify themselves, distrustfully, behind the solid ramparts of Ferdinand's autonomous legislation"[14]—and not only the Catalans. There had been antifiscal risings in Oporto in 1628 and in Santarém in 1629 and the "Salt Mutiny" in Basque country in 1632, the primary cause of which was new taxes—"the last drop of water which caused the patience of the people, already exhausted from other forms of exploitation, to overflow."[15] What was particular to Catalonia was not that popular resentments "burst suddenly and explosively to life,"[16] but that this popular resentment combined with the "disenchantment of the bourgeoisie," and the ambivalence of the "governing classes of Catalonia."[17] These combined sources of discontent were what made the Revolt of the Catalans so long and so threatening.[18]

It was precisely at this moment of reorientation of the European world-economy from an era of expansion and inflation to one of stagnation that Portugal became legally part of Spain—in the Iberian Union, or what the Portuguese would later call the Sixty Years' Captivity. A dynastic gap in succession plus a military defeat of the Portuguese by the Moroccans in 1578 at Alcazar-el-Kebir permitted the King of Spain to enter Portugal with his army and become the King of Portugal in 1580. Opposition had been weak because the Union had some clear advantages to the Portuguese. One was the abolition of customs frontiers on the peninsula, giving Portugal duty-free access to Spanish wheat.[19] A second was that the Union gave the Portuguese bourgeoisie access to the Spanish empire, which in 1580 "had reached its zenith and strongly appealed to the Portuguese initiatives, accustomed as they were to different cultures and odd methods of trading, eager to expand their markets everywhere, well aware of the immense

in particular that Catalonia and Portugal, which were *allegedly* the two wealthiest States in the peninsula, must be induced to play a part commensurate with their *presumed* resources. Both of these States seemed to Olivares dangerously 'separated' from the rest of the Monarchy" (Elliott, 1966, 333, italics added).

[14] Vicens Vives (1970, 107). See also Pierre Vilar: "the central government, in great financial distress, fixed its eye upon Catalonian resources, which the local councils ardently defended against levies" (1962b, I, 627).

[15] Emiliano Fernández de Pinedo cites this phrase of Porchnev about France as being precisely applicable to Vizcaya at this time (1974, 76).

[16] Elliott (1963, 463), who identifies these popular resentments as "the hatred of lesser peasantry and landless for the wealthy peasant and the noble; the bitterness of the rural unemployed; the desire for revenge of the bandit element against those who had repressed it; the old feuds of town against country, of the poorer citizens against the municipal

oligarchs" (pp. 462–463).

[17] Elliott (1963, 127, 465).

[18] "The war would bring upon the principality the worst evils from which the domains of Castile had been suffering since 1600: enormous public expenses, monetary inflation, paralysis of production, depopulation resulting from a terrible epidemic, and finally, as a conclusion of the international struggle, loss of part of the Catalan lands, including the very rich plains of Roussillon" (Vilar, 1962b, I, 633). Those who suffered most were the small independent peasants. See Vilar (1962a, 80–81). Note again the parallel with peripheral countries. This, of course, sharpened the revolt and made it take on "social overtones which threatened to subject the aristocracy to the rule of the mob" (Elliott, 1966, 349). For this reason, the unity of Catalonia disintegrated and the Catalans were brought back into the Spanish fold by 1652.

[19] A. H. de Oliveira Marques calls this abolition of customs duties "a long-cherished dream, particularly among the Portuguese" (1976, I, 308).

possibilities such ties offered them."[20] From the Spanish point of view, the Union had the economic advantage of allowing access to new financial networks at the moment of an increasingly greater financial squeeze on the Castilian state administration. Portuguese bankers were now able to enter the Castilian financial circuit—officially after 1606 but unofficially before that.

The Portuguese were favored by Olivares, who was seeking to solve the financial problems of the monarchy. Portuguese bankers were linked to the Amsterdam exchange and may have been using Dutch funds.[21] (They were in fact almost all *marranos,* that is, Jewish *conversos.*)[22] They were, further-more, merchant-bankers,[23] and for them access to Spain was access as well to Hispanic America—Buenos Aires, Rio de la Plata, Terraferma, the Antil-les.[24] In addition, the Portuguese could profit from their flourishing Brazi-lian sugar colony[25] with the protection of the Spanish flotillas.[26] Thus, partly through the advantages of the Union, the Portuguese protected themselves against the first chill winds of the seventeenth century; but it could not last. On the one side, the Spanish began to react against this Portuguese advan-tage,[27] which easily took the cover of anti-Jewish xenophobia.[28] On the other side, the Portuguese also came to be unhappy, since the Spanish were

[20] Marques (1976, **I,** 308). The Portuguese took ample advantage. Israel estimates that by 1640 they were 6% of the population of New Spain, and that there were similar groups throughout the Spanish Indies. He speaks of "a truly massive exodus from Portugal . . . [which] reflected the drift of popula-tion from the Portuguese countryside and small towns and the flight of Portuguese entrepreneurs from a depressed Portugal, a declining Spain, and a stricken Italy" (1974b, 32).

[21] See Castillo's discussion (1964, especially pp. 311–314).

[22] This was also true in other non-Castilian areas of Iberia: "In the marginal zones of the Iberian peninsula [Portugal, the coastal areas of Catalonia, Valencia], . . . there was a high correlation between the status of bourgeois and that of 'converso'" (Chaunu, 1963a, 82). Mauro makes the same point: "Portugal was not the only country, in the seven-teenth century, to have a bourgeoisie and a group of new Christians. But what distinguished it from the others was the *de facto* confusion of the two statuses" (1970, 34).

[23] See Mauro's description of these merchant-bankers: "There are no technical grounds to distin-guish among them. Wholesale, semiwholesale, re-tail? They all do all. Long-distance trade, national trade, local trade? They all partake in each more or less. Commodity trade, trade in money? They are inseparable" (1961c, 20).

[24] See Huguette and Pierre Chaunu (1954, 53). Revah points out that in these regions, "the proper

noun, *Portuguese,* became synonomous with 'new-Christian' and, often, with 'crypto-Jew'" (1959–1960, 37; cf. p. 48, n. 4). See, however, Israel's care-ful distinction among the *judaizantes,* the effectively assimilated *Cristãos novos,* and an in-between group, the *conversos,* "who were non-judaizing but whose Jewishness nevertheless impinged strongly on their careers (1974b, 24 and *passim,* 19–32).

[25] Mauro reminds us "not to confuse the fate of the Portuguese and Spanish empires [toward the end of] the sixteenth century, for Brazil and its enormous sugar development make a difference, and not a small one" (1959, 183).

[26] Huguette and Pierre Chaunu (1954, 52).

[27] See the suggestion by J. Elliott in "Seven-teenth-Century Revolutions" (1958, 68). Disney, in explaining why Portuguese entrepreneurs were unwilling to invest in the Portuguese East India Company (founded in 1628) adduces one fac-tor: "Some Portuguese saw in it an insidious attempt by Madrid to circumvent the administrative inde-pendence that had been granted to Portugal by Philip II in 1580" (1977, 252).

[28] Huguette and Pierre Chaunu (1954, 54), who note that the Jews were made the target and speak of "these edicts of Nantes which one accords in a phase A to revoke in a phase B." See also Chaunu (1963d). Some of these new Christians simply moved to Hamburg, where they played an impor-tant role in its commercial expansion in the eighteenth century. See Kellenbenz (1958).

increasingly less able to offer them the protection they needed. The Dutch occupation of Brazil was attributed by the Portuguese in part to the continuing Dutch–Spanish conflict.[29] In any case, the Luso–Atlantic trade, which had in the period from 1600 to 1630 maintained itself far better than the Seville–Atlantic trade, began to turn down.[30] These difficulties in Brazil were compounded by the loss of the West African maritime gold trade to the English and Dutch as of 1638.[31]

The Portuguese rose up in 1640, at the same time as the Catalans but without the internal class divisions of the latter, which "made it easier for [the Portuguese bourgeoisie] to accept the transition from the Spanish connection to independence."[32] Portugal reclaimed its independence and started down the road to the English connection. It lost its trade empire in Asia to the Dutch in the beginning of the seventeenth century, says Boxer, because the latter "were vastly superior in actual and potential strength to the impoverished Kingdom of Portugal."[33] As we have seen, it had found some compensation in union with Spain; however, the squeeze of the downturn of the European world-economy was eliminating even the compensation. For Braudel, "the big question is: was not Portugal for Spain the companion of good times, economically speaking?"[34] While Spain was thus tearing itself apart to little material profit, it was simultaneously suffering the beginning of the bleeding of the colonies. First of all, there was the great recession of American traffic with Spain, which Chaunu dates from 1622 to 1680.[35] Secondly, there was the development of contraband as a major facet of European-American exchanges, first by the Dutch,[36] then by

[29] Boxer gives the occupation as "one of the chief reasons why [the Portuguese] rebelled against the Spanish Crown in 1640," but he notes that "they were disappointed in the hope that the Dutch would cease their aggression against the Portuguese *conquistas* as soon as these and the mother-country severed their connection with Spain. On the contrary . . ." (1961, 52).

[30] See Chaunu (1961, 1194). Mauro speaks of the "splendor" of the Portuguese Atlantic economy up to 1670 (1960, 513); but Chaunu is more prudent: "In comparison to the Seville sector, where the reversal of the secular trend at the beginning of the seventeenth century is more visible than anywhere else, the Brazilian Atlantic is made up of shadows and of nuances." He also speaks of a "late turning-point, in the late 1630s, perhaps 1650; a slowdown of growth rather than a crash." May not the Portuguese revolt explain the ability of Brazil to have recovered at least until 1670? Conversely, as Elliott argues, the recovery was "the salvation of Portugal," in that it "helped to stimulate foreign [English in particular] interest in its survival as an independent state" (1966, 351).

[31] See Godinho (1950a, 34).

[32] Elliott (1963, 543).

[33] Boxer (1961, 53).

[34] Braudel (1956, 196).

[35] Chaunu (1959, **VIII**, 2*bis*, 1568). See also Helmer: "Beginning in 1630, there are numerous bankruptcies among the *cargadoras de Indias*" (1967, 405). Chaunu notes, "without trying to decide the delicate issue of causality," that this period correlates with the inflation of *billón* and remarks: "Perhaps a mere coincidence? A disturbing coincidence, nonetheless" (1959, **VIII**, 2*bis*, 1568–1569).

[36] Indeed, Jaime Vicens Vives lectures retrospectively to the Spanish government of the time: "Instead of involving himself in the troublesome European conflicts, where the full power of France and Holland awaited him, Olivares should have stanched the first wounds of empire inflicted by the Dutch in the Caribbean Sea, and should have placed the American colonies on a war footing. Instead, with the gold he had collected in Andalusia to carry out that sound policy, he paid for the military operations of the Thirty Years' War. The result was that the future of Spanish America was liquidated in Europe" (1970, 106).

the English and French.[37] Gradually, through the seventeenth century, it came to be the case that the direct relations of the core states with Hispanic America "supplied the largest part of the basic needs of the latter via the route of contraband."[38]

Thus over the seventeenth century Spain came to be at best a rather passive conveyor belt between the core countries and Spain's colonies. Spain imported textiles and dried Newfoundland fish from core countries, consuming them at home and, when not bypassed entirely by the contraband trade, passing them on to the colonies. Spain paid partly in exports of raw materials from the peninsula, in dyes from the colonies and, above all, in American bullion—"the essential attraction of the trade with Old Spain."[39] The constant wars—with the United Provinces, France, Catalonia, Portugal—in a time of financial squeeze led to successive inflationary coinages of vellon, especially acute after 1650. This resulted by the 1680s in "Castile's total administrative and economic collapse."[40] In such circumstances, the Spanish monarchy was scarcely in a position to resist the encroachments and depradations of the core powers in the Americas or of even the steady expansion of the sale of manufactures from northwest Europe in Spain itself.[41] Rambert summarizes: "At the end of the seventeenth century, Spain occupied a special place in the world economy: it was a vast and virtually unexploited market upon which converged all the covetous European powers. . . . [Spain] lived in a narrow dependence [on the more advanced countries]."[42]

Portugal faced, more or less, the same situation. From the perspective of English textiles in the Restoration period, both Portugal and Spain "opened up prospects of vast overseas markets, though English merchants could only trade with South America through intermediaries."[43] In fact, the successive Anglo-Portuguese Treaties of 1642, 1654, and 1661 involved England even more heavily in Brazil than in Spanish America.[44] English insertion into Portuguese triangular trade (making it quadrangular) would make Portugal "more and more peripherical."[45] When the temporary economic uplift

[37] Vignols points out that, though the transatlantic contraband varied in intensity at different moments, it was always greater than inter-European contraband and contraband internal to any European country (1925, 240).

[38] Larraz (1943, 98). Trade in contraband was aided and abetted by corrupt Spanish officials and Spanish colonists. See Pantaleão (1946, 127–129, 235–236).

[39] See McLachlan (1940, 13); see also Christelow (1941, 516).

[40] Elliott (1966, 360), who says Castile's collapse "was accompanied by the paralysis of its cultural and intellectual life" (p. 361). See also Larraz (1943, 96). Kamen, in recounting the crisis between 1677 and 1686, calls the inflation of vellon coinage "little short of catastrophic" (1964, 75). A further reflec-

tion of the difficulties was the "ever-growing intensity throughout the seventeenth century" of banditry, particularly in Valencia (Kamen, 1974, 654).

[41] Delumeau speaks of this trade as "the great providence of France" (1966, 100). Pantaleão says that "the commerce with the Spanish empire interested the entire British empire" (1946, 272).

[42] Rambert (1959, 269).

[43] Francis (1966, 187).

[44] See Pantaleão (1946, 15). Furthermore, the Treaty of 1661, which registered the bethrothal of Catherine of Bragança and Charles II, ceded Bombay and Tangiers to England as Catherine's dowry. Boxer explains this in terms of Portugal's "seeking the protection of an English alliance" against the Dutch (1961, 52).

[45] Sideri (1970, 21).

that began circa 1650 in Europe generally and in Portugal in particular came to an end in 1670,[46] Portugal made a valiant effort to extricate itself from this middleman, conveyor-belt position by adopting the universal remedy of the seventeenth century—mercantilism—the avowed policy of the Marquis of Fronteira and the Duke of Ericeira, Secretaries of State from 1675 to 1690. The Portuguese consciously thought of this as an imitation of Colbert's policies. They imported French technicians to help them build industries that could compete with English and French industries[47] and created a merchant company for African slave trade to try to get Spanish business. At one point, they raised the nominal value of currency by 20%, hoping to attract bullion, especially from Spain.[48]

It was also as a result of this crisis of the 1670s that Portugal renewed the search for bullion in Brazil,[49] although it would not be until 1693–1695 that a significant amount of gold was in fact discovered.[50] The crisis led in addition to a search for new export markets, and it was just at this time that a wide export market opened for madeira wine. The English discovered that "madeira was the best wine for keeping and for carrying to a hot climate.[51] The English thought so well of it, in fact, that in the Navigation Act of 1663 wine imported from Madeira and the Azores was one of three exceptions to the requirement of staple, which stated that goods from Europe had to pass through England to get to British colonies in the Americas.[52] The British West Indies and New England rapidly became the major market for these wines,[53] and the importance of wine growing steadily in-

[46] Mauro dates it as 1680 (1975, 9); but here he seems to be at odds with most others. See Vilar (1974, 280) who speaks of a crisis from 1670 to 1703; V. M. Godinho who speaks of one from 1670 to 1690 (1974, 266; also 1950b, 186); and Sideri who speaks of a "difficult economic situation" as of 1670 (1970, 26). The crisis was in fact precipitated by a downturn in silver imports and the increasing exclusion of Portuguese colonial sugar and tobacco from French, English, and Dutch markets. In addition, Dutch competition with the Portuguese in the Gulf of Guinea caused the price of slaves to rise; this was compounded by partial exhaustion of the Angolan supply. All this began to occur as of 1670, making it difficult for Portugal to play its part in the previous structure of trade. It was what we would call today a balance of payments crisis. See Godinho (1950b, 184–185).

[47] One consequence was that in the period from 1670 to 1680 France became the leading trade partner of Portugal. When Mauro seeks to explain why this ceased later to be true, he emphasizes the degree to which French and Portuguese products were competitive on the world market (1961b). But is not this the consequence, rather than the cause, of the renewed Anglo–Portuguese link?

[48] See Godinho (1950b, 186–187). They were not unsuccessful in these policies. For example, Godinho notes of the currency operation: "In 1688, it had been impossible to arrange payments; in 1689, specie circulated normally in Lisbon. Hence, successful operation."

[49] Godinho (1950b, 191); cf. Vilar (1974, 280–281).

[50] Sideri (1970, 40).

[51] Francis (1972, 64); see also Silbert (1954, 413–419).

[52] See Andrews (1929, I, 275); Beer (1912, I, 78–79).

[53] See T. Bentley Duncan (1972, 46), who notes: "Considering the small population of the British and Portuguese colonies, the madeira wine trade, even if modest by general European standards, was an important business in the Americas" (1972, 48). But note also that the wine trade to the Americas "was entirely in the hands of English merchants of Funchal, who bought their wine cargoes with the proceeds from the sale of English textiles and other imported commodities (salted fish, pickled herring, English manufactures, Azorean wheat, etc.)" (pp. 50–51).

creased in Portugal.[54] Ericeira died in 1690, and by 1692, Portuguese mercantilism had collapsed. What had happened? Godinho gives three explanations:[55] first, the fact that the general commercial crisis in 1690, which raised the overall price of sugar and tobacco, and the advantage to the Portuguese of the temporary difficulties of the Dutch both came to an end; second, there was a constant rise in the sale of wines to the British Americas, reinforced by the fact that, as a result of the Anglo–French war, England prohibited the import of French wines and turned to Portuguese wines as a substitute;[56] third the Brazilian gold rush began.[57]

Mercantilism had been adopted as a policy response to an acute commercial crisis;[58] but the indigenous antimercantilist forces were already too strongly entrenched, and it was impossible to prevent them from reasserting themselves politically the minute the climate was slightly favorable to their interests once again.[59] The Portuguese eased into the Treaties of Methuen in 1703 and 1713 which, in Godinho's words, "essentially confirmed a *de facto* situation[60] already created in 1692 and deriving from all the developments of the seventeenth century. The famous treaties, the model for Ricardo's theory of the blessings of the international division of labor, did not create English privileges, but *re*created those enshrined in the treaties of 1642, 1654, and 1661.[61] English cloth for Portuguese wine was to become the glorious symbol of Whig commercial policy.[62]

If the period of mercantilism under Ericeira (1675 to 1690) was the brief moment of resistance by the Portuguese to their increasingly subordinate

---

[54] Godinho argues that the increase in wine production is "directly linked to the expansion of markets in the Americas" (1953, 70).

[55] See Godinho (1950b, 188–190).

[56] See also Boxer who says that the increased demand for Portuguese wines during King William's war reduced Portugal's adverse balance of trade and therefore "rendered the substitution of imported English cloth-goods by nationally manufactured products less urgent" (1958, 34). The English did not really *prefer* Portuguese to French wines. Sideri has revealing figures. In 1683, French wines were prohibited in England. That year, the English imported 65 gallons from France and 16,772 from Portugal. When the prohibition was lifted in 1686, they imported 289 gallons from Portugal and 12,750 from France (see 1970, 64).

[57] Cardoso notes that an effect of the gold rush was to increase the "illegal introduction of foreign products in Brazil," which was the "only market that gave [Portugal] any profit" (1946, 146).

[58] "Personally, I believe this policy of encouraging manufactures may be explained precisely by the crisis" (Godinho, 1953, 76). In the end, says Godinho, the mercantilist period was nothing but a "turntable" between the cycle of sugar, tobacco, and salt and the cycle of Brazilian gold, port, and

madeira (1950b, 190).

[59] "The 'industrialists' gave way to the seigniors of the vineyards" (Godinho, 1950b, 189). This would be justified subsequently by ideology: "In later years even the Portuguese were inclined to agree that the English had been responsible for the development of the vineyards of the Upper Douro and to believe that before their coming nothing had grown there but broom and furze" (Francis, 1972, 109).

[60] Godinho (1950b, 188).

[61] See Macedo (1963b, 53); Sideri (1970, 42).

[62] "The Whigs, who in 1713 voted [against Tory opposition] for trade with Portugal rather than France, came into power and stayed there a long time. During their first years of government, Anglo–Portuguese trade reached unprecedented heights" (Francis, 1966, 185).

In a private communication, E. Fernández de Pinedo pointed out to me that from 1650 onward, the Dutch and English, not wishing their ships that brought textiles, salted fish, and wheat to Spain to return empty, stimulated the production of brandy (*aguardiente*) in Catalonia and dried grapes and almonds off the Malaga coast. He calls this "a silver Methuen Treaty," especially since the trade deficit was balanced by American bullion.

role in the world-economy in this epoch, the War of the Spanish Succession may be interpreted as a parallel, equally frustrated, attempt at resistance by the Spanish. The Spanish state had become so weak in the seventeenth century that, beginning with the Peace of Rijswijk in 1697, France, Austria, England, and the United Provinces dickered over the partition of the Spanish empire. By 1702 Spain had cast its lot with France against all the rest of Europe, including Portugal, who signed the Methuen Treaty the following year.[63] From the British point of view, the French had long had too large a share of the Spanish pie, and a Bourbon succession threatened to cut the British share further—not so much in the Americas, where the British already had outmaneuvered the French, but in Spain itself and in the Mediterranean generally.[64] The war as fought by France and Britain ranged far beyond Spain and represented an attempt to destroy each other's trade networks, especially by privateering.[65] As Arsène Legrelle put it, "the history of the War of the Spanish Succession [was] not the internal history of Spain.[66] The French found out soon enough that the prime concern of their Spanish allies was not to promote the interests of France, but to get Spain out from under the economic constraints in which it found itself.[67]

The revolt in Catalonia must be seen in this same light. Catalonia had undergone a slow recovery economically after 1670, largely because "the burden of taxation was lighter and . . . economic prostration had been less complete" than in Castile.[68] This moderate prosperity was based on a commercial intermediary role. A mercantilist and centralized Spain would not have served "this developing class who . . . dreamed of 'free trade' and of

---

[63] See Kamen (1969, 1–5).

[64] See Temperley (1940, ix–x); cf. McLachlan, who reports that English merchants were opposed to the partition treaties of 1698 and 1700 because they felt that, were they signed, the Mediterranean "would have become a French lake" (1940, 30). Clark shares this view: "If the French succeeded, the Dutch and the English, the two outstanding Maritime Powers, stood to lose much of their trade" (1928, 262).

[65] The French would eventually lose this battle of the high seas. "The British not only succeeded in stemming the danger from French privateers; they also did well as aggressors in the same branch of warfare" (Clark, 1928, 264).

[66] Arsène Legrelle, *La diplomatie française et la succession d'Espagne* (Paris, 1888–1892), **III,** 332, cited in Kamen (1969, 9).

[67] Kamen remarks: "To promote Franco–Spanish trade, tariffs [had to] be kept low and commerce with the [Anglo–Dutch] enemy prohibited. The French, to their annoyance, found that it was no easy matter to get their way on these two points, which threatened to diminish the value of the trade

privileges they officially enjoyed" (1969, 127). Still, the French did enjoy privileges in Spain. It was these privileges that aroused the British; France was more interested in gaining access to the Spanish Indies. However, "despite French naval superiority, despite the Asiento, despite the volume of illicit trade carried on through Saint-Malo, for France the whole question ended in failure. Louis XIV never managed to break into the monopoly exercised by Cádiz over the Indies" (Kamen, 1969, 155).

See Rambert: "The Spanish Bourbons might constantly remember their origins; they didn't appear the less to be, from the outset, one hundred percent Spaniards" (1959, 272).

[68] Elliott (1966, 365). Vilar thinks it was more than slow recovery. He argues that "the reign of Charles II of Spain (1665–1700) was for Catalonia a happy period. . . . For the rich peasants, the merchants, businessmen of all sorts, . . . the last third of the seventeenth century was a time of prosperity. . . . The crisis of 1700–1715 was not at all preceded, as had been the secession of 1640, by severe attacks against the Crown" (1962a, 101).

becoming another Holland.[69] In addition, "France, as a power, was the enemy,"[70] that had seized Catalonian territory in the Treaty of the Pyrenees in 1659. Hence the Catalan Movement—a movement of the ruling groups and not a popular revolt as in 1640—"offered itself to the Anglo–Austrian 'allies' to bring about the reconquest of the French-aligned Peninsula."[71] This time it was less a separatist movement from Spain than a movement that wished to preserve the Catalan bourgeoisie's economic interests by preventing the coming to power within Spain of groups with a mercantilist outlook.[72] And a mercantilist outlook was in this context a progressive, worldly outlook.[73] What was the outcome of the War of the Spanish Succession? Spain was forced to give up her territories outside the peninsula. Even more important, Spain had to sign the Asiento Treaty with England, giving England the right, formerly held by France, to bring slaves (a minimum of 4800 per year) to the Spanish Indies; two features not part of the previous French Asiento were an English settlement on Rio de la Plata and an annual English "permission ship" of 500 tons, which was allowed to carry a general trade in Hispanic America.[74] The multiple treaties that settled the war were "an incontestable victory for the coalition against Louis XIV,"[75] but in particular for England.[76]

However, internally in Spain, the Catalans were abandoned by their allies, and Philip V could proceed to the centralization of Spain. Aragon and Catalonia lost their privileges and institutions with the *Nueva Planta* enunciated in 1716.[77] The *furs* of Valencia had already been revoked in 1707.[78] Only Navarre and the Basque country, which had remained loyal to Philip

[69] Vilar (1969a, 104)

[70] Vilar (1962a, 103).

[71] Vilar (1962b, I, 672). For a time the Catalan Movement was very successful. As Kamen notes, this time, unlike in the 1640 crisis, "instead of Castilian troops quartering themselves in Lisbon and Barcelona, we witness Portuguese and Catalan troops quartering themselves in Madrid" (1969, 248).

[72] See Vilar (1962b, I, 678).

[73] Chaunu captures the cultural implications of the economic choice: "The Spain of Philip V was to open up, but it could only do so slowly. . . . What did it mean to open up? It meant to open up to France, to the north. . . . The German party which, at the end of the reign of Charles II, rallied around the Queen, Marie-Anne de Neubourg, was unquestionably the party of Italian influence in art, the party of the past" (1963c, 468–469). On the role of the Spanish Bourbons as cultural "modernizers" after the War of the Spanish Succession, see Vicens Vives (1970, 116–120).

[74] See Pitt (1970, 475–476).

[75] Veenendaal (1970, 444). It is in this sense that Vilar sees Utrecht as a turning point. It accomplished the "liquidation of the old Spanish empire in Europe, ended French hegemony, and an-nounced the dawn of English preponderance in the maritime and colonial world, symbolized among other ways by the occupation of Gibraltar" (1962a, 12).

[76] G. N. Clark points that although the English and Dutch had been allies, the "general nature of the peace . . . was that the British used their political preponderance to establish themselves in a position of advantage for their competition with Dutch commerce" (1928, 279). See also A. W. Ward: "The United Provinces gained a strong Barrier, firmly planted in Allied territory, against any renewal of the aggression of France. But though they continued to secure, in addition, some commercial advantages from the Peace, their political position as a Great Power had gone from them, forever, passing, without any real resistance on their part, to the Power which had been their rival; . . . and their mercantile supremacy was likewise at an end" (1908, 438).

[77] Elliott (1966, 370–371). Jaime Vicens Vives poignantly argues: "The Catalans were fighting against the current of history, and the price for this is usually very high" (1970, 111).

[78] See Kamen (1974, 687).

V, conserved their *fueros,* and were henceforth known as the Exempt Provinces.[79] In the context of the overall interstate settlement and the Asiento Treaty, this centralization of Spain could not accomplish the objectives that were intended.[80] By the provisions of the Treaty of Utrecht, Spain was not permitted to alter duties to the disadvantage of Great Britain. Furthermore, the conversion ratio of silver duties into current money (vellon) was fixed at that prevailing at the end of the reign of Charles II in 1700. This "effectively precluded genuinely protective duties."[81]

There is no doubt, as Romero de Solís emphasizes, that the triumph of the Bourbons in the War of the Spanish Succession "was the triumph of the middle classes and of the lower nobility against the Church and the seigniorial aristocracy."[82] Nor is there any doubt that Philip V would try "within the limits permitted by the Treaty of Utrecht" to end Spain's semiperipheral role.[83] But is it true, as Kamen argues, that: "Shorn at Utrecht of the burden of Italy and the Netherlands, the country could devote itself to internal recuperation and external resurgence?"[84] No doubt the Bourbons tried. But, as Kamen himself argues, the credit for starting the attempt goes back to Charles II and 1680, the same time that Portugal was making its attempt. "Philip V entered a Spain substantially removed from the monetary chaos that had been its hallmark for nearly a century."[85] It is clear that, whatever the vigor of Bourbon efforts, Spain would not substantially change its economic role in the eighteenth century; it would, in fact, during the renewed expansion of the world-economy after 1750, lose its American empire. Should one not compare what the Bourbons accomplished with what they might have accomplished if Utrecht had not ended with the Asiento Treaty and the crippling of Spain's ability to pursue mercantilist tactics? Philip V may *perhaps* be credited with halting a still further decline in Spain's world-economic role, at least for a time; but it can hardly be said that he reversed the trend. To the extent that Spain achieved any success in redeveloping an industrial base, it was at the expense of France, not England.[86]

[79] See Vicens Vives (1970, 114).

[80] For Vicens Vives, "the mystique of regional charters was merely replaced by the mystique of centralization at any cost. . . . And in this enterprise the Bourbon dynasty and its collaborators (like their predecessors) would fail" (1970, 113).

[81] E. J. Hamilton (1935, 116).

[82] Romero de Solís (1973, 54), who speaks of the "new middle class, agrarian capitalists and national bourgeoisie" (p. 66) and of the partisans of Philip V being "the middle sectors of the landed nobility in the process of transforming themselves into agrarian capitalists, and the national bourgeoisie plus its agents (*servidores*), the state bourgeoisie" (p. 67, n. 108). However, Dominguez Ortiz says: "Bourbon absolutism, although opposed to any weakening of central sovereignty, did make deals with the seig-

niories (*señorios*) once they had stripped them of their last political significance, which was already almost nil in the last days of the Austrian Hapsburgs" (1955, 301). Kamen agrees: "It should be emphasized that the fall of the grandees, though of fundamental political and administrative importance, is of lesser significance in the social history of Spain. As in previous reigns, the nobility remained entrenched in their privileges and estates" (1969, 115).

[83] See the description of these efforts by E. J. Hamilton (1943, 206); see also La Force (1964, 337–338).

[84] Kamen (1969, 391–392).

[85] Kamen (1969, 34).

[86] See Rambert: "Their customs policies, ceaselessly watchful, would succeed [through the

The key problem was the Asiento. There was immense profit for the English in the slave trade to be sure. In addition, the Asiento made it possible for this legal trade to "be used as a screen behind which to import forbidden commodities into the Spanish colonies."[87] The extent of this illegal trade under the aegis of the South Sea Company became immense by the 1730s.[88] "Contraband trade was an integral part of every phase of the South Sea Company's operations."[89] It became a major cause of the War of Jenkin's Ear in the 1740s.[90] The contraband trade operated primarily from Jamaica and from Barbados and Buenos Aires as well.[91] It succeeded in significantly diminishing the traffic through Cádiz.[92] What advantage the English did not get out of the direct English–Hispanic American trade,[93] they got through indirect trade via Cádiz, in which Spain ultimately used American bullion to cover their payments deficit with England.[94] Spain's bullion loss was matched by a chronically and increasingly unbalanced state budget that resulted precisely from Bourbon centralization, which involved a threefold rise in Crown expenditure from 1701 to 1745.[95] French efforts to counter the British in Spain and worldwide gave Spain some small breathing space; but finally, at the end of the Seven Years' War in 1763, when France was "practically eliminated as a factor in the American colonial situation, Spain was left to face the English menace for the next two decades alone."[96] In the long sweep from 1600 to 1750 or 1763, Spain proved itself unable to stem the tide of what has come to be known as Spanish "decadence."

Alongside their flourishing licit and illicit trade with Spain and Hispanic America, England's licit and illicit trade with Portugal and Brazil was even greater yet.[97] The effects of Methuen were immediate. In one decade, Portuguese imports from England more than doubled—but her exports went

---

eighteenth century] little by little in raising barriers, in the shelter of which national industries could grow and the country partially liberate itself from foreign control. France, for a long time leading the competition, was to be the principal victim of this evolution" (1959, 270).

[87] Nelson (1945, 55).

[88] Nelson cites a value of 5.5 million pounds between 1730 and 1739 and says that it was "of such magnitude that it was a real threat to Spanish mercantilism" (1945, 64).

[89] V. L. Brown (1928, 179). Nelson points out that the South Sea Company used every conceivable means to engage in illicit trade: Secrecy (which was possible because, although the Spanish government had a member on the Board of Directors, most communications did not pass through the Board); bribery of Spanish officials; the slave trade as a blind; deception; and force, the protection offered by British men-of-war. (see Nelson, 1945, 56–60).

[90] See Nelson (1945, 55).

[91] See Christelow (1941, 532); Nelson (1945, 57).

[92] Godinho (1948, 552).

[93] For a list of products exchanged, see Nelson (1945, 61) and Godinho (1948, 553).

[94] Godinho notes that the flow of Hispano-American bullion at this time, if not as great as that from Minas Gerais in Brazil, "was nonetheless of great importance in the monetary life of Europe" (1948, 553). See also H. E. S. Fisher (1971, 4–5). The licit and illicit trade with Hispanic America probably benefited two different groups of Englishmen to some extent. The Spanish state tried to use their interlocutors of the licit trade to constrain the illicit trade, but not very successfully. See Godinho (1948, 552).

[95] See E. J. Hamilton (1949, 316).

[96] V. L. Brown (1928, 187); see also Christelow (1941, 519–520) for the period leading up to 1763.

[97] In the period from 1700 to 1750, Portugal was the third greatest consumer of British exports (after the United Provinces and the Germanies); and English shipping in Lisbon almost never fell below 50% of the total. See Maxwell (1968, 612).

up only 40%. The treaty wiped out the "infant" textile industry.[98] This was paralleled by a fivefold increase in Portuguese wine production from 1670 to 1710, which "absorbed most of the available Portuguese capital, and even more important, an increasing amount of Portuguese labor."[99] The advantages to England of Portuguese wine over French wine was that, although it was more expensive, it did not have to be paid for in bullion, as in France, because of the quantity of English textile exports to Portugal.[100] It may have cost the English customer more, but the bourgeois interests located in England were better off. The wine trade was not in fact very advantageous to Portugal. In addition to its negative impact on manufactures, the trade itself was "largely controlled by English interests which took most of the profits.[101] It was thus not without reason that the Duc de Choiseul, France's Minister of Foreign Affairs, would say in 1760 that Portugal "must be regarded as an English colony."[102]

Still, there was far less wine exported, in terms of value, than textiles imported. The balance of trade deficit with England, negligible as late as 1700, grew to about one million pounds annually.[103] Fortunately for Portugal, she was still at least a semiperipheral country. She had her own colony, Brazil, and it was a wealthy one.[104] It was Brazilian gold that permitted Portugal to balance its trade with England from after 1710 until mid-century.[105] The Portuguese historian J. P. Oliveira Martins noted acerbically in 1908: "The gold of Brazil merely passed through Portugal and cast anchor in England to pay for flour and textiles with which England fed and clothed us. Our industry consisted of operas and devotions."[106] England, on the other hand, got a very much needed infusion of bullion that allowed her money supply to be adequate for her growing share in the overall

[98] See Sideri (1970, 44–46). Macedo (1963a) argues that despite this British advantage, the competition of other foreign manufactures forced British prices down and nullified the monopoly; but Sideri denies this, pointing to this contradictory statement in Macedo's own account: "Dutch or French textiles could never offset British advantages, because they did not benefit from a distribution network and an established influence as that behind the British merchants" (Macedo, p. 51, cited in Sideri, p. 46). H. E. S. Fisher claims that English textile merchants had an advantage over their French, Dutch, and German competitors because they were "more specialized . . . [in] light woollen and worsted textiles in the low to medium price range," and also could "ship . . . more cheaply" (1971, 36–37). A close reading of Fisher reveals that this is circular since cheaper shipping was a function of greater quantity of trade, and sale of textiles was a function of purchase of wine, "and the English merchants in Portugal controlled both the purchase and shipment of

the wines sent to England" (p. 36).

[99] Sideri (1970, 46).

[100] Sideri (1970, 41, 48), who on page 41 says the English negative balance with France was made up in silver but on page 48 says it was in gold.

[101] Sideri (1970, 46).

[102] Cited in Christelow (1946, 27). G. Young, writing in 1917, similarly observed: "The Douro port district became a sort of hinterland to a British colony" *Portugal Old and Young* (Oxford, 1917, 185), cited in Sideri (1970, 56).

[103] Sideri (1970, 45).

[104] Boxer asserts that in the eighteenth century "there can be no doubt but that [Brazil] was in most ways more prosperous than the mother country" (1969b, 323).

[105] See Francis (1972, 179–180).

[106] J. P. Oliveira Martins, *História de Portugal* (London, 1908), 2 vols., pp. 149–151, cited in Sideri (1970, 67).

production and trade of the world-economy.[107] Furthermore, England thereby got a corner not only on the licit gold trade, but on the bullion-smuggling trade as well.[108] The English historian, Charles Boxer, finds in these arrangements one solace for Portugal: "One benefit which Portugal did derive from her overseas possessions was that, by virtue of them, and the resources she derived from them, she was able to escape the fate of Scotland and of Catalonia."[109] From the vantage point of the twentieth century, Portugal might have been better off to have been poorer (by Brazil) in the seventeenth and eighteenth centuries. The story of Scotland and Catalonia is complex, and their later development of industry is beyond the bounds of this discussion, but it may not have hurt these two countries that they did not have a Brazil that permitted the unequal exchange with England, profitable to certain Portuguese groups, to occur without political upheaval at home. It was the Brazilian direct producer who paid the price, but there was then less internal pressure within Portugal to seek structural changes.

If the Iberian states, which in the sixteenth century were the glorious colonizers and controllers of bullion, were in the seventeenth century to decline so ignominiously into the role of mere conveyor belts of northwestern European manufactures, what of the areas that had been the great industrial centers in the fifteenth and sixteenth centuries? The dorsal spine of Europe—northern Italy, the southern and western Germanies, and the southern (Spanish) Netherlands also declined, and dramatically, but in a different way. Having no colonies and therefore no bullion sources or indeed tropical raw materials with which to buy imported goods, they had only their own industry and agriculture on which to survive, and their long-cultivated commercial and financial expertise.

The key to their survival was the putting-out system (*Verlagssystem*). This system was basically defined by the following features. The actual producer worked in his domicile with his own equipment. He used his own tools. Either he was a master with a few apprentices, or he worked alone or in small family groups. He received the necessary raw materials for his transformational task from a merchant-entrepreneur (*Verleger*), who thereby received the right to "purchase" the transformed product at a fixed price and who took charge of transporting the product to a market. If the producer worked alone or in a small family group, he normally worked only part-time

---

[107] See Sideri (1970, 49). Morineau wants to temper this judgment: Though Brazilian gold had a "circumscribed but certain influence" on British exports to Portugal, it was neither "essential" nor "irreplaceable"; in general, in terms of British economic growth in the eighteenth century, "Brazilian gold . . . was neither the sole agent of growth, nor the strongest" (1978h, 44, 47). This is tilting at a windmill, however. The bullion was necessary, and

it was from Brazil that it was in fact largely obtained at this juncture.

[108] Francis notes that "the Dutch and Hamburgers, who also needed precious metals, had not the same facilities [as the English] and received their share [of smuggled bullion] by way of London" (1966, 217).

[109] Boxer (1961, 90).

and combined this productive activity with some other economic role. Often the operation of the system resulted in the chronic indebtedness of the producer to the merchant-entrepreneur, which resembled the debt-bondage situation prevalent at the time in various kinds of agricultural production.

The putting-out system was already known in the Middle Ages, but it first spread significantly in the sixteenth century, primarily at that time in urban industry.[110] This system has often been identified with the textile industry, but it was used in almost every kind of industrial production.[111] In the stagnation of the seventeenth century, the putting-out system spread even more than it had in the sixteenth, with one important modification. Everywhere in Europe the putting-out industries shifted location into the rural areas. The primary motive was to increase the profits of the merchant-entrepreneur. Braudel tells us: "Wherever [the putting-out system] was introduced, it struck a blow against the guilds.[112] As long as the production process remained in the towns, however, the guilds were in a political position to fight back *within* the putting-out system, especially in good years, by regulating through contracts the relationship between merchant-entrepreneur and artisan-producer.[113]

Once the industry was located in the rural areas, the merchant-entrepreneur escaped the guilds,[114] replacing guild craftsmen with the peasantry who "constituted a much cheaper labor force."[115] A rural location

---

[110] See Braudel (1972, **I**, 430–432).

[111] See for example Friedrichs: "In Nuremberg by the early sixteenth century the *Verlagssystem* had been introduced into numerous branches of the metal industry and in the manufacture of purses, gloves, brushes, paper and books as well as linen and fustian. In late seventeenth-century Nuremberg even the production of pencils was organized on the basis of *Verlag*" (1975, 32–33). Kellenbenz makes the same point and adds: "In the mining of ferrous and non-ferrous ores, the purchase of pumps, furnaces and other indispensable technical equipment often ran the small workshop into debt, and the help of a merchant was needed. This happened especially when the man who regularly bought the product was an obvious potential source of credit" (1977a, 469).

[112] Braudel (1972, **I**, 431). Craeybeckx observes for Ghent and Bruges: "In the seventeenth century, the 'guild' links became looser, especially in the second half. The worker, 'master' or 'journeyman', knew that his fate lay in the hands of the merchants, alone capable of ensuring the disposition of his products" (1962, 427).

[113] See Friedrichs, who notes that "the guild could terminate the arrangement when the relationship proved detrimental to its members" (1975, 33).

[114] See Kellenbenz (1965, **II**, 420).

[115] Kellenbenz (1977a, **V**, 470). Sella thinks the shift to the rural areas, at least from Venice, was due more to the inefficiency of the work of guild members than to their high wages, but this seems to me the same thing. See Sella (1968, 122–123). In the rural areas, not all peasants were equally anxious to play this role. E. L. Jones points out that cottage (putting-out) industries were particularly to be found in those lowland districts that had "infertile sandlands, and heavy clays" as well as in certain "highland districts." He suggests it was the fact that these districts "could not feed their populations from internal agricultural resources" that led them to seek to supplement their income in this way (1975, 339, 341). In a similar vein, Mendels points out: "There is evidence . . . that the peasants who became weavers were at the bottom of the social scale and remained there" (1972, 242). Peter Kriedte argues: "The less [income obtained from agriculture] because of the lack of arable land, the more there grew a tendency among the small manufacturers to neglect agriculture, and to concentrate their skills on industrial production" (in Kriedte *et al.*, 1977, 68). Klíma and Macůrek note that in the Czech lands, workers on rural manufactures were drawn from "the poor of the countryside" (1960, 90). See also Thirsk's discussion of the link of handicrafts industries to certain types of farming communities (1961).

also guaranteed the physical dispersal of the work force, minimizing the risk of worker organization while still concentrating distribution in a few big merchant-entrepreneurs.[116] Kellenbenz stresses how important it is to realize that this system was in no way static,[117] but responded to the evolution of the economic situation. One of the ways in which it evolved was toward an ever-spreading permanent dependence[118] of the workers on their merchant-entrepreneurs. In semiperipheral countries especially, the putting-out system had a further feature that should be noted. It was often in the hands of *foreign* merchant-entrepreneurs. The Dutch, as befit the hegemonic power, were everywhere: in the North Sea and Baltic city-states; in Brandenburg, Scandinavia, Kurland, and Russia; in the Rhineland and northern Italy. But the English and the French were also installed in many of these areas. In the seventeenth century, old entrepreneurial groups like the Italians were playing a diminished but still significant role. And "minority" foreign groups also flourished: the Huguenots in the Germanies, North America, Switzerland, Holland, and England; the Jews everywhere; the Mennonites in a number of key German areas.[119]

The putting-out system marked the beginning of proletarianization in the same way that the venality of office and the use of mercenary troops marked the beginning of bureaucratization (that is, proletarianization) of state employment. Under putting-out, the direct producer formally owned the means of production but *de facto* became an employee of the merchant-entrepreneur, who controlled the producer's real income and appropriated his surplus-value without being yet in a position to ensure his maximal efficiency by direct supervision at the workplace.[120] (By analogy,

[116] See Kulischer (1931, 11).

[117] Kellenbenz (1965, **II,** 427 and *passim*).

[118] Friedrichs (1975, 33). Bulferetti and Constantini point out: "Through the second half of the sixteenth century and the first half of the seventeenth century, the ancient antagonism between commercial capital and independent artisans became transformed in Genoa . . . into a uniform subordination of the artisanal groups (*corpi di mestiere*) to the direction of the merchant-entrepreneurs" (1966, 73). Peter Kriedte points out that even in the *Kaufsystem*, where unlike in the *Verlagssystem* work was not done on commission, there was "the beginning of an economic dependence" through the according of credit and that despite the formal independence of the producers there was "exploitation via trade" (in Kriedte *et al.,* 1977, 202–203). *A fortiori*, this was so in the *Verlagssystem*, where the merchant-entrepreneur could "determine the whether, what, how, and how much of production, from first to last" (p. 214).

[119] See the survey by Treue (1957, 41–42). On the Jews in Germany, see Treue (1955, 398–399); on the Anglo–Dutch in Italy, see Fanfani (1959, 57–58, 128); on the English and Dutch in Bohemia, see

Klíma (1959) and Míka (1970, 201–205); on the link between the *Verlagssystem* in central Europe and the export trade, see Klíma & Macůrek (1960, 96) and Kriedte in Kriedte *et al.* (1977, 64).

[120] See Sombart (1900, 1138–1140). Even home-industry producers who were not tributary to a merchant–entrepreneur were, by the workings of the market, reduced to an analogous *de facto* situation, as Hans Medick underlines: "Whether the home-industrial weaver, knitter, nailer or scythemaker entered the market as buyer and seller himself and so worked with the 'Kaufsystem', or whether he was organized in the 'putting-out system', he was always directly or indirectly dependent upon merchant capital" (1976, 296). The putting-out system (*Verlagssystem*) was of course more profitable to the merchant entrepreneur than the *Kaufsystem*, since under the latter the direct producer retained a larger proportion of the surplus-value. Although the *Verlagssystem* did not compare with the factory system in terms of managerial control, it was an advance over the *Kaufsystem* and thereby increased productivity, the profits of which went largely to the merchant-entrepreneur. While the piecework income of a direct producer

the situation was the same in the state bureaucracy.) That semiperipheral states had putting-out industries at all was what marked them off at this time from peripheral areas. The fact that the putting-out industries of the semiperipheral areas tended to be partly under the control of nonindigenous groups and so found it difficult to secure protectionist legislation was what marked them off from the industries of the core areas at this time. The putting-out system is what is described in Mendel's popular phrase as protoindustrialization,[121] although I do not think it useful to think of this industrialization as proto-, which implies it is not the real thing. The putting-out system was less efficient but in fact more exploitative of labor than a factory system,[122] and hence it was ideal for an era of relative stagnation.

The old industries of the dorsal spine areas all underwent a decline in the seventeenth century. This was particularly dramatic in northern Italy, but substantially the case in the Germanies and in the southern Netherlands as well. Romano sees the situation in northern Italy in bleak terms. He sums it up as four trends: decline in urban (but not total) population; decline in industrial production in classic centers (Florence, Milan, Venice; and also Naples), especially in the cheaper textiles; decline in distributive trades; and decline of prices and money in circulation but fairly static wages (resulting in unemployment and therefore in an increase in the number of paupers and vagrants). Thus the *urban* economy is said by Romano to have been in "an extremely depressed state" between 1620 and 1740. In addition, Romano speaks of "the general involution of Italian agrarian economy."[123] He sees Italy as unquestionably part of that majority in seveenth-century Europe who (unlike those in England, the United Provinces, and to some

was less under the *Verlagssystem* than under the *Kaufsystem*, his annual income could be bigger through more sustained employment. See Schlumbohm in Kriedte *et al.* (1977, 215–216, including n. 56).

[121] Mendels (1972). See the discussion of the historiographic roots of the concept in Kriedte *et al.* (1977, 13–35), who consider protoindustrialization to be of "strategic importance" in determining the eventual economic role of given areas in the world-economy (pp. 30–31, n. 52). Klíma and Macůrek make the case for seeing manufacture, that is the putting-out system, as a "stepping-stone [*jalon*] in the evolutionary road from the guild-system via manufacture to large-scale mechanized production." Their explanation as to why manufacture and the factory system shouuld be regarded as links in an evolutionary process rather than as opposite shores of a deep rupture is that manufacture "deepened the division of labor" and "brought into production a large number of unskilled or low-skilled workers" (1960, **IV,** 96–97). Myška makes basically the same point in discussing the centralized

iron manufactories of the Czech lands (see 1979, 44–49 and *passim*). See also Redlich (1955, 93–97).

[122] Medick gives a very good account of how this worked and sums it up by saying: "The logic of family economic production became effective above all because of the inclination of the poor, landless laborers to fall back on 'self-exploitation' in the production of craft goods, if this was necessary to ensure customary family subsistence and economic self-sufficiency." This resulted in a "differential profit" for the merchant-entrepreneur that "surpassed both the profits that could be gained from the social relations of production in the guild system, and the profits that could be derived from comparable wage-labor relations in manufactures" (1976, 299). Medick is particularly interested in the "symbiotic relationship of family economy and merchant capital." He argues that the "norms and rules of behavior of the traditional family subsistence economy" were more important in permitting the genesis of capitalism [I would rather say its growth] than the Protestant ethic (1976, 300).

[123] Romano (1974, 188–189).

extent France) were living "under the sign of involution."[124] For Romano, Italy therefore missed a "great historical opportunity for renewal," just as it had in the fourteenth century, because it had a "whole ruling class ready to withstand" the crisis and "come through the long night" weakened but intact.[125] Procacci attacks the voluntarist assumptions of the concept of missed opportunity;[126] and Sella atacks the empirical description, arguing that it is overstated. Sella believes that by the end of the seventeenth century the northern Italian industrial scene was "far from barren" and that manufactured goods still had a "conspicuous place" in export trade.[127] Furthermore, he argues, the countryside (at least in Lombardy) fared better still—the seventeenth-century story being one of "remarkable endurance, adaptation, and resilience" in the face of adversity.[128]

We find a similar mixed evaluation in the literature on the western and southern Germanies. Already in the nineteenth century, Schmoller had emphasized the "unconditional dependence" of this area on Holland in the period from 1600 to 1750.[129] A 1770 source cited by Beutin notes that at that time Frankfurt was "nothing but a big entrepôt, dominated by the Dutch."[130] Anderson speaks of a "thwarted Rhenish economy,"[131] the result of Dutch control of its outlets to the sea. Kuske sees an "era of passivity" in the Rhineland beginning at the end of the sixteenth century,[132] and Liebel describes the "devastating effect" of seventeenth-century wars on the imperial towns of Swabia—Augsburg, Ulm, Nuremburg.[133] Kisch speaks rather of "the leavening influence of neighboring Dutch buoyancy,"[134] viewing this

[124] Romano (1971, 201).

[125] Romano (1974, 195).

[126] Procacci (1975, 28), who calls the idea too simplistic and radical." Borelli gives a good instance of why it was not merely a matter of will. He notes the efforts of Venice to save its silk industry by forbidding the export of raw silk in 1588. Since this led to a lower price for raw silk on the internal market, it encouraged contraband export. By 1694, two-thirds of Venetian raw silk was exported clandestinely (see Borelli, 1974, 27–28). It was not enough to proclaim mercantilist policies. One had to be strong enough, politically, to enforce them. In this case, the competitive margin offered by mercantilist measures was not enough to overcome the very high costs of Venetian production.

[127] Sella (1969, 244). Rapp's reservation on the empirical situation is somewhat different. He agrees that Venice shifted from export-oriented industries to domestic service industries. He sees this as an attempt, somewhat successful, to preserve employment and hence levels of prosperity (see Rapp, 1975, 523–524).

[128] Sella (1975, 12). One form of resilience was in fact the increased economic linkage between city and surrounding countryside, as in the case of Venice and the Terraferma. See Marino: "The

increased fiscal burden on production of the Terraferma, investments in agriculture and the regional market made of Venice and its hinterland an organic entity. . . . The most important consequence of the [seventeenth-century] crisis was itself the sudden emergence of an integrated regional economy and a coordinated economic policy (1978, 100).

[129] Schmoller (1897, 74). J. de Vries gives a good example of this dependence. In the period up to 1650, the clothiers of Haarlem depended on their hinterlands for female weavers; but by 1650, this task had moved geographically outward to households in Westphalia (and the southern Netherlands). "Haarlem now acted as a focal point for a network of cloth factors who sent linen there for bleaching and final sale" (1976, 97).

[130] *Die Handlung von Holland* (Frankfurt and Leipzig, 1770, 251–252) cited in Beutin (1939, 120). Beutin cites Friedrich List as sharing this view, about which he himself has "no doubt" (1939, 127).

[131] P. Anderson (1974a, 249).

[132] Kuske (1922, 189).

[133] Liebel (1965a, 287). These towns of course had already begun a secular decline in the sixteenth century.

[134] Kisch (1968, 3).

as an explanation of why the Rhineland "escaped the depression" that hit most regions in Germany in the seventeenth century.[135]

When we turn to the southern Netherlands, we find the same debate. We have the classic view of Pirenne—economic decline resulting from the closing of the Scheldt and the inability to procure protectionist measures from either the Spaniards or the Austrians.[136] This is reinforced by Stols who argues that the Flemish were unable to profit vis-à-vis the Dutch even with their continued Spanish link in the seventeenth century because of Spanish suspicions about their possible pro-Dutch sentiments.[137] Brulez, on the other hand, insists that the situation in Antwerp in the seventeenth century was "less bad than we have believed up to now."[138] Brulez explains this in terms of Antwerp's continuing role as a *Dispositionshandel,* where decisions about European trade and commercial deals were made and Flemish merchants profited from their historically acquired business connections.[139]

---

[135] Kisch (1959, 555).

[136] See Pirenne (1920, **V,** 65–69, 129–130, 193–201). There is of course one mercantilist interlude, and that in itself is instructive. The so-called Belgian Colbert, Jean de (Jan van) Brouchaven, Count of Bergeyck, managed in 1698 to persuade the Elector Maximilien Emmanuel of Bavaria, governor of the Spanish Netherlands, to institute tariffs, to create the *Compagnie d'Ostende* for trade in the Indies, to plan the improvement of internal navigable routes, and in 1699, even, to prohibit the export of wool and the entry of foreign textiles. But the reprisals of the English and Dutch, combined with interprovincial jealousies, led Maximilien to retreat (pp. 64–69). When, in the wake of the accession of Philip V, Maximilien was ousted and his troops replaced by French troops, Bergeyck was once again authorized to proceed with his Colbertist reforms. This was the so-called "régime anjouin" (pp. 94–105). When French troops were defeated by Marlborough at Ramillies in 1706, French occupation was replaced by Anglo–Dutch occupation. The tariffs were immediately abolished, and the centralization of administration ended. Pirenne observes: "Thus disappeared the last vestiges of the reforms instituted to tear the country from the sluggish state into which it had fallen at the end of the seventeenth century. And no one noticed it. The particularism which had opposed the projects of Bergeyck now served the interests of the Conference [of Anglo–Dutch authorities]. No more central government. Each province was abandoned to itself and thought only of its immediate interests. England and the United Provinces did nothing but stand by and let this happen complacently. They knew that once peace came, they would not keep Belgium, and it was therefore best to turn it over to Charles III [of Austria] in a state of political and economic impotence and quietude" (p. 114). See also Hasquin (1971, 125–

126).

Even Craeybeckx, who insists on the noninferiority of southern Netherlands production vis-à-vis Anglo–Dutch competitors in this period, explains the crisis of the late seventeenth century in terms of the *general* downward conjuncture in Europe which "was felt with particular severity in the southern Netherlands because they were extremely bereft of means to react again to the ever more frenetic protectionism of neighboring countries" (1962, 465). Van der Wee argues that the revival of the southern Netherlands in the seventeenth century is in fact accompanied by "clear de-urbanisation" and a "return to a self-sufficient, *traditional* agriculture" (1978, 14, 17).

[137] This was true especially before 1648. Stols quotes a Jesuit from Bruges in 1617 who, speaking of Hispanic America, said: "Henceforth the access to India seems to become difficult for the Flemish and this because of the Dutch traitors" (cited in Stols, 1976, 40).

[138] Brulez (1967, 89). This view is shared by Craeybeckx (1962, 413–418), who nonetheless admits a "slide in the center of economic gravity to the countryside" (p. 419). There was also a slide to Liège. See Kellenbenz: "It has been said that the misfortune of the Spanish Netherlands was the fortune of Liège" (1965, **II,** 393). See also Jeannin (1969, 70).

[139] See Brulez (1967, 94–99); Craeybeckx (1962, 416). This is reinforced by Baetens's discussion of Flemish privateering, a flourishing business in the seventeenth century up to the War of the Spanish Succession. Baetens speaks of its *negative* impact on the Antwerp merchant community, which used Dutch carriers for their extensive trade; this indicates the main channel by which the Flemish circumvented the legal constraints on their economy (see Baetens, 1976, 74).

Let us look more closely, therefore, at what we know of the actual economic structures in these zones at this time. The decline of *urban* industry was indeed unmistakable in the northern Italian centers. Whether the breaking point should be taken at 1619 or 1636 is a matter of debate.[140] In any case, Milan wool production went from 60 to 70 enterprises producing 15,000 *panni* annually in 1619, to 15 producing 3,000 *panni* in 1640, to 5 in 1682, to 1 in 1709 producing 100 *panni*.[141] Bulferetti attributes this decline to French mercantilism in the seventeenth century, which he sees as having "struck a vital blow" to both manufacturing and artisanal activity in Lombardy (and Tuscany as well); but he also blames the resistance of the workers to technological change.[142] De Maddalena adds that the *de facto* incorporation of Milan into the Austrian empire in 1706 can be considered the definitive "widening of the secular downward tendency."[143] Lombardy, having emerged from Spanish domination, was "reduced to extremities [*stremata*]."[144] The same was true of the wool industry in Genoa,[145] and of the industrial sectors of Venice.[146] Liebel reports a similar decline of crafts in Württemberg, "the most bourgeois territory of the Holy Roman Empire" as of the Thirty Years' War, especially in woolen and linen weaving.[147]

As for the Swiss, they seem to have made a virtue out of necessity, and transformed their special link with France into a mechanism of semiperipheralization. The origins of this special link began in the sixteenth century with the Swiss role of supplying mercenaries, which Swiss authorities used to bargain exemptions from French tariff walls. The French market thus became "the principal stimulant of Swiss industry."[148] In spite of being fortified by this link, the Swiss, during the Thirty Years' War, commenced their classic stance of neutrality, which enabled them "to oust France from the German market"[149] and use this as a basis of developing an export industry.[150] When France incorporated Franche-Comté in 1678, however, the dependence of the Swiss dairy industry on salt imported this region reinforced Switzerland's *political* dependence on France.[151] Accept-

[140] Meuvret argues that it was 1636 (1953, 216); Cipolla argues that it was 1619 (1958, **I**, 392).

[141] See Cipolla (1958, **I**, 392, 394).

[142] Bulferetti (1953, 53).

[143] De Maddalena (1974b, 77). "The Milanese economy entered undeniably into a phase of standstill, of stagnation" (p. 79).

[144] Caizzi (1968, 6).

[145] See Bulferetti and Constantini (1966, 35).

[146] Rapp asserts that the total employment in the exporting sector was reduced by the latter half of the seventeenth century to the absolute level of 1539, "before the industrial spurt began" (1976, 104). He adds: "The port of Venice did not collapse with the economic troubles of the seventeenth century but its character changed from that of the fulcrum of world trade to that of a regional service port" (p. 105). Lane points out that Venice was no longer able to keep rival fleets out of the Adriatic or prevent the rise of rival ports (see 1973, 417).

[147] Liebel (1965a, 295, 300).

[148] Bürgin (1969, 220), who says that by the end of the seventeenth century, Switzerland "emerged as the world center" of clockmaking (p. 227).

[149] Bürgin (1969, 221).

[150] "The political basis for an unbroken development of export trade," as well as of transit trade, which "was very important in the seventeenth and eighteenth centuries, was the political neutrality of the state" (Bodmer, 1951, 574). Furthermore, Switzerland attracted refugee entrepreneurs because of her neutrality (p. 598).

[151] "The French government, true to the principle of Colbertism, placed the newly-won mineral wealth [of Franche-Comté] at the service of their power politics and delivered salt at advantageous conditions

ing the combination of economic antimercantilism[152] and political protection by France and parlaying their growing cottage industry in clockmaking and dairy products, Switzerland became by the end of the eighteenth century "the most industrialized land on the European continent."[153]

As the foregoing discussion indicates, it cannot be said that industry disappeared from the dorsal spine of Europe in the seventeenth century. What happened was that industry, especially wool and cotton textiles, moved into the countryside. This is reported to have been true everywhere: in Venice, Genoa, Aachen, Flanders, Zurich, and, in the late seventeenth century, even in Holland.[154] In each case, reduction of the high wage costs, resulting from the strength of urban guilds, is adduced as a key motive. On the other hand, the *luxury* silk industry continued to flourish in the cities, where silk mills became veritable factories.[155] A second urban luxury "industry" that expanded in this period was the production and export of art.[156] In the countryside, we find that simultaneously and in the same places there was a trend toward the worsening of peasant exploitation and the creation of putting-out industries. There was a usurpation of communal lands in northern Italy in the seventeenth century.[157] Beltrami characterized noble property in the Terraferma as having "henceforth the character of true latifundia."[158] The Venetian Senate in 1633 expressly forbade peasants to emigrate, even without their animals and tools of production. Borelli asks: "How can one not think . . . of the resurrection in more modern dress of the old institution of serfdom of the glebe?"[159]

Throughout the seventeenth century, as the power of landowners over peasantry was strengthened in northern Italy (a result of "downward"

only to those places which showed themselves pliable to their wishes" (Bodmer, 1951, 576).

[152] "It was, as paradoxical as this seems for the seventeenth and eighteenth century, precisely the lack of a well-defined mercantilist trade policy, that helped this particular place achieve a positive balance of payments" (Bodmer, 1951, 575). To be sure, antimercantilism did not exclude state loans to entrepreneurs, and the absence of tariffs was opposed—for example, by the Genevan guilds (see Piuz, 1970a, 9).

[153] Bodmer (1951, 598), who says Switzerland "exported not only industrial goods in great quantity but also certain products of their mountain economy [*Alpwirtschaft*], among others cheese and beef."

[154] See Rapp on Venice (1976, 159); Bulferetti and Constantini on Genoa (1966, 48–50); Kisch on Aachen (1964, 524); Mendels on Flanders (1975, 203); and J. de Vries on Zurich (1976, 97). In Holland, textiles went from Haarlem and Leyden to Twente and North Brabant. Delft pottery went to Friesland. Biscuit baking moved beyond the frontiers of North Holland. Van der Woude calls this the

"ruralization of [Dutch] trade and industry" (1975, 239).

[155] "While wool-making declined, silk-making rose" (Borelli, 1974, 25). See also Bulferetti and Constantini (1966, 70) and Rapp (1976, 105–106). Piuz speaks of the rise of an "urban *Verlagssystem*" in Genevan silk (1970a, 5). Kisch notes a shift from linen to silk in Krefeld in the early eighteenth century (1968, 28). However, Gino Luzzatto insists that all was not well even for silk, since French protectionism hurt sales—not only in France but elsewhere in Europe (see Luzzatto, 1974, 161–162). On the silk mills as factories, see Poni (1976, 490–496).

[156] Haskell (1959, 48). The other side of the export of art was the import of tourists. Venice became probably the first modern tourist center in the seventeenth century (see J. de Vries, 1976, 27).

[157] See Romano (1962, 510–513), Borelli (1974, 20), and Sereni (1961, 207). Along with this went the continued spread in the period from 1600 to 1750 of sharecropping (*mezzadria*) throughout northern and central Italy (see Sereni, 1961, 205).

[158] Cited in Romano (1968, 733).

[159] Borelli (1974, 15).

semiperipheralization) and as the power of the state was strengthened in east Elbia (a result of "upward" semiperipheralization), the social structures of the two areas grew closer, so that by the early eighteenth century, Piedmont and Brandenburg-Prussia, the organizing units of the future Italian and German states, showed some remarkable similarities.[160] Similar developments seem to have occurred in the southern Netherlands (and Liège), where the power of the large landowners grew in the seventeenth and early eighteenth century and where many peasants lost a degree of independence by moving from the status of tenant to that of sharecropper.[161] The literature on the southern and western Germanies often emphasizes the degree to which peasants retained control over the land;[162] however, one should not overlook *changes* in rural structures in these areas that led German scholars to invent a new term, *Wirtschaftsherrschaft,* designating new structures somewhere between the traditional *Grundherrschaft* and the east Elbian *Gutsherrschaft.*[163] As noted earlier, *Wirtschaftsherrschaft* was a system prevalent in the more semiperipheral zones of central Europe.

[160] Stuart Woolf spells out these similarities: "In both countries, the reforming activities of the rulers (Vittorio Amadeo II, Carlo Emanuele II—the Great Elector, Frederick William I) were consciously directed against a nobility regarded as the prime obstacle to the creation of a centralized absolutist monarchy; a new central administration was created, the fiscal privileges of the nobility were attacked; but in both instances a substantial element of fiscal immunity was retained by the nobility, while their control of local administration remained virtually untouched" (1964, 285).

[161] Regarding the increasing power of the landowners, see Jeannin (1969, 69); regarding the rise of sharecropping in Liège, see Ruwet (1957, 69).

[162] See, for example, Weis (1970), who compares the situation in western Germany (except the Rhineland) and France. Peasants owned 35% of the land in France and 90% of the land in Germany west of the Elbe; therefore the French peasants' "economic, social, legal, and psychological situation . . . in the seventeenth and first half of the eighteenth century [was] far more unfavorable . . . in spite of the greater fecundity of French soil and the overall progress in agricultural methods" (p. 14). See also Blaschke (1955, 116) on Saxony.

[163] See the discussion in Lütge (1963, 139, and 1965, 685). The concept, *Wirtschaftsherrschaft,* was invented by Alfred Hoffmann, who explicitly conceived of it as midway between the old *Rentenherrschaft* and the new *Gutsherrschaft* developing in the sixteenth and seventeenth centuries. He defines *Wirtschaftsherrschaft* thus: "In this form the overwhelming majority of arable land remains, as previously, divided into individual, independent peasant-type farms [*bäuerlichen Wirtschaften*]. How-

ever, by means of greater centralization of tax-deliveries [*Abgaben*] and greater involvement in services for the lord, the peasant farms are linked [to each other] more closely than before into an economic association [*Verband*]. This association encompassed not only the purely peasant agricultural economic activities but a series of craft activities as well, and was closely linked to a firm [*selbständingen Organisation*] oriented to the export market" (1952, 98). Hoffmann believes that the shift from the *Rentenherrschaft* to the more modern and capitalist *Wirtschaftsherrschaft* "resulted in a significant rise in the profitability of *grundherrlichen* property" (pp. 166–167).

T. M. Barker says that *Wirtschaftherrschaft* means a "centralized, managerially-rationalized 'farm manor' . . . which combined demesne agriculture and craft production with a host of techniques for profiting from the husbandman's private labours" (1974, 27). Makkai suggests the key feature is that the landlord "exploited his monopolistic rights (tavern, mills, slaughterhouse, and so forth) and also engaged in commercial ventures on his own to increase his income" (1975, 230). Makkai believes it is "untenable" to consider this as a third type of economic system (p. 231). To the extent that the emphasis is on the lord's commercial activities, he is right and can cite Alfred Hoffmann himself, who wrote a whole article on the *Grundherr* as an entrepreneur (1958). But to the extent that *Wirtschaftsherrschaft* was "managerially rationalized," it is different from the traditional *Grundwirtschaft.* It may well be however that all the *Grundwirtschaft* demesnes were moving in the direction of *Wirtschaftsherrschaft* at this time.

The decline of a geographical area normally means that holders of capital in these areas begin to shift the location of their investments, so that collective geographical decline does not mean personal or family decline. There are two forms of capital transfer—transfer to a geographical zone with better economic prospects, which frequently takes the form of physical movement, and transfer in the same zone to units of production with a higher rate of return, often because of higher rates of exploitation. During the seventeenth-century stagnation, capital transfer within a zone took the form of investments in the land. Capitalists located in the dorsal spine engaged in both kinds of transfer at this time. Banking operations gradually moved from such centers as Genoa to Amsterdam,[164] and industrial tradesmen emigrated—the Flemish to England, the Germans to Holland, The Venetians to Lyons, and so on. Rapp is quite right to insist that these industrial workers were not searching for higher pay since they were emigrating after all from the high-wage zones. This movement represented an "entrepreneurial exodus" of small capitalists who risked emigration in order "to gain enormous profits."[165]

The transfer of capital from industry to land at this time has been studied most extensively for northern Italy, perhaps because it occurred most dramatically there. Bulferetti calls this a shift to "safe investments on the land"[166] but this gives, I believe, a false image. Woolf reminds us that the evidence in Piedmont "points fairly conclusively to efficient methods of estate management"[167] of both old and new landowners in this period. Sereni speaks of the "relative continuity" of agricultural improvements in Italian agriculture and indicates that from the sixteenth to the eighteenth century, there was "a mercantile development of agriculture, which the economic depression [of the seventeenth century] was not great enough to interrupt."[168] Clearly capitalist agriculture in northern Italy was an intelligent place for an entrepreneur to place his money when the wool industry was doing badly. The greater self-sufficiency of the northern Italian food supply, aided and abetted by the "march of rice"[169] planted in otherwise unused land, was part of the world overproduction of staple foods that led to the dramatic decline in eastern European grain exports in the seventeenth century.

---

[164] On the decline of Genoa's old financial role as banker of Spain as of the 1620s, see van der Wee (1977, 333, 375). On Genoa's new role as the banker of Europe through investment in state bonds (*titoli pubblici*), first of France and the Hapsburg states, then of England, Scandinavia, Saxony, etc., see Dermigny (1974, 549). Dermigny says Genoese financial investments were so caricatural that "one might, stretching terms only slightly, talk of parasitism, the highest stage of capitalism" (p. 562).

[165] Rapp (1976, 37). Fanfani also notes that there was net emigration from Italy in the seventeenth

century (1959, 130–131).

[166] Bulferetti (1953, 47).

[167] Woolf (1964, 283).

[168] Sereni (1961, 188, 210). Villani says the same thing: "In the seventeenth century there was not regression [in the agricultural sector in Italy], but continuity in development" (1968, 124).

[169] Sereni sees rice as "a force of decisive propulsion for the development of capitalist agriculture" (1961, 187). See also Glamann (1977, 201), who considers the introduction of maize in the Iberian peninsula a parallel phenomenon.

Northern Italian capital found other ways to protect itself. One was the rise, particularly in Tuscan silk production, of the *commenda* (or *commandite*), a form of limited responsibility partnership, that da Silva says we should regard as "a form of centralization of capital.[170] A second was the rise of tax-farming (*appalti di gabelle*), which was linked to state loans.[171] The rise of state debts in northern Italy is seen by some to have served over the seventeenth and eighteenth century as an "incessant drainage of money out of productive activity.[172] Perhaps, but into whose hands? Into the hands of the entrepreneurs who made the loans in the first place—collective decline, but individual capitalist survival (even flourishing).

Let us now turn to the noncore areas that found the long stagnation of the seventeenth century a moment of opportunity rather than of decline. Of these, Sweden clearly heads the list. Sweden was a minor state and was backward politically, economically, and culturally when Sigismund was dethroned in 1599 and Charles (later Charles IX) became Regent. Yet by 1697, and the accession of Charles XII, Sweden had become a great military power in Europe and, relatively speaking, an important industrial power. How had such a transformation come about? In the later Middle Ages, Stockholm was listed as a Hanseatic town, and in general, up to the sixteenth century, Sweden "occupied the position almost of a German colony."[173] Although this had begun to change during the reign of Gustav Vasa (1523–1560), as late as 1612 political demands were still being made to exclude Germans from municipal offices.[174] The other side of this coin was, however, that the guilds never quite took root in Sweden. They were an "exotic growth imported from Germany," and to the extent they did exist, they were restricted to Stockholm.[175]

Somewhere in the middle of the sixteenth century, the volume of trade began to increase. The German monopoly was broken and Dutch and Scots trades entered the picture. Foreign textile imports expanded.[176] Swedish exports grew too, with particular emphasis on minerals.[177] The process of peripheralization seemed to be occurring, and yet the outcome was different from the one in eastern Europe.[178] It is well known that in Sweden the peasantry was juridically very strong. The term for *Estate* (*stånd*) first came into common Swedish usage during the reign of Erik XIV in the mid-

[170] da Silva (1964a, 485); see also pp. 490–491; Carmona (1964, 106–107).

[171] See Romano (1968, 735).

[172] Ventura (1968, 719).

[173] Roberts (1958, **II**, 20).

[174] See Roberts (1958, **II**, 21).

[175] Roberts (1958, **II**, 21).

[176] Karl-Gustav Hidebrand says that the main advantage imported broadcloth had over domestic produce was not durability or elegance but the fact that "the qualities were comparatively uniform" (1954, 101).

[177] See Roberts (1958, **II**, 139–142).

[178] Hans-Edvard Roos refers to my discussion of the "tipping mechanism" in Volume I of this work (1974) and says: "This does not correspond to conditions in Sweden. Despite that the state finances were characterized by big deficits during the second half of the sixteenth century this did not result in a 'downward spiral' with a weaker state and a peripheral position as a consequence. On the contrary. A fundamental point in this essay is that new paths were found out of this dilemma, paths which eventually led to an expansion of the national state and new forms of a national economy" (1976, 65, n. 35).

sixteenth century,[179] as did the term for *parliament* (*riksdag*). When after long
negotiations the arrangements concerning these houses were finally fixed in
1617 by the *riksdagsordning,* Sweden emerged with the unique number of
four, the fourth being the Peasantry, defined as those who owned their
farms.[180] I have previously explained this curiosity as being a result of the
economic weakness of Swedish agriculture due to pedological and climatic
reasons, which meant that the aristocracy saw relatively little profit in "(re)-
feudalizing" land relations in the sixteenth-century expansion of the
European world-economy.[181] As a result, the interests of the aristocracy
were not as directly opposed to the state-building centralization of the Vasa
dynasty as the great landowners of eastern Europe were to their rulers.[182]

   When the first signs of economic downturn began to hit Europe in the
seventeenth century, a strong personality like Gustavus Adolphus (1611–
1632) was able to use the crisis to strengthen the Swedish state still further
and launch an economic transformation. He mobilized Sweden's resources
to fight the Thirty Years' War. He increased taxation and made taxes pay-
able in coin. He instituted tax-farming. He squeezed money out of Prussia
(the so-called Prussian licences, or tolls at ports). He created royal
monopolies, which failed in the salt and grain trades and more or less
succeeded in copper and iron. In short, as Michael Roberts sums it up:

> The peripheral and primitive position which Sweden had occupied under Gustav
> Vasa . . . was now forever abandoned; with Gustavus Adolphus, Sweden's economic
> interests became fully European, and his policy in economic matters conformed to the
> mercantilist patterns of the age.[183]

The secret in many ways was copper. "Copper was the poor man's gold;[184]
and the poor man who needed copper most was that rich man, Spain, which
had largely monopolized silver sources in the sixteenth century. The financial strains for Castile of trying to maintain Hapsburg domination in the
Netherlands led the Duke of Lerma, who led Philip III's government, to
authorize in 1599 a vellon coinage of pure copper. Thus began the great

---

[179] The term was "imported, like so much else,
from Germany to describe any body of men possessing common privileges and duties, common claims
upon society and common function in society"
(Roberts, 1953, **I**, 285).

[180] See Roberts (1958, **II**, 48).

[181] See Wallerstein (1974, 312–313). Perry Anderson makes a similar argument, arguing that "the
index of commercialization in agriculture was probably the lowest anywhere in the continent" (1974a,
179).

[182] Indeed, P. Anderson argues that "the Vasa Reformation [expropriation of the Church, under the
timely banner of the Reformation, by Gustav Vasa
between 1527 and 1542] was undoubtedly the most
successful economic operation of its kind accom-

plished by any dynasty in Europe" (1974a, 173).
Anderson details the economic acquisitions of the
monarchy as well as the measures of administrative
centralization. He concludes that nonetheless these
measures "did not antagonize the aristocracy, which
evinced a basic solidarity with the regime throughout [Gustav Vasa's] rule" (p. 174).

[183] Roberts (1958, **II**, 120), who gives an overall
picture of economic transformation under Gustavus
Adolphus (chap. 2, *passim*). There had in fact been
earlier monopolies in the 1580s in which Willem van
Wijck played an important role; however they had
not lasted.

[184] Glamann (1977, 242). On the primacy of copper among metals (after silver and gold) in the
seventeenth century, see Kellenbenz (1977b, 290).

Spanish inflation, born of the fact that "the temptation to make money out of money proved to be too strong for a perennially bankrupt Government."[185] The issuance of vellon started and stopped throughout the seventeenth century in continuing devaluations, until the inflation was finally halted in 1686.[186]

Though Spain was the main victim of copper-based devaluations and therefore the main stimulus to an augmented world demand for copper,[187] it was not the only victim. There was the *Kipper- und Wipperzeit* in the Germanies from 1621 to 1623 and an extensive French copper coinage from 1607 to 1621.[188] Sweden itself sent on a copper–silver standard in 1625.[189] Furthermore, currency was not the only use to which copper was put at the time. It was needed for the kettles and brassware produced in Holland; and since the mid-fifteenth century, it had been used for bronze cannon founding. Bronze cannon, which gave way to iron cannon in the course of the seventeenth century, was at the height of its use in 1600.[190] In the sixteenth century, the main sources for copper had been the Tyrol, Upper Hungary, and Thuringia. Whether these sources declined because of exhaustion or were effaced by Swedish output,[191] Sweden rapidly became Europe's leading producer, and copper mining became the key economic activity of Sweden.[192]

In this first great leap forward—starting in the time of Gustavus Adolphus and continuing under the administrative hand of Axel Oxenstierna during the reign of Queen Christina—the link to the Dutch was crucial. We can talk of Swedish economic development being largely (at least up to 1660) "under Dutch auspices," as does de Vries;[193] but this is a bit ambiguous. Treue expresses the phenomenon more carefully: "It was very meaningful in world-historical terms . . . that Sweden in the various years of its

[185] Elliott (1966, 300). One of the consequences of this inflation, begun in the sixteenth but culminating in the seventeenth century, was a sharp internal concentration of capital (see Ruiz Martín, 1970, 60).

[186] See Elliott (1966, 300, 329, 344, 352–353, 361, 365). The minting of vellon in Castile only ended in 1693.

[187] P. Anderson, for example, argues that "it was the issue of the new copper *vellón* by Lerma in the devaluation of 1599 that created a soaring international demand for the output of the Kopparberg at Falun" (1974a, 183). It is surely no accident that it was in 1599 that there was a "change in the monetary policy of the Swedish government"; they began in that year "to issue a pure copper vellón currency in enormous quantities, [which] led to a sudden increase in the price of copper after 1600" (Roberts, 1958, **II**, 33).

[188] See van der Wee (1977, 299).

[189] Heckscher argues that the point of this was both to raise the price of copper and to reduce the need to import silver (1954, 88–89).

[190] See Glamann (1977, 243).

[191] Glamann argues that the central European mines had been declining in output in the last half of the sixteenth century (1977, 189). Roberts argues that it was the Thirty Years' War that cut off the Hungarian mines and disabled the Thuringian mines (1958, **II**, 90). Kellenbenz rejects both these explanations and sees the decline in Hungarian production and hence in the central German copper market, as due to the "glut of Swedish copper" (1974, 262; see also 1977b, 340).

[192] See Roberts (1958, **II**, 90). See Heckscher: "The copper industry was the strongest link between Sweden's political expansion and her economic development" (1954, 85). Eventually it would be challenged by Japanese copper, which first appeared on the Amsterdam market in 1623, but whether the competition was significant before 1650 is a matter of controversy. See the references to the debate in Roberts (1958, **II**, 97, n. 3); see also Nordmann (1964, 474–475).

[193] J. de Vries (1976, 21).

struggle for existence and of becoming a great power had the international merchants and entrepreneurs of Holland and Hamburg on its side."[194] It was Amsterdam (and also Hamburg) that bought Swedish copper, both for reexport as the basis of coinage and to supply the "considerable copper-working industry in the towns of the Netherlands."[195] Under Gustavus Adolphus, we see the start of foreign investments (largely Dutch and Flemish) and a considerable direct foreign managerial involvement in the Swedish mining and metallurgical industries.[196] Extensive Dutch loans were made on the condition that "repayment was effective in copper."[197] The familiar pattern of international debt peonage was taking hold.

Gustavus Adolphus tried to eliminate this threat in 1619 by creating the Swedish Trading Company to control the marketing of Swedish copper.[198] The king sought to combine the fiscal advantages of greater short-run income and structural change. The original charter granted a monopoly to the Company on condition that it establish brassworks and copper refineries in Sweden within three years. Foreign capital was to be welcomed in the company, and indeed it was successfully attracted. The Company tried to play off the Hamburg against the Amsterdam markets; but the world copper market suddenly fell, and by 1627 the Company was dissolved. Was this perhaps manipulated by Dutch capitalists? We do know that the Trip firm, a major investor in Swedish copper, also had links with the VOC (Dutch East India Company), which ordered copper from Japan in 1624. Trip purchased the whole of the VOC's Japanese copper imports in 1626 and 1627. We also know that the Trips after 1627 granted new loans to the Swedes, again repayable in copper, and hence recreated the Amsterdam copper staple.[199]

The failure of this putative attempt to effect Swedish economic independence from the Dutch will not stretch our credibility if we remember Alderman Cockayne's Project, a comparable English failure, that was roughly contemporaneous (1614–1617). We are, after all, discussing the era of Dutch hegemony. What is striking about the efforts of Gustavus Adolphus

[194] Treue (1957, 28). See Polišenský: "Gothenburg and other towns were just outposts of Holland on Swedish soil while its copper and steel had become commodities controlled by mixed Dutch–Swedish entrepreneurship as represented by families like the Trips and De Geer" (1971, 175). See also Roberts: "The growth of the new Göteborg that arose after 1619 is the visible sign of this changing orientation [westward]. For Göteborg's trade was all outside the Baltic; the most important of her markets was Amsterdam; and Dutch skippers settled in Göteborg, as they settled in Hamburg, in order that they might trade freely with Spain, in defiance of the prohibition of the States General" (1958, II, 122).

[195] Glamann (1977, 244).

[196] See Roberts (1958, II, 28). There had been the

instance of Willem van Wijck's involvement earlier, in the 1580s.

[197] Glamann (1977, 245).

[198] The timing was intriguing. The Company was founded on July 24, 1619. 1619 was a year of acute commercial crisis. It was also a year of political crisis in Holland. On April 23, the Synod of Dordrecht formally condemned the Arminian five points, the *Sententia Remonstrantium*, and on May 13, Oldenbarnevelt was executed. Did Gustavus Adolphus deliberately try to seize the conjuncture of political weakness of those Regents most involved in Baltic trade, who tended to be in the Arminian camp, a weakness compounded by generalized commercial crisis?

[199] See the discussions in Roberts (1958, II, 92–98) and Glamann (1977, 245–246).

was not his inability to best Dutch entrepreneurs but the degree of his success in building Sweden's military strength and industrial strength—and the two went together, for as Nordmann says, Sweden in the seventeenth century was "a nation in arms, living off war, and making [war] its national industry."[200] Gustavus Adolphus was the leading military innovator of his time. He took the organizational methods of Maurice of Nassau, improved them, and created a pattern for European armies that would last until the French Revolution. He emphasized training and discipline and made tactical reforms that restored to all the arms an emphasis on offensive action. Perhaps his most important innovation was that his army consisted of peasants in arms. "Its modernity," says Nordmann, "lay in its being a national army and not an army of mercenaries."[201]

Mercenaries, let us not forget, were the great advance of the sixteenth century. Gustavus Adolphus was not able to dispense with mercenaries altogether, but he reduced their role. He was able to build on the weakness of the feudal tradition in Sweden and on the fact that the heavily armed cavalry of the Middle Ages had never been adopted in Sweden, due partly to topographical considerations and partly to the strength of the peasantry, which was, in part, also a consequence of soil conditions.

> Here, more than anywhere else in Europe, the primitive Germanic military tradition had persisted; and the invader who ventured into the Swedish forests was met by a *levée en masse* of the population, fighting mainly on foot, and grouped, if the country were open, in large irregular masses.[202]

The conscript army was based on provincial regiments, which preferred craftsmen and young peasants, and, unlike other armies of the time, rejected "scum." Central clothing depots were created. The army was paid regularly in a decentralized system of assigning income from taxpaying households. Weapons and munitions were standardized and great emphasis was placed on artillery.

Gustavus Adolphus built up an arms industry so that Sweden became self-supporting.[203] One crucial feature he added to his military organization was to shift a large part of the costs outside of Sweden. A famous instance is the role of the so-called Prussian licences in the financing of Sweden's military role in the Thirty Years' War. These licences were authorized by the Truce of Altmark, signed by Poland and Sweden in 1629. They permitted Sweden to lay tolls on ports in Brandenburg and Courland, and what was most valuable, on Gdańsk. The yield was large, equivalent to

[200] Nordmann (1972, 133).

[201] Nordmann (1972, 133). The Swedish army was therefore the first modern nonlooting army (see Hutton, 1968, 524).

[202] Roberts (1958, **II,** 189). The other country that had maintained this infantry tradition was Switzerland.

[203] This description is based on a chapter in Roberts called "The Army", see also "The Navy" (1958, **II,** chaps. 3 and 4). Given these achievements, it is no wonder that the Swedish army served as a model for Cromwell, for the *Roi-Sergent* (Frederick William I of Prussia, the "soldier-king"), and for Peter the Great (see Nordmann, 1972, 147).

about 20% of Sweden's recorded war costs. When these privileges ended in 1635, they were replaced in the Treaty of Stuhmsdorf with the right to secure tolls in Livonia.[204] Essentially, Sweden was getting a cut of the surplus-value being transferred from eastern to northwestern Europe and using it to create a semiperipheral status for herself.

The army was a crucial tool for this rising semiperipheral state, but the payoff was to be in industrialization—and copper was not enough. Over the seventeenth century, copper gave way to iron as the pivot of Swedish mining and industrial production. For one thing, iron was replacing copper as a material in the world market—not only in artillery,[205] but also in household ware.[206] From Sweden's vantage point, however, the difference between copper and iron was that she owned a disproportionate share of the available world copper ore at this time, whereas iron deposits were widespread in Europe. To compete as an iron producer, Sweden could not bank on having a near monopoly of ores and on techniques of protection alone. Yet compete it did, very effectively, by taking a piece of resource luck and transforming it into a socioeconomic advantage. The luck was that Swedish iron ore was "of unusually high purity," which, given the technology of the time, made a great deal of difference and put Sweden in an "extremely strong marginal position."[207] Sweden's "emphasis on quality" in production[208] was the chief selling point of Swedish iron throughout the seventeenth and eighteenth centuries.

Swedish iron mining went back at least to the twelfth century. Even then, the fine quality of her malleable iron, *osmund,* was known throughout Europe.[209] It was Gustav Vasa in the first half of the sixteenth century who

[204] See Bowman (1936, 343–344) and Åström (1973, 92–94). The costs of war had escalated dramatically between 1630 and 1635, the period of the licences. Before 1630, it had cost the Swedes 500,000 rixdalers annually; after that, 20–30 million. Jeannin says: "The essential precondition of this jump [in expenditure] was that war nourishes war" (1969, 324). He cites Gustavus Adolphus who wrote in 1628: "If we cannot say that *bellum se ipsum alet* [war sustains war], I do not see how we can successfully accomplish what we have begun." The key question is whether the Prussian licences made it possible for the Swedes to respond to independently escalating war costs or the Treaty of Altmark and the consequent Prussian licences made it possible for them to escalate war costs—for themselves and for others? In analyzing Sweden's solvency, attained *without* the sale of offices, an achievement to be compared to France's inability to do the same, Roberts comments: "One possible answer to this difficulty [the weakness of the Swedish tax base] lay in the paradox that security and solvency might be found in what to Sweden's victims appeared to be aggression. War might be made to sustain war, and might bring rich rewards besides: a war economy,

rather than a peace economy, was what suited Sweden's needs." Furthermore, when later "her armies ceased to strike fear into her neighbours, the real inadequacy of her resources became increasingly apparent" (1973a, 12, 14).

[205] "The Swedish entrepreneur Louis de Geer [actually a Dutchman who invested and lived in Sweden] declared in 1644 that iron cannon could be procured for the war fleet at one-third the price of bronze cannon. . . . In the subsequent decades, iron cannon, now improved to such an extent as to stand comparison with the older ordnance even from the technical standpoint, gained ground everywhere" (Glamann, 1977, 243).

[206] "A shift can be detected away from utensils fabricated from copper and towards those manufactured from iron. A cheapening of the price of iron products was partly responsible for this, but so was the fact that iron pots and pans were easier to clean and did not taint the taste of food" (Glamann, 1977, 203).

[207] Samuelsson (1968, 28).

[208] Samuelsson (1968, 30). See also the discussion of iron ore technology in Sweden (pp. 30–31).

[209] See Roberts (1958, **II,** 29).

first chafed when low-priced *osmund* was exported to Germany for hammering into high-priced bar iron. To end this resource outflow, he imported German technicians and established Swedish forges. Nonetheless, more *osmund* continued to be produced than bar iron. *Osmund* accounted for two-thirds of the production until between 1600 and 1650, when the ratio changed to equal amounts of each. A steel industry was launched. The shift from mining *osmund* to forging bar iron required a considerable amount of capital investment, much of which the king provided. This investment, in turn, required the expansion of mines and the concomitant colonization of remote areas that had large ore deposits, such as Varmland.[210] By now, the Swedish iron industry was of sufficient importance to tempt Dutch entrepreneurs. In the 1580s, Willem van Wijck had acquired a lease of the royal mines in Uppland and an interest in the copper monopoly. Under Gustavus Adolphus, the state divested itself of direct management, and with the rise of the arms industry, foreign capital became even more interested. In the early seventeenth century, the Dutchman, Louis de Geer, played a central role.[211] While the actual control of the industry moved back and forth between the state and foreign entrepreneurs, the relationship was more one of symbiosis than of conflict.

Nordmann speaks of a take-off in iron production and a "first industrial revolution."[212] The state encouraged iron production and was the chief customer, using the products for its military equipment. The role of traditional small ironmakers was preserved—that is, to engage in iron mining and the making of pig iron—while foreign entrepreneurs with large ironworks were "given a monopoly of refining processes plus guaranteed access to cheap raw materials and semimanufactures."[213] In these large ironworks, the labor power was largely made up of persons recruited from Sweden's peripheral zones—Finns, and peasants from Swedish regions where there was grain deficiency—as well as of persons seeking exemption from military service and fugitives from justice. In short, the foreign entrepreneurs were

---

[210] Roberts cites the colonization of Varmland by Charles IX (1599–1611) as "a famous example of the truth of [Swedish historian Erik Gustav] Geijer's dictum that 'iron opens up the country' ('*järnet bryter bygd*')" (1958, **II,** 36); Roberts also discusses the history of state intervention in the iron industry (29–31, 35–36).

[211] Here, and in footnote 205, de Geer is identified as a Dutchman, for he was so viewed in Sweden. But the de Geer family illustrates the mobility of capital. For reasons of politico-economic opportunity, the de Geer family of Liège moved its "headquarters" to Amsterdam only at the end of the sixteenth century (see Yernaux, 1939, 101, 120–124). See also the reference (p. 195) to Dutch investments in putting-out industries in central Europe and northern Italy. Kamen claims that these

investors were Flemish and Walloons or Belgians, that is, from the southern Netherlands—and Liège? (see 1972, 92–99). This is true for the last half of the sixteenth century, which is the period from which he draws his specific references; but in the course of the Revolt of the Netherlands, many of these Flemish settled in Holland, and subsequently invested elsewhere. In these other countries, in the seventeenth century, they were perceived as Dutchmen, and not only by the "English contemporaries" to whom Kamen attributes "the use of the word . . . [which] hid" the fact that they were Flemish (1972, 95). Word usage more often reveals rather than hides a social reality.

[212] Nordmann (1972, 137).

[213] Samuelsson (1968, 31).

supplied with cheap labor.[214] The role reserved for small ironmakers did not constitute the preservation of space for Swedish entrepreneurs, but quite the opposite, the reduction of these ironmakers to semiproletarian status through a *Verlagssystem,* by which they were indebted to foreign merchants. The Swedish iron story paralleled the general European story in textiles:

> Foreign importers made advances to the exporting merchants in Stockholm and Göteborg, who in turn gave credit to the ironmasters who, as the last link in the chain, made advances to the workers. . . . All parties were bound to their creditors. . . . The workers generally drew their credits in the form of commodities from the master's store. That could hardly be avoided as the works usually were situated in isolated places in the country.[215]

It may be wondered whether the picture of copper and iron production that has been drawn is one to boast about, for foreign domination seems to be the *leitmotiv.* Two things must be borne in mind however. First, for Sweden, unlike let us say for Poland, the seventeenth century was a time of the development of new export industries. This was in addition to the export of tar and other naval stores, which would be more comparable to Polish grain and wood exports.[216] Second, Sweden could eventually "nationalize" the industries by ennobling the entrepreneurs.[217] The crucial element was the conscious use of the state machinery. In effect the Swedish state had three near monopolies in the European world-economy of the seventeenth century—copper, high quality iron, and tar. Linking itself at

[214] See Roberts (1958, **II,** 37–38). Birgitta Odén, in a private communication, wrote me she doubts this, since, other than for charcoaling, "the labor force was highly skilled and hierarchically organized."

[215] Heckscher (1954, 99). A study by Munktell (1934) indicates that the workers engaged both in mining and first-stage smelting in their huts and that the ironmasters provided them primarily with wood. I had access to this study with the assistance of John Flint. The putting-out system, under the name *utarbetningsträtt,* was also extensively used in copper production. See Roos (1976, 59) and also Boëthius (1958, 148–149).

[216] See Samuelsson (1968, 28–29). Grain export declined to virtually zero in the seventeenth century. See Åström (1973, 67, Table 5). Lumber export was curtailed both by Norwegian competition and a government embargo on the export of oak, needed for Sweden's own navy. See Samuelsson (1968, 29).

[217] See Samuelsson: "The seventeenth-century struggle for a 'national' merchant marine, not to mention other Swedish endeavours on behalf of domestic industry and commerce generally, may be compared to the aspirations of an ex-colony which,

having achieved political autonomy, also seeks to throw off the economic yoke. Perhaps the parallel may be even more boldly drawn. . . . Just as some of the newly emergent African states have been concerned to retain former colonial officials to help run their economy and public administration, so Sweden during the seventeenth century was concerned to persuade erstwhile financiers and other businessmen from abroad to become Swedish subjects. The idea was to 'Swedify' their capital and capabilities by 'adopting' them" (1968, 41).

See also Heckscher: "The Hansards regarded themselves as agents of a more advanced civilization and Sweden as a colonial territory; they remained thoroughly German and were never assimilated. But it did not even occur to the aliens of the seventeenth century that the country might have belonged to them, and they, or at least their children, acclimatized with almost incredible speed. As a rule, the second generation was Swedish by language as well as by custom. . . . The governments of the seventeenth century also pursued a deliberate policy aimed at absorbing foreigners" (1954, 107–108). The policy to which Heckscher refers was that of ennoblement.

first to the hegemonic power, and later profiting from and maneuvering between rival core states, the Swedish state machinery pursued a mercantilist policy comparable to that of England and France at the time.[218] Sweden was in a sense the OPEC of its day. It used the three quasimonopolies to create a strong bargaining position, "without which the political–military expansion would have been unattainable."[219] The political–military expansion in turn made it possible to develop the transformation industries.

Gustavus Adolphus laid the base for Swedish military power, and allowed his successors to reign over what Anderson calls the "Hammer of the East,"[220] at least until Sweden reached the limits of its power by its recognition in 1721 of nonvictory in the Great Northern War. As long as the Dutch remained a hegemonic power, Sweden did well.[221] Sweden acquired Scania from Denmark by the Treaty of Roskilde in 1658. Not only was Scania the "key to the Baltic," by virtue of having command of the Sound (Öresund), but a century later it turned out to be Sweden's breadbasket.[222] By midcentury, Sweden had acquired Estonia, Livonia, Ingria, and Kexholm, turning this eastern Baltic area into "colonies of the Swedish–Finnish motherland";[223] it also acquired Bremen-Verden, Pommern, Halland, and Jämtland farther west. In short, by the 1650s, the only way to describe Sweden's Baltic policy was that it was one of "conscious economic imperialism."[224]

[218] See Deyon (1969, 36–37). Nonetheless, Deyon also suggests that unlike England and France, Sweden was "too tied to the economy of the United Provinces" to have a coherent economic policy (p. 22).

[219] Samuelsson (1968, 29). Actually Samuelsson calls the three monopolies a "commercial supremacy," but this seems to me to be verbal inflation.

[220] P. Anderson (1974a, 198), who compares Sweden's military role vis-à-vis eastern Europe in the seventeenth century to Spain's military role in western Europe in the sixteenth century. He dates Sweden's time as a great power from 1630 to 1720. Roberts dates it from the capture of Riga by Gustavus Adolphus in 1621 to the Peace of Nystad in 1721, "exactly a century" (1973a, 1).

[221] Roberts dates Sweden's comparative success story as going up to the 1670s—exactly our dating for the end of Dutch hegemony. This of course explains why "Sweden does not exactly fit any of the generalizations which have been put forward to explain 'the crisis of the seventeenth century'" (Roberts, 1962, 53).

[222] See Samuelsson (1968, 75).

[223] Åström (1973, 68). The imperial structure was stratified, as Åström indicates: "Their ancient aristocracy, organized as a knightly corporation, was German in language and ways of thought. This was true also of the burghers in the most important trading entrepôts, in stable Riga, stagnating Reval and flourishing Narva. . . . Governors-general and

governors, with their little courts and staffs of officials and servants from Sweden and Finland, administered the duchies on behalf of the Swedish crown; garrisons from Sweden and Finland formed the basis of their authority. The Estonian and Livonian nobility lived on their estates, encompassed by an enserfed peasantry which spoke another tongue than that of their masters." From the point of view of these east Baltic areas, the seventeenth century represented a constant struggle, not too successful, against the incursion of foreign capital. See Arnold Soom: "Doubtless the lack of capital played a large role [in this matter]. In order to be successfully competitive with the Dutch, one needed very large sums of capital" (1962, 458).

[224] Roberts (1973a, 1), who also argues that the attempt thereby to secure "a permanently stable financial situation" was one that failed, but there "can be no doubt of the economic importance of the empire to Sweden herself" (pp. 4, 5, 6). Lundkvist also sees Sweden's "commercial aspirations" in her Baltic empire as failing, except for the advantages deriving from the control of Riga, and the consequent access to the flax and hemp grown in its hinterland. "The statistics for the trade of Riga show an unmistakable upward trend in the latter part of the seventeenth century; and the importance of the town steadily increased" (1973, 47). Dunsdorfs says that for trade with points outside the Baltic, there were only three important harbors in the seventeenth century: Danzig (Gdańsk), Königsberg, and Riga

Side by side with the politico-commercial expansion went the rise in size and importance of Swedish merchant shipping[225] and naval fleets[226] in the Baltic.

The creation of a relatively strong and efficacious Swedish state-machinery depended on curbing the power of the nobility. This was possible because of Sweden's class structure at the time and because of her roles in the world division of labor and the interstate system. The policy of *avsöndring* (severance) of Crown properties and revenues to the nobility, which had begun in the sixteenth century, accelerated in the first half of the seventeenth century. This policy "encompasse[d] a rather wide range of historical phenomena in terms of state finance."[227] It included the process of tax-farming, started by Gustavus Adolphus, as well as the alienation of Crown land and of the revenue of freehold land to nobility by sale and donation in return for civil or military service.[228] These were means of obtaining rapidly liquid resources for the Crown, as well as of enlarging the monetized area of the Swedish economy; but the advantages for the Crown were bought at the price of increasing politico-economic power for the upper nobility. The new power was codified in the *ridderhusordningen* (Nobility Matriculation Law) of 1626 (reconfirmed in 1644), which limited the right to vote in the Estate of the Nobility (created in the *riksdagsordning* of 1617) to 126 matriculated noble families, thus excluding the poor petty nobility (*knapar*). This "high nobility were by Swedish standards extremely wealthy, and were probably growing wealthier—both absolutely, and relatively to the crown."[229]

The peasantry was strong too, however, and it had also been organized as an Estate in the *riksdagsordning* of 1617. There were in fact three kinds of peasants: *kronobönder,* or peasants on Crown lands; *frälsebönder,* or peasants on noble lands; and *skattebönder,* or taxpaying, that is, freehold, peasants. The freehold peasants paid in taxes approximately what the Crown–peasants paid in rent, but they of course had a more secure legal position. The *frälsebönder* were exempt from state taxation and paid to the noble only about half of what the other two types paid, but their position was highly insecure. They could be evicted easily, were subject to the lord's juridical authority, and had to do about 30 days service a year for the noble.[230]

(see 1947, 2). Jensch shows an increase in ships coming into the Riga harbor—from 96 in 1600–1609 to 263 in 1650–1657, of which Dutch ships went from 65 to 221 (see 1930, 88).

[225] The number of ships went from some 40 to some 300 annually by the second half of the century. See Dunsdorfs (1947, 6).

[226] See Jeannin (1969, 95).

[227] Ågren (1973a, 9).

[228] See Carr (1964, 20–21).

[229] Roberts (1958, **II,** 1958, 59; and see the discussion on pp. 57–60). See also Samuelsson (1968, 53–54).

[230] See Roberts (1958, **II,** 1958, 50–52). See also Kàre D. Tonnesson: "It is among the tenants of the nobility [*frälsebönder*] that one finds the large majority of peasants who were subject to the corvée. The corvée spread and became more burdensome in the seventeenth century following the creation of large agricultural estates [*exploitations*] centered around noble castles, which were constructed with new splendor in this period" (1971, 307). Tonnesson observes that these were regional differences: There were few estates in the north, doubtless because a cash crop was more difficult to grow profitably, and there was a high concentration west of Stockholm

Furthermore, when the Estate of the Peasantry was established, the *frälse-bönder* were excluded from membership.[231] In general, although there seemed to be little overall difference in the economic rewards of the three kinds of peasant status, it was generally felt that the insecurity of tenure of the *frälsebönder* was "a considerable disadvantage."[232] The *avsöndring* had the effect of making some former Crown–peasants into *frälsebönder*; and *de facto*, if not *de jure*, this was also happening to many freeholders.[233] The figures are dramatic. By 1654 land controlled by the nobility had risen from 21.4% to 63%.[234] The peasants reacted. By 1634 the Estate of the Peasantry, fearing that the peasantry was on the road to *servitus*, was "clamouring for a curtailment of noble privileges." A peasant spokesman in 1650 said: "They know that in other lands the commonalty are slaves; they fear the like fate for themselves, who are nevertheless born a free people."[235]

The problem with the sale of tax income to raise revenue is that it solves one year's budgetary crisis at the cost of exacerbating budget crises of future years. We must bear in mind that while Sweden's mercantilist efforts involved heavy military expenditures for constant expansion,[236] she was a country poor in natural resources (which were being used up) and small in population (which was about a million Swedes and a half-million Finns and others in the mid-seventeenth century). This led to a "condition of strain" on state finances, which prevailed throughout the seventeenth century.[237] The need to finance the Polish War in 1655 precipitated the first so-called *reduktion,* or return of land from the control of the nobles to the crown.[238] The *reduktion* of 1655 was relatively minor. Former crown lands in so-called inalienable areas were taken back, and exactly one-quarter of other lands donated since 1632 were handed back (*fjardepartsrafsten*). Any land given away in allodial tenure since 1604 in defiance of the decisions of the Diet of Norrköping that donations could only be made on "feudal" terms were to be redesignated as being held on such "feudal" terms. Although the 1655 *reduktion* was neither massive in scope nor vigorously enforced,[239] it was nonetheless a start; and combined with the demographic growth of the nobility, it put a squeeze on them that pushed them to seek a larger proportion of income through government office.[240]

and in the former Danish provinces of Scania and Halland.

[231] See Carlsson (1972, 575).

[232] Dahlgren (1973a, 109).

[233] See Roberts (1958, **II**, 55–56).

[234] Hatton (1974, 4, n. 2). Tonnesson (1971, 308) says noble land went from 15% in 1560 to 60% in 1655. Jutikkala says that from 1600 to mid-century, the increase in Sweden was from one-fourth to two-thirds, and in Finland from 5% to one-half (1975, 159–160).

[235] Roberts (1958, **II**, 153). The statement by a peasant spokesman is cited by Roberts from G. Wittrock (1927).

[236] "The Swedish empire in the seventeenth cen-

tury could continue to exist only as long as it continued to expand" (Dahlgren, 1973b, 175).

[237] Åström (1973, 58; see also pp. 65–75).

[238] See Dahlgren, who believes the war to have been only the immediate excuse: "Charles X had in fact planned a *reduktion* even before his accession [in 1654]. He considered the *reduktion* a necessary measure quite irrespective of whether Sweden were at war or not" (1973b, 178).

[239] See Ågren (1973b, 240–241) and Dahlgren (1973a, 120).

[240] See Ågren (1973a, 27; also 1973b, 237–241). This squeeze was even more severe after the *reduktion* of 1680. See Dahlgren (1973a, 126–131).

We have already mentioned the role of the Prussian licences in the search for revenue sources. They came to an end in 1635, and they were replaced between 1637 and 1679 by French subsidies. These subsidies were so important that Åström calls Sweden in this period "virtually a French satellite" and Swedish armies a "direct instrument of French foreign policy in central and eastern Europe." The sums involved in French subsidies were less than those involved in the Prussian licences, however; no doubt, as Åström observes, "the mulcting of the Baltic trade was to be preferred to dependence on French subsidies,"[241] but they were better than nothing. Of course the French, whose Baltic trade was minimal,[242] were quite willing to build Sweden up as a potential commercial rival to the Dutch and English. This dependence on French subsidies also served the interests of the high aristocracy, who sustained their "expensive aristocratic style of living" by use of revenue from the subsidies plus revenues from the hypothecation or sale of royal lands. In effect, the high aristocracy bought the royal lands and then spent the revenue on themselves in their capacity as members of the council of state during the *de jure* and *de facto* regencies of the middle and late seventeenth centuries—more than half the period between the death of Gustavus Adolphus in 1632 and the effective assumption of power by Charles XI in the late 1670s.[243]

The "great" *reduktion* came in 1680, and it does not seem difficult to explain it in economic terms. Growing state expenditures in a time of overall stagnation,[244] increasing diversion of state revenue to the nobility,[245] and

[241] Åström (1973, 94), who notes that Sweden also obtained small subsidies on occasion from Holland, England, Spain, and some German states but that these were "of quite subordinate importance." In general, Sweden attempted to channel west European trade with Poland and Russia via its customs ports at Narva, Gothenburg, and Stockholm. See Åström (1963, 50).

[242] See Bamford (1954).

[243] See Åström (1973, 73, 86–87). It was the Finnish peasant more than the Swedish who paid the price of this grab by the nobility. Finland (and also Kexholm) constituted the Promised Land because the donations along the shores of the Gulf of Bothnia and Lake Ladoga offered good transport access "for the export of the produce of the great estates of the high council nobility" (Åström, 1973, 87). When it came to providing military fodder, Finland also contributed more than its share. "It is perhaps an unhistorical parallel, or an eccentric exaggeration, to say that at the opening of the Age of Greatness the Finnish cavalry formed a kind of analogue to the Cossacks. But there is truth in it nevertheless" (Åström, 1973, 64).

[244] Nordmann reminds us of the importance of the general European price decline; the decline in Sweden was "late" (post-1650), "but nonetheless ap-

preciable" (1971, 454). It was "late" in Sweden in the same sense that it had been late in England and the United Provinces. See Jeannin (1969, 95). The effects of the price decline on state revenue was exacerbated by the fact that shortly after a moderate rise in prices began (in 1672), Sweden entered the Franco-Dutch war (in 1675). Rosén argues: "By threatening not to pay subsidies Louis XIV forced Sweden to attack Brandenburg, the ally of the United Provinces, and in June 1675 the Swedish army suffered a defeat at Fehrbellin. Against her will Sweden had been dragged into the struggle of the great powers. . . . The battle of Fehrbellin, an insignificant clash of arms, robbed the Swedish army of that nimbus of strength which had surrounded it since the Thirty Years' War" (1961, 529). See Roberts: "By 1679, . . . the power which thirty years before had terrified and astonished Europe had been reduced to a position of considerable ignominy. . . . The heirs of Gustav Adolf had become the vassals of France: French and Dutch diplomats debated the fate of Swedish territories in the same tone as they discussed the possessions of Spain, as pieces of booty or objects of exchange" (1967, 230). Rosén adds: "Exactly as the war of 1657–1660 gave the impetus to the introduction of absolutism in Denmark-Norway, the war of 1675–

the ending of the French subsidies[246] combined to produce a financial crisis for the Crown, which was resolved by a political decision, made possible by the fact that the Crown had far more allies than the high aristocracy. The decision was two successive acts of *reduktion*. In 1680 the Diet resolved to return the so-called Norrköping-resolution estates, which were held on "feudal" terms from the Crown, (except for those worth less than 600 silver *daler,* which thus exempted the property of the lesser nobility). In 1682 the Diet further agreed that the medieval Land Law gave the king not only the power to create fiefs but to revoke them; this in effect gave the king carte blanche to proceed on *reduktions* as he wished.[247] There seems little doubt that much land was in fact transferred to the Crown and that the Crown emerged richer and with gains that were the nobility's loss.[248] Furthermore, much of this land was later sold by Charles XII to civil servants, to bourgeois, to nobility—but under terms such that it became taxable land.[249]

1679 led to absolutism in Sweden" (1961, 531). See also Østerud: "Absolute monarchy was established in Sweden about 1680 as a response to a severe financial and military crisis" (1976, 8).

[245] Dahlgren feels that the Swedish nobility were doing distinctly better economically than their counterparts elsewhere in Europe: "In other European countries, and even in a country as close to Sweden as Denmark, it was frequently the case that the landowning nobility found itself passing through a period of acute economic crisis. . . . One gets the distinct impression that there is no trace of any such crisis in the period before 1680 as far as the Swedish nobility is concerned. One circumstance which seems to indicate that they were doing reasonably well is the fact that so very many of them, not least those belonging to the higher aristocracy, took advantage of opportunities for involvement in many lucrative ventures of various kinds, or in shipping, or in the trading companies. . . . It was not until after 1680 that the Swedish nobility was confronted with a crisis, and when it came it was the result of political decisions rather than economic factors" (1973a, 124–125).

It should not be forgotten that the *avsöndring* had particularly benefitted the high aristocracy (the so-called *högadel* as opposed to the *lågadel*) and that the increasing dependence of the aristocracy on state service for revenue was, until 1680, largely a phenomenon of the *lågadel.* One explanation of the *reduktion* is that the latter found their salaries unpaid in the war of 1675–1679 and wished to ensure their income by increasing state revenues through confiscations of the lands of the *högadel.* See the discussion of the theories of J. Rosén and C. A. Hessler in Ågren (1976, 56–58, 79–80). Åström adds an ethnic consideration to the discussion of the split in the aristocracy. He points out that both Christina and even Charles XI had raised into the ranks of the

högadel many German Balts, and that the "zealots" for the *reduktion* were "men from Finland—such as Creutz, Fleming or Wrede; or men from central Sweden whose families had only recently risen in the social scale" (1973, 77). Within Finland, too, the "champions" of the *reduktion* were those whose baronies were "the most unfavorably situated," that is, on the Gulf of Bothnia and Lake Ladoga (p. 87). Liiv's research on Estonia tends to confirm Åström. In Livland, the aristocracy lost five-sixths of its land, in Estland two-fifths, in Saaremaa almost a third. See Liiv (1935, 35).

[246] The Franco–Dutch war ended with the Treaties of Nijmegen in 1678–1679. "Louis XIV, without any real consultation, make peace on Sweden's behalf with her enemies. . . . Louis XIV's failure to consult Charles XI was resented. France had also given Charles XI the promise, given in the alliance of 1672, not to make peace with the United Provinces till Sweden had received certain concessions in respect of tolls, and had included in the peace treaty with the Dutch a trade agreement so disadvantageous that Charles XI refused to ratify it" (Rosén, 1961, 530). Hatton sees the *reduktion* as primarily "a largely successful attempt to solve 'the problem of the peace,' to rid Sweden of alliances and subsidy treaties which limited her freedom of choice in European affairs and hindered the 'balancing policy'" (1968a, 74).

[247] See Ågren (1973b, 243).

[248] Ågren (1973b, 257). In addition, this land transfer had an indirect effect on agricultural productivity, as Heckscher points out: "Deprived of their extensive land holdings, the nobles tended to become gentlemen farmers rather than *rentiers.* . . . They were more productive . . . than previously" (1954, 128).

[249] See Aspvall (1966, 3–4).

On the other hand, one should not exaggerate the decline of the nobility. For in the period prior to the *reduktion,* in addition to the steady rise in the percentage of noble-owned (*frälse*) land at the expense of both crown land and freeholds, a second shift had been occurring. Within the category of *frälse* land, there was a subcategory of *ypperligt* (or supremely) *frälse* land, which referred to the manorial home farm, the *säteri,* and its immediate surroundings as opposed to *strögods,* or scattered lands, farmed by *frälsebön-der.* Although the latter lands had some minor obligations to the Crown, the former had none whatsoever. In the century prior to the *reduktion, ypperligt frälse* land had been growing as a percentage of *frälse* land; that is, there had been increasing concentration of noble land.[250] When the *reduktion* occurred, the nobles had the right to choose which lands to return. In general, they chose the *strögods* and retained the manors, thus increasing still further the concentration of their land at the expense of the *frälsebönder.*[251]

The state nonetheless secured more from the *reduktion* than increased income in general. Specifically, it achieved a more secure basis for financing the army through the revision in 1682 of the system of payment known as *indelningsverket* (allotment system). The farms of the whole country were now divided into groups of from three to four farms (*rote*), out of whose revenues the soldiers would be paid and on whose area they would be quartered in cottages (*soldattorp*). The officers were settled on land confiscated from the nobility in the *reduktion.* Bigger farms (*rusthåll*) had to maintain a cavalryman; farms on the coast had to support seamen (*båtsmän*). A system of "substitution" for conscription meant that the soldiers, cavalrymen, and sailors were no longer recruited from the class of peasant land-

---

[250] See Østerud (1976, 13–14).

[251] See Rosén (1961, 534), Østerud (1976, 14), and Dahlgren (1973a, 125). Land concentration was further abetted by the fact that "some of the leading servants of the crown [used] the drop in the price of land which was a consequence of the *reduktion* to acquire great landed estates for themselves" (Dahlgren, 1973a, 125). Ågren agrees that the nobility salvaged the manors, but about the presumed acquisition of land by leading crown servants he says: "The assertion that there was a fall in land prices—a point fundamental to the whole line of argument—is no more than an assumption, and has not been proved" (1973b, 256).

The scholarly quarrel over the relative strength of new versus old high aristocracy is not to be ignored, especially since there were "exceptionally frequent ennoblements [in] the 1680s and 1690s" (Carlsson, 1972, 580). The important factor is the increasing symbiosis of large landowner and nonhereditary bureaucrat. In 1700, 25% of the higher civil service were noblemen by birth and 44% were ennobled. During the Great Northern War (1700–1721), Charles XII ennobled many officers of the army,

often of foreign noble families (Carlsson, 1972, 586); after the war, many civil servants were ennobled rather than being given separate political rights (p. 610). At the same time, the large place reserved for the old nobility in the state structure kept the old nobility loyal to the Crown during the war, despite the *reduktion.* See Hatton (1974, 4).

The whole affair amounted to harnessing the upper strata, old and new, together under the leadership of the state machinery. The relative strength of the state was reflected in the polarization of the class structure circa 1700; a "sharp distinction" was made between nobles and commoners. "Noblemen were *both* office-holders *and* landowners, whereas the commoners were *either* only office-holders (clergymen, civil servants, army and navy officers), only landowners (peasants) *or* only merchants or artisans" (Carlsson, 1972, 608). See Ågren for great skepticism about the nineteenth-century Swedish historiographical view that by the *reduktion,* the king intended to rescue the peasants from noble oppression (1973b, 244, 257–263). Roberts, on the other hand, gives it credence: "The freedom of the peasant would never be threatened again" (1967, 249).

owners but rather from among unpropertied rural laborers "accustomed from childhood to obey their temporal and spiritual superiors"; and the officers were now "paid servants of the crown, with no other profession than the army."[252] This more rational system was made possible by the *reduktion*; before this the Crown did not have sufficient farms to form the basis of such a system.[253]

In terms of the degree to which the state–machinery was consistently strengthened over the seventeenth century, the Swedish state stands out among noncore areas. It created an army to be feared. It contained the rapacity of the landowning classes and channeled them into state service.[254] It built up an iron industry of some importance and a respectable merchant fleet. It prevented England from succeeding, at least immediately, to all the prerogatives of a declining United Provinces in the Baltic.[255] Compared to Spain and Portugal, not to speak of Poland and Hungary, the Swedish state was strong—in many ways almost as strong as the French state although still far weaker than the English state or that of the United Provinces. In fact, from the point of view of the latter two, it was Sweden and France who were the two great expansionist military states of the seventeenth century. Yet just when the strength of Sweden seemed to reach its apex under Charles XII, it was revealed as "a colossus on feet of clay."[256]

Sweden had a quite small population by European standards and hence basically a small financial base for its state machinery. As Lundkvist puts it, the resources of the Swedish empire "were inadequate to sustain its position in the long run."[257] Economically, Sweden *rose* to the position to which Spain and Portugal *declined*—that of a middleman between the periphery and the core. She profited not merely from her strategic location in the Baltic but from the *increased* weakness of the peripheral zones of eastern Europe in

[252] Aberg (1972, 272). The universality of the system was popular. In the war of 1675–1679, "conscription for the infantry was particularly obnoxious to most peasants because servants and tenants of the nobility were often exempted" (Stoye, 1970b, 770).

[253] See Dahlgren (1973a, 129). Ågren points out that the rationality extended beyond the army: "Strictly speaking, the use of the term *indelningsverk* to describe a purely military organization is too narrow; in a wider sense it implied that every item of expenditure was linked to a definite source of revenue, so that the organization came to apply not only to military but also to civil expenditures" (1973b, 248n.).

[254] "Henceforward the members of the *Råd* (Council) would be ministers—servants of the king, or of the Estates, as it might happen—but for all their ermined hats and velvet robes, their grave eloquence, composed countenances, and traditional senatorial dignity, they would never be what they had been in the period of Charles XI's minority"

(Roberts, 1967, 242–243).

[255] As England's need for grain declined and need for timber increased in the seventeenth century, her trade increasingly shifted from Poland to Sweden, because Polish timber was too expensive. See Fedorowicz (1976). The shift was dramatic after the Polish–Swedish war of 1655–1656 (see Fedorowicz, 1967, 377, Fig. 1), but Sweden was able to prevent the peripheralization that had been Poland's fate. "The eternal theme of [English] complaints was the curtailment of the foreign factors' freedom of movement and trade [within Sweden]" (Åström, 1962, 101). England was so frustrated by Swedish ability to dictate terms of trade that she moved, as we shall see, strenuously to subvert her by attempting to create, without too great success, a rival source of naval stores in British North America in the early eighteenth century.

[256] Samuelsson (1968, 13).

[257] Lundkvist (1973, 57).

the seventeenth century. Marian Małowist, looking at it from the perspective of a Pole, saw Sweden as a parasite:

> In the seventeenth century, Sweden profited from industrial weakness of her neighbors and also from the weakness of their governments, a consequence of the enormous growth in the power of the nobility. In fine, Sweden was something of a parasite living on the weakness of her neighbours, and it was largely due to this weakness that, for a hundred years, she would become the most powerful country in the Baltic region. But she, in turn, had to give way to Russia.[258]

To Russia, and be it added, to Prussia.

In 1696–1697, before the onset of the Great Northern War, Finland had been decimated by famine and lost perhaps a third of its population. Nonetheless, the state was not strong enough to prevent the burghers of Scania from exporting grain to outside the kingdom.[259] Furthermore, Sweden's role as middleman was for the first time attacked not only by the core powers, but by Russia—the other end of the commodity chains. England, the United Provinces, and Sweden had limited success, at best, in their attempts throughout the seventeenth century[260] to incorporate Russia into the world-economy. In 1695 Tsar Peter I (Peter the Great) assumed the reins of power in Russia and started on his great campaign of reform and "Westernization," which included his visit ("great embassy") to western Europe (where he concentrated on learning shipbuilding), his foundation of St. Petersburg in 1703 (to be Russia's Baltic port), and his challenge to Sweden. From the point of view of the world-system as a whole, Peter's efforts may be seen as an attempt to participate fully in the world-economy—but as a semiperipheral rather than a peripheral area (which Poland had become). To do this, it was essential, though clearly not sufficient, to break Sweden's intermediary role. Sweden saw this as clearly as did Peter: "Sweden's conquests along the eastern Baltic were, with good reason, regarded as the bastions of her great-power position, to be defended at all costs."[261]

The Great Northern War started in 1700 with an attack on Livonia by the

---

[258] Małowist (1959, 189). See also Hatton (1970, 648–650).

[259] See Jutikkala (1955, 48, 63).

[260] Kellenbenz treats seventeenth-century Russia as being already incorporated into the world-economy in the seventeenth century. See Kellenbenz (1973). For the views of Soviet scholars in the seventeenth century, see Cherepnin (1964, especially 18–22). Åström believes that the turning point in the economic relations between Russia and the western countries only occurred in "the middle of the eighteenth century, when the *major share* in English imports of iron, hemp, flax, pitch and tar, and potash came from Russian-owned ports" (1962, 113).

[261] Hatton (1970, 648). This was scarcely an economically irrational position—as Ohberg points out: "It can thus be said that there was a certain real justification for the shaping of Sweden's commercial policy along these monopolistic lines. Sweden as a country was not rich in capital and could not with means possessed by her own citizens compete for the Russian market against such rich countries as the Netherlands and England. If, however, Sweden could achieve a monopoly position by military or political means, she might make a rich financial profit out of the Russian market" (1955, 161). This, of course, is why England and the Netherlands "pursued a common Baltic policy during the war of the 1690s" (Åström, 1962, 45).

Polish–Saxon King, Augustus II. Peter joined the war. Seeking to use the occasion to break the Russians, Sweden resisted attempts to end the war,[262] but she was nowhere near strong enough to break Russia militarily. Peter employed the scorched-earth retreat policy, which was destined to become Russia's classic defense against invasion; eventually, logistics plus the onset of winter led to disaster for the Swedes at Poltava in the Ukraine in 1709.[263] Charles XII's political imperialism, says Nordmann, "upset the equilibrium" established by Charles XI.[264] What equilibrium? The excessive internal costs of Charles XII's imperial drive were not acceptable to the Swedish people; it was the same equilibrium Charles V had upset in Castile in an earlier century. The *indelningsverk* system had created an "indissoluble tie between the source of revenue and the item of expenditure,[265] and while this balanced the state budget more or less, it was difficult to sustain the system in a long war, especially without foreign subsidies and recruits. In the Great Northern War, the army of 80,000 "had mostly to be raised from the heart of the empire"; and once the Russians had really mobilized for war, "Sweden had no choice but to give up the game."[266]

Does it make sense to debate whether continuing the war was bad judgment on Charles XII's part? whether it was hybris that brought disaster? Scarcely, since Sweden had little choice.[267] In a sense, her bluff was her strength; but once her bluff had been called, her position was "revolutionized."[268] In 1721, Sweden lost Livonia, Estonia, Ingria, Karelia—most of the eastern Baltic—to Russia. She also ceded parts of her possessions in Germany to Prussia. Sweden thus lost land, population, state revenue, control over her "breadbasket"[269]—and most of all, her monopolistic position in

[262] "The Maritime Powers, anxious to end the war and so use Swedish troops in their imminent struggle with France [the War of the Spanish Succession], offered mediation in 1700 to both Peter and Charles. Such offers, repeated more than once in after years, were consistently accepted by the tsar and as consistently refused by the king of Sweden, flushed with success and inspired by the idea of a righteous vengeance to be exacted from the States which had attacked him" (M. S. Anderson, 1970, 734).

[263] See Chandler (1970, 754).

[264] Nordmann (1972, 147).

[265] Lundkvist (1973, 26).

[266] Åström (1973, 100).

[267] "The reasons for the loss of Sweden's extraordinary empire have been debated even since 1721 [the Peace of Nystad, which formally ended the war]. Was it the fault of Charles XII, who refused peace in the years when luck was with him? . . . On the contrary, it can be argued that the only hope of keeping the great-power position died with Charles XII" (Hatton, 1970, 679).

[268] "Poltava, which transformed Charles XII from a conqueror into a fugitive, revolutionized the whole position. . . . It enormously increased Peter's influence in western Europe, besides endowing him with the prestige which military success alone could give. 'Now', wrote Urbich (the Russian minister in Vienna) to Leibniz in August 1709, 'people begin to fear the Tsar as formerly they feared Sweden.' The philosopher agreed that 'it is commonly said that the Tsar will be formidable to all Europe, and that he will be a kind of northern Turk'" (M. S. Anderson, 1970, 735) Note the comparison to Turkey, which, like Russia, was a world-empire in the external arena of the European world-economy and was *threatened with* incorporation and peripheralization in the seventeenth century.

[269] Actually, "Livonia did not really become a 'Swedish breadbasket' until after its assimilation [into] Russia in 1721" (Samuelsson, 1968, 76). The Treaty of 1721 specifically permitted Sweden to import grain from her former provinces duty-free, up to the value of 50,000 rubles a year. See Lundkvist (1973, 56).

the Baltic.[270] Since the strength of the Swedish colossus was based on her being a quasi-monopoly, this "German–Slav push" succeeded in turning Sweden into a second-rank power.[271] The internal consequences for Sweden were dramatic. On the surface, it seemed that absolutism had given way to parliamentary freedom. The period from 1718 to 1772[272] is known in Sweden as *Frihetstiden,* the Age of Liberty. The essential compromise of 1680–1682 had consisted of a strong central government and the politico-economic merger of old aristocracies, newer nobilities, and bourgeois, and this compromise was consummated and fulfilled by the Age of Liberty in the same way that the Glorious Revolution of 1688–1689 and the Age of Walpole in England consummated and fulfilled the English Revolution. The only difference was that in the eighteenth century, England was on the way to becoming a world hegemonic power, whereas Sweden was beset by the dilemmas of her failure to make it as a strong semiperipheral state with pretensions to eventual core status. Hence England enjoyed stability under what was *de facto* a one-party regime, and Sweden publicly displayed an intrabourgeois quarrel of the finest two-party variety.

During the first years of the Age of Liberty, Sweden's key problem was state bankruptcy. Count Arvid Horn led a government that concentrated on peace[273] and "moderate mercantilism."[274] In 1738 a strong mercantilist party known as the Hats emerged and overthrew Horn, but in essence they continued the same policies.[275] The Hats remained in power until 1765, being replaced in the moment of British world triumph by their opponents, the Caps. The policies of Hats were pro-French, mercantilist, and inflationary; they represented the large exporting, ironmaking, and textile manufacturing interests, and their slogan was *Svensker man i svensk dräkt* (Swedish men in Swedish clothing). The policies of Caps were pro-English, free trade, and deflationary; they represented the importing sector and the smaller merchants and industrialists, and they presented themselves as the

[270] "After 1720 an increasing amount of products which had hitherto been almost entirely Swedish monopolies—iron, tar and pitch—could be directly fetched from Russia" (Åström, 1962, 106).

[271] Nordmann (1971, 455).

[272] The year 1718 marked the death of Charles XII. He had left no heirs, and it was in the course of the complicated succession issue that the "anti-absolutist party, a loose grouping of influential landowners, officers of the armed forces and administrators, . . . won the day," by imposing on Ulrika, prior to her crowning in May 1719, a declaration "to sign and keep a constitution to be formulated by the Estates" (Hatton, 1966, 351).Ulrika reneged and was forced to abdicate, and her successor, Frederick I, signed the Constitution of 1720, which essentially created a constitutional monarchy governed by a cabinet eventually responsible to the

Diet (see Hatton, 1966, 352–355).

[273] Samuelsson compares Horn's efforts to "unravel the great bankruptcy" as comparable to those of Cardinal Fleury under Louis XV "at about the same time" (1968, 14). Hatton points out that during the years when Horn was most powerful in the *Råd* (Council), "it seemed as if Sweden was once more governed by an oligarchic council in the interests of the landed nobility, the higher bureaucracy and the higher clergy" (1966, 352).

[274] Hatton (1966, 357).

[275] Their self-designation as Hats was a "hint of military headgear," hence an implied criticism of Horn's lack of military backbone. They called their opponents Nightcaps or Caps, suggesting they were "sleepy cowards, old men in nightcaps" (Hatton, 1966, 356).

radical party of the socially underprivileged.[276] But did real choices lie behind this game of what Anderson calls "corrupt aristocratic parliamentarianism"?[277] Probably no more than in Bourbon Spain. The Great Northern War was for Sweden what the War of the Spanish Succession was for Spain: an attempt to break out of the structural constraints the world-economy had imposed on her. Neither effort succeeded, but each may have prevented worse things from happening.

As long as it was not entirely clear who would win the competition between England and France, that is, up to 1763, Sweden (like Spain) could still utilize her margin of maneuver and reach for a greater role than she could grasp.[278] Sweden's moment of reckoning came later, in the period between 1763 and 1815, when England called in its chips, due to the last-stage resistance of France. Sweden was as strong a state as her economy would permit. That the strength of the state machinery had little to do with the formal powers of the king can be seen by comparing Sweden to Denmark, which was absolutist earlier and longer than Sweden but nonetheless far weaker, reflecting Denmark's peripheral economic role as compared with the semiperipheral role Sweden's policies enabled her to assume. Denmark is often thought of as a "unique constellation,"[279] not fitting into any general model of the division of labor of early modern Europe. We indicated in chapter IV that we considered Denmark a part of the periphery, which was primarily oriented to the export of low-wage commodities, in Denmark's case, grain and cattle exports. Unlike most other peripheral areas in the seventeenth century, however, Denmark instituted an absolutist monarchy in 1660. What we must explain is why this political change was

---

[276] See Samuelsson (1968, 107, 119–120); Eagly (1969, 748, 752; 1971, 13–14, 18–20); Hovde (1948, 23–25).

[277] P. Anderson (1974a, 190).

[278] There was little real debate about this between the Hats and the Caps. Hatton says that "the strict mercantilism . . . of the 1720s [was] exemplified by the *Produktplakatet* of 1724," which was "modeled on the English navigation acts [and] hit hard at Dutch and English shipping in the Baltic." The strict mercantilism, Hatton says, was also exemplified by the importation ordinances of 1726 which were revived by the Hats after 1738, who were "intensifying support for Sweden's industrial undertakings and accompanying it with an ever stronger protection against foreign competition." Hatton says: "In retrospect it can easily be seen that only the profits deriving from Sweden's and Finland's well-established exports, above all from Swedish iron, allowed the Hats for so long to continue mercantilist experiments with new manufactures, but until the crisis of 1762–1763 (brought about partly by Sweden's participation in the Seven Years' War and partly by the effects of an international financial crisis) the Caps raised no strong protests against the

theory of Hat economic policy, though they continually urged moderation on the party in power. Similarly the two parties were in some measure of agreement on agricultural policy" (Hatton 1966, 357).

The precondition of this mercantilist policy was slipping away, not only because of England's growing strength vis-à-vis France, but because of Russia's steadily increasing competitive role as an exporter of iron manufactures. Sweden went from producing 75–90% of world output in the beginning of the eighteenth century to producing about one-third by the 1760s, when Russian output passed that of Sweden. As Swedish sales declined in the depressed conditions circa 1730–1745, the Swedes restricted output to maintain prices. Samuelsson sees this not as foolishness but as "making a virtue of necessity" (1968, 89). See also Heckscher (1932, 134–135, 139); Boëthius (1958, 151–152); Hildebrand (1958, 13).

[279] Østerud (1976, 24), whose "unique constellation" consisted of "an Absolutist state raised above the social foundation of a semiservile peasantry and ascendant towns."

not sufficient to catapult Denmark into the category of semiperipheral countries like Sweden and Brandenburg-Prussia, and also why the change occurred at all.

How did the economic structures in Denmark compare to those in eastern Europe on the one hand and Sweden on the other? Petersen emphasizes the advantages Denmark had over eastern European countries
because it exported *both* grain and cattle, which meant it had greater flexibility in difficult times.[280] This may explain in part why Denmark was less
affected than eastern European countries by the first phase of European
regression (1600–1650); indeed the 1630s and early 1640s were an "Indian
summer" for Danish profits on the world market.[281] The extreme closure
plus the tax exemption of the Danish nobility enabled them to increase land
concentration steadily in this period.[282] The king, however, was a very large
landowner[283] himself, and this plus his ability to increase Sound dues during the Thirty Years' War assured him of a considerable state income.[284]
Sweden's economic system was different in that agriculture was not the main
source of income and its production and export items were primarily minerals, which, as we have seen, were the basis of Sweden's industrial growth.
Furthermore, the ecological weakness of agriculture in Sweden reinforced
the social strength of the peasantry and prevented the growth of anything
resembling a *Gutswirtschaft*.

Denmark was the opposite extreme in terms of the social structure of the
countryside. The organization of Danish agriculture involved large demesnes surrounded by peasant farms that owed the demesne owner not
rent but labor services. The groups owing such services, the *ugedagsbønder,*
or weekday farmers, were expanding in number, accounting for 40% of all
bønder by the mid-seventeenth century: "Boon work [corvée] was used not
only in the fields but for cartage, building, handicraft labor, and even for
loading and discharging in port."[285] During this same period, the role of
Danish merchants was diminishing radically. German and Dutch merchants
were ousting Danes from the export trade, especially during the "Indian

---

[280] See Petersen (1967, 20–21, and 1968, 1249).

[281] Petersen (1967, 30). Of course, as in any such
situation, the misfortune of a competitor is a positive
advantage for the one not struck by the misfortune.
Petersen notes "Denmark's relatively favorable position in the prevalent war-boom" in terms of "safe
provisions." He says: "Commercial and monetary
crises in Germany and Poland in 1617–1623 and
Sweden's Baltic politics until the mid-1630s offered
exceptional opportunities to Danish agriculture;
Swedish war operations and restrictive grain trade
politics . . . once more forced up grain prices at the
stock exchange of Amsterdam, thus allowing Dutch
producers to carry home extraordinary marginal
profits."

[282] See Petersen (1967, 6–7) and Østerud (1976,
19).

[283] Of the nondomain land, 56% belonged to the
Crown. See Petersen (1968, 1238).

[284] See C. E. Hill (1926, 102–152) and Roberts
(1970, 402–403).

[285] Jutikkala (1975, 164). It always depends on
what side of a percentage one perceives. Petersen,
obviously looking at the 60% percent, wishes to
stress that Danish agriculture was based on *Grundherrschaft* (see 1967, 23; 1968, 1251–1252). Petersen
does note that the Danish nobility was "radically different" from that of Sweden (and England and
France) in the degree of closure to mobility by the
bourgeoisie (1968, 1237).

summer" from 1630 to 1645.[286] In the Peace of Christianopel in 1645, the Swedes (in concert with the Dutch) forced a reduction in Sound dues so that Crown revenues became "an inconsiderable remnant"[287] of their former size. Thus when the good times of the Thirty Years' War came to an end,[288] Denmark was the very model of a peripheral area: it had export-oriented demesne farming with widespread corvée; its commerce was in the hands of foreigners; its state-machinery had a weak financial base (the wealthiest land being tax-exempt; and the Sound dues were no longer significant).

The Danish crown made an attempt to recover its lost strategic–economic advantage by declaring war on Sweden in 1657, when Sweden was already engaged in other wars. It hoped for aid from the Netherlands, which it did not get. The Treaty of Roskilde in 1658, which brought the war with Sweden to an end, precipitated Denmark's political crisis. Denmark had to cede to Sweden the provinces of Scania, Halland, and Bohuslän—that is, the whole right bank of the Sound itself and the approaches on each side of the Sound.[289] However, later that year, when Charles X of Sweden renewed the war and tried to incorporate all of Denmark into Sweden, he was rapidly faced by the opposition of the Dutch, the English, and the French, who joined together in the so-called Concert of the Hague (May 11, 1659), in which the three core powers dictated peace to the combatants and vetoed "the sealing of the Baltic against the fleets of non-riparian States.[290] Denmark was saved from extinction because the core powers wanted to check Sweden. The core powers were thus interested in ensuring that Denmark had the tax base to maintain an army strong enough to play this geopolitical role which was obviously not the case in 1657–1660.

Furthermore, Denmark's state debt was considerable. It was over four million *rigsdaler* in 1660, of which 38% was owed to foreign interests, a quarter of this to the States–General of the Netherlands, another quarter to Dutch houses, and the remainder to merchant houses in Hamburg and Lübeck. The Dutch state and foreign private creditors thus had consider-

---

[286] See Jørgensen (1963, 78, 107), Glamann (1977, 240), and Petersen (1970, 84).

[287] Reddaway (1906, 573). Østerud speaks of "a grave financial crisis" (1978, 15).

[288] Denmark was hit by epidemics in the 1650s which had great demographic consequences. See Petersen (1967, 31) and Jørgensen (1963, 79).

[289] The Treaty of Roskilde also turned over the Trondheim District in Norway and the island of Bornholm in the Baltic Sea to Sweden; but they were returned to Denmark in the Treaty of Copenhagen in 1660. See Rosén (1961, 552); C. E. Hill (1926, 184); and the map in Darby and Fullard (1970, 36).

[290] Reddaway (1906, 588); see also C. E. Hill (1926, 174–175). The Swedish advance had already

been implemented by sending the Dutch fleet on October 29, 1658, to engage the Swedish fleet in the Sound, and despite a tactical draw, the Swedes entered Copenhagen in strategic triumph. Hill points out that the squadron was under the command of De Witt, "the same admiral that forced the Sound against Christian IV [of Denmark] in 1645" (1926, 170). In this earlier phase, Sweden aided by Holland had obtained extremely favorable terms in the Treaty of Brömsebro, whose terms "marked clearly the degradation of Denmark from the primacy of the North" (Reddaway, 1906, 572). This treaty reconfirmed Sweden's ancient exemption from Sound dues, and more importantly, extended this privilege to Sweden's new provinces in the eastern Baltic and Germany.

able direct and immediate interest in the ability of the Danish state to get out of its extremely difficult financial situation, as Jørgensen notes:

> The precise role played by the creditors of the State in the constitutional upheaval of 1660 and immediately afterwards is difficult to define . . . but in the short run it must have had a considerable bearing on political developments. . . . Danish state bankruptcy would have had unpleasant consequences for considerable sections of the merchant class of northern Europe. . . . To a large extent, settlement was in fact achieved by giving creditors a charge on crown land.[291]

This was the setting for the seemingly hard-to-explain sudden introduction of absolutism in Denmark. What did absolutism mean? It meant the monarchy had became hereditary and "sovereign," and it meant administrative reforms—which involved the creation of a privy council and more direct control over local bureaucratic structures. It meant the end of the closure of the nobility, and it meant increased taxation. It meant, in short, a state able to play some role in paying its external debts and checking Swedish expansion.

Did it, however, mean changing the basic economic structures? Not to any significant degree. The nobility still had a tax exemption, although now they were required to aid the state in collecting taxes from the free peasants. The king could now sell his own land to the newly immigrated German service nobility, who promptly emulated the old nobility in creating export-oriented demesne structures. The emphasis was now toward monoculture (grain rather than cattle), thus reducing the previous small difference between the economic structures of Denmark and eastern Europe.[292] Within 30 years, the amount of land owned by the nobility had increased—at the expense of both the Crown and the free peasants.[293] The economic and legal position of the peasants, on the other hand, worsened, culminating in a decree in 1733 binding peasants to the land.[294] As for the state, to be sure, it had more purchasing power[295] than before; but while Sweden reinforced the role of its indigenous militia, Denmark abandoned it in favor of relying upon mercenaries.[296] There was some feeble effort at mercantilist legislation,[297] but the strength of Denmark's state was largely a facade and bolstered by outside interests. The economic role of Denmark remained the same. Indeed, if anything, it became increasingly peripheral in the period from 1650 to 1750.

It is not really surprising that Denmark remained a peripheral zone de-

---

[291] Jørgensen (1963, 97–98). At the same time the price declines of the agricultural depression in 1660 were a "total catastrophe for the Danish aristocracy, socially, economically, and demographically" (S. A. Hansen, 1972, 101). This obviously made the aristocracy less able to resist the new absolutist measures.

[292] See Rosén (1961, 523–526). On the tendency to monoculture, see Jensen (1937, 41–42).

[293] See Rosén (1961, 536) and Jutikkala (1975, 160).

[294] See Jensen (1937, 45), Rosén (1961, 526), Imhof (1974, *passim*), and Munck (1977, *passim*).

[295] Jørgensen (1963, 96).

[296] See Rosén (1961, 538).

[297] See Kent (1973, 6–8).

spite the formal institution of an absolute monarchy. What is far more surprising is that Brandenburg, an insignificant peripheral zone, was able, first, to develop into a semiperipheral power, Prussia, by the eighteenth century,[298] and then to surpass and eventually leave behind far more likely candidates—Sweden to the north and Saxony and Austria to the south. There is no reasonable explanation of this unless one takes into account (1) the continuous interaction within the interstate system as an expression of economic forces and (2) the range of economic roles (a limited range, however) that particular areas are able to play at given points in history. The key to Prussia's development was that, from the perspective of the core powers, there was room for one major semiperipheral power in central Europe. When Sweden faltered, Prussia fit into that slot. How and why are questions we must explore. But we cannot understand the process unless we realize in advance that *two* states in the same region could not simultaneously have succeeded in doing what Prussia did.

In the seventeenth century, the German lands east of the Elbe underwent most of the same processes as Poland and other regions of eastern Europe did in terms of the social organization of agricultural production. This was the zone of *Gutswirtsschaft* and *Gutsherrschaft,* as opposed to *Grundherrschaft* (and/or *Wirtschaftherrschaft*) in the western and southern Germanies.[299] The

---

[298] The evolution of state nomenclature reflected the process. The Elector of Brandenburg, the area surrounding Berlin, added a few noncontiguous territories to his domains in the fifteenth and sixteenth centuries, and still more in the seventeenth. With the domains went additional titles. He was, for example, Duke of Pomerania, of Magdeburg, of Cleves. He was Prince of Halberstadt and Minden. He was Count of Mark and Ravensberg. He became Duke of Prussia in 1618, but this was East Prussia only, and it was still under Polish suzerainty until 1657–1660. In 1701 he was named King *in* Prussia, and only in 1772, when, with the First Partition of Poland, he acquired West Prussia was he called King *of* Prussia. Although in international diplomacy, the state was known as "la Prusse" as late as 1794, the *Allgemeines Landrecht* was proclaimed for "the Prussian states." Only in 1807, amidst the Napoleonic upheaval, was the process crystallized such that Prussia became the name of the Hohenzollern monarchy as a whole, until, of course, it became Germany. It should be noted that it was only in 1804 that "the lands of the House of Hapsburg" became "the Austrian Empire." See Rosenberg (1958, 27–28); Darby and Fullard (1970, 138–144, 146).

[299] The exact definition of *Gutsherrschaft* as opposed to *Grundherrschaft* is a matter of extensive debate in the literature. (One possible English approximation might be demesne [*Gut*] versus manor economy.) Three definitions will do.

Otto Hintze says: "[The] chief feature [of *Gut-* *sherrschaft*] was that the landlord himself farmed the estate, living off the revenues gained by selling its product in distant markets, and using the services of serfs, who were therefore bound to the soil. The estate formed a legal administrative unit (*Gutsbezirk*), and the landlord held political and judicial powers over the peasants. . . . [The] chief feature [of *Grundherrschaft*] was that the landlord did not himself farm the estate but lived off the payments of cash and kind received from his peasant tenants. Because they were less under the economic control of their lord, peasants under this system enjoyed a greater degree of freedom than those under the system of *Gutsherrschaft*" (1975a, 39).

Joachim Freiherr von Braun says: "*Gutswirtschaft* is a large agricultural enterprise and thus an independent organism based on managerial [*Betriebsleiters*] initiative and it therefore can be operated without regard to laws and indirect obligations as maximally market-oriented production" (*Zur ostdeutschen Agrargeschichte*, 1960, 10).

Friedrich Lütge says: "*Gutswirtschaft* . . . is an economic phenomenon [*Tatbestand*]. The *Gut* belongs to a lord, who operates it by hiring and assigning non-family laborers to do the work. *Grundherrschaft* occurs in two forms. One is *Rentengrundherrschaft,* in which the *Grundherr* [landlord] maintains only a small land unit for himself [*Eigenbetrieb*], and lives primarily off rents, etc. The other is *Wirtschaftgrundherrschaft,* . . . in which within a *grundherrlichen* framework [that is, a legal system

large estates developed in east Elbia in the sixteenth century through a process of engrossment (often forced purchases) combined with the removal of peasants from the land, *Bauernlegen*.[300] This process was considerably accelerated in Mecklenburg, Brandenburg, and Pomerania[301] after the Thirty Years' War. The corvée was increased, going from an average of two to three days a week to six.[302] As the land shifted hands from peasant to noble lord, it became tax-exempt which meant that the remaining peasants became "all the more heavily burdened."[303] In the Hapsburg lands, there were similar developments in Hungary and Bohemia, but Austria proper remained a zone of *Grundherrschaft*.[304] If one compares east Elbia with other peripheral zones in eastern Europe, the oppression of the peasantry was the same; indeed, if anything, worse.[305]

How then did eighteenth-century Prussia come into existence? One consideration is that although the oppression of the peasant was greater in east Elbia than in Poland, the concentration of land was less. It was more *Gutsherrschaft* than *Gutswirtschaft*. Lütge reminds us of the aphorism of G. N.

corresponding to *Grundherrschaft*], a larger *Gutswirtschaft* (*Eigenwirtschaft*) [that is, a demesne under the direct control of the landlord] is kept" (*Zur ostdeutschen Agrargeschichte*, 1960, 83).

One must bear in mind that *herrschaft* refers to political-legal structures, and *wirtschaft* to the social relations of production, and that it was possible to have "mixed" forms such as in Lower Saxony where *Grundherrschaft* and *Gutswirtschaft* prevailed. See the discussion between Joachim Freiherr von Braun and Freidrich Lütge (*Zur ostdeutschen Agrargeschichte*, 1960, 84–85).

We will not review here the question, discussed at length in Wallerstein (1974), as to whether a *Gutswirtschaft* is simply another version of feudalism or is a capitalist phenomenon. We simply point out that there has been a long debate in the *Zeitschrift für Geschichtswissenschaft*, a journal of the German Democratic Republic, on this specific topic. In 1953 Johannes Nichtweiss argued that since *Gutswirtschaft* involved market-oriented production on a large scale, it was different from a feudal economy. He also pointed out that "in the case of a feudal vassal-economy [*Fronwirtschaft*], it is typical that the peasant is bound to the *peasant's land*, not to the lord's land [as in the case of *Gutswirtschaft*]" (1953, 705). Jürgen Kuczynski responded (1954). There followed a whole series of articles Nichtweiss (1954), Manfred Hamann (1954), Gerhard Heitz (1955), Nichtweiss (1956), Willi Boelcke (1956), Heitz (1957), and Nichtweiss (1957). As Nichtweiss points out, Kuczynski's position is similar on this question to that of Lütge (1957, 805). A. J. P. Taylor takes a position similar to that of Nichtweiss, comparing Junker estates to "the great capitalist farms of the American prairie" (1946, 29).

[300] See Carsten (1947, 145, 157); Kuhn (*Zur ostdeutschen Agrargeschichte*, 1960, 40–41); Lütge (1963, 101–102); Slicher van Bath (1977, 111–112). *Gutswirtschaft* is clearly linked to *Wüstungen*, or vacant lands (see Schlesinger in *Zur ostdeutschen Agrargeschichte*, 1960, 48); but what is the link? Siegmund Wolf argues that *Bauernlegen* led to *Wüstungen* which made possible the creation of a *Gutswirtschaft*. See Wolf (1957, 323–324). Berthold, however, argues that peasant flight was a reaction to increased exploitation (1964, 16, 19).

[301] See Treue (1955, 413); Barraclough (1962, 394); Harnisch (1968, 130–31); Slicher van Bath (1977, 111).

[302] See Kulischer (1932, 12).

[303] Carsten (1954, 198).

[304] See Tapié (1971, 123–124). Indeed, the Hapsburgs stopped granting tax exemptions for dominical (seigniorial) land that was engrossed rustical (common) land as of 1654 (Tapié, 1971, 120).

[305] For one thing, in east Elbia, there was the additional institution of *Gesindezwangdienst*, which was the requirement that the children of serfs had to serve as domestics for from 1 to 4 years in the lord's mansion. See Kulischer (1932, 14); Slicher van Bath (1977, 115). Rutkowski (1926, 496) points out that *Gesindezwangdienst* involved such bad treatment that serfs "preferred to spend ten years in prison than two in service," despite the fact that such service was salaried (a low salary, to be sure). Rutkowski sees the overall obligations of the east Elbian peasant (services plus taxes) as greater than those of the Polish peasant (1927a, 97). *Gesindezwangdienst* also existed in Bohemia, Moravia, and Silesia. See Śpiesz (1969, 53).

Knapp: "The lord [*Gutsherr*] did not become more well-endowed economically [*begüterer*]; he became more powerful." Lütge draws the inference that this was the source of the rise of the prince's power (*Fürsten-
macht*).[306] The lack of real land concentration, the medium size of most
estates, and the absence, therefore, of a "stratum of great magnates" were
striking differences between east Elbia and other peripheral areas, including
most of Europe.[307] It meant that vis-à-vis potential central authorities, the
Junker class was economically less able to seize the political reins than were
landlords elsewhere in the peripheral areas of seventeenth-century Europe.
This weakness, a necessary condition for the rise of Prussia, was scarcely a
sufficient one. It was combined, however, with a favorable geopolitical conjuncture.

Prior to the end of the Thirty Years' War, the Elector of Brandenburg
was "scarcely more than a super Junker,"[308] in a dispersed, defenseless land
without great resources or commercial wealth and containing "some of the
most stubbornly independent towns and insubordinate nobility in
Europe."[309] The Thirty Years' War was at one and the same time the nadir
of Hohenzollern power and its great opportunity, partly through sheer
luck.[310] The luck was that the Elector of Brandenburg inherited certain
lands collaterally: in 1609, the Duchy of Cleves (an area adjoining the
United Provinces at the northern end of the Rhine); in 1625, Prussia (which
was on the Baltic Sea, adjoining and indeed under the suzerainty of Poland);
and in 1637, Pomerania. Thus Brandenburg found itself in two of the main
war arenas, the Rhineland and the Baltic. Brandenburg had acquired lands
of "great strategical importance" that were "coveted" by various European
states, and had done this "without any military exertions" of its own, of

[306] Lütge (1963, 117). The statement cited from
Knapp is from "Die Bauernbefreiung in Österreich
und in Preussen," reprinted in *Grundherrschaft und
Rittergut* (1897, I, 34). See also Gorlitz, speaking of
the social transformation in Brandenburg-Prussia
in the seventeenth and eighteenth centuries: "The
peasant is no longer simply the vassal [*Untertan*] of
the nobleman; as an Estate, noblemen stand parallel
to the Prince's court. Both become vassals of the
Prince. The nobility no longer delimits the arena of
social action [*Lebenswelt*]. It has become rather a
functional part of society" (1956, 86). This fits in
with Rutkowski's explanation for the plight of the
east Elbian peasant. He argues that the rise of industry and the royal *Bauernschutz* (protection of the
peasants) made it difficult to obtain agricultural
manpower by the eighteenth century. Ergo the
conditions of *Gesindezwangdienst* became worse, since
it was only by the further exploitation of the peasants subject to their control that the lords could survive economically. See Rutkowski (1926, 497).

Spiesz argues that east Elbian estates used corvée
less than other parts of eastern Europe did, despite
legal possibilities, and that estate work was based
more "on mercenary labour of families employed
on the basis of forced or voluntary hire" (1969,
23).

[307] P. Anderson (1974a, 262). Furthermore, relative strength was further eroded in the Thirty
Years' War, which "certainly marked a decisive
change [for the worse] in the fortunes of the Estates
in many German lands" (Carsten, 1959, 437).

[308] Rosenberg (1958, 31).

[309] Howard (1976, 67). See also Carsten: "It is one
of the marvels of German history that suddenly, in
the later seventeenth century, a strong centralized
state arose on such an unpropitious basis, for Brandenburg seemed to be predestined to go the way of
Poland or of Mecklenburg" (1969, 544).

[310] Carsten (1954, 179), who says the war presented "fortuitous circumstances" (1950, 177).

which, at the time, it was incapable.[311] Furthermore, Brandenburg was allowed by the great powers to keep these coveted lands. Farther Pomerania, which had been under Swedish occupation at the moment of Brandenburg's claim in 1637, was recognized as part of the Brandenburg domains as a result of French support at the Peace of Westphalia.[312] Brandenburg was in this way the beneficiary—one of the first—of the balance of power. It was in order to check Swedish power that other states supported the expansion of Brandenburg; and it was in order to prevent the Swedish king from ending this happy state of affairs that Elector Frederick William of Brandenburg, the Great Elector, turned his thoughts to creating a bureaucracy and an army that could maintain this expanded territory.[313]

At this moment, the Junkers may not have been economically strong enough to create mini-armies, although their compeers, the Polish magnates were. However the Elector of Brandenburg was not strong either; and he was seeking taxes to build up an army powerful enough to tax the Junkers against their will.[314] The Great Recess of 1653 was the first step in an ingenious compromise in which the Great Elector in effect gave the Junker class the full incomes from their estates (which were not, remember, all that much) plus new incomes, via the state bureaucracy, in return for the power to squeeze the peasantry and the urban populations heavily. He was thus allowed to establish a strong bureaucracy and army, which safeguarded the state externally and eventually allowed his successors to institute a policy of industrial growth at home (without the Junker class wanting or being able to prevent it). Such a compromise might have seemed reasonable to princes elsewhere—the King of Poland, the Hapsburgs in Austria, the Bourbons in Spain. Why could Brandenburg alone make it work? Let us review what happened. Up to 1653, the major tax was the so-called (military) contribution, a land tax. The nobles were exempt from this tax. In the rural areas, one noble appointed by the others assigned rates among the peasants to meet the gross tax for the district. The income derived for the state in this fashion was rather small.

In 1650 the Elector convened the Estates, hoping to persuade them to let him imitate the Dutch and institute an excise tax (that is, an indirect tax on commodities) from which no one would be exempt. However, what a core state, such as the United Provinces, could do proved politically impossible for a peripheral state, even one led by an intelligent, ambitious ruler. The

---

[311] Carsten (1950, 178). Cleve, and nearby Mark and Ravensburg were, furthermore, areas with a considerable amount of industry prior to the Thirty Years' War.

[312] "The Hohenzollerns emerged from the Thirty Years' War as the most important German ruling house after the Habsburgs" (Carsten, 1969, 544); but Hither Pomerania went to Sweden.

[313] P. Anderson places particular stress on Sweden's role as "the Hammer of the East" which

created Prussian absolutism as "a direct response to the impending Swedish menace" (1974a, 198–199).

[314] Franz Mehring put it quite succinctly: "If the Elector Frederick William . . . was to continue to be a prince at all after the Thirty Years' War, then he obviously needed an army. But it is no less obvious that he could not keep a single company under arms without the Junkers, not to speak of doing it in opposition to the Junkers" (1975, 47).

nobility refused to vote an excise. Still, the need for an army in those troubled times seemed obvious. Both sides thus agreed on the Recess of 1653, which was an interim solution. The Elector got an additional half-million thalers in taxes over six years, but no excise; and he conceded to the Junkers, to a considerable degree, the further institutionalization of serf-dom. The most important clause was that making a legal presumption that peasants were *leibeigen* (serfs), unless they could prove to the contrary. Had this been all, we would scarcely remember today the Recess of 1653. It would have seemed one more noble victory in one more peripheral state of the seventeenth century. But the Recess of 1653 represented for the Great Elector "the thin edge of the wedge,"[315] which was then utilized during the Northern War of 1655–1660. We have already discussed this war as the moment in which the Swedish military role in the Baltic reached its high point. Sweden defeated Poland and Denmark, stopped Russian expansion, and acquired Scania and thereby one side of the Sound.

Where did Brandenburg fit into these events? Brandenburg sided with Sweden against Poland until 1657 and then switched sides—with Dutch encouragement. Hence it prevented Sweden from swallowing up Poland, or at least the Polish coast, and acquired for itself full sovereignty over Prussia. Thus Brandenburg served the Dutch (and the English) by setting limits to Swedish power. Brandenburg was the only state able to do this at the time because it had an army created with the taxes obtained by the Recess of 1653. Within Brandenburg, the Great Elector could turn this geopolitical success to his immediate advantage, which is why Carsten considers the Northern War, rather than the Recess of 1653, the turning point in the increase of state power.[316] To review the details of the Great Elector's successive political moves thereafter—various meetings of the Estates of various areas, various decrees, the crushing of the burghers revolt in Königsberg in 1674—is less important than to review what had changed by the time the reign of the Great Elector ended in 1688, on the eve of the Glorious Revolution and the Nine Years' War.[317]

The Great Elector had reorganized the Privy Council as an agency of central administration and created three bureaucracies—financial, military, and judicial—to implement central decisions.[318] These bureaucracies, while comprehensive in scope, were and would remain in the eighteenth century

[315] Carsten (1950, 188).

[316] Carsten (1954, 189), who says: "By internal evidence . . . it seems unlikely that Frederick William at this juncture had any plan of making himself absolute and of ruling against the Estates. It was much more circumstances which forced him onto this road, above all the impact of foreign affairs on internal developments."

[317] A detailed account of this political history is to be found in Carsten (1954, Pt. III).

[318] See Dorwart (1953, 17); Braun (1975, 134–140). Otto Hintze argues that "there is a striking analogy between the process that created the administrative structure of the French *Ancien régime* and the emergence of the Prussian commissary. . . . The [provincial] intendants occupied the same place in the administrative system of old France as did the Boards for War and Domains in old Prussia" (1975b, 275).

"surprisingly small"[319] in size. The increased revenue, 3.3 million thalers in 1688 as compared with 1 million in 1640,[320] was spent primarily on maintaining a paid volunteer army, partially composed of foreigners. In 1653 the permanent force was 4,000 men; in 1688, 30,000.[321] The authority of these bureaucracies, however, ended at the gate of the Junker estates, within which the *Landrat* (County Commissioner), elected by fellow Junkers, reigned supreme.[322] The Brandenburg-Prussian state had however one ʹlever vis-à-vis the estate owners that rulers in Poland, Austria, Denmark, and Sweden did not have—the fact there were few *large*-scale estates. This, combined with bad times,[323] extensive war devastation,[324] and the meager natural resources of the soil,[325] meant that "work for the King of Prussia could be most gratifying to material ambition. . . . Under the conditions of the seventeenth and eighteenth centuries it was one of the best and shortest ways either of getting rich or of adding to one's riches."[326] Since there were no owners of *great* estates it was not merely the "best and shortest" way, it was virtually the only way.

Hence, the Junkers were both hard-working on their estates[327] and desir-

---

[319] Dorn (1932, 261). "In the entire kingdom there were no more than 14,000 officers of every category. While in the France of the old regime the persistent popular complaint was that there were too many officials, in Prussia it was that there were not enough. The Prussian king could not afford to employ superfluous officials." Dorn is speaking here of the already extended bureaucratic structure of the eighteenth century. It is *a fortiori* true of the time of the Great Elector. Similarly, Barraclough, also referring to the eighteenth century, observes: "The frugality, the rigid checks on expenditure, the careful management which produced this result, were the mark of Prussian administration" (1962, 400).

[320] See Finer (1975, 140). On tax collection, see Rachel (1911, 507–508), Rosenberg (1958, 49–50), and Braun (1975, 271–273). Carsten argues that the urban excise tax was so lopsided in its effects that it "became a barrier to the economic development of the towns" (1954, 198).

[321] See Finer (1975, 139). Frederick William I (1713–1740) increased the standing army to 80,000 (half foreigners) and made it "in drill and discipline, incomparable in Europe" (E. Barker, 1966, 42).

[322] See Craig (1955, 16) and Braun (1975, 273).

[323] "The wintry economic climate of the later seventeenth century provided another incentive for the landowning class to rally to the political edifice of princely power that was now going up in the Hohenzollern lands" (P. Anderson, 1974a, 243).

[324] "Above all, Prussia was terribly devastated [in the Northern War] by the marches of ill-disciplined troops, by booty, burning, and foreign invasion" (Carsten, 1954, 208). Of course, Brandenburg and

Cleves had already been devastated in the Thirty Years' War.

[325] Mehring speaks of the "sandy patrimonies in the Mark and Pomerania" and points out that for the Junkers, "every new company was as good as a new estate," earning them, "even without swindling," an annual income of a few thousand thalers (1975, 54).

[326] Rosenberg (1958, 102). Mehring notes how the army established by the Great Elector solved the problem of a wandering lumpenproletariat created by the Thirty Years' War as well as the problem of the poor nobility known as the *Krippenreiter*, "knights on wooden horses." They became soldiers and officers respectively (1975, 48–49). See also Craig (1955, 11). Rosenberg points out that the role of the army in the promotion of the poor nobility was interrupted in the reign of Frederick I (1688–1733), by the incorporation of Huguenots and German commoners into officer rank, but was resumed under the soldier-king, Frederick William I, who "methodically neutralized the political restlessness, allayed the fears, and reconciled most of the Junker class to the growth of autocratic central power by inviting the noble ʹreserve army' to regain a secure and highly honored position in society by joining the ranks of the professional service aristocracy" (1958, 59–60).

[327] A. J. P. Taylor asserts that the virtues of efficiency and hard work "were the very virtues possessed by the Junkers and not possessed to the same degree by the German burghers of the eighteenth century" (1946, 29). P. Anderson makes a similar point: "The Prussian Junkers of the late seventeenth and early eighteenth centuries were . . . a

ous of strengthening the state bureaucracy of Brandenburg-Prussia as a necessary employment outlet for them.[328] This in turn made it possible for the state to create a modern bureaucracy without any significant use of the expensive intermediate form of venality of office.[329] It permitted the retention of some closure[330] of the nobility (which France could not do) while still maintaining a frugal, efficient state machinery. Brandenburg-Prussia went as far as any state in Europe in this period, both in augmenting the "feudal" rights of nobles over peasants and in incorporating the nobles into the state bureaucracy. Yet because the Junker estates were only medium in size at best and comparatively poor, the state structure[331] steadily grew stronger—first as a military force and later as a force acting on the world-economy—so that by the early eighteenth century, Prussia became a semiperipheral state.

In some ways, of course, Austria was much better placed to play the role Prussia was seeking to play. At the start of the seventeenth century it was a major military power. The Hapsburgs incarnated the Counter-Reformation and achieved the reconversion of Austria, Czechia, and most of Hungary to Catholicism by the mid-seventeenth century. After the Battle of the White Mountain in 1620, the Hapsburgs crushed the Bohemian state, and "reduced [it] to the status of a province."[332] The upheaval transformed the Bohemian aristocracy from an independent landed class to a court nobility and liquidated the indigenous bourgeoisie.[333] Furthermore,

compact social class, in a small country, with rough rural business traditions" (1974a, 263). Hard work on the estates, furthermore, fit in very closely with the needs of the army. "The wheat trade was determined by the fast-growing consumption stratum, military demand, rising production costs and trade margins. Frederick William I established a close link, in that project rich time, between the wheat trade policy, Army provisioning, the Estate-economy and army reform" (Treue, 1955, 423).

[328] "Especially in the area of personnel recruitment, there was no hard and fast line between the old entrenched *officiers* and the upstart 'commissars'. From the outset, some of those who merged with the new administration came from the disturbed army of *Ständestaat* officials" (Rosenberg, 1958, 56)

[329] See Rosenberg (1958, 79, 83). Given the economic situation of the Junkers, there was not much money with which to buy offices.

[330] Closure did not mean that bourgeois could not become landowners. Treue observes: "In Pomerania, Mecklenburg, Brandenburg, Bohemia, Lower Saxony, and Westphalia, many colonels and generals who became rich as entrepreneurs of regiments and divisions, became members of the landowning class by purchasing land from a nobleman in debt" (1955, 414).

[331] Rosenberg points out that in France after the Fronde the *noblesse de race* were virtually excluded

from the state machinery for two generations and that in Bohemia and Moravia, a whole new stratum rose with the victorious Catholic Counter-Reformation; but in Prussia, noble resistance to monarchical authority did not flare up in organized rebellion and bloody civil war. The three great Hohenzollerns never pushed the Junkers too far" (1958, 44). See also Carsten (1954, 273) on the comparison with France. In Prussia, Frederick William I put a further twist on the arrangement. He opened the civil bureaucracy to commoners (creating "chances for advancement unmatched in Prussian government employment until the 1920s when the Prussian state was a stronghold of the Social Democrats"), while converting the army into "a closely knit corps of aristocrats" (Rosenberg, 1958, 67, 70). The two groups thus checked each other, yet had reason to be content with the state.

[332] Kavke (1964, 59).

[333] See Kavke (1964, 55, 57). To be sure, the position of the aristocracy recovered somewhat. Wright speaks of its going "from the nadir of 1627 to the zenith of 1740" (1966, 25). After 1740 came Maria Theresa and new centralization. However, one should not exaggerate. Wright himself tells us that: "As the Habsburgs' expenses grew [in the latter half of the seventeenth and eighteenth centuries] their tax demands became greater and more insistent, and the tax burden on the serf became heavier.

the Hapsburgs were able to recruit an officer corps that was not confined to the nobility, as in Brandenburg-Prussia.[334] Yet the Hapsburgs could never transform their domains into a coherently integrated state that could function adequately within the interstate system. Only a relatively homogeneous state structure was likely to thrive in the capitalist world-economy.[335] The Austrian Hapsburgs suffered from the same dilemmas faced on a larger scale by their ancestor, Charles V.

The key stumbling block to achieving such integration in the Hapsburg domains was Turkish military power. The seventeenth century was a century of Austrian struggle with the Ottomans culminating in the *Türkenjahr* of 1683 when the Hapsburgs successfully resisted the second siege of Vienna.[336] While the Hapsburgs emerged triumphant, the victory involved a price—concessions over this period to the Hungarian nobility, who always had a Turkish card to play and thus laid claim to their autonomous rights within the Hapsburg realms.[337] The Turkish threat with its direct economic implications, plus its indirect consequences for the structure of the state, made the Hapsburgs suffer, "more perhaps than any other sovereigns"[338] in the seventeenth century, from an inability to raise sufficient money for their treasury, making them "distinctly underendowed."[339] By the reign of Charles VI (1711–1740), Austria could sustain, on the basis of its revenue, an army only half the size of France, and indeed only slightly larger than that of Prussia.[340] Consequently, in terms of the efficacy of its mercantilist

When the serf began to falter under the weight of taxes, the state took an interest in him as a producer of revenue and began to intervene in his favor against the lords who bade fair to ruin him" (1966, 21). Thus the peasant revolt in Bohemia in 1679 was followed by the *Robotpatent* of 1680, limiting *robota* (corvée) to a maximum of three days a week. Polišenský sees 1680 as a "watershed" (1978, 200). There were, in addition, two further *Robotpatents* in 1717 and 1738. This pattern is not really different from that of Brandenburg-Prussia. See Špiesz (1969, 33–34); von Hippel (1971, 293–295); Slicher van Bath (1977, 117).

[334] See Kann (1973, 9) and cf. T. M. Barker (1978).

[335] Brandenburg, by contrast, had transformed an initially very heterogeneous population (see Treue, 1955, 355) into an ethnically very homogeneous realm already by the beginning of the modern era. See Carsten (1941, 75, and 1947, 147).

[336] See T. M. Barker (1967) for a detailed account.

[337] P. Anderson calls Hungary the "unsurmountable obstacle to a military royal state," and the "proximity of Turkish military power . . . a decisive objective hindrance to the extension of a centralized Austrian Absolutism into Hungary" (1974a, 314–315).

[338] Bérenger (1973, 657), whose article spells out the consequent dependence on public loans. He in-

dicates that these loans were indeed available and thus the financial situation of Emperor Leopold I (1657–1705) "was not so desperate as is generally assumed, and as the Emperor himself liked to declare" (p. 669). But the long-run consequences of dependence on private financiers was not conducive to strengthening the state machinery. It should be noted, however, that the Turkish wars had a positive effect on the agrarian economy (and thus presumably on the tax base) insofar as it became necessary to victual troops. Bog (1971) credits the wars as a major factor in the recovery of all the Germanies after the Thirty Years' War, which had not served the same function, because of war devastation. But did not devastation also affect the agrarian economy in the Turkish wars? See T. M. Barker (1967, 282–284).

[339] Wangermann (1973, 12), who compares the Hapsburgs unfavorably to the French monarchs. The territorial extent of their domains were roughly the same, but "far more important were homogeneity, compactness, a regular revenue from taxation and facilities for profitable commercial enterprise." The net product of corvée labor in Austria was the marvelous Baroque architecture, for which perhaps we should be grateful. See Zollner (1970, 279–280).

[340] See Wangermann (1973, 14).

endeavors, Austria, with twice the army and far greater wealth and population, could achieve little more than Prussia.

One should have clearly in mind the difference between the mercantilism
of core powers, such as England and France, and the mercantilism of
semiperipheral powers. Treue points this out:

> While [mercantilism] corresponds basically and among the great powers to an eco-
> nomic policy of aggressiveness and expansion, it bore in Germany the defensive
> objective of self-assertion; more holding onto markets than conquering them; more
> repelling the domination of others, most especially that of the Western neighbors,
> than the aspiration to dominate.[341]

The whole period from the Thirty Year's War until the end of the
Napoleonic era was an age of mercantilism (cameralism) in all the Germanies, indeed in all of central Europe.[342] The Hapsburg mercantilist policies can be traced to about 1660.[343] The Hohenzollerns, beginning with the
Great Elector, made it central to their governmental practice.[344] The real
question is what was achieved by these mercantilist policies. On the one
hand, it is probably true that the results of state encouragement of manufacture in the period from 1650 to 1750 were "not very satisfying" anywhere.[345] Indeed, von Klaveren argues that mercantilism in backward countries was "*pseudo*mercantilism", whose true objective was "the enrichment of
local dignitaries," and that "nobody really expected mercantilism to succeed."[346] To say nothing but this, which is to some extent true, is to ignore
the difference between the semiperipheral countries, which could be at least
pseudomercantilist, and the peripheral countries, which could not even be
that.

It is equally clear that the mercantilism of semiperipheral countries in this
long period of downturn laid the foundations[347] for the significant development of manufacturing activities in the period of the expansion of the

[341] Treue (1974, 106–107). For evidence that mercantilism is never totally defensive, see Dorwart's
discussion of why a new tolerance was shown for
Jews in Germany. He speaks of "the almost desperate recruiting of Jews by German princes to aid in
recovery from the commercial ruin caused by the
Thirty Years' War" (1971, 212). How admitting the
Jews would help is made clear in Dorwart's description of the Great Elector's decision in 1650 to allow
Jews to reenter Brandenburg from Poland: "With
the mouth of the Oder in Swedish hands, reopening
trade directly with Poland could be a useful function of the Jewish merchants" (1971, 122). For the
view that mercantilism was "natural" in France in
terms of the socioeconomic structure of the country,
but not so in Brandenburg-Prussia, see Kruger
(1958, 65). Kruger's view is part of a polemic against
what he calls the "Hohenzollern legend" of the "social kingdom" propagated by German bourgeois

historians since the time of Schmoller (1958, 13).

[342] See Lütge (1966, 321–322); Bog (1961, 134–
135, 139); Klíma and Macůrek (1960, 98).

[343] See Tremel (1961, 176); Klíma (1965, 107);
Zollner (1970, 283).

[344] See von Braun (1959, 611–614) and Kisch
(1968, 4).

[345] Kulischer (1931, 13).

[346] Van Klaveren (1969b, 149–150). Deyon points
out that "mercantilist projects were universal," but
were "often merely impulses, purely formal decisions, recommendations deprived of all efficacity"
(1978a, 208).

[347] Klíma (1965, 119). Kulischer asks whether
after the mid-eighteenth century "the rapid rise of
industry in France, Prussia, Austria, the Rhineland,
and Russia would have been achieved, had it not
been prepared in the preceding era, that is, the Colbertist period" (1931, 13–14).

world-economy after circa 1750. What should be looked at closely, there-
fore, is what was happening in the first half of the eighteenth century, when
Sweden had been knocked out of the competition, so to speak, and when
Prussia and Austria were in fact vying for being the power in central
Europe that could most take advantage of a further expansion of Europe.
Charles VI ascended the Hapsburg throne in 1711; Frederick William I
came to the Prussian throne in 1713. In 1713–1714, with the Treaties of
Utrecht and Rastatt, the War of the Spanish Succession came to an end.
Austria acquired the Spanish (now Austrian) Netherlands, Milan, Naples,
and Sardinia (traded with Savoy in 1720 for Sicily). In 1718 Austria obtained from the Ottomans, in the Peace of Passarowitz, Serbia, Banat, and
Lesser Wallachia (having already obtained Hungary and Transylvania in
the Treaty of Carlowitz of 1699). Austria recreated the *Wiener orientalisch
Handelskompagnie* (the first one having failed in 1683) in order to profit
from the new possibilities of Balkan trade. In 1719, Charles VI finally was
able to have Trieste and Fiume declared free ports, the idea having first
been broached in 1675.[348]

In Austria's "Drang Nach Meer," 1719 was thus the turning point. Austria now had access both to the Atlantic (at Ostend) and the Mediterranean
(at Trieste). It could pretend to compete with Venice and Hamburg.[349] It
seemed at last to be a great power.[350] Suddenly it found itself "at odds
simultaneously"[351] with England, Holland, France, and Spain—for they all
were threatened by Austria's new commercial pretensions. Prussia, to be
sure, also emerged greatly strengthened at this time. In the Treaty of Stockholm (1719), it had acquired the last of Sweden's German possessions. It
was now stronger militarily than Sweden, and by the reign of Frederick the
Great, it would succeed to the "reputation for military prowess in Europe"
that had been Sweden's until the death of Charles XII.[352] Still, as of 1713,
Prussia was still "a mainly agricultural country"[353] whose resources were
"contemptibly small."[354] By the middle of the eighteenth century, nonetheless, Austria was confined to being the kind of second-rate world power it
would remain up to 1918, while Prussia was on the road to being a real
world power. The particular internal structure of Prussia that made this

[348] See Hassinger (1942, 36–37).

[349] See Kaltenstadler (1969, 489–498) and also
Kaltenstadler (1972). This access to the sea explains, in turn, the rapid growth of the woollen-
goods industry in Bohemia, Moravia, and Silesia
in this period. See Freudenberger (1960b, 389–
393).

[350] J. W. Stoye cites approvingly the title of O.
Reddich's book on Austria between 1700 and 1740:
"The Development of a Great Power" (see 1970a,
598).

[351] Macartney (1966, 397).

[352] Samuelsson (1968, 69).

[353] Bruford (1966, 293). "Before Prussia could
really count as an independent Power in Europe,
serious difficulties had to be overcome which resulted
from the geographic disposition of its provinces,
their low economic development, and their lack of
manpower."

[354] A. J. P. Taylor (1946, 27), who adds the words:
"no industrial areas, no important cities, no outlet to
the sea, the land barren and unyielding, the nobility
poor and ignorant, cultural life virtually non-
existent."

possible we have already reviewed;[355] but the tilt of the Prussian–Austrian rivalry in favor of Prussia cannot be explained without taking into account the course of English–French rivalry, which we shall discuss in the next chapter.

Barraclough feels that at this time the two rivals "tended to cancel each other out;"[356] This is not quite the way to put it. Prussia was used to cancel Austria out, and got Silesia as its reward. Silesia was valuable politically, economically, and strategically. It had been fought over since the tenth century, and in the seventeenth and eighteenth centuries, it was what preoccupied most of Brandenburg's diplomacy.[357] Silesia was the "true industrial zone of the East, . . . [the] 'jewel' among the [Austrian] Hereditary Lands."[358] To be sure, Silesian linens were marketed by English, Dutch, and Hamburg merchants, and Silesia may be said to have reflected "a classic pattern of colonial penetration."[359] Production was local, however. It developed especially after the Thirty Year's War in a *Kaufsystem* form at the village level, the village merchants then selling to larger merchants who engaged in centralized quality control.[360] In many cases, there were manufactories on the estates, with the landowner as entrepreneur and serfs working for wages.[361] The extensiveness of these industrial activities may be what accounts for the fact that among the three Bohemian Lands of the Hapsburgs—Bohemia, Moravia, and Silesia—Silesia was known for "the relative mildness of its serf–lord regulations."[362] When in 1748 Prussia acquired Silesia as its prize in the War of the Austrian Succession, it therefore acquired "the most prosperous and industrialized province"[363] of the Hapsburg domains.

[355] The superiority of Prussia over Austria in terms of state structure at this time is made clear in the descriptions by Behrens and Rosenberg Behrens says: "In the Habsburg dominions at Maria Theresa's accession in 1740 there was nothing in the way of a central administration, let alone a nation. A central administration only began to come into existence after 1748, and then only in the so-called German hereditary lands of Austria and Bohemia" (1977, 551). Prussian administrative unification only dates to the reign of Frederick William I, that is, 30 years earlier (see Behrens, 1977, 557). However, "in the basic direction of development under the Old Regime, Hohenzollern Prussia moved in harmony with the other absolute polities of Europe. Perhaps its most distinguishing characteristic was the fact that . . . many political innovations, administrative reforms, and fiscal measures were carried to extremes by overzealous leaders" (Rosenberg, 1958, 23).

[356] Barraclough (1962, 386).

[357] Leszczyński (1970, 104).

[358] Tremel (1961, 177). "Silesian linen found export markets in Holland and England, Poland and Russia. Dutch merchants needed it for Spain, Portugal, and the Levant. Silesian *Schleier* [light, sheer women's headwear made of linen or linenlike cotton] were exported to Africa, Curaçao and Indonesia. Silesian wool played a dominant role on the wool market." Another reason why Silesia was the "jewel" was the key role of its capital, Breslau, in land transit with the east, in which it came to have a monopoly (Wolański, 1971, 126). See also Hroch (1971, 72).

[359] Kisch (1959, 544). The rising importance of Hamburg's role in the eighteenth century at the expense of the Dutch is discussed by Liebel (1965b, 210–216).

[360] See Klíma (1959, 37–38).

[361] See Aubin (1942, 169) and Klíma (1957, 92).

[362] Wright (1966, 20). Despite this mildness, there were several peasant revolts in the late seventeenth and eighteenth centuries; they were put down by military force. See Kisch (1959, 549) and cf. Michalkjewicz (1958) and Tapié (1971, 121).

[363] P. Anderson (1974a, 317). See also von Braun (1959, 614–616) on the importance to Prussia of acquiring Silesia.

This was a "staggering blow" to Austria, not only because of Silesia's industrial output, but because it was the "principal commercial intermediary" of the Hapsburg monarchy with the outside world.[364] The effects of its loss reached also to Bohemia and Moravia, since the spinners and weavers of the latter had sold their wares up to 1742 to Silesian merchants. Were this to have continued, as permitted by the peace treaty, it would have made these laws "economically dependent on the whims of Prussia."[365] Austria was forced into reconversion. The acquisition of Silesia by Prussia was thus a major event, aiding substantially the industrialization of the nineteenth century.[366] It had been made possible by the creation of a Prussian army and state plus the needs of the English (and Dutch) to check Sweden and then frustrate Austria; and the creation of the Prussian army and state had been rendered possible by the peculiar weaknesses of the landed nobility as compared to other peripheral states. It was this sequence of conjunctures over a century that made it possible for Brandenburg, a very insignificant peripheral area, to become by 1750 the semiperipheral power in Europe with the greatest potential for transforming its role in the world-economy.

The last semiperipheral area created in this era, one rather different from the others, was that composed of the New England and Middle Atlantic colonies of British North America. Their colonization only began in 1620, and with the exception perhaps of New Amsterdam as a strategic and commercial outpost of the Dutch world network, these areas were not even part of the capitalist world-economy before 1660.[367] Indeed, New Jersey, Pennsylvania, and Delaware were only colonized by the English in the Restoration period.[368] The turning point in North America was 1660 because that was the turning point in England. It marked the institutionalization of the mercantilist doctrine that "the interests of the colonies [were to be subordinated] to the good of the nation."[369] The various English Navigation Acts of the 1660s, by making the most important colonial products—sugar, tobacco, dyewoods, and so on—"enumerated" products, which therefore had to be shipped on English ships and sold to English buyers, affected markedly the West Indian and Chesapeake Valley producers. At first, these

[364] Freudenberger (1960b, 384).

[365] Freudenberger (1960a, 351).

[366] See Kula (1965, 221).

[367] See Craven's description of New England as of 1660: "The economy . . . rested basically upon agriculture. . . . The typical New England town was a farming village. . . . But outside Boston, now a town of possibly 3000 souls, subsistence farming was so basic to all other activity that even the minister at times had to be found in the field" (Craven, 1968, 18).

[368] See Craven (1968, 68–103) on the "Restoration Colonies," which also include the two Carolinas and

New York, which was captured from the Dutch in 1664.

[369] Bailyn (1955, 112–113). *Institutionalization* is the key term. Cromwell was mercantilist too; but, "the English colonists had tried to use the Civil War as an opportunity to assert a measure of independence, and the Commonwealth had tolerated many pretensions so long as loyalty to the Stuarts was not involved. . . . The period of accomplishment [of the English government vis-à-vis the colonies] . . . was rather that of the restored Stuarts than that of the Cromwellian republicans" (Rich, 1961, 330–331).

acts had hardly any negative affect on the northern colonies, partly because they were little enforced, and partly because these colonies did not produce many enumerated products.[370] Indeed, the impact might be said to have been positive, in that the Navigation Acts stimulated shipbuilding in these colonies by driving the Dutch out of North America "before English shipping could meet the full needs of the colonies."[371]

These colonies produced little of use to sell to England in the seventeenth century and were too small to be much of a market for English goods, but they competed in the carrying trade and thus seemed to be almost a liability to England. If England held on to them, it was partly for fear of France's taking hold of them. It was in a sense preemptive retention.[372] The Stuarts moved to revoke charters and gain most effective control over these problem child colonies by the creation in 1684 of the Dominion of New England. These areas might have been effectively peripheralized had not New England resistance to Stuart policies coincided with the internal revolt in England that culminated in the Glorious Revolution, which "ended, or at least postponed, the threat to the colonists."[373] Thus it was that because of what Eleanor Lord calls the "inadvertent neglect of these colonies," but what might better be called the internal difficulties of carrying out England's mercantilist grand design, New England and Middle Atlantic merchants were by 1700 "making great strides" not only as shipbuilders but as commercial middlemen.[374]

These merchants were involved in the so-called triangular trade, of which there were in fact many variants. In the triangle with Africa and the West Indies, West Indian molasses went to the northern colonies, whose rum and trinkets went to Africa, and African slaves went to the West Indies. In the triangle with England and the West Indies, provisions and lumber went from the northern colonies to the West Indies, West Indian sugar and tobacco went to England, and English manufactures went to the northern colonies (or the northern-colony ship was sold in England). In a third and lesser triangle with southern Europe and England, wheat,[375] fish, and lumber from the northern colonies went to southern Europe; southern European wine, salt, and fruits went to England; and again English manufactures went to the northern colonies. Two things must be underlined

---

[370] Craven says they suffered "no adverse effects" (1968, 39). Nettels says that between 1685 and 1720, New England and New York had "little in the way of exports to England" (1933, 326). Bailyn notes that a provision in 1673 that required double taxation for New England merchants—at port of clearance and at port of entry—but only single taxation for English merchants were protested as "gross discrimination" (1955, 151). Kammen discusses the beginnings of the consciousness by New Englanders that they were a "special interest separate from other competing groups in London" by the late 1670s (1970, 37).

[371] Nettels (1952, 109; see also 1931b, 9–10).

[372] See the discussion in Beer (1912, I, 51–53).

[373] Barrow (1967, 34–35). See also Bailyn (1953, 386) and Craven (1968, 246).

[374] Lord (1898, 105).

[375] Slicher van Bath goes so far as to claim that in the last half of the seventeenth and first half of the eighteenth centuries "only large [European] land owners could grow cereals cheaply enough to compete with the grain from Pennsylvania" (1963a, 220).

about these famous triangles. They are in large part analytic constructs. They represent flows of commodities far more than movements of ships. The ships from the northern colonies concentrated on the West Indian shuttle run, doing only a little travel across the Atlantic to England, and very little to Africa.[376]

Secondly, the English pressed the northern colonies to maintain an unfavorable balance of direct trade, which meant the latter had to procure coin if they wished to obtain manufactures. To the extent that the triangular trade did not procure the bullion necessary, they had either to expand their own manufactures (and hence reduce imports from England) or find a staple.[377] The political struggle of the northern colonies with England in the first half of the eighteenth century centered around which of these two alternatives was to be pursued. In the seventeenth century, the northern colonists came to be competitors of English producers as shipbuilers, ship conveyors, and suppliers of provsions to the West Indies and Europe. They were, by mercantilist doctrine, "more a competitor . . . [than] an asset" and thus "the least valuable of British possessions."[378] After 1689 the English made a conscious effort[379] to redress the situation; they tried to expand their function as a market for English manufactures by encouraging a new staple (naval stores) and by stifling the incipient industrial production.[380]

---

[376] Walton (1968b, 365–371). The reason was economic. Familiarity between the merchant and his agents reduced risks considerably, which led to route specialization. Crews in ships on triangular routes were paid while in port, whereas crews on shuttle ships were not (Walton, 1968b, 386–389). Ostrander goes further and doubts that the construct is valid since the ships did not in fact make the voyage. He attributes the concept to the ideological needs of the nineteenth century (see 1973, 642).

[377] Lord (1898, 124–125).

[378] Barrow (1967, 8). Nettels feels such an analysis neglects the "invisible returns" to England from the northern colonies—the coin and bullion flows, the fruits of piracy, the "purchase" of crown services, even shipbuilding for English purchasers; but the invisible returns were precisely that, less visible, and hence may not have been able to alter English consciousness substantially regarding the value of the northern colonies (see 1933, 344–347).

[379] However conscious the effort to increase the value of the northern colonies to England, there is no doubt that relative to their attitude toward the colonies of the extended Caribbean, the English attitude in this case was one of neglect. A. G. Frank thinks that such neglect, caused by "the relative *poverty* of the land and climate, as well as . . . the nonexistence of mines," was the good fortune of these colonies because it permitted them to develop differently as compared with the tropical and semitropical colonies (Frank, 1979b, 60). Barrow discus-

ses the "policy of 'salutary neglect'" from another angle. He points out that at least in the eighteenth century "to keep the colonists [of British North America] content required a policy of appeasement, not of coercion. Consequently for Walpole and his successors the guiding principle became to let well enough alone. 'Quieta non movere' thus became Walpole's political maxim in colonial administration" (1967, 116, 134).

[380] See Nettels (1931a, 233). On the timing, Nettels refers to G. L. Beer's view that the northern colonies only became valued as a market after 1745. Nettels argues that this view is wrong, and that they were so valued as of the end of the seventeenth century (See 1931a, 230–231). Kammen gives 1713 as the year after which "all colonial resources [including those of the northern colonies] were regarded [by the English] as important in contributing to a self-sufficient empire" (1970, 46). Bruchey speaks of this occurring "in the later colonial period" (1966, 8). Coleman gives the earliest date. He says that "England's North American colonies offered the most striking net increase in demand after 1650, thereby opening up an exclusive market for English industrial output precisely when intra-European trade was depressed and competition intensifying" (1977, 197–198).

Perhaps what we have here is intent (beginning in the 1690s) becoming realization (by mid-eighteenth century). Farnie's data for the colonies in the Americas taken together show that, as a market for Eng-

How does one "create" a market in a particular zone? By involving the people therein in production for the world-economy; and if there aren't enough such people of a high enough income level, one encourages "settlement." It is the latter tack that the English took, and which distinguished them significantly from the French, the Dutch, even the Spanish and Portuguese in the Americas.[381]

There is in fact a particularly important stream of migrants, especially to the Middle Atlantic states, between 1713–1739. Since Englishmen were not willing to emigrate in significant numbers, at that time the English accomplished this by opening up British North America to non-Englishmen: Scots, Ulstermen, and the so-called Dutch (who were in fact Germans and Swiss).[382] The English hoped these new migrants would be engaged in the production of the new staple—naval stores. This promised not only economic advantage to the English, but also a military advantage. The one "serious deficiency"[383] of English colonial trade had long been naval stores, and it had been a "standing aim"[384] of her policy throughout the seventeenth century to remedy this. This deficiency was made more acute by the outbreak of the Nine Years' War in 1689. Almost all the production or transiting of English naval stores were in the hands of the Swedes, who were neutral but pro-French; and this was a "constant cause of uneasiness."[385] The obvious alternative source was the northern colonies (and also Ireland). In 1696 England created the Board of Trade and Plantations, and one of their first concerns was to free England from dependence on Sweden. They attempted to create a monopoly to do this, but this approach ran into much resistance.[386]

The War of the Spanish Succession made the issue once again acute, and the situation was compounded by the formation of the Stockholm Tar Company as a monopoly. This led to the Naval Stores Act of 1705, in which it was decided to rely on bounties as an inducement for production in the

---

lish goods, the colonies went from about 10% in 1701–1705 to 23% in 1766–1770, and as a source of imports to England from 19% to 34%. The role of the continental colonies (but this includes both north and south) exceeded that of the West Indies for the first time in 1726–1730. Farnie suggests that this "Americanization" of English foreign trade—he borrows the phrase from Schlote—resulted in an "eventual over-dependence," which accounts for English economic difficulties in the latter half of the eighteenth century (1962, 214). This strikes me as highly dubious—indeed, as mercantilist ideology carried to an extreme. The point is rather, as we shall see, that England was unable to keep the northern colonies from being a semiperipheral area, and to this extent England created some of its own future difficulties. But if not from there, then from elsewhere.

[381] See Nettels (1933, 322).

[382] See M. L. Hansen (1945, 48–50).

[383] McLachlan (1940, 4).

[384] Åström (1962, 15).

[385] Åström (1962, 20). Of imports to England including all items from northern Europe as of 1699-1700—hemp, flax, pitch, tar, iron, potash—48.0% originated primarily from Sweden; 26.4% came from Russia; 24.1% from the East Country; and only 1.5% from Denmark–Norway. However, Russian goods transited via Narva, which was in Swedish hands, and East Country goods via Riga, also in Swedish hands (See Åström, 1962, 99).

[386] The resistance was triple. The traders in the northern colonies were opposed. The Navy, whose primary concern was to get the best and cheapest naval stores, were opposed. English public opinion had turned suspicious of monopolies. See Lord (1898, 38–39).

northern colonies.[387] Extrication of England from dependence on Sweden was clearly not the only motive for the Naval Stores Act. Nettels gives three reasons that the creation of markets in the northern colonies was a central objective, even the primary motive. First, while the dependence on Sweden really applied only to pitch and tar, the Naval Stores Act gave bounties as well for resin, turpentine, hemp, and ship lumber—all of which could be obtained from a number of countries. Second, Navy officials seemed most unconcerned by this dependence, which throws doubt on the reality of the shortages. They consistently opposed obtaining pitch and tar from the northern colonies because of poor quality. (Nettels reminds us, however, that officials of the Board of Trade accused Navy officials of interested collusion with Eastland merchants.) Third, the Board of Trade was *not* interested in obtaining pitch and tar from the Carolinas, even though the quality was superior to that from the northern colonies. (The Carolinas, of course, already produced staples.)

Nettels argues further that the most consistent supporters of the naval-stores program were precisely those English merchants trading with the northern colonies.[388] In any case, the northern colonists remained more interested in the production of lumber than of tar and pitch;[389] and the lumber went not to England but into the indigenous shipbuilding industry.[390] The fact is that the development of a shipbuilding industry did at least as much for the development of a market for English goods, as a successful naval-stores production program would have done. This may be the fundamental reason that under the Navigation Acts, "for most practical purposes," the ships owned by the colonists were never excluded from the privileges of British-owned vessels.[391] Because of this, it made economic sense to build the ships in the northern colonies, where wages were high, but the costs of lumber were low enough to more than compensate the wage factor.[392] This comparative advantage was intensified by steady increases in the productivity of American colonial shipping in the period from 1675 to 1775.[393] The result was that by 1775 nearly a third of all ships that were

---

[387] See Lord (1898, 56) and Nettels (1931a, 247).

[388] See Nettels (1931a, 255–264). Rees provides one piece of evidence that freedom from dependence on Sweden was a consideration. He reports that despite the long-standing opposition of English ironmasters to the production of wrought iron and hardware in North America, when the price of iron soared in 1717 because of strained relations with Sweden, it was "proposed to find a new source of supply by including bar and pig iron in the list of goods the production of which was to be encouraged in the colonies under the head of naval stores" (1929, 586). The law was not enacted, however, because of the death of Charles XII of Sweden and the subsequent improvement of Anglo–Swedish re-

lations.

[389] Nettels says they did *not* produce "the commodities most desired" (1931a, 269; see also 1952, 112). Åström, however, dates the end of the Swedish tar and pitch monopoly about 1728 and explains this by increased production in the nothern colonies (1962, 111; 1973, 101).

[390] See Lord (1898, 101–123) for the colonists' consistent ability to evade restrictive laws.

[391] Harper (1939a, 9).

[392] See K. G. Davies (1974, 193).

[393] See Walton (1967 and 1968a) for a discussion of the various factors that went into higher productivity.

registered in Britain as British-owned were built in the northern colonies—
"an important source of colonial prosperity."[394]

As for colonial manufactures other than shipbuilding, the English did
indeed try to discourage them, but in a desultory way. In 1699 they passed
the Woollens Act, forbidding shipment beyond the borders of a colony. In
1732 they passed the Hat Act, with similar constraints. In 1733 the Molasses
Act sought to restrict the production of rum. In 1750 the Iron Act forbade
the erection of further mills.[395] All these acts were largely unenforced.[396]
For one thing, the English were far more actively concerned with Dutch,
German, and French competition than with colonial manufactures.[397] In
addition, as Bruchey argues, "the shortage of skilled labor and both the
scarcity and preferred allocations of capital funds" in the northern colonies
acted as a "natural" constraint.[398] Whether natural or not, this factor did
contribute to the low intensity of English enforcement, at least until the era
after 1763. How can we summarize the experience of the northern colonies? They were triply fortunate. They were poor in natural resources, yet
they were a colony of the rising world industrial and commercial power with
enough geographic distance to make it economically highly profitable to
exploit their one major resource, lumber, for a shipbuilding industry.
Shipbuilding was a start, and a crucial one. The conditions were created
whereby in the changed situation of the last half of the eighteenth century
there could be an American Revolution, and in the nineteenth century, the
rise of a major industrial power.

The period from 1600 to 1750 was dominated by the efforts of England
and France first to destroy Dutch hegemony and then to succeed to the top
position. In this long period of relative stagnation (relative, that is, to the
marked economic expansion of the long sixteenth century), the peripheral
areas suffered greatly exacerbated exploitation of the direct producers and
reduced advantage of the indigenous exploiting strata (reduced, that is, by
comparison with similar strata in the core countries). The story of the
semiperipheral countries was a far more complex one. The core countries
sought to make them intermediaries with the periphery, conveyor-belts of
surplus value. They largely succeeded; but in a situation where there was
great inter-core rivalry, some zones could improve their relative status. This
was the case at first of Sweden and later of Brandenburg-Prussia, and on a
lesser scale this was true also of the northern colonies of British North
America.

---

[394] Dickerson (1951, 32).

[395] See Bruchey (1966, 9) and Ostrander (1956,
77–79). The Molasses Act elicited the most protest.
"Molasses and rum . . . were vital factors in the
colonial economy" (Harper, 1942, 11). The chief
purpose of this act seemed to be to aid West Indian
producers.

[396] See Dickerson (1951, 46–47), who notes that,
at most, there was some effect on the hat industry.
See Ostrander (1956, 77) on the Molasses Act.

[397] See Harper (1942, 6–8).

[398] See Bruchey (1965, 69).

W. Hogarth inv. et sculp.

Wine Hall

THIS MONUMENT
WAS ERECTED IN
MEMORY OF THE
DESTRUCTION OF
THIS CITY BY THE
SOUTH SEA
IN
1720

See here ye Causes why in London,— Inspiring their Rude with Lottery Chances— Leaving, their strife Religious bustle,
So many Men are made & undone,— That venges from the Garters down— Since Money serves to bind an issue.
That Arts & honest Trading drop,— To all Blue Apron in the Town,— Thus when the Sheepherds are at play
To Swarm about ye Devils Shopp,— Here all Religous— flock together,— Their flocks must needs go astray,
Who Cuts out (B.) Fortunes Golden Haunches, Like Lambs of a Feather,— The woeful Cause y in these Times,—

(E.) Honour & Honesty, are Crimes,
That boldickly are punished by,—
(G.) Self-Interest & its
(F.) Villany,—
So much ye Worsas magick power
To amuse & Cheat you find out more,
Gues at ye Rest you find one more,
poor & Ruin.

6

STRUGGLE IN THE CORE —
PHASE II: 1689–1763

Figure 7: "The South Sea Scheme," by William Hogarth (1697–1764), an engraving and etching done in 1721. The Guildhall, London Monument, and St. Paul's Church can be recognized. The fortune wheel is a merry-go-round, with South Sea directors turning the passengers who consist of subscribers, a prostitute, and a clergyman. A devil cuts off pieces of Fortune's body while clergyman gamble. The whole scene represents, in Hogarth's description below the engraving, Self-Interest and Villainy overcoming Honor and Honesty.

One cannot analyze social phenomena unless one bounds them in space and time. We have made the concept of spatial boundaries a central axis of the analysis in this book; but what of time and the perennial issues of periodization on which the writers of history are so much divided? We have asserted that the meaningful unit of time to cover in this volume is approximately from 1600 to 1750. This is seen as a period in which the European world-economy went through a long relative stagnation of the total production of the system as a whole. (Stagnation was correspondingly manifested in the relative stability of overall population growth, physical expansion, and velocity of transactions and in a global price deflation.) To sustain this assertion, we have presented throughout this book such evidence as we have.[1] In our analysis, we have subdivided the discussion of core rivalries into two phases, 1651 to 1689 and 1689 to 1763. This set of dates is not perfectly consonant with the 1600 to 1750 period mentioned above. Unfortunately, the real world does not consist of clearly etched dividing lines that serve all purposes. While the dates 1651 to 1689 and 1689 to 1763 reflect a changing world economic situation, they emphasize the political consequences of these changes.

In the first period (1651–1689), as we have already discussed, Dutch hegemony was successfully challenged by the English and the French, who by 1672 came to feel that the Dutch state was no longer the unquestioned giant it had been. I believe that by 1689 even the Dutch agreed. The accession of William and Mary to the throne of England seems, therefore, a reasonable breaking point.[2] It follows then that the period of 1689 to 1763 is chosen because it bounds a time of unbroken Anglo–French rivalry. One might regard 1763 as the moment of the definitive triumph of England after what has been called the second Hundred Years' War, even if the

---

[1] Of course, these dates for the European world-economy are the subject of unending debate. While Pierre Chaunu argues, on the one hand, that "from 1580 to 1760, there is no fundamental modification" in the relation of man and land in Europe (1966a, 242), he also states: "It is between 1680 and 1690 that we must date the beginning, in Manila as in America, furthermore in the Dutch East Indies, of the long phase of expansion of the eighteenth century. An upturn then which precedes by 40 or 50 years more or less the long-deferred upturn of continental Europe" (1960a, 213) Pierre Goubert and Pierre Vilar both date the upturn from 1733 (Goubert, 1970g, 333; Vilar, 1962b, I, 708); but Vilar also states: "Economically, the so-called great élan of the eighteenth century began, it is widely felt, in 1733, but only takes off after 1760 and continues to 1817" (1962a, 11). Similarly, C. E. Labrousse sees a slow upturn from 1726 to 1763, but an "élan" only after that (1970, 388).

[2] Christopher Hill argues: "The Revolution of 1688 was no less a turning point in the economic than in the political and constitutional history of England. A week before James fled, the Royal Africa Company was still, as a routine matter, issuing commissions authorizing the seizure of interlopers who had infringed the Charter of 1672. With no recorded decision, the Company abandoned this claim to enforce its monopoly by coercive measures. Free trade was established formally by Act of Parliament later; but the real change was recognized to have taken place with the fall of James II" (1961a, 262). Heckscher (1935, I, 262–263) also uses 1688 as a dividing point, the great point of divergence between England (liberal) and France (Colbertian); but I have already indicated my skepticism of such an interpretation.

French were not ready to acknowledge defeat until 1815.[3] It was by no means clear as of 1689 that England was going to succeed in its struggle with France. France had four times the population of England and a far larger army. She was rich in natural resources with excellent ports and naval bases. Furthermore, her industrial production was growing, whereas "in England the rate of growth slackened after the Civil War."[4] Thus it is not unreasonable to argue, as Charles Wilson does, that "from 1689 [England] was faced by a hostile power [France] far more formidable than Spain or Holland had ever been."[5] The rivalry seemed a round of almost unending wars over the issues of land, allies, and markets in Europe and over supplies (of slaves, of tropical and semitropical products such as sugar, and of furs and naval stores) in the periphery and the external arena (the Americas, West Africa, India).[6]

In 1689 William of Orange became King William III of England, Scotland, and Ireland.[7] France's war with the Dutch, which had begun in November 1688, thus became France's war with England.[8] This marked for England the resumption of a "foreign policy of Cromwellian scope."[9] This was only possible because of the political settlement of the Glorious Revolution, a settlement further entrenched during the era of Walpole and the Whigs. In the struggle against France, the English military needed larger sums than they had been allotted in the past. This required parliamentary assent, ultimately in the form of guaranteeing public loans. The settlement of 1689, which ended the antagonistic relationship of Crown and Parliament, made the necessary cooperation possible. The question for England in 1689, one that would remain a question throughout the eighteenth century, was whether the central military effort was to be on land or on sea. This was a debate between two schools of thought, the Maritime School and the Continental (or Military) School. In analyzing strategy, they debated

[3] See Sheridan (1969, 13). See also Seeley (1971, 64). Braudel dates England's victory over France "as early as the Treaty of Utrecht of 1713," but he says England only "triumphed in 1815" (1977, 102).

[4] Nef (1968, 149). See also Goubert, who says that "the force of numbers, demographic primacy, was the characteristic feature of the *Ancien Régime*" (1970b, 21). Fred Cottrell, on the other hand, argues that England had an "energy" advantage: "It was in England that the sailing ship produced the full revolution of which it was capable. As an island, England had certain advantages over the continental powers. Her principal protection was obtained by the use of the sailing ship, itself a surplus-producer [of energy], instead of an army. The surplus necessary for defense against invasion was smaller than that required by her neighbors, so that energy could be used in producing more converters without endangering the survival of the country. The armies of the Continent were a constant drain

upon their surpluses" (1955, 69–70).

[5] Wilson (1965, 282).

[6] See Andrews (1915, 546).

[7] This is sometimes dated as 1688. The anomaly is due to the fact that England until 1752 still used the Julian Calendar. The New Year 1689 thus began in England on March 25. William became "Administrator" on January 7 and jointly with Mary accepted the crown and the Declaration of Rights on February 23. Hence the Glorious Revolution was either 1688 or 1689. See Murray (1961, 162) and de Beer (1970, 206–208).

[8] In theory, this was one-sided. Although William, as King of England, Scotland, and Ireland, declared war against France on May 17, 1689, France never declared war on England; Louis XIV continued to recognize James II as the legitimate king until 1697 and the Treaty of Rijswijk. See Clark (1970, 226, n. 2).

[9] C. Hill (1961a, 257).

whether entering the Continent with land forces during war would strengthen the English cause (because it would bolster allies) or weaken the English cause (their armies being basically too weak to win over French armies but their navy being more than a good match for the French navy).

Behind the debate on strategy lay a debate on economics. Since the Maritime School saw the wars primarily as a struggle for new markets and for the removal of competitors, they said the wars had to be fought on the seas and in the periphery. They saw land warfare as leading to taxation that was too high and thus indirectly hurting commerce. The Continental School argued that unless the English committed themselves to land warfare in Europe, the French would bring the other European states (and their colonies) within their orbit and thus be able to exclude England from a continental tariff system.[10] The economic debate was reflected in a sociopolitical one. The Whigs were the heirs of those who had made the Glorious Revolution, and one of its tenets had been "no standing army." Yet by 1694 the Whigs had ceased mouthing such a slogan and had in fact become the protagonists of the dramatic expansion of the army (which increased its numbers from 10,000 in 1689 to at least 70,000 by 1711).[11] As J. H. Plumb says: "A strange Whiggery this! . . . From [1694] the Whigs, in constitutional principles, became deeply conservative. . . . They wanted to capture the government machine and run it. . . . They felt that, given the King's full patronage, they could make the government work both in the national interest and their own."[12]

What the Whig Parliaments did not explicitly authorize, they would come at least to condone. By simple mechanisms, the Army and the Navy began to avoid Parliamentary limits during the Anglo–French Wars. The Army withheld pay and diverted the sums, presenting Parliament with *post hoc* deficits that the latter felt forced to meet; the Navy ran up debts for goods, services, and victuals, and also presented Parliament with *faits accomplis*. Roseveare says of this system, somewhat disingenuously, "It seems remarkable that Parliament should have tolerated these practices, but it did."[13] The early acceptance of this system was facilitated by a shift in social structure. After 1689 the Whig forces represented a coalition of the larger landlords, the growing bureaucracy, and the merchant classes as against a primarily "country party" of minor gentry who were hostile to taxes, to a standing army, and to a "corrupt" government. In the expanding army, commissions were bought; and those who had the money to buy them were mostly

---

[10] See the discussion by Fayle (1923, 285), who points out that the Continental School thus foresaw the Duc de Choiseul's proposal to the Spanish in 1762 as well as Napoleon's Continental Blockade.

[11] See Plumb (1967, 120, 134).

[12] Plumb (1967, 135).

[13] Roseveare (1969, 93). See also Barnett, speaking of the *annual* renewal of "guards and garrisons" in Georgian Britain: "The supposedly temporary basis of such forces in peacetime was carefully cherished, and each year the mutiny bill provided an opportunity for diehard Members of Parliament to demand the reduction or destruction of what they horridly referred to as 'a standing army'. It was not until 1755 that 'the army' achieved official recognition when the first of the continuous Army lists was published" (1974, 166).

the younger sons of Whig families. Thus this army "was officered and commanded by an extension of the very same families who controlled Parliament."[14]

That England created a large army is not the point however. The point is that in the Nine Years' War, that "national ordeal"[15] for England, a qualitative transformation occurred in both army and navy.[16] Of course the transformation was even greater for the navy than for the army since European statesmen now felt that unlike the land, where a balance of power was possible, "the sea is one."[17] The sea, as we shall discover, became England's. Yet in 1689 the French navy was as strong as the navies of either England or Holland, and it was expanding at a more rapid rate. Colbert, in the 20 preceding years, had created it "virtually *ex nihilo.*"[18] He had built a chain of naval bases in the Atlantic (the principal one at Brest) and in the Mediterranean (the principal one at Toulon); and he had divided the navy into two squadrons for the two zones.[19] Furthermore, the French navy at this time was technologically more advanced than the navies of either England or Holland. The ships had larger and heavier guns, yet they were less weighed down, faster, and more maneuverable. The French had developed a new, advanced ship, the bomb ketch, a small vessel good for bombarding coastal cities and fortresses. (It had already served Louis XIV well in the attack on Algiers in 1682.)

Even though the English navy had been neglected under the Stuarts and the Dutch navy had become obsolescent,[20] in the crucial Battle of Barfleur in 1694, the French fleet found itself outnumbered (44 French to the 99 Anglo–Dutch line ships), outgunned (3240 to 6756),[21] and outmaneuvered.[22] In Admiral Mahan's pungent prose, the French navy "shrivelled away like a leaf in the fire."[23] It was a turning point, not only for this war but for wars in the century to come: "Command of the sea had passed in one

[14] Finer (1975, 123–124). See also Barnett: "The Tories were 'maritime', the Whigs 'continental'" (1974, 148).

[15] This is a phrase from J. R. Jones (1966, 85).

[16] Graham says: "Until the eighteenth century, British naval operations rarely strayed outside the European theatre. . . . Disease and gales were almost the worst enemies. . . . By the end of the seventeenth century, however, improvements in naval architecture and [in] the technique of navigation, as well as [in] the methods of presenting and protecting health, enabled ships to keep at sea for larger periods, and at greater distances from their home ports" (1948, 95).

[17] "When the stronger fleet secured control of sea communications, it had acquired what amounted to an exclusive monopoly" (Graham, 1958, viii)

[18] Symcox (1974, 1).

[19] See Symcox (1974, 43, 49).

[20] See Symcox (1974, 37–40). Carter, however, argues: "William [of Orange] gained one other great advantage in 1686, as a result of the better climate prevailing between him and his domestic opponents. This was the means to rebuild the Dutch navy, accomplished through a decision to form some Dutch customs duties and to pay over the proceeds, a not inconsiderable sum, to the prince for this purpose. By 1688 therefore, the naval forces of the Republic were relatively strong" (1975a, 24–25)

[21] See Ehrman (1953, 395).

[22] Symcox points out that though the major naval tactics of this and previous battles had been one of "pounding matches" between "ships of the line" designed for them, the "naval guns were woefully inaccurate"; naval combat, he says, was therefore "a clumsy and ill-coordinated affair." In such a situation, victories depended on "advantage of position and direction of the wind" (1974, 56, 60–61, 64, 67)

[23] Mahan (1889, 225).

blow to the Allies, and in particular to England"[24]—and one wonders why. Symcox suggests that the agrarian crisis of 1693 and the languishing of French overseas trade led to a fiscal crisis in the French state that made it impossible for the French to "maintain something close to parity with the Allies."[25] Part of the fleet had to be laid up to save money for the army. This points to the same problem the English grappled with in the debate between the Maritime and Continental Schools. Neither England nor France, in this time of overall world economic stagnation, could bear the costs of military preparations on all fronts at once. A choice had to be made. It was natural for the English to tilt to the navy and the French to the army.

Given France's sprawling size and relative lack of internal integration, both in political and economic terms, she seemed to have had little choice,[26] even though control of the seas in the capitalist world-economy has consistently been the "central link [in] the chain of exchange by which wealth accumulates."[27] Whatever the explanation of this great naval defeat, it changed the naval tactics of France from being those of a *guerre d'escadre* to being those of a *guerre de course*. No longer was destroying the enemy's fleet and winning control of the seas the primary objective; now the focus was on capturing and destroying the enemy's merchantmen and harassing the enemy's commerce, and both naval vessels and vessels of privateers were used toward this end. Such tactics were not unknown before 1694, but now they became the primary mode of operation.[28] "Commerce destroying," G. N. Clark says "is the natural weapon of the weaker party in a naval war."[29] The natural weapon yes, but a second-best one; for it was difficult to coordinate the actions of ships commanded by individual entrepreneurs. Symcox calls the overall French effort "only a qualified success" and points to the underlying contradiction of the mode: "If the government could not pay the piper, it would not be permitted to call the tune."[30] Furthermore two could play at the game. For example, during the War of the Spanish Succession, the privateers of England's Channel Islands operated so effec-

---

[24] Ehrman (1953, 398). Bromley and Ryan point out: "The Dutch, who in 1689 had contested English command of the combined sea forces, were hard-pressed to get eight ships together in 1714 as an escort for King George I" (1970, 790).

[25] Symcox (1974, 147).

[26] Often an explanation is given in terms of the economic stagnation of France in the period from 1683 to 1717, presumably caused by the emigration of the Huguenots following the Revocation of the Edict of Nantes. As Scoville says, this is a good example of *post hoc propter hoc* fallacy. Of course, the Revocation "did not help matters" (1960, 218–219), but most Protestants in fact remained, as new converts. Indeed, "instead of weakening and reducing their energies, religious persecution seems to have strengthened their resolve" (1960, 252). Scoville presents evidence of this in all arenas—

manufactures, trade, shipbuilding, agriculture. On the economic crisis of France in this period see also Léon (1956, 152).

[27] Mahan (1889, 226), who argues that it was in the *union* of a great navy and a prosperous commerce that "England made the gain of sea power over and beyond all other States" (p. 225).

[28] See Symcox (1974, 5–6, 187–220).

[29] Clark (1960, 123–124). See also Symcox (1974, 68–69). Clark continues: "That side which had the stronger fleet would be able to close the seas to the commerce of its enemies, but its own merchant shipping would invite attack from the swift sailing corsairs which had escaped the vigilance of fleets. The greater the volume of a nation's commerce, the more it rewarded this form of attack. For these reasons privateering reached a great height in France."

[30] Symcox (1974, 222–223).

tively that they "caused serious alarm to the French [and] were able, above all, to inflict wounds on French port-to-port trade."[31]

The Treaty of Rijswijk in 1697, which ended the Nine Years' War, marked only a respite. It was important largely because it marked "the first retrograde step France had taken" since Richelieu.[32] France was forced to recognize William III as King of England, Scotland, and Ireland and to recognize Anne as his heiress. This recognition had been the primary war aim of William III. Furthermore, all lands that had been acquired by France since the Treaty of Nijmegen were to be restored (except Strasbourg and the Alsatian "Reunions"). Thus France yielded zones on all her frontiers—parts or all of Flanders, Luxembourg, Lorraine, the Rhineland, Pinerolo, and Catalonia.[33] In the minor adjustments overseas, Fort Albany was restored by France to the Hudson Bay Company, and Pondicherry and Nova Scotia were regained by the French—*status quo ante bellum*. The Dutch also got what they wanted: a favorable commercial treaty with the French restoring the French tariff of 1664, and the acceptance by the French of the so-called Netherlands Barrier.

The concept of a military barrier between the United Provinces and France has a long history. It started, perhaps as early as 1635, as the idea that the southern (Spanish) Netherlands should be a *scheidingszone,* or buffer state. The Treaty of Nijmegen in 1678, however, ceded 16 fortresses in the southern Netherlands to France, although small contingents of Dutch troops were permitted to be placed in adjoining areas. By 1684 the French had seized Luxembourg, a situation that the Dutch were forced to accept in a Treaty of Truce. All this changed as a result of the Nine Years' War; and in the Treaty of Rijswijk the concept of a barrier took a new clear form, the Dutch receiving the right to garrison a series of fortresses returned by the French.[34] The Nine Years' War confirmed the new alignment of power in Europe. After the Treaty of Westphalia in 1648, the power struggle between the states had been essentially a three-sided one between the United Provinces, England, and France. But the three sides were now, for all effects and purposes, reduced to two, with the Dutch becoming a more or less permanent ally of the English, indeed a junior partner.

J. R. Jones dates the Dutch "abdication of great power status"[35] as occurring already in May 1689, when William III arranged for the Dutch fleet to be subordinated to the English. It is not that the Dutch did not chafe at this new role—the Dutch–English alliance was "from the beginning, an uneasy

---

[31] Bromley (1950, 465).

[32] Henri Martin, *History of France* (Boston, 1865), **II,** 167, cited in Morgan (1968, 174). Morgan observes: "Ryswick marks the beginning of the end for Louis XIV. Ryswick laid the egg of his destruction, and Utrecht hatched it" (p. 195). Hazard says of the treaty: "How the pride of the *Grand Monarque* must have been humbled!" (1964, 84).

[33] Bromley says that in keeping Alsace and Strasbourg, Louis "retained . . . the strategic key to his kingdom when Franco–Imperial relations were habitually at the centre of his calculations" (1970, 26).

[34] See Carter (1975a, 25–26).

[35] J. R. Jones (1972, 329).

partnership."[36] On the one hand, they did not want the mere fact that they were allied with the English to disturb their trade relations with France, especially since their profitable Baltic trade "depended on a continued supply of French goods."[37] The Dutch consistently argued throughout the seventeenth century that neutral states (as they often were) should not be interfered with in their maritime commerce. Their slogan had been "free ships, free goods," whereas the English had maintained the right to search neutrals' ships and the French had even argued for the right to confiscate a neutral's ship that was carrying goods to the enemy.[38] War was an undesirable last resort for the Dutch. When in 1702 the war resumed as the War of the Spanish Succession, it was the Dutch who kept pushing the English to arrange for peace, provided the Dutch could keep the Netherlands Barrier.[39] In the end, the English were willing to support the Dutch drive for the Barrier, even though it involved commercial dangers for them, as the necessary *quid pro quo* for the Dutch guarantee of English Protestant succession, the issue that hung over English (and Scottish) politics.[40]

It was in the middle of the War of the Spanish Succession that the crisis in English–Scottish relations came to a head and was resolved. By the settlement of 1688, France had effectively lost its ability to interfere in the internal politics of England, and by the so-called Union of Parliaments of 1707,[41] it would lose the same ability regarding Scotland. The political negotiations and maneuvering of the final arrangements in 1707 were complex,[42] but the real story is how core rivalry in the world-economy created pressures on Scotland that led to the Union of the Parliaments. For Scotland (as for other peripheral zones), the whole second half of the seventeenth century had been a long period of "economic stagnation punctuated by crisis and decline."[43] Scotland's main trading partner was England; but this was scarcely true vice versa, and as stagnation continued, Scotland moved toward ever-greater dependence on England.[44] The Scots, like others, tried mercantile measures of resistance. In 1681 the Duke of York, as

[36] Stork-Penning (1967, 113).

[37] J. R. Jones (1966, 93).

[38] See Clark (1923, 4–6, 121).

[39] See Stork-Penning (1967, 113–114). As Wilson says, the Dutch attitude was one of "empirical, self-interested and qualified pacifism" (1968, 165).

[40] See Carter (1975a, 30–31).

[41] Murray points out that the conventional account of the Union of the Crowns of 1603 being augmented by a Union of the Parliaments "may be good history but [it] is doubtful law." The correct legal statement, he argues, is this: "The succession to the crown of each Kingdom continued to depend upon the law of that Kingdom. The Scottish and the English succession laws differed, though only slightly, and had an appropriate contingency occurred, the crowns could have diverged again, each following its own succession. . . . The coincidence

of the English and Scottish crowns continued (apart from Cromwell's intervention) until 1707, when the Treaty of Union came into force. Until that time the 'Union of the Crowns' was a temporary association rather than a permanent union. What the Articles of Union created in 1707 was essentially an indissoluble union of the crowns" (1961, 162). It was as a result of the Union of 1707 that England and Scotland became Great Britain. H. R. Trevor-Roper points out that in fact the Union of 1652 was closer than that of 1707, but of course it didn't last (1964, 79).

[42] For a detailed political history, see Brown (1914).

[43] Smout (1963, 256). See also Trevor-Roper (1964, 78).

[44] See Smout (1963, 29, 238).

the king's representative in Scotland, summoned various merchants to consult with him and the Committee of Trade that he had created in the Privy Council about Scottish foreign trade patterns (with England, Norway, France, and the Baltic), inland trade, shipping, and Scottish desires for a Carribbean colony. The Scottish Estates then enacted various protectionist measures. Soon thereafter, the New Mills Cloth Manufactory was created, which led the Estates that same year to pass the Act for the Encouraging of Trade. The shelter of the act allowed the company to thrive—until the Treaty of Union.[45]

In 1695 the Estates passed an Act for a Company Tradeing to Affrica and the Indies, which created the Company of Scotland. The Company represented a conjuncture of three interests: Edinburgh merchants seeking to participate in the Africa trade; Glasgow merchants hoping to find a market for their linen in a new Caribbean colony; and some London merchants, who were eager to circumvent the monopoly of the English East India Company.[46] The creation of this new company, which came to be known as the Darien Company, probably had much to do with building up the pressures that led to Union in 1707. On the one side, it had become clear that "an independent Scotland endangered the whole [English mercantile] system."[47] The dangers of the Jacobite claims of the Old Pretender were real.[48] Furthermore, it was not Scotland alone that was at stake, but Ireland as well.[49] Thus England had long-term interests in pressing for Union.

[45] See Insh (1952, 32–37, 51–55). "But when the trading barriers that had during this time warded off the competition of the English cloth manufacturers were cast down by the Treaty of Union, the pioneer Scottish company gradually fell into a decline. On 16th February, 1713, the hall in which their cloth had been stored in Edinburgh was sold. A month later came the sale of the machinery and remaining stock of material" (p. 55).

[46] See Insh (1952, 69–71). T. Keith points out that the Act of 1695 "created some alarm [in England]. It was feared that . . . the Scots would gradually engross more and more of the American trade, in which they already had a large illicit share" (1909, 54). See also H. Hamilton, who speaks of Glasgow's "rapidly growing in inportance" in the Atlantic trade in the second half of the seventeenth century (1963, 249). Indeed, T. C. Smout explains the opposition of Glasgow merchants to Union on precisely these grounds: "Just because Glasgow was already progressing [in terms of overseas trade, they] felt she would be better off without Union" (1960, 211–212).

[47] T. Keith (1909, 60). Insh says: "In the autumn of 1706 the pressure of events in Europe was once again to exert its all-powerful influence on the cause of Anglo–Scottish relations" (1952, 80). England's allies, Holland and Austria, were quarreling over control of the southern Netherlands, newly retaken

from the French. Charles XII of Sweden had just defeated Peter the Great, conquered Poland, and occupied Saxony, and he was menacing Bohemia; Louis XIV was trying to persuade him to strike southward against Austria. "Meantime it was all important, with the situation so clouded both in the East and in the West, that there should not be an angry and potentially independent Scotland to provide a threat for Jacobite intrigues and to offer a base for Franco–Jacobite campaigns" (1952, 81).

[48] The Old Pretender, James Francis Edward, Chevalier de St. Georges, was an active soldier on the French side. He laid claim to the thrones of both Scotland and England. No doubt he would have accepted Scotland's alone, had he been able to get it. G. H. Jones argues: "It was because of Jacobite conduct in the Scottish Parliament that the Union of England and Scotland became such a pressing matter, . . . second to no other. . . . [An act of the Scottish Parliament in 1704] provided that Anne's successor in Scotland should be of the royal line of Scotland, but *not* the same person as should succeed her in England. . . . If Union alone could extinguish [the] possibility [of the Jacobite succession in Scotland], there must be a Union, and quickly" (1954, 73).

[49] The Jacobite cause was even more popular in Ireland than in Scotland. In Scotland "the religion of James II and VII was a perpetual cause of offence,

On the Scottish side, on the other hand, while feelings were very divided, the Darien scheme turned out to be a fiasco. The Company of Scotland sought to establish a major entrepôt of world trade on the Isthmus of Darien (located in what is today Panama). It was to be more than a mere haven for interlopers. The Company intended to create an overland route (secured by a colony to be named Caledonia) that would substitute for the Cape of Good Hope route (a foreshadowing of the function of the Panama Canal). The ambitious scheme failed because neither Amsterdam nor Hamburg merchants would invest the necessary capital, and the actual expeditions of 1698–1700 collapsed.[50] Lenman argues that the Scots had aimed too high:

> Scotland did not have the power to protect an empire of monopolistic trade or settlement against rival European powers, all predatory, most much larger. The only worthwhile objective for her in the colonial field was other nations' colonists. Trade with these was feasible and could be so lucrative as to easily cover the marginal risk of its technical illegality [i.e., the fact that Spain had legal claims to Darien]. Glasgow in the late seventeenth century was flourishing partly because of a brisk illegal trade with the English Empire. A fraction of the capital thrown away in Darien, applied to honest smuggling to semi-independent American colonies, would have yielded solid dividends.[51]

Once again, we are seeing that mercantilism in a time of stagnation is a weapon that can be employed successfully only by the fairly strong.

Perhaps it is true, as Riley argues, that the Union of 1707 was due "di-

---

[but] the Irish naturally liked him the better for being a Roman Catholic" (Petrie, 1958, 100). The English put down with difficulty the Irish Expedition of the Royal exile of 1689–1691 (see Petrie, 1958, 100–135). Still the English won and not a minor victory. "The Treaty of Limerick marked the end of Old Ireland as completely as Appotomax meant the end of the Old South" (James, 1973, 17). Subsequent Penal Laws, excluding Catholics from office and landholding, were so "numbing" that the Irish did not rise up during the Jacobite rebellions of 1715 and 1745. Petrie observes: "No such vindictive treatment was meted out to the opponents of the [Glorious] Revolution in the other two Kingdoms, and after their betrayal at Limerick [of the terms of surrender] the Irish had as much hope of successfully resisting their conquerors by force of arms as had the Jews in more recent times of overthrowing the not dissimilar tyranny of Hitler" (1958, 133). For a description of the Penal Laws, see James (1973, 22–25). Given the fact that until the Treaty of Utrecht in 1713 there were eight or nine Irish regiments fighting as part of the French army, the English must have nonetheless feared that any success of the Jacobite cause in Scotland would have reopened the issue in Ireland.

[50] See Insh (1952, 74–77), who says: "The losses and vexations of the expeditions to the Isthmus of Darien led to that demand for freedom of trade, for access to English colonial markets, which was the strongest Scottish incentive toward the acceptance of the terms of the incorporating Union of 1707" (p. 50). But Lenman deprecates the importance of access to the English colonies in the Scottish debate (see 1977, 55). There were, in addition, major subsistence crises in Scotland in 1696 and 1699, part of what the Jacobites called "King William's Seven Ill Years" (see Lenman, 1977, 45–52).

[51] Lenman (1977, 51). See also Smout: "A great power might conceivably have pulled the [Darien] attempt off, if it had had sufficient resources of courage, experience, money, men, and seapower. The Scots possessed only the courage: everything else, including a knowledge of their own limitations, was sadly lacking" (1963, 252). Smout further argues that the Darien failure was only one of four disasters of the 1690s, the other three being the negative effects of the Anglo–French Wars, four years of famine, and severe tariff battles that affected trade everywhere—England, the United Provinces, the southern Netherlands, France, North America, and Norway (see pp. 244–253).

rectly to English rather than Scottish politics;"[52] but the English would not have been able to carry it off without substantial Scottish acquiescence. Where did this come from? There was strong support from that large segment of the aristocracy in Scotland who were Episcopalians, or those who had been involved in the Glorious Revolution and were anti-Jacobite, or those who had those with land interests in England who had been threatened by the English Alien Act of 1705. Another even more important Scottish group were the burgh merchants. Daniel Defoe had led a pamphlet campaign designed by the English government to persuade the burgh merchants that England was and should continue to be the main market for Scottish export and that the road to prosperity was to emphasize the export to England of Scottish cattle and linen (and potentially of corn, wool, and salt) because the balance of trade with England would then be favorable. In 1704, the Scottish Parliament passed the Act of Security, providing for the ending of an automatically unified monarchy after the death of Queen Anne. In retaliation, the English Parliament passed the Alien Act providing that unless the Scots repealed their Act, all their exports would be excluded from England.[53] History never tested English resolve in this regard.[54]

As might have been predicted, the burghs were split between those whose trading interests lay primarily in the English trade and those who did a large amount of trading outside of England and her colonies; and of course the craft guilds felt threatened by English competition. Smout adjures us to note that an increasing number of landowners, particularly the nobility, were in fact "trading men" involved in the export trade. As we have seen time and again, the dividing line between aristocracy and bourgeoisie was more blurred than we usually think. So it was in Scotland at this time. "The coincidence that for a large number of the nobility an enlarged trade with England was important and that, when it came to vote, 70 percent of them were found in favor of Union is too striking to be overlooked."[55] What actually were the economic provisions of the Act of Union, and *cui bono?* The Act contained two economic provisions of advantage to Scotland. First, the shareholders of the Company of Scotland were to be bought out at cost plus interest by the English Parliament in return for the dissolution of the Company, which of course encouraged business revival in areas affected by the previous loss of investments in the Darien scheme, particularly in Edinburgh.

Secondly, the so-called plantation trade was for the first time legally

---

[52] Riley (1969, 498). Carstairs puts it differently. He says that from the very long-term view, the pressure for Union came from the English side but that in the short term, "economic interests provide a plausible explanation of the assent at last given by the Scots to a union which they had resisted with arms for centuries" (1955, 65). Smout makes the distinction between English political reasons and Scots economic reasons (see 1964b, 462).

[53] See R. W. Harris (1963, 68–70).

[54] Lenman shares my skepticism: "It would have required stronger will and nerve than the Scots' leadership possessed to sit out the crisis and see if England really was foolish enough to hazard war on her northern frontier when she was deep in a great conflict in Europe" (1977, 57).

[55] Smout (1963, 273).

opened to the Scots, which particularly benefited the merchants of Glasgow and elsewhere on the Clyde in the west of Scotland. In addition, and presumably as an outgrowth of Union, Parliament in 1727 created a Board of Trustees for Fisheries and Manufactures, which promoted the expansion of the Scottish linen industry.[56] Was all this Scotland's bitter cup or her opportunity? Therein lies a still-burning debate. Union in any case it was, and the new state of Great Britain went on to win the War of the Spanish Succession. The war had been fought of course over who would rule in Spain, but more fundamentally over what would happen to the commerce of the Spanish empire. In 1701 the King of Spain turned over the *Asiento,* the monopoly for slave trading in Spanish America, to the French Guinea Company, whose shares were owned by the Kings of France and Spain as well as by leading French capitalists. The *Asiento* had been previously held by a Portuguese company. It was this act, more than any other, which outraged English and Dutch merchants and led to the resumption of war.[57]

The Peace of Utrecht gave the Spanish succession to the Bourbons but the *Asiento* to the British.[58] The South Sea Company obtained the sale rights to import 4800 slaves annually to Spanish America for 30 years. In addition, the Company could send one vessel and 500 tons of goods each year to sell in Spanish America. As for the Dutch, the Emperor of Austria may have gotten the Spanish Netherlands, but the Dutch got their Barrier. According to the Treaty, Dutch troops were to be stationed in all the districts restored by France to the House of Austria—Namur, Tournay, Menin, Furnes, Warneton, Ypres, Knoque, and Dendermonde (and 60% of the costs of the garrisons were to be borne by the Austrians). This arrangement not only gave the Dutch security, but it "acted also as a cover for Dutch penetration into southern Netherlands markets."[59] Each of the maritime powers had thus gotten their share of the Spanish pie. It remained for them to profit

---

[56] See Insh (1952, 84–89) and Lenman (1977, 58–60). Carstairs is skeptical about how immediate these advantages were. He argues that the expansion of trade to British North America and the West Indies came only after 1750. He says that Union did *not* account for the expansion of the linen industry, since up to mid-century, it was largely German and Austrian linen manufactures that were the major imports of the American colonies and that these came via England by means of "drawbacks". It was only after 1742, with the creation of a bounty system, that the Scottish linen export trade began to expand (see 1955, 69–70). Lenman splits the difference. He agrees with Carstairs that the Scots had very little advantage of Union at first, but he sees 1727 as the turning point, "as indicating the arrival of the first few swallows of this particular summer" (1977, 66).

[57] "Never did French projects appear as threatening to England and the United Provinces as in the immediate aftermath of the acceptance by Louis XIV of the testament of Charles II of Spain. . . . Was the immense market of the Spanish empire to become the private hunting-grounds of French merchants?" (Deyon, 1978b, 235). Goubert notes how rapidly the English and Dutch responded: "The signature of the *Asiento* was followed only a few days later by the Grand Alliance of The Hague. At The Hague, the emperor and the maritime powers came together strongly and gave Louis XIV two months to come to terms. If not, it would be war, the aims of which would be to undo the Spanish succession, to close the Netherlands to the French, to gain control of Italy and the Mediterranean, and to give the allies an entry into the Spanish colonies and at the same time to keep French trade out" (1970a, 237–238).

[58] The details of the various treaties are spelled out in A. W. Ward (1908, 440–450).

[59] Carter (1975a, 26).

from it. In the 25 years of relative peace that followed, the victorious English were not sure that peace was serving their interests—as Plumb points out:

> From 1713 to 1739 there was peace; peace which to many was degrading, a peace which made Britain the dupe of France which, under the cloak of friendship, was steadily rebuilding its maritime and industrial strength for inevitable clash. Large sections of mercantile opinion howled for war.[60]

The war did come. It was the War of the Austrian Succession between Prussia, allied to France, against Austria, which was eventually allied to Britain and the Netherlands. When it ended in 1748, with the Treaty of Aix-la-Chapelle, "the settlement was very nearly a return to the *status quo ante bellum.*"[61] Yet this fruitless war served British commercial interests very well. Temperley goes so far as to say that it was "the first of English wars in which trade interest absolutely predominated, in which war was waged solely for the balance of trade rather than for balance of power."[62] This could be seen on many fronts. Despite their alliance, the British and the Dutch carried on a running quarrel over the southern (now Austrian) Netherlands. The Austrians were tired of paying for the Netherlands Barrier and of not being allowed an expansion of their own trade at the Barrier, in Britain, and in the Netherlands. Indeed, Britain was threatening to remove the drawback whereby Silesian (still Austrian) linens were allowed to be sold in the West Indies via Britain. Furthermore, Flemish merchants were tired of the political constraints on their competing with Dutch merchants.[63]

As for Spain, it was tired of the excessive British illicit trade in their colonies—"the real secret of the Spanish fury against English vessels";[64] while the British government was wary of reviving an active Bourbon alliance of Spain and France.[65] The South Sea Company, on the other hand,

[60] Plumb (1966, 29), who says: "To vast numbers of eighteenth-century Englishmen wars were . . . golden opportunities to beggar their neighbors, to seize the wealth of the world, and to demonstrate the contempt in which the nation held those Pope-ridden, food-eating, puny, wooden-shoed slaves, the French" (p. 14). See also Sutherland (1956, 56–57).

[61] Thomson (1966, 436).

[62] Temperley (1909b, 197). Seeley shares these views: "It seems to me to be the principal characteristic of this phase of England that she is at once commercial and warlike" (1971, 88).

[63] See Dickson: "The incompatibility of the Austrian and Anglo–Dutch negotiating positions [in 1739] is clear. The English and Dutch wished to retain the Austrian Netherlands as an economic colony, partly defended by Dutch garrisons paid for by Austria, the position reached in the Barrier Trea-

ty of 1715. . . . Economically, [in 1746] England wanted to retain her pre-1746 tariff advantages, and the favorable trade balance with the Netherlands which was thought to depend on them. She treated Flemish pretensions to lower duties in England, or to direct entry into the East Indian trade, with glacial dismay" (1973, 83, 107).

[64] Temperley (1909b, 204). See V. L. Brown: "Contraband trade was an integral part of every phase of the South Sea Company's operations" (1928, 179). See also Nelson (1945, 55).

[65] Temperley notes that, throughout the eighteenth century, Spain was "sometimes a passive spectator, oftener an active enemy, never the friend of England." However, the government view in 1739 was that "to drive Spain into the arms of France was to imperil the future of English predominance in the New World" (1909b, 198).

was powerfully and narrowly defending its own interests and serving as a vigorous pressure group in Britain.[66] Nor was the South Sea Company the only beneficiary of an aggressive policy. The sugar planters of the British West Indies found that the war ended the acute sugar depression of the 1730s;[67] and English marine insurance companies "insured French vessels against capture at sea by the British navy."[68] Indeed, so central were commercial interests to the policies of the British government that a convoy system was applied throughout the war and "the safety of the convoy was to be made the first consideration" of the accompanying vessels.[69] While on the land the French and Prussians outnumbered the British and the Austrians at this time,[70] the British navy was twice the size of the French navy. The Spanish navy plus the French navy was the same size as the navy of Britain, but if one added Dutch ships to those of the British, the latter pair had a slight numerical superiority, and more importantly, a unified command. The war reconfirmed British command of the sea, despite the French maritime rebuilding that had been going on since 1713. France lost half her ships of the line in the war and over 1000 merchant ships. "The sea-power of France had been shattered to its foundations."[71]

Peace once again was a short respite, and war broke out again in 1754 in the Americas and 1756 in Europe. The continual commercial conflict of Britain and France in the Americas "merged almost imperceptibly, but none the less certainly,"[72] into the culminating struggle that was the Seven Years' War. The Dutch tried to remain neutral but were constrained by British force to limit their trade with France.[73] The Spanish were tempted into joining France as a way to abolish British privileges at last,[74] but it did France no good. The Treaty of Paris of 1763 marked Britain's definitive achievement of superiority in the 100 years struggle with France. "In Europe, a long period of sickness, comparable to Spain's, was in store for France."[75] The British thus won a century-long struggle for the eventual

---

[66] See Temperley again: "A study of the documents does not confirm the popular view that England's desire to maintain the illicit trade of the interlopers and private individuals weighed deeply with the Ministry. Their tenderness was reserved for the South Sea Company—that body so closely connected with the Government by financial ties, which was to repay Walpole for saving it in 1720 by ruining him in 1739" (1909b, 222).

[65] See K. G. Davies: "On the whole I am inclined to think that (the American War apart) the Atlantic Wars of Britain and France did more good than harm to the British planter, though numerous exceptions would have to be admitted" (1960, 109). Davies singles out the wars of 1739–1748 and 1689–1713 in this regard.

[68] Viner (1969, 84). "Parliament, after protracted debate, refused to make the practice illegal."

[69] Fayle (1923, 288). To be sure, the French went

even further, "and tied the escort to a rigidly defensive role. . . . What is still more surprising . . . is that French ships of war were actually hired to the merchants . . . for a percentage commission on the values of cargoes safely brought in."

[70] Léonard (1958, 192) gives the following figures for 1740: France, 160,000; Prussia, 84,000; Austria, 107,000; England, 59,000 (including Hanoverians).

[71] Richmond (1928, 173).

[72] Andrews (1915, 780).

[73] See Carter (1963, 820–821).

[74] See Christelow (1946, 24, 29). It was, however, an error on the part of the Spanish. "Spain's injudicious entrance into the Seven Years' War enabled the English to consolidate at the close of that conflict the gains they had made in the preceding years and to open up new avenues of approach to the riches of the Spanish colonial world" (Brown, 1928, 186).

[75] Dehio (1962, 117).

succession to the Dutch hegemony of the mid-seventeenth century. This victory of certain segments of the world bourgeoisie, who were rooted in England, with the aid of the British state, can be adequately accounted for only by an analysis of how the state of Britain was politically able to help create and enlarge the socioeconomic margin British entrepreneurs had over competitive forces rooted in France.

Let us start with a demographic overview. The problem is that a great debate rages, not only about the causes of demographic shifts but also about the data to be explained. Some believe that the rate of population growth in England from 1600 to 1750 was slow[76] and some even believe that it was "practically stationary";[77] others argue that it rose by 50% in that period.[78] For France there seems to be a consensus that population remained more or less stable from 1500 to 1750,[79] and at a figure over three times as great as that for England and more than double that of Great Britain. Some see a low point for France in 1700 and a slight rise between 1700 and 1750.[80] Some see all of the years between 1700 and 1750 as "abnormally low"[81] for England. The presumed rise for France between 1700 and 1750 is all the more surprising in that France suffered a very severe famine in 1693–1694 unlike England but like most of Europe,[82] and another in 1709–1710[83] Furthermore, in 1720 Marseille experienced the last great European plague.[84] By 1740, however, the population figures for England and France, and indeed for most of Europe, turn upward quite definitively.[85]

The crucial variable, Hufton argues, was overall food supply. "A starving population, generally speaking, cannot reproduce itself; an under-nourished one has no difficulty in so doing."[86] Whence the increase in overall food supply? It was not a result of climatic change, or at least not

[76] Darby (1973, 304).

[77] Tucker (1963, 214).

[78] See Wilson (1977b, 116).

[79] See Goubert (1965, 473).

[80] See Goubert (1965, 473), Henry (1965, 455), and C. E. Labrousse (1953, 22).

[81] Tucker (1963, 214).

[82] See Flinn :"There was probably never again in western Europe a famine so severe and so widespread as that of the 1690s" (1974, 301). Flinn notes England as an exception. In France, however, "the great majority of the population . . . were threatened with, suffered or actually died from starvation" (Goubert, 1970a, 216). Pentland has a complicated explanation for England. England had a high population growth rate from 1690 to 1710, a time of high prices for agriculture (presumably because of general European famine). Because of this and also because young adults were rare in this period (due to previously low rates of population growth), the opportunities for farm employment led to early marriage and a high birthrate, which in turn led to a falloff in opportunity and a downturn after

1705–1710. With the downturn in prices after 1720, mortality rose, which accounts for the great epidemics of the 1720s—"the logical consequence of a decade of worsening conditions, brought on by the excess (not dearth) of agricultural output relative to demand and the accompanying excess (not dearth) of manpower" (1972, 174).

[83] See Goubert (1970d, 60) and Jacquart (1975, 187).

[84] See Rambert (1954, 606–617). For Reinhard and Armengaud, the last great plague was in 1668, after which plagues were "rare" (1961, 131); but they mention one in Spain in 1694 (1961, 143). Despite the Marseille plague, Le Roy Ladurie speaks of a French demographic thrust between 1720 and 1737 (1975a, 364).

[85] Deprez calls 1740 the "great turning-point in the demographic history of Europe" (1965, 626). The usual explanation is the end of plagues and famines. See Le Roy Ladurie (1975a, 388) and Helleiner, who speaks of the absence of catastrophe (1967, 95).

[86] Hufton (1974, 15).

that alone. Since the whole period from the middle of the sixteenth to the middle of the nineteenth century is known as the little ice age,[87] it is unlikely that any great improvement occurred circa 1750. It is more probable that developments in the agricultural production systems of England and France (the north and the southeast) were the crucial elements in the picture. The potato is given high credit by some, who argue that population increase in the eighteenth century varied "according to [the potato's] diffusion and consumption."[88] Others see the potato as only one element in a generally better diet. Tea replaced alcohol, and rice and, above all, sugar were increasingly consumed, the latter in fruits, jams, and desserts that helped vary the diet, especially in winter.[89] We have described the social context of agricultural improvement, that is, the increased concentration of agricultural land by the squeeze on nonprosperous producers.[90] Enclosure, an important technique that had begun well before 1750,[91] was made possible partly by legislation and partly by the owners' efficiency and profits.[92] What kinds of efficiency could larger landowners effect? For one thing, there was the improvement of agricultural implements, primarily because iron was used in place of wood.[93] In addition, temporary grasses and fodder were found particularly useful to owners of livestock, who tended also to be the larger farmers.[94]

What was central, however, to the picture of the steady trend toward concentration was the long-term low price of cereals.[95] In the whole period

[87] Jacquart (1975, 187). However, Goubert attributes the end of famines in France to better climate, warmer and with less rain (see 1970d, 63). Le Roy Ladurie emphasizes the crucial variable of generally wet but not cold climate, at least in France (see 1967, 281). The same point is made by Reinhard and Armengaud (1961, 115).

[88] Vandenbrocke (1971, 38). The argument is that, compared with grains, the potato more than doubled the food supply in calories per person. While the caloric content of potatoes is about one-fifth that of grains per quintal, yield is ten times as great. "Moreover, potatoes are a summer crop and therefore less dependent upon weather. Cereal cultivation was always a hazardous undertaking because so much depended on weather conditions." However, Salaman (1949, 455–456) argues that the potato was not widespread in the diet of the English poor until the last quarter of the eighteenth century, although for two centuries before that its use had been steadily spreading. He says that until circa 1775 it was primarily used as animal food: "Before the potato could play the part of fodder for the poor, it was necessary that it should prove its worth as food for swine."

[89] See C. Hill (1969, 256).

[90] See also Coleman (1977, 125), Mingay (1963, 81–82), and Lavrovsky (1960, 354–355). Mingay notes a major decline in small landowners between 1660 and 1750 (1968, 31).

[91] "From the standpoint of 1750 it is obvious that a good deal of England was already inclosed" (Holderness, 1976, 52). "Even in villages which throughout the [eighteenth] century remained in open field there was often a strong bias in favor of fewer and larger units" (Mingay, 1962, 480). This seems to have occurred in England despite the fact that the "high productivity of the potato crop made it possible to gain a livelihood even on very small plots of land" (Vanderbrocke, 1971, 38). This may mean that grain production was the financially crucial variable.

[93] Who could afford this? Presumably those who already had a higher total income. Bairoch argues, in perhaps a circular manner, that the possibility of paying for the new tools resulted from the increase in agricultural productivity (see 1966, 16).

[94] "Without the aid of turnips the mere support of livestock had been in winter and spring a difficult problem" (Ernle, 1912, 176). Not only turnips but clover, sainfoin, trefoil, nonsuch, and rye-grass were all well known throughout England by 1720 (see Holderness, 1976, 65).

[95] "What happens is that the small farmer, producing in good years only a small market surplus, loses money income in bad years, but his loss is the gain of larger-scale farmers who enjoy an added

from 1600 to 1750 there were very few prosperous years for grain.[96] It has been argued that the misfortune of low prices was in fact the fortune of England, since it led to agricultural innovation.[97] One wonders why this should be true only or primarily in England when low grain prices were a pan-European constant in this period. What is remarkable is that it was precisely when prices were at their lowest, in the first half of the eighteenth century, that Britain became the leading exporter of grain in Europe. The most obvious explanation is that the Corn Bounty Act enacted by the British government in 1688 to encourage the export of grain[98] created the "generally propitious"[99] conditions for agricultural expansion. There is little doubt that the bounty led to increased grain production in England, and it may indeed have contributed to the further depression of domestic grain prices by causing more grain to be available on the home market than would otherwise have been the case.[100] The obvious intent was to help the British agricultural entrepreneur increase his profit margin.

Where was the market for this increased British grain supply? Outlets were in the making of gin and brewing; and the market for these products was the urban work force, which in a period of secular stagnation had seen an increase in real wages.[101] Gilboy, for example, notes that the rise of real wages in London was used up, so to speak, by the "gin epidemic."[102] This

windfall by the withdrawal from competition of these smaller producers" (Gould, 1962, 321).

[96] Ernle (1912, 168–169), Gould (1962, 323), and Hartwell (1969, 25).

[97] John (1969, 171). See also Wilson (1965, 245) and Holderness (1976, 74–75).

[98] See R. Ashton (1969, 49–50).

[99] Mingay (1960, 337). Grain rose from 3.7% to 19.6% of English exports between 1700 and 1750. See T. S. Ashton (1960, 12). Slicher van Bath asserts that between 1690 and 1720 the "weighted average price ratio between agricultural and non-agricultural products" was temporarily reversed in favor of agriculture, within the context of an unfavorable ratio running from 1620 to 1740 (1963a, 211).

[100] See Gould (1962, 331–332).

[101] "The improvement (in real wages in England] between 1660 and 1760 was substantial but not spectacular. . . . By 1750 things were nevertheless notably better than in 1600. The lower rate of price inflation after 1670, a slow-down of population growth before 1750, the accumulation of agricultural (especially food) surpluses, and the revival of economic activity, especially in labor-intensive trades, were responsible for the increment to real wages before 1750" (Holderness, 1976, 204).

Even if real wages went up, was there not increased unemployment? Yes, there was, but it was at least partly compensated for by the alternative employment of such periods. Workers became

smugglers and highwaymen. The women took to spinning. There was an increase in the fishing industry ("one of the last resorts of the poor"), men being more willing to accept the hardship of life at sea in small boats. The number of itinerant salesmen rose. Even construction seemed to flourish, almost varying inversely with the prosperity of exports (see T. S. Ashton, 1959, 138). In spite of a rise in real wages in this period, the quality of urban life was scarcely one that would have turned workers away from the taverns. "In the midst of the elegance and luxury, dirt and disease abounded. In the reign of George I, and for the early part of that of George II, London was a stinking, muddy, filth-bespattered metropolis, pullulating with slums" (Plumb, 1966, 17).

[102] Gilboy (1930, 613). The process was, to be sure, circular. Higher real wages led to increased production of gin, which required an increased supply of grain. If grain supply was too much for any reason, further sales of gin could resolve the dilemma. See Chambers: "The Gin Age [was] something more than the inexplicable aberration of the besotted London populace. . . . A succession of good harvests enhanced the supply of grain while a series of epidemics was thinning the ranks of those who should have consumed it. When in 1739 the War of the Austrian Succession began, and the export of grain fell off, a further outlet of grain was partially closed. . . . The race suicide of London was coming to the aid of midland farmers suffering

was also true in the Netherlands, where the increased import of British grains was in particular that of malt and barley for the use of Dutch distillers and brewers.[103] British bounties led to an ever-greater export to the Dutch,[104] who in turn inspired more British production because of the rise in grain prices in the Netherlands from 1700 to 1720.[105] The British were able to squeeze the Baltic producers out of the Dutch market[106] because they could outsell them. This was not only because of lower British transport costs (which existed, after all, previously), but because of the bounty that accounted for about 16.5% of the real value of cereals shipped abroad.[107] A London pamphlet on bounties written in 1768 explained it as follows: "We took upon ourselves to rival the Polanders in their employment as ploughmen to the Dutch. . . . And at the same time we likewise allowed our bretheren the Irish to rival the Danes in the office of being cowkeepers to them."[108] That the bounty was effective overall and its impact felt in all zones of British agricultural production is indicated by the increased uniformity in the prices of wheat throughout Britain in this period of high export.[109]

The British state thus sought to capture a Dutch grain market for its entrepreneurs, both as a supplement to other opportunities for profit (in an era when such opportunities were constrained) and as a way of providing profit through linkage effects. For example, the British supplanted the Dutch in the grain-carrying trade as a result of having supplanted Baltic producers.[110] Others, of course, also sought to do the same. Indeed, in the half-century from 1650 to 1700, the southern Netherlands and France had augmented their exports to the Dutch, and the Dutch had increased their

from the pinch of plenty; the superfluities of which they complained were being partially taken off by the excesses of Gin Lane" (1957, 44).

Midland farmers, however, payed the middle-run costs of short-run gains. London distilling and brewing industries developed the linked activity of using the waste products in the feeding of cattle and pigs. This activity became widespread. As more and more of the meat and milk of Londoners came from hogs and milch cows within the town area of London in the eighteenth century, Home County farmers suffered acute competition from what "was now 'capitalist' meat production in a systematic way" (Mathias, 1952, 254).

[103] See Ormrod (1975, 39–40). The bounty was paid for bulk. Barley could be "blown-up," which encouraged its export over other grains. This was also the Gin Age in Holland. See John (1976, 53).

[104] "Perhaps the Dutch were vulnerable in being hooked on [English grain] imports, but one might as well be hooked on cheap, or subsidized, as on unsubsidized grain" (de Vries, 1975, 55). The Dutch were not the only export market. The Portuguese were an important secondary market. See Fisher (1971, 64).

[105] See Slicher van Bath (1963a, 212). If the prices went down again from 1720 to 1740, was it not partly in response to increased British production?

[106] John has striking figures on the average annual exports of grain from Great Britain and the Baltic. From 1650 to 1699, the Baltic area exported 58,800 lasts of approximately 10½ quarters and Great Britain exported about 2500; between 1700 and 1749, Baltic exports went down to 31,000 and British up to 42,000. The total of the two went up from 58,300 to 73,000 (see John, 1976, 56, Table 6). See also Lipson (1956, **II**, 460), Jeannin (1964, 332), and Ormrod (1975, 38).

[107] John (1976, 59).

[108] *Considerations on the Effects which Bounties Granted on Exported Corn, Malt and Flour have on the Manufactures of this Kingdom* (London, 1768, 61–62, footnote), cited in John (1976, 56).

[109] "As undogmatically as befits a complex and uncertain field . . . we tend to the view that, in wheat at least, the autonomy of markets can be seriously overstated" (Granger and Elliott, 1967, 262).

[110] See Ormrod (1975, 40).

own production;[111] but the British bounty caused these producers to lose ground in the period from 1700 to 1750 by underselling them.[112] Thus Britain secured its own position by capitalizing on the world grain market, in some ways *faute de mieux,* and contributed to the recuperation throughout Europe of the *ager* over the *saltus* between 1700 and 1750.[113] However, since the overall world-economy was still weak, it led rapidly to an overproduction of cereals and another agricultural depression between 1730 and 1750.[114] In the general world upturn after 1750, Britain would once again reduce its role as a world grain producer in favor of a greater specialization in industrial production.[115]

The French picture, as we have already argued, was less different from the English than we think. When we examine the changes that occurred in the period after 1690, we ask, first of all, why the French did not institute bounties. France may not have needed them because it was so much larger than England. The wars from 1688 to 1713 had cut off such grain imports as France had previously made and thereby "created a situation that favored cereal farming in southern France."[116] In addition, the wars having caused destruction in Spain and thus cut off the Spanish market for cattle and wine products, and the blockade having cut off the English and Dutch markets for linseed, producers in southwest France returned markedly to wheat production.[117] There was a steady concentration in land from this period on, until by the mid-eighteenth century, the Midi-Pyrénées area had become a "zone of cereals monoculture producing for export in the Mediterranean."[118] Meanwhile, agriculture was flourishing in Languedoc because of the transport revolution (the Canal du Midi was opened in 1680 and new roads were built beginning in 1725); improved transportation made it possible for wheat products to reach Marseille at prices that were low enough to be competitive in the Mediterranean market.[119] Thus the increased production of cereals in France paralleled the increased production of wheat in England and had roughly the same effects in terms of rural social structure and in terms of its meaning for the world-economy. That is, core zones were reclaiming profit-making "peripheral" tasks in an era of overall stagnation.

[111] See J. de Vries (1974, 171).

[112] See Abel who notes that English exports from 1711 to 1740 closed the world market to French and German producers (1973, 265). J. C. G. M. Jansen notes that in the period from 1680 to 1740, agricultural producers in South Limburg, faced with a fall in prices, cut back on the ordinary cereals (*kortkoren* and spelt) and turned to "expensive wheat" (as well as oats-growing) "to compensate for the fall in corn prices" (1971, 255).

[113] See Chaunu (1966a, 242). *Ager* are surfaces that are worked upon as opposed to *saltus*, which is land covered by a natural vegetation (1966a, 640).

[114] See Mingay (1956, 324, 336).

[115] See T. S. Ashton on the second half of the eighteenth century: "The change from an export to an import surplus could hardly be avoided at a time when population was growing rapidly and when England was turning from agriculture to manufacture" (1969, 50).

[116] See Slicher van Bath (1977, 75).

[117] See Enjalbert (1950, 116) and Braudel (1951, 71).

[118] Frêche (1974, 835).

[119] See Le Roy Ladurie (1975a, 397–400).

In view of the foregoing, why is there a widespread historiographic impression that the English had an agricultural revolution circa 1650 to 1750 and the French did not? To answer this, we must look at what happened in the nonagricultural industries. Metallurgy and textile production in England after 1700 showed "a general tendency towards recovery, but not yet clear growth."[120] The price trend of manufactures, like that of agriculture, would remain "mildly downward" until 1750, with a "mildly upward trend in both real wages and market demand."[121] This increased demand represented, first of all, export demand, especially colonial demand, which we have previously argued was one of the main objectives of British policy in the northern states of British North America. It also represented domestic demand, a result of the increase in agricultural wealth in this period.[122] The large landowners were among the first to profit from their own increased demand. Between 1700 and 1750, the usually low land rents were compensated for by increasing sources of estate profits from the sale of timber and from the leasing of land for coal and other mining as well as for quarrying, ironworks, and limekilns.[123]

The expansion of agricultural production was a major impetus to the metallurgical industries,[124] and the constant wars with France were also a significant stimulus.[125] The wars created a demand for metals in armament, made imports more difficult (at least in wartime), and used up wood through expanded shipbuilding. The increased level of domestic demand brought about an expansion in construction that stimulated lead production; lead prices remained low, however, which may indicate that output was in fact expanding too fast for the slowly rising demand.[126] Gould makes the guess that the real importance of low food prices in the period from

---

[120] Kellenbenz (1977a, 547), who says: "There were still too many handicaps, especially in metallurgy, in spite of the economic shifts in favor of Russia, rich in iron and forests." See East: "As with coal, so with iron, *large-scale* developments which were to leave their mark on the map awaited the nineteenth century" (1951, 512, italics added).

[121] Coleman (1977, 151), who says that the period from 1650 to 1750 "was an age of investment and enterprise in English industry, not manifested in any spectacular changes as in the succeeding century, but vitally important in providing the stronger and more flexible bases from which the later revolution could be launched."

[122] See Wilson (1977a, 8).

[123] See Mingay (1960, 373).

[124] Bairoch (1966) analyzes this at length, in terms of both the use of iron in tools and the expansion of the number of tools used. He also places emphasis on the increased use of horses and the new practice of shoeing them. He sees 1720 to 1760 as the key period for England in this regard and 1760 to 1790

or even 1790 to 1820 as the key period for France. See also Chambers, who sees agriculture in England in the seventeenth and eighteenth century as making three contributions to industry: the provision of capital and the leadership in the development of the lead, iron, and coal industries; the consumption of industrial products; and the promotion of transport changes, especially the turnpikes (1957, 36).

[125] John argues that these factors "quickened the search for methods of using coal for smelting purposes," which led to the invention of the reverberating furnace between 1688 and 1698. He also reminds us that "between 1714 and 1763, the size of the Navy doubled" (1955, 330, 333). Kellenbenz points out that once one substituted coal for charcoal in iron smelting, the incompatibility between iron production and dense population disappeared, which, he asserts, accounts for the noticeable shift of production from Sweden to England (see 1974, 206–207).

[126] See Burt (1969, 266).

1600 to 1750 lay in the reduction of the costs of producing textiles.[127] Here, as in the case of wheat export, the crucial element in the expansion of production was government intervention in the world market. The British government initiated what would today be called an "import substitution" policy.[128] As early as 1675, the competition that English weavers felt from the India trade had been discussed in Parliament, and some duties had been placed on calicoes.

The particular economic crisis of the 1690s led to the so-called calico controversy of 1696 to 1700, which culminated in an act in 1700 prohibiting imports of printed calicoes from Persia, India, and China. This was done despite opposition from the East India Company and from those who sold or worked up Indian goods for the English market. This did not aid woollens manufacturers, however, since calicoes could be printed in England. Weavers' riots in 1719 (resulting from unemployment) led to the sumptuary law of 1720 prohibiting the use and the wear of printed calicoes (with a few exceptions). To be sure, the efficiency of enforcement was limited. Since muslins could still be imported, many calicoes were imported under the name of muslins, and chintz was smuggled in. In 1735 the Manchester Act backtracked and specifically excluded from the sumptuary laws printed goods of linen yarn and cotton wool manufactured in Great Britain, in effect at last giving cotton and linen textiles *droit de cité* provided they were manufactured in England.[129] The overall impact of the legislation was thus that it "encouraged the manufacture of calico substitutes"[130] within England.

We still had not arrived at the age of cotton, however, because until 1773 so-called English cottons were in fact a fabric in which a cotton weft, or transverse thread of the web, was combined with a linen warp, or longitudinal thread.[131] The linen continued to be largely imported, principally from Germany, Ireland, and Scotland.[132] German linens steadily lost place over

[127] Gould (1962, 320). By contrast, Gould rejects as "hazardous" (p. 319) any attempt to discern a direct and constant significance of harvest fluctuations for the state of economic activity; he points to the opposite effects such fluctuations could cause. Wilson is less sure of Gould's point: "But how much the proliferation of manufactures in the years between the Restoration and the industrialization of the late eighteenth century owed to the levelling off and even the fall in the general price level of necessities remains an unsolved problem" (1977a, 13).

[128] See Ormrod (1975, 40). The great Prohibition of 1678, aimed primarily at France, was thought of at the time as a turning point (Ashley, 1897, 338).

[129] See P. J. Thomas (1963, 68, 101, 125, 139, 150, 163–164). Despite this, woollens remained the major English manufacturing industry throughout the eighteenth century (Deane, 1957, 207) and went

through a period of "marked growth" from 1700 to 1740–1750 (p. 221).

[130] Smelser (1959, 53). Heckscher argues that the difference between French and English mercantilist policies was that England encouraged the import substitution. He feels it necessary to add that what was "perhaps most important" was that England really did not strictly enforce its import prohibitions whereas France did (1935, **I**, 174–145). Do we have evidence for this, or is this merely liberal (anti-French) prejudice?

[131] See Warden (1864, 373).

[132] The degree of reliance on linen imports is a matter of debate. Harte argues: "It is probable . . . that more linen was produced in England itself for domestic consumption in the eighteenth century than was imported from Scotland and Ireland altogether" (1973, 107). Perhaps, but more was im-

the eighteenth century to Scottish and Irish linens, again the result of government policy that began in 1660 and was made steadily more stringent thereafter.[133] After 1707, of course, Scotland was part of Great Britain. The basic effect of the Union was that English woollens displaced Scottish woollens (except for the most coarse variety); but in return, Scottish linen was allowed to thrive in England.[134] How beneficial this was to Scottish landowner–entrepreneurs[135] has long been a matter of debate. The Irish situation was more one-sided. The Williamite War of 1689–1691 had ended with the Treaty of Limerick, which asserted that the Crown's authority was the same over Ireland as it was over the colonies.[136] The impact on Irish productive activity had been immediate. The Restoration period had already seen measures to reduce Irish industries by forbidding most direct trade relations with the American colonies.[137] The Great Cattle Act of 1666, by excluding Irish produce from the English market, had forced a concentration on wool exports to England.[138]

In the period after the Glorious Revolution, the British went much further. They destroyed the Irish woollen manufactures by the Irish Woollen Act of 1699.[139] This act pushed the Irish toward linen production via the medium of cottage industries with very low wage structures.[140] James claims this was not so bad for Ireland because they were permitted in the eighteenth century, as was Scotland, to export to England *and* to the British colonies, the West Indies becoming a prime market for Irish provisions.[141]

ported from all sources than was produced locally, and Scottish and Irish linens played an increasing role.

[133] Harte (1973, 76). See also Davis (1962, 287–288). "The duties on most kinds of linen were . . . nominally doubled roughly twice over in the century after 1690" (Harte, 1973, 78). Harte argues that French linens were hit for reasons of direct competition, while German, Flemish, and Dutch linens were hit "for purely fiscal reasons" (p. 97). No doubt, but as he himself admits, the "side-effect of the exigencies of national finance, of the increasing need for revenue to pay for warfare" (p. 76) was almost as great as the punitive duties on the French.

[134] See Gulvin (1971), H. Hamilton (1963, 255), and Durie (1973, 17). Campbell asserts: "It is sufficient economic justification to say that the Union of 1707 ensured that, when in due course other developments took place, the economy of Scotland [would specialize] in those fields where, because of her English annexations, a market for her product would be guaranteed" (1964, 477).

[135] This combination is insisted upon by Smout who points to Scotland as giving an "ironical twist" to the "old fashioned simplification" that the Industrial Revolution was a triumph of the bourgeoisie over the aristocracy. "The eighteenth-century [Scottish] landowners strove side by side with the middle classes to develop a new kind of dynamic economy

. . .—and when they had succeeded, it became a Frankenstein to rend off their limbs of privilege and leadership" (1964a, 234).

[136] See James (1973, 277), who suggests that Ireland was even more of a colony than the American colonies since "the Irish government rested on conquest and could not readily escape its military origins" (p. 290). Cullen calls Ireland's role in the English system "in some respects colonial," already in the seventeenth century, and speaks of the "growing dependence on England" in the eighteenth century (1968, 2, 46).

[137] See James (1973, 191–192).

[138] See Cullen (1968, 53).

[139] See Kearny (1959). Cullen considers the Woollens Act less serious in its consequences and more notorious than the Cattle Act and the various Navigation Acts only because unlike the latter, which were English acts to regulate English trade, the Woollens Act legislated about Irish exports and was a "flagrant example of the pretensions of the British parliament to legislate for Ireland" (1967, 2).

[140] See Kellenbenz (1965, 385–386), Gill (1925, 31), and Warden (1864, 393).

[141] "Instead of selling cattle to English dealers, the Irish were now selling beef, pork, and butter to customers all over the world" (James, 1963, 576). See also James (1973, 190–217). Cullen points out, however, an important negative side effect of the

This leaves out the fact, however, that the chief beneficiaries of this export trade were the large *English* landowners in Ireland. Hill's assessment seems more reasonable: "After Negro slaves, Ireland was the principal victim of the navigation system which gave England her world hegemony."[142] What we see then is a pattern whereby the British government actively used mercantilist measures in the period from 1650 to 1750 (and especially after 1689) to expand Britain's share of world metallurgical and textile production.[143] Woollens and cottons were reserved for England, but Scotland and Ireland were allowed to share in linen production.[144] The question remains, how does this undoubted growth in British industrial production compare with what happened in France?

Imbert says that French industrial capital made unquestioned progress in the three last centuries of the *Ancien Régime,* but less progress than English industrial capital made.[145] France had been ahead at the outset, and Mendels thinks that in the period from 1700 to 1750 it was still the first industrial power in the world.[146] Léon points out that although the percentage of French exports that were manufactures remained the same during the course of the eighteenth century, the absolute amount quadrupled, and he says that this export-oriented industry was the most technologically advanced sector.[147] Nef argues that the volume of French production grew at a more rapid rate between 1640 and 1740 than between 1540 and 1640 and that the English rate of growth slackened with the Civil War and only picked up again in the 1750s. He thus feels that the two rates of economic growth converged.[148] The quantitative data are weak, and the scholars contradict each other, which means we should proceed with caution. Perhaps it is best to make a qualitative or structural comparison of English and French production in this post-Restoration, post-Colbert period. Cunningham in 1892 made this comparison:

Navigation Acts: "the lack of a direct colonial trade and of a re-export trade reduced the need for sophisticated financial institutions" (1977, 171).

[142] Hill (1969, 164).

[143] Ralph Davis argues that the 1690s were the years when protection began in England, that "by 1722 industrial protection had clearly arrived and been recognized," and that over the 50 years thereafter it was extended (1966, 306, 313, 317).

[144] Even so, the period 1740 and 1790 was a "remarkable period of expansion" for English linen production (Harte, 1973, 107). Durie, however, points out that English linen was not a competitor to Scots linen at this point in the *export* market (1973, 37).

[145] J. Imbert (1965, 385).

[146] See Mendels (1972, 258–259); cf. Markovitch (1968b, 579). Léon, however, sees France as behind England in terms of the *percentage* of total produc-

tion that was industrial—one-fifth versus one-fourth in the eighteenth century (1970c, 528). Heckscher, great partisan of England against France, admits England's superiority is not quantitative but "technological." Why not quantitative? Because "even in England industrialization at the outbreak of the French Revolution had hardly emerged from its chrysalis stage and the innovations were potential rather than actual" (1935, **I,** 202–203).

[147] See Léon (1970b, 229–230). C. E. Labrousse says: "In the race, the already full-blown capitalism of the eighteenth century easily beat out the old feudal sector and its traditional revenue" (1970, 704).

[148] Nef (1968, 149). Crouzet agrees for the period of 1700 to 1750, but finds the English–French picture reversed from 1750 to 1800 (1966, 268).

> During the greater part of [the period from 1689 to 1776] a very remarkable policy [the system of bounties] was in force [in England] with regard to the export and import of corn. . . . A great interest attaches to this masterful stroke of policy, since it appears to have occasioned the great advance in agricultural improvement which took place while it was maintained. . . . This appears to have been the one point of the scheme known as the Mercantile System which was original to England. The French had fostered industry, and the Dutch shipping. The English took a line which promoted the development of agriculture. . . . In the eighteenth century this measure was proving itself the cornerstone of English prosperity.[149]

Two questions spring to mind. Is it correct to see the difference between English and French governmental policy in this period as a difference in emphasis on agriculture as opposed to industry? Does this account for Britain's later greater prosperity? A recent study by Markovitch tends to confirm Cunningham's generalization by looking at the terms of trade of agriculture and industry in the two countries in the eighteenth century. He finds that in France industrial prices were high in relation to agricultural prices and that precisely the reverse was true in England.[150] Why should this have been so? Perhaps it was because the respective governments wanted it so; and if they did, may it not have had something to do with the size of the two countries in the context of the long-term stagnation of the world economy? Neither the domestic market of England nor the domestic market of the Five Great Farms of France was large enough to sustain a major drive toward the mechanization of industry. For England, this meant conquering external markets; for France this meant achieving the economic integration of the state.[151]

Given the slack in world demand in this period, exporting grain rather than manufactured goods may have seemed to the English a surer way to gain access to, and ultimate control of, major foreign markets. The government thus emphasized the corn bounty, although not to the exclusion of other tactics. The French situation was different. A good portion of French industry was in the Ponant, an area outside the Five Great Farms and one that had the closest commercial ties to the Americas. Entrepreneurs of the Ponant found selling their goods in the rest of France more difficult than selling in Holland. In order to maintain commercial links with Holland, they began to renounce such industries as sugar refining and sell Holland West Indian unrefined sugar in return for printed cottons and hardwares.[152] This began to put the Ponant in a position vis-à-vis Holland that was analogous to the position of Portugal vis-à-vis England.

---

[149] Cunningham (1892, **II**, 371–372).

[150] Markovitch (1968b, 578).

[151] See Richard Roehl: "In England, the domestic market was too small, the level of aggregate demand generated internally was inadequate, to spontaneously generate and sustain an industrial revolution. France was a much larger nation. There, domestic demand was sufficient to the needs of an industrial revolution, and France did not need to rely substantially upon the world market to supplement aggregate demand. England was compelled to substitute international demand as a supplement to what was, had it to stand by itself, a domestic market too small to sustain an extended drive to industrialization" (1976, 272).

[152] See Boulle (1975, 73). The Dutch, in turn,

The Colbertian policy did not succeed in "incorporating" the Ponant, but it did rescue France from Portugal's fate by picking up in other regions the industry the Ponant was dropping. In the beginning of the seventeenth century, the Ponant was the rich region, a region of cloths and linens; with Colbert this began to shift, and industry rose both in the northeast (within the Five Great Farms) and in Languedoc.[153] In the period from 1700 to 1750, 55% of the wool industry was in the northeast, 28% was in the south, and the west was down to 4%.[154] The French emphasis on industry responded to an urgent need, and in the long run it was successful. When Colbert's policies were finally fully implemented in the Napoleonic era, the industrial base needed to make such policies feasible had been preserved. "Laissez-faire, laissez-passer" referred originally to the ideal of abolishing barriers *within mercantilist* France.[155]

Can Britain's greater emphasis on agricultural exports in the period from 1700 to 1750 be what accounts for her economic triumphs in the century thereafter?[156] Perhaps, but only indirectly. It was the emphasis on foreign trade (which happened to be mostly grain trade at this moment) that led to Britain's emphasis on the navy and the colonies, which, in turn, permitted her the military triumphs of the long struggle with France. While the French state strained to overcome its internal obstacles, it was outmaneuvered by the British state. Far from being the triumph of liberalism, it was the triumph of the strong state, whose strength, however, was the result of necessity. The productive strength of Britain and France can best be appreciated in relation to that of the former hegemonic power, the Dutch Republic. Throughout the seventeenth century, the costs of Dutch production rose relative to those of England and of France, and a difference was clearly visible by 1700.[157] Rising costs were a result of two features that normally accompany hegemony: rising taxes[158] and rising wage levels,[159] the

helped the Nantes merchants with the slave trade (see Boulle, 1972, 76–80). Huetz de Lemps notes the same phenomenon for the merchants of Bordeaux. "Never perhaps had the economic life of Bordeaux depended as much upon the Dutch" (1975, 614). Morineau talks of the key role of the French Basque country, Bayonne in particular, as a legal and contraband way station for the Dutch trading with Spain (1969a, 326).

[153] See Léon (1970c, 525–526) and also Le Roy Ladurie (1974a, 155). Of course Languedoc, like the Ponant, was outside the Five Great Farms, but its export market was primarily the Mediterranean, where France was better able, for geographical reasons, to compete with Britain and the Netherlands. Carrière speaks of the symbiosis between Languedoc and Marseilles after 1689 (1974, 169).

[154] See Markovitch (1968b, 556).

[155] See Bosher (1964, 66–69).

[156] The eventual wealth of the British nation must be appreciated in relation to J. H. Plumb's assess-

ment of where things stood at the beginning of the eighteenth century: "In 1714 England was a country of small towns and scattered population; the wealth of its people did not compare with that of the French or Dutch" (1966, 28).

[157] See Wilson, who says that in "about 1700, the English began to complain of the costs and quality of Dutch goods" (1968, 236). Roessingh dates the decline of Dutch tobacco manufacture vis-à-vis England's as of 1720 (1976, 501–502). Boxer says that by the 1730s the English shipwrights were teaching improved techniques to the Dutch (1964, 149). Carrière asserts that the rise of production in southern France as of 1700 is the counterpart of the decline of the Dutch (and also of the English) in the Mediterranean (1974, 172).

[158] See Barkhausen (1974, 246). See also Wilson, who offers data to show that the Dutch in this period paid roughly three times as much in the taxes as the English and French (1969b, 120).

[159] See Swart (1975, 47) and J. de Vries (1975, 56),

latter especially hurting the labor intensive sector (in this case, textiles, shipbuilding, breweries).[160] To the degree that Dutch products were less competitive in the world market, Dutch capitalism could still live off its income from foreign investments. Thus Dutch decline was not absolute, but only relative to England and France.[161]

The slow shift in the production patterns of Britain and France (and the continued relative decline of the Netherlands, not to speak of that of Spain and Portugal) led to new commercial patterns, or at least to the accentuation of some previous tendencies. In the period from 1660 to 1700 England emerged as a major entrepôt for the reexport of colonial products; but it was still the case that seaborne commerce in the world-economy was "preponderantly European in character" and was still largely in the hands of the Dutch. However, the direction of economic expansion, especially after 1700, was markedly westward in the new colonial trades, and in this way England was seeking to be successful in supplanting the Dutch.[162] The period of the English–French wars, from 1689 to 1713, marked the emergence of open debate in England on the benefits of mercantilist policies for trade. On the one hand, the English Navigation Act of 1696 and the establishment of the Board of Trade marked a new level of seriousness in government direction of the trade process.[163] On the other hand, demands were being made for freer trade and for modification of mercantilist policies.[164] Neither position was strong enough to prevail, reflecting precisely the fact that England was getting stronger in the world-economy but was still far from hegemonic.[165]

In the westward trade in the first half of the eighteenth century was first

who says: "Large-scale charitable relief in the Republic, providing a floor for wages higher than many employers would pay for certain types of jobs, [allowed] unemployment and a labor shortage to coexist."

[160] Kossmann (1975a, 53). This was compounded by environmental disasters—shipworms (*T. Navalis*) that destroyed the pilings in dikes and water pollution that forced cloth finishers to import fresh water for dyeing. See Knoppers (1975b), Carter (1975a, 67), and Van Veen (1950, 73). After 1731 the Dutch invested in stone defenses, but this was a considerable expense.

[161] See Morineau (1965, 170) and Klein (1970, 33). Hazard paints the picture well: "Holland was prosperous, and Holland was powerful. If, in the commercial field, she had a rival in England; if, after 1688, she began to look like a dinghy alongside a big ship; if she gradually lost that fighting, adventurous spirit that had made her a great maritime and colonial power, it must not be supposed that she was impoverished by her altered circumstances. She

was wealthy, and she was tasting the sweets of wealth" (1964, 96).

[162] Wilson (1957b, 27–28). "The principal dynamic element in English export trade during all the middle decades of the eighteenth century was . . . colonial trade." (Davis, 1962, 290).

[163] See Clark (1923, 135–137), Andrews (1929, 285), Ogg (1970, 261), and Hoffenden (1970, 490–491).

[164] See Cherry (1953, 119).

[165] The wavering political position of British governmental opinion reflected no doubt the wavering economic realities. "It is probable that most of the rather modest progress made [in world trade] in the first half of the eighteenth century took place in the first twenty to twenty-five years, and that the movement was then checked for about twenty years before the much stronger, many-sided wave of expansion which began in the 1740s and gathered increasing momentum with the ensuing decades" (Deane and Cole, 1962, 61).

of all sugar,[166] and second of all the slaves who made the sugar possible.[167] Britain clearly dominated world commerce in sugar as of 1700, but by 1750 primacy had passed to France.[168] This change can probably best be explained by comparing Jamaican production, where there was an increase in costs because of the exhaustion of the coastal zones, and French-controlled production sites, which were relatively new.[169] Does this mean that France was out-competing Britain? Not quite, for as Vilar notes, while French foreign trade became "Americanized" in the eighteenth century, British foreign trade became "globalized."[170] What Britain lost on the sugar trade, she made up elsewhere—and first of all, on the slave trade. In the seventeenth century scramble for the African slave trade, the Dutch were initially the most powerful contender,[171] as befit their role then. The key market was the Spanish colonies; hence the competition for the *Asiento,* an institution revived in 1662.[172]

In England, the Royal Africa Company had a monopoly of slave trading beginning in 1663.[173] At first, the profits were low because of the depression in world sugar, but this changed as a result of the war in 1689.[174] This English company had a monopoly for sales in English colonies and also an exemption from the Navigation Act that allowed them to sell slaves in English Caribbean ports to Spanish purchasers (Spanish ports being closed to the English slave traders), who took away their purchases in Spanish ships. This opened the Company to attacks by English planters who saw Spanish sales as raising the price of slaves and increasing the Spanish ability to compete.[175] The planters called for free trade in slaves, and the Company's monopoly was in fact ended in 1698 despite its claim that the African

[166] Moreno Fraginals calls sugar the "primary basic world product, that is, the commodity which occupied top place in terms of the total value of the transactions in international commerce" (1978, **I,** 22).

[167] "The importance of the slave trade to Europe and America lay not in unusual profitability—which was probably mythical—but in its indispensable support for the tropical economy of the Caribbean" (Davis, 1973b, 137).

[168] "Between 1701 and 1725, the advance [of France] was so rapid that . . . the French were not only supplying France, but were underselling the British in the continental market, notably at Hamburg, in Flanders, Holland, and Spain, and at the Straits, [the French, along] with Portugal, furnished the Levant with sugar from Brazil" (Andrews, 1915, 550). England's reexports of sugar declined steadily. They were 37.5% of all reexports in 1698–1700 and down to 4.2% by 1733–1737 (see Sheridan, 1957, 64). Meanwhile, it was "the most dynamic economic sector of France" (Boulle, 1972, 71). See also Moreno Fraginals (1978, **I,** 27) and Léon and Carrière (1970, 197).

[169] Moreno Fraginals dates the turning point of

these "economic and technical" factors as about 1730 (1978, **I,** 32–34), which correlates well with Andrews's landmark turning point in British policy: 1731, when the bill to forbid the importation of non-British sugar into Britain or its colonies was not passed (1915, 772). What L. P. May bemoans as the slow collapse of France's protectionism in Martinique between 1673 and 1757 may be the sign of the strength of sugar (1930, 163).

[170] Vilar (1974, 323). In absolute terms, however, French trade was expanding. Romano speaks of the "substantial and structurally good condition of French commercial life" in the eighteenth century—except in the periods of wars (1957, **II,** 1278).

[171] K. G. Davies (1957, 2). The other contenders were Portugal, France, England, Sweden, Denmark, Brandenburg, and Scotland.

[172] See K. G. Davies (1957, 13).

[173] The monopoly was that of the Company of Royal Adventures into Africa, which was succeeded by the Royal Africa Company in 1672 (see Dunn 1972, 20).

[174] See K. G. Davies (1957, 335–343).

[175] See Parry (1961, 175).

slave trade was in the nature of a public utility.[176] Still, the profits from slave trading seemed as legitimate a cause for the British government to defend as were profits from sugar growing. The only way the government could please both sides was by securing "a separate contract for the supply of slaves to Spanish America"[177]—in short, the *Asiento*, which, as we have seen, was acquired in 1713.

English planters got their free trade in slaves but English slavers got their Spanish market. The planters felt that this compromise leaned to the side of the slavers.[178] Furthermore, all those on the island of Jamaica who had benefited from the fact that it had been the slave entrepôt now bewailed the direct access of the South Sea Company to Spanish ports.[179] The *Asiento* also cut seriously into French illicit trade in the Americas, and the French were forced back into an earlier and less profitable mode of trade with Spanish America, the consignment of goods to merchants in Spain who reexported them in Spanish bottoms.[180] By contrast, the English had three different

[176] Waddell (1960, 9).

[177] Parry (1961, 176).

[178] See Rich (1967, 356), who cites Malachi Postlethwayte on the *Asiento* clauses of the Treaty of Utrecht: "a treaty could scarce have been contrived of so little benefit to the nation." What should be borne in mind is that the planters got what they wanted—abolition of the monopoly—in 1648, whereas the slavers got the *Asiento* in 1713. In the intervening period, the import of slaves to Jamaica tripled and the total population doubled. "Thus when the Peace of Utrecht closed the French wars, Jamaica emerged at last as a classically proportioned sugar society, totally dominated by the big planters" (Dunn, 1972, 165). They therefore needed only to defend their position of strength.

[179] The *Asiento* "interfered with a trade regarded by [Jamaica] as her own prerogative" (Donnan, 1930, 442). Donnan cites a London book of 1731, entitled *Importance of the British Plantations in America to this Kingdom:* "The island of Jamaica flourished till the Year 1716; and a considerable Trade was carried on, to near as great a value as ever was before: and they employed from twelve to fifteen hundred Men in that Trade, which was a great Defence upon Occasion, as well as a Benefit accruing to them from so many Men spending their Money there. And indeed no small Number of these were properly Inhabitants, as being either married, or born there. But in the Year 1716, when the Assiento Factors settled in the West Indies, that Trade, which was of such prodigious Advantage to that Island, and by which they could gain from twenty-five to thirty per cent. Monthly and which was generally allowed to bring in from three to four hundred thousand Pistoles a Year, was tho' not quite destroyed, yet so affected thereby, as to be rendered very inconsiderable and affected thereby, as to be rendered very

inconsiderable and more precarious. So that it is thought at present, that by the Assiento Company, and private Traders together, there are not near one half of the People now employed that used to be. The ill effects of this upon the Island of Jamaica are visible and palpable."

In addition to benefiting the elements in Jamaica who legally engaged in the slave trade, the *Asiento* also interfered with the profits of the privateers: "Since their livelihood depended upon the chance of seizing Spanish ships, the privateers saw with alarm the growth of the protected and semi-legal [slave] trade between the Jamaicans and the Spaniards" (Rich, 1901b, 8). They therefore joined forces with the planters in opposing the "assientists." This discontent of the privateers had serious consequences, as Pares notes: "It is generally admitted that unemployment among privateers caused the almost world-wide outbreaks of piracy after King William's War and the War of the Spanish Succession. Moreover, after the Peace of Utrecht the seamen of England and Spain in America were asked to forget, not merely the tradition of two long wars, but that of a century of skirmishing and marauding. Indeed, the remarkable thing is, not that they should have continued for a time the hostilities and pillage to which they had become accustomed, but that they should finally have been put down at all" (1963, 17).

[180] See Penson (1929, 345). In any case, the French had not been doing too well in the contraband trade. See Pares: "Perhaps the comparative failure of the French in the smuggling trade is best accounted for by supposing that they were undersold by the Dutch and English. . . . It was not so much a love of excessive profit as high overhead charges which hindered the French competitor. French shipping seems to have been less cheaply

modes of tapping Spanish trade. Like the French, they traded via Spain, but they also traded by means of the annual ship of the South Seas Company, and through the illicit but semiprotected trade via Jamaica.[181] The Spanish commercial fleet was disappearing,[182] and to the extent it survived, the English now profited from the invisible item of bottomry loans.[183]

In the beginning of the seventeenth century, the French played a larger role than the English in Mediterranean commerce (Masson calls it preponderant[184]). England's participation steadily increased throughout the century,[185] but declined in the war period of 1689 to 1713. On the one hand, there was France's successful diplomacy. In 1690, France signed a treaty with Algiers that eliminated attacks on French commerce by Barbary corsairs, who continued at the same time to menace the trade of other European powers.[186] France also acquired a privileged position in Egypt (which they lost when Louis XIV signed the Treaty of Rijswijk in 1697 without consulting his Turkish allies).[187] Overall, there was a clear upsurge of French participation in the Levant trade.[188] The basic reason seems to have been the good quality of French textiles, or at least the higher quality of French as compared with English middle-level textiles being offered in Levant at this time.[189] The French trade was monopolized, both formally and *de facto,* by Marseille,[190] which thereupon could also become a center for reexport of various products of the Levant and North Africa.[191] Despite this, the Ottoman Empire was still basically an external arena,[192] and its trade was therefore growing less rather than more important as a percent-

navigated than English, and if . . . it was heavier armed and manned in this trade, the difference in favour of the English must have been accentuated, especially as the English were sometimes saved by convoys from the counter-balancing risks of the *Guarda-Costas*" (1960, 132). The high costs of French shipping remained a constraint throughout the eighteenth century. Knoppers notes that in 1785 "French merchants, having secured the timber supply contract for the Frency navy, founded a new company, the 'Compagnie francaise du Nord'. But nationalistic considerations could not overcome the fact that non-French shippers offered much lower freight prices. The French navy annulled the contract with the Compagnie in 1786 and awarded it instead to Dutch shippers" (1977b, 1).

[181] See H. E. S. Fisher (1963, 219).

[182] See Haring (1947, 335–347).

[183] See John (1953, 154). Still, some argue that the commercial advantages were exaggerated. McLachlan goes so far as to call them a delusion (1940, 28). If this were the case, however, it is difficult to see why the Spanish were so continuously upset by the gains of the South Sea Company. See Hildner (1938, 322–323). Moreover, once the *Asiento* was surrendered after the Treaties of

Aixla-Chapelle in 1748 and Madrid in 1750, the English seemed to retain their by then well-established trade advantages (see Scelle, 1910, 658).

[184] Masson (1967a, 522).

[185] See Cernovodeanu (1967, 457).

[186] See Bono (1964, 51–61). The French had also made a treaty with Tripoli in 1687.

[187] See Paris (1957, 91). Diplomatic relations between France and the Sublime Porte went up and down then for a century to come (see Paris, 1957, 91–100).

[188] Stoianovich speaks of a "collapse of English commerce in Aleppo from 1680–1720" (1974, 80). Masson calls it a "most unexpected turnabout, which surprised even the French" (1967b, 367).

[189] See Stoianovich (1974, 86, 100), Masson (1967b, 370), and Paris (1957, 100).

[190] See Paris (1957, 12–15, 30–36).

[191] See Paris (1957, 5–6).

[192] Neguev dates the inclusion of the area in the world-economy as only from the end of the eighteenth century (1975, 11). Paris points out that before that "European merchants depended heavily on the Porte, and therefore on the latter's relations with their sovereigns" (1957, 80).

age of France's (and indeed western Europe's) overall commercial activity.[193]

In late seventeenth-century Asian trade with Europe, a slow shift began from pepper and spices to other luxury products: Indian textiles; Chinese, Bengal, and Persian silks; chinoiserie (lacquer, porcelain, etc);[194] and tea and coffee, which were also luxury products at first.[195] This growing trade still did not in itself peripheralize the Indian ocean area. For one thing, the increase in textile production was not "accompanied by any significant changes in the technique of manufacture"[196] or therefore by any significant change (as yet) in the social relations of production. To be sure, the European powers were beginning to place themselves in a position to force a change. In 1674 the English East India Company entered into an alliance with the Mahrattas; and in 1684 they fortified Bombay, ending the policy of "fenceless factories," (factories in the sense of trading posts). Sutherland says this was "the thin edge of a great wedge."[197] This increased European interest led to increased intra-European competition, which took a warlike form after 1746 with the capture of Madras by the French from the English. After this, and despite momentary peace in Europe, underground conflict was continuous;[198] it ended with definitive British supremacy only after the Treaty of Paris in 1763.

Nonetheless, despite the growing European interest in Asian trade,[199] Asia remained an external arena. The core states were all dragged bit by bit into becoming colonial or semicolonial powers in vast regions of the world from 1600 to 1750. While they were positive about North America (being able to expand their markets via settler colonies)[200] and about the West

[193] Whereas in the beginning of the seventeenth century, the Levant trade represented 50% of France's external trade, by 1789 it was 5%. As of 1750 it ranked far below that with the Americas and Spain, although about the same as that with Holland (see Masson, 1967b, 429).

[194] See Boxer (1965, 199), Vilar (1974, 345), and Glamann (1974, 447ff.). Vilar speaks of one-way commerce until circa 1765 (see pp. 345, 354).

[195] See Boxer (1965, 174–178) and Glamann (1958, 14). As these items became popular in Europe, they begin to be imitated more cheaply there: Delft potteries by the mid-seventeenth century, Meissen porcelain in 1709, and calicoes in England in the eighteenth century. Tea and coffee could of course not be grown in Europe, but the tea boom dates from 1734, and coffee still later.

[196] Boxer (1965, 197). The increase in quantity had nonetheless a momentum. It was, for one thing, actively encouraged by the English East India Company, which was strongly attacked for this in Parliament in 1696 and 1699 by English woollen and silk manufacturers (see P. J. Thomas, 1963, 39). Leuilliot points to the consequences of this momentum: "If the introduction in Europe of Indian cottons

and muslins provoked at first a protectionist response—prohibition in France in 1686, in Venice and Flanders in 1700, in England in 1701 (and for printed calicoes in 1721), in Prussia about the same time—it also stimulated the cotton industry, influenced also by the colonization in the New World, linked to the African slave trade. The rise of this imitation of Indian products was more or less simultaneous in England, in Germany, in the Netherlands, and in France" (1970, 260).

[197] Sutherland (1952, 3).

[198] Sutherland (1952, 48).

[199] Léon seems to me to overstate the reality when he says that in the period from 1650 to 1750, "the center of interest of [European] large-scale commerce shifted to Asia" (1970a, 128).

[200] I would, however, put the North American fur-trading areas, largely Canada, in the external arena. Lawson speaks of fur as a "luxury demand" (1943, 2). See also Glenday (1975, especially 24–35). K. G. Davies says it started as a luxury, but he sees the beaver hat as "democratizing fur," that is, bringing it in the price range of the bourgeois (1974, 168). The "trickle" of 1600 became, he says, the "stream" of 1650 and the "flood" of 1700 (p. 174).

Indies (being able to obtain lucrative sugar supplies), they were most reluctant about the Indian Ocean area, the coasts of Africa, and the Moslem Mediterranean. Even in these latter areas, direct European political authority sometimes intruded, usually to preempt a rival's claim or threat. Slowly the produce exchanged became less of a luxury from the European perspective. It would not be, however, until the world economic upsurge of the mid-eighteenth century that true peripheralization would begin, and even then it first occurred in the most economically promising areas such as India and Indonesia.[201] It is in the Baltic and White Sea trade that one sees most sharply what it means to speak of the end of Dutch commercial hegemony in the world-economy in the period after 1689. To be sure, the Dutch position declined elsewhere as well, in the Caribbean and Atlantic, generally, and in the Asian trade;[202] but the northern trade was Holland's mother trade, and it was here that English and French rivalry hurt Holland most.

As with India, trade with Russia was becoming more intense without yet peripheralizing Russia.[203] The bulk trade (items such as grain, hemp, and potash) was distinctive for its irregularity at this time, grain being imported to western Europe from Archangel only when prices in the European market were particularly high; but the luxury items such as wax, caviar, and furs, "in the selling price of which the cost of transport was of subordinate importance," were regularly shipped.[204] The Dutch, to be sure, retained an important segment of Russian trade,[205] but slowly, after 1700, the English took over the Dutch role,[206] particularly as an importer of timber masts.[207] The English also began to dominate the import of Swedish iron.[208] France increased her trade in the north at this time, less than England did, but once again at the expense of Holland.[209] Wilson says that Holland's "practical

Rich sees overproduction by 1696 (1966, 26). Still, we must bear in mind the view of Cobbett in the British Parliament in the eighteenth century. He noted that a military expense of 800,000 pounds had been spent fighting the French to preserve a trade worth 50,000: "Suppose the entire fur trade sunk into the sea, where is the detriment to this country?" (cited in Innis, 1943, xx).

[201] "The European economy in the Indian Ocean becomes colonial, in the true sense . . . only after 1750. By that we mean the moment when it reexports to Europe entrepreneurial profits" (Chaunu, 1966b, 893). "It must be emphasized that although the Dutch East India Company became [in the seventeenth and eighteenth centuries] a territorial power in Java, Ceylon, and the Moluccas, it always remained an alien body on the fringe of Asian society, even in the regions which it administered directly" (Boxer, 1965, 194).

[202] On the English–Dutch rivalry in textile imports from Asia, Glamann says that after 1700 "the English trade managed to surpass that of the Dutch

rival" (1977, 251).

[203] Chaunu dates the critical shift as of the mid-eighteenth century, after which he sees Russia as part of European politics (1966a, 639).

[204] Ohberg (1955, 131–133). However, bulk items produced in the immediate vicinity of Archangel—tar, pitch, and leather—and tallow, a monopoly article, were also regularly shipped.

[205] Indeed, Knoppers regards the period from 1716–1717 to the early 1740s as a high point, after which there was a sharp decline (1977b, 12).

[206] See Åström (1963, 188, 196–198).

[207] See Bamford (1956, 141) and W. S. Unger (1959), who notes also an expansion in the import of iron.

[208] See Birch (1955).

[209] Morineau says French exports to the north became equal to Dutch exports in 1742 (1965, 206). Jeannin, however, points out: "Direct commerce of France with the north benefited in the eighteenth century from an expansion resulting in part from a diminution of the role of the Dutch as intermediary.

monopoly" of European transport and commerce "stood intact until about 1730"[210] and that only after 1740 was there a serious attack on the Dutch entrepôt function.[211]

Perhaps Wilson is right, but there are two facts that might induce us to see the end of the practical monopoly as even earlier. First, in the seventeenth century, English goods were stapled in Amsterdam and Rotterdam and sold on commission, but by the eighteenth century the situation was reversed: London was the entrepôt and Dutch linen was accepted in England only on commission.[212] Second, there is evidence that perceptive English people of the eighteenth century no longer thought of the Dutch as hegemonic; rightfully, in our view, they saw the French as more serious competitors than the Dutch.[213] It was, of course, in the realm of finance that the Dutch lead still held. But even here, striking changes eventually occurred in the English and French positions. The second Hundred Years' War, which began in 1689, posed great financial problems to both England and France, but especially to the latter.[214] As the "continental" power, France had to supply endless funds to sustain its mercenary forces and its diplomacy throughout Europe. The French state first sought to meet these growing costs by a series of devaluations[215] effectuated between 1690 and

But if Hamburg was substituted more or less for Amsterdam, was this change so consequential from the point of view of French merchants?" (1975, 71).

[210] Wilson (1954, 254).

[211] See Wilson (1941, 137).

[212] Ormrod points out: "This meant that the Dutch merchant effectively paid the duties and bore all the risk, with his capital tied up until the linen was actually sold. The English merchant made his 2% [commission] without any risk attached, and his capital was free for other, more lucrative pursuits" (1975, 72).

[213] See Andrews: "Contemporary opinion regarding the effectiveness of Dutch rivalry can be inferred from the fact that in 1713 John Withers found it necessary to write a letter 'from a Citizen to a Country Gentleman,' entitled *The Dutch better Friends than the French,* in which he argued against a prevailing opinion that the Dutch were 'rivals with us in our trade, and undermine us in our commerce; and that if these Englanders were once crushed, the trade of the world would be our own.' . . . He endeavored to show that in reality the French were England's great rivals and the Dutch England's friends" (1915, 545–546, n. 18).

The Dutch recognition of and mode of handling the loss of commercial advantage is to be found in their retreat into neutrality, to the degree possible, in Anglo–French wars. The explanations are curiously internally contradictory. See for example Alice Carter and David Horn. Dutch neutrality in the eighteenth century, Carter says, "was due partly

to constitutional forms and to a political system which made rapid decision virtually impossible, but nevertheless served her interests reasonably well" (1963, 818). Horn says: "The sudden disappearance after the Utrecht settlement of the United Provinces as a Great Power must be attributed not to failure of economic strength but to paralysis of the will. . . . Non interventism and neutral rôles and stratagems, if they made the Dutch unpopular with both sides, at least helped to postpone the day of final reckoning" (1967, 24, 88). Both authors offer a purely political explanation (constitutional forms, paralysis of the will) and end by admitting that the policy of neutrality was economically advantageous. In a situation of increasing comparative costs of their products, the Dutch remained competitive by reducing their "protection costs".

[214] Pierre Goubert notes of the first of the wars: "To feed, arm and equip 200,000 men and two fleets for nine years on four main fronts and as many distant theatres of war, against almost the whole of Europe, the Bank of Amsterdam and, before long (in 1694) the Bank of England as well, was a gigantic task, the cost of which, in terms of money, was literally beyond measure" (1970a, 205).

[215] What we today call a devaluation, meaning reduction of the value of paper money (the money of account) in terms of metallic money, was thought of in early modern times as a "crying-up of money" (*augmentation des espèces*), meaning that the metallic money was now worth more in terms of the money of account, since the ratio of coin to other

1725.[216] These devaluations aided the state in several ways in the short run,[217] but the cost was high in the medium run,[218] since the nominal price rise papered over acute cyclical crises, a general reduction of production, and an increase of taxation.[219]

The English were able to weather the financial pressures of these wars better, partly because their sheer military costs were lower and partly because their bullion situation was more favorable. In the late seventeenth century, all of Europe suffered a silver crisis. England, to be sure, was no exception, and in the 1690s they imposed a partial prohibition on exports, exemptions being permitted for trading with the East Indies and the Baltic.[220] We have already argued that since French production was largely sold on a French market and required the currency of internal commerce (silver) and since England (because of its size) was oriented significantly to an export market that required the currency of international clearance (gold), England moved toward *de facto* gold monometallism and France toward silver.[221] This was reinforced by the nature of the bullion trade links: France obtained silver from Mexico via Spain, whereas England would monopolize the gold coming via Portugal from Brazil.[222] England used the

---

kinds of money was substantially on the side of coin during this period. For France, see Lüthy (1959, 99); for England, see T. S. Ashton (1959, 106).

[216] See Lüthy (1959, 114–120).

[217] Lüthy notes three advantages to the state: the tax revenue (*droit de seigneurage*) from minting new coins; the reduction in state debt; and the increased number of coins in hand, since the state in fact returned fewer coins than it received in each such operation (1959, 101). Besnier adds as a fourth advantage the fact that the French state mixed the major devaluations with constant minor revaluations, which had the effect of creating pressure on holders of specie to lend them to the state: "For example in 1703, Chamillart announced several successive revaluations and thus got the *rentiers* to accept a conversion of their debt-papers (*titres*) to a lower rate of interest, since they were threatened with being reimbursed in specie, whose diminution of value, the forerunner of demonetization, was imminent" (1961, 83).

[218] Each devaluation resulted in a "bloodletting of metallic currency to the detriment of France" (Lüthy, 1959, 118). Lüthy argues that "the French Treasury finally paid dearly for the illusion of not having to pay" (p. 120). Braudel and Spooner, looking back on the period from the standpoint of 1750, assert that: "Over the whole of Europe in 1750, the devaluations appear in retrospect to have been particularly severe in three huge political systems: in Poland, Turkey and France" (1967, 382). By the nineteenth century, Poland had ceased to exist and

Turkey was the "sick man of Europe"—and France . . . ? Still, devaluations had another side. Over the long run, they weakened the seigniors. "Each weakening of the money of account was a step in a millenary evolution which ate away at, and finally extinguished, hereditary payments (*charges*)" (Lüthy, 1959, 101).

[219] See Jacquart (1975, 211). See also Richet's skeptical views of the state of the French economy from 1690 to 1720. He doubts that it was an upturn of the Colbertian contraction (1660–1690). In money of account, cereal prices went up sharply, as did wine and olive oil; but in metallic content, they continued low. "It was a 'nominal' rise, artificially provoked by monetary depreciation, a sign of poverty and not a symptom of prosperity" (1968, 762).

[220] See Wilson (1951, 240–241). The exceptions are explained by Sperling in terms of profitability. "Silver went eastward not because the trade depended upon it in any ultimate sense, but because it was profitable" (1962, 62). The reason was the difference in the silver to gold ratio in various parts of the world: 17:1 in Spanish America, 15:1 in Europe, 12:1 in India, 9:1 in Japan. Blitz gives similar ratios: 16:1 in Spain, 15:1 in England, 9/10:1 in the East (1967, 53).

[221] Mertens (1944, 56) finds the origin of the English gold standard in the acute shortage of silver of the seventeenth century; but how can this be, since the same logic would then apply to France?

[222] See Bouvier (1970, 308–309).

period of wars, from 1689 to 1714, to ensure its gold supply.[223] Thus the silver crisis affected England less severely than France. At the very moment when France was weakening its state structure through manipulations of an overburdened silver stock, England was strengthening its state structure through its commercial control over an expanding gold stock.

No doubt, the importance of bullion was not intrinsic but the reflection of the price weakness of other commodities;[224] but in such an era, control of an adequate bullion stock was nonetheless a crucial variable in the struggle between core powers. Both countries sought to place their state finances on a sounder basis. In both states there was the growth of specialized organisms, an expansion of taxation, the rise of paper money, an increase in public borrowing.[225] However, the wars of 1689 to 1714 led to "impossible chaos"[226] in French public finances by 1715 and to relative solvency in English public finances. What was the difference? Van der Wee says French mercantilism "was placed too much at the service of a policy of *military* expansion during the *politique de grandeur* of Louis XIV," whereas English mercantilism "was systematically made to serve a policy of *economic* expansion."[227] Van der Wee thus contrasts a military expansion (implicitly an unproductive use of state funds) with an economic expansion (more meritorious). This is a standard view, but it does not explain why such a difference should exist.

We have already argued that the different geographies of France and England forced the former into their costly efforts at land-based economic expansion—first of all, the effective economic unification of France itself. France's relative success as a land power is to be measured not by comparison with England but by comparison with Austria. "At the beginning of the eighteenth century, although the Austrian monarchy had territories as extensive and almost as heavily populated as those of the French Kingdom, his revenue from taxes was five times less."[228] It was not France alone but both England and France that were required to live beyond their incomes,

---

[223] See Vilar (1974, 278–279). See also Wilson: "The Anglo–Portuguese Treaty of 1703 . . . had the effect of redirecting the gold stream from Brazil to London" (1941, 8). Redirecting it, that is, from the former flow to Amsterdam. Gold was 60% of Brazilian cargo in 1713 (see Morineau, 1978h, 32). Over the eighteenth century, Brazil exported about 800 tons of pure gold (Morineau, 1978h, 24).

[224] Vilar says: "We must always remember that a time of very low prices for commodities overall means a time of high purchasing power for precious metals, and thereby an incitement to prospect them" (1974, 247). On the other hand, this advantage dissipates as the economy recovers, as Morineau notes: "At its zenith in 1730, the commercial significance [of gold] had singularly diminished on the verge of the nineteenth century. To give only one example, a kilogram of pure gold, which in 1740 was 'worth' in Lisbon 12¼ cases of sugar (about 7,200 kg.), was worth in 1778 less than seven (3,900 kg.) and in 1796 less than 3½ (1,950 kg.). Who would have believed that between gold and sugar it would be the former which had the biggest price collapse?" (1978h, 40).

[225] See Mousnier (1951, 1–8), who insists nonetheless that the differences between England and France are greater than the similarities. He offers, however, less a demonstration than an ideological argument *a priori*. England is "more capitalist, more bourgeois" (p. 8). "In 1713, France has a government dictatorial in nature with totalitarian tendencies. England has a plutocratic government with liberal tendencies" (pp. 13–14).

[226] Van der Wee (1977, 378).

[227] Van der Wee (1977, 391–392).

[228] Ardant (1975, 200).

which in a capitalist system is always possible provided confidence reigns. Confidence largely reflects economic reality. Success breeds success, and failure breeds failure. The French state, as we have seen, used devaluations as a mechanism of debit-financing. Even more important, the French state developed a form of borrowing against future tax income. In the late 1690s, merchant bankers began to sell discounted securities based on Treasury expectations of future tax income. As this process extended itself, the reality was that the merchant-bankers were in fact issuing a form of fiduciary currency based on unreliable wartime government promises. This credit edifice collapsed in 1709. The state authorized a moratorium on repayments to the merchant-bankers. As Lüthy says, "the state was in reality according itself the moratorium."[229]

Meanwhile *affermage*, or tax-farming, became a central mechanism of raising royal revenue; it accounted for half the total from the time of Colbert to the French Revolution.[230] *Affermage* was an expensive mechanism from the point of view of the state; Léon says the *financiers*, an expensive corps of intermediaries, were indispensable "in a weakly developed state," where direct appeal for public loans "seemed difficult, if not impossible."[231] In England, the developments in this period were quite different. It is true that there were similar difficulties of state financing in earlier times. Clapham speaks of "the hand-to-mouth finance of the late Stuart period."[232] Yet in the period of wars, 1689 to 1714, which in England was during the reign of William and Mary and then of Queen Anne, the English took the decisive step of creating a system of long-term public borrowing, and therefore of public debt, which placed the state on a secure financial base at relatively low cost. The Bank of England was founded in 1694. In addition, this period saw the establishment of a reorganized United East India Company and a newly established South Sea Company. All three companies were granted their privileges in return for long-term loans to the state.[233] The loans of those three corporations "played a crucial role . . . in the transition from floating to consolidated national debt."[234]

[229] Lüthy (1959, 112). Compare van der Wee (1977, 378) and Harsin (1970, 272–273).

[230] See Y. Durand (1976, 21).

[231] Léon (1970d, 623), who says that in the period from 1685 to 1715, "the 'reign' of finance was absolute in France." As of that period, we mean by *financiers* the *traitants* who were both royal bureaucrats and bankers lending to the state and who were still limited in how much they could extract from the surplus. "These men, seemingly all-powerful, remained feeble and dependent before the Powers that be, who were no doubt 'controlled' by them, but who also 'controlled' them" (Léon, 1970d, 624). As the eighteenth century went on, the *traitants* gave way to the *fermiers-généraux* who operated in a more stable, less speculative manner. They could no longer make wild fortunes, but over the century

they were able to cream off still more surplus. See Léon (1970d, 628–630) and Y. Durand (1976, 13–16).

[232] Clapham (1944, 25).

[233] See Clapham (1944, 1–2) and van der Wee (1977, 352, 387).

[234] Van der Wee (1977, 388). Deyon and Jacquart offer this empirical indicator of the advantage of the new English mode of financing the state over the French system. "The financial effort imposed on England by the Wars [1688–1713] was comparable to that of France. Taxes, especially indirect taxes, and the volume of loans rose in both countries at analogous rates. Nonetheless, at the moment of signing the Treaties of Utrecht, the French national debt was some five or six times as great as that of the English" (1978, 500).

To be sure, these loans were a good trade-off. For the authorities, the loans were perpetual though redeemable, and for the shareholders the rates of interest were good and the shares could increase in value. It still required a certain confidence. Carter says that after William and Mary came to power, the moneyed interests felt they could trust government. "The effects on financial development were dramatic."[235] Who was it that invested? Besides city dwellers (and even a certain country element), Carter speaks of a foreign element, a Sephardic element, and a Huguenot element.[236] It seems quite clear on closer investigation that the crucial confidence on which the English National Debt could be built was the confidence of Dutch bankers and their financial allies, including those who made up what has been called the Huguenot international.[237] It is obvious why Huguenots preferred to bank in England rather than in France in the immediate aftermath of the Revocation of the Edict of Nantes[238] and why the Dutch who were allied with England against France in wars would feel the same. But why not invest the money in Holland? The English may have taken the risk, after 1689, of living beyond their income by borrowing, and it may be true, as Charles Wilson puts it, that "with the borrowed profits from Holland's Golden Age, Britain gambled on an imperial future, and gambled successfully";[239] but the Dutch had to be willing to lend.

If Dutch banking showed a "particularly lively"[240] interest in the English national debt in the eighteenth century, there must have been a reason. I

[235] Carter (1955, 21). See also Roseveare: "The parliamentary revolution had relieved the City of anxieties it had traditionally felt about making large loans to government, and the moneyed community, headed by the King and Queen, had no hesitation in subscribing [in 1694] the £1.2 million capital required to qualify for incorporation" (1969, 69). Not everyone was so sanguine. On the opposition of some landed interests who saw the Bank of England as providing a source of income independent of parliament, see Rubini (1970, 697–701).

[236] Carter (1955, 22, 30, 39–41; see also 1959).

[237] See Monter on Swiss investments in England, the second most important source of foreign funds after the Dutch: "If Swiss investors were basically Genevans and if Genevans were predominantly Huguenots (and if other investors in English stocks were predominantly Huguenots in the early eighteenth century), then the real subject which needs to be unearthed and if possible quantified is the activity of the 'Huguenot international' on the London exchange of the early eighteenth century" (1969, 298). Monter points out that the Berlin and Hamburg investors in England were "almost to a man Huguenots." See also, on the Huguenot international, Bouvier (1970, 312). Marrès points out

that the emigration of the Huguenots created "a network of business and of clients for the industrial products of Languedoc. Those of their brothers who remained in Languedoc, having been eliminated from public service, took over some of the most prosperous industries, notably textiles" (1966, 152–153). See also Lüthy (1959, 424).

[238] Later on, after the death of Louis XIV, the Huguenots would once again return to investment in France, particularly in French external commerce (see Bouvier, 1970, 312–313). "It was certainly more than a mere coincidence that the Financial Revolution followed the arrival of the Dutch monarch and his advisors, who were skilled in handling fiscal and financial affairs, particularly long-term government borrowing, and were connected with Dutch banking circles" (Braun, 1975, 292).

[239] Wilson (1949, 161). One piece of evidence for the success of the key institution, the Bank of England, was the fact that, although *de jure* its notes were not legal tender until 1833, *de facto*, "quite early in the eighteenth century, Bank of England notes had established themselves as generally acceptable in final settlement of debts"—that is, as money (Horsefield, 1977, 131).

[240] Van der Wee (1977, 389).

think the reason has less to do with England than with Holland.[241] We start with two facts. In the eighteenth century, the English national debt was largely owed to foreigners,[242] and after 1689, England came to be the "preferred field of investment of Amsterdam capital."[243] The net result of English and French mercantilist policies in the seventeenth century was to eliminate Dutch advantage in the spheres of production and even to a large extent in commerce. Dutch wage costs had risen. The Dutch technological lead had disappeared, and state taxation rates were exceptionally high, partly because of the high cost of debt servicing.[244] The low interest rates, which had been a consequence of the strength of the Dutch position in the world-economy, now seemed to be maintained by a "languishing business climate that would justify transferring funds to foreign assets."[245] With an interest rate in the United Provinces that had dropped from $6\frac{1}{4}\%$ in the early seventeenth century to $2\frac{1}{2}\%$ by the mid-eighteenth, the 6% offered by the Bank of England (and the 5% in annuities and colonial mortgages) seemed very attractive to Dutch investors.[246]

There was, in short, no real choice. It was neither a "feudal business" mentality nor of a lack of patriotism that caused the Dutch placed their money in England. "Comparative costs, comparative returns on capital, and fiscal policy all favored [Dutch] investment in rentier stocks, home and foreign, as against industry."[247] Sombart analyzed this shift as evidence that the bourgeois always "degenerates," but the Dutch liberal historian, A. N. Klein, takes issue with this "debatable" expression of Sombart, preferring Marx's explanation that every capitalist is a "Fanatiker der Verwertung des Werts," a fanatic of the valorization or self-expansion of capital. Klein argues that this characterization fits the Dutch case perfectly:

> The Dutch merchant of the seventeenth century and his rentier descendant of the eighteenth century fit this conception, provided we realized that the economic possibilities of the latter had been limited to the much less spectacular terrain of financial investments. If one fanatic attains his objectives more rapidly and effectively than

[241] "It seems that Dutch capital, except perhaps for a few years of war, found employment in English funds less from England's need for capital than for a lack of investment opportunities at home" (John, 1953, 158).

[242] Wilson (1941, 72–73). The Dutch in particular held three-sevenths of the public debt (Wilson, 1941, 78, 190). Carter argues, however, that the evidence for this is "extremely dubious" (1953a, 159). Her impression from the ledgers was that the Dutch had only between a one-eighth and a one-sixth interest (p. 161). She admits nonetheless that just before the War of the Austrian Succession, Dutch investment had come to be a "fairly considerable interest, relative to the total" in the English public debt (1953b, 338).

[243] Barbour (1963, 125).

[244] Klein points out that the fastest growth of public debt for the United Provinces was in the seventeenth century, which is to be expected given their hegemony. They tried to keep taxation rates low, in part because one of the ideological motifs of the war against Spain had been the revolt of taxation; but the costs eventually had to be met. "In this way it may be said that it is not unlikely that the Dutch liberty of the sixteenth century had been bought at the cost of later generations" (1969, 19).

[245] Morineau (1974, 775). See also Carter (1971, 131–135).

[246] See Wilson (1954, 263–264).

[247] Wilson (1960b, 439).

another, that is perhaps due to his greater possibilities, but certainly not to his greater determination.[248]

The Dutch financial shift was neither sudden nor total. Rather it was a gradual process. Dutch banks were still a solid conservative place in which others could place their bullion,[249] and the rate of minting continued to rise in the eighteenth century.[250]

It would not be until 1763 that European confidence in Amsterdam as the financial center of the world would be shaken;[251] but already at the turn of the eighteenth century, the Dutch were moving their money to where it could be most remunerated, and this was England. It was "a straightforward business arrangement,"[252] in which the high return for the Dutch investor helped the English state keep down its cost of borrowing. Ultimately, the English could have raised their money at home as the French did, but Dutch investments "enabled England to fight [its] wars with a minimum of dislocation to her economy."[253] The symbiotic arrangement between a formerly hegemonic power and the new rising star provided graceful retirement income for the one and a crucial push forward against its rival for the other. The pattern was repeated later, in the period from 1873 to 1945, with Great Britain playing the Dutch role and the United States in the English role.

After Utrecht, the French made one strong effort to undo the incipient English advantage in world finance. Harsin puts his finger on France's problem. "The absence of true public credit up to 1715 had been the most serious lacuna in the French financial system."[254] John Law's "private" bank[255] was intended to fill this lacuna. What Law attempted was to reestablish the credit of the French state by creating a bank that would be the recipient of state income; on this basis it would issue valid currency notes convertible into gold. The long-run object was to ensure monetary stability, increase liquid currency, lower the interest rate, improve the rate of exchange with foreign currencies, and perhaps above all, reduce state expenditures (in terms of both the public debt and the continuing drain by the intermediate bureaucratic strata on state income). All this would make pos-

---

[248] Klein (1970, 34). That this was a deliberate decision can be seen in the fact that the Dutch pioneered the financial innovation in the eighteenth century of investment trusts, an idea not to reach England until the 1870s, when England would be reaching the stage the United Provinces had reached in 1689 (see Klein, 1969, 12).

[249] See van Dillen (1926, 199–200).

[250] See Morineau (1972, 4).

[251] See Wilson (1954, 264–265).

[252] Carter (1953b, 323).

[253] John (1955, 343).

[254] Harsin (1970, 276).

[255] Because of objections by various interests to John Law's proposal for a public bank, the bank "had to camouflage itself under the appearances of a private bank in order to be authorized"(Harsin, 1970, 277–278). On Law's attempt to establish a bank of France, see E. J. Hamilton (1969, 140–149). Hamilton calls Law's original plan, submitted in 1702, "one of the very best plans for a national bank that I have seen in any country for that period" (p. 143). That the private nature of the bank was camouflage is indicated by the fact that when on December 4, 1718, it finally became formally the Royal Bank, "all of the outstanding shares had already been purchased secretly by the government." (E. J. Hamilton, 1969, 145).

sible a program of considerable maritime and colonial expansion. To achieve these ends, Law proposed primarily two things: the expansion of money in the form of paper and fiscal reform.[256] It seemed an attempt to complete Colbert's work, an imaginative leap forward that might restore to France a clear lead in the struggle with England. The project failed abysmally. After obtaining its initial capital, Law's bank created the *Compagnie d'Occident* to explore and exploit the Mississippi Valley (known as Louisiana) with a state monopoly. The bank proceeded to absorb other trading companies (*Sénégal, Indes orientales, Chine*) and to create in 1719 the *Compagnie des Indes.*

At the same time, Law's bank took over the payment of public debts against repayment out of tax receipts. Law also sought to reorganize and rationalize the tax system, but was never able to carry out this program amidst the immense speculative fever the inflation of the stocks and paper money had aroused. Suddenly there was a crisis of confidence. Attempts to deflate the stock backfired, and the system collapsed in the so-called Mississippi Bubble. Why? Deyon and Jacquart say that despite the "admiration" that the "scope of the project" arouses, Law did not possess "the art of execution, the patient mastery of time, on which depends the success of even the most brilliant strategies."[257] Harsin says that Law had constructed a system that was "sturdy [but] probably premature" and that it failed in the last analysis because of "the temerity of his initiatives and the too fast implementation of his proposals, rather than to their lack of logic and the coalition of his enemies."[258] For Max Weber, however, Law's fall was inevitable simply because "neither Louisiana nor the Chinese or East India trade had yielded sufficient profit to pay interest on even a fraction of his capital."[259]

Perhaps we can appreciate Law's failure better if we look at the concurrent speculation in England, which led to a similar crisis called the South Sea Bubble. (Of course, speculation was not limited to England and France but was actively abetted by bankers and investors in Geneva, the United Provinces, Hamburg, and northern Italy.)[260] John Law's "system" had in-

---

[256] This description of Law's intent is drawn from Harsin (1970, 279). Carswell says: "The idea of a national paper currency which would be universally accepted because it was backed by the authority of the State and controlled through a network of local agencies was the heart of Law's plan for increasing the world's wealth. He was so sure such a currency would be preferred to metal that in his original pattern of the project he thought it necessary to set a limit to the premium paper should enjoy over gold and silver and provide that a debt of 100 should not require more than 110 in gold to discharge it" (1960, 78–79).

[257] Deyon and Jacquart (1978, 502).

[258] Harsin (1970, 280).

[259] Weber (1950, 288), who gives the identical explanation for the South Sea Bubble: "Here also bankruptcy was unavoidable because the South Sea trade was not sufficient to pay interest on the sums advanced" (p. 289).

[260] See Åkerman (1957, **II**, Pt. I, 254–255); Harsin (1970, 294); Kindelberger (1978, 120–122). T. S. Ashton adds Denmark, Spain, and Portugal (1959, 120). On Geneva, see Sayous (1937). Åkerman calls the crisis of 1720 "the first international crisis" (p. 255). Weber calls the pair of bubbles "the first great speculative crises," differentiating them from the great tulip craze of Holland in the 1630s (1950, 286). Parker uses almost the same phrase: "the first financial crisis of modern times" (1974a, 582).

volved a putting together of three state monopolies: a bank of issue (*Banque Royale*), a trading company (*Compagnie des Indes*), and a centralized depot for indirect taxes (*Ferme générale des impôts*). In October 1719, when Law offered to refund the remaining national debt of 1.5 billion francs, the demand for stocks was far more than anticipated, in England as well as in France. The English thereupon copied the scheme, using the already existent South Sea Company.[261] There too, the demand exceeded expectations. In both cases, the crucial element was that the individual government creditor was induced, not forced, to purchase the stock.[262] However, in France, after such inducement under pressure, the rules of the game were changed and the bank notes were reduced in terms of money of account by 50%. As Hamilton notes:

> Inasmuch as both Law and the Regent had solemnly and repeatedly promised that Bank notes would never be changed in terms of money of account, panic reigned. Since one stroke of a pen that the Crown was honor-bound not to make had taken away half the nominal value of Bank notes, holders tried to spend or invest them before the second stroke![263]

The "Great Crash" spread from Paris to London. No doubt it "provided a graphic demonstration of the fragility of the new financial edifice," but no doubt too it showed "the resilience of the new financial techniques."[264] Both England and France then emerged into a period of long-term financial stability that continued right up to the French Revolution.[265] In this sense, the outcome was happy. However, the attempt by France to use the System of John Law to overcome the growing gap in the financial power of the two states had backfired. England's previously created central bank survived the South Sea Bubble, but the similar structure in France led to the Mississippi Bubble and therefore died with it. "The reign of Law, extremely brief, had shook up everything without achieving anything."[266] In England, Parliament backed the bankrupt South Sea Company; it "saved appearances," and thereby saved English credit.[267] This was not politically possible in

[261] The original use of the South Sea Company in 1711 to refund short-term obligations was highly successful. "This intelligent move enabled Britain to emerge from the Peace of Utrecht in 1713 with her credit virtually intact, even though her public debt was enormous" (Parker, 1974a, 581). Flinn (1960) is more skeptical of the success. But B. W. Hill argues that it was a *politically* crucial act, even more than an economically crucial one: "A Tory Parliament had been persuaded to undertake maintenance of the national debt, and the Whig City to resume its role as the nation's creditor. Both politically and financially these were important developments for the future; politically because they removed a fear that public credit could crumble as the result of change in government [in 1710 there had been a shift from

Whig to Tory], financially because the form of organization developed by the 'monied interest' since the Revolution [the Bank of England] was acknowledged and even protected by a ministry which represented the City's greatest critics, the landed gentry" (1971, 411).

[262] See Parker (1974a, 583).

[263] E. J. Hamilton (1969, 147).

[264] Parker (1974a, 586).

[265] For England, see Vilar (1974, 285); for France, see Lüthy (1961, 31) and Bouvier (1970, 307).

[266] Lüthy (1959, 414)

[267] Harsin (1970, 279). Plumb's view of the government's action is even stronger. Walpole, he says, "saved the court" (1950, 59)—and thereby, two years later, became prime minister.

France. The direct negative effects of John Law's System have been much exaggerated,[268] and there were even positive effects.[269] The true negative was the failure to succeed, and thereby to recoup the process of falling behind.

As the eighteenth century proceeded, the financial centrality of England in the world-economy increased while France's decreased[270] because the French state was not as strong as the English state. The question before us then is how the English state became so much stronger than the French state. For those who measure the strength of a state by the degree to which individuals are protected against arbitrary decisions of the government or by the size of the public bureaucracy, this may seem an absurd question. But we have already made clear our position that a state is strong to the extent that those who govern can make their will prevail against the will of others outside or inside the realm. Using such a criterion, we believe the English state had clearly outstripped the French state by the early eighteenth century. The truly strong state seldom has need to show its iron fist. Temperley notes that, if the Age of Walpole was "one of peace [and] uneventful," it was because of past prowess: "The Methuen Treaty with Portugal in 1703, the commercial clauses of the Peace of Utrecht in 1713, were universally regarded as concessions to English trade which only arms, or the threat of arms, could have extorted."[271] Nor was strength of arms sufficient; there also had to be efficiency of administration. Plumb says that "by 1714, Britain probably enjoyed the most efficient government machinery in Europe."[272]

We have taken the position that the social compromises effectuated in late seventeenth-century England and France were less different than is sometimes suggested and that in both cases they resulted in relative internal stability during the Anglo–French wars between 1689 and 1763. The eighteenth century was the "epoch of reconciliation between monarchy and nobility throughout Europe,"[273] and this reconciliation was based on strong government support for the incomes of the landed classes. While this is

[268] See Poisson (1974, 266).

[269] J. Imbert speaks the beneficial "whiplash to the French economy between 1718 and 1721" (1965, 354). E. J. Hamilton notes that it got France out of her commercial crisis but that this was not "costless" (1969, 147–148).

[270] On the decline of Lyon as a financial center after 1720, see Lüthy (1959, 55).

[271] Temperley (1909a, 40, 49). With strength came conservatism. "[Walpole's] policy was exceedingly simple—the avoidance of war, the encouragement of trade, reduction of taxation, and for the rest, *status quo*—no innovations. As he rightly said, 'I am no saint, no Spartan, no reformer.'" (Plumb, 1966, 78–79).

[272] Plumb (1967, 13). Efficiency is more important than numbers, but it is well to note that numbers were not neglected in England. "The number of men employed by the government grew faster between 1689 and 1715 than in any previous period of English history" (Plumb, 1967, 112)—until the nineteenth century. See also Aylmer: "In terms of the sheer growth of government, the crucial epochs . . . seem to have been the years 1642–1652 and 1689–1697 (possibly also 1702–1713)" (1974, 24). Contrast Plumb's description with Berger's assessment of the presumed upsurge of French administrative efficiency after 1689: "There is no impression left after studying the famine of 1693 [and how the French government handled it] of that great administrative offensive supposedly prompted by the needs of the war" (1978, 120).

[273] P. Anderson (1974a, 232).

commonly admitted for France, was not England the home of a triumphant merchant capital? No doubt, but was this so separate from landed income?[274] Quite aside from the overlap of personnel, the governments on the one hand aided commercial, industrial, and financial enterprises in all the ways we have already described; but they simultaneously allowed the landed classes to appropriate a vast part of the surplus. Once again, this is commonly admitted for France. The nobility, which paid no taxes, and the venal *noblesse de robe* are central to our image of the *Ancien Régime*,[275] but was this so unknown in England? In this "age of the great estate" with an "aristocratic monopoly of land,"[276] what was the effect of Walpolian stability? E. P. Thompson suggests acerbically:

> Political life in England in the 1720s had something of the sick quality of a 'banana republic'. . . . Each politician, by nepotism, interest and purchase, gathered around him a following of loyal dependents. The aim was to reward them by giving them some post in which they could milk part of the public revenue: army finances, the Church, excise. . . . The great gentry, speculators and politicians were men of huge wealth, whose income towered like the Andes above the rain forests of the common man's poverty.[277]

Was this version of "state banditry"[278] in England so markedly different in its consequences for landed wealth than the slightly different version in France? We must return to our question of what made the English state stronger than the French. Perhaps the simplest answer is that it was the result of their military ability to contain France in the wars of 1689 to 1714; and their ability to win those wars was the result of the Anglo–Dutch alliance, not so much because of the military assistance of the Dutch (though this was not unimportant), but because of the financial underpinning Dutch investment gave the English state. The Dutch interest created a level of confidence that made it possible to create the Bank of England, and that made it possible for the Bank of England to survive the South Sea Bubble. Above all, it was finally possible to resolve in the Walpolian one-party state the split in the English ruling classes that had begun in the period of the early Stuarts and had continued in a different form in the acute Tory–Whig

---

[274] On England and landed wealth, see Habakkuk: "There is no reasonable doubt that circumstances were more favorable to landed incomes in the century after 1715 than they had been between 1640 and 1715" (1967b, 9). See also Plumb: "The landed gentleman was being increasingly stitched into the new economic fabric of the society; trade, speculation, [and] a venture ceased, at last, to be alien to them" (1967, 8). On France and merchant capital, see McManners: "Money is the key to the understanding of French society in the eighteenth century. With the power of money behind it, the plutocracy was infiltrating into the aristocracy" (1967, 26). See also Grassby (1960), for some of the

ways in which the concept of *dérogation* was evaded and hence unable to maintain the strict barriers between the nobility and the merchants it was intended to foster.

[275] G. V. Taylor calls this "court capitalism": "Nobles, financiers, bankers, and professional speculators brought the government into questionable speculative operations and used their influence to procure official decisions that raised or depressed prices or released speculators from disadvantageous future commitments" (1964, 488).

[276] Mingay (1963, 15, 26).

[277] E. P. Thompson (1975, 197–198).

[278] The phrase is E. P. Thompson's (1975, 294).

party struggles of 1689 to 1715.[279] It was not because England was more democratic than France, but because in some sense it was less[280] that the English state waxed strong and the English entrepreneur went on to conquer the economic world. Overnight, the atmosphere changed from one of political violence to one of political stability.[281]

The political reconciliation of the upper strata, the stuff of English eighteenth-century stability, was accomplished only partly in France. Just as in England, the newer segments of the upper strata had gained *droit de cité* in the political structure and had ceased to be an oppositional force;[282] so had the comparable group, the *noblesse de robe,* in France.[283] Nonetheless, unlike in England, the executive never came to be in total control of the state. The "gulf between theory and practice [of absolutism] remained extraordinarily wide."[284] To explain the incompleteness of the reconciliation of the upper strata in France, let us return to the question of the Huguenots and the Revocation of the Edict of Nantes. The "Protestant party" in the sixteenth century had the support of half the French nobility, especially its medium and lower ranks. The curious consequence of this was that the lesser nobility, suffering the pressures of the officers of the king, fell back on "a relative and paradoxical tolerance for their peasants." When the political compromise of 1598 was turned into the royal victory of 1629, however, the social consequences were immense: "The defeat of the Protestant party was first of all the defeat of the nobility,"[285] Slowly after 1598 and

---

[279] The Dutch financial role in English politics was of course mediated through the City of London. Sutherland makes the City's support one of the four bases of Walpole's system, both directly and through the connected East India Company (see 1952, 18–23).

[280] Plumb argues persuasively that 1715 marked the final taming of the popular thrust that England knew since 1640. "The freeholder had become in seventeenth-century England a political animal. . . . By the middle of the eighteenth century, much of that birthright had been lost" (1969, 115–116). After 1715 England's stability was, Plumb argues, a function of "three major factors: single-party government, the legislature being firmly under executive control, and a sense of common identity in those who wielded economic, social, and political power" (1967, xviii).

[281] "There was a tradition of conspiracy, riot, plot, and revolt *among the ruling class* that stretches back to the Normans. By 1685 violence in politics was an Englishman's birthright" (Plumb, 1967, 19, italics added). "Political stability, when it comes, often happens to a society quite quickly, as suddenly as water becomes ice" (p. xvii). Christopher Hill has a similar image, but dates the turning point at 1688 rather than 1715: "England was notorious throughout Europe for the violence of its politics. . . . After 1688 the heroic age of English politics is over. The

violent oscillations of the preceding fifty years were succeeded by a relative calm" (1969, 119, 213).

[282] "[The Junto and Walpole] separated Whiggery from radicalism. . . . The party fused the interests of aristocracy, high finance, and executive government, a process extended by Walpole to embrace the bulk of the landed gentry" (Plumb, 1967, 187).

[283] Franklin Ford observes that whereas in the meeting of the Estates General in 1614, the high *noblesse de robe* had still figured among the commoners, "the most important single fact about the high robe's nobility in 1715 was that in legal terms there was no longer any doubt about it" (1953, 59). Indeed, he goes on, "in 1715 the high robe, secure in its nobility and with its political rights restored, was the most potent force within the aristocracy" (1953, 188).

Not even all those who were still formally *roturiers,* that is, the bourgeoisie, were negatively affected by the so-called feudal reaction. Elinor Barber points out that whereas the "middle" bourgeoisie found career paths blocked, the "big" bourgeoisie, by using their wealth, were "much less affected" (1955, 143).

[284] Bromley (1957, 135), who says: "The emancipation of government from historic restraints was a slow process, often interrupted and never complete" (p. 137).

[285] Chaunu (1965b, 26–27).

precipitately after 1630, the nobility abandoned Protestantism; this is what made possible the Revocation in 1685.[286]

With the Revocation, there was a dispersion, largely of urban burgher elements;[287] but this amounted to only 10% of the French Protestants. Many others converted.[288] What was left?

> Royal severity had thus destroyed that Protestantism—centralized, institutional, cleri-
> cal, and bourgeois—which had covered over, during the seventeenth century, the
> Protestantism of the Reformation. In adversity, the latter was recreated. Without
> pastors at first, following simple laymen, the predicants. . . . Thanks to those noble-
> men and peasants [*ruraux*] who had been the principle strength of the Reformed
> Churches in the sixteenth century. When the Revocation forced them to reinvent a
> technique of resistance, their first instinct was to rebel.[289]

The crucial features of this reconstituted Protestant church were "con-gregationalist, federalist, secular, parliamentary, and egalitarian."[290] Egalitarian and rebellious! The French state had on its hands a potential class uprising of middle strata—poorer nobles and richer peasants—which was serious. It had got into this difficulty because of the historic dilemmas posed in the sixteenth century by a state size that was too large and too economically disparate to permit the rapid creation of a strong state struc-ture.

The sectors that might cause an upheaval had to be mollified and con-tained, and so they were, partly by the lowering of taxes on the peasantry after 1720[291] and partly by the spread of primary school education in the rural areas as a mode of acculturation by a triumphant Counter-Reformation.[292] However, lowering taxes simply expanded the already growing gap between the strength of the English and French states.[293] The

---

[286] "If carefully considered, the conversion of [Marshal-General] Turenne [in 1668] was more im-portant than the Revocation of the Edict of Nantes. Without the conversion of Turenne, the edict of Fontainebleau would have been unthinkable. The king could not have constrained half his gentlemen, had they been resolute. A century and a half later, La Fayette, La Rochefoucauld-Liancourt, and 90 other liberal nobles did more than the speeches of Mirabeau to ensure the success of the Third Estate on June 23, 1789" (Chaunu, 1965b, 27).

[287] About 200,000 Huguenots left between 1680 and 1720, going primarily to England, the United Provinces, Geneva, and the Germanies (see Scoville, 1952, 409–410).

[288] See Scoville (1960, 3–5, 118). Some converts were in fact dissimulators, "new marranos" (see Leonard, 1948, 177–178).

[289] Léonard (1948, 178). Hence the war of the Camisards, hence Antoine Court and the Synod of the Desert in the Basses-Cévennes in 1715.

[290] Léonard (1948, 179).

[291] See Le Roy Ladurie (1975c, 35–37).

[292] See Le Roy Ladurie (1975a, 528). The eighteenth century, by contrast with the seven-teenth, was "the great epoch of peasant schooling" (1975a, 538).

[293] See Mousnier's figures for comparative re-ceipts from customs, excise, posts, and stamps in the period from 1690 to 1715. Whereas French income from the *Fermes-Unies*, went from about 70 million livres tournois in 1690 to 47 in 1715, English in-come went from 20.5 in 1700 to 59.5 in 1713 (1951, 18). As the century proceeded, the gap got steadily worse. Mathias and O'Brien (1976), after a careful consideration of comparative tax burdens for the whole of the century, say that "in France the burden of taxation was less than in England" (p. 634); they point out that "it is perhaps not just coincidence" that English tax burdens were exceeded only by those in the United Provinces, the only country "where internal markets were even more highly ar-ticulated than in Britain" (p. 640).

educational and religious evolution, although it may have held in check
"radicalism" and "criminality"[294] in eighteenth-century rural France was
clearly insufficient to eradicate the sense of political exclusion of the larger
farmers, the group who in England were called the gentry, or at least the
lesser gentry. Without the political incorporation of this group, the state was
unable to grow really strong.[295] France's internal struggles were not totally
unrelated to the creation of the crucial Anglo–Dutch alliance. It was by no
means obvious in the mid-seventeenth century that in the eighteenth the
Dutch would prefer an alliance with the English to one with the French.
The English were their major commercial foe, whereas they had many links
with France. Indeed, as we have seen, they were in the process of turning
the Ponant into an economic conveyor belt similar to the one that Portugal
and Spain were becoming.

French internal dilemmas, however, forced them into their position as a
land-oriented militarily expansionist power that suppressed its Protestants.
To the Dutch holders of capital, whether republican or royalist, a deal with
England must have seemed less disconcerting than did a deal with France.
France threatened to embrace the Dutch and smother them. The English
offered the slow osmosis of two capitalist strata. The accession of the House
of Orange to the English throne only confirmed the Dutch preference for
the English. Thus, as often happens, strength led to strength and weakness
to weakness. The difficulties of creating a state structure in the sixteenth
century tore France apart, festered, and ultimately resulted in the incom-
plete integration of eighteenth-century France. Sixteenth-century England
was a compact state. Having been forced by the turmoil of the Civil War to
recreate a unified ruling class, England was able to absorb and incorporate
its Celtic fringe; and it was able to attract enough Dutch capital to support
the creation in the eighteenth century of a stable Walpolian one-party state.
It was this steady increase in the relative strength of the English state—
rather than significant differences in how French and English production
was organized in the period from 1600 to 1750 or in their value systems—
that accounted for the ability of England to outdistance France decisively in
the period from 1750 to 1815.

Throughout this volume, we have stressed the similarities in the organization of English and French production. As for technological and intellectual innovation, it all depends on whose history books you read. Bourgeois,
capitalist values no doubt began to pervade the United Provinces and England; but we must not forget Paul Hazard's classic demonstration that the
ideas of the Enlightenment came to dominate France not with the Revolu-

---

[294] Le Roy Ladurie (1975a, 550, 552).

[295] Le Roy Ladurie contrasts the political coali-
tions of rural England and rural France in the
eighteenth century: seigniors and well-off farmers

(*gros fermiers*) in England as against the "historical
bloc" in France of the poor and middle peasants,
even the well-off farmers, against the *féodalité*
(1975a, 584–585).

tion or even with the Encyclopedists, but in the period from 1680 to 1715.[296]
As Labrousse says, "the eighteenth century [in France] thought
bourgeois."[297] This was true not only of France. Although the ideological
facades of an earlier world still reigned throughout the European world-
economy, more and more groups tended to act primarily and ultimately in
the manner of bourgeois and proletarians pursuing their interests and
defending their stakes in a capitalist system. This is indeed the heart of
what we have been arguing. Neither bourgeois nor proletarian culture had
yet emerged; but bourgeois and proletarian praxis were already forming
the central constraints on social action.

[296] "Never was there a greater contrast, never a more sudden transition than this. . . . One day the French people, almost to a man, were thinking like Bossuet. The day after, . . . like Voltaire. No ordinary swing of the pendulum, that. It was a revolution" (Hazard, 1964, 7).

[297] C. E. Labrousse (1970, 716).

BIBLIOGRAPHY

Aalbers, J., "Holland's Financial Problems (1713–1733) and the Wars against Louis XIV," in A. C. Duke & C. A. Tamse, eds., *Britain and the Netherlands,* **VI:** *War and Society.* The Hague: Martinus Nijhoff, 1977, 79–93.

Abel, Wilhelm, *Die Drei Epochen der deutschen Agrargeschichte,* 2nd ed., Schriftenreihe für Ländliche Sozialfragen, **XXXVII.** Hannover: Verlag M. & H. Schaper, 1964.

Abel, Wilhelm, *Geschichte der deutschen Landwirtschaft vom fruhen Mittelalter bis zum 19. Jahrhundert,* 2nd rev. ed. Stuttgart: Verlag Eugen Ulmer, 1967.

Abel, Wilhelm, *Massenarmut und Hungerkrisen in vorindustriellen Deutschland.* Gottingen: Vandenhoeck & Ruprecht, 1972.

Abel, Wilhelm, *Crises agraires en Europe* (*XIIIe–XXe siècle*), traduit de la 2ème édition allemande, revue et augmentée. Paris: Flammarion, 1973.

Aberg, Alf, "The Swedish Army, from Lutzen to Narva," in M. Roberts, ed., *Sweden's Age of Greatness, 1632–1718.* New York: St. Martin's Press, 1973, 265–287.

Achilles, Walter, "Getreidepreise und Getreidehandelsbeziehungen europäischer Raume im 16. und 17. Jahrhundert," *Zietschrift für Agrargeschichte und Agrarsoziologie,* **VII,** 1, 1959, 32–55.

Adams, Geoffrey, "Myths and Misconceptions: The Philosophic View of the Hugenots in the Age of Louis XV," *Historical Reflections,* **I,** 1, June 1974, 59–79.

Ågren, Kurt, "Breadwinners and Dependents: An Economic Crisis in the Swedish Aristocrary during the 1600's?" in K. Ågren *et al., Aristocrats, Farmers, Proletarians,* Studia Historica Uppsaliensia **XLVII.** Uppsala: Almquist & Wiksell, 1973, 9–27. (a)

Ågren, Kurt, "The *reduktion,*" in M. Roberts, ed., *Sweden's Age of Greatness, 1632–1718.* New York: St. Martin's Press, 1973, 237–264. (b)

Ågren, Kurt, "Rise and Decline of an Aristocracy," *Scandinavian Journal of History,* **I,** 1–2, 1976, 55–80.

Åkerman, Johan, *Structure et cycles économiques,* 2 vols. Paris: Presses Univ. de France, 1957.

Allen, Theodore, "'. . . They Would Have Destroyed Me': Slavery and the Origins of Racism," *Radical America,* **IX,** 3, May–June 1975, 41–64.

Anderson, M. S., "Russia Under Peter the Great and the Changed Relations of East and West," in *New Cambridge Modern History,* **VI:** J. S. Bromley, ed., *The Rise of Great Britain and Russia, 1688–1725.* Cambridge: University Press, 1970, 716–740.

Anderson, Perry, *Lineages of the Absolutist State.* London: New Left Books, 1974. (a)

Anderson, Perry, *Passages from Antiquity to Feudalism.* London: New Left Books, 1974. (b)

Andrews, Charles M., "Anglo-French Commercial Rivalry, 1700–1750: The Western Phase," *American Historical Review,* Part I: **XX,** 3, Apr. 1915, 539–556; Part II: **XX,** 4, July 1915, 761–780.

Andrews, Charles M., "The Acts of Trade," in J. Holland Rose *et al.,* eds., *Cambridge History of the British Empire.* Cambridge: University Press, 1929, **I,** 268–299.

Anes Alvarez, Gonzalo, & le Flem, Jean-Paul, "Las crisis del siglo XVII: Producción agrícola, precios e ingresos en tierras de Segovia," *Moneda y Credito,* No. 93, junio 1965, 3–55.

Appleby, Andrew B., "Agrarian Capitalism or Seigneurial Reaction? The Northwest of England, 1500–1700," *American Historical Review,* **LXXX,** 3, June 1975, 574–594.

Ardant, Gabriel, "Financial Policy and Economic Infrastructure of Modern States and Nations," in Charles Tilly, ed., *The Formation of National States in Western Europe.* Princeton, New Jersey: Princeton Univ. Press, 1975, 164–242.

Ariès, Philippe, "Nationalisme d'hier et nationalisme d'aujourd'hui," *La table ronde,* No. 147, mars 1960, 46–51.

Asher, Eugene L., *The Resistance to the Maritime Classes: The Survival of Feudalism in the France of Colbert.* Berkeley & Los Angeles: Univ. of California Press, 1960.

Ashley, M. P., *Financial and Commercial Policy under the Cromwellian Protectorate.* London & New York: Oxford Univ. Press, 1934.

Ashley, W. J., "The Tory Origin of Free Trade Policy," *Quarterly Journal of Economics,* **XI,** 4, July 1897, 335–371.

Ashton, Robert, "Cavaliers and Capitalists," *Renaissance and Modern Studies,* **V,** 1961, 149–175.

Ashton, Robert, "Puritanism and Progress," *Economic History Review,* 2nd ser., **XVIII,** 3, Apr. 1965, 579–587.

Ashton, Robert, "The Parliamentary Agitation for Free Trade in the Opening Years of the Reign of James I," *Past and Present,* No. 38, 1967, 40–55.

Ashton, Robert, "Jacobean Free Trade Again," *Past and Present,* No. 43, 1969, 151–157.

Ashton, T. S., *Economic Fluctuations in England, 1700–1800.* Oxford: Clarendon Press, 1959.

Ashton, T. S., "Introduction" to Elizabeth Boody Schumpeter, *English Overseas Trade Statistics, 1697–1808.* Oxford: Clarendon Press, 1960, 1–14.

Ashton, T. S., *An Economic History of England: The 18th Century.* London: Methuen, 1969, reprinted with minor corrections.

Aspvall, G., "The Sale of Crown Land in Sweden: The Introductory Epoch, 1701–1723," *Economy and History,* **IX,** 1966, 3–28.

Åström, Sven-Erik, "The English Navigation Laws and the Baltic Trade, 1660–1700," *Scandinavian Economic History Review,* **VIII,** 1, 1960, 3–18.

Åström, Sven-Erik, *From Stockholm to St. Petersburg,* Studia Historica, **II.** Helsinki: Finnish Historical Society, 1962.

Åström, Sven-Erik, "From Cloth to Iron: The Anglo–Baltic Trade in the Late 17th Century," Part I: "The Growth, Structure and Organization of the Trade," *Commentationes Humanum Litterarum,* **XXIII,** 1, 1963, 1–260.

Åström, Sven-Erik, "From Cloth to Iron: The Anglo–Baltic Trade in the Late 17th Century," Part II: "The Customs Accounts as Sources for the Study of Trade," *Commentationes Humanum Litterarum,* **XXXVII,** 3, 1965, 1–86.

Åström, Sven-Erik, "The Swedish Economy and Sweden's Role as a Great Power, 1632–1697," in M. Roberts, ed., *Sweden's Age of Greatness, 1632–1718.* New York: St. Martin's Press, 1973, 58–101.

Attman, Artur, *The Russian and Polish Markets in International Trade, 1500–1650.* Publications of the Institute of Economic History of Gothenburg University, No. 26, Göteborg, 1973.

Aubin, Hermann, "Die Anfänge der grossen schlesischen Leineweberei und -handlung," *Vierteljahrschrift für Sozial- und Wirtschaftsgeschichte,* **XXXV,** 2, 1942, 105–178.

Aylmer, Gerald E., "Office-holding, Wealth and Social Structure in England, c. 1580–c. 1720," paper at Istituto Internazionale di Storia Economica "Francesco Datini", Prato, 30 apr. 1974.

Aymard, Maurice, "Commerce et production de la soie sicilienne, aux XVIe–XVIIe siècles," *Mélanges d'archéologie et d'histoire,* **LXXVII,** 1965, 609–640.

Aymard, Maurice, *Venise, Raguse et le commerce du blé pendant la seconde moitié du XVIe siècle.* Paris: S.E.V.P.E.N., 1966.

Aymard, Maurice, "Une croissance sélective: la population sicilienne au XVIIe siècle," *Mélanges de la Casa de Velázguez,* **IV,** 1968, 203–227.

Aymard, Maurice, "Production, commerce et consommation des draps de laine," *Revue Historique,* No. 499, juil.–sept. 1971, 5–12. (a)

Aymard, Maurice, "In Sicilia: Sviluppo demografico e sue differenzatione geografiche, 1500–1800," *Quaderni storici,* No. 17, magg.–agosto 1971, 417–446.

Aymard, Maurice, "Economie rurale, économie marchande," in *Commerce de gros, commerce de detail dans les pays méditerranéens (XVIe–XIXe siècles),* Actes des Journées d'Etudes Bendor, 25–26 avr. 1975. Univ. de Nice: Centre de la Méditerranée Moderne et Contemporaine, 1976, 131–144.

Baehrel, René, "Economie et histoire à propos des prix," in *Eventail de l'histoire vivante: hommage à Lucien Febvre.* Paris: Lib. Armand Colin, 1953, **I,** 287–310.

Baehrel, René, "Histoire statistique et prix italiens," *Annales* E.S.C., **IX,** 2, avr.–juin 1954, 213–226.

Baehrel, René, *Une croissance: La Basse-Provence rurale (fin du XVIe siècle—1789).* Paris: S.E.V.P.E.N., 1961.

Baetens, R., "The Organization and Effects of Flemish Privateering in the Seventeenth Century," *Acta Historiae Neerlandicae,* **IX,** 1976, 48–75.

Bailyn, Bernard, "Communications and Trade: The Atlantic in the Seventeenth Century," *Journal of Economic History,* **XIII,** 4, Fall 1953, 378–387.

Bailyn, Bernard, *The New England Merchants in the Seventeenth Century.* Cambridge, Massachusetts: Harvard Univ. Press, 1955.

Bairoch, Paul, "Le rôle de l'agriculture dans la création de la sidérurgie moderne," *Revue d'historie économique et sociale,* **XLIV,** 1, 1966, 5–23.

Bairoch, Paul, "Le rôle du secteur tertiaire dans l'attenuation des fluctuations économiques," *Revue d'économie politique,* No. 1, 1968, 31–49.

Bairoch, Paul, "Agriculture and the Industrial Revolution, 1700–1914," in C. M. Cipolla, ed., *The Fontana Economic History of Europe,* **III:** *The Industrial Revolution.* London: Collins, 1973, 452–506.

Baker, Dennis, "The Marketing of Corn in the First Half of the Eighteenth Century: North-East Kent," *Agricultural History Review,* **XVIII,** 2, 1970, 126–150.

Baker, Norman, "Changing Attitudes towards Government in Eighteenth-Century Britain," in A. Whiteman, J. S. Bromley, & P. G. M. Dickson, eds., *Statesmen, Scholars and Merchants.* Oxford: Clarendon Press, 1973, 202–219.

Bakewell, P. J., *Silver Mining and Society in Colonial Mexico: Zacatecas, 1546–1700.* Cambridge: University Press, 1971.

Bakewell, P. J., "Zacatecas: An Economic and Social Outline of a Silver Mining District, 1547–1700," in Ida Altman & James Lockhart, eds., *Provinces of Early Mexico.* Los Angeles: UCLA Latin American Center Publication, 1976, 199–229.

Balibar, Etienne, "Sur les concepts fondamentaux du matérialisme historique," in Louis Althusser & Etienne Balibar, *Lire Le Capital,* nouv éd. entièrement refondue. Paris: Maspéro, 1968, **II,** 79–226.

Bamford, Paul Walden, "French Shipping in Northern European Trade, 1660–1789," *Journal of Modern History,* **XXVI,** 3, Sept. 1954, 207–219.

Bamford, Paul Walden, *Forests and French Sea Power, 1660–1789.* Toronto: Univ. of Toronto Press, 1956.

Bamford, Paul Walden, "Entrepreneurship in Seventeenth- and Eighteenth-Century France," *Explorations in Entrepreneurial History,* **IX,** 4, Apr. 1957, 204–213.

Bangs, Carl, "Dutch Theology, Trade and War: 1590–1610," *Church History,* **XXXIX,** 4, Dec. 1970, 470–482.

Baranowski, B. *et al., Histoire de l'économie rurale en Pologne jusqu'à 1864.* Wrocław: Zakład Narodowy Imienia Ossolinskich, Wydawnictwo Poskiej Akademii Nauk, 1966.

Barber, Elinor G., *The Bourgeoisie in 18th Century France.* Princeton, New Jersey: Princeton Univ. Press, 1955.

Barbour, Violet, "Marine Risks and Insurance in the Seventeenth Century," *Journal of Economic and Business History,* **I,** 1929, 561–596.

Barbour, Violet, "Dutch and English Merchant Shipping in the Seventeenth Century," in E. M. Carus-Wilson, ed., *Essays in Economic History,* **I.** London: Edw. Arnold, 1954, 227–253. (Originally in *Economic History Review,* **II,** 2, 1930.)

Barbour, Violet, *Capitalism in Amsterdam in the Seventeenth Century.* Ann Arbor: Univ. of Michigan Press, Ann Arbor Paperbacks, 1963.

Bargalló, Modesto, *La minería y la metalúrgica en la América Española durante la época colonial.* Mexico: Fondo de Cultura Económica, 1955.

Barker, Ernest, *The Development of Public Services in Western Europe, 1660–1930.* Hamden, Conn.: Archon Books, 1966.

Barker, Thomas M., *Double Eagle and Crescent.* Albany: State Univ. of New York Press, 1967.

Barker, Thomas M., "Military Entrepreneurship and Absolutism: Habsburg Models," *Journal of European Studies,* **IV,** 1, 1974, 19–42.

Barker, Thomas M., "Armed Service and Nobility in the Holy Roman Empire: General Aspects and Habsburg Particulars," *Armed Forces and Society,* **IV,** 3, May 1978, 449–500.

Barkhausen, Max, "Government Control and Free Enterprise in Western Germany and the Low Countries in the Eighteenth Century," in Peter Earle, ed., *Essays in European Economic History, 1500–1800.* Oxford: Clarendon Press, 1974, 212–273. (Translated from *Vierteljahrschrift fur Sozial- und Wirtschaftsgeschichte,* 1958.)

Barnett, Correlli, *Britain and Her Army, 1509–1970.* London: Pelican, 1974.

Baron, Salo W., *A Social and Religious History of the Jews,* **XV,** *Late Middle Ages and Era of European Expansion (1200–1650): Resettlement and Exploration.* New York: Columbia Univ. Press, 1973.

Barraclough, Geoffrey, *The Origins of Modern Germany.* Oxford: Basil Blackwell, 1962.

Barral, Pierre, "Note historique sur l'emploi du terme 'paysan'," *Etudes rurales,* No. 21, avr.–juin 1966, 72–80.

Barrett, Elinore M., *"Enconiendas, Mercedes,* and *Haciendas* in the *Tierra Caliente* of Michoacán," *Jahrbuch für Geschichte von Staat, Wirtschaft und Gesellschaft Lateinamerikas,* **X,** 1973, 71–111.

Barrett, Ward, "Caribbean Sugar Production Standards in the Seventeenth and Eighteenth Centuries," in J. Parker, ed., *Merchants and Scholars. Essays in the History of Exploration and Trade.* Minneapolis: Univ. of Minnesota Press, 1965, 145–170.

Barrow, Thomas C., *Trade and Empire: The British Customs Service in Colonial America, 1660–1775.* Cambridge, Mass.: Harvard Univ. Press, 1967.

Bassett, D. K., "Early English Trade and Settlement in Asia, 1602–1690," in J. S. Bromley and E. H. Kossmann, eds., *Britain and the Netherlands in Europe and Asia.* London: Macmillan, 1968, 83–109.

Batie, Robert Carlyle, "Why Sugar? Economic Cycles and the Changing of Staples in the English and French Antilles, 1624–54," *Journal of Caribbean History,* **VIII,** 1, Nov. 1976, 3–41.

Baynes, John, *The Jacobite Rising of 1715.* London: Cassell, 1970.

Bazant, Jan, "Feudalismo y capitalismo en la historia económica de México," *Trimestre económico,* **XVII,** 1, enero–marzo 1950, 84–98.

Bazant, Jan, "Evolution of the Textile Industry of Puebla: 1544–1845," *Comparative Studies in Society and History,* **VII,** 1, Oct. 1964, 56–69.

Beaujon, A., *History of the Dutch Sea Fisheries: Their Progress, Decline and Revival.* London: William Clowes & Sons, 1884.

Beer, George Louis, *The Old Colonial System 1660–1754,* Part I: *The Establishment of the System, 1660–1668,* 2 vols. New York: Macmillan, 1912.

Behrens, Betty, "Government and Society," *Cambridge Economic History of Europe,* **V:** E. E. Rich & C. H. Wilson, eds., *The Economic Organization of Early Modern Europe.* Cambridge: University Press, 1977, 549–620.

Beiguelman, Paula, "A destruição do escravismo capitalista," *Revista da História,* **XXIV,** 69, 1967, 149–160.

Bérenger, Jean, "Public Loans and Austrian Policy in the Second Half of the Seventeenth Century," *Journal of European Economic History,* **II,** 3, Winter 1973, 657–669.

Berengo, Marimo, & Diaz, Furio, "Noblesse et administration dans l'Italie de la Renaissance: la formation de la bureaucratie moderne," paper at XIII International Congress of Historical Sciences, Moscow, Apr. 16–23, 1970.

Berger, Patrice, "French Administration in the Famine of 1693," *European Studies Review,* **VIII,** 1, Jan. 1978, 101–127.

Bergier, Jean-François, "Il XVI secolo segnò l'inizio di una nuova concezione dei salari," *Revista storica italiana,* **LXXVIII,** 2, 1966, 431–438.

Bernard, Léon, "French Society and Popular Uprisings under Louis XIV," *French Historical Studies,* **III,** 4, Fall 1964, 454–474.

Berthe, Jean-Pierre, "Xochimancas: Les travaux et les jours dans une *hacienda* sucrière de Nouvelle-Espagne au XVIIe siècle," *Jahrbuch für Geschichte von Staat, Wirtschaft und Gesellschaft Lateinamerikas,* **III,** 1966, 88–117.

Berthold, Rudolf, "Wachstumprobleme der landwirtschaftlichen Nutzfläche in Spätfeudalismus (zirka 1500 bis 1800)," *Jahrbuch für Wirtschaftsgeschichte,* **II–III,** 1964, 5–23.

Besnier, R., *Histoire des faits économiques: La fin de la croissance et les prodromes d'une révolution économique en Europe au XVIIe siècle.* Cours de Doctorat, 1960–1961. Paris: Les Cours de Droit, polyc., 1961.

Beutin, Ludwig, "Nordwestdeutschland und die Niederlande seit dem Dressigjährigen Krieg," *Vierteljahrschrift für Sozial- und Wirtschaftsgeschichte,* **XXXII,** 2, 1939, 105–147.

Birch, Alan, "Foreign Observers of the British Iron Industry During the Eighteenth Century," *Journal of Economic History,* **XV,** 1, 1955, 23–33.

Blanchard, Marcel, "Le sel de France en Savoie (XVIIe et XVIIIe siècles)," *Annales d'histoire économique et sociale,* **IX,** 47, sept. 1937, 417–428.

Blaschke, Karlheinz, "Das Bauernlegen in Sachsen," *Vierteljahrschrift für Sozial- und Wirtschaftsgeschichte,* **XLII,** 2, 1955, 97–116.

Blitz, Rudolph C., "Mercantilist Policies and the Pattern of World Trade, 1500–1750," *Journal of Economic History,* **XXVII,** 1, Mar. 1967, 39–55.

Bloch, Marc, "La lutte pour d'individualisme agraire dans la France du XVIIIe siècle," *Annales d'histoire économique et social,* **II,** 7, juil. 1930, 329–383; **II,** 8, oct. 1930, 511–556.

Bloch, Marc, *French Rural History.* Berkeley: University of California Press, 1966.

Bluche, François, "L'origine sociale des Secrétaires d'État de Louis XIV (1661–1715), *XVIIe siècle,* Nos. 42–43, 1ᵉʳ trimestre 1959, 8–22.

Bodmer, Walter, "Tendenzen der Wirtschaftspolitik der eidgenossischen Orte in Zeitalter des Merkantilismus," *Schweizerische Zeitschrift für Geschichte,* **I,** 4, 1951, 562–598.

Boelcke, Willi, "Zur Geschichte der Gutscherrschaft und der zweiten Leibeigenschaft in der Oberlausitz," *Zeitschrift für Geschichtswissenschaft,* **IV,** 6, 1956, 1223–1232.

Boëthius, B., "Swedish Iron and Steel, 1600–1955," *Scandinavian Economic History Review,* **VI,** 2, 1958, 144–179.

Bog, Ingomar, *Der Reichsmerkantilismus.* Stuttgart: Gustav Fischer Verlag, 1959.

Bog, Ingomar, "Der Merkantilismus in Deutschland," *Jahrbuch für Nationalökonomie und Statistik,* **CLXXIII,** 9, Mai 1961, 125–145.

Bog, Ingomar, "Türkenkrieg und Agrarwirtschaft," in O. Pickl, her., *Die Wirtschaftlichen Auswirkungen der Türkenkriege,* Grazer Forschungen zur Wirtschafts- und Sozialgeschichte, **I.** Graz: 1971, 13–26.

Bogucka, Maria, "Merchants' Profits in Gdansk Foreign Trade in the First Half of the 17th Century," *Acta Poloniae Historica,* No. 23, 1971, 73–90.

Bogucka, Maria, "Le marché monétaire de Gdańsk et les problèmes de crédit public au cours de la première moitié du XVIIe siècle," Quarta settimana di studio, Istituto Internazionale di Storia Economica "Francesco Datini", Prato, 20 apr. 1972.

Bogucka, Maria, "Amsterdam and the Baltic in the First Half of the Seventeenth Century," *Economic History Review,* 2nd ser., **XXVI,** 3, Aug. 1973, 433–447.

Bogucka, Maria, "The Monetary Crisis of the XVIIth Century and its Social and Psychological Consequences in Poland," *Journal of European Economic History,* **VI,** 1, Spring 1975, 137–152.

Boissonade, P., *Le socialisme d'état: L'industrie et les classes industrielles pendant les deux premières siècles de l'ère moderne (1453–1661).* Paris: Lib. Ancienne Honoré Champion, 1927.

Bonney, Richard J., "The French Civil War, 1649–53," *European Studies Review,* **VIII,** 1, Jan. 1978, 71–100.

Bono, Salvatore, *I corsari barbareschi.* Torino: Ed. Rai, 1964.

Borelli, Giorgio, *Un patriazato della terraferma veneta tra XVII e XVIII secolo*. Milano: Dott. A. Giuffrè–Ed., 1974.

Bosher, J. F., *The Single Duty Project: A Study of the Movement for a French Customs Union in the Eighteenth Century*. London: Athlone Press, 1964.

Boswell, A. Bruce, "Poland," in A. Goodwin, ed., *The European Nobility in the Eighteenth Century*. New York: Harper & Row (Torchbooks), 1967, 154–171.

Boulle, Pierre H., "Slave Trade, Commercial Organization, and Industrial Growth in Eighteenth-Century Nantes," *Revue française d'histoire d'outre-mer*, **LIX**, 214, 1er trimestre 1972, 70–112.

Boulle, Pierre H., " 'Failed Transition,' Lombardy and France: General Comments," in Frederick Krantz & Paul M. Hohenberg, eds., *Failed Transitions to Modern Industrial Society: Renaissance Italy and Seventeenth Century Holland*. Montreal: Interuniversity Centre for European Studies, 1975, 72–74.

Bourde, André-J., "Louis XIV et l'Angleterre," *XVIIe siècle*, Nos. 46–47, 1er–2e trimestres 1960, 54–83.

Bouvier, Jean, "Vers le capitalisme bancaire: l'expansion du crédit après Law," in Fernand Braudel & Ernest Labrousse, dir., *Histoire économique et sociale de la France*, **II**: Ernest Labrousse *et al.*, *Des derniers temps de l'age seigneurial aux préludes de l'age industriel (1660–1789)*. Paris: Presses Univ. de France, 1970, 301–321.

Bouwsma, William J., "The Secularization of Society in the Seventeenth Century," paper delivered at XII International Congress of Historical Sciences, Moscow, Aug. 16–23, 1970. Moscow: Nauka, 1970.

Bowman, Francis, J., "Dutch Diplomacy and the Baltic Grain Trade, 1600–1660," *Pacific Historical Review*, **V**, 4, 1936, 337–348.

Boxer, C. R., *Salvador de Sá and the Struggle for Brazil and Angola*. London: Athlone Press, 1952.

Boxer, C. R., "Vicissitudes of the Anglo-Portuguese Alliance, 1600–1700," *Revista da faculdade de letras* (Univ. de Lisboa), ser. 3, 1958, 15–46.

Boxer, C. R., *Four Centuries of Portuguese Expansion, 1415–1825*. Johannesburg: Witswatersrand Univ. Press, 1961. (Reprinted by Univ. of California Press, 1969.)

Boxer, C. R., "Sedentary Workers and Seafaring Folk in the Dutch Republic," in J. S. Bromley & E. H. Kossman, eds., *Britain and the Netherlands*, **II**. Groningen: J. B. Wolters, 1964, 148–168.

Boxer, C. R., *The Dutch Seaborne Empire, 1600–1800*. New York: Knopf, 1965.

Boxer, C. R., "Brazilian Gold and British Traders in the First Half of the Eighteenth Century," *Hispanic American Historical Review*, **XLIX**, 3, Aug. 1969, 454–472. (a)

Boxer, C. R., *The Golden Age of Brazil, 1695–1750*. Berkeley: Univ. of California Press, 1969. (b)

Boxer, C. R., *The Portuguese Seaborne Empire, 1415–1825*. New York: Knopf, 1969. (c)

Boyer, Richard, "Mexico in the Seventeenth Century: Transition of Colonial Society," *Hispanic American Historical Review*, **LVII**, 3, Aug. 1977, 455–478.

Brading, D. A. & Cross, Harry E., "Colonial Silver Mining: Mexico and Peru," *Hispanic American Historical Review*, **LII**, 2, Nov. 1972, 545–579.

Braudel, Fernand, "L'économie française au XVIIe siècle," *Annales E.S.C.*, **VI**, 1, janv.–mars 1951, 65–71.

Braudel, Fernand, "L'économie de la Méditerranée au XVIIe siècle," *Les Cahiers de Tunisie*, **IV**, No. 14, 2e trimestre 1956, 175–197.

Braudel, Fernand, "L'histoire des civilisations: le passé explique le présent," in *Ecrits sur l'histoire*. Paris: Flammarion, 1969, 255–314. (Originally chap. V, in *Encyclopédie française*, **XX**, "Le Monde en devenir [Histoire, évolution, prospective]," 1959.)

Braudel, Fernand, *The Mediterranean and the Mediterranean World in the Age of Philip II*, 2 vol. New York: Harper & Row, 1973.

Braudel, Fernand, "Discorso inaugurale," in *La Lána come materia prima*, Atti della 'Prima

Settimana di Studio' (18–24 aprile 1969). Firenze: Istituto Internazionale di Storia Economica "F. Datini", Prato, 1974, 5–8.

Braudel, Fernand, *Afterthoughts on Material Civilization and Capitalism.* Baltimore: Johns Hopkins Univ. Press, 1977.

Braudel, Fernand, "The Expansion of Europe and the 'Longue Durée'," in H. L. Wesseling, ed., *Expansion and Reaction: Essays on European Expansion and Reaction in Asia and Africa.* Leiden: Leiden Univ. Press, 1978, 1–27.

Braudel, Fernand, Jeannin, Pierre, Meuvret, Jean, & Romano, Ruggiero, "Le déclin de Venise au XVIIe siècle," *Aspetti e cause della decandenza economica veneziana nel secolo XVII,* Atti del Convegno 27 giugno–2 luglio 1957. Venezia-Roma: Istituto per la Collaborazione Culturale, 1961, 23–86.

Braudel, Fernand & Spooner, Frank, "Prices in Europe from 1450 to 1750," in *The Cambridge Economic History of Europe,* **IV:** E. E. Rich & C. H. Wilson, eds., *The Economy of Expanding Europe in the Sixteenth and Seventeenth Centuries.* Cambridge: University Press, 1967, 374–480.

Braun, Rudolf, "Taxation, Sociopolitical Structure, and State-Building: Great Britain and Braudenburg-Prussia," in Charles Tilly, ed., *The Formation of National States in Western Europe.* Princeton, New Jersey: Princeton Univ. Press, 1975, 243–327.

Braure, Maurice, "Quelques aspects des relations commerciales entre la France et l'Angleterre au XVIIIe siècle," *Annales du Midi,* **LXV,** 21, janv. 1953, 67–89.

Breen, T. H., "A Changing Labor Force and Race Relations in Virginia, 1660–1710," *Journal of Social History,* **VII,** 1, Fall 1973, 3–25.

Brenner, Robert, "The Social Basis of English Commercial Expansion, 1550–1650," *Journal of Economic History,* **XXXII,** 1, Mar. 1972, 361–384.

Brenner, Robert, "England, Eastern Europe, and France: Socio-Historical versus 'Economic' Interpretation: General Conclusions," in Frederick Krantz & Paul M. Hohenberg, eds., *Failed Transitions to Modern Industrial Society: Renaissance Italy and Seventeenth Century Holland.* Montreal: Interuniversity Centre for European Studies, 1975, 68–71.

Brenner, Robert, "Agrarian Class Structure and Economic Development in Pre-Industrial Europe," *Past and Present,* No. 70, Feb. 1976, 30–75.

Briggs, Martin S., "Building Construction," in C. Singer, *et al., A History of Technology,* **III:** *From the Renaissance to the Industrial Revolution, c 1500–c 1750.* Oxford: Clarendon Press, 1957, 245–268.

Bromley, J. S., "The Channel Island Privateers in the War of the Spanish Succession," *La Société Guernesiaise, Report and Transactions for the Year 1949, XIV, 4, 1950, 444–478.*

Bromley, J. S., "The Decline of Absolute Monarchy (1638–1774)," in J. M. Wallace-Hadrill & John McManners, eds., *France: Government and Society.* London: Methuen, 1957, 134–160.

Bromley, J. S., "The French Privateering War, 1702–1713," in H. E. Bell & R. L. Ollard, eds., *Historical Essays 1600–1750 presented to David Ogg.* London: Adam & Charles Black, 1964, 203–231.

Bromley, J. S., "Introduction," in *New Cambridge Modern History,* **VI:** *The Rise of Great Britain and Russia, 1688–1725.* Cambridge: University Press, 1970, 1–36.

Bromley, J. S. & Ryan, A. N., "Armies and Navies: (3) Navies," in *New Cambridge Modern History,* **VI:** J. S. Bromley, ed., *The Rise of Great Britain and Russia, 1688–1725.* Cambridge: University Press, 1970, 790–833.

Brown, P. Hume, *The Legislative Union of England and Scotland.* Oxford: Clarendon Press, 1914.

Brown, Vera Lee, "Contraband Trade as a Factor in the Decline of Spain's Empire in America," *Hispanic American Historical Review,* **VIII,** 2, May 1928, 178–189.

Bruchey, Stuart, *The Roots of American Economic Growth, 1607–1861.* New York: Harper & Row, 1965.

Bruchey, Stuart, ed., *The Colonial Merchant. Sources and Readings.* New York: Harcourt, Brace & World, 1966.

Bruford, W. H., "The Organisation and Rise of Prussia," in *New Cambridge Modern History*, **VII:** J. O. Lindsay, ed., *The Old Regime, 1713–63*. Cambridge: University Press, 1966, 292–317.

Brulez, W., "Anvers de 1585 à 1650," *Vierteljahrschrift für Sozial- und Wirtschaftsgeschichte*, **LIV,** 1, 1967, 75–99.

Bulferetti, Luigi, "L'oro, la terra e la società: una interpretazione del nostro Seicento," *Archivio storico lombardo*, 8th ser., **IV**, 1953, 5–66.

Bulferetti, Luigi & Constantini, Claudio, *Industria e commercio in Liguria nell'età del Risorgimento (1700–1860)*. Milano: Banca Commerciale Italiana, 1966.

Burckhardt, Jacob, *Fragments historiques*. Geneve: Lib. Droz. 1965.

Bürgin, Alfred, "The Growth of the Swiss National Economy," in Hugh G. T. Aitken, ed., *The State and Economic Growth*. New York: Social Science Research Council, 1959, 213–236.

Burke, Peter, *Venice and Amsterdam: A Study of Seventeenth-Century Elites*. London: Temple Smith, 1974.

Burt, Roger, "Lead Production in England and Wales, 1700–1770," *Economic History Review*, 2nd ser., **XXII,** 2, Aug. 1969, 249–267.

Busquet, Raoul, Bourrilly, V.-L., & Agulhon, M., *Histoire de la Provence*. Paris: Presses Univ. de France, 1972.

Caizzi, Bruno. *Industria, commercio e banca in Lombardia nel XVIII secolo*. Milano: Banca Commerciale Italiana, 1968.

Campbell, R. H., "Anglo-Scottish Union of 1717: the Economic Consequences," *Economic History Review*, 2d ser., **XVI,** 3, Apr. 1964, 468–477.

Cancilo, Orazio, "I dazi sull'esportazione dei cereali e il commercio dei grani nel Regno di Sicilia," *Nuovi quaderni del meridione*, No. 28, ott.-dic. 1969, 1–36.

Cardozo, Manoel, "The Brazilian Gold Rush," *The Americas*, **III,** 2, Oct. 1946, 137–160.

Carlsson, Sten, "The Dissolution of the Swedish Estates, 1700–1865," *Journal of European Economic History*, **I,** 3, Winter 1972, 574–624.

Carmagnani, Marcello, *Les mécanismes de la vie économique dans une société coloniale: Le Chili (1680–1830)*. Paris: S.E.V.P.E.N., 1973.

Carmona, Maurice, "Aspects du capitalisme toscan au XVIe et XVIIe siècles," *Revue d'histoire moderne et contemporaine*, **XI,** 2, avr.-juin 1964, 81–108.

Carr, Raymond, "Two Swedish Financiers: Louis de Geer and Joel Gripenstierna," in H. E. Bell & R. L. Ollard, eds., *Historical Essays 1600–1750 presented to David Ogg*. London: Adam & Charles Black, 1964, 18–34.

Carrière, Charles, "La draperie languedocienne dans la seconde moitié du XVIII siècle (contribution à l'étude de la conjoncture levantine)," in *Conjoncture économique, structures sociales; Hommage à Ernest Labrousse*. Paris & La Haye: Mouton, 1974, 157–172.

Carstairs, A. M., "Some Economic Aspects of the Union of Parliaments," *Scottish Journal of Political Economy*, **II,** 1, Feb. 1955, 64–72.

Carsten, F. L., "Slaves in North-Eastern Germany," *Economic History Review*, **XI,** 1, 1941, 61–76.

Carsten, F. L., "The Origins of the Junkers," *English Historical Review*, **LXII,** No. 243, Apr. 1947, 145–178.

Carsten, F. L., "The Great Elector and the Foundation of the Hohenzollern Despotism," *English Historical Review*, **LXV,** No. 255, Apr. 1950, 175–202.

Carsten, F. L., *The Origins of Prussia*. Oxford: Clarendon Press, 1954.

Carsten, F. L., "Was There an Economic Decline in Germany Before the 30 Years War?" *English Historical Review*, **LXXI,** No. 279, Apr. 1956, 240–247.

Carsten, F. L., *Princes and Parliaments in Germany, from the Fifteenth to the Eighteenth Century*. Oxford: Clarendon Press, 1959.

Carsten, F. L., "Introduction: The Age of Louix XIV," in *The New Cambridge Modern History*, **V:** F. L. Carsten, ed., *The Ascendancy of France, 1648–88*. Cambridge: University Press, 1961, 1–18.

Carsten, F. L., "The Rise of Brandenburg," in *The New Cambridge Modern History*, **V**: F. L. Carsten, ed., *The Ascendancy of France, 1648–88.* Cambridge: University Press, 1969, 543–558.

Carswell, John, *The South Sea Bubble.* Stanford: Stanford Univ. Press, 1960.

Carswell, John, *The Descent on England.* New York: John Day, 1969.

Carter, Alice C., "The Dutch and the English Public Debt in 1777," *Economica*, n.s., **XX**, No. 78, May, 1953, 159–161. (a)

Carter, Alice C., "Dutch Foreign Investment, 1738–1800," *Economica*, n.s., **XX**, Nov., 1953, 322–340. (b)

Carter, Alice C., "The Huguenot Contribution to the Early Years of the Funded Debt, 1694–1714," *Proceedings of the Huguenot Society of London*, **XIX**, 3, 1955, 21–41.

Carter, Alice C., "Financial Activities of the Huguenots in London and Amsterdam in the Mid-Eighteenth Century," *Proceedings of the Huguenot Society of London*, **XIX**, 6, 1959, 313–333.

Carter, Alice C., "Note on *A Note on Yardsticks*," *Economic History Review*, 2nd. ser., **XII**, 3, Apr. 1960, 440–444.

Carter, Alice C., "The Dutch as Neutrals in the Seven Years War," *International and Comparative Law Quarterly*, **XII**, 3, July 1963, 818–834.

Carter, Alice C., "Britain as a European Power from her Glorious Revolution to the French Revolutionary War," in J. S. Bromley & E. H. Kossmann, eds., *Britain and the Netherlands in Europe and Asia.* London: Macmillan, 1968, 110–137.

Carter, Alice C., *The Dutch Republic in the Seven Years War.* Coral Gables, Fla.,: Univ. of Miami Press, 1971.

Carter, Alice C., ed., "Survey of Recent Dutch Historiography," *Acta Historiae Neerlandica*, **VI**, 1973, 175–200.

Carter, Alice C., *Neutrality or Commitment: The Evolution of Dutch Foreign Policy, 1667–1795.* London: Edw. Arnold, 1975. (a)

Carter, Alice C., *Getting, Spending and Investing in Early Modern Times.* Assen, Netherlands: Van Gorcum & Comp B. V., 1975. (b)

Castillo, Alvaro, "Dans la monarchie espagnole du XVIIe siècle: Les banquiers portugais et le circuit d'Amsterdam," *Annales E.S.C.*, **XIX**, 2, mars–avr. 1964, 311–316.

Castillo, Alvaro, "La coyuntura de la economía valenciana en los siglos XVI y XVII," *Anuario de historia económica y social*, **II**, 2, enero–dic. 1969, 239–288.

Cavignac, Jean, "Carrières et carriers du Bourgeois au XVIIIe siècle," in *Carrières, mines et métallurgie de 1610 à nos jours*, Actes du 98e Congrès National des Societes Savantes, Saint-Etienne, 1973, Section d'histoire moderne et contemporaine, **I.** Paris: Bibliothèque Nationale, 1975, 205–226.

Cernovodeanu, Paul, "The General Condition of English Trade in the Second Half of the 17th Century and at the Beginning of the 18th Century," *Revue des études du sud-est européen*, **V**, 3–4, 1967, 447–460.

Cernovodeanu, Paul, *England's Trade Policy in the Levant, 1660–1714.* Bibliotheca Historica Romaniae, Economic History Section Studies, **41**(2). Bucharest: Publishing House of the Academy of the Socialist Rep. of Romania, 1972.

Céspedes del Castillo, Guillermo, *Lima y Buenos Aires. Repercusiones económicas y políticas de la creación del Virreinato de La Plata.* Publicaciones de la Escuela de Estudios Hispano-Americanos de Sevilla, **XXIV.** Sevilla, 1947.

Chambers, J. D., "The Vale of Trent, 1670–1800," *Economic History Review Supplements*, No. 3. Cambridge: University Press, 1957.

Chambers, J. D., "Industrialization as a Factor in Economic Growth in England, 1700–1900," *First International Conference of Economic History*, Stockholm, Aug. 1960. Paris & La Haye: Mouton, 1960, 205–215.

Chambers, J. D., "The Rural Domestic Industries during the Period of Transition to the Factory System, with Special Reference to the Midland Counties of England," *Second International Conference of Economic History,* Aix-en-Provence, 1968, **II:** *Middle Ages and Modern Times,* Paris & La Haye: Mouton, 1965, 429–455.

Chandler, David G., "Armies and Navies, I: The Act of War on Land," in *New Cambridge Modern History,* **IV:** J. S. Bromley, ed., *The Rise of Great Britain and Russia, 1688–1725.* Cambridge: University Press, 1970, 741–762.

Chaudhuri, K. N., "The East India Company and the Export of Treasure in the Early Seventeenth Century," *Economic History Review,* 2d ser., **XVI,** 1, Aug. 1963, 23–38.

Chaudhuri, K. N., "Treasure and Trade Balances: the East India Company's Export Trade, 1660–1720," *Economic History Review,* **XXI,** 3, Dec. 1968, 480–502.

Chaunu, Huguette & Pierre, "Autour de 1640: politiques et économies atlantiques," *Annales E.S.C.,* **IX,** 1, janv.–mars 1954, 44–54.

Chaunu, Pierre, *Séville et l'Atlantique,* **VIII** (2bis): *La conjoncture (1593–1650).* Paris: S.E.V.P.E.N., 1959.

Chaunu, Pierre, "Les échanges entre l'Amérique espagnole et les anciens mondes aux XVIe, XVIIe, et XVIIIe siècles," *Information historique,* No. 5, nov.–déc. 1960, 207–216. (a)

Chaunu, Pierre, *Les Philippines et le Pacific des Ibériques (XVIe, XVIIe, XVIIIe siècles).* Paris: S.E.V.P.E.N., 1960. (b)

Chaunu, Pierre, "Brésil et l'Atlantique au XVIIe siècle," *Annales E.S.C.,* **XVII,** 6, nov.–déc. 1961, 1176–1207.

Chaunu, Pierre, "Jansénisme et frontière de catholicité (XVIIe et XVIIIe siècles): A propos du Jansénisme lorrain," *Revue historique, 86e année,* **CCXXVII,** 1, fasc. 461, 1er trimestre 1962, 115–138. (a)

Chaunu, Pierre, "Le renversement de la tendance majeure des prix et des activités au XVIIe siècle," *Studi in onore di Amintore Fanfani,* **IV:** *Evo moderno.* Milano: Dott. A. Giuffrè-Ed., 1962, 219–255. (b)

Chaunu, Pierre, "Manille et Macao, face à la conjoncture des XVIe et XVIIe siècles," *Annales E.S.C.,* **XVII,** 3, mai–juin 1962, 555–580. (c)

Chaunu, Pierre, "Las Casas et la première crise structurelle de la colonisation espagnole (1515–1523)," *Revue historique,* 87e année, **CCXXIX,** 1, fasc. 465, 1er trimestre 1963, 59–102. (a)

Chaunu, Pierre, "Le XVIIe siècle. Problèmes de conjoncture. Conjoncture globale et conjonctures rurales françaises," in *Mélanges d'histoire économique et social en hommage au professeur Antony Babel à l'occasion de son soixante-quinzième anniversaire.* Genève: La Tribune, 1963, **I,** 337–355. (b)

Chanu, Pierre, "Notes sur l'Espagne de Philippe V (1700–1746)," *Revue d'histoire économique et social,* **XLI,** 4, 1963, 448–470. (c)

Chaunu, Pierre, "Les 'Cristãos Novos' et l'effondrement de l'empire portugais dans l'Océan Indien au début du XVIIe siècle," *Revue des études juives,* 4e ser., **II** (CXXII), fasc. 1-2, janv.–juin 1963, 188–190. (d)

Chaunu, Pierre, *L'Amérique et les Amériques.* Paris: Lib. Armand Colin, 1964. (a)

Chaunu, Pierre, "La population de l'Amérique indienne," *Revue historique,* **CCXXXII,** 1, juil.–sept. 1964, 111–118. (b)

Chaunu, Pierre, "Les crises au XVIIe siècle de l'Europe reformée," *Revue historique,* **CCXXXIII,** 1, janv.–mars 1965, 23–60. (a)

Chaunu, Pierre, "Une histoire religieuse sérielle: A propos du diocèse de La Rochelle (1648–1724) et sur quelques exemples normands," *Revue d'histoire moderne et contemporaine,* **XII,** 1965, 5–34. (b)

Chaunu, Pierre, *La civilisation de l'Europe classique.* Paris: Arthaud, 1966. (a)

Chaunu, Pierre, "Le rythme trentenaire de l'expansion européenne," *Annales E.S.C.,* **XXI,** 4, juil.–août 1966, 886–893. (b)

Chaunu, Pierre, "Reflexions sur le tournant des années 1630–1650," *Cahiers d'histoire*, **XII**, 3, 1967, 249–268. (a)

Chaunu, Pierre, "A partir du Languedoc, De la peste noire à Malthus. Cinq siècles d'histoire sérielle," *Revue historique*, **CCXXXVII**, 2, fasc. 482, avr.–juin 1967, 359–380. (b)

Checkland, S. G., "Finance for the West Indies, 1780–1815," *Economic History Review*, 2d ser., **X**, 3, 1958, 461–469.

Cherepnin, L. V., "Russian Seventeenth-Century Baltic Trade in Soviet Historiography," *Slavonic and East European Review*, **XLIII**, No. 100, Dec. 1964, 1–22.

Cherry, George L., "The Development of the English Free-Trade Movement in Parliament, 1689–1702," *Journal of Modern History*, **XXV**, 2, June 1953, 103–119.

Chevalier, François, "Pour l'histoire du travail en Nouvelle Espagne: Une oeuvre fundamentale," *Annales E.S.C.*, **III**, 4, oct.–déc. 1948, 484–487.

Chevalier, François, *Land and Society in Colonial Mexico*. Berkeley: Univ. of California Press, 1970.

Christelow, Allen, "French Interest in the Spanish Empire during the Ministry of the Duc de Choiseul, 1759–1771," *Hispanic American Historical Review*, **XXI**, 4, Nov. 1941, 515–537.

Christelow, Allen, "Contraband Trade between Jamaica and the Spanish Main, and the Free Port Act of 1766," *Hispanic American Historical Review*, **XXII**, 2, May 1942, 309–343.

Christelow, Allen, "Economic Background of the Anglo-Spanish War of 1762," *Journal of Modern History*, **XVIII**, 1, Mar. 1946, 22–36.

Cipolla, Carlo M., "Aspetti e problemi nell'economia milanese e lombarda nei secoli XVI e XVII," in *Storia di Milano*, **XI.** *Il declino spagnolo (1630–1706)*, 1st ed. Milano: Fond. Treccani degli Alfieri per la Storia di Milano, 1958, 377–399.

Cipolla, Carlo M., *The Economic History of World Population*. rev. ed. Baltimore: Penguin Books, 1964.

Cipolla, Carlo M., *Guns, Sails and Empires*. New York: Pantheon, 1966.

Cipolla, Carlo M., "Introduction" to *The Fontana Economic History of Europe*, **IV:** *The Sixteenth and Seventeenth Centuries*. Glasgow: Collins, 1974, 7–13.

Clapham, (Sir) John, "The Growth of an Agrarian Proletariat, 1688–1832: A Statistical Note," *The Cambridge Historical Journal*, **I**, 1, 1923, 92–95.

Clapham, Sir John, *The Bank of England, I: 1694–1797*. Cambridge: University Press, 1944.

Clark, G. N., *The Dutch Alliance & the War Against French Trade, 1688–1697*. Univ. of Manchester Historical Series No. 42, Manchester, England: University Press, 1923.

Clark, G. N., "War, Trade and Trade War, 1701–13," *Economic History Review*, **I**, 2, Jan. 1928, 262–280.

Clark, G. N., "Early Capitalism and Invention," *Economic History Review*, **VI**, 2, Apr. 1936, 143–156.

Clark, G. N., *The Seventeenth Century*. 2nd ed. Oxford: Clarendon Press, 1960.

Clark, G. N., "The Nine Years War, 1688–1697," in *New Cambridge Modern History*, **VI:** J. S. Bromley, ed., *The Rise of Great Britain and Russia, 1688–1725*. Cambridge: University Press, 1970, 223–253.

Coats, A. W., "Changing Attitudes to Labour in the Mid-Eighteenth Century," *Economic History Review*, 2nd ser., **XI**, 1, Aug. 1958, 35–51.

Cohen, Jacob, "The Element of Lottery in British Government Bonds, 1684–1919," *Economica*, n.s., **XX**, No. 79, Aug. 1953, 237–246.

Coleman, D. C., "Labour in the English Economy of the Seventeenth Century," *Economic History Review*, 2nd ser., **VIII**, 3, Apr. 1956, 280–295.

Coleman, D. C., "Eli Heckscher and the Idea of Mercantilism," *Scandinavian Economic History Review*, **V**, 1, 1957, 3–25.

Coleman, D. C., "Technology and Economic History, 1500–1750," *Economic History Review*, 2d ser., **XI**, 3, 1959, 506–514.

Coleman, D. C., *Revisions in Mercantilism.* London: Methuen, 1969.

Coleman, D. C., *The Economy of England, 1450–1750.* London & New York: Oxford Univ. Press, 1977.

Cook, Sherburne F., & Borah, Woodrow, *Essays in Population History,* **I:** *Mexico and the Caribbean.* Berkeley: Univ. of California Press, 1971.

Cooper, J. P., "Sea Power," *The New Cambridge Modern History,* **IV.** J. P. Cooper, ed., *The Decline of Spain and the Thirty Years War, 1609–48/59.* Cambridge: University Press, 1970, 226–238.

Coornaert, E. L. J., "European Economic Institutions and the New World: the Chartered Companies," in E. E. Rich & C. H. Wilson, eds., *Cambridge Economic History of Europe,* **IV:** *The Economy of Expanding Europe in the Sixteenth & Seventeenth Centuries.* Cambridge: University Press, 1967, 220–274.

Corvisier, André, "Les généraux de Louis XIV et leur origine sociale," *XVIIe siècle,* Nos. 42–43, 1er trimestre 1959, 23–53.

Cottrell, Fred, *Energy and Society.* New York: McGraw-Hill, 1955.

Craeybeckx, Jan, "Les industries d'exportation dans les villes flamandes au XVIIe siècle, particulièrement à Gand et à Bruges," *Studi in onore di Amintore Fanfani,* **IV:** *Evo moderno.* Milano: Dott. A. Giuffrè–Ed., 1962, 411–468.

Craig, Gordon A., *The Politics of the Prussian Army, 1640–1945.* Oxford: Clarendon Press, 1955.

Craven, Wesley Frank, *The Colonies in Transition, 1660–1713.* New York: Harper & Row, 1968.

Croft, Pauline, "Free Trade and the House of Commons, 1605–6," *Economic History Review,* 2nd. ser., **XXVIII,** 1, Feb. 1975, 17–27.

Croot, Patricia & Parker, David, "Agrarian Class Structure and Economic Development," *Past and Present,* No. 78, Feb. 1968, 37–47.

Crosby, Alfred W., "Conquistador y Pestilencia: The First New World Pandemic and the Fall of the Great Indian Empires," *Hispanic American Historical Review,* **XLVII,** 3, Aug. 1967, 321–337.

Crouzet, François, "Angleterre et France au XVIII siècle. Essai d'analyse comparée de deux croissances économiques," *Annales E.S.C.,* **XXI,** 2, mars–avr. 1966, 254–291.

Crouzet, François, "The Economic History of Modern Europe," *Journal of Economic History,* **XXXI,** 1, Mar. 1971, 135–152.

Crouzet, François, "England and France in the Eighteenth Century," in Marc Ferro, ed., *Social Historians in Contemporary France.* New York: Harper & Row, 1972, 59–86. (Translated from *Annales E.S.C.,* 1966.)

Cullen, L. M., "Problems in the Interpretation and Revision of Eighteenth-Century Irish Economic History," *Transactions of the Royal Historical Society,* 5th ser., **XVII,** 1967, 1–22.

Cullen, L. M., *Anglo-Irish Trade, 1660–1800.* Manchester, England: Manchester Univ. Press, 1968.

Cullen, L. M., "Merchant Communities Overseas, the Navigation Acts and Irish and Scotish Responses," in L. M. Cullen & T. C. Smout, eds., *Comparative Aspects of Scottish and Irish Economic and Social History, 1600–1900.* Edinburgh: John Donald Publ., 1977, 165–176.

Cunningham, W., *The Growth of English Industry & Commerce in Modern Times,* 2 vol. Cambridge: University Press, 1892.

Cunningham, W., *Alien Immigrants to England.* London: Swan Sonnenschein, 1897.

Curtin, Philip D., "Epidemology and the Slave Trade," *Political Science Quarterly,* **LXXXIII,** 2, June 1968, 190–216.

Curtin, Philip D., *The Atlantic Slave Trade: A Census.* Madison: Univ. of Wisconsin Press, 1969.

Curtin, Philip D., "The Atlantic Slave Trade, 1600–1800," in J. F. A. Ajayi & M. Crowder, eds., *History of West Africa.* London: Longmans, 1971, **I,** 240–268.

Dahlgren, Stellan, "Estates and Classes," in M. Roberts, ed., *Sweden's Age of Greatness, 1632–1718.* New York: St. Martin's Press, 1973, 102–131. (a)

Dahlgren, Stellan, "Charles X and the Constitution," in M. Roberts, ed., *Sweden's Age of Greatness, 1632–1718.* New York: St. Martin's Press, 1973, 174–202. (b)

Dales, J. H., "The Discoveries and Mercantilism: An Essay in History and Theory," *Canadian Journal of Economics and Political Science,* **XXI,** 2, May 1955, 141–153.

Darby, H. C., "The Age of the Improver: 1600–1800," in H. C. Darby, ed., *A New Historical Geography of England.* Cambridge: University Press, 1973, 302–388.

Darby, H. C. & Fullard, Harold, eds., *Atlas,* Vol. **XIV** of *New Cambridge Modern History.* Cambridge: University Press, 1970.

da Silva, José-Gentil, "Au XVIIe siècle: la stratégie du capital florentin," *Annales E.S.C.,* **XIX,** 3, mai–juin 1964, 480–491. (a)

da Silva, José-Gentil, "Degradazione economica e ristagno secolare. Linee di sviluppo dell' economia spagnola dopo il secolo XVI," *Studi storici,* **V,** 2, 1964, 241–261. (b)

da Silva, José-Gentil, *En Espagne: développement économique, subsistance, déclin.* Paris & La Haye: Mouton, 1965.

da Silva, José-Gentil, "Les sociétés commerciales, la fructification du capital et la dynamique sociale, XVI-XVIIIe siècles," *Anuario de historia economica y social,* **II,** 2, enero–dic. 1969, 117–190.

Davies, C. S. L., "Peasant Revolt in France and England: A Comparison," *Agricultural History Review,* **XXI,** 2, 1973, 122–134.

Davies, K. G., "Joint-Stock Investment in the Later Seventeenth Century," *Economic History Review,* 2nd ser., **IV,** 3, 1952, 283–301. (a)

Davies, K. G., "The Origin of the Commission System in the West India Trade," *Transactions of the Royal Historical Society,* 5th ser., **II,** 1952, 89–107. (b)

Davies, K. G., *The Royal African Company.* London: Longmans, Green & Co., 1957.

Davies, K. G., "Empire and Capital," *Economic History Review,* 2nd ser., **XIII,** 1, Aug. 1960, 105–110.

Davies, K. G., *The North Atlantic World in the Seventeenth Century.* Minneapolis: Univ. of Minnesota Press, 1974.

Davis, Ralph, "English Foreign Trade, 1660–1700," *Economic History Review,* 2nd ser., **VII,** 2, Dec. 1954, 150–166.

Davis, Ralph, "Merchant Shipping in the Economy of the Late Seventeenth Century," *Economic History Review,* 2nd ser., **IX,** 1, Aug. 1956, 59–73.

Davis, Ralph, "Earnings of Capital in the English Shipping Industry, 1670–1730," *Journal of Economic History,* **XVII,** 3, 1957, 409–425.

Davis, Ralph, "England and the Mediterranean, 1570–1670," in F. J. Fisher, ed., *Essays in the Economic and Social History of Tudor and Stuart England.* Cambridge: University Press, 1961, 117–137.

Davis, Ralph, "English Foreign Trade, 1700–1774," *Economic History Review,* 2nd ser., **XV,** 2, Dec. 1962, 285–303.

Davis, Ralph, "The Rise of Protection in England, 1669–1786," *Economic History Review,* 2nd ser., **XIX,** 2, Aug. 1966, 306–317.

Davis, Ralph, review of Pierre Jeannin, *L'Europe du Nord-Ouest et du Nord aux XVII et XVIII siècles* (Paris: Presses Univ. de France, 1969) in *Economic History Review,* **XXIII,** 2, Aug. 1970, 387–388.

Davis, Ralph, *English Overseas Trade, 1500–1700, Studies in Economic History.* London: Macmillan, 1973. (a)

Davis, Ralph, *The Rise of the Atlantic Economies.* London: Weidenfeld & Nicolson, 1973. (b)

Davis, Ralph, *English Merchant Shipping and Anglo-Dutch Rivalry in the Seventeenth Century.* London: H.M.S.O., National Maritime Museum, 1975.

Deane, Phyllis, "The Output of the British Woollen Industry in the Eighteenth Century," *Journal of Economic History,* **XVII,** 2, 1957, 207–223.

Deane, Phyllis & Cole, W. A., *British Economic Growth, 1688–1959.* Cambridge: University Press, 1962.

de Beer, E. S., "The English Revolution," in *New Cambridge Modern History,* **VI:** J. S. Bromley, ed., *The Rise of Great Britain and Russia, 1688–1725.* Cambridge: University Press, 1970, 193–222.

Debien, Gabriel, *Le peuplement des Antilles françaises au XVIIe siècle: Les engagés partis de La Rochelle (1683–1715), Notes d'histoire coloniale,* **II.** Cairo: Institut Français d'Archéologie Orientale du Caire, 1942.

de Castro, Antonio Barros, "The Hands and Feet of the Planter: The Dynamics of Colonial Slavery," unpubl. ms., c. 1976.

Dechêne, Louise, *Habitants et marchands de Montréal au XVIIe siècle.* Paris, Plon, 1974.

Dehio, Ludwig, *The Precarious Balance.* New York: Vintage, 1962.

Delille, Gerard, review of M. Morineau, *Les faux semblemts d'un démarrage économique* in *Journal of European Economic History,* I, 3, Winter 1972, 809–812.

Delumeau, Jean, "Le commerce extérieur français au XVIIe siècle," *XVIIe siècle,* No. 70–71, 1966, 81–105.

de Maddalena, Aldo, "Rural Europe, 1500–1750," in C. M. Cipolla, ed., *The Fontana Economic History of Europe,* **II:** *The Sixteenth and Seventeenth Centuries.* Glasgow: Collins, 1974, 273–353. (a)

de Maddalena, Aldo, *Prezzi e mercedi a Milano dal 1701 al 1860.* Milano: Banco Commerciale Italiano, 1974. (b)

Dent, Julian, "An Aspect of the Crisis of the Seventeenth Century: The Collapse of the Financial Administration of the French Monarchy (1653–61)," *Economic History Review,* 2nd ser., **XX,** 2, Aug. 1967, 241–256.

Deprez, P., "The Demographic Development of Flanders in the Eighteenth Century," in D. V. Glass & D. E. C. Eversley, eds., *Population in History.* London: Edw. Arnold, 1965, 608–630.

Dermigny, Louis, "Saint-Domingue aux XVIIe et XVIIIe siècles," *Revue historique,* No. 204, oct.–déc. 1950, 234–239.

Dermigny, Louis, "Circuits de l'argent et milieux d'affaires au XVIIIe siècle," *Revue historique,* 78e année, No. 212, oct.–déc. 1954, 239–277.

Dermigny, Louis, "Le fonctionnement des Compagnies des Indes, I: L'organisation et le rôle des Compagnies," in M. Mollat, réd., *Sociétés et compagnies en Orient et dans l'Océan Indien.* Paris: S.E.V.P.E.N., 1970, 443–451. (a)

Dermigny, Louis, "Le fonctionnement des Compagnies des Indes, II. East India Company et Compagnie des Indes," in M. Mollat, réd., *Sociétés et compagnies en Orient et dans l'Océan Indien.* Paris: S.E.V.P.E.N., 1970, 453–466. (b)

Dermigny, Louis, "Gênes et le capitalisme financier," *Revue d'histoire économique et social,* **LII,** 4, 1974, 547–567.

de Roover, Raymond, *L'évolution de la lettre de change, XIVe–XVIIIe siècles.* Paris: Lib. Armand Colin, 1953.

de Roover, Raymond, "What is Dry Exchange? A Contribution to the Study of English Mercantilism," in Julius Kirshner, ed., *Business, Banking and Economic Thought in Late and Early Modern Europe: Selected Studies of Raymond de Roover.* Chicago, Illinois: Univ. of Chicago Press, 1974, 183–199. (a) (Originally in *Journal of Political Economics,* **LII,** 3, 1944, 250–266.)

de Roover, Raymond, "New Interpretations in the History of Banking," *Business, Banking, and Economic Thought in Late Medieval and Early Modern Europe.* Chicago, Illinois: Univ. of Chicago Press, 1974, 200–238. (b) (Originally in *Journal of World History,* **II,** 1954, 38–76.)

Deschamps, Hubert, *Pirates et flibustiers,* "Que sais-je?," No. 554. Paris: Presses Univ. de France, 1973.

Desdevises du Dézert, G., "Les institutions de l'Espagne," *Revue hispanique,* **LXX,** 1927, 1–556.

Dessert, Daniel & Journet, Jean-Louis, "Le lobby Colbert: Un royaume, ou une affaire de famille?," *Annales E.S.C.,* **XXX,** 6, nov.–déc. 1975, 1303–1336.

Devine, T. M., "Colonial Commerce and the Scottish Economy, c. 1730–1815," in L. M. Cullen & T. C. Smout, eds., *Comparative Aspects of Scottish and Irish Economic and Social History, 1600–1900.* Edinburgh: John Donald Publ., 1977, 177–190.

de Vries, Jan, "On the Modernity of the Dutch Republic," *Journal of Economic History,* **XXXIII,** 1, Mar. 1973, 191–202.

de Vries, Jan, *The Dutch Rural Economy in the Golden Age, 1500–1700.* New Haven, Connecticut: Yale Univ. Press, 1974.

de Vries, Jan, "Holland: Commentary," in Frederick Krantz & Paul M. Hohenberg, eds., *Failed Transitions to Modern Industrial Society: Renaissance Italy and Seventeenth Century Holland.* Montreal: Interuniversity Centre for European Studies, 1975, 55–57.

de Vries, Jan, *The Economy of Europe in an Age of Crisis, 1600–1750.* Cambridge: University Press, 1976.

de Vries, Jan, "Barges and Capitalism: Passenger Transportation in the Dutch Economy, 1632–1839," *A.A.G. Bijdragen,* No. 21, 1978, 33–398.

de Vries, Philip, "L'animosité anglo-hollandaise au XVIIe siècle," *Annales E.S.C.,* **V,** 1, janv.–mars 1950, 42–47.

Deyon, Pierre, "Variations de la production textile aux XVIe et XVIIe siècles: sources et premiers résultats," *Annales E.S.C.,* **XVIII,** 5, sept.–oct. 1963, 939–955.

Deyon, Pierre, "A propos des rapports entre la noblesse française et la monarchie absolue pendant la première moitié du XVIIe siècle," *Revue historique,* **CCXXI,** 2, fasc. 470, avr.–juin 1964, 341–356.

Deyon, Pierre, "La production manufacturière en France au XVIIe siècle et ses problèmes," *XVIIe siècle,* Nos. 70–71, 1966, 47–63.

Deyon, Pierre, *Amiens, capitale provinciale.* Paris & La Haye: Mouton, 1967.

Deyon, Pierre, *Le mercantilisme,* Questions d'histoire, 11. Paris: Flammarion, 1969.

Deyon, Pierre, "La concurrence internationale des manufactures lainières aux XVIe et XVIIe siècles," *Annales E.S.C.,* **XXVII,** 1, janv.–févr. 1972, 20–32.

Deyon, Pierre, "Théorie et pratique de mercantilisme," in Pierre Deyon & Jean Jacquart, *Les hésitations de la croissance, 1580–1740,* Vol. **II** of Pierre Léon, réd., *Histoire économique et sociale du monde.* Paris: Lib. Armand Colin, 1978, 197–218. (a)

Deyon, Pierre, "Compétitions commerciales et coloniales," in Pierre Deyon & Jean Jacquart, *Les hésitations de la croissance, 1580–1740,* Vol. **II** of Pierre Léon, réd., *Histoire économique et sociale du monde.* Paris: Lib. Armand Colin, 1978, 219–247. (b)

Deyon, Pierre, "Le rôle animateur des marchands," in Pierre Deyon & Jean Jacquart, *Les hésitations de la croissance, 1580–1740,* Vol. **II** of Pierre Léon, réd., *Histoire économique et sociale du monde.* Paris: Lib. Armand Colin, 1978, 263–289. (c)

Deyon, Pierre, "La production manufacturière," in Pierre Deyon & Jean Jacquart, *Les hésitations de la croissance, 1580–1740,* Vol. **II** of Pierre Léon, réd., *Histoire économique et sociale du monde.* Paris: Lib. Armand Colin, 1978, 263–289. (d)

Deyon, Pierre, "Les sociétés urbaines," in Pierre Deyon & Jean Jacquart, *Les hésitations de la croissance, 1580–1740,* Vol. **II** of Pierre Léon, réd., *Histoire économique et sociale du monde.* Paris: Lib. Armand Colin, 1978, 291–316. (e)

Deyon, Pierre & Jacquart, Jean, "L'Europe: gagnants et perdants," in Pierre Deyon & Jean Jacquart, *Les hésitations de la croissance, 1580–1740,* Vol. **II** of Pierre Léon, réd., *Histoire économique et sociale du monde.* Paris: Lib. Armand Colin, 1978, 497–519.

de Zeeuw, J. W., "Peat and the Dutch Golden Age: The Historical Meaning of Energy Attainability," *A.A.G. Bijdragen,* No. 21, 1978, 3–31.

Dickens, A. G., "Preface," *The Anglo-Dutch Contribution to the Civilization of Early Modern Society.* London & New York: Published for The British Academy by Oxford Univ. Press, 1976, 8–10.

Dickerson, Oliver M., *The Navigation Acts and the American Revolution.* Philadelphia: Univ. of Pennsylvania Press, 1951.

Dickson, P. G. M., *The Financial Revolution in England: A Study in the Development of Public Credit, 1688–1756.* London: Macmillan, 1967.

Dickson, P. G. M., "English Commercial Negotiations with Austria, 1737–1752," in A. Whiteman, J. S. Bromley, & P. G. M. Dickson, eds., *Statesmen, Scholars and Merchants.* Oxford: Clarendon Press, 1973, 81–112.

Disney, A. R., "The First Portuguese India Company, 1628–33," *Economic History Review,* 2nd ser., **XXX,** 2, May 1977, 242–258.

Dobb, Maurice H., "The English Revolution, II," *Labour Monthly,* **XXIII,** 2, Feb. 1941, 92–93.

Dobb, Maurice H., *Studies in the Development of Capitalism.* London: Routledge & Kegan Paul, 1946.

Dobb, Maurice H., "A Reply," in Rodney Hilton, ed., *The Transition from Feudalism to Capitalism.* London: New Left Books, 1976, 57–67. (Originally in *Science and Society,* Spring 1958.)

Dobyns, Henry F., "An Outline of Andean Epidemic History to 1720," *Bulletin of the History of Medicine,* **XXXVII,** 6, Nov.–Dec. 1963, 493–515.

Dominguez Ortiz, Antonio, *La sociedad española en el siglo XVII,* Monografias historico-sociales, **I.** Madrid: Instituto Balmes de Sociologia, Depto. de Historia Social, 1955.

Dominguez Ortiz, Antonio, *The Golden Age of Spain, 1516–1659.* New York: Basic Books, 1971.

Donnan, Elizabeth, "The Early Days of the South Sea Company, 1711–1718," *Journal of Economic and Business History,* **II,** 3, May 1930, 419–450.

Dorn, Walter L., "The Prussian Bureaucracy in the Eighteenth Century," *Political Science Quarterly,* **XLVI,** 3, Sept. 1931, 403–423; **XLVII,** 1, Mar. 1932, 75–94; **XLVII,** 2, June 1932, 259–273.

Dorwart, Reinhold A., *The Administrative Reforms of Frederick William I of Prussia.* Cambridge, Massachusetts: Harvard Univ. Press, 1953.

Dorwart, Reinhold A., *The Prussian Welfare State before 1740.* Cambridge, Massachusetts: Harvard Univ. Press, 1971.

Duckham, Baron F., *A History of the Scottish Coal Industry,* **I:** *1700–1815.* Newton Abbot: David & Charles, 1970.

Duncan, T. Bentley, *Atlantic Islands: Madeira, the Azores and the Cape Verdes in Seventeenth-Century Commerce and Navigation.* Chicago, Illinois: Univ. of Chicago Press, 1972.

Duncan, T. Bentley, "Neils Steensgaard and the Europe-Asia Trade of the Early Seventeenth Century," *Journal of Modern History,* **XLVII,** 3, Sept. 1975, 512–518.

Dunn, Richard S., *Sugar and Slaves.* Chapel Hill: Univ. of North Carolina Press, 1972.

Dunsdorfs, Edgars, *Merchant Shipping in the Baltic During the 17th Century,* Contributions of Baltic University, No. 40, Pinneberg, 1947.

Dunsdorfs, Edgars, *Der grosse schwedische Kataster in Livland, 1681–1710,* Kungl. Vitterhets Historie och Antikvitets Akademiens Handlingar, del 72. Stockholm: Wahlstrom & Widstrand, 1950.

Dupâquier, J. (& Jacquart, J.), "Les rapports sociaux dans les campagnes françaises au XVIIe siècle: quelques exemples," in D. Roche, réd., *Ordres et classes,* Colloque d'histoire sociale, Saint-Cloud, 24–25 mai 1967. Paris & La Haye: Mouton, 1973, 167–179.

Dupuy, Alex, "Spanish Colonialism and the Origin of Underdevelopment in Haiti," *Latin American Perspectives,* **III,** 2, Spring 1976, 5–29.

Durand, Georges, "Vin, vigne et vignerons en Lyonnais et Beaujolais (XVIe–XVIIIe siècles)," *Cahiers d'histoire,* **XXII,** 2, 1977, 123–133.

Durand, Yves, *Finance et mécénat: Les fermiers généraux au XVIIIe siècle.* Paris: Lib. Hachette, 1976.

Durie, Alastair J., "The Markets for Scottish Linen, 1730–1775," *Scottish Historical Review,* **LII,** Nos. 153–154, 1973, 30–49.

Dworzaczek, Włodzimierz, "La mobilité sociale de la noblesse polonaise aux XVIe et XVIIe siècles," *Acta Poloniae Historica,* No. 36, 1977, 147–161.

Eagly, Robert V., "Monetary Policy and Politics in Mid-Eighteenth Century Sweden," *Journal of Economic History,* **XXIX,** 4, Dec. 1969, 739–757.

Eagly, Robert V., "Monetary Policy and Politics in Mid Eighteenth Century Sweden: A Reply," *Journal of Economic History,* **XXX,** 3, Sept. 1970, 655–656.

Eagly, Robert V., "Introductory Essay," to *The Swedish Bullionist Controversy: P. N. Christiernin's Lectures on the High Price of Foreign Exchange in Sweden (1761).* Philadelphia, Pennsylvania: Amer. Philosophical Soc., 1971, 1–37.

East, W. G., "England in the Eighteenth Century," in H. C. Darby, *Historical Geography of England before A.D. 1800.* Cambridge: University Press, 1951, 465–528.

Edel, Matthew, "The Brazilian Sugar Cycle of the Seventeenth Century and the Rise of West Indian Competition," *Caribbean Studies,* **IX,** 1, Apr. 1969, 24–44.

Ehrman, John, *The Navy in the War of William III, 1689–1697.* Cambridge: University Press, 1953.

Elliott, J. H., *The Revolt of the Catalans.* Cambridge: University Press, 1963.

Elliott, J. H., *Imperial Spain, 1469–1716.* New York: Mentor Books, 1966.

Elliott, J. H., "Revolution and Continuity in Early Modern Europe," *Past and Present,* No. 42, Feb. 1969, 35–56.

Elliott, J. H., "Self-Perception and Decline in Early Seventeenth-Century Spain," *Past and Present,* No. 74, Feb. 1977, 41–61.

Emmanuel, Arghiri, *Unequal Exchange.* New York: Monthly Review Press, 1972.

Emmer, Pieter C., "The History of the Dutch Slave Trade: A Bibliographical Survey," *Journal of Economic History,* **XXXII,** 3, Sept. 1972, 728–747.

Endelman, Todd M., *The Jews of Georgian England, 1714–1830.* Philadelphia, Pennsylvania: Jewish Publ. Soc. of America, 1979.

Endrei, Walter G., "English Kersey in Eastern Europe with special reference to Hungary," *Textile History,* **V,** 1974, 90–99.

Enjalbert, Henry, "Le commerce de Bordeaux et la vie économique dans le Bassin Aquitaine au XVIIe siècle," *Annales du Midi,* **LXII,** 9, janv. 1950, 21–35.

Ernle, Lord (Prothero, Rowland E.), *English Farming, Past and Present.* London: Longmans, Green & Co., 1912.

Everitt, Alan, "The Food Market of the English Town, 1660–1760," *Third International Conference of Economic History,* **I,** Munich, 1956. Paris & La Haye: Mouton, 1968, 57–71.

Eversley, D. C. E., "Demography and Economics. A Summary Report," *Third International Conference of Economic History,* Munich, 1965, *Demography and Economy.* Paris & La Haye: Mouton, 1972, 15–35.

Faber, J. A., "Cattle Plague in the Netherlands During the Eighteenth Century," *Mededelingen van de Landbouwgeschool te Wageningen,* **LXII,** 11, 1962, 1–7.

Faber, J. A., "The Decline of the Baltic Grain Trade in the Second Half of the Seventeenth Century," *Acta Historiae Neerlandica,* **I,** 1966, 108–131.

Faber, J. A., Diedericks, H. A., & Hart, S., "Urbanization, Industrialization, and Pollution in the Netherlands, 1500–1800," paper prepared for VIth International Congress on Economic History, Copenhagen, 1974, 21 p., mimeographed. Published in Dutch in *A.A.G. Bijdragen,* No. 18, 1973, 251 271.

Faber, J. A., Roessingh, H. K., Slicher Van Bath, B. H., Van der Woude, A. M., & Van Xanten, H. J., "Population Changes & Economic Developments in the Netherlands, A Historical Survey," *A.A.G. Bijdragen,* No. 12, 1965, 47–114.

Fairlie, Susan, "Dyestuffs in the Eighteenth Century," *Economic History Review,* 2nd ser., **XVII,** 3, Apr. 1965, 488–510.

Fanfani, Amintore, *Storia del lavoro in Italia dalla fine del secolo XV agli inizi del XVIII.* 2a ed. accresc. ed illus., Vol. **III** of A. Fanfani, ed., *Storia del lavoro in Italia.* Milano: Dott. A. Giuffrè–Ed., 1959.

Farnell, J. E., "The Navigation Act of 1651, the First Dutch War, and the London Merchant Community," *Economic History Review,* 2nd ser., **XVI,** 3, Apr. 1964, 439–454.

Farnie, D. A., "The Commercial Empire of the Atlantic, 1607–1783," *Economic History Review,* 2d ser., **XV,** 2, Dec. 1962, 205–218.

Fayle, C. Ernest, "The Deflection of Strategy by Commerce in the Eighteenth Century," *Journal of the Royal United Service Institution,* **LXVIII,** 1923, 281–290.

Febvre, Lucien, "De l'histoire-tableau: Essais de critique constructive," *Annales d'histoire économique et sociale,* **V,** No. 21, 31 mai 1933, 267–281.

Fedorowicz, Jan K., "Anglo-Polish Commercial Relations in the First Half of the Seventeenth Century," *Journal of European Economic History,* **V,** 2, Fall 1976, 359–378.

Fernández de Pinedo, Emiliano, *Crecimiento económico y transformaciones sociales del país vasco (1100–1850).* Madrid, Siglo XXI de España, 1974.

F[ield], P[eter], "England's Revolution," review of Christopher Hill, ed., *The English Revolution, 1640,* in *Labour Monthly,* **XXII,** 10, Oct. 1940, 558–559. (a)

F[ield], P[eter], "The English Revolution, 1640: II. A Rejoinder," *Labour Monthly,* **XXII,** 12, Dec. 1940, 653–655. (b)

Finer, Samuel E., "State and Nation-Building in Europe: The Role of the Military," in Charles Tilly, ed., *The Formation of National States in Western Europe.* Princeton, New Jersey: Princeton Univ. Press, 1975, 84–163.

Fischer, Wolfram & Lundgreen, Peter, "The Recruitment and Training of Administrative and Technical Personnel," in Charles Tilly, ed., *The Formation of National States in Western Europe.* Princeton, New Jersey: Princeton Univ. Press, 1975, 456–561.

Fisher, F. J., "London's Export Trade in the Early Seventeenth Century," *Economic History Review,* 2d ser., **III,** 2, 1950, 151–161.

Fisher, F. J., "Tawney's Century," in F. J. Fisher, ed., *Essays in the Economic and Social History of Tudor and Stuart England.* London & New York: Cambridge Univ. Press, 1961, 1–14.

Fisher, Sir Godfrey, *Barbary Legend: War, Trade and Piracy in North Africa, 1475–1830.* Oxford: Clarendon Press, 1957.

Fisher, H. E. S., "Anglo-Portuguese Trade, 1700–1770," *Economic History Review,* 2d ser., **XVI,** 2, 1963, 219–233.

Fisher, H. E. S., *The Portugal Trade: A Study of Anglo-Portuguese Commerce, 1700–1770.* London: Methuen, 1971.

Flinn, M. W., "The Growth of the English Iron Industry, 1660–1760," *Economic History Review,* **XI,** 1, Aug. 1958, 144–153.

Flinn, M. W., "Sir Ambrose Crowley and the South Sea Scheme of 1711," *Journal of Economic History,* **XX,** 1, Mar. 1960, 51–66.

Flinn, M. W., "Agricultural Productivity and Economic Growth in England, 1700–1760: A Comment," *Journal of Economic History,* **XXVI,** 1, Mar. 1966, 93–98.

Flinn, M. W., "The Stabilisation of Mortality in Pre-industrial Western Europe," *Journal of European Economic History,* **III,** 2, Fall 1974, 285–318.

Florescano, Enrique, *Precios del maíz y crisis agrícolas en México (1708–1810).* México: El Colegio de México, 1969.

Floyd, Troy S., *The Anglo-Spanish Struggle for Mosquita.* Albuquerque: Univ. of New Mexico Press, 1967.

Forbes, R. J., "Food and Drink," in C. Singer *et al., A History of Technology.* **III:** *From the Renaissance to the Industrial Revolution, c1500–c1700.* Oxford: Clarendon Press, 1957, 1–26.

Ford, Franklin L., *Robe and Sword: The Regrouping of the French Aristocracy After Louis XIV,* Harvard Historical Studies, Vol. **XXIV.** Cambridge, Massachussetts: Harvard Univ. Press, 1953.

Forster, Robert, "Obstacles to Agricultural Growth in Eighteenth-Century France," *American Historical Review,* **LXXV,** 6, Oct. 1970, 1600–1615.

Forster, Robert & Litchfield, R. Burr, "Four Nobilities of the Old Regime (review article)," *Comparative Studies in Society and History,* **VII,** 3, Apr. 1965, 324–332.

Fourastié, Jean & Grandamy, René, "Remarques sur les prix salariaux des céréales et la productivité du travailleur agricole en Europe du XVe et XVIe siècles," *Third International Conference of Economic History,* **I,** Munich, 1965. Paris & La Haye: Mouton, 1968, 647–656.

Francis, A. D., *The Methuens and Portugal, 1691–1708.* Cambridge: University Press, 1966.

Francis, A. D., *The Wine Trade.* Edinburgh: T. & A. Constable, 1972.

Frank, André Gunder, *Mexican Agriculture: Transformation of Mode of Production, 1521–1630.* Cambridge: Cambridge Univ. Press, 1979. (a)

Frank, André Gunder, *Dependent Accumulation and Underdevelopment.* New York: Monthly Review Press, 1979. (b)

Franken, M. A. M., "The General Tendencies and Structural Aspects of the Foreign Policy and Diplomacy of the Dutch Republic in the Latter Half of the 17th Century," *Acta Historiae Neerlandica,* **III,** 1968, 1–42.

Frèche, Georges, *Toulouse et la région, Midi-Pyrénées au siècle des lumières vers 1670–1789.* Mayenne: Ed. Cujas, 1974.

Freudenberger, Herman, "Industrialization in Bohemia and Moravia in the Eighteenth Century," *Journal of Central European Affairs,* **XIX,** 4, Jan. 1960, 347–356. (a)

Freudenberger, Herman, "The Woolen-Goods Industry of the Habsburg Monarchy in the Eighteenth Century," *Journal of Economic History,* **XX,** 3, Sept. 1960, 383–406. (b)

Friedrichs, Christopher R., "Capitalism, Mobility and Class Formation in the Early Modern German City," *Past and Present,* No. 69, Nov. 1975, 24–49.

Furniss, Edgar S., *The Position of the Labourer in a System of Nationalism.* New York: Kelley & Millman, 1957. (Original publication, Boston, 1920.)

Furtado, Celso, *The Economic Growth of Brazil.* Berkeley: Univ. of California Press, 1963.

Fussell, G. E., "Low Countries: Influence on English Farming," *English Historical Review,* **LXXIV,** No. 293, Oct. 1959, 611–622.

Fussell, G. E., "Dairy Farming, 1600–1900," *Third International Conference of Economic History,* Munich, 1965, **II:** *Production et productivité agricoles.* Paris & La Haye: Mouton, 1968, 31–36.

Gaastra, F., Summary of paper delivered at Nederlands Historisch Genootschap, 24–25 Oct. 1975, title translated as "The Dutch East India Company in the Seventeenth and Eighteenth Centuries: the Growth of the Concern; Money for Goods; A Structural Change in Dutch-Asian Trading Relations, in *Newsletter,* Centre for the Study of European Expansion, **I,** 0, 1976, 18–19.

Galenson, David, "The Slave Trade to the English West Indies, 1673–1724," *Economic History Review,* 2nd ser., **XXXII,** 2, May 1979, 241–249.

Galloway, J. H., "Northeast Brazil, 1700–50: The Agricultural Crisis Re-examined," *Journal of Historical Geography,* **I,** 1, Jan. 1975, 21–38.

Garman, Douglas, "The English Revolution, 1640: I, A Reply to P. F.," *Labour Monthly,* **XXII,** 12, Dec. 1940, 651–653.

Gately, Michael O., Moote, A. Lloyd, & Wills, John E., Jr., "Seventeenth-Century Peasant 'Furies': Some Problems of Comparative History," *Past and Present,* No. 51, May 1971, 63–80.

George, C. H., "The Making of the English Bourgeoisie, 1500–1750," *Science and Society,* **XXXV,** 4, Winter 1971, 385–414.

George, Dorothy, *England in Transition.* London: Penguin, 1953, published with additions.

Georgelin, J., "Ordres et classes à Venise aux XVIIe et XVIIIe siècles," in D. Roche, réd., *Ordres et classes,* Colloque d'histoire sociale, Saint-Cloud, 24–25 mai 1967. Paris & La Haye: Mouton, 1973, 193–197.

Geremek, Bronisław, review of Jerzy Topolski, *O tak zwanym kryzysic gospodarczym w. w Europie* (Sur la pretendu crise économique du XVIIe siècle en Europe), *Kwartalnik Historyczny,* **LXIX,** 2, 1962, 364–379, in *Annales E. S. C.,* **XVIII,** 6, nov.–déc. 1963, 1206–1207.

Geremek, Bronisław, "La populazione marginale tra il medioevo e l'èra moderna," *Studi storici,* **IX,** 3–4, lugl.-dic. 1968, 623–640.

Geyl, Pieter, *The Netherlands in the Seventeenth Century,* Part One: *1609–1648.* London: Ernest Benn, 1961.

Geyl, Pieter, *The Netherlands in the Seventeenth Century,* Part Two: *1648–1715.* London: Ernest Benn, 1964.

Gibbs, F. W., "Invention in Chemical Industries," in C. Singer *et al., A History of Technology,* **III:** *From the Renaissance to the Industrial Revolution, c1500–c1700.* Oxford: Clarendon Press, 1957, 676–708.

Gierowski, Józef, "Les recherches sur l'histoire de Pologne du XVIe au XVIIIe siècle au cours de 1945–1965," in *La Pologne au XIIe Congrès International des Sciences Historiques à Vienne.* Warszawa: PWN, 1965, 229–263.

Giesey, Ralph E., "National Stability and Hereditary Transmission of Political and Economic Power," paper delivered at XIV International Congress of Historical Sciences, San Francisco, Aug. 22–29, 1975, 19 pp.

Gieysztorowa, Irena, "Guerre et régression en Masovie aux XVI et XVIIIe siècles," *Annales E.S.C.,* **XIII,** 4, oct.–déc. 1958, 651–668.

Gilboy, Elizabeth Waterman, "Wages in Eighteenth-Century England," *Journal of Economic and Business History,* **II,** 1930, 603–629.

Gill, Conrad, *The Rise of the Irish Linen Industry.* Oxford: Clarendon Press, 1925.

Glamann, Kristof, *Dutch-Asiatic Trade 1620–1740.* Copenhagen, Denmark: Danish Science Press, 1958.

Glamann, Kristof, "European Trade 1500–1750," in C. M. Cipolla, ed., *The Fontana Economic History of Europe,* **II:** *The Sixteenth and Seventeenth Centuries.* Glasgow: Collins, 1974, 427–526.

Glamann, Kristof, "The Changing Patterns of Trade," in *Cambridge Economic History of Europe,* **V:** E. E. Rich & C. H. Wilson, eds., *The Economic Organization of Early Modern Europe.* Cambridge: Cambridge Univ. Press, 1977, 185–289.

Glass, D. V., "Two Papers on Gregory King," in D. V. Glass & D. E. C. Eversley, eds., *Population in History.* London: Edw. Arnold, 1965, 159–220.

Glenday, Daniel G., "French Mercantilism and the Atlantic Colonies (With Specific Reference to New France), 1494–1672," unpubl. M. A. thesis, McGill University, January 1975.

Godinho, Vitorino Magalhães, "Le commerce anglais et l'Amérique espagnole au XVIIIe siècle," *Annales E.S.C.,* **III,** 4, oct.–déc. 1948, 551–554.

Godinho, Vitorino Magalhães, "Création et dynamisme économique du monde atlantique (1420–1670)," *Annales E.S.C.,* **V,** l, janv.–mars 1950, 32–36. (a)

Godinho, Vitorino Magalhães, "Le Portugal, les flottes du sucre et les flottes de l'or (1670–1770)," *Annales E.S.C.,* V, 2, avr.–juin 1950, 184–197. (b)

Godinho, Vitorino Magalhães, "Portugal, as frotas do açúcar e as frotas do ouro 1670–1770," *Revista de história,* **XV,** 1953, 69–88.

Godinho, Vitorino Magalhães, "L'émigration portugaise du XV siècle à nos jours: Histoire d'une constante structurale," in *Conjoncture économique, structures sociales,* Hommage à Ernest Labrousse. Paris & La Haye: Mouton, 1974.

Gongora, Mario, "Vagabondage et société pastorale en Amérique latine (spécialement au Chili central)," *Annales E.S.C.,* **XXI,** 1, janv.–févr. 1966, 159–177.

Goodwin, Albert, "The Social Structure and Economic and Political Attitudes of the French Nobility in the Eighteenth Century," *XIIe Congrès International des Sciences Historiques: Rapports,* **I:** *Grands thèmes.* Wien: Verlag Ferdinand Berger & Söhne, 1975, 356–368.

Gorlitz, Walter, *Die Junker: Adel und Bauer in deutschen Osten.* Glücksburg/Ostsee: Verlag von C. A. Starke, 1956.

Goslinga, Cornelis Ch., *The Dutch in the Caribbean and on the Wild Coast, 1580–1680.* Gainesville, Florida: Univ. of Florida Press, 1971.

Goubert, Pierre, "Les officiers royaux des Présidiaux, Bailliages et Elections dans la société française du XVIIe siècle," *XVIIe siècle,* Nos. 42–43, 1er trimestre 1959, 54–75.

Goubert, Pierre, *Beauvais et le Beauvaisis de 1600 à 1730,* 2 vols. Paris: S.E.V.P.E.N., 1960.

Goubert, Pierre, "Recent Theories and Research in French Population Between 1500 and 1700," in D. V. Glass & D. E. C. Eversley, eds., *Population in History*. London: Edw. Arnold, 1965, 457–473.

Goubert, Pierre, *Louis XIV and Twenty Million Frenchmen*. New York: Pantheon, 1970. (a)

Goubert, Pierre, "La force du nombre," in Fernand Braudel & Ernest Labrousse, dir., *Histoire économique et sociale de la France*, **II:** Ernest Labrousse *et al., Des derniers temps de l'age seigneurial aux préludes de l'age industriel (1660–1789)*. Paris: Presses Univ. de France, 1970, 9–21. (b)

Goubert, Pierre, "Le régime démographique français au temps de Louis XIV," in Fernand Braudel & Ernest Labrousse, dir., *Histoire économique et sociale de la France*, **II:** Ernest Labrousse *et al., Des derniers temps de l'age seigneurial aux préludes de l'age industriel (1660–1789)*. Paris: Presses Univ. de France, 1970, 23–54. (c)

Goubert, Pierre, "Révolution demographique au XVIIIe siècle?," in Fernand Braudel & Ernest Labrousse, dir., *Histoire économique et sociale de la France, II:* Ernest Labrousse, *et al., Des derniers temps de l'age seigneurial aux préludes de l'age industriel (1660–1789)*. Paris: Presses Univ. de France, 1970, 55–84. (d)

Goubert, Pierre, "Les cadres de la vie rurale," in Fernand Braudel & Ernest Labrousse, dir., *Histoire économique et sociale de la France, II:* Ernest Labrousse *et al., Des derniers temps de l'age seigneurial aux préludes de l'age industriel (1660–1789)*. Paris: Presses Univ. de France, 1970, 87–118. (e)

Goubert, Pierre, "Le paysan et la terre: seigneurie, tenure, exploitation," in Fernand Braudel & Ernest Labrousse, dir., *Histoire économique et sociale de la France, II:* Ernest Labrousse *et al., Des derniers temps de l'age seigneurial aux préludes de l'age industriel (1660–1789)*. Paris: Presses Univ. de France, 1970, 119–158. (f)

Goubert, Pierre, "Le tragique XVIIe siècle," in Fernand Braudel & Ernest Labrousse, dir., *Histoire économique et sociale de la France, II:* Ernest Labrousse *et al., Des derniers temps de l'age seigneurial aux préludes de l'age industriel (1660–1789)*. Paris: Presses Univ. de France, 1970, 329–365. (g)

Goubert, Pierre, "Remarques sur le vocabulaire social de l'Ancien Régime," in D. Roche, red., *Ordres et classes,* Colloque d'histoire sociale, Saint-Cloud, 24–25 mai 1967. Paris & La Haye: Mouton, 1973, 135–140.

Goubert, Pierre, "Sociétés rurales françaises du XVIII siècle: vingt paysanneries contrastées, quelques problèmes," in *Conjoncture économique, structures sociales,* Hommage à Ernest Labrousse. Paris & La Haye: Mouton, 1974.

Gould, J. D., "The Trade Depression of the Early 1620's," *Economic History Review,* 2nd ser., **VII,** 1, Aug. 1954, 81–90.

Gould, J. D., "The Date of England's Treasure by Forraign Trade," *Journal of Economic History,* **XV,** 2, 1955, 160–161. (a)

Gould, J. D., "The Trade Crisis of the Early 1620's and English Economic Thought," *Journal of Economic History,* **XV,** 2, 1955, 121–133. (b)

Gould, J. D., "Agricultural Fluctuations and the English Economy in the Eighteenth Century," *Journal of Economic History,* **XXII,** 3, Sept. 1962, 313–333.

Goyhenetche, Manex, *Histoire de la colonisation française au pays basque.* Bayonne, France: Ed. E.L.K.A.R., 1975.

Graham, Gerald S., "The Naval Defense of British North America, 1739–1763," *Transactions of the Royal Historical Society,* 4th ser., **XXX,** 1948, 95–110.

Graham, Gerald S., *Empire of the North Atlantic: The Maritime Struggle for North America,* 2nd ed. London & New York: Oxford Univ. Press, 1958.

Grampp, W. D., "The Liberal Elements in English Mercantilism," *Quarterly Journal of Economics,* **LXVI,** 4, Nov. 1952, 465–501.

Granger, C. W. J. & Elliott, C. M., "A Fresh Look at Wheat Prices and Markets in the Eighteenth Century," *Economic History Review,* 2nd ser., **XX,** 2, Aug. 1967, 257–265.

Grantham, G., in "Holland: Participant's Discussion," in Frederick Krantz & Paul M. Hohenberg, eds., *Failed Transitions to Modern Industrial Society: Renaissance Italy and Seventeenth Century Holland.* Montreal: Interuniversity Centre for European Studies, 1975, 64–66.

Grassby, R. B., "Social Status and Commercial Enterprise under Louis XIV," *Economic History Review,* 2nd ser., **XIII,** 1, 1960, 19–38.

Gray, Stanley & Wyckoff, V. J., "The International Tobacco Trade in the Seventeenth Century," *Southern Economic Journal,* **VII,** 1, July 1940, 1–26.

Grycz, Marian, "Handelsbeziehungen der Stadt Poznán bis Ende des XVII Jahrhunderts," *Studia Historiae Economicae,* **II,** 1967, 43–55.

Grycz, Marian, "Die Rolle der Stadt Poznań im Innen- und Aussenhandel bis Ende des XVII Jahrhunderts," in Ingomar Bog, her., *Der Aussenhandel Ostmitteleuropas 1450–1650.* Köln-Wien: Böhlau Verlag, 1971, 105–119.

Guerrero B., Andres "La *hacienda* précapitaliste en Amérique latine," *Etudes rurales,* No. 62, avr.–juin 1976, 5–38.

Gulvin, G., "The Union and the Scottish Woollen Industry," *Scottish Historical Review,* **L,** Nos. 149–150, 1971, 121–137.

Guthrie, Chester L., "Colonial Economy, Trade, Industry and Labor in Seventeenth Century Mexico City," *Revista de historia de América,* No. 7, dic. 1939, 103–134.

Habakkuk, H. John, "The English Land Market in the Eighteenth Century," in J. S. Bromley & E. H. Kossman, eds., *Britain and the Netherlands.* London: Chatto and Windus, 1960, 154–173.

Habbakkuk, H. John, "La disparition du paysan anglais," *Annales E.S.C.,* **XX,** 4, juil.–août 1965, 649–663. (a)

Habakkuk, H. John, "The Economic History of Modern Britain," in D. V. Glass & D. E. C. Eversley, eds., *Population in History.* London: Edw. Arnold, 1965, 147–158. (b) (Originally in *Journal of Economic History,* 1958.)

Habakkuk, H. John, "Land-owners and the Civil War," *Economic History Review,* 2nd ser., **XVIII,** 1, Aug. 1965, 130–151. (c)

Habakkuk, H. John, "Economic Functions of English Landowners in the Seventeenth and Eighteenth Centuries," in Hugh G. J. Aitken, ed., *Explorations in Enterprise.* Cambridge, Massachusetts: Harvard Univ. Press, 1965, 327–340. (d) (Originally in *Explorations in Entrepreneurial History,* 1953.)

Habakkuk, H. John, "England," in Albert Goodwin, ed., *The European Nobility in the Eighteenth Century.* New York: Harper & Row (Torchbooks), 1967, 1–21.

Haley, K. H. D., "The Anglo-Dutch Rapprochement of 1677," *English Historical Review,* **LXXIII,** 1958, 614–648.

Haley, K. H. D., *The Dutch in the Seventeenth Century.* London: Thames & Hudson, 1972.

Haley, K. H. D., "Holland: Commentary," in Frederick Krantz & Paul M. Hohenberg, eds., *Failed Transitions to Modern Industrial Society: Renaissance Italy and Seventeenth-Century Holland.* Montreal: Interuniversity Centre for European Studies, 1975, 58–60.

Hall, A. Rupert, "Military Technology," in C. Singer *et al., A History of Technology.* **III,** *From the Renaissance to the Industrial Revolution, c1500–c1700.* Oxford: Clarendon Press, 1957, 347–376. (a)

Hall, A. Rupert, "The Rise of the West," in C. Singer *et al., A History of Technology.* **III,** *From the Renaissance to the Industrial Revolution, c1500–c1700.* Oxford: Clarendon Press, 1957, 709–721. (b)

Hall, A. Rupert, "Scientific Method and the Progress of Techniques," in E. E. Rich & C. H. Wilson, eds., *Cambridge Economic History of Europe,* **IV:** *The Economy of Expanding Europe in the Sixteenth and Seventeenth Centuries.* Cambridge: University Press, 1967, 96–154.

Hall, Douglas, "Slaves and Slavery in the British West Indies," *Social and Economic Studies,* **XI,** 4, Dec. 1962, 305–318.

Hamann, Manfred, "Archivfunde zur Geschichte der zweiten Leibeigenschaft," *Zeitschrift für Geschichtswissenschaft,* **II,** 3, 1954, 476–480.

Hamilton, Earl J., "The Mercantilism of Gerónimo de Uztariz: A Reexamination," in Norman E. Hines, ed., *Economics, Sociology and the Modern World*. Cambridge, Massachusetts: Harvard Univ. Press, 1935, 111–129.

Hamilton, Earl J., "Prices and Wages in Southern France under John Law's System," *Economic History*, **III**, 12, Feb. 1937, 441–461.

Hamilton, Earl J., "Money and Economic Recovery in Spain under the First Bourbon, 1701–1746," *Journal of Modern History*, **XV**, 3, Sept. 1943, 192–206.

Hamilton, Earl J., *War and Prices in Spain, 1651–1800*. Cambridge, Massachusetts: Harvard Univ. Press, 1947.

Hamilton, Earl J., "The Role of Monopoly in the Overseas Expansion and Colonial Trade of Europe before 1800," *American Economic Review*, Proceedings, **XXXVIII**, 2, May 1948, 33–53.

Hamilton, Earl J., "Plans for a National Bank in Spain, 1701–83," *Journal of Political Economy*, **LVII**, 4, Aug. 1949, 315–336.

Hamilton, Earl J., "The History of Prices before 1750," in *International Congress of Historical Sciences*, Stockholm, 1960, *Rapports*, **I**: *Methodologie, histoire des universités, histoire des prix avant 1750*. Göteborg, Sweden: Almqvist & Wiksell, 1960, 144–164.

Hamilton, Earl J., "The Political Economy of France at the Time of John Law," *History of Political Economy*, **I**, 1, Spring 1969, 123–149.

Hamilton, Earl J., "The Role of War in Modern Inflation," *Journal of Economic History*, **XXXVII**, 1, Mar. 1977, 13–19.

Hamilton, Henry, *An Economic History of Scotland in the Eighteenth Century*. Oxford: Clarendon Press, 1963.

Hansen, Marcus Lee, *The Atlantic Migration, 1607–1860*. Cambridge, Massachusetts: Harvard Univ. Press, 1945.

Hansen, S. A., "Changes in the Wealth and the Demographic Characteristics of the Danish Aristocracy, 1470–1720," *Third International Conference of Economic History*, Munich, 1965, **IV**: J. E. C. Eversley, ed., *Demography and History*. Paris & La Haye: Mouton, 1972, 91–122.

Harkness, D. A. E., "The Opposition to the 8th and 9th Articles of the Commercial Treaty of Utrecht," *Scottish Historical Review*, **XXI**, No. 83, Apr. 1924, 219–226.

Haring, Clarence Henry, *The Spanish Empire in America*. London & New York: Oxford Univ. Press, 1947.

Haring, Clarence Henry, *Trade and Navigation Between Spain and the Indies in the Time of the Hapsburgs*. Gloucester, Massachusetts: Peter Smith, 1964. (Original publication, 1918.)

Harlow, Vincent T., *A History of Barbados, 1625–1685*. Oxford: Clarendon Press, 1926.

Harnisch, Helmut, *Die Herrschaft Boitzenburg: Untersuchungen zur Entwicklung der sozialökonomischen Struktur ländlicher Gebiete in der Mark Brandenburg vom 14. bis zum 19. Jahrhundert*. Weimar: Hermann Böhlaus Nachfolger, 1968.

Harper, Lawrence A., "The Effect of the Navigation Acts on the Thirteen Colonies," in Richard B. Morris, ed., *The Era of the American Revolution*. New York: Columbia Univ. Press, 1939, 3–39. (a)

Harper, Lawrence A., *The English Navigation Laws*. New York: Columbia Univ. Press, 1939. (b)

Harper, Lawrence A., "Mercantilism and the American Revolution," *Canadian Historical Review*, **XXIII**, 1, Mar. 1942, 1–15.

Harris, L. E., "Land Drainage and Reclamation," in C. Singer *et al.*, *A History of Technology*, **III**: *From the Renaissance to the Industrial Revolution, c1500–c1750*. Oxford: Clarendon Press, 1957, 300–323.

Harris, R. W., *England in the Eighteenth Century—1689–1793: A Balanced Constitution and New Horizons*. London: Blandford Press, 1963.

Harsin, Paul, "La finance et l'état jusqu'au système de Law," in Fernand Braudel & Ernest Labrousse, dir., *Histoire économique et sociale de la France*, **II**: Ernest Labrousse *et al.*, *Des derniers temps de l'age seigneurial aux préludes de l'age industriel (1660–1789)*. Paris: Presses Univ. de France, 1970, 267–299.

Harte, N. B., "The Rise of Protection and the English Linen Trade, 1690–1790," in N. B. Harte & K. G. Ponting, eds., *Textile History and Economic History.* Manchester, England: Manchester Univ. Press, 1973, 74–112.

Hartwell, Richard M., "Economic Growth in England Before the Industrial Revolution: Some Methodological Issues," *Journal of Economic History,* **XXIX,** 1, Mar. 1969, 13–31.

Haskell, Francis, "The Market for Italian Art in the 17th Century," *Past and Present,* No. 15, Apr. 1959, 48–59.

Hasquin, Hervé, *Une mutation: Le "Pays de Charleroi" aux XVIIe et XVIIIe siècles.* Bruxelles: Ed. de l'Institut de Sociologie, 1971.

Hassinger, Herbert, "Die erste Wiener orientalische Handelskompanie, 1667–1683," *Vierteljahrschrift für Sozial–und Wirtschaftgeschichte,* **XXXV,** 1, 1942, 1–53.

Hatton, Ragnhild M., "Scandinavia and the Baltic," in *New Cambridge Modern History,* **VII:** J. O. Lindsay, ed., *The Old Regime, 1713–1763.* Cambridge: University Press, 1966, 339–364.

Hatton, Ragnhild M., "Gratifications and Foreign Policy: Anglo-French Rivalry in Sweden During the Nine Years War," in R. Hatton & J. S. Bromley, eds., *William III and Louis XIV, Essays 1680–1720, by and for M. A. Thomson.* Toronto: Univ. of Toronto Press, 1968, 68–94. (a)

Hatton, Ragnhild M., *Charles XII of Sweden.* London: Weidenfeld & Nicolson, 1968. (b)

Hatton, Ragnhild M., "Charles XII and the Great Northern War," in *New Cambridge Modern History,* **VI:** J. S. Bromley, ed., *The Rise of Great Britain and Russia, 1688–1725.* Cambridge: University Press, 1970, 648–680.

Hatton, Ragnhild M. *Charles XII.* London: The Historical Association, 1974.

Haudricourt, André G. & Delamarre, Mariel Jean-Brunhes, *L'homme et la charrue à travers le monde.* Paris: Gallimard, 1955, 3rd ed.

Hauser, H., "Réflections sur l'histoire des banques à l'èpoque moderne de la fin du XVe siècle à la fin du XVIIIe siècle," *Annales d'histoire économique et sociale,* 1er année, No. 3, 15 juil. 1929, 335–351.

Havinden, M. A., "Agricultural Progress in Open-Field Oxfordshire," in E. L. Jones, ed., *Agriculture and Economic Growth in England, 1650–1815.* London: Methuen, 1967, 66–79. (Originally in *Agricultural History Review,* 1961.)

Hazard, Paul, *The European Mind, 1680–1715.* London: Penguin, 1964.

Heaton, Herbert, "Heckscher on Mercantilism," *Journal of Political Economy,* **XLV,** 3, June 1937, 370–393.

Heckscher, Eli F., "Un grand chapitre de l'histoire du fer: le monopole suédois," *Annales d'histoire économique et sociale,* **IV,** 14, 31 mars 1932, 127–139; 15, 31 mai 1932, 225–241.

Heckscher, Eli F., *Mercantilism,* 2 vol. London: Geo. Allen & Unwin, 1935.

Heckscher, Eli F., "Mercantilism," *Economic History Review,* **VII,** 1, Nov. 1936, 44–54.

Heckscher, Eli F., "Multilateralism, Baltic Trade, and the Mercantilists," *Economic History Review,* 2d. ser., **III,** 2, 1950, 219–228.

Heckscher, Eli F., *An Economic History of Sweden.* Cambridge, Massachusetts: Harvard Univ. Press, 1954.

Heitz, Gerhard, review of Johannes Nichtweiss, *Das Bauernlegen in Mecklenburg,* in *Zeitschrift für Geschichtswissenschaft,* **II,** 4, 1955, 643–649.

Heitz, Gerhard, "Zur Diskussion über Gutsherrschaft und Bauernlegen in Mecklenburg," *Zeitschrift für Geschichtswissenschaft,* **V,** 2, 1957, 278–296.

Helleiner, Karl F., "The Population of Europe from the Black Death to the Eve of the Vital Revolution," in E. G. Rich & C. H. Wilson, eds., *The Cambridge Economic History of Europe.* **IV:** *The Economy of Expanding Europe in the Sixteenth and Seventeenth Centuries.* Cambridge: University Press, 1967, 1–95.

Helmer, Marie, "Economie et société au XVIIe siècle: Un *Cargador de Indias,*" *Jahrbuch für Geschichte von Staat, Wirtschaft und Gesellschaft Lateinamerikas,* **IV,** 1967, 399–409.

Henry, Louis, "The Population of France in the Eighteenth Century," in D. V. Glass & D. E. C. Eversley, eds., *Population in History.* London: Edw. Arnold, 1965, 434–456.

Herlihy, David, "Population, Plague and Social Change in Rural Pistoia, 1201–1430," *Economic History Review,* 2nd ser., **XVIII,** 2, Aug. 1965, 225–244.

Hildebrand, Karl-Gustaf, "Salt and Cloth in Swedish Economic History," *Scandinavian Economic History Review,* **II,** 2, 1954, 74–102.

Hildebrand, Karl-Gustaf, "Foreign Markets for Swedish Iron in the 18th Century," *Scandinavian Economic History Review,* **VI,** 1, 1958, 3–52.

Hildner, Ernest G., Jr., "The Role of the South Sea Company in the Diplomacy Leading to the War of Jenkins' Ear, 1729–1739," *Hispanic American Historical Review,* **XVIII,** 3, Aug. 1938, 322–341.

Hill, B. W., "The Change of Government and the 'Loss of the City', 1710–1711," *Economic History Review,* 2nd ser., **XXIV,** 3, Aug. 1971, 395–413.

Hill, Charles E., *The Danish Sound Dues and the Command of the Baltic.* Durham, North Carolina: Duke Univ. Press, 1926.

Hill, Christopher, "The English Civil War Interpreted by Marx and Engels," *Science and Society,* **XII,** 1, Winter 1948, 130–156.

Hill, Christopher, "Land in the English Revolution," *Science and Society,* **XIII,** 1, Winter 1948–1949, 22–49.

Hill, Christopher, *The Century of Revolution, 1603–1714.* New York: W. W. Norton, 1961. (a)

Hill, Christopher, "Protestantism and the Rise of Capitalism," in F. J. Fisher, ed., *Essays in the Economic and Social History of Tudor and Stuart England.* Cambridge: University Press, 1961, 15–39. (b)

Hill, Christopher, *1530–1780, Reformation to Industrial Revolution,* Vol. 2 of *The Pelican Economic History of Britain.* Baltimore: Penguin, 1969, published with revisions.

Hill, Christopher, "Conclusion," in *Change and Continuity in Seventeenth-Century England.* Cambridge, Massachusetts: Harvard Univ. Press, 1975, 278–284. (a)

Hill, Christopher, "The Many-Headed Monster," in *Change and Continuity in Seventeenth-Century England.* Cambridge, Massachusetts: Harvard Univ. Press, 1975, 181–204. (b) (Originally in C. H. Carter, ed., *From the Renaissance to the Counter-Reformation: Essays in Honor of Garrett Mattingly* New York, 1965.)

Hilton, R. H., "Capitalism. What's in a Name?," *Past and Present,* No. 1, 1952, 32–43.

Hinton, R. W. K., "The Mercantile System in the Time of Thomas Mun," *Economic History Review,* 2nd ser., **VII,** 3, Apr. 1955, 277–290.

Hinton, R. W. K., *The Eastland Trade and the Common Weal in the Seventeenth Century.* Cambridge: University Press, 1959.

Hintze, Otto, "The Hohenzollern and the Nobility," in *Historical Essays.* London and New York: Oxford Univ. Press, 1975, 33–63. (a) (Translated from *Historische Zeitschrift,* 1914.)

Hintze, Otto, "The Commissary and His Significance in General Administrative History: A Comparative Study," in *Historical Essays.* London & New York: Oxford Univ. Press, 1975, 267–301. (b) (Originally published in 1919.)

Hobsbawm, E. J., "Seventeenth Century Revolutions," a discussion with others in *Past and Present,* No. 13, Apr. 1958, 63–72.

Hobsbawm, E. J., "The Seventeenth Century in the Development of Capitalism," *Science and Society,* **XXIV,** 2, Spring 1960, 97–112.

Hobsbawm, E. J., "The Crisis of the Seventeenth Century," in Trevor Aston, ed., *Crisis in Europe, 1560–1660.* London: Routledge & Kegan Paul, 1965, 5–58. (Originally in *Past and Present,* 1954.)

Hoffenden, Philip S., "France and England in North America, 1689–1713," in *New Cambridge Modern History,* **VI:** J. S. Bromley, ed., *The Rise of Great Britain and Russia, 1688–1725.* Cambridge: University Press, 1970, 480–508.

Hoffman, Alfred, *Wirtschaftsgeschichte des Landes Oberösterreich,* **I:** *Werden, Wachsen, Reifen von der Frühzeit bis zum Jahre 1848.* Salzburg: Otto Müller Verlag, & Linz: Verlag F. Winter'sche Buchhandlung H. Fürstelberger, 1952.

Hoffman, Alfred, "Die Grundherrschaft als Unternehmen," *Zeitschrift für Agrargesehichte und Agrarsoziologie,* **VI,** 2, 1958, 123–131.

Holderness, B. A., *Pre-Industrial England: Economy and Society, 1500–1750.* London: J. M. Dent & Sons, 1976.

Homer, Sidney, *A History of Interest Rates.* New Brunswick, New Jersey: Rutgers Univ. Press, 1963.

Horn, David Bayne, *Great Britain and Europe in the Eighteenth Century.* Oxford: Clarendon Press, 1967.

Horner, John, *The Linen Trade of Europe during the Spinning Wheel Period.* Belfast: McCaw, Stevenson & Orr, 1920.

Horsefield, J. Keith, "The Beginnings of Paper Money in England," *Journal of European Economic History,* **VI,** 1, Spring 1977, 117–132.

Hoskins, W. G., "English Agriculture in the 17th and 18th Centuries," *X Congresso Internazionale di Scienze Storiche,* Roma 4-11 settembre 1955, *Relazioni,* **IV:** *Storia moderna.* Firenze: G. C. Sansoni-Ed., 1955, 205–226.

Hoskins, W. G., "Harvest Fluctuations and English Economic History, 1620–1759," *Agricultural History Review,* **XVI,** 1, 1968, 15–31.

Hovde, B. J., *The Scandinavian Countries, 1720–1865,* **I:** *The Rise of the Middle Classes.* Ithaca, New York: Cornell Univ. Press, 1948.

Howard, Michael, *War in European History.* London & New York: Oxford Univ. Press, 1976.

Hroch, Miroslav, "Der Dreissigjährige Krieg und die europäischen Handelsbeziehungen," *Wissenschaftliche Zeitschrift der Ernst-Moritz-Arndt-Universitat Greifswald,* **XII,** 5/6, 1963, 533–543.

Hroch, Miroslav, "Die Rolle des zentraleuropäischen Handels im Ausgleich der Handelsbilanz Zwischen Ost- und Westeuropa, 1550–1650," in Ingomar Bog, her., *Der Aussenhandel Ostmitteleuropas, 1450–1650.* Köln-Wein: Böhlau Verlag, 1971, 1–27.

Hubert, Eugene, "Joseph II," in *Cambridge Modern History,* A. W. Ward *et al.,* eds., **VI:** *The Eighteenth Century.* Cambridge: University Press, 1909, 626–656.

Huetz de Lemps, Christian, *Géographie du commerce de Bordeaux à la fin du règne de Louis XIV.* Paris & La Haye: Mouton, 1975.

Hufton, Olwen H., *The Poor of Eighteenth-Century France.* Oxford: Clarendon Press, 1974.

Hughes, Edward, *North Country Life in the Eighteenth Century. The North-East, 1700–1750.* London & New York: Oxford Univ. Press, 1952.

Hutchison, E. P., *The Population Debate.* Boston, Massachusetts: Houghton Mifflin, 1967.

Hymer, Stephen & Resnick, Stephen, "A Model of an Agrarian Economy with Non-agricultural Activities," *American Economic Review,* **LIX,** 3, Sept. 1969, 493–506.

Imbert, Gaston, *Des mouvements de longue durée Kondratieff.* Aix-en-Provence: La Pensée Universitaire, 1959.

Imbert, Jean, *Histoire économique (des origines à 1789),* Collection Thémis. Paris: Presses Univ. de France, 1965.

Imhof, Arthur E., "Der Arbeitszwang für das landwirtschaftliche Dientsvolk in den nordischen Ländern im 18. Jahrhundert," *Zeitschrift für Agrargeschichte und Agrarsoziologie,* **XXII,** 1, 1974, 59–74.

Innis, H. A., "Preface" to M. G. Lawson, *Fur: A Study in English Mercantilism, 1700–1775.* Toronto: Univ. of Toronto Press, 1943, vii–xx.

Insh, George Pratt, *The Scottish Jacobite Movement: A Study in Economic and Social Forces.* London: Moray Press, 1952.

Israel, J. I., "Mexico and the 'General Crisis' of the Seventeenth Century," *Past and Present,* No. 63, May 1974, 33–57. (a)

Israel, J. I., "The Portuguese in Seventeenth-Century Mexico," *Jahrbuch für Geschichte von Staat, Wirtschaft und Gesellschaft Lateinamerikas,* **XI,** 1974, 12–32. (b)

Israel, J. I., "A Conflict of Empires: Spain and the Netherlands 1618–1648," *Past and Present*, No. 76, Aug. 1977, 34–74.

Issawi, Charles, "The Ottoman Empire in the European Economy, 1600–1914. Some Observations and Many Questions," in Kemal H. Karpat, ed., *The Ottoman State and Its Place in World History.* Leiden: E. J. Brill, 1974, 107–117.

Jacquart, Jean, "La production agricole dans la France du XVIIe siècle," *XVIIe siècle,* Nos. 70–71, 1966, 21–46.

Jacquart, Jean, "La productivité agricole dans la France due Nord du XVIe et XVIIe siècles," *Third International Conference of Economic History,* Munich, 1965, **II.** *Production et productivité agricole.* Paris & LaHaye: Mouton, 1968, 65–74.

Jacquart, Jean (& Dupâquier, J.), "Les rapports sociaux dans les campagnes françaises au XVIIe siècle: quelques exemples," in D. Roche, réd., *Ordres et classes,* Colloque d'histoire sociale, Saint-Cloud, 24–25 mai 1967. Paris & La Haye: Mouton, 1973, 167–179.

Jacquart, Jean, "French Agriculture in the Seventeenth Century," in Peter Earle, ed., *Essays in European Economic History, 1500–1800.* Oxford: Clarendon Press, 1974. (Translated from *XVII siècle,* 1966.)

Jacquart, Jean, "Immobilisme et catastrophes," in Emmanuel Le Roy Ladurie, réd., *L'age classique des paysans de 1340 à 1789,* Vol. **II** of *Histoire de la France rurale.* Paris: Seuil, 1975, 185–353.

Jacquart, Jean, "Les inerties terriennes," in Pierre Deyon & Jean Jacquart, *Les hésitations de la croissance, 1580–1740,* Vol. **II** of Pierre Léon, réd., *Histoire économique et sociale du monde.* Paris: Lib. Armand Colin, 1978, 345–388. (a)

Jacquart, Jean, "L'offensive des dominants," in Pierre Deyon & Jean Jacquart, *Les hésitations de la croissance, 1580–1740,* Vol. **II** of Pierre Léon, réd., *Histoire économique et sociale du monde.* Paris: Lib. Armand Colin, 1978, 389–430. (b)

Jacquart, Jean, "Des sociétés en crise," in Pierre Deyon & Jean Jacquart, *Les hésitations de la croissance, 1580–1740,* Vol. **II** of Pierre Léon, réd., *Histoire économique et sociale du monde.* Paris: Lib. Armand Colin, 1978, 455–494. (c)

Jago, Charles, "The Influence of Debt on the Relations between Crown and Aristocracy in Seventeenth-Century Castile," *Economic History Review,* 2nd ser., **XXVI,** 2, May 1973, 218–230.

James, Francis Godwin, "Irish Colonial Trade in the Eighteenth Century," *William and Mary Quarterly,* 3rd ser., **XX,** 4, Oct. 1963, 574–582.

James, Francis Godwin, *Ireland in the Empire, 1688–1770.* Cambridge, Massachusettes: Harvard Univ. Press, 1973.

Jansen, H. P. H., "Holland's Advance," *Acta Historiae Neerlandicae,* **X,** 1978, 1–19.

Jansen, J. C. G. M., "Agrarian Development and Exploitation in South Limburg in the Years 1650–1850," *Acta Historiae Neerlandica,* **V,** 1971, 243–270.

Jeannin, Pierre, "Les comptes du Sund comme source pour la construction d'indices généraux de l'activité économique en Europe (XVIe–XVIIIe siècles)," *Revue historique,* 88e année, No. 231, 1er partie, janv.–mars 1964, 55–102; 2e partie, avr.–juin 1964, 307–340.

Jeannin, Pierre, *L'Europe du Nord-Ouest et du Nord aux XVIIe et XVIIIe siècles,* Nouvelle Clio 34. Paris: Presses Univ. de France, 1969.

Jeannin, Pierre, "Preis-, Kosten- und Gewinnunterschiede im Handel mit Ostseegetriede (1550–1650)," in *Wirtschaftliche und soziale Strukturen im saekularen Wandel,* **II:** Ingomar Bog *et al.,* her., *Die vorindustrielle Zeit: Ausseragrarische Probleme.* Hannover: Verlag M. & H. Schaper, 1974, 494–518.

Jeannin, Pierre, "Les marché du Nord dans le commerce français au XVIIIe siècle," in Pierre Léon, réd., *Aires et structures du commerce français au XVIIIe siècle,* Colloque national de l'Association Française des Historiens Economistes, Paris, CNRS, 4–6 oct. 1973. Lyon: Centre d'histoire économique et social de la region lyonnaise, 1975, 47–73.

Jensch, Georg, "Der Handel Rigas im 17. Jarhundert," *Mitteilungen aus der livländischen Geschichte,* **XXIV,** 2, 1930.

Jensen, Einar, *Danish Agriculture: Its Economic Development.* Copenhagen: J. H. Schultz Forlag, 1937.

John, A. H., "Insurance Investment and the Land on Money Market of the 18th Century," *Economica,* n.s., **XX,** No. 78, May 1953, 137–158.

John, A. H., "War and the English Economy, 1700–1763," *Economic History Review,* 2d ser., **VII,** 3, Apr. 1955, 329–344.

John, A. H., "Agricultural Productivity and Economic Growth in England," *Journal of Economic History,* **XXV,** 1, Mar. 1965, 19–34.

John, A. H., "Aspects of English Economic Growth in the First Half of the Eighteenth Century," in W. E. Minchinton, ed., *The Growth of English Overseas Trade in the Seventeenth and Eighteenth Centuries.* London: Methuen, 1969, 164–183. (Originally in *Economica,* 1961.)

John, A. H., "English Agricultural Improvement and Grain Exports, 1660–1765," in D. C. Coleman & A. H. John, eds., *Trade, Government and Economy in Pre-Industrial England.* London: Weidenfeld & Nicolson, 1976, 45–67.

Johnsen, Oscar Albert, *Norwegische Wirtschaftsgeschichte.* Jena: Verlag von Gustav Fischer, 1939.

Jones, E. L., "Agriculture and Economic Growth in England, 1660–1750: Agricultural Change," *Journal of Economic History,* **XXV,** 1, Mar. 1965, 1–18.

Jones, E. L., "Editor's Introduction," in *Agriculture and Economic Growth in England, 1650–1815.* London: Methuen, 1967, 1–48.

Jones, E. L., "Afterword," in William N. Parker & Eric L. Jones, eds., *European Peasants and Their Markets: Essays in Agrarian Economic History.* Princeton, New Jersey: Princeton Univ. Press, 1975, 327–360.

Jones, E. L. & Woolf, S. J., *Agrarian Change and Economic Development: The Historical Problems.* London: Methuen, 1969.

Jones, George Hilton, *The Main Stream of Jacobitism.* Cambridge, Massachusetts: Harvard Univ. Press, 1954.

Jones, Sir Harold Spencer, "The Calendar," in C. Singer *et al., A History of Technology.* **III:** *From the Renaissance to the Industrial Revolution, c1500–c1700.* Oxford: Clarendon Press, 1957, 558–581.

Jones, J. R., *Britain and Europe in the Seventeenth Century.* London: Edw. Arnold, 1966.

Jones, J. R., "English Attitudes to Europe in the Seventeenth Century," in J. S. Bromley & E. H. Kossmann, eds., *Britain and the Netherlands in Europe and Asia.* London: Macmillan, 1968, 37–55.

Jones, J. R., *The Revolution of 1688 in England.* London: Weidenfeld & Nicolson, 1972.

Jørgensen, Johan, "Denmark's Relations with Lubeck and Hamburg in the Seventeenth Century," *Scandinavian Economic History Review,* **IX,** 2, 1963, 73–116.

Joslin, D. M., "London Private Bankers, 1720–1785," *Economic History Review,* 2nd ser., **VII,** 2, 1954, 167–186.

Judges, A. V., "The Idea of a Mercantile State," in D. C. Coleman, ed., *Revisions in Mercantilism.* London: Methuen, 1969, 35–60. (Originally in *Transactions of the Royal Historical Society,* 1939.)

Jutikkala, Eino, "The Great Finnish Famine in 1696–97," *Scandinavian Economic History Review,* **III,** 1, 1955, 48–63.

Jutikkala, Eino, "Large Scale Farming in Scandinavia in the Seventeenth Century," *Scandinavian Economic History Review,* **XXIII,** 2, 1975, 159–166.

Kaltenstadler, Wilhelm, "Der österreichisch Seehandel über Triest im 18. Jahrhundert," *Vierteljahrschrift für Sozial- und Wirtschaftsgeschichte,* **LV,** 4, Marz 1969, 481–500; **LVI,** 1, Juni 1969, 1–104.

Kaltenstadler, Wilhelm, "European Economic History in Recent German Historiography," *Journal of European Economic History,* **I,** 1, Spring 1972, 193–218.

Kamen, Henry, "The Decline of Castile: The Last Crisis," *Economic History Review,* 2nd ser., **XVII,** 1, Aug. 1964, 63–76.

Kamen, Henry, "The Economic and Social Consequences of the Thirty Years' War," *Past and Present,* No. 39, Apr. 1968, 44–61.

Kamen, Henry, *The War of Succession in Spain, 1700–15.* Bloomington: Indiana Univ. Press, 1969.

Kamen, Henry, *The Iron Century: Social Change in Europe, 1550–1660.* New York: Praeger, 1972.

Kamen, Henry, "Public Authority and Popular Crime: Banditry in Valencia, 1660–1714," *Journal of European Economic History,* **III,** 3, Winter 1974, 654–687.

Kamen, Henry, "The Decline of Spain: A Historical Myth?," *Past and Present,* No. 81, Nov. 1978, 24–50.

Kammen, Michael, *Empire and Interest: The American Colonies and the Politics of Mercantilism.* Philadelphia, Pennsylvania: J. B. Lippincott, 1970.

Kann, Robert A., "Aristocracy in the Eighteenth Century Habsburg Empire," *East European Quarterly,* **VII,** 1, 1973, 1–13.

Kavke, František, "Die habsburger und der böhmische Staat bis zur Mitte des 18. Jahrhunderts," *Historica,* **VIII,** 1964, 35–64.

Kearney, H. F., "The Political Background to English Mercantilism, 1695–1700," *Economic History Review,* 2nd ser., **XI,** 3, Apr. 1959, 484–496.

Kearney, H. F., "Puritanism, Capitalism and the Scientific Revolution," *Past and Present,* No. 28, July 1964, 81–101.

Keith, Robert G., "Encomienda, Hacienda and Corregimiento in Spanish America: A Structural Analysis," *Hispanic American Historical Review,* **LI,** 3, Aug. 1971, 431–446.

Keith, Theodora, "The Economic Causes for the Scottish Union," *English Historical Review,* **XXIV,** No. 93, Jan. 1909, 44–60.

Kellenbenz, Hermann, *Sephardim an der unteren Elbe. Ihre wirtschaftliche und politische Bedeutung vom Ende des 16. bis zum Beginn des 18. Jahrhunderts.* Vierteljahrschrift für Sozial- und Wirtschaftsgeschichte, Beiheft 40. Wiesbaden: Franz Steiner Verlag GMBH, 1958.

Kellenbenz, Hermann, "Händliches Gewerbe und bäuerliches Unternehmertum in Westeuropa von Spätmittelalter bis ins XVIII. Jahrhundert," *Second International Conference of Economic History, Aix-en-Provence, 1962. II: Middle Ages and Modern Times.* Paris & La Haye: Mouton, 1965, 377–427.

Kellenbenz, Hermann, "Les industries rurales en Occident de la fin du Moyen Age au XVIIIe siècle," *Annales E.S.C.,* **LXIII,** 5, sept.–oct. 1963, 833–882.

Kellenbenz, Hermann, "The Economic Significance of the Archangel Route (from the late 16th to the late 18th century)," *Journal of European Economic History,* **II,** 3, Winter 1973, 541–581.

Kellenbenz, Hermann, "Technology in the Age of the Scientific Revolution, 1500–1700," in C. M. Cipolla, ed., *The Fontana History of Europe,* **II:** *The Sixteenth and Seventeenth Centuries.* Glasgow: Collins, 1974, 177–272.

Kellenbenz, Hermann, *The Rise of the European Economy.* London: Weidenfeld & Nicolson, 1976.

Kellenbenz, Hermann, "The Organization of Industrial Production," in *Cambridge Economic History of Europe,* **V:** E. E. Rich & C. H. Wilson, eds., *The Economic Organization of Early Modern Europe.* Cambridge: Cambridge Univ. Press, 1977, 462–548. (a)

Kellenbenz, Hermann, "Europaisches Kupfer, Ende 15. bis Mitte 17. Jahrhundert. Ergebnisse eines Kolloquiums," in H. Kellenbenz, her., *Schwerpunkte der Kupferproduktion und des Kupferhandels in Europa, 1500–1650.* Köln-Wien: Böhlau Verlag, 1977, 290–351. (b)

Kemp, Tom, "Structural Factors in the Retardation of French Economic Growth," *Kyklos,* **XV,** 2, 1962, 325–350.

Kent, H. S. K., "The Anglo-Norwegian Timber Trade in the Eighteenth Century," *Economic History Review,* 2nd ser., **VIII,** 1, Aug. 1955, 62–74.

Kent, H. S. K., *War and Trade in Northern Seas.* Cambridge: University Press, 1973.

Kepler, J. S., "Fiscal Aspects of the English Carrying Trade during the Thirty Years' War," *Economic History Review,* 2nd ser., **XXV,** 2, May 1972, 261–283.

Kerridge, Eric, *Agrarian Problems in the Sixteenth Century and After.* London: Geo. Allen & Unwin, Ltd., 1969.

Kerridge, Eric, *The Farmers of Old England.* London: Geo. Allen & Unwin, 1973.

Kersten, Adam, "Les magnats—élite de la société nobiliaire," *Acta Poloniae Historica,* No. 36, 1977, 119–133.

Kindleberger, Charles P., "Commercial Expansion and the Industrial Revolution," *Journal of European Economic History,* **IV,** 3, Winter 1975, 613–654.

Kindleberger, Charles P., *Manias, Panics, and Crashes.* New York: Basic Books, 1978.

Kirchner, Walther, "Emigration: Some Eighteenth Century Considerations," *Comparative Studies in Society and History,* **V,** 3, Apr. 1963, 346–356.

Kirilly, Zs., "Examen au point de vue de rendement de la production du blé des serfs," in Mme. Zs. Kirilly *et al.,* "Production et productivité agricoles en Hongrie à l'époque du féodalisme tardif, (1550–1850)," *Nouvelles études historiques,* publiées à l'occasion du XIIe Congrès International des Sciences Historiques par la Commission Nationale des Historiens Hongrois. Budapest: Akademiai Kiado, 1965, 615–622.

Kirilly, Zs. & Kiss, I. N., "Production de céréales et exploitations paysannes: En Hongrie aux XVIe et XVIIe siècles," *Annales E.S.C.,* **XXIII,** 6, nov.–déc. 1968, 1211–1236.

Kisch, Herbert, "The Textile Industries in Silesia and the Rhineland: A Comparative Study in Industrialization," *Journal of Economic History,* **XIX,** 4, Dec. 1959, 541–564.

Kisch, Herbert, "Growth Deterrents of a Medieval Heritage: The Aachen-area Woolen Trades before 1790," *Journal of Economic History,* **XXIV,** 4, Dec. 1964, 517–537.

Kisch, Herbert, *Prussian Mercantilism and the Rise of the Krefeld Silk Industry: Variations upon an Eighteenth-Century Theme,* Transactions of the American Philosophical Society, **LVIII,** Pt. 7, 1968. Philadelphia, Pennsylvania: Amer. Phil. Soc., 1968.

Kiss, Istvan, "Die Rolle der Magnaten-Gutswirtschaft im Grosshandel Ungarns im 17. Jahrhundert," in Ingomar Bog, red., *Der Aussenhandel Ostmitteleuropas, 1450–1650.* Köln-Wien: Böhlau Verlag, 1971, 450–482.

Klein, Peter W., "The Trip Family in the 17th Century: A Study of the Behavior of the Entrepreneur on the Dutch Staple Market," *Acta Historiae Neerlandica,* **I,** 1966, 187–211.

Klein, Peter W., "Entrepreneurial Behavior and the Economic Rise and Decline of the Netherlands in the 17th and 18th Centuries," *Annales cisalpines d'histoire sociale,* **I,** 1, 1969, 7–19.

Klein, Peter W., "Stagnation économique et emploi du capital dans la Hollande des XVIIIe et XIXe siècles," *Revue du Nord,* **LII,** No. 204, janv.–mars 1970, 33–41.

Klíma, Arnošt, "Industrial Development in Bohemia, 1648–1781," *Past and Present,* No. 11, Apr. 1957, 87–99.

Klíma, Arnošt, "English Merchant Capital in Bohemia in the Eighteenth Century," *Economic History Review,* 2nd ser., **XII,** 1, Aug. 1959, 34–48.

Klíma, Arnošt, "Mercantilism in the Habsburg Monarchy—with special reference to the Bohemian Lands," *Historica,* **XI,** 1965, 95–119.

Klíma, Arnošt & Macůrek, J., "La question de la transition du féodalisme au capitalisme en Europe centrale (16e-18e siècles)," *International Congress of Historical Sciences,* Stockholm, 1960, **IV:** *Histoire moderne.* Göteborg, Sweden: Almqvist & Wiksell, 1960, 84–105.

Knoppers, Jake, "A Quantitative Study of Dutch Shipping from Russia in the Eighteenth Century," paper presented to Canadian Historical Association, Edmonton, June 7, 1975. (a)

Knoppers, Jake, "Discussion," in F. Krantz & P. M. Hohenberg, eds., *Failed Transitions to Modern*

Industrial Society: Renaissance Italy and Seventeenth Century Holland. Montreal: Interuniversity Centre for European Studies, 1975, 65. (b)

Knoppers, Jake, "Patterns in Dutch Trade with Russia from the Nine Years' War to the End of the Republic," paper presented at the Annual Meeting of the Canadian Association for the Advancement of Netherlandic Studies, Univ. of New Brunswick, Fredericton, 28–29 May 1977. (a)

Knoppers, Jake, "Ships and Shipping Towards the End of the Eighteenth Century: Trends and Developments in Europe," paper presented at Annual Meeting of the Canadian Historical Association, Univ. of New Brunswick, Fredericton, 2–6 June 1977. (b)

Koeningsberger, H. G., "English Merchants in Naples and Sicily in the Seventeenth Century," *English Historical Review,* **LXII,** No. 244, July 1947, 304–326.

Kossmann, E. H., "Discussion of H. R. Trevor-Roper: 'The General Crisis of the Seventeenth Century,'" *Past and Present,* No. 18, Nov. 1960, 8–11.

Kossmann, E. H., "The Low Countries," *New Cambridge Modern History,* **IV:** J. P. Cooper, ed., *The Decline of Spain and the Thirty Years' War, 1609–48/59.* Cambridge: University Press, 1970, 359–384.

Kossmann, E. H., "Some Meditations on Dutch Eighteenth-Century Decline," in Frederick Krantz & Paul M. Hohenberg, eds., *Failed Transitions to Modern Industrial Society: Renaissance Italy and Seventeenth Century Holland.* Montreal: Interuniversity Centre for European Studies, 1975, 49–54. (a)

Kossmann, E. H., "Some Late 17th-Century Dutch Writings on Raison d'Etat," in R. Schnur, her., *Staatsräson: Studien zur Geschichte eines politischen Begriffs.* Berlin: Duncker & Humblot, 1975, 497–504. (b)

Kossmann, E. H., "The Singularity of Absolutism," in R. Hatton, ed., *Louis XIV and Absolutism.* Columbus: Ohio State Univ. Press, 1976, 3–17.

Kowecki, Jerzy, "Les transformations de la structure sociale en Pologne au XVIIIe siècle: La noblesse et la bourgeoisie," *Acta Poloniae Historica,* No. 26, 1972, 5–30.

Kriedte, Peter, Medick, Hans, & Schlumbohm, Jürgen, *Industrialisierung vor der Industrialisierung.* Göttingen: Vandenhoeck & Ruprecht, 1977.

Kruger, Horst, *Zur Geschichte der Manufakturen und der Manufakturarbeiter in Preussen,* Vol. **III** of Schriftenreihe des Institut für allgemeine Geschichte an der Humboldt Universität Berlin, ed. by Gerhard Schilfert. Berlin: Rütten & Loening, 1958.

Kuczynski, Jürgen, "Zum Aufsatz von Johannes Nichtweiss über die zweite Leibeigenschaft," *Zeitschrift für Geschichtswissenschaft,* **II,** 3, 1954, 467–471.

Kula, Witold, "L'histoire économique de la Pologne du dix-huitieme Siecle," *Acta Poloniae Historica,* No. 4, 1961, 133–146.

Kula, Witold, "La métrologie historique et la lutte des classes: Exemple de la Pologne au XVIIIe siècle," *Studi in onore di Amintore Fanfani,* **V:** *Evi moderno e contemporaneo.* Milano: Dott. A. Giuffrè-Ed., 1962, 273–288.

Kula, Witold, "Gli studi sulla formazione del capitalismo in Polonia," in A. Caracciolo, red., *Problemi storici della industrializzazione e dello sviluppo.* Urbino, Italy: Argalia Ed., 1965, **VI,** 205–228.

Kula, Witold, *Theorie économique du systeme féodal.* Paris & La Haye: Mouton, 1970.

Kulischer (Koulischer), Joseph, "La grande industrie aux XVIIe et XVIIIe siècles: France, Allemagne, Russie," *Annales d'histoire économique et sociale,* **III,** 9, janv. 1931, 11–46.

Kulischer, Joseph, "Liebeigenschaft in Russland und die Agrarverfassung Preussens in 18. Jahrhundert: Eine vergleichende Studie," *Jahrbucher für Nationalökonomie und Statistik,* 3rd ser., **LXXXII,** 1, 1932, 1–62.

Kuske, Bruno, "Gewerbe, Handel und Verkehr," in H. Aubin *et al.,* her., *Geschichte des Rheinlandes von der altesten Zeit bis zur Gegenwart,* **II:** *Kulturgeschichte.* Essen: G. D. Baedeker, Verlagsbuchhandlung, 1922, 149–248.

Kuske, Bruno, "Die wirtschaftliche und soziale Verflechtung zwischen Deutschland und den

Niederlanden bis zum 18. Jahrhundert," in *Köln, Der Rhein und das Reich.* Köln-Graz: Böhlau-Verlag, 1956, 200–256. (Originally in *Deutsches Archiv für Landes- und Volksforschung,* 1937.)

Labrousse, C.-E. *Esquisse du mouvement des prix et des revenus en France au XVIIIe siècle.* Paris: Lib. Dalloz, 1932, 2 vol.

Labrousse, C.-E., "La révolution démographique du premier tiers du XVIIIe siècle," Bulletin semestriel, *Association pour l'histoire de la civilisation,* Association Marc Bloch, Toulouse, séance du 17 mai 1953, 21–23.

Labrousse, C.-E., "Les 'bons prix' agricoles du XVIIIe siècle," in Fernand Braudel & Ernest Labrousse, dir., *Histoire économique et sociale de la France,* **II:** Ernest Labrousse *et al., Des derniers temps de l'age seigneurial aux préludes de l'age industriel (1660–1789).* Paris: Presses Univ. de France, 1970, 367–416.

Labrousse, Elisabeth, "Le refuge hollandais: Bayle et Jurieu," *XVIIe siècle,* No. 76–77, 1967, 75–93.

La Force, J. Clayburn, "Royal Textile Factories in Spain, 1700–1800," *Journal of Economic History,* **XXIV,** 3, Sept. 1964, 337–363.

Land, Aubrey C., "Economic Base and Social Structure: The Northern Chesapeake in the Eighteenth Century," *Journal of Economic History,* **XXV,** 4, Dec. 1965, 639–654.

Land, Aubrey C., "The Tobacco Staple and the Planter's Problems: Technology, Labor and Crops," *Agricultural History,* **XLIII,** 1, Jan. 1969, 69–81.

Lane, Frederic C., "Oceanic Expansion: Force and Enterprise in the Creation of Oceanic Commerce," *Journal of Economic History,* **X,** Supplement, 1950, 19–39.

Lane, Frederic C., *Venice: A Maritime Republic.* Baltimore, Maryland: Johns Hopkins Univ. Press, 1973.

Lang, James, *Conquest and Commerce: Spain and England in the Americas.* New York: Academic Press, 1975.

Lang, M. F., "New Spain's Mining Depression and the Supply of Quicksilver from Peru," *American Historical Review,* **XLVIII,** 4, Nov. 1968, 632–641.

Langton, John, "Coal Output in South-West Lancashire, 1590–1799," *Economic History Review,* 2nd ser., **XXV,** 1, Feb. 1972, 28–54.

Larquié, Cl., "Les esclaves de Madrid à l'époque de la décadence (1650–1700)," *Revue historique,* **CCXLIV,** 1, juil.–sept. 1970, 41–74.

Larraz, José, *La época del mercantilismo en Castilla (1500–1700).* 2nd ed. Madrid: Atlas, 1943.

Laslett, Peter, "John Locke, the Great Recoinage, and the Origins of the Board of Trade: 1695–1698," *William and Mary Quarterly,* **XIV,** 3, July 1957, 370–402.

Lavrovsky, V. M., "Expropriation of the English Peasantry in the Eighteenth Century," *Economic History Review,* n.s., **IX,** 2, Aug. 1957, 271–282.

Lavrosky, V. M., "The Great Estate in England from the 16th to the 18th Centuries," *First International Conference of Economic History,* Stockholm, August 1960, Paris & La Haye: Mouton, 1960, 353–365.

Lawson, Murray G., *Fur: A Study in English Mercantilism, 1700–1775.* Univ. of Toronto Studies, History and Economics Series, Vol. **IX.** Toronto: Univ. of Toronto Press, 1943.

Lenman, Bruce, *An Economic History of Modern Scotland, 1660–1976.* Hamden, Conneticut: Archon Books, 1977.

Léon, Pierre, "La crise de l'économie française à la fin du règne de Louis XIV (1685–1715)," *Information historique.* **XVIII,** 4, sept.–oct. 1956, 127–137.

Léon, Pierre, "Points de vue sur le monde ouvrier dans la France du XVIIIe siècle," *Third International Conference of Economic History,* Munich, 1965. **I.** Paris & La Haye: Mouton, 1968, 181–185.

Léon, Pierre, *Economies et societes préindustrielles,* **II:** *1650–1780: Les origines d'une accélération de l'histoire.* Paris: Lib. Armand Colin, 1970. (a)

Léon, Pierre, "La réponse de l'industrie," in Fernand Braudel & Ernest Labrousse, dir., *Histoire économique et sociale de la France*, **II:** Ernest Labrousse, *et al., Des derniers temps de l'age seigneurial aux préludes de l'age industriel (1660–1789)*. Paris: Presses Univ. de France, 1970, 217–266. (b)

Léon, Pierre, "L'élan industriel et commercial," in Fernand Braudel & Ernest Labrousse, dir., *Histoire économique et sociale de la France*, **II:** Ernest Labrousse *et al., Des derniers temps de l'age seigneurial aux préludes de l'age industriel (1660–1789)*. Paris: Presses Univ. de France, 1970, 499–528. (c)

Léon, Pierre, "Les nouvelles élites," in Fernand Braudel & Ernest Labrousse, dir., *Histoire économique et sociale de la France*, **II:** Ernest Labrousse *et al., Des derniers temps de l'age seigneurial aux préludes de l'age industriel (1660–1789)*. Paris: Presses Univ. de France, 1970, 601–649. (d)

Léon, Pierre, "Morcellement et émergence du monde ouvrier," in Fernand Braudel & Ernest Labrousse, dir., *Histoire économique et social de la France*, **II:** Ernest Labrousse *et al., Des derniers temps de l'age seigneurial aux préludes de l'age industriel (1660–1789)*. Paris: Presses Univ. de France, 1970, 651–689. (e)

Léon, Pierre, "Structures du commerce extérieur et évolution industrielle de la France à la fin du XVIII siècle," in *Conjonture économique, structures sociales*. Hommage à Ernest Labrousse. Paris & La Haye: Mouton, 1974.

Léon, Pierre & Carrière, Charles, "L'appel des marchés," in Fernand Braudel & Ernest Labrousse, dir., *Histoire économique et sociale de la France*, **II:** Ernest Labrousse *et al., Des derniers temps de l'age seigneurial aux préludes de l'age industriel (1660–1789)*. Paris: Presses Univ. de France, 1970, 161–215.

Léonard, Emile–G., "Economie et religion. Les protestants français au XVIIIe siècle," *Annales d'histoire sociale,* **II,** 1, janv. 1940, 5–20.

Léonard, Emile–G., "Le protestantisme français au XVIIe siècle," *Revue historique,* **CC,** 2, oct.–dec. 1948, 153–179.

Léonard, Emile–G., *L'Armée et ses problèmes au XVIIIe siècle*. Paris: Lib. Plon, 1958.

Le Roy Ladurie, Emmanuel, "Climat et récoltes aux XVIIe et XVIIIe siècles," *Annales E.S.C.,* **XV,** 3, mai–juin 1960, 434–465.

Le Roy Ladurie, Emmanuel, *Histoire du Languedoc*. Paris: Presses Univ. de France, 1962.

Le Roy Ladurie, Emmanuel, "Voies nouvelles pour l'histoire rurale (XVIe–XVIIIe siècles)," *Etudes rurales*, No. 13–14, avr.–sept., 1964, 79–95.

Le Roy Ladurie, Emmanuel, *Histoire du climat depuis l'an mil*. Paris: Flammarion, 1967.

Le Roy Ladurie, Emmanuel, "Les rendements du blé en Languedoc," *Third International Conference of Economic History*, Munich, 1965, **II.** *Production et productivité agricole*. Paris & La Haye: Mouton, 1968, 75–84.

Le Roy Ladurie, Emmanuel, "L'amenorrhée de famine (XVIIe-XXe siècles)," *Annales E.S.C.,* **XXIV,** 6, nov.–dec. 1969, 1589–1601.

Le Roy Ladurie, Emmanuel, "Les insurgés de l'impôt," *Le Nouvel Observateur*, 28 juin 1971, 26–28.

Le Roy Laduire, Emmanuel, "Sur quelques types de revenus réels (16e–18e siècles)," *Fourth International Conference of Economic History*, Bloomington, 1968. Paris & La Haye: Mouton, 1973, 419–435.

Le Roy Ladurie, Emmanuel, "A Long Agrarian Cycle: Languedoc, 1500–1700," in Peter Earle, ed., *Essays in European Economic History, 1500–1800*. Oxford: Clarendon Press, 1974. (a) (Translated from *Les Paysans de Languedoc*, 1969.)

Le Roy Ladurie, Emmanuel, "Pour un modèle de l'économie rurale française au XVIII siècle," *Cahiers d'histoire,* **XIV,** 1, 1974, 5–27. (b)

Le Roy Ladurie, Emmanuel, "Révoltes et contestations rurales en France de 1675 à 1788," *Annales E.S.C.,* **XXIX,** 1, janv.–févr. 1974, 6–22. (c)

Le Roy Ladurie, Emmanuel, "De la crise ultime à la vraie croissance," in Emmanuel Le Roy Ladurie, réd., *L'age classique des paysans de 1340 à 1789,* Vol. **II** of *Histoire de la France rurale.* Paris: Seuil, 1975, 359–591. (a)

Le Roy Ladurie, Emmanuel, "Un 'modele septentrional': Les campagnes parisiennes (XVIe–XVIIe siècles)," *Annales E.S.C.,* **XXX,** 6, nov.–dec. 1975, 1397–1413. (b)

Le Roy Ladurie, Emmanuel, "Un cas de méthodologie dans l'histoire rurale: Les grandes monographies des révoltes et des contestations rurales en France de 1675 à 1788," in *Metodología de la historia moderna: economía y demografía,* Actas de las I Jornadas de Metodología Aplicada de las Ciencias Históricas, Univ. de Santiago de Compostala. Segovia: Artes Graficas Galicia, **III,** 1975, 33–50. (c)

Le Roy Ladurie, Emmanuel, "Motionless History," *Social Science History,* **I,** 2, Winter 1977, 115–136. (Translated from *Annales E.S.C.,* 1974.)

Leśkiewicz, Janina, "Sur le niveau et les composantes du revenu foncier en Pologne du XVIe siècle au XVIIIe siècle," in *First International Conference of Economic History,* Stockholm, August, 1960, *Contributions.* Paris & La Haye: Mouton, 1960, 409–414.

Leśnodorski, Bogusław, "Les Partages de la Pologne. Analyse des causes et essai d'une théorie," *Acta Poloniae Historica,* No. 8, 1963, 7–30.

Leszczyński, Józef, "La Silésie dans la politique européenne au XVIe–XVIIIe siècles," *Acta Poloniae Historica,* No. 22, 1970, 90–107.

Leuilliot, Paul, "Influence du commerce oriental sur l'économie occidentale," in M. Mollat, réd., *Sociétés et compagnies en Orient et dans l'Ocean Indien.* Paris: S.E.V.P.E.N., 1970, 611–627.

Lichtheim, George, *Imperialism.* London: Penguin, 1974.

Liebel, Helen P., "The Bourgeoisie in Southwestern Germany, 1500–1789: A Rising Class?", *International Review of Social History,* **X,** 2, 1965, 283–307. (a)

Liebel, Helen P., "Laissez-faire vs. Mercantilism: The Rise of Hamburg and the Hamburg Bourgeoisie vs. Frederick the Great in the Crisis of 1763," *Vierteljahrschrift für Sozial- und Wirtschaftgeschichte,* **LII,** 2, 1965, 206–238. (b)

Liiv, Otto, "Die wirtschaftliche Lage des estnischen Gebietes am Ausgang des XVII Jahrhunderts," *I. Verhandlungen der Gelehrten Estnischen Gesellschaft,* **XXVII,** 1935, 1–336.

Lipson, Ephraim, *The Economic History of England,* Vols. II–III: *The Age of Mercantilism,* 6th ed. London: Adam & Charles Black, 1956.

Lira, Andrés & Muro, Luis, "El siglo de la integración," in Centro de Estudios Históricos, *Historia General de Mexico,* **II.** Mexico: El Colegio de Mexico, 1976, 83–181.

Litchfield, R. Burr, "Les investissements commerciaux des patriciens florentins au XVIIIe siècle," *Annales E.S.C.,* **XXIV,** 3, mai–juin 1969, 685–721.

Lockhart, James, "Encomienda and Hacienda: The Evolution of the Great Estate in the Spanish Indies," *Hispanic American Historical Review,* **LXIX,** 3, Aug. 1969, 411–429.

Lom, František, "Die Arbeitsproduktivitat in der Geschichte der tschechoslowakischen Landwirtschaft," *Zeitschrift für Agrargeschichte und Agrarsoziologie,* **XIX,** 1, Apr. 1971, 1–25.

López, Adalberto, "The Economics of Yerba Mate in Seventeenth-Century South America," *Agricultural History,* **XLVIII,** 4, Oct. 1974, 493–509.

Lord, Eleanor Louisa, *Industrial Experiments in the British Colonies of North America.* Studies in History and Political Science, **XVII,** Baltimore, Maryland: Johns Hopkins Univ., 1898.

Lunde, Johs., *Handelshuset bak "Garman & Worse": Jacob Kielland & Son.* Bergen: Universitetsforlaget, 1963.

Lundkvist, Sven, "The Experience of Empire: Sweden as a Great Power," in M. Roberts, ed., *Sweden's Age of Greatness, 1632–1718.* New York: St. Martin's Press, 1973, 20–57.

Lütge, Friedrich, "Strukturelle und konjunkturelle Wandlungen in der deutschen Wirtschaft vor Ausbruch des Dreissigjährigen Krieges," in *Bayerische Akademie der Wissenschaften, Phil.-Hist. Kl., Sitzungsberichte,* No. 5, 1958.

Lütge, Freidrich, *Geschichte der deutschen Agrarverfassung vom frühen Mittelalter bis zum 19. Jahrhundert.* Stuttgart: Verlag Eugen Ulmer, 1963.

Lütge, Friedrich, "Grundherrschaft und Gutsherrschaft," *Handwörterbuch des Sozialwissenschaften*. Stuttgart: Gustav Fischer; Tubingen: J. C. B. Mohr (Paul Siebeck); Göttingen: Vandenhoeck & Ruprecht, 1965, **IV,** 682–688.

Lütge, Friedrich, *Deutsche Sozial- und Wirtschaftsgeschichte,* 3rd enlarged and improved ed. Berlin: Springer-Verlag, 1966.

Lüthy, Herbert, *La Banque Protestante en France de la Révocation de l'Edit de Nantes à la Révolution,* **I:** *Dispersion et regroupement (1685–1730).* Paris: S.E.V.P.E.N., 1959.

Lüthy, Herbert, *La Banque Protestante en France de la Révocation de l'Edit de Nantes à la Révolution,* **II:** *De la Banque aux Finances (1730–1794).* Paris: S.E.V.P.E.N., 1961.

Luzac, Elie, *La richesse de la Hollande.* London: aux dépens de la Compagnie, 1778, 2 vol.

Luzzatto, Gino, *Per una storia economica d'Italia,* 2nd ed. Bari, Italy: Ed. Laterza, 1974.

Lynch, John, *Spain Under the Habsburgs.* **II:** *Spain and America: 1598–1700.* Oxford: Basil Blackwell, 1969.

Macartney, C. A., "The Habsburg Dominions," in *New Cambridge Modern History,* **VII:** J. O. Lindsay, ed., *The Old Regime, 1713–63.* Cambridge: University Press, 1966, 391–415.

Macartney, C. A., "Hungary," in A. Goodwin, ed., *The European Nobility in the Eighteenth Century.* New York: Harper & Row (Torchbooks), 1967, 118–135.

Macedo, Jorge Borges de, "O Tratado de Methuen," *Dicionário de história de Portugal,* **II,** edited by Joël Serrão. Lisboa: 1963. (a)

Macedo, Jorge Borges de, *Problemas de Historia da Industria Portuguesa no Século XVIII.* Lisboa: Assoc. Industrial Portuguesa, Estudos de Economia Aplicada, 1963. (b)

Macera, Pablo, "Feudalismo colonial americano: el caso de las haciendas peruanas," *Acta Historica* (Acta Universitatis Szegediensis de Attila Josef Nominatae), **XXXV,** 1971, 3–43.

MacLeod, Murdo J., *Spanish Central America: A Socioeconomic History, 1520–1720.* Berkeley: Univ. of California Press, 1973.

Mączak, Antoni, "Export of Grain and the Problem of Distribution of National Income in the Years 1550–1650," *Acta Poloniae Historica,* No. 18, 1968, 75–98.

Mączak, Antoni, "The Balance of Polish Sea Trade with the West, 1565–1646," *Scandinavian Economic History Review,* **XVIII,** 2, 1970, 107–142.

Mączak, Antoni, "Agricultural and Livestock Production in Poland: Internal and Foreign Markets," *Journal of European Economic History,* **I,** 3, Winter 1972, 671–680.

Mączak, Antoni, review of A. Attman, *The Russian and Polish Markets in International Trade, 1500–1650,* in *Journal of European Economic History,* **III,** 2, Fall 1974, 505–508.

Mączak, Antoni, "Money and Society in Poland-Lithuania of the 16th–17th Centuries," Settima Settimana di Studio, Istituto Internazionale di Storia Economica "Francesco Datini", 15 apr. 1975.

Mączak, Antoni, "Money and Society in Poland and Lithuania in the 16th and 17th Centuries," *Journal of European Economic History,* **V,** 1, Spring 1976, 69–104. (a)

Mączak, Antoni, "State Revenues and National Income: Poland in the Crisis of the Seventeenth Century," Ottava Settimana di Studio, Istituto Internazionale di Storia Economica "Francesco Datini", Prato, 8 magg. 1976. (b)

Mączak, Antoni & Samsonowicz, Henry K., "La zone baltique; l'un des éléments du marché européen," *Acta Poloniae Historica,* No. 11, 1965, 71–99.

Mahan, A. T., *Influence of Sea Power Upon History, 1600–1783.* London: Sampson Low, Marston, Searle & Rivington, 1889.

Makkai, László, "Die Hauptzuge der wirtschaftlichsozialen Entwicklung Ungarns im 15–17. Jh." in *Studia Historica,* No. 53. Budapest: Akademiai Kiado, 1963, 27–46.

Makkai, László, "Der Ungarische Viehhandel, 1550–1650," in Ingomar Bog, her., *Der Aussenhandel Ostmitteleuropas, 1450–1650.* Köln-Wien: Böhlau Verlag, 1971, 483–506.

Makkai, László, "La structure et la productivité de l'économie agraire de la Hongrie au milieu du XVIIe siècle," in S. Herbst *et al.,* eds., *Spoleczenstwo Gospodarka Kultura.* Studia ofiarowane

Marianowi Małowistowi w czterdziestolecie pracy naukowej. Warszawa: PWN, 1974, 197–209.

Makkai, László, "Neo-Serfdom: Its Origin and Nature in East Central Europe," *Slavic Review,* **XXXIV,** 2, June 1975, 225–238.

Małecki, Jan M., "Le rôle de Cracovie dans l'économie polonaise aux XVIe, XVIIe et XVIIIe siècles," *Acta Poloniae Historica,* No. 21, 1970, 108–122.

Małecki, Jan M., "Die Wandlungen im Krakauer und polnischen Handel zur Zeit der Türkenkriege des 16. und 17. Jahrhunderts," in O. Pickl, her., *Die wirtschaftlichen Auswirkungen der Türkenkriege,* Grazer Forschungen zur Wirtschafts- und Sozialgeschichte, **I.** Graz: 1971, 145–151.

Małowist, Marian, "The Economic and Social Development of the Baltic Countries from the 15th to the 17th Centuries," *Economic History Review,* 2nd ser., **XII,** 2, 1959, 177–189.

Małowist, Marian, "L'évolution industrielle en Pologne du XIVe au XVIIe siècle," in *Croissance et regression en Europe, XIVe–XVIIe siècles,* Cahiers des Annales, 34. Paris: Lib. Armand Colin, 1972, 191–215.

Małowist, Marian, "Problems of the Growth of the National Economy of Central-Eastern Europe in the Late Middle Ages," *Journal of European Economic History,* **III,** 2, Fall 1974, 319–357.

Małowist, Marian, "Quelques remarques sur le déclin des états de l'Europe de l'est au XVIe jusqu'au XVIIIe siècle," paper delivered at Seminar of Fernand Braudel, Paris, 4 mars 1976.

Mandrou, Robert, "Le baroque européen: mentalité pathétique et révolution sociale," *Annales E.S.C.,* **XV,** 5, sept.–oct. 1960, 898–914.

Mandrou, Robert, "L'agriculture hors du développement capitaliste: Le cas des Fugger," *Studi storici,* **IX,** 3/4, lugl.-dic. 1968, 784–793.

Marino, John A., "La crisi di Venezia e la New Economic History," *Studi storici,* **XIX,** 1, genn.–marzo 1978, 79–107.

Markovitch, Tihomir J., "L'industrie française au XVIIIe siècle: l'industrie lainière à la fin du regne de Louis XIV et sous la Régence," *Economies et sociétés,* Cahiers de l'I.S.E.A., **II,** 8, août 1968, 1517–1697. (a)

Markovitch, Tihomir J., "L'industrie lainière française au début du XVIIIe siècle," *Revue d'histoire économique et sociale,* **XLVI,** 4, 1968, 550–579. (b)

Marques, A. H. de Oliveira, *History of Portugal,* 2nd ed. New York: Columbia Univ. Press, 1976.

Marrès, P., "Le Languedoc méditerranéen aux XVIIe et XVIIIe siècles," *Annales de l'Institut d'Etudes Occitanes,* 4e ser., No. 2, aut. 1966, 151–156.

Martin Saint-Léon, Etienne, *Histoire des corporations de métiers.* Genève: Slatkine–Megariotis Reprints, 1976. (Originally published, Paris, 1922).

Marx, Karl, *Secret Diplomatic History of the Eighteenth Century.* New York: International Publ., 1969.

Masefield, G. B., "Crops and Livestock," in *Cambridge Economic History of Europe,* **IV:** E. E. Rich & C. H. Wilson, eds., *The Economy of Expanding Europe in the Sixteenth and Seventeenth Centuries.* Cambridge: University Press, 1967, 275–301.

Masselman, George, "Dutch Colonial Policy in the Seventeenth Century," *Journal of Economic History,* **XXI,** 4, Dec. 1961, 455–468.

Masselman, George, *The Cradle of Colonialism.* New Haven, Connecticut: Yale Univ. Press, 1963.

Masson, Paul, *Histoire du commerce français dans le Levant au XVIIe siècle.* New York: Burt Franklin, 1967. (a) (Originally published, Paris, 1911).

Masson, Paul, *Histoire du commerce français dans le Levant au XVIIIe siècle.* New York: Burt Franklin, 1967. (b) (Originally published, Paris 1896.)

Mata, Eugénia & Valério, Nuno, "Alguns dados e notas sobre o comércio europeu e mundial nos finais do século XVII," *Revista de história económica e social,* No. 2, julho–dez. de 1978, 105–122.

Matejek, František, "La production agricole dans les pays tchécoslovaques à partir du XVIe siècle jusqu'a la première guerre mondiale," *Troisième Conférence Internationale d'Histoire Economique*, Munich, 1965, **II.** Paris & La Haye: Mouton, 1968, 205–219.

Mathias, Peter, "Agriculture and the Brewing and Distilling Industries in the Eighteenth Century," *Economic History Review*, n.s., **V,** 2, Aug. 1952, 249–257.

Mathias, Peter & O'Brien, Patrick, "Taxation in Britain and France, 1715–1810. A Comparison of the Social and Economic Incidence of Taxes Collected by the Central Government," *Journal of European Economic History*, **V,** 3, Winter 1976, 601–650.

Mathiex, Jean, "Trafic et prix de l'homme en Méditerranée aux XVIIe et XVIIIe siècles," *Annales E.S.C.*, **IX,** 2, avr. juin 1954, 157 164.

Mauro, Frédéric, "Pour une théorie du capitalisme commercial," *Vierteljahrschrift fur Sozial- und Wirtschaftsgeschichte*, **XLII,** 2, 1955, 117–131.

Mauro, Frédéric, "Sur la 'crise' du XVIIe siècle," *Annales E.S.C.*, **XIV,** 1, janv.–mars 1959, 181–185.

Mauro, Frédéric, *Le Portugal et l'Atlantique au XVIIe siècle (1570–1670). Etude économique.* Paris: S.E.V.P.E.N., 1960.

Mauro, Frédéric, "Toward an 'Intercontinental Model': European Overseas Expansion between 1500 and 1800," *Economic History Review*, 2nd ser., **XIV,** 1 1961, 1–17. (a)

Mauro, Frédéric, "L'empire portugais et le commerce franco-portugais au milieu du XVIIIe siècle," *Actas do Congresso Internacional de Historia dos Descobrimentos*, **V.** Lisboa: 1961, 1–16. (b)

Mauro, Frédéric, "Marchands et marchands-banquiers portugais au XVIIe siècle," *Revista portuguesa de história*, **IX,** 1961, 5–20. (c)

Mauro, Frédéric, "La bourgeoisie portugaise au XVIIe siècle," in *Etudes économiques sur l'expansion portugaise (1500–1900).* Paris: Fund. Calouste Gulbenkian, 1970, 15–35. (Originally in *Le XVIIe siècle,* 1958.)

Mauro, Frédéric, "Existence et persistance d'un régime féodal ou scigneurial au Brésil," in *L'abolition de la "féodalité" dans le monde occidental,* Colloques internationaux du C.N.R.S., Toulouse 12–16 nov. 1968. Paris: Ed. du C.N.R.S., **I,** 1971, 385–391.

Mauro, Frédéric, "Conjoncture economique et structure sociale en Amérique latine depuis l'époque coloniale," in *Conjoncture économique, structures sociales.* Hommage á Ernest Labrousse. Paris & La Haye: Mouton, 1974, 237–251.

Mauro, Frédéric, "Le rôle de la monnaie dans les décollages manqués de l'économie portugaise du XVe au XVIIIe siècles." Paper presented at VII Settimana di Studio, Prato, 17 apr. 1975.

Maxwell, Kenneth, "Pombal and the Nationalization of the Luso-Brazilian Economy," *Hispanic American Historical Review*, **XLVIII,** 4, Nov. 1968, 608–631.

May, Louis–Philippe, *Histoire économique de la Martinique (1635–1763).* Paris: Les Presses Modernes, 1930.

McLachlan, Jean O., *Trade and Peace with Old Spain, 1667–1750.* Cambridge: University Press, 1940.

McManners, J., "France," in Albert Goodwin, ed., *The European Nobility in the Eighteenth Century.* New York: Harper & Row (Torchbooks), 1967, 22–42.

McNeill, William H., *The Shape of European History.* London & New York: Oxford Univ. Press, 1974.

Medick, Hans, "The Proto-Industrial Family Economy: The Structural Function of Household and Family during the Transition from Peasant Society to Industrial Capitalism, *Social History*, No. 3, Oct. 1976, 291–315.

Mehring, Franz, *Absolutism and Revolution in Germany, 1525–1848.* London: New Park Publ., 1975. (Originally published in 1892, 1897, 1910)

Meilink-Roelofsz, M. A. P., "Aspects of Dutch Colonial Development in Asia in the Seventeenth Century," in J. S. Bromley & E. H. Kossmann, eds., *Britain and the Netherlands in Europe and Asia.* London: Macmillan, 1968, 56–82.

Mejdricka, Kveta, "L'état du régime féodal à la veille de son abolition et les conditions de sa supression en Bohème," in *L'abolition de la "féodalité" dans le monde occidental.* Colloques internationaux du C.N.R.S., Toulouse 12–16 nov. 1968. Paris: Ed. du C.N.R.S., **I**, 1971, 393–409.

Mellafe, Rolando, *La introducción de la esclavitud negra en Chile: tráficos y nitas.* Estudios de Historia Económica Americana: Trabajo y Salario en el Periodo Colonial, **II.** Santiago: Univ. de Chile, 1959.

Menard, Russell R., "Secular Trends in the Chesapeake Tobacco Industry," *Working Papers from the Regional Economic History Research Center,* **I,** 3, 1978, 1–34.

Menashe, Louis, "Historians Define the Baroque: Notes on a Problem of Art and Social History," *Comparative Studies in Society and History,* **VII,** 3, Apr. 1965, 333–342.

Mendels, Franklin F., "Proto-Industrialization: The First Phase of the Industrialization Process," *Journal of Economic History,* **XXXII,** 1, Mar. 1972, 241–261.

Mendels, Franklin F., "Agriculture and Peasant Industry in Eighteenth-Century Flanders," in William N. Parker & Eric L. Jones, eds., *European Peasants and Their Markets.* Princeton, New Jersey: Princeton Univ. Press, 1975, 179–204.

Merrington, John, "Town and Country in the Transition to Capitalism," in Rodney Hilton, ed., *The Transition from Feudalism to Capitalism.* London: New Left Books, 1976, 170–195. (Originally in *New Left Review,* 1975.)

Mertens, Jacques E., *La naissance et le développement de l'étalon-or, 1692–1922,* Univ. de Louvain, Collection de l'Ecole des Sciences Politiques et Sociales, No. 131. Louvain: Ed. Em. Warny, 1944.

Meuvret, Jean, "Les mouvements des prix de 1661 à 1715 et leurs répercussions," *Journal de la Société de Statistique de Paris,* **LXXXV,** 5–6, mai–juin 1944, 109–119.

Meuvret, Jean, "Circulation monétaire et utilisation économique de la monnaie dans la France du XVIe et du XVIIe siècles," *Etudes d'histoire moderne et contemporaine,* **I,** 1947, 15–18.

Meuvret, Jean, "La géographie des prix des céréales et les anciennes économies européennes: Prix méditerranéens, prix continentaux, prix atlantiques à la fin du XVIIe siècle," *Revista de economia,* **IV,** 2, 1951, 63–69.

Meuvret, Jean, "Conjoncture et crise au XVIIe siècle: L'exemple des prix milanais," *Annales E.S.C.,* **VII,** 2, avr.–juin 1953, 215–219.

Meuvret, Jean, "L'agriculture en Europe au XVIIe et XVIIIe siècles," *X Congresso Internazionale di Scienze Storiche,* Roma, 4–11 sett. 1955, *Relazioni,* **IV:** *Storia moderna.* Firenze: G. C. Sansoni-Ed., 1955, 139–168.

Meuvret, Jean, "Circuits d'échange et travail rural dans la France du XVIIe siècle," *Studi in onore di Armando Sapori.* Milano: Istituto Edit. Cisalpino, **II,** 1957, 1127–1142.

Meuvret, Jean, "Domaines ou ensembles territoriaux?," *First International Conference of Economic History,* Stockholm, August 1960. Paris & La Haye: Mouton, 1960, 343–352.

Meuvret, Jean, "Production et productivité agricoles," *Third International Conference of Economic History,* Munich, 1965, **II:** *Production et productivités agricoles.* Paris & La Haye: Mouton, 1968, 11–22.

Meuvret, Jean, "La France au temps de Louis XIV: des temps difficiles," in *Etudes d'histoire économique.* Paris: Lib. Armand Colin, 1971, 17–37. (a) (Originally in *La France au temps de Louis XIV,* 1965.)

Meuvret, Jean, "Les oscillations des prix de céréales aux XVIIe et XVIIIe siècles en Angleterre et dans les pays du bassin parisien," in *Etudes d'histoire économique.* Paris: Lib. Armand Colin, 1971, 113–124. (b) (Originally in *Revue d'histoire moderne et contemporaine,* 1969.)

Michalkjewicz, Stanislas, "Einige Episoden der Geschichte der schleisischen Bauernkämpfer, im 17. und 18, Jh.," in Eva Maleczyńska, her., *Beitrage zür Geschichte Schlesiens.* Berlin: Rütten & Loening, 1958, 356–400.

Michell, A. R., "The European Fisheries in Early Modern History," in *Cambridge Economic History of Europe,* **V:** E. E. Rich & C. H. Wilson, eds., *The Economic Organization of Early Modern Europe.* Cambridge: University Press, 1977, 134–184.

Mika, Alois, "On the Economic Status of Czech Towns in the Period of Late Feudalism," *Economic History,* **II,** published on the occasion of the VIIth International Economic History Congress in Edinburgh, 1978. Prague: Institute of Czechoslovak and World History of the Czechoslovak Academy of Sciences, 1978, 225–256.

Mims, Stewart L., *Colbert's West India Policy.* New Haven, Connecticut: Yale Univ. Press, 1912.

Minchinton, Walter, "Patterns and Structure of Demand 1500–1750," in C. M. Cipolla, ed., *The Fontana Economic History of Europe,* **II:** *The Sixteenth and Seventeenth Centuries.* Glasgow: Collins, 1974, 82–176.

Mingay, G. E., "The Agricultural Depression, 1730–1750," *Economic History Review,* 2nd ser., **VIII,** 3, 1956, 323–338.

Mingay, G. E., "The Large Estate in Eighteenth-Century England," *First International Conference of Economic History,* Stockholm, August 1960. Paris & La Haye: Mouton, 1960, 367–383.

Mingay, G. E., "The Size of Farms in the Eighteenth Century," *Economic History Review,* 2nd ser., **XIV,** 3, Apr. 1962, 469–488.

Mingay, G. E., *English Landed Society in the Eighteenth Century.* London: Routledge & Kegan Paul, 1963.

Mingay, G. E., "The Land Tax Assessments and the Small Landowner," *Economic History Review,* 2nd ser., **XVII,** 2, Dec. 1964, 381–388.

Mingay, G. E., *Enclosure and the Small Farmer in the Age of the Industrial Revolution.* London: Macmillan, 1968.

Mintz, Sidney W., "Currency Problems in Eighteenth Century Jamaica and Gresham's Law," in Robert A. Manners, ed., *Process and Pattern in Culture.* Chicago, Illinois: Aldine, 1964, 248–265.

Mintz, Sidney W. & Wolf, Eric R., "Haciendas and Plantations in Middle America and the Antilles," *Social and Economic Studies,* **VI,** 3, Sept. 1957, 380–412.

Molenda, Danuta, "Investments in Ore Mining in Poland from the 13th to the 17th Centuries," *Journal of European Economic History,* **V,** 1, Spring 1976, 151–169.

Mollat, Michel, réd., *Sociétés et compagnies de commerce en Orient et dans l'Océan Indien,* Actes du Huitième Colloque International d'Histoire Maritime, Beyrouth, 5–10 sept. 1966. Paris: S.E.V.P.E.N., 1970.

Molnar, Erik, "Les fondements économiques et sociaux de l'absolutisme," *XII Congrès International des Sciences Historiques, Rapports,* **IV.** *Methodologie et histoire contemporaine.* Wien: Verlag Ferdinand Berge & Söhne, 1965, 155–169.

Mols, Roger, O. J., "Population in Europe 1500–1700," in C. M. Cipolla, ed. *The Fontana Economic History of Europe,* **II:** *The Sixteenth and Seventeenth Centuries.* Glasgow: Collins, 1974, 15–82.

Monter, E. William, "Swiss Investment in England, 1697–1720," *Revue internationale d'histoire de la banque,* **II,** 1969, 285–298.

Moreno Fraginals, Manuel, *El Ingenio,* 3 vol. La Habana: Ed. de Ciencias Sociales, 1978.

Morgan, W. T., "Economic Aspects of the Negotiations at Ryswick," in Ian R. Christie, ed., *Essays in Modern History.* London: Macmillan, 1968, 172–195. (Originally in *Transactions of the Royal Historical Society,* read 14 May 1931.)

Morineau, Michel, "Le balance du commerce franco-néerlandais et le resserrement économique des Provinces-Unies au XVIIIe siècle," *Economisch-Historisch Jaarboek,* **XXX,** 4, 1965, 170–233.

Morineau, Michel, "Y a-t-il eu une révolution agricole en France au XVIIIe siècle?," *Revue historique,* **CCXXXIX,** 1, avr.–juin 1968, 299–326.

Morineau, Michel, "Gazettes hollandais et trésors américains," *Anuario de historia económica y social,* **II,** 2, enero–dic. 1969, 289–361. (a)

Morineau, Michel, "Histoire sans frontières: prix et 'révolution agricole'," *Annales E.S.C.,* **XXIV,** 2, mars–avr. 1969, 403–423. (b)

Morineau, Michel, "En Hollande au XVIIe siècle," in Jean-Jacques Hemardinquier, réd., *Pour une histoire de l'alimentation,* Cahiers des Annales, 28. Paris: Lib. Armand Colin, 1970, 107–114. (a) (Originally in *Annales E.S.C.,* 1963.)

Morineau, Michel, "Post-scriptum. De la Hollande à la France," in Jean-Jacques Hémardinquier, réd., *Pour une histoire de l'alimentation,* Cahiers des Annales, 28. Paris: Lib. Armand Colin, 1970, 115–125. (b)

Morineau, Michel, "Flottes de commerce et trafics français en Méditerranée au XVIIe siècle (jusqu'en 1669)," *XVIIe siècle,* No. 86–87, 1970, 135–171. (c)

Morineau, Michel, "Bayonne et Saint-Jean-de-Lux, relais du commerce néerlandais vers l'Espagne au début du XVIIe siècle," *Actes du Quatre-Vingt-Quatorzième Congrès National des Sociétés Savantes,* Pau 1969, **II,** Section d'histoire moderne et contemporaine. Paris: Bibliothèque Nationale, 1971, 309–330.

Morineau, Michel, "Quelques remarques touchant le financement de l'économie des Provinces-Unies au XVIIe et au XVIIIe siècle," paper at Cuarta Settimana di Studio, Istituto Internazionale di Storia Economica "Francesco Datini", Prato, 16 apr. 1972.

Morineau, Michel, "Quelques remarques sur l'abondance monétaire aux Provinces-Unies," *Annales E.S.C.,* **XXIX,** 3, mai–juin 1974, 767–776.

Morineau, Michel, "Quelques recherches relatives à la balance du commerce extérieur français au XVIIIe siècle: ou cette fois un égale deux," in Pierre Léon, réd., *Aires et structures du commerce français au XVIIIe siècle,* Colloque National de l'Association Française des Historiens Economistes, Paris, C.N.R.S., 4–6 oct. 1973. Lyon: Centre d'Histoire Economique et Social de la Region Lyonnaise, 1975, 1–45.

Morineau, Michel, "La terre," in Pierre Deyon & Jean Jacquart, *Les hésitations de la croissance, 1580–1740,* Vol. **II** of Pierre Léon, réd., *Histoire économique et sociale du monde.* Paris: Lib. Armand Colin, 1978, 11–39. (a)

Morineau, Michel, "Le siècle," in Pierre Deyon & Jean Jacquart, *Les hésitations de la croissance, 1580–1740, Vol.* **II** of Pierre Léon, réd., *Histoire économique et sociale du monde.* Paris: Lib. Armand Colin, 1978, 63–106. (b)

Morineau, Michel, "Un siècle après la conquête: Les empires ibériques," in Pierre Deyon & Jean Jacquart, *Les hésitations de la croissance, 1580–1740,* Vol. **II** of Pierre Léon, réd., *Histoire économique et sociale du monde.* Paris: Lib. Armand Colin, 1978, 109–138. (c)

Morineau, Michel, "Les mancenilliers de l'Europe," in Pierre Deyon & Jean Jacquart, *Les hésitations de la croissance, 1580–1740,* Vol. **II** of Pierre Léon, réd., *Histoire économique et sociale du monde.* Paris: Lib. Armand Colin, 1978, 139–162. (d)

Morineau, Michel, "La 'substitution' aux Indes Orientales," in Pierre Deyon & Jean Jacquart, *Les hésitations de la croissance, 1580–1740,* Vol. **II** of Pierre Léon, réd., *Histoire économique et sociale du monde.* Paris: Lib. Armand Colin, 1978, 163–176. (e)

Morineau, Michel, "Jeune Amérique et vieille Afrique," in Pierre Deyon & Jean Jacquart, *Les hésitations de la croissance, 1580–1740,* Vol. **II** of Pierre Léon, réd., *Histoire économique et sociale du monde.* Paris: Lib. Armand Colin, 1978, 521–546. (f)

Morineau, Michel, "Le challenge Europe-Asie," in Pierre Deyon & Jean Jacquart, *Les hésitations de la croissance, 1580–1740,* Vol. **II** of Pierre Léon, réd., *Histoire économique de sociale du monde.* Paris: Lib. Armand Colin, 1978, 547–579. (g)

Morineau, Michel, "Or brésilien et gazettes hollandaises," *Revue d'histoire moderne et contemporaine,* **XXV,** 1, janv.–mars, 1978, 3–60. (h)

Mörner, Magnus, "The Spanish American Hacienda: A Survey of Recent Research and Debate," *Hispanic American Historical Review,* **LIII,** 2, May 1973, 183–216.

Mousnier, Roland, "L'évolution des finances publiques en France et en Angleterre pendant les guerres de la Ligue d'Augsbourg et de la Succession d'Espagne," *Revue historique,* **XLIV,** No. 205, janv.–mars 1951, 1–23.

Mousnier, Roland, *Les XVIe et XVIIe siècles,* 5e ed., revue, corrigée et augmentée, Vol. **IV** of Maurice Crouzet, réd., *Histoire Générale des Civilisations.* Paris: Presses Univ. de France, 1967.

Mukherjee, Ramkrishna, *The Rise and Fall of the East India Company.* New York: Monthly Review Press, 1974.

Munck, Thomas, "The Economic and Social Position of Peasant Freeholders in Late Seventeenth-Century Denmark," *Scandinavian Economic History Review,* **XXV**, 1, 1977, 37–61.

Munktell, Henrik, *Bergsmans- och Bruksförlag intill 1748 års Förlags-Förordning.* Uppsala, Sweden: Almqvist & Wiksells, 1934.

Murray, R. K., "The Anglo-Scottish Union," *Scots Law Times,* Nov. 4, 1961, 161–164.

Myška, Milan, "Pre-Industrial Iron-Making in the Czech Lands," *Past and Present,* No. 82, Feb. 1979, 44–72.

Nadal, J. & Giralt, E., *La population catalane de 1553 à 1717.* Paris: S.E.V.P.E.N., 1960.

Naish, G. P. B., "Ships and Shipbuilding," in C. Singer, *et al., A History of Technology.* **III:** *From the Renaissance to the Industrial Revolution, c1500–c1700.* Oxford: Clarendon Press, 1957, 471–500.

Nef, John U., *War and Human Progress: An Essay on the Rise of Industrial Civilisation.* New York: W. W. Norton, 1968.

Nef, John U., "Impact of War on Science and Technology," *Fourth International Conference on Economic History,* Bloomington, 1968. Paris & La Haye: Mouton, 1973, 237–243.

Neguev, S., "Le Proche-Orient précapitaliste," *Khamsin,* No. 2, 1975, 7–14.

Nelson, George H., "Contraband Trade under the Asiento, 1730–1739," *American Historical Review,* **LI**, 1, Oct. 1945, 55–67.

Neto, Paulo Elpídio de Menezes, "Patrimonialisme rural et structure de domination au Brésil, à l'époque coloniale," *Revista de ciências sociais,* **IV**, 1, 1973, 93–107.

Nettels, Curtis P., "The Manace of Colonial Manufacturing," *New England Quarterly,* **IV**, 2, Apr. 1931, 230–269. (a)

Nettels, Curtis P., "England and the Spanish American Trade, 1670–1775," *Journal of Modern History,* **III**, 1, Mar. 1931, 1–32. (b)

Nettels, Curtis P., "England's Trade with New England and New York, 1685–1720," *Publications of the Colonial Society of Massachusetts,* **XXVIII**, Feb. 1933, 322–350.

Nettels, Curtis P., "British Mercantilism and the Economic Development of the Thirteen Colonies," *Journal of Economic History,* **XII**, 2, Spring 1952, 105–114.

Nichtweiss, Johannes, "Zur Frage des zweiten Liebeigenschaft und des sogennanten preussischen Weges der Entwicklung des Kapitalismus in der Landwirtschaft Ostdeutschlands," *Zeitschrift für Geschichtswissenshaft,* **I**, 5, 1953, 687–717.

Nichtweiss, Johannes, "Antwort an Jurgen Kuczynski," *Zeitschrift für Geschichtswissenschaft,* **II**, 3, 1954, 471–476.

Nichtweiss, Johannes, "Zu strittigen Fragen der sogenannten zweiten Leibeigenschaft in Mitteleuropa: Zusammenfassung eines Artikels von Benedykt Zientara," *Zeitschrift für Geschichtswissenschaft,* **IV**, 4, 1956, 750–754.

Nichtweiss, Johannes, "Einige Bemerkungen zum Artikel von G. Heitz 'Zur Diskussion über Gutscherrschaft und Bauernlegen in Mecklenburg'," *Zeitschrift für Wirtschaftgeschichte,* **V**, 4, 1957, 804–817.

Nielsen, Axel, *Dänische Wirtschaftsgeschichte.* Jena: Gustav Fischer Verlag, 1933.

Nordmann, Claude J., "Monnaies et finances suédoises au XVIIe siècle," *Revue du Nord,* **XLVI**, No. 183, oct.–déc. 1964, 469–488.

Nordmann, Claude J., *Grandeur et liberté de la Suède (1660–1792).* Paris: Béatrice-Nauwelaerts, 1971.

Nordmann, Claude J., "L'armée suédoise au XVIIe siècle," *Revue du nord,* **LIV**, No. 213, avr.–juin 1972, 133–147.

North, Douglass C., "Innovation and Diffusion of Technology. A Theoretical Framework," *Fourth International Conference on Economic History,* Bloomington 1968. Paris & La Haye: Mouton, 1973, 223–231.

North, Douglas C. & Thomas, Robert Paul, *The Rise of the Western World.* Cambridge: University Press, 1973.

Oberem, U., "Zur Geschichte des Lateinamerikanschen Landarbeiters: Conciertos und Huasipungueros in Ecuador," *Anthropos,* **LXII,** 5/6, 1967, 759–788.

Ochmański, Jerzy, "La situation économico-sociale et la lutte de classes des paysans dans les domaines royaux (*Ekonomie*) de Kobryń dans la deuxième moitié du XVI–ème et dans la première moitié du XVII–ème siècle," *Roczniki dziejów społecznych i gospodarczych,* **XIX,** 1957, 89–90.

O'Farrell, Patrick, *Ireland's English Question.* New York: Schocken, 1971.

Ogg, David, "The Emergence of Great Britain as a World Power," in *New Cambridge Modern History,* **VI:** J. S. Bromley, ed., *The Rise of Great Britain and Russia, 1688–1725.* Cambridge: University Press, 1970, 254–283.

Öhberg, Arne, "Russia and the World Market in the Seventeenth Century," *Scandinavian Economic History Review,* **III,** 2, 1955, 123–162.

Ónody, Oliver, "Quelques aspects historiques de l'économie de l'or brésilien," *Revue internationale d'histoire de la banque,* **IV,** 1971, 173–316.

Ormrod, David, "Dutch Commercial and Industrial Decline and British Growth in the Late Seventeenth and Early Eighteenth Centuries," in Frederick Krantz & Paul M. Hohenberg, eds., *Failed Transitions to Modern Industrial Society: Renaissance Italy and Seventeenth Century Holland.* Montreal: Interuniversity Centre for European Studies, 1975, 36–43.

Ortiz, Fernando, *Cuban Counterpoint: Tobacco and Sugar.* New York: Knopf, 1947.

Osborn, Wayne S., "Indian Land Retention in Colonial Metztitlán," *Hispanic American Historical Review,* **LIII,** 2, May 1973, 217–238.

Østerud, Øyvind, "Configurations of Scandinavian Absolutism: The 17th Century in Comparative Perspective," paper given at the ISSC/MSH Symposium on "Capitalism and the Rise of the National State in Europe, 16th–18th Centuries," Bellagio, Oct. 14–16, 1976.

Østerud, Øyvind, "Agrarian Structures, Urban Networks and Political Development: The Cases of Early Modern Scandinavia," paper at IX World Congress of Sociology, Uppsala, August 14–19, 1978.

Ostrander, Gilman M., "The Colonial Molasses Trade," *Agricultural History,* **XXX,** 2, Apr. 1956, 77–84.

Ostrander, Gilman M., "The Making of the Triangular Trade Myth," *William and Mary Quarterly,* **XXX,** 4, Oct. 1973, 635–644.

Pach, Zsigmond Pál, "Uber einige Probleme der Gutswirtschaft in Ungarn in der ersten Hälfte des XVII. Jahrhunderts," in *Second International Conference of Economic History,* Aix-en-Provence, 1962. Paris & La Haye: Mouton, 1965, 222–235.

Pach, Zsigmond Pál, "The Shifting of International Trade Routes in the 15th–17th Centuries," *Acta Historica Academiae Scientiarum Hungaricae,* **XIV,** 1968, 287–321.

Pach, Zsigmond Pál, "Diminishing Share of East-Central Europe in the 17th Century International Trade," *Acta Historica Academiae Scientarum Hungaricae,* **XVI,** 1970, 289–306. (a)

Pach, Zsigmond Pál, "The Role of East-Central Europe in International Trade (16th and 17th Centuries)," in *Etudes historiques 1970.* **I,** Budapest: Akademiai Kiado, 1970, 217–264. (b)

Pach, Zsigmond Pál, "Favourable and Unfavourable Conditions for Capitalist Growth: The Shift of International Trade Routes in the 15th to 17th Centuries," in F. C. Lane, ed., *Fourth International Conference on Economic History,* Bloomington, 1968. Paris & La Haye: Mouton, 1973, 53–68.

Palmer, R. R., "Questions de féodalité aux Etats-Unis," in *L'abolition de la "féodalité" dans le monde occidental.* Colloques internationaux du C.N.R.S., Toulouse 12–16 nov. 1968. Paris: Ed. du C.N.R.S., **I,** 1971, 348–356.

Pantaleão, Olga, *A penetração comercial da Inglaterra na América Espanhola de 1713 a 1783.* São Paulo: n.p., 1946.

Pares, Richard, "The Economic Factors in the History of the Empire," *Economic History Review*, **VII**, 2, May 1937, 119–144.

Pares, Richard, *Yankees and Creoles: The Trade between North America and the West Indies before the American Revolution*. London: Longmans, Green & Co., 1956.

Pares, Richard, *Merchants and Planters*, Economic History Review Supplement No. 4. Cambridge: University Press, 1960.

Pares, Richard, *War and Trade in the West Indies, 1739–63*. London: Frank Cass, 1963. (Original publication, 1936.)

Paris, Robert, *Histoire du commerce de Marseille*, **V**: *De 1600 à 1789, Le Levant*, gen. ed., Gaston Rambert. Paris: Lib. Plon, 1957.

Parker, Geoffrey, *The Army of Flanders and the Spanish Road, 1567–1659*. Cambridge: University Press, 1972.

Parker, Geoffrey, "The Emergence of Modern Finance in Europe," in C. M. Cipolla, ed., *The Fontana History of Europe*. **II**: *The Sixteenth and Seventeenth Centuries*. Glasgow: Collins, 1974, 527–594. (a)

Parker, Geoffrey, "War and Economic Change: The Economic Costs of the Dutch Revolt," paper at Sesta Settimana di Studio, Istituto Internazionale di Storia Economica "Francesco Datini", Prato, 3 magg. 1974. (b)

Parker, Geoffrey, "Why Did the Dutch Revolt Last Eighty Years?," *Transactions of the Royal Historical Society*, 5th ser., **XXVI**, 1976, 53–72. (a)

Parker, Geoffrey, "The 'Military Revolution,' 1560–1660—A Myth?," *Journal of Modern History*, **XLVIII**, 2, June 1976, 195–214. (b)

Parry, J. H., *The Establishment of the European Hegemony: 1415–1715*. New York: Harper & Row (Torchbooks), 1961.

Parry, J. H., "Transport and Trade Routes," in E. E. Rich & C. H. Wilson, eds., *Cambridge Economic History of Europe*. **IV**: *The Economy of Expanding Europe in the Sixteenth and Seventeenth Centuries*. Cambridge: University Press, 1967, 155–219.

Patterson, R., "Spinning and Weaving," in C. Singer *et al., A History of Technology*. **III**: *From the Renaissance to the Industrial Revolution, c1500–c1700*. Oxford: Clarendon Press, 1957, 151–180.

Penson, Lillian M., "The West Indies and the Spanish American Trade, 1713–1748," in J. Holland Rose *et al.*, eds., *Cambridge History of the British Empire*, **I**. Cambridge: University Press, 1929, 330–345.

Pentland, H. C., "Population and Labour Growth in Britain in the Eighteenth Century," *Third International Conference of Economic History*, Munich, 1965, **IV**: J. E. C. Eversley, ed., *Demography and History*. Paris & La Haye: Mouton, 1972, 157–189.

Perjés, G., "Army Provisioning, Logistics and Strategy in the Second Half of the 17th Century," *Acta Historica Academiae Scientarum Hungaricae*, **XVI**, 1–2, 1970, 1–52.

Perrot, Jean-Claude, *Genèse d'une ville moderne: Caen au XVIIIe siècle*. Lille: Service de reproduction des thèses, Univ. de Lille III, 2 vol. 1974.

Petersen, E. Ladewig, *The Crisis of the Danish Nobility, 1580–1660*. Odense, Denmark: Odense Univ. Press, 1967.

Petersen, E. Ladewig, "La crise de noblesse danoise entre 1580 et 1660," *Annales E.S.C.*, **XXIII**, 6, nov.–déc. 1968, 1237–1261.

Petersen, E. Ladewig, "The Danish Cattle Trade During the Sixteenth and Seventeenth Centuries," *Scandinavian Economic History Review*, **XVIII**, 1, 1970, 69–85.

Peterson, Mendel, *The Funnel of Gold*. Boston: Little-Brown, 1975.

Petraccone, Claudia, *Napoli dal 1500 all'800: problemi di storia demografica e sociale*. Napoli: Guida Ed., 1974.

Petrie, Sir Charles, *The Jacobite Movement*, 3rd ed., revised one volume. London: Eyre & Spottiswoode, 1958.

Phelan, John L., "Free Versus Compulsory Labor. Mexico and the Philippines 1540–1648," *Comparative Studies in Society and History,* I, 2, 1959, 189–201.

Phelan, John L., *The Hispanization of the Philippines: Spanish Aims and Filipino Responses, 1565–1700.* Madison: Univ. of Wisconsin Press, 1967.

Phelan, John L., review of John Lynch, *Spain Under the Habsburgs.* **II:** *Spain and America, 1598–1700* in *Journal of Latin American Studies,* **II,** 2, Nov. 1970, 211–213.

Piel, Jean, *Capitalisme agraire au Pérou.* **I:** *Originalité de la société agraire péruvienne au XIXe siècle.* Paris: Ed. Anthropos, 1975.

Pillorget, René, "Les problèmes monétaires français de 1602 à 1689," *XVIIe siècle,* No. 70–71, 1966, 107–130.

Pillorget, René, *Les mouvements insurrectionnels de Provence entre 1596 et 1715.* Paris: Ed. A. Pedone, 1975.

Pinkham, Lucille, "William of Orange: Prime Mover of the Revolution," in Gerald M. Straka, ed., *The Revolution of 1688: Whig Triumph or Palace Revolution?* Boston: D. C. Heath, 1963, 77–85. (Originally in *William III and the Respectable Revolution,* 1954.)

Pirenne, Henri, *Histoire de Belgique,* Vols. **IV, V.** Bruxelles: Henri Lamertin, Libr.-Ed., 1920.

Pitt, H. G., "The Pacification of Utrecht," in *New Cambridge Modern History,* **VI:** J. S. Bromley, ed., *The Rise of Great Britain and Russia, 1688–1715/25.* Cambridge: University Press, 1970, 446–479.

Piuz, Anne-Marie, "Politique économique à Geneve et doctrine mercantiliste (vers 1690–1740)," paper delivered at V International Congress of Economic History, Leningrad, 10–14 Aug. 1970. (a)

Piuz, Anne-Marie, "Alimentation populaire et sous-alimentation au XVIIe siècle: Le cas de Genève et sa région," in Jean-Jacques Hémardinquier, réd., *Pour une histoire de l'alimentation.* Paris: Lib. Armand Colin, 1970, 129–145. (Originally in *Revue suisse d'histoire,* 1968.)

Plumb, J. H., *England in the Eighteenth Century (1714–1815),* Vol. 7 of *The Pelican History of England.* London: Penguin, 1950.

Plumb, J. H., "Introduction," to C. R. Boxer, *The Dutch Seaborne Empire, 1600–1800.* New York: Knopf, 1965, xiii–xxvi.

Plumb, J. H., *The First Four Georges.* Glasgow: Fontana Collins, 1966.

Plumb, J. H., *The Origins of Political Stability: England, 1675–1725.* Boston:, Massachusetts: Houghton Mifflin, 1967.

Plumb, J. H., "The Growth of the Electorate in England from 1600 to 1715," *Past and Present,* No. 45, Nov. 1969, 90–116.

Pohl, Hans, "Das Textilgewerbe in Hispanoamerika während der Kolonialzeit," *Vierteljahrschrift für Sozial- und Wirtschaftsgeschichte,* **LVI,** 4, Dez. 1969, 438–477.

Poisson, Jean-Paul, "Introduction à une étude quantitative des effects socio-économiques du système de Law," *Journal de la Société de Statistique de Paris,* 115e annee, No. 3, 3e trimestre 1974, 260–280.

Poitrineau, Abel, "L'alimentation populaire en Auvergne au XVIIIe siècle," in Jean-Jacques Hémandinquier, réd., *Pour une histoire de l'alimentation.* Paris: Lib. Armand Colin, 1970, 146–193. (Originally in *Annales E.S.C.,* 1962.)

Polišenský, J. V., "The Thirty Years' War," *Past and Present,* No. 6, Nov. 1954, 31–43.

Polišenský, J. V., "The Thirty Years' War and the Crises and Revolutions of Seventeenth-Century Europe," *Past and Present,* No. 39, Apr. 1968, 34–43.

Polišenský, J. V., *The Thirty Years' War.* Berkeley: Univ. of California Press, 1971.

Polišenský, J. V., *War and Society in Europe, 1618–1648.* Cambridge: Cambridge Univ. Press, 1978.

Poni, Carlo, "All'origine del sistema di fabbrica: tecnologia e organizzazione produttiva dei mulini da seta nell'Italia settentrionale (sec. XVII–XVIII)," *Rivista storica italiana,* **LXXXVIII,** 3, 1976, 444–497.

Ponsot, Pierre, "En Andalousie occidentale: Les fluctuations de la production du blé sous l'Ancien Régime," *Etudes rurales*, No. 34, avr.–juin 1969, 97–112.

Postel-Vinay, Gilles, *La rente foncière dans le capitalisme agricole*. Paris: Maspéro, 1974.

Price, Derek J., "The Manufacture of Scientific Instruments from c1500–c1700," in C. Singer, *et al.*, *A History of Technology*. **III:** *From the Renaissance to the Industrial Revolution, c1500–c1700*. Oxford: Clarendon Press, 1957, 620–647.

Price, Jacob M., "The Rise of Glasgow in the Chesapeake Tobacco Trade, 1707–1775," *William and Mary Quarterly*, 3rd ser., **XI,** 2, Apr. 1954, 179–199.

Price, Jacob M., "Multilateralism and/or Bilateralism: The Settlement of British Trade Balances with 'The North', c1700," *Economic History Review*, 2nd ser., **XIV,** 2, 1961, 254–274. (a)

Price, Jacob M., "The Tobacco Adventure to Russia: Enterprise, Politics and Diplomacy in the Quest for a Northern Market for English Colonial Tobacco, 1676–1722," *Transactions of the American Philosophical Society*, n.s., **LI,** 1, Mar. 1961. (b)

Price, Jacob M., "The Economic Growth of the Chesapeake and the European Market, 1697–1775," *Journal of Economic History*, **XXIV,** 4, Dec. 1964, 496–511.

Prickler, Harald, "Das Volumen des westlichen ungarischen Aussenhandels vom 16. Jahrhundert bis 1700," in O. Pickl, her., *Die wirtschaftlichen Auswirkungen der Türkenkriege*, Grazer Forschungen zur Wirtschafts- und Sozialgeschichte, **I.** Graz: 1971, 131–144.

Priestley, Margaret, "Anglo-French Trade and the 'Unfavorable Balance' Controversy, 1600–1685," *Economic History Review*, 2nd ser., **IV,** 1, 1951, 37–52.

Procacci, Giulio, "Italy: Commentary," in Frederick Krantz & Paul M. Hohenberg, eds., *Failed Transitions to Modern Industrial Society: Renaissance Italy and Seventeenth-Century Holland*. Montreal: Interuniversity Centre for European Studies, 1975, 27–28.

Quencez, G., *Vocabularum geographicum*. Bruxelles: Presses Académiques Européennes, 1968.

Rabb, Theodore K., "Puritanism and the Rise of Experimental Science in England," review article, *Cahiers d'histoire mondiale*, **VII,** 1, 1962, 46–67. (a)

Rabb, Theodore K., "The Effects of the Thirty Years' War on the German Economy," *Journal of Modern History*, **XXXIV,** 1, Mar. 1962, 40–51. (b)

Rabb, Theodore K., "On Edwin Sandys and the Parliament of 1604," *American Historical Review*, **LXIX,** 3, Apr. 1964, 646–670.

Rabb, Theodore K., "Free Trade and the Gentry in the Parliament of 1604," *Past and Present*, No. 40, 1968, 165–173.

Rabb, Theodore K., *The Struggle for Stability in Early Modern Europe*. London & New York: Oxford Univ. Press, 1975.

Rabe, Hannah, "Aktienkapital und Handelsinvestitionen im Überseehandel des 17. Jahrhunderts," *Vierteljahrschrift für Sozial- und Wirtschaftsgeschichte*, **XLIX,** 3, 1962, 320–368.

Rachel, Hugo, *Die Handels-, Zoll- und Akzisepolitik Brandenburg–Preussens bis 1713*. Acta Borussica. Die einzelnen gebilte des verwaltung. Handels-, Zoll- und Akzisepolitik, **I,** Berlin: P. Parey, 1911.

Rambert, Gaston, "De 1660 à 1789," in *Histoire du commerce de Marseille*, **IV:** *De 1599 à 1789*, gen. ed., Gaston Rambert. Paris: Lib. Plon, 1954, 193–683.

Rambert, Gaston, "Préface" to Robert Paris, *Histoire du commerce de Marseille*, **V:** *De 1660 à 1789*, *Le Levant*. Paris: Lib. Plon, 1957, i–vi.

Rambert, Gaston, "La France et la politique de l'Espagne au XVIIIe siècle," *Revue d'histoire moderne et contemporaine*, **VI,** oct.–déc. 1959, 269–288.

Rapp, Richard Tilden, "The Unmaking of the Mediterranean Trade Hegemony: International Trade Rivalry and the Commercial Revolution," *Journal of Economic History*, **XXXV,** 3, Sept. 1975, 499–525.

Rapp, Richard Tilden, *Industry and Economic Decline in Seventeenth-Century Venice*. Cambridge, Massachusetts: Harvard Univ. Press, 1976.

Raychaudhuri, Tapan, *Jan Company in Coromandel, 1605–1690. A Study in the Interrelations of European Commerce and Traditional Economics*, Verhandelingen van het Koninklijk Instituut voor Taal-, Land- en Volkenkunde, Vol. 38. 's-Gravenhage: Martinus Nijhoff, 1962.

Reddaway, W. F., "The Scandinavian North," in A. W. Ward *et al.*, eds., *Cambridge Modern History*, **IV:** *The Thirty Years' War.* Cambridge: University Press, 1906, 560–591.

Redlich, Fritz, "Entrepreneurship in the Initial Stages of Industrialization," *Weltwirtschaftliches Archiv,* **LXXV,** 1955, 59–106.

Redlich, Fritz, "Contributions in the Thirty Years' War," *Economic History Review,* 2nd ser., **XII,** 2, 1959, 247–254.

Reed, Clyde G., "Transactions Costs and Differential Growth in Seventeenth-Century Western Europe," *Journal of Economic History,* **XXXIII,** 1, Mar. 1973, 177–190.

Rees, J. F., "The Phases of British Commercial Policy in the Eighteenth Century," *Economica,* **V,** No. 14, June 1925, 130–150.

Rees, J. F., "Mercantilism and the Colonies," in J. Holland Rose *et al., Cambridge History of the British Empire,* **I,** Cambridge: University Press, 1929, 561–602.

Reinhard, Marcel R. & Armengaud, Armand, *Histoire générale de la population mondiale.* Paris: Ed. Montchrestien, 1961.

Renier, G. J., *The Dutch Nation: An Historical Study.* London: Geo. Allen & Unwin, 1944.

Revah, I. S., "Les marranes," *Revue des études juives,* 3e ser., **I** (CXVIII), 1959–1960, 29–77.

Rich, E. E., "The First Earl of Shaftsbury's Colonial Policy," *Transactions of the Royal Historical Society,* 5th ser., **VII,** 1957, 47–70.

Rich, E. E., "Europe and North America," in *New Cambridge Modern History,* **V:** F. L. Carsten, ed., *The Ascendancy of France, 1648–88.* Cambridge: University Press, 1961, 330–368.

Rich, E. E., *Montreal and the Fur Trade.* Montreal: McGill Univ. Press, 1966.

Rich, E. E., "Colonial Settlement and Its Labour Problems," in E. E. Rich & C. H. Wilson, eds., *The Cambridge Economic History of Europe.* **IV:** *The Economy of Expanding Europe in the Sixteenth and Seventeenth Centuries.* Cambridge: University Press, 1967, 308–373.

Richet, Denis, "Croissance et blocages en France du XVe au XVIIIe siècle," *Annales E.S.C.,* **XXIII,** 4, juil.–août 1968, 759–787.

Richet, Denis, "Economic Growth and its Setbacks in France from the Fifteenth to the Eighteenth Century," in Marc Ferro, ed., *Social Historians in Contemporary France.* New York: Harper & Row, 1972, 180–211. (Translated from *Annales E.S.C.,* 1968.)

Richmond, Vice-Admiral Sir H., *National Policy and Naval Strength and Other Essays.* London: Longmans, Green & Co., 1928.

Riemersma, Jelle C., "Government Influence on Company Organization in Holland and England (1550–1650)," *Journal of Economic History,* Supplement X, 1950, 31–39.

Riley, P. W. J., "The Union of 1707 as an Episode in English Politics," *English Historical Review,* **LXXXIV,** No. 332, July 1969, 498–527.

Ringrose, D. R., "European Economic Growth: Comments on the North-Thomas Theory," *Economic History Review,* 2nd ser., **XXVI,** 2, May 1973, 285–292.

Robert, Daniel, "Louis XIV et les protestants," *XVIIe siècle,* No. 76–77, 1967, 39–52.

Roberts, Michael, *Gustavus Adolphus,* 2 vol. London: Longmans, Green, & Co., 1953, 1958.

Roberts, Michael, "Cromwell and the Baltic," *English Historical Review,* **LXXVI,** No. 300, July 1961, 402–446.

Roberts, Michael, "Queen Christina and the General Crisis of the Seventeenth Century," *Past and Present,* No. 22, July 1962, 36–59.

Roberts, Michael, "Charles XI," in *Essays in Swedish History.* London: Weidenfeld & Nicolson, 1967, 226–268. (Originally in *History,* 1965.)

Roberts, Michael, "Sweden and the Baltic, 1611–54," in *New Cambridge Modern History,* **IV:** J. P. Cooper, ed., *The Decline of Spain and the Thirty Years' War, 1609–49/59.* Cambridge: University Press, 1970, 385–410.

Roberts, Michael, "Introduction," in M. Roberts, ed., *Sweden's Age of Greatness, 1632–1718.* New York: St. Martin's Press, 1973, 1–19. (a)

Roberts, Michael, "The Swedish Church," in M. Roberts, ed., *Sweden's Age of Greatness, 1632– 1718.* New York: St. Martin's Press, 1973, 132–173. (b)

Roebuck, P., "Absentee Landownership in the Late Seventeenth and Early Eighteenth Centuries: A Neglected Factor in English Agrarian History," *Agricultural History Review,* **XXI,** 1, 1973, 1–17.

Roehl, Richard, "French Industrialization: A Reconsideration," *Explorations in Economic History,* **XIII,** 3, July 1976, 233–281.

Roessingh, H. K., "Inland Tobacco: Expansion and Contraction of a Cash Crop in the 17th and 18th Centuries in the Netherlands," *A.A.G. Bijdragen,* No. 20, 1976, 498–503.

Romano, Ruggiero, "Documenti e prime considerazioni intorno alla 'Balance du commerce' della Francia dal 1716 al 1780," *Studi in onore di Armando Sapori,* **II,** Milano: Istituto Edit. Cisalpino, 1957, 1265–1300.

Romano, Ruggiero, "Une économie coloniale: le Chili au XVIIIe siècle," *Annales E.S.C.,* **XV,** 2, mars–avr. 1960, 259–285.

Romano, Ruggiero, "Tra XVI e XVII secolo, una crisi economica: 1619–1622," *Rivista storica italiana,* **LXXIV,** 3, 1962, 480–531.

Romano, Ruggiero, "L'Italia nella crisi del secolo XVII," *Studi storici,* **IX,** 3–4, lugl.–dic. 1968, 723–741.

Romano, Ruggiero, "Sens et limites de l'industrie' minière en Amérique espagnole du XVIe au XVIIIe siècle," *Journal de la Société des Américanistes,* **LIX,** 1970, 129–143.

Romano, Ruggiero, "L'Italia nella crisi del secolo XVII," in *Tra due crisi: L'Italia del Rinascimento.* Torino: Piccola Bibl. Einaudi, 1971, 186–206. (Originally in *Studi storici,* 1968.)

Romano, Ruggiero, "Italy in the Crisis of the Seventeenth Century," in Peter Earle, ed., *Essays in European Economic History 1500–1800.* Oxford: Clarendon Press, 1974, 185–198. (Translated from *Studi storici,* 1968.)

Romero de Solís, Pedro, *La población española en los siglos XVIII y XIX.* Madrid: Siglo XXI de España, 1973.

Roorda, D. J., "The Ruling Classes in Holland in the Seventeenth Century," in J. S. Bromley & E. H. Kossmann, eds., *Britain and the Netherlands,* **II.** Groningen: J. B. Wolters, 1964, 109–132.

Roorda, D. J., "Party and Faction," *Acta Historiae Neerlandica,* **II,** 1967, 188–221.

Roos, Hans-Edvard, "Origin of Swedish Capitalism," *Economy and History,* **XIX,** 1, 1976, 49–65.

Rosén, Jerker, "Scandinavia and the Baltic," in *New Cambridge Modern History.* **V:** F. L. Carsten, ed., *The Ascendancy of France, 1648–88.* Cambridge: University Press, 1961, 519–42.

Rosenberg, Hans, *Bureaucracy, Aristocracy and Autocracy: The Prussian Experience, 1660–1815.* Cambridge, Massachusetts: Harvard Univ. Press, 1958.

Roseveare, Henry, *The Treasury: The Evolution of a British Institition.* New York: Columbia Univ. Press, 1969.

Roseveare, Henry, "Government Financial Policy and the Market in Late Seventeenth-Century England," Ottava VIII. Settimana di Studio, Istituto Internazionale di Storia Economica "Francesco Datini", Prato, 8 magg. 1976.

Rostworowski, Emanuel, "The Crisis of Sovereignty (1697–1763)," in A. Gieysztor *et al., History of Poland.* Warszawa: PWN, 1968, 313–337.

Rowen, Herbert H., "The Revolution That Wasn't: The *Coup d'Etat* of 1650 in Holland," *European Studies Review,* **IV,** 2, Oct. 1974, 99–117.

Rubini, Dennis, "Politics and the Battle for the Banks, 1688–1697," *English Historical Review,* **LXXXV,** No. 337, Oct. 1970, 693–714.

Ruiz Martín, Felipe, "La banca en España hasta 1782," in F. Ruiz Martín *et al., El banco de España: Una historia económica.* Madrid: Banco de España, 1970, 1–196.

Rule, John C., "Louis XIV, Roi-Bureaucrate," in John C. Rule, ed., *Louis XIV and the Craft of Kingship*. Columbus: Ohio State Univ. Press, 1969, 3–101.

Rusche, G. and Otto Kirchheimer, *Punishment and Social Structure*. New York: Columbia Univ. Press, 1939.

Rusiński, Władysław, "Hauptprobleme der Fronwirtschaft im 16. bis 18, Jhd. in Polen und den Nachbarländern," in *First International Conference of Economic History*, Stockholm, August 1960. *Contributions*. Paris & La Haye: Mouton, 1960, 415–423.

Rusiński, Władysław, "Strukturwandlungen der bäuerlichen Bevölkerung Polens im 16.–18. Jahrhundert," *Studia Historiae Oeconomicae*, **VII,** 1972, 99–119.

Rusiński, Władysław, "Über die Entwicklungsetappen der Fronwirtschaft in Mittel- und Osteuropa," *Studia Historiae Oeconomicae*, **IX,** 1974, 27–45.

Rutkowski, Jan, "Le régime agraire en Pologne au XVIIIe siècle," *Revue d'histoire économique et social*, **XIV,** 4, 1926, 473–505; **XV,** 1, 1927, 66–103. (a)

Rutkowski, Jan, *Histoire économique de la Pologne avant les partages*. Paris: H. Champion, 1927. (b)

Ruwet, Joseph, "Prix, production et bénéfices agricoles. Le pays de Liège au XVIII siècle," *Cahiers d'histoire des prix*, **II,** 1957, 69–108.

Saalfeld, Diedrich, *Bauernwirtschaft und Gutsbetrieb in der vorindustriellen Zeit*. Stuttgart: Gustav Fischer Verlag, 1960.

Sagnac, Philippe, "Le crédit de l'Etat et les banquiers à la fin du XVIIe et au commencement du XVIIIe siècle," *Revue d'histoire moderne et contemporaine*, **X,** No. 4–5, juin–juil. 1908, 257–272.

Salaman, Redcliffe N., *The History and Social Influence of the Potato*. Cambridge: University Press, 1949.

Salin, Edgar, "European Entrepreneurship," *Economic History Review*, 2nd ser., **XII,** 4, Fall 1952, 366–377.

Salmon, J. H. M., "Venality of Office and Popular Sedition in Seventeenth-Century France," *Past and Present*, No. 37, July 1967, 21–43.

Samuelsson, Kurt, *From Great Power to Welfare State*. London: Geo. Allen & Unwin, 1968.

Sandberg, Lars S., "Monetary Policy and Politics in Mid-Eighteenth Century Sweden: A Comment," *Journal of Economic History*, **XXX,** 3, Sept. 1970, 653–654.

Sayous, André-E., "L'affaire de Law et les Génevois," *Zeitschrift für schweizerische Geschichte*, **XVII,** 3, 1937, 310–340.

Scammell, G. V., "Shipowning in the Economy and Politics of Early Modern England," *Historical Journal*, **XV,** 3, 1972, 385–407.

Scelle, Georges, "The Slave-Trade in the Spanish Colonies of America: the Assiento," *American Journal of International Law*, **IV,** 3, July 1910, 612–661.

Schmoller, Gustav, *The Mercantile System and its Historical Significance*. New York: MacMillan, 1897. (Reprinted Augustus M. Kelley Publ., 1967).

Schöffer, Ivo, "Did Holland's Golden Age Coincide With a Period of Crisis?" *Acta Historiae Neerlandica*, **I,** 1966, 82–107.

Schöffer, Ivo, *A Short History of the Netherlands*. 2nd rev. ed. Amsterdam: Allert de Lange bv, 1973.

Schumpeter, Joseph A., *Capitalism, Socialism, and Democracy*. London: Geo. Allen & Unwin, 1943.

Schwartz, Stuart B., "The Mocambo: Slave Resistance in Colonial Bahia," *Journal of Social History*, **III,** 4, Summer 1970, 313–333.

Schwartz, Stuart B., "Free Labor in a Slave Economy: The *Lavradores de Cana* of Colonial Bahia," in Dauril Alden, ed., *Colonial Roots of Modern Brazil*. Berkeley: Univ. of California Press, 1973, 147–197.

Schwartz, Stuart B., "The Manumission of Slaves in Colonial Brazil: Bahia, 1684–1745," *Hispanic American Historical Review*, **LVII,** 4, Nov. 1974, 603–635.

Scoville, Warren C., "The Huguenots and the Diffusion of Technology," *Journal of Political Economy,* **LX,** 4, Aug. 1952, 294–311; **LX,** 5, Oct. 1952, 392–411.

Scoville, Warren C., *The Persecution of Huguenots and French Economic Development, 1680–1720.* Berkeley: Univ. of California Press, 1960.

Sée, Henri, "Remarques sur le caractère de l'industrie rurale en France et les causes de son extension au XVIIIe siècle," *Revue historique,* **CXLII,** 1, janv.–févr. 1923, 47–53.

Seeley, J. A., *The Expansion of England,* ed. by John Gross. Chicago, Illinois: Univ. of Chicago Press, 1971. (Originally published in 1883.)

Sella, Domenico, "The Rise and Fall of the Venetian Woollen Industry," in Brian Pullan, ed., *Crisis and Change in the Venetian Economy in the Sixteenth and Seventeenth Centuries.* London: Methuen, 1968, 106–126.

Sella, Domenico, "Industrial Production in Seventeenth-Century Italy: A Reappraisal," *Explorations in Entrepreneurial History,* **VI,** 3, Spring–Summer 1969, 235–253.

Sella, Domenico, "European Industries 1500–1700," in C. M. Cipolla, ed., *The Sixteenth and Seventeenth Centuries,* **II,** Glasgow: Collins, 1974, 354–412.

Sella, Domenico, "The Two Faces of the Lombard Economy in the Seventeenth Century," in Frederick Krantz & Paul M. Hohenberg, eds., *Failed Transitions to Modern Industrial Society: Renaissance Italy and Seventeenth-Century Holland.* Montreal: Interuniversity Centre for European Studies, 1975, 11–15.

Semo, Enrique, *Historia del capitalismo en México: Los orígenes/1521–1763.* Mexico City: Ed. Era, 1973.

Sereni, Emilio, *Storia del paesaggio agrario italiano.* Bari, Italy: Laterza, 1961.

Sheridan, Richard B., "The Molasses Act and the Market Strategy of the British Sugar Planters," *Journal of Economic History,* **XVII,** 1, 1957, 62–83.

Sheridan, Richard B., "The Wealth of Jamaica in the Eighteenth Century," *Economic History Review,* 2nd ser., **XVIII,** 2, Aug. 1965, 292–311.

Sheridan, Richard B., "The Wealth of Jamaica in the Eighteenth Century: A Rejoinder," *Economic History Review,* 2nd ser., **XXI,** 1, Apr. 1968, 46–61.

Sheridan, Richard B., "The Plantation Revolution and the Industrial Revolution, 1625–1775," *Caribbean Studies,* **IX,** 3, Oct. 1969, 5–25.

Sideri, S., *Trade and Power: Informal Colonialism in Anglo-Portuguese Relations.* Rotterdam: Rotterdam Univ. Press, 1970.

Silbert, Albert, "Un carrefour de l'Atlantique: Madère (1640–1820)," *Economias e Finanças,* ser. 2, **XXII,** 1954, 389–443.

Simiand, François, *Les fluctuations économiques à longue période et la crise mondiale.* Paris: Lib. Felix Alcan, 1932. (a)

Simiand, François, *Recherches anciennes et nouvelles sur le mouvement général des prix du 16e au 19e siècle.* Paris: Ed. Domat-Montchrestien, 1932. (b)

Simpson, Leslie Boyd, "Mexico's Forgotten Century," *Pacific Historical Review,* **XXII,** 2, May 1953, 113–121.

Singh, O. P., *Surat and its Trade in the Second Half of the 17th Century.* Delhi: Univ. of Delhi, 1977.

Skazkine, S., "Sur la genèse du capitalisme dans l'agriculture de l'Europe occidentale," *Recherches internationales à la lumière du marxisme.* No. 37, *Le féodalisme,* mai–juin 1963, 191–202.

Slicher van Bath, B. H., "Agriculture in the Low Countries (ca. 1600–1800)", *X Congresso Internazionale di Scienze Storiche,* Roma, 4–11 settembre 1955. *Relazioni,* **IV:** *Storia Moderna.* Firenze: G. C. Sansoni-Ed., 1955, 169–203.

Slicher van Bath, B. H., "The Rise of Intensive Husbandry in the Low Countries," in J. S. Bromley & E. H. Kossman, eds., *Britain and the Netherlands.* London: Chatto & Windus, 1960, 130–153.

Slicher van Bath, B. H., *The Agrarian History of Western Europe, A.D. 500–1850.* London: Edw. Arnold, 1963. (a)

Slicher van Bath, B. H., "Yield Ratios, 810–1820," *A.A.G. Bijdragen,* No. 10, 1963. (b)

Slicher van Bath, B. H., "Les problèmes fondamentaux de la société préindustrielle en Europe occidentale: Une orientation et un programme," *A.A.G. Bijdragen,* No. 12, 1965, 3–46. (a)

Slicher van Bath, B. H., "Die europäischen Agrarverhältnisse im 17. und der ersten Hälfte des 18. Jahrhunderts," *A.A.G. Bijdragen,* No. 13, 1965, 134–148. (b)

Slicher van Bath, B. H., "Eighteenth-Century Agriculture on the Continent of Europe: Evolution or Revolution?" *Agricultural History,* **XLIII,** 1, Jan. 1969, 169–179.

Slicher van Bath, B. H., "Agriculture in the Vital Revolution," in *Cambridge Economic History of Europe,* **V:** E. E. Rich & C. H. Wilson, eds., *The Economic Organization of Early Modern Europe.* Cambridge: University Press, 1977, 42–132.

Sluiter, Engel, "Dutch-Spanish Rivalry in the Caribbean Area, 1594–1609," *Hispanic American Historical Review,* **XXVIII,** 2, May 1948, 165–196.

Smelser, Neil J., *Social Change in the Industrial Revolution.* London: Routledge & Kegan Paul, 1959.

Smit, J. W., "The Netherlands and Europe in the Seventeenth and Eighteenth Centuries," in J. S. Bromley & E. H. Kossmann, eds., *Britain and the Netherlands in Europe and Asia.* London: Macmillan, 1968, 13–36.

Smit, J. W., "Holland: Commentary," in Frederick Krantz & Paul W. Hohenberg, eds., *Failed Transitions to Modern Industrial Society: Renaissance Italy and Seventeenth Century Holland.* Montreal: Interuniversity Centre for European Studies, 1975, 61–63.

Smith, C. T., *An Historical Geography of Western Europe Before 1800.* London: Longmans, 1967.

Smout, T. C., "The Development and Enterprise of Glasgow, 1556–1707," *Scottish Journal of Political Economy,* **VII,** 3, 1960, 194–212.

Smout, T. C., *Scottish Trade on the Eve of the Union, 1660–1707.* Edinburgh: Oliver & Boyd, 1963.

Smout, T. C., "Scottish Landowners and Economic Growth, 1650–1850," *Scottish Journal of Political Economy,* **XI,** 1, Feb. 1964, 218–234. (a)

Smout, T. C., "The Anglo-Scottish Union of 1707. I: The Economic Background," *Economic History Review,* 2nd ser., **XVI,** 3, Apr. 1964, 455–467. (b)

Smout, T. C. & Alexander Fenton, "Scottish Agriculture Before the Improvers—An Exploration," *Agricultural History Review,* **XIII,** 2, 1965, 73–93.

Sombart, Werner, "Hausindustrie," *Handwörterbuch der Staatswissenschaften,* 2nd ed. Jena: Verlag von Gustav Fischer, 1900, **IV,** 1138–1169.

Soom, Arnold, "Der Kampf der baltischen Städte gegen das Fremdkapital im 17. Jahrhundert," *Vierteljahrschrift für Sozial- und Wirtschaftsgeschichte,* **XLIX,** 4, 1962, 433–458.

Spengler, Joseph, J., "Mercantilist and Physiocratic Growth Theory," in Bert F. Hoselitz, ed., *Theories of Economic Growth.* New York: Free Press, 1960, 3–64.

Sperling, J., "The International Payments Mechanism in the Seventeenth and Eighteenth Centuries," *Economic History Review,* 2d ser., **XIV,** 3, 1962, 446–468.

Špiesz, Anton, "Czechoslovakia's Place in the Agrarian Development of Middle and East Europe of Modern Times," *Studia Historica Slovaca,* **VI,** 1969, 7–62.

Spooner, Frank C., *L'économie mondiale et les frappes monétaires en France 1493–1680.* Paris: Lib. Armand Colin, 1956.

Spooner, Frank C., "The European Economy, 1609–50," *New Cambridge Modern History.* **IV:** J. P. Cooper, ed., *The Decline of Spain and the Thirty Years War, 1609–48/59.* Cambridge: University Press, 1970, 67–103.

Stark, Werner, "Die Abhängigkeitsverhältnisse der gutsherrlichen Bauern Böhmens im 17. und 18. Jahrhundert," *Jahrbucher für Nationalökonomie und Statistik,* **CLXIV,** 4, Juli 1952, 270–92; 5, Sept. 1952, 348–374.

Steensgaard, Niels, "The Economic and Political Crisis of the Seventeenth Century," paper delivered at XIII International Congress of Historical Sciences, Moscow, Aug. 16–23, 1970.

Stefanescu, St., Mioc, D. & Chirca, H., "L'évolution de la rente féodale en travail en Valachie et en Moldavie aux XIVe–XVIIIe siècles," *Revue roumaine d'histoire,* **I,** 1, 1962, 39–60.

Stolanovich, Traian, "Pour un modèle du commerce du Levant: Economie concurrentielle et économie de bazar, 1500–1800," *Bulletin de l'Association Internationale d'Etudes du Sud-Est Européen,* **XII,** 2, 1974, 61–120.

Stols, E., "The Southern Netherlands and the Foundation of the Dutch East and West India Companies," *Acta Historiae Neerlandicae,* **IX,** 1976, 30–47

Stone, Lawrence, "Social Mobility in England, 1500–1700," *Past and Present,* No. 33, Apr. 1966, 16–55.

Stone, Lawrence, "Literacy & Education in England, 1640–1900," *Past and Present,* No. 42, Feb. 1969, 69–139.

Stone, Lawrence, *The Causes of the English Revolution, 1529–1642.* London: Routledge & Kegan Paul, 1972.

Stork-Penning, J. G., "The Ordeal of the States—Some Remarks on Dutch Politics During the War of the Spanish Succession," *Acta Historiae Neelandica,* **II,** 1967, 107–141.

Stoye, J. W., "The Austrian Habsburgs," in *New Cambridge Modern History,* **VI:** J. S. Bromley, ed., *The Rise of Great Britain and Russia, 1688–1725.* Cambridge: University Press, 1970, 572–607. (a)

Stoye, J. W., "Armies and Navies. 2. Soldiers and Civilians," in *New Cambridge Modern History,* **VI:** J. S. Bromley, ed., *The Rise of Great Britain and Russia, 1688–1725.* Cambridge: University Press, 1970, 762–790. (b)

Stradling, R. A., "Seventeenth Century Spain: Decline or Survival?," *European Studies Review,* **IX,** 2, Apr. 1979, 157–194.

Strong, Frank, "The Causes of Cromwell's West Indian Expedition," *American Historical Review,* **IV,** 2, Jan. 1899, 228–245.

Supple, Barry E., "Thoman Mun and the Commercial Crisis, 1623," *Bulletin of the Institute of Historical Research,* **XXVII,** No. 75, May 1954, 91–94.

Supple, Barry E., "Currency and Commerce in the Early Seventeenth Century," *Economic History Review,* 2nd ser., **X,** 2, 1957, 239–255.

Supple, Barry E., *Commercial Crisis and Change in England 1600 42.* Cambridge: University Press, 1959.

Supple, Barry E., "The State and the Industrial Revolution," in C. M. Cipolla, ed., *The Fontana Economic History of Europe,* **III.** *The Industrial Revolution.* Glasgow: Collins, 1973, 301–357.

Supple, Barry E., "The Nature of Enterprise," in *Cambridge Economic History of Europe,* **V:** E. E. Rich & C. H. Wilson, eds., *The Economic Organization of Early Modern Europe.* Cambridge: University Press, 1977, 394–461.

Sutherland, Lucy S., *The East India Company in Eighteenth Century Politics.* Oxford: Clarendon Press, 1952.

Sutherland, Lucy S. "The City of London in Eighteenth-Century Politics," in Richard Pares & A. J. P. Taylor, eds., *Essays Presented to Sir Lewis Namier.* London: Macmillan, 1956, 49–74.

Swart, K. W., "Holland's Bourgeoisie and the Retarded Industrialization of the Netherlands," in Frederick Krantz & Paul M. Hohenberg, eds., *Failed Transitions to Modern Industrial Society: Renaissance Italy and Seventeenth Century Holland.* Montreal: Interuniversity Centre for European Studies, 1975, 44–48.

Sweezy, Paul, "Karl Marx and the Industrial Revolution," in *Modern Capitalism and Other Essays.* New York: Monthly Review Press, 1972, 127–146. (a) (Originally in Robert V. Eagly, ed., *Events, Ideology and Economic Theory,* 1968.)

Sweezy, Paul, "Marx and the Proletariat," in *Modern Capitalism and Other Essays.* New York: Monthly Review Press, 1972, 147–165. (b) (Originally in *Monthly Review,* 1967.)

Symcox, Geoffrey, *The Crisis of the French Sea Power 1688–1697. From the Guerre d'Escadre to the Guerre de Course.* The Hague: Martinus Nijhoff, 1974.

Szczygielski, Wojciech, "Le rendement de la production agricole en Pologne du XVIe au XVIIe siècle sur le fond européen," *Ergon,* **V,** supplement to *Kwartalnik historii kultury materialnej,* **XIV,** 4, 1966, 745–803.

Szczygielski, Wojciech, "Die ökonomische Aktivität des polnischen Adels im 16.–18. Jahrhundert," *Studia Historiae Economicae,* **II,** 1967, 83–101.

Takahashi, H. K., "The Transition from Feudalism to Capitalism; A Contribution to the Sweezy-Dobb Controversy," *Science and Society,* **XVI,** 4, Fall 1952, 313–345.

Tapié, Victor-Lucien, "Les officiers seigneuriaux dans la société française du XVIIe siècle," *XVIIe siècle,* Nos. 42–43, 1er trimestre 1959, 118–140.

Tapié, Victor-Lucien, "Quelques aspects généraux de la politique étrangère de Louis XIV," *XVIIe siècle,* Nos. 46–47, 1er–2e trimestres 1960, 1–28.

Tapié, Victor-Lucien, *The Rise and Fall of the Habsburg Monarchy.* New York: Praeger, 1971.

Tawney, R. H., "A History of Capitalism", review of M. H. Dobb, *Studies in the Development of Capitalism, in Economic History Review,* 2nd ser., **II,** 3, 1950, 307–316.

Taylor, A. J. P., *The Course of German History.* New York: Coward-McCann, 1946.

Taylor, George V., "Types of Capitalism in Eighteenth–Century France," *English Historical Review,* **LXXIX,** No. 312, July 1964, 478–497.

Taylor, Harland, "Trade, Neutrality and the 'English Road', 1630–1648," *Economic History Review,* 2nd ser., **XXV,** 2, May 1972, 236–260.

Tazbir, Janusz, "Recherches sur la conscience nationale en Pologne au XVIe siècle," *Acta Poloniae Historica,* No. 14, 1966, 5–22.

Tazbir, Janusz, "The Commonwealth at the Turning Point (1586–1648)," in A. Gieysztor *et al., History of Poland.* Warszawa: PWN, 1968, 208–241. (a)

Tazbir, Janusz, "The Commonwealth in the Years of Crisis (1648–1696)," in A. Gieysztor *et al., History of Poland.* Warszawa: PWN, 1968, 242–312. (b)

Temperley, Harold W. V., "The Age of Walpole and the Pelhams," *Cambridge Modern History.* **VI:** *The Eighteenth Century.* Cambridge: University Press, 1909, 40–89. (a)

Temperley, Harold W. V., "The Causes of the War of Jenkins' Ear, 1739," *Transactions of the Royal Historical Society,* 3rd ser., **III,** 1909, 197–236. (b) (Reprinted in Ian R. Christie, ed., *Essays in Modern History,* 1968.)

Temperley, Harold W. V., "Foreword" to Jean O. McLachlan, *Trade and Peace with Old Spain, 1667–1750.* Cambridge: University Press, 1940, ix–xi.

Teuteberg, H. J., "The General Relationship between Diet and Industrialization," in Elborg & Robert Forster, eds., *European Diet from Pre-Industrial to Modern Times.* New York: Harper & Row (Torchbooks), 1975, 61–109.

Thirsk, Joan, "The Restoration Land Settlement," *Journal of Modern History,* **XXVI,** 4, Dec. 1954, 315–328.

Thirsk, Joan, "Industries in the Countryside," in F. J. Fisher, ed., *Essays in the Economic and Social History of Tudor and Stuart England.* Cambridge: University Press, 1961, 70–88.

Thirsk, Joan, "Seventeenth-Century Agriculture and Social Change," *Agricultural History Review,* **XVIII,** 1970, Supplement: Joan Thirsk, ed., *Land, Church and People,* 148–177.

Thirsk, Joan, "New Crops and Their Diffusion: Tobacco-growing in Seventeenth-century England," in C. W. Chalklin & M. A. Havinden, eds.,   *Rural Change and Urban Growth. 1500–1800.* London: Longmans, 1974, 76–103.

Thirsk, Joan, *The Restoration.* London: Longmans, 1976.

Thomas, P. J., *Mercantilism and the East India Trade.* London: Frank Cass, 1963.

Thomas, Robert Paul, "The Sugar Colonies of the Old Empire: Profit or Loss for Great Britain?," *Economic History Review,* 2nd ser., **XXI,** 1, Apr. 1968, 30–45.

Thompson, E. P., "Time, Work-Discipline and Industrial Capitalism," *Past and Present,* No. 38, Dec. 1967, 56–97.

Thompson, E. P., *Whigs and Hunters: The Origin of the Black Act.* New York: Pantheon, 1975.

Thompson, F. M. L., "The Social Distribution of Landed Property since the Sixteenth Century," *Economic History Review,* 2nd ser., **XIX,** 3, Dec. 1966, 505–517.

Thomson, Mark A., "The War of the Austrian Succession," in *New Cambridge Modern History,*

VII: J. O. Lindsay, ed., *The Old Regime, 1713–1763*. Cambridge: University Press, 1966, 416–439.

Tilly, Charles, "Reflections on the History of European State-Making," in Charles Tilly, ed., *The Formation of National States in Western Europe*. Princeton, New Jersey: Princeton Univ. Press, 1975, 3–83.

Tomkiewicz, Władysław, "Varsovie au XVIIe siècle,"*Acta Poloniae Historica*, No. 15, 1967, 39–64.

Tonnesson, Kàre D., "Les pays scandinaves," in *L'abolition de la "féodalité" dans le monde occidental*. Colloques internationaux du C.N.R.S., Toulouse 12–16 nov. 1968. Paris: Ed. du C.N.R.S., **I**, 1971, 303–313 (plus Discussion, **II**, 719–721).

Topolska, Maria Barbara, "Peculiarities of the Economic Structure of Eastern White Russia in the Sixteenth–Eighteenth Centuries," *Studia Historiae Oeconomicae*, **VI**, 1971, 37–49.

Topolski, Jerzy, "Les tendances de l'évolution agraire de l'Europe Centrale et Orientale aux XVIe–XVIIIe siècles," *Rivista di storia dell'agricoltura*, **VII**, 2, giug. 1967, 107–119.

Topolski, Jerzy, "L'économie rurale dans les biens de l'archévêché de Gniezno depuis le 16e jusqu'au 18e siècle," *Recherches internationales à la lumière du marxisme*, No. 63–64, 2e et 3e trimestre, 1970, 86–98.

Topolski, Jerzy, "La reféodalisation dans l'économie des grands domaines en Europe centrale et orientale (XVIe–XVIIIe ss.)," *Studia Historiae Oeconomicae*, **VI**, 1971, 51–63.

Topolski, Jerzy, "Economic Decline in Poland from the Sixteenth to the Eighteenth Centuries," in Peter M. Earle, ed., *Essays in European Economic History, 1500–1800*. Oxford: Clarendon Press, 1974, 127–142. (a) (Translated from *Acta Poloniae Historica,* 1962.)

Topolski, Jerzy, "The Manorial Serf Economy in Central and Eastern Europe in the 16th and 17th Centuries," *Agricultural History*, **XLVIII**, 3, July 1974, 341–352. (b)

Topolski, Jerzy, "Commerce des denrées agricoles et croissance économique de la zone baltique aux XVIe et XVIIe siècles," *Annales E.S.C.*, **XXIX**, 2, mars–avr. 1974, 425–436. (c)

Torr, Dona, "The English Revolution, I," *Labour Monthly*, **XXIII**, 2, Feb. 1941, 90–92.

Tremel, Ferdinand, "Die österreichische Wirtschaft zwischen 1620 und 1740," *Österreich in Geschichte und Literatur*, 1961, **V**, 166–181.

Treue, Wilhelm, "Wirtschafts- und Sozialgeschichte vom 16. bis zum 18. Jahrhundert," in Bruno Gebhardt, her., *Handbuch der deutschen Geschichte*. **II:** *Von der Reformation bis zum Ende des Absolutismus*, 8th rev. ed. Stuttgart: Union Verlag, 1955, 366–436.

Treue, Wilhelm, "Das Verhältnis von Fürst, Staat und Unternehmer in der Zeit des Merkantilismus," *Vierteljahrschrift für Sozial- und Wirtschaftsgeschichte*, **XLIV**, 1, 1957, 26–56.

Treue, Wilhelm, *Wirtschaft, Gesellschaft und Technik in Deutschland von 16. bis zum 18. Jahrhundert*. München: Deutscher Taschenbuch Verlag, 1974.

Trevelyan, George Macauley, "The Revolution as a Movement for Democratic Unification," in Gerald M. Straka, ed., *The Revolution of 1688: Whig Triumph or Palace Revolution?* Boston: D. C. Heath, 1963, 43–49. (Originally in *The English Revolution, 1688–1689,* 1938.)

Trevor-Roper, Hugh R., "The General Crisis of the 17th Century," *Past and Present*, No. 16, Nov. 1959, 31–66.

Trevor-Roper, Hugh R., "Scotland and the Puritan Revolution," in H. E. Bell & R. L. Ollard, eds., *Historical Essays 1600–1750 presented to David Ogg*. London: Adam & Charles Black, 1964, 78–130.

Trevor-Roper, Hugh R., "The Union of Britain in the 17th Century," in *Homenaje a Jaime Vicens Vives*. Barcelona: Facultad de Filosofía y Letras, 1967, **II**, 703–715.

Tucker, G. S. L., "English Pre-Industrial Population Trends,"*Economic History Review*, 2nd ser., **XVI**, 2, Dec. 1963, 205–218.

Unger, Richard W., *Dutch Shipbuilding Before 1800*. Assen/Amsterdam: Van Gorcum, 1978.

Unger, W. S., "Trade through the Sound in the Seventeenth and Eighteenth Centuries," *Economic History Review*, 2nd ser., **XII**, 2, Dec. 1959, 206–221.

Unwin, George, *Industrial Organization in the Sixteenth and Seventeenth Centuries*. Oxford: Clarendon Press, 1904.

Usher, Abbott Payson, *The History of the Grain Trade in France, 1400–1710.* Harvard Economic Studies, Vol. **IX.** Cambridge, Massachusetts: Harvard Univ. Press, 1913.

Usher, Abbott Payson, "The Growth of English Shipping, 1572–1922," *Quarterly Journal of Economics,* **XLII,** 3, May 1928, 465–478.

Usher, Abbott Payson, "Machines and Mechanisms," in C. Singer *et al., A History of Technology.* **III:** *From the Renaissance to the Industrial Revolution, c1500–c1700.* Oxford: Clarendon Press, 1959, 324–346.

Utterström, Gustav, "An Outline of Some Population Changes in Sweden ca. 1660–1750 and a Discussion of Some Current Issues," in D. V. Glass & D. E. C. Eversley, eds., *Population in History.* London: Edw. Arnold, 1965, 536–548.

Vandenbroeke, Chr., "Cultivation and Consumption of the Potato in the 17th and 18th Century," *Acta Historiae Neerlandica,* **V,** 1971, 15–39.

Van der Wee, H., "Introduction—The Agricultural Development of the Low Countries as Revealed by the Tithe and Rent Statistics, 1250–1800," in H. van der Wee & E. van Cauwenberghe, eds., *Productivity of Land and Agricultural Innovation in the Low Countries (1250–1800).* Leuven: Leuven Univ. Press, 1978, 1–23.

Van der Woude, A. M., "Discussion," in *Third International Conference of Economic History,* Munich, 1965, **IV:** J. E. C. Eversley, ed., *Demography and History.* Paris & La Haye: Mouton, 1972, 232–234.

Van der Woude, A. M., "The A. A. G. Bijdragen and the Study of Dutch Rural History," *Journal of European Economic History,* **IV,** 1, Spring 1975, 215–241.

Van der Woude, A. M. & Mentink, G. J., "La population de Rotterdam au XVIIe et au XVIIIe siècle," *Population,* **XXI,** 6, Nov.–Deç. 1966, 1165–1190.

Van Dijk, H. & Roorda, D. J., "Social Mobility under the Regents of the Republic," *Acta Historiae Neerlandicae,* **IX,** 1976, 76–102.

Van Dillen, J. G., "Stukken betreffende den Amsterdamschen graanhandel omstreeks het jaar 1681," *Economisch-Historisch Jaarboek,* **III,** 1917, 70–106.

Van Dillen, J. G., "Eenige stukken aangaande den Amsterdamschen graanhandel in de tweede helfte der zeventiende eeuw," *Economisch-Historisch Jaarboek,* **IX,** 1923, 221–230.

Van Dillen, J. G., "Amsterdam, marché mondial des métaux précieux au XVIIe et au XVIIIe siècle," *Revue historique,* 51e annee, **CLII,** 2, juil.–aôut 1926, 194–201.

Van Dillen, J. G., "Amsterdam's Role in Seventeenth-Century Dutch Politics and its Economic Background," in J. S. Bromley & E. H. Kossman, eds., *Britain and the Netherlands,* **II.** Groningen: J. B. Wolters, 1964, 133–147.

Van Dillen, J. G., "Economic Fluctuations and Trade in the Netherlands, 1650–1750," in Peter Earle, ed., *Essays in European Economic History, 1500–1800.* Oxford: Clarendon Press, 1974. 199–211. (a) (Translated from *Van rijkdom en regenten: handboek tot de economische en sociale geschiedenis van nederland tijdens de republiek,* 1970.)

Van Dillen, J. G., "La banque de changes et les banquiers privés à Amsterdam aux XVIIe et XVIIIe siècles," *Third International Conference of Economic History.* Munich, 1965, Paris: Mouton, **V,** 1974, 177–185. (b)

Van Hoboken, W. J., "The Dutch West India Company: The Political Background of its Rise and Decline," in J. S. Bromley & E. H. Kossman, eds., *Britain and the Netherlands.* London: Chatto & Windus, 1960, 41–61.

Van Houtte, Jean A., "Déclin et survivance d'Anvers (1550–1700)," *Studi in onore di Amintore Fanfani,* V: *Evi moderno e contemporaneo.* Milano: Dott. A. Giuffrè–Ed., 1962, 703–726.

Van Klaveren, Jacob, *General Economic History, 100–1760.* München: Gerhard Kieckens, 1969. (a)

Van Klaveren, Jacob, "Fiscalism, Mercantilism and Corruption," in D. C. Coleman, ed., *Revisions in Mercantilism.* London: Methuen, 1969, 140–161. (b) (Translated from *Vierteljahrschrift für Sozial- und Wirtschaftsgeschichte,* 1960.)

Van Veen, Joh., *Dredge, Drain, Reclaim.* The Hague: Martinus Nijhoff, 1950.

Várkonyi, Ágnes R., "Historical Personality, Crisis and Progress in 17th Century Hungary,"

Etudes historiques, 1970, publiées à l'occasion du VIIIe Congrès International des Sciences Historiques par la Commission National des Historiens Hongrois. Budapest: Akademiai Kiado, 1970, 295–299.

Veenendaal, A. J., "The War of the Spanish Succession in Europe," in *New Cambridge Modern History,* **VI:** J. S. Bromley, ed., *The Rise of Great Britain and Russia, 1688–1715/25.* Cambridge: University Press, 1970, 410–445.

Ventura, Angelo, "Considerazioni sull'agricoltura veneta e sulla accumulazione originaria del capitale nei secoli XVI e XVII," *Studi storici,* **IX,** 3–4, lugl.–dic. 1968, 674–722.

Verlinden, Charles, "Schiavitù ed economia nel mezzogiorno agli inizi dell'età moderna," *Annali del mezziogiorno,* **III,** 1963, 11–38.

Verlinden, Charles, "Amsterdam," in Amintore Fanfani, red., *Città mercanti doctrine nell'economia europea dal IV al XVIII secolo.* Milano: Dott. A. Giuffrè–Ed., 1964, 321–340.

Verlinden, Charles, "Les conditions de l'introduction et de l'abolition du régime feódal dans les deux Amériques," in *L'abolition de la "féodalité" dans le monde occidental,* Colloques internationaux du C.N.R.S., Toulouse 12–16 nov. 1968. Paris: Ed. du C.N.R.S., **I,** 1971, 341–348.

Verlinden, Charles, "Dal Mediterraneo all'Atlantico," in *Contributi per la storia economica.* Prato: Istituto Internazionale di Storia Economica "F. Datini", 1975, 27–51.

Viana, Luis Filho, "O trabalho do engenho e a reacção do Indio—Estabelecimento de escravatura africans," in *Congresso do Mundo Portugues,* **X,** Lisboa: Publicações Lisboa, 1940, 11–29.

Vicens Vives, Jaime, *Approaches to the History of Spain,* 2nd ed. Berkeley: Univ. of California Press, 1970.

Vignols, Léon, "L'ancien concept monopole et la contrebande universelle, I. Le 'commerce interlope' français, à la mer du sud, aux débuts du XVIIIe siècle, type de ce contrebande. Et textes inédits sur ce sujet," *Revue d'histoire économique et social,* **XIII,** 3, 1925, 239–299.

Vigo, Giovanni, "Real Wages of the Working Class in Italy: Building Workers' Wages (14th to 18th Century)," *Journal of European Economic History,* **III,** 2, Fall 1974, 378–399.

Vilar, Pierre M., "Problems of the Formation of Capitalism," *Past and Present,* No. 10, Nov. 1956, 15–38.

Vilar, Pierre M., "Remarques sur l'histoire des prix," *Annales E.S.C.,* **XVI,** 1, janv.–févr. 1961, 110–115.

Vilar, Pierre M., *Le "Manuel de la Companya Nova" de Gibraltar, 1709–1723,* Affaires et Gens d'Affaires, **XXVI.** Paris: S.E.V.P.E.N., 1962. (a)

Vilar, Pierre M., *La Catalogne dans l'Espagne moderne,* 3 vol. Paris: S.E.V.P.E.N., 1962. (b)

Vilar, Pierre M., *Or et monnaie dans l'histoire, 1450–1920.* Paris: Flammarion, 1974.

Villani, Pasquale, *Feudalità, riforme, capitalismo agrario.* Bari: Ed. Laterza, 1968.

Villani, Pasquale, "Note sullo sviluppo economico–sociale del Regno di Napoli nel settecento," *Rassegna economica,* **XXXVI,** 1, 1972, 29–55.

Villari, Rosario, "Baronaggio e finanza a Napoli alla vigilia della rivoluzione del 1647–48," *Studi storici,* **III,** 2, apr.–giug. 1962, 259–306.

Villari, Rosario, "Note sulla rifeudalizzazione del Regno di Napoli alla vigilia della rivoluzione di Masaniello, *Studi storici,* **IV,** 4, ott.–dic. 1963, 637–668; **VI,** 2, apr.–giug. 1965, 295–328. Continued as "Cogiura aristocratica e rivoluzione popolare," *Studi storici,* **VII,** 1, genn.–marzo 1967, 37–112.

Villari, Rosario, "Rivolte e coscienza rivoluzionaria nel secolo XVII," *Studi storici,* **XII,** 2, apr.–giug. 1971, 235–264.

Viner, Jacob, "Power versus Plenty as Objectives of Foreign Policy in the Seventeenth and Eighteenth Centuries," in D. C. Coleman, ed., *Revisions in Mercantilism.* London: Methuen, 1969, 61–91. (Originally in *World Politics,* 1948.)

Visconti, Alessandro, *L'Italia nell'epoca della controriforma dal 1576 al 1773,* Vol. **VI** of *Storia d'Italia.* Milano: Arnoldo Mondadori Ed., 1958.

Vivanti, Corrado, "La storia politica e sociale: Dall'avvento delle signorie all'Italia spagnola," in R. Romano & C. Vivanti, coordinators, *Storia d'Italia,* **II,** Part 1, 277–427. Torino: Einaudi, 1974.

Vlachovič, Jozef, "Produktion und Handel mit ungarischen Kupfer im 16. und im ersten Viertel des 17. Jahrhunderts," in Ingomar Bog, her., *Der Aussenhandel Ostmitteleuropas, 1450–1650.* Köln-Wien: Böhlau Verlag, 1971, 600–627.

von Braun, Joachim Freiherr, "Die ostdeutsche Wirtschaft in ihrer vorindustriellen Entwicklung," in Göttinger Arbeitskreis, *Das östliche Deutschland: Ein Handbuch.* Würzburg: Holzner Verlag, 1959, 603–639.

von Hippel, W., "Le régime féodal en Allemagne au XVIIIe siècle et sa dissolution," in *L'abolition de la "féodalité" dans le monde occidental,* Colloques internationaux du C.N.R.S., Toulouse 12–16 nov. 1968. Paris: Ed. du C.N.R.S., **I,** 1971, 289–301.

Waddell, David A. G., "Queen Anne's Government and the Slave Trade," *Caribbean Quarterly,* **VI,** 1, 1960, 7–10.

Wallerstein, Immanuel, *The Modern World-System.* New York: Academic Press, 1974.

Walton, Gary M., "Sources of Productivity Change in American Colonial Shipping, 1675–1775," *Economic History Review,* 2nd ser., **XX,** 1, Apr. 1967, 67–78.

Walton, Gary M., "A Measure of Productivity Change in Colonial Shipping," *Economic History Review,* 2nd ser., **XX,** 2, Aug. 1968, 268–282. (a)

Walton, Gary M., "New Evidence on Colonial Commerce," *Journal of Economic History,* **XXVIII,** 3, Sept. 1968, 363–389. (b)

Walzer, Michael, "Puritanism as a Revolutionary Ideology," *History and Theory,* **III,** 1964, 75–90.

Wangermann, Ernst, *The Austrian Achievement, 1700–1800.* New York: Harcourt, Brace & Jovanovich, 1973.

Wansink, N., "Holland and Six Allies: The Republic of the Seven United Provinces," in J. S. Bromley & E. H. Kossman, eds., *Britain and the Netherlands,* **IV:** *Metropolis, Dominion and Province.* The Hague: Nijhoff, 1971, 133–155.

Ward, A. W., "The War of the Spanish Succession. (2) The Peace of Utrecht and the Supplementary Pacifications," in *Cambridge Modern History,* **V:** *The Age of Louis XIV.* Cambridge: University Press, 1908, 437–459.

Ward, J. R., "The Profitability of Sugar Planting in the British West Indies, 1650–1834," *Economic History Review,* 2nd ser., **XXXI,** 2, May 1978, 197–209.

Warden, Alexander J., *The Linen Trade Ancient and Modern.* London: Longmans, Green & Co., 1864. (Reprinted New York: Augustus Kelley, 1968.)

Wätjen, Hermann, "Zür statistik der Höllandischen Heringsfischerei im 17. und 18. Jahrhundert," *Hansische Geschichtsblatter,* **XVI,** 1910, 129–185.

Weber, Max, *General Economic History.* Glencoe, Illinois: Free Press, 1950.

Weinryb, Bernard D., *The Jews of Poland.* Philadelphia, Pennsylvania: Jewish Publ. Society of America, 1973.

Weis, Eberhard, "Ergebnisse eines Vergleichs der grundherrschaftlichen Strukturen Deutschlands und Frankreichs vom 13. bis Zum Ausgang des 18. Jahrhundert," *Vierteljahrschrift für Sozial- und Wirtschaftsgeschichte,* **LVII,** 1, 1970, 1–14.

Weise, Heinz, "Der Rinderhandel in nordwesteuropäischen Küstengebiet vom 15. bis zum Beginn des 19. Jahrhunderts," in H. Wiese & J. Bölts, *Rinderhandel und Rinderhaltung im nordwesteuropäischen Küstengeibiet vom 15. bis zum 19. Jahrhundert.* Stuttgart: Gustav Fischer Verlag, 1966, 1–129.

Wiese, Heinz, "Die Fleischversorgung der nordwesteuropäischen Grossstädte unter besonderer Berücksichtigung des interterritorialen Rinderhandels," *Third International Conference of Economic History,* Munich 1965, Paris & La Haye: Mouton, 1974, **V,** 453–458.

Weisser, Michael, "The Decline of Toledo Revisited: The Case of Toledo," *Journal of European Economic History,* **II,** 3, Winter 1973, 614–640.

Westergaard, Waldemar, *The Danish West Indies under Company Rule (1671–1754).* New York: Macmillan, 1917.

Wiles, Richard C., "The Theory of Wages in Later English Mercantilism," *Economic History Review,* 2nd ser., **XXI**, 1, Apr. 1968, 113–126.

Williamson, J. A., "The Colonies after the Restoration, 1660–1713," in *The Cambridge History of the British Empire,* **I.** J. Holland Rose *et al.,* eds., *The Old Empire from the Beginnings to 1763.* Cambridge: University Press, 1929, 239–267.

Wilson, Charles Henry, *Anglo-Dutch Commerce and Finance in the Eighteenth Century.* Cambridge: University Press, 1941.

Wilson, Charles Henry, "Treasure and Trade Balances: The Mercantilist Problem," *Economic History Review,* 2nd ser., **II**, 2, 1949, 152–161.

Wilson, Charles Henry, "Treasure and Trade Balances: Further Evidence," *Economic History Review,* 2nd ser., **IV,** 2, 1951, 231–242.

Wilson, Charles Henry, "The Economic Decline of the Netherlands," in E. M. Carus-Wilson, ed., *Essays in Economic History,* **I.** London: Edw. Arnold, 1954, 254–269. (Originally in *Economic History Review,* 1939.)

Wilson, Charles Henry, *Profit and Power: A Study of England and the Dutch Wars.* London: Longmans, Green & Co., 1957. (a)

Wilson, Charles Henry, "The Growth of Overseas Commerce and European Manufacture," in *New Cambridge Modern History,* **VII:** J. O. Lindsay, ed., *The Old Regime, 1713–63.* Cambridge: University Press, 1957, 27–49. (b)

Wilson, Charles Henry, "Cloth Production and International Competition in the Seventeenth Century," *Economic History Review,* 2nd ser., **XIII**, 2, Dec. 1960, 209–221. (a)

Wilson, Charles Henry, "Dutch Investment in Eighteenth Century England. A Note on Yardsticks," *Economic History Review,* 2nd ser., **XII**, 3, Apr. 1960, 434–439. (b)

Wilson, Charles Henry, *England's Apprenticeship, 1603–1763.* London: Longmans, 1965.

Wilson, Charles Henry, "Trade, Society and the State," in E. E. Rich & C. H. Wilson, eds., *Cambridge Economic History of Europe,* **IV:** *The Economy of Expanding Europe in the Sixteenth and Seventeenth Centuries.* Cambridge: University Press, 1967, 487–575.

Wilson, Charles Henry, *The Dutch Republic and the Civilisation of the Seventeenth Century,* World University Library. London: Weidenfeld & Nicolson, 1968.

Wilson, Charles Henry, "The Other Face of Mercantilism," in D. C. Coleman, ed., *Revisions in Mercantilism.* London: Methuen, 1969, 118–139. (a) (Originally in *Transactions of the Royal Historical Society,* 1959.)

Wilson, Charles Henry, "Taxation and the Decline of Empires, an Unfashionable Theme," in *Economic History and the Historian.* London: Weidenfeld & Nicolson, 1969, 114–127. (b) (Originally in *Bijdragen en Mededelingen van het Historisch Genootschap,* 1963.)

Wilson, Charles Henry, *Queen Elizabeth and the Revolt of the Netherlands.* Berkeley: Univ. of California Press, 1970.

Wilson, Charles Henry, "Transport as a Factor in the History of Economic Development," *Journal of European Economic History,* **II,** 2, Fall 1973, 320–337.

Wilson, Charles Henry, "The Historical Study of Economic Growth and Decline in Early Modern History," in *Cambridge Economic History of Europe,* **V:** E. E. Rich & C. H. Wilson, eds., *The Economic Organization of Early Modern Europe.* Cambridge: University Press, 1977, 1–41. (a)

Wilson, Charles Henry, "The British Isles," in Charles Wilson & Geoffrey Parker, eds., *An Introduction to the Sources of European Economic History, 1500–1800,* Vol. **I:** *Western Europe.* London: Weidenfeld & Nicolson, 1977, 115–154. (b)

Wittman, T., "Apuntes sobre los métodos de investigación de la decadencia castellana (siglos XVI–XVII)," in *Nouvelles études historiques,* publiées à l'occasion du XIIᵉ Congrès International des Sciences Historiques par la Commission Nationale des Historiens Hongrois, **I.** Budapest: Akadémiai Kiadó, 1965, 243–250.

Wolański, Marian, *Związki handlowe Śląska z Rzecząpospolitą w XVII Wieku.* Wydawnictwa

Wrooławskiego Towarzystwa Naukowego, No. 77, 1961. Germany summary, pp. 303–39: "Die Handelbeziehungen Schlesiens mit dem Königreich Polen im XVII. Jahrhundert unter besonderer Berücksichtigung der Stadt Wroclaw."

Wolański, Marian, "Schlesiens Stellung im Osthandel vom 15. bis zum 17. Jahrhundert," in Ingomar Bog, her., *Der Aussenhandel Ostmittelemopas, 1450–1650*. Köln-Wien: Böhlau Verlag, 1971, 120–138.

Wolf, Siegmund A., "Das Entstehen von Wüstungen durch Bauernlegen," *Zeitschrift für Wirtschaftsgeschichte*, **V**, 2, 1957, 319–324.

Wolfe, Martin, "French Views on Wealth and Taxes from the Middle Ages to the Old Regime," *Journal of Economic History*, **XXVI**, 4, Dec. 1966, 466–483.

Woolf, Stuart J., "Economic Problems of the Nobility in the Early Modern Period: The Example of Piedmont," *Economic History Review*, 2nd ser., **XVII**, 2, Dec. 1964, 267–283.

Woolf, Stuart J., "The Aristocracy in Transition: A Continental Comparison," *Economic History Review*, 2nd ser., **XXIII**, 3, Dec. 1970, 520–531.

Wright, William E., *Serf, Seigneur and Sovereign: Agrarian Reform in Eighteenth Century Bohemia*. Minneapolis: Univ. of Minnesota Press, 1966.

Wrigley, E. A., "Family Limitation in Pre-Industrial England," *Economic History Review*, 2nd ser., **XIX**, 1, Apr. 1966, 82–109.

Wrigley, E. A., "A Simple Model of London's Importance in Changing English Society and Economy, 1650–1750," *Past and Present*, No. 37, July 1967, 44–70.

Wyczański, Andrzej, "Le niveau de la récolte des céréales en Pologne du XVIe au XVIIIe siècle," in *First International Conference of Economic History*, Stockholm, August 1960. *Contributions*. Paris & La Haye: Mouton, 1960, 585–590.

Wyczański, Andrzej, "La campagne polonaise dans le cadre des transformations du marché des XVIe–XVIIe siècles. L'économie de la Starostie de Korczyn, 1500–1600," *Studia Historiae Oeconomicae*, **II**, 1967, 57–81.

Wyrobisz, Andrzej, "Mining in Medieval and Modern Poland," *Journal of European Economic History*, **V**, 3, Winter 1976, 757–762.

Yates, Frances A., *Astraea: The Imperial Theme in the Sixteenth Century*. London: Routledge & Kegan Paul, 1975.

Yernaux, Jean, *La métallurgie liégeoise et son expansion au XVIIe siècle*. Liège: Georges Thone, 1939.

Zagorin, Perez, "The Social Interpretation of the French Revolution," *Journal of Economic History*, **XIX**, 3, Sept. 1959, 376–401.

Závala, Silvio, "The Evolving Labor System," in John Francis Bannon, ed., *Indian Labor in the Spanish Indies*. Boston: D. C. Heath, 1966, 76–81. (Originally in *New Viewpoints on the Spanish Colonization of America*, 1943.)

Zhukov, E. M., "The Periodization of World History," in *International Congress of Historical Sciences*, Stockholm, 1960, *Rapports*, **I**: *Methodologie, histoire des prix avant 1750*. Göteborg, Sweden: Almqvist & Wiksell, 1960, 74–88.

Zientara, Benedykt, "Eisenproduktion und Eisenhandel in Polen im 16. und 17. Jahrhundert," in Ingomar Bog, her., *Der Aussenhandel Ostmitteleuropas, 1450–1650*. Köln-Wien: Böhlau Verlag, 1971, 270–285.

Zimányi, Vera, "Mouvements des prix hongrois et l'évolution européenne (XVIe–XVIIIe s.)," *Acta Historica Academiae Scientarum Hungaricae*, **XIX**, 1973, 305–333.

Zollner, Erich, *Geschichte Österreichs*, 4th ed. München: R. Oldenbourg Verlag, 1970.

Żytkowicz, Leonid, "An Investigation into Agricultural Production in Masovia in the First Half of the Seventeenth Century," *Acta Poloniae Historica*, No. 18, 1968, 99–118.

Żytkowicz, Leonid, "Grain Yields in Poland, Bohemia, Hungary, and Slovakia in the 16th to 18th Centuries," *Acta Poloniae Historica*, No. 24, 1971, 51–72.

Żytkowicz, Leonid, "The Peasant's Farm and the Landlord's Farm in Poland from the 16th to the Middle of the 18th Century," *Journal of European Economic History*, **I**, 1, 1972, 135–154.

Żvtkowicz, Leonid, review of A. Piatkowski, *Agricultural Estates Belonging to the Town of Elblag in the XVIIth and XVIIIth Centuries*, in *Journal of European Economic History*, **III**, 1, Spring 1974, 249–251.

"'Failed Transitions': Concluding Participants' Discussions," in Frederick Krantz & Paul M. Hohenberg, eds., *Failed Transitions to Modern Industrial Society: Renaissance Italy and Seventeenth-Century Holland*. Montreal: Interuniversity Centre for European Studies, 1975, 81–84.

"Holland: Participants' Discussion," in Frederick Krantz & Paul M. Hohenberg, eds., *Failed Transitions to Modern Industrial Society: Renaissance Italy and Seventeenth-Century Holland*. Montreal: Interuniversity Centre for European Studies, 1975, 64–66.

L'abolition de la "féodalité" dans le monde occidental, **II:** *Discussion des rapports*. Colloques internationaux du C.N.R.S., Toulouse, 12–16 nov. 1968. Paris: Editions du C.N.R.S., 1971.

"Seventeenth-Century Revolutions," a discussion, *Past and Present*, No. 13, 1958, 63–72.

"Summary of the Discussion: Population Change in Relation to the Economy," *Third International Conference of Economic History*, Munich 1965, **IV:** *Demography and History*. Paris & La Haye: Mouton, 1972, 227–235.

Zur Ostdeutschen Agrargeschichte: Ein Kolloquium, Vol. **XVI** of Ostdeutsche Beiträge: Aus dem Göttinger Arbeitskreis. Würzburg: Holzner-Verlag, 1960.

INDEX

STUDIES IN SOCIAL DISCONTINUITY

Under the Consulting Editorship of:

CHARLES TILLY
University of Michigan

EDWARD SHORTER
University of Toronto

In preparation

Evelyne Huber Stephens. The Politics of Workers' Participation: The Peruvian Approach in Comparative Perspective

Paul Oquist. Violence, Conflict, and Politics in Columbia

John R. Hanson II. Trade in Transition: Exports From The Third World, 1840-1900

Fred Weinstein. Germany's Discontents, Hitler's Visions: The Claims of Leadership and Ideology in the Nazi Movement

Published

Albert Bergesen (Ed.). Studies of the Modern World-System

Lucile H. Brockway. Science and Colonial Expansion: The Role of the British Royal Botanic Gardens

James Lang. Portuguese Brazil: The King's Plantation

Elizabeth Hafkin Pleck. Black Migration and Poverty: Boston 1865-1900

Harvey J. Graff. The Literacy Myth: Literacy and Social Structure in the Nineteenth-Century City

Michael Haines. Fertility and Occupation: Population Patterns in Industrialization

Keith Wrightson and David Levine. Poverty and Piety in an English Village: Terling, 1525-1700

Henry A. Gemery and Jan S. Hogendorn (Eds.). The Uncommon Market: Essays in the Economic History of the Atlantic Slave Trade

Tamara K. Hareven (Ed.). Transitions: The Family and the Life Course in Historical Perspective

Randolph Trumbach. The Rise of the Egalitarian Family: Aristocratic Kinship and Domestic Relations in Eighteenth-Century England

Arthur L. Stinchcombe. Theoretical Methods in Social History

Juan G. Espinosa and Andrew S. Zimbalist. Economic Democracy: Workers' Participation in Chilean Industry 1970-1973

Richard Maxwell Brown and Don E. Fehrenbacher (Eds.). Tradition, Conflict, and Modernization: Perspectives on the American Revolution

Harry W. Pearson. The Livelihood of Man by Karl Polanyi

Frederic L. Pryor. The Origins of the Economy: A Comparative Study of Distribution in Primitive and Peasant Economies

Charles P. Cell. Revolution at Work: Mobilization Campaigns in China